OREGON'S MAIN STREET: U.S. Highway 99

"The Folk History"

Painting by Karen Pidgeon

by Jo-Brew and Pat Edwards

About the Cover Art...

The cover art for *U.S. Highway 99, "The Stories,"* was such a hit, we wanted to find something equally as impressive for "The Folk History." We thought that it should relate to Highway 99 and be based on one of the pictures that we've included in the books. We both agreed that the photograph submitted to us by historian, Curt Deatherage of Creswell, Oregon, was an ideal subject. It shows Highway 99 as it passes in front of the old wigwam burner at Drain, Oregon.

The road sign that is prominently displayed in the photograph was set up as a prop for the photograph. Curt Deatherage rescued the old Highway 99 sign from the trash several years ago. He mounted it on a well-used wooden post and when no traffic was coming, set it up long enough to shoot this picture.

Because the first book's cover art was a painting, we decided to get Curt's permission to use his photo as a model for a commissioned piece. He graciously accepted, so I approached Lorane wildlife artist, Karen Pidgeon to do the artwork. We are thrilled with the quality of her work and hope that our readers agree.

Thank you to both Karen and Curt for helping to make this book an enjoyable experience for our readers.

About the Artist:

Cover artist, Karen Pidgeon, has lived in Lorane, Oregon for 44 years. She raised two children there and continues to enjoy riding the forested hills on her horse. Her artwork is inspired by the forest and the animals who live there. She specializes in Wildlife and Nature art and her home-based studio and art gallery displays her diverse creations featuring flora and fauna of all kinds.

Karen will have prints of this cover painting available for those who would like to purchase copies.

For more information, visit Karen's website at http://www.karenpidgeon.com or give her a call at 541-942-1566 to schedule a visit.

Copyright © 2014
by Jo-Brew and Patricia Ann Edwards

All rights reserved. No part of the material protected by this
copyright notice may be reproduced or
utilized in any form or by any means, electronic or mechanical,
including photocopying,
recording or by any informational storage and retrieval system
without written permission from the copyright owner.

ISBN-13: 978-1500948337
ISBN-10: 1500948330

First Edition, September 2014

Published by
Groundwaters Publishing, LLC

P.O. Box 50, Lorane, Oregon 97451
http://www.groundwaterspublishing.com

Acknowledgments

How do we thank so many people who have lent so much of their time and talents to our endeavor? We're going to list a few on these pages, but we cannot begin to mention all of those who were willing to share their stories, photos and information. Just look at the contributor and photo credit pages and you'll get some idea of the debt of gratitude that we owe.

Jo-Brew and I want to begin by putting at the very head of our lists our own personal thank yous.

In Jo's case, her personal wish is heartfelt: *"I'd like to dedicate my work on this book to my mother, Irene Roach, who traveled all the ordinary and secret places of Oregon with me for more than a decade. I also want to thank my family, husband, children and grandchildren, who have been forced to listen to stories of Highway 99 at every gathering for what must have seemed like an eternity."*

For my own personal acknowledgments, I put at the very top of my list the loving support and patience of my husband of 50 years, Jim Edwards. He spent many evenings by himself over the past year and a half as I worked at my computer until midnight every night. There were few complaints and I could not have done this without his total support.

In addition, the rest of my family deserves my undivided attention now that we've finished the book. Maybe they can now walk in our house at noon and find me actually dressed in street clothes and doing something other than typing at my computer.

Together, Jo and I wish to thank some other very special individuals. Each provided us their generosity and talent without expectations of payment and their contributions have touched our hearts.

Michael J. "Hoss" Barker: "Hoss" is a logger-poet and author who has freely contributed not only his poetry, but his insightful stories of his experiences as a logger and as the handyman at Paradise Lodge on the wild and scenic Rogue River. His love and respect for the beauty of nature adds to various segments of this book. Besides being a talented writer, he is a good friend.

Curt Deatherage: Curt, who is researching his own book, has been a willing supporter of our project, donating pictures and stories for both Highway 99 books with an "eager-to-help" willingness. It's his photo that inspired our cover art for this book.

Gary Richards: Gary has been a much-valued resource on the history of Camp Adair. In addition, Gary volunteered to proof the book for us before it went to press. Jo and I have stared at these 550 or so pages for so long that we needed a new pair of eyes to pick out the little typos and inconsistencies. He did it for us on the first book, *"The Stories,"* too. That means so much to both of us!

We especially want to thank all of those who were willing to share their old photographs with us free of charge. Writing a book on history is an expensive proposition that will never really be recovered by book sales. We do it because we love history and want to record special parts of it for future reference, and your support has been invaluable to us.

There are others that we want to thank individually who provided a much-needed and appreciated service in the making of this book.

Jill Livingston: Jill designed the maps that were used at the beginning of each of the sections in both of our books. They help to give our readers a visual idea of where the Pacific Highway / U.S. Highway 99 routes led us in those early years before Interstate 5 was built

Karen Pidgeon: Karen is a professional artist and friend who designed the cover for my first book on the history of Lorane called *Sawdust and Cider; A History of Lorane, Oregon and the Siuslaw Valley*. I've always loved and appreciated her art and was thrilled when she agreed to do the cover art for this book.

Jo has been the historian and "front person" for both books. The concept to write a book on the history of Highway 99 was hers and she was the one who has traveled the road innumerable times, recording the routes and all of the sights and interesting spots along the way. She interviewed dozens of people at their homes across Oregon. She visited most of the historical societies and museums in each of the communities that she passed through, searching out information and photos she could use. By the time I came along to help organize the material, she had probably logged well over 1,000 miles on her car. She made friends and acquaintances on these trips and many of them were tremendous help in locating and providing information on their respective communities.

For that reason, we want to give perhaps our biggest "thank you" to the friendly people who staff those museums and who've been so helpful and interested in our project. There's a list of them at the back of this book. I hope that our readers will visit and lend their support to each of these wonderful organizations.

Now that I have been unchained from my computer, it is my hope, as the "mechanic" of these books, to make a personal journey with my husband Jim to visit each one of these museums and historical societies so that I can thank and meet in person all of the people whose names I've been working and corresponding with. Thanks to each of you!

Last, but certainly not least, is my appreciation and gratitude for Jo-Brew. She had enough faith in me to take me on originally as her editor, then collaborator, and now co-author. I think that we've done an amazing job with both books. Thank you, Jo, for allowing me to come on this ride.

And, from Jo... *"I especially want to thank Pat Edwards, co-author and collaborator for both books in the series."*

TABLE OF CONTENTS

Introduction 1
    Staging Days Through the Oregon Territory 2
    The Impact of the Railroad on the Eventual Route of Pacific
        Highway 9
    The Pacific Highway Through Oregon 10

Section 1 - Over the Siskiyous to Ashland 13
    The Siskiyou Pass 13
    Pacific Highway - A Dream Come True 21
    Ashland Mills / Ashland 28

Section 2 - Talent to Grants Pass 46
    Eden / Warner Creek / Talent 46
    Gasburg / Phoenix 55
    Jacksonville 58
    Medford 60
    Central Point 77
    Gold Hill 79
    Rock Point 84
    Gold River / Tailholt / Woodville / Rogue River 86

Section 3 - Grants Pass to Wolf Creek 89
    Perkinsville / Grant's Pass / Grants Pass 89
    Grave Creek / Leland / Sunny Valley 107
    Almaden / Wolf Creek 110

Section 4 - Wolf Creek to Winchester 115
    Galesville 117
    Stump Town / Julia / Glendale 118
    New Odessa 119

Section 4 - Wolf Creek to Winchester *(continued)*
- Starvout / Booth / Azalea 120
- Canyonville 125
- Days Creek & Tiller 129
- Riddleburg / Riddle 138
- Tri-City 140
- Myrtle Creek 141
- Oak Grove / Dole / Ruckles 149
- Dillard / Willis Creek 149
- Civil Bend / Brockway / Coos Junction / Winston 150
- Deer Creek / Roseburg 151
- Winchester 163

Section 5 - Winchester to Curtin 165
- Bunton's Gap / Wilbur 165
- Camas Swale / Sutherlin 171
- Oakland 174
- Rice Valley / Ricehill / Rice Hill 176
- Yoncalla 177
- Drain 186
- Leona 192
- Anlauf 192
- Curtin 194
- Comstock 197

Section 6 - Divide to Junction City 203
- Divide 203
- Latham 210
- Slab Town / Lemati / Cottage Grove 210
- Saginaw 233
- Walkers / Walker 235
- Creswell 236
- Goshen 241

Section 6 - Divide to Junction City *(continued)*
Springfield 243
Glenwood 244
Skinner's / Eugene City / Eugene 245
River Road/Highway 99 Through Eugene to
    Junction City (before 1936) 265
6th & 7th Streets/Highway 99 Through Eugene to
    Junction City (from 1936) 269
Luper 272
Junction City 273

Section 7 - Junction City to Albany 284
Woody's Landing / Woodyville / Freedom / Lancaster 284
Crow's Nest / Prairie City / Thurston / Harrisburg 287
Halsey 298
Boston / Boston Mills / Shedd's Station / Shedd 299
Tangent 300
Takenah / New Albany / Albany 302

Section 8 - Albany to Salem 310
Millersburg 310
Jefferson 311
Sunnyside 318
Chemeketa / Salem 318

Section 9 - Salem through East Portland 337
Hayesville 337
Brooks 338
Waconda / Hopmere / Quinaby / Chemawa / Concomly ... 344
Gervais 345
Belpassi / Belle Passi 346
Halsey / Woodburn 347
Hubbard 351

Section 9 - Salem through East Portland *(continued)*

- Aurora Colony / Aurora 353
- Barlows / Barlow 361
- Baker Prairie / Canby 364
- New Era 367
- Canemah 371
- Oregon City 373
- Gladstone 383
- Creighton / Center / Oak Grove 386
- Milwaukie 387
- Stumptown / Portland (East Side of the Willamette River) 395

Section 10 - Junction City to Camp Adair 405

- Lick Skillet / Starr's Point / Monroe 409
- Jennyopolis 415
- Greenberry 416
- Marysville / Corvallis 418
- Lewiston / Lewisburg 428
- Camp Adair 431
- Tampico 437
- Soap Creek / Suver / New Suver / Suver Junction / 438

Section 11 - Camp Adair to Tigard 441

- Monmouth 441
- Thorp's Town / Henry Hill's Town of Independence /
  Independence 446
- Dixie / Rickreal / Rickreall 448
- Amity 452
- McMinnville 455
- Lafayette 460
- Ekins / Dundee Junction / Dundee 465

Section 11 - Camp Adair to Tigard *(continued)*
    Grubby End of the Nehalem Valley / Chehalem / Roger's
        Landing / Neuberg / Newburgh / Newburg 467
    Butte / East Butte / Tigardville / Tigard 469

Section 12 - Tigard to the Interstate Bridge 472
    Stump Town / Portland (West Side of the Willamette River) 472
    Kaiserville / Vanport / Vanport City 496

**Epilogue: Traveling the Pacific Highway in 1913 from
        North to South** 504

Bibliography 509
Webliography 514
List of Contributors 518
Photo Credits 519
Museums & Historical Societies Along the Way 521
About the Authors 523

INDEX 525

OREGON'S MAIN STREET: U.S. HIGHWAY 99
"The Folk History"

Foreword

by Pat Edwards

Jo-Brew had already spent several years researching her book, *OREGON'S MAIN STREET: U.S. Highway 99 "The Stories"* when I came on-board as her editor. She had gathered so much material, the job of organizing it had become overwhelming. As the author and researcher of an area history of my own, my interest in her dilemma was immediately piqued and we began working together to try to bring it all together. About halfway through, however, we came to the realization that there was just too much material to put into one book – the logistics of trying to blend contributors' stories, historical details and Jo's narrative were just not working. We went through some rocky periods trying to figure out how to proceed. Jo wanted her book to be a reflection of her own "voice" and personality, telling her own stories while showcasing the remembrances of the many people whom she had interviewed and talked to over the past several years. I was concerned that, although history was being included, it was secondary to the stories in many cases and even seemed to be in the way at times, overshadowing the real purpose of the book.

At one point, I mentioned to Jo that the charm of her book was in the stories that she was telling and that she might consider pulling much of the historical data out and perhaps save it for a second book.

The suggestion appealed to both of us, but Jo wasn't sure she wanted to tackle a second book alone. She asked me to take the lead on compiling the history of the communities lying along the route of Pacific Highway / U.S. Highway 99 through Oregon that she had already collected. We knew that we would also need to do a great deal more research to flesh out the details, so we agreed that we'd work on it together as co-authors.

So, here we are. Because it would be prohibitive to try and write a comprehensive history on each of the communities along the route, and since we both were unwilling to merely repeat history that has already been well-covered, we decided to seek out some of the more interesting and obscure happenings, remembrances and legends of those same communities... or, as we are labeling it, the "Folk History."

So, if you have picked up this book hoping for extensive biographies and historical data on each community along the highway, you will be sorely disappointed.

As we have traveled along the route, south to north, we have found that frequently, some of the smaller communities and towns have much larger segments than the larger urban areas. The more obscure the community, the harder we dug for information on it. And, you may find that we occasionally give much more space to certain smaller aspects of a community's history than what it is best known for. That's our intent.

Of course, we have included the history of the highway and automobile travel as well as other transportation systems used through Oregon's history – stagecoaches, railroads, electric railways, trolleys, buses – along the various paths that the builders of the Pacific Highway took. And, yes, we have mined the material that we include from various sources. Much of it was found in Jo's extensive personal library of Oregon history books, local museums, historical societies, libraries and, of course, the internet. Our most treasured resources, however, are the personal family histories and stories that people we have met along the way have been willing to share with us.

We have painstakingly tried to run down and gain permissions for the pieces that we prefer to include as direct quotes. For those more recent ones which we have not been able to contact the author or owner for permission, we have written our own accounts, compiling it from whatever sources we can find. We have also included quotes from many of the wonderful WPA interviews that were done in the late 1930s which relate directly to the areas we are writing about.

Of course, not all of this history is as comprehensive as it could be because of our space limitations, but we're hoping that by whetting your appetite for more, you will seek out the historical societies, museums and the original reference sources that are listed in the book's bibliography and webliography to learn more.

So, sit back and enjoy your trip through Oregon's heartland. You just may decide that you want to actually get in your car and follow the original paths taken by the old Pacific Highway and visit some of the remarkable communities and sites along the way. Get off the Interstate 5 freeway for awhile and you will discover a whole, not-so-new Oregon that awaits rediscovery.

> The maps we've used to divide the sections of the road are by Jill Livingston. They have been adapted from *That Ribbon of Highway III: Highway 99 through the Pacific Northwest*. Klamath River, CA: Living Gold Press, 2003.

TIME LINE– U.S. HIGHWAY 99

1860   Only one year after becoming a state, the Oregon legislature passes the law that every male between 21 and 50 years of age, except persons who are public charges too infirm to perform labor, had to do two days' work on the public roads of the county in which they lived, or pay $2 for every $200 of taxable property they owned, or go to jail.

1890   The Good Roads Movement with its Automobile Clubs begins. Localities build some short stretches of road. Pressure for more roads increases.

1899   The Oregon State Legislature provides that "all able-bodied persons sentenced to the county jail should be liable to work on the public roads. Any prisoner refusing to work was to be denied all food other than bread and water until he complies."

1901   The Oregon State Legislature passes a law providing for the construction of "...bicycle paths on either or both sides of all public highways of the state for the use of pedestrians and bicycles." $1 annual tax levied on bicycle riders.

1901   The Oregon State Legislature authorizes the counties to levy, annually, not to exceed 10 mills on each $1 of assessed values on real property within the county to finance county road construction.

1910   Jackson County issues bonds to begin Pacific Highway. The first stretches of the great Pacific Highway laid in Oregon were begun in 1913, and connected the California state line, Ashland, Medford and Central Point.

1913   The Oregon State Highway Department is formed. There are only 25 miles of paved roads in the whole state. The Federal government offers some funding to build roads for rural post delivery.

1916   Federal money is granted for short sections of Pacific Highway in rural areas.

1919   The State of Oregon passes the first gasoline tax to use for road building. Vehicle licenses provide more funds.

1921   The Federal Highway Act provides one half the cost for the building of the road from the border of Mexico to the border of Canada

1926   Pacific Highway becomes U.S. Highway 99 as Federal dollars help with improvements.

1928   U.S. Highway 99 is declared the longest improved highway in the country.

1956   The Federal Interstate System Act creates the Interstate Highway system, a network that will allow travel from coast to coast without traffic light stops.

1966   The U.S. Highway 99 is decommissioned.

INTRODUCTION

The Pacific Highway, later known as U.S. Highway 99, had its beginnings long before the gold-rush and westward expansion of white settlers. The Native American tribes roamed throughout the area for centuries, establishing their own routes to winter and summer lodgings and areas where fish and game were plentiful and their favorite plants – camas roots, acorns, hazelnuts, fruits and berries – could readily be found during their seasons of harvest.

Once the French Canadian fur traders of the Hudson's Bay Company, the gold miners and, eventually, the white settlers arrived, they also used many of the Indian trails to find the easiest ways to travel over hills and mountains and through valleys with their wagons and on horseback.

Supplies and mail were originally brought by ships along the Oregon Coast to Portland and then by pack train. Southern Oregon mail primarily traveled by ship to and from the tidewater landing at Scottsburg, Oregon on the Umpqua River or by mule or packhorse trains to and from Yreka, California. These early trails eventually became stagecoach roads when the increasing need to transport the settlers, commodities and mail from one locale to another became necessary. The most prominent north-to-south – or in this case, south-to-north – route was part of the Applegate Trail. It was a component of the system of trails that connected the Oregon Trail in the north to the California Trail to the south and also was frequently called the Oregon-California Trail or "The Great Road."

The Applegate Trail, which formed the southern part of what was also called the California Trail through Oregon, is rich in the history of the emigration and settling of the southern part of the state and the Applegate family, for which it is named, impacted that history.

Southern Oregon historian, Dr. Jeffrey M. LaLande, shares his considerable knowledge about the Applegate Trail as part of the extensive on-line Oregon Encyclopedia Project:

"Conceived as being safer, quicker, and more secure from possible British control should war break out over the Oregon Question, the trail (which was also known to Oregonians as Applegate's Cut-off, the Southern Emigrant Road, and simply as the South Road or Southern Road during its main period of use in 1846-1860) was intended to bring wagon trains of settlers into the Willamette Valley. Although the number of emigrants who used the Applegate Trail was comparatively modest, it had particular significance in the settling of the Rogue River Valley during the 1850s.

"...Jackson County's Emigrant Creek was named for the trail's several crossings of that stream as travelers descended the Cascade Range into the Rogue River

Valley near Ashland. Today, portions of the Applegate Trail in Oregon are closely paralleled by Interstate Highway 5 and State Highway 66. The National Park Service designated the Applegate Trail as a National Historic Trail in 1992 (as a part of the larger California Trail)..."

Staging Days through the Oregon Territory

In 1852, as part of its banking service, Wells, Fargo & Co. began buying and transporting gold by the quickest means possible.

In 1858, they started their Overland Mail Company to deliver mail. The company bought out the western leg of the Pony Express in 1861 and added stagecoach service to the settlers flooding the Oregon Territory seeking donation land claims.

These Oregon stagecoach routes set the main pathway for later roads and highways through Oregon.

Wells, Fargo & Co. expanded slowly in rural Oregon during the 1850s, keeping pace with the lumber trade and coastal steamer stops. The company itself ran its own stagelines only from 1866 to 1869, from Nebraska to California, and north from Utah into Montana and Idaho, so the stages in Oregon were run under various independent names.

In 1857, the first Oregon stagecoach line that contracted with Wells Fargo was the California & Oregon Stage Company. It ran between Portland and Salem. Wells, Fargo & Co. then contracted out its express service with independent stage companies throughout Oregon.

To maintain their teams of horses and to provide needed services, the stage lines that contracted with Wells Fargo set up stagecoach stops along the way. Because the stages were pulled by teams of horses through all kinds of terrain and conditions, the maximum amount of distance the horses were allowed to travel before a fresh hitch took over was 19 miles, although 12 or 13 was the norm. In the hilly areas of the state, the distance was much shorter.

The California & Oregon Stage Company kept about 6,000 horses. Because these horses were such a valuable commodity, care was taken to feed and treat them well.

Although the stagecoach drivers carried and used the long 16-20 foot whips to urge their teams on, they were ordered to never allow them to touch the horses. The sound – the crack of the whip – was to be the only part the whip was to play. If a horse was traumatized by the bite and sting of the whip on his flesh, it was ordered to be either sold

> "... 'On the afternoon of the 8th of October, I left Portland for San Francisco by the overland route ... I took a seat in a coach of the California and Oregon Stage Company to commence my long ride ...Four gentlemen and two ladies with children occupied the inside while the driver had plenty of company on top ...Careful driving is required on these mountain roads, necessarily narrow in the most dangerous places, so that a few inches' divergence from the single track would be a sure upset into the ragged abysses of darkness below. The night was radiant. I never saw more brilliant heavens, even in the tropics, than on the Oregon Mountains.' — Frances Fuller Victor, 1870 (Steve Greenwood, *"Stagecoaching in Oregon"* Wells Fargo blog)

A Wells Fargo Stage.
Courtesy of the Wells Fargo archives

or destroyed because he could no longer be relied upon to work as a dependable part of the team.

The stages were Concord coaches that used four- or six-horse teams, depending on the incline and route they would be going over and the weather they would be traveling through. The coaches were painted gold with olive-green trim. "California-Oregon Stage Company" and "U.S. Mail – Wells Fargo and Company" were stenciled on the sides. A canvas rack at the back carried the baggage, but the driver carried the Wells Fargo money box and valuables. Hard seats and canvas curtains that did little to keep out the dust or rain made for an uncomfortable trip, but it was still much improved from a farm wagon.

The stage stops soon not only provided fresh horses, but also rest areas where the weary travelers could stop and eat and, in some cases, spend the night, along their route.

Thirty-five drivers were employed to drive 28 coaches and 30 stage wagons. They were to travel at eight miles per hour with ten minutes at each stop to pick up and deliver passengers and change horses.

The driver was changed every 45 miles. There were 14 district agents along the route and usually 75 hostlers. When November came, the Concord coaches had to be replaced by more substantial coaches and the schedule lengthened. This continued until the railroad was in operation between California and Oregon. By 1880, there were 50 offices throughout Oregon and 75 express offices that linked the stages with steamers and the railroad. The stagecoaches continued to operate until the north/south rail lines met and joined at the Oregon/California border in December of 1887.

Joseph Gaston, in his *The Centennial History of Oregon 1811-1912* gives an overall picture of how the stage routes developed:

"The stage line service followed on soon after the establishment of the express business, the first service of its kind being on the line between Portland and Salem in 1857, where the Concord stage made the fifty-five miles in one day. In 1859, a

Postcard of a California & Oregon Stagecoach passing Mt. Shasta, California in the 1850s

mail and passenger coach line was put on the road from Salem to Eugene, and shortly after, extended from Eugene to Jacksonville. And, this was the extent of the accommodations until 1860. In June 1860, the California Stage Company placed its stock on the line from Red Bluffs on the Sacramento River to Oakland in Douglas County, Oregon, where it connected with the line of Chase & Co., running stages to Corvallis and where Chase & Co. connected with the Oregon Stage Company's line to Portland, thus making a through mail and passenger line from Red Bluffs, California to Portland, Oregon."

Henry W. Corbett, a prominent Portland businessman and philanthropist, and later U.S. Senator from Oregon, owned the Oregon Stage Company in 1865 and contracted with Wells Fargo for the transportation of the U.S. mail from Oregon to California. In about 1869, he bought out the California Stage Company and combined the two, calling it the California & Oregon Stage Company. At 710 miles, it was the second longest stageline in the nation.

He generally used 4-horse stages that ran daily between Portland, Oregon and Sacramento, California. The runs took seven days, and eventually, six days, in the months of April through December. The winter and spring months of January through March took 12 days per run. It was a faster means of transportation for both mail and passengers.

Even though the steamships that plied the coast to and from San Francisco took only five days, they only ran every two weeks.

He gave up the mail contract after his election to the United States Senate when it conflicted with his Senate responsibilities.

From a newspaper article written for a Salem newspaper in the early 1900s:

"Old Cal. Mail Carrier Reminisces. Colonel Scovell, now of Salem. The Man

Who Drove the First Stage Out of The City – Portland-Sacramento Route."

"SALEM, Oct. 5. Colonel (L.C.) Scovell, who began carrying the United States mail to the Salem post office in 1854 is still engaged in that occupation. He drove the first stage out of Portland on the through line to Sacramento in 1860, drove the last stage out on that line in 1868?(date unclear), and has had the Government contract for carrying mail from the depot to the post office ever since the railroad was completed to Salem in 1870. He expects to have the privilege of delivering the first mail sacks at the new post office building now. In course of construction, 'Old Cal,' as he is familiarly known in Salem, may well be accorded the honor of being called Oregon's pioneer stage driver. Though he is 65 years old, and has endured the hardships of many a midnight ride through wind and rain, when the roads were almost impassable, he still performs his exacting duties with never-failing promptness. Except for a stiffness in his right hip, due to the continued cramped position necessary in holding his foot on the brake lever of his stage, he is wonderfully active, and hopes to see many more years of work in the mail service.

"Scovell came to Oregon from Iowa in 1833, and settled on a ranch near Corvallis. Soon thereafter, he fell in with a man whom he remembers by the name of Thompson – D.P. Thompson, of Portland – and who was planning the establishment of a stage line between Oregon City and Corvallis. As Scovel had driven a stage for many years in Iowa, he soon showed by his intelligent discussion of the practical features of staging that he was just the man Thompson needed. He was immediately engaged to assist in establishing the line, and to take charge of the details of operation.

"The stage line between Oregon City and Corvallis was started in 1854, the service being very irregular, and the route sometimes indirect. The stage ran where business called and made as good time as was convenient. As compared with the present, there were practically no wagon roads, and in some places the stage was driven through the almost trackless woods. Yet this was an improvement over previous facilities, and the stage was appreciated by the early inhabitants of the territory covered by the stage service.

"**On Portland-Sacramento Route**. In 1850 the Government provided for the carrying of mails from Portland to Sacramento, and the contract for this service was secured by a company formed for the purpose. Scovel was one of their first drivers and it was he who drove the first stage out of Portland on the new line. The stages were of the old-fashioned type, known to the present generation only by the pictures that may be found in pioneer newspapers or early books. The horses were large and powerful, and, according to Old Cal, ready to run at the crack of the whip. 'You bet everybody stood clear when the stage drove into town in those days,' says this old veteran, as he recalls with a merry twinkle in his eye the events of his more exciting labors. 'You don't see any such horses nowadays, because there is no use for them. The horses were wild. They had to be held until everything was ready, and when they were turned loose they started off at a gallop. When we came into town on a dead run, the stage horn blowing, everybody turned out to see who had come

> **"Snow in the Siskiyou"** *The Oregon Sentinel,* Jacksonville, Oregon, Saturday morning, December 12, 1863.
>
> "On Monday morning last, snow commenced falling fast in the Siskiyou mountains, on the line of the stage road between this place and Yreka, and by twelve o'clock of that night, four or five feet of snow lay upon the road. As a consequence, the stage due here from Yreka, on Tuesday evening, did not arrive until the following night. Mr. Louis Tucker, the driver, tells us that he was eleven hours struggling through the snow on the mountain. Mr. John Anderson, the energetic stage agent, has put an extra driver and teams on the route, and it is not probable that the stages will again fail to connect at this place this winter. Tucker drives to Cole's 'Mountain House and back each day, while Bell and King drive to and from Cole's and Yreka."

on the stage. We dashed up to the stage office and stopped quicker than an airbrake express. It took mighty fine horses to stand that kind of work and those that couldn't stand it didn't last long.'

"The stage under this new system made regular trips and had a time table that was closely followed. The company, known as the California Stage Company, had a contract by which it received $90,000 per year from the Government, and made a good profit besides from carrying passengers and small freight. The stage left Portland at 5 o'clock in the morning and reached Salem at 4 o'clock in the afternoon. Horses were changed at Oregon City, Dutch Town (Aurora) *and* Waconda, near the present site of Gervais. The stage left Salem for Eugene at 4 o'clock in the afternoon and reached the latter place at 3 o'clock next morning. The fare from Portland to Salem was $5 and this included the transportation of 150 pounds of baggage.

"The Portland-Sacramento stage line was operated by the California Company until 1860, when H.W. Corbett bought the line for $100,000 and conducted it until he was elected United States Senator in 1866. Scovel was a witness to the transfer and saw the money counted out in gold. He continued with the stage line until 1870 when the northern terminus of the route was Salem.

"In 1868 the railroad had been completed to Lake Labish, and regular train service to that point was commenced. Under the federal law the railroad then had the right to carry the mails, and the stage ran only to Labish. Two years later the train and stage met at Salem, and in 1872 Eugene became the connecting point."

The north/south route was not the only one that Wells Fargo contracted for. It established express lines in Oregon between The Dalles and Canyon City, and from Umatilla to Baker City and on into Idaho. Wells Fargo's Express rode in other stageline routes across Oregon, as well. It also had offices in the towns of Butteville, Dayton, Forest Grove, Hillsboro, Lafayette and McMinnville.

Livery businesses sprung up all over the state to make short runs between smaller towns and areas of Oregon not served by the major north/south route.

This is an approximation of where the known northern stage stops along the U.S. Highway 99 route were. **(Note:** the pre-1865 routes leading from the Welsh Changing Station are uncertain. It appears that when the route was changed in 1865 from going over the mountains to the Cartwright House in Lorane to going through the Pass Creek area south of Cottage Grove, it may have occurred about the same time as the move from Milliorn's near Junction City to Lancaster.)

These maps were created by Pat Edwards and are not meant to be official and should be considered a rough placement of the stage routes

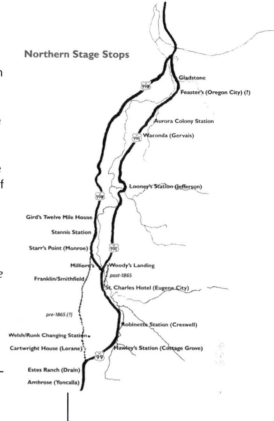

The approximate locations for the southern stage stops along the U.S. Highway 99 route.

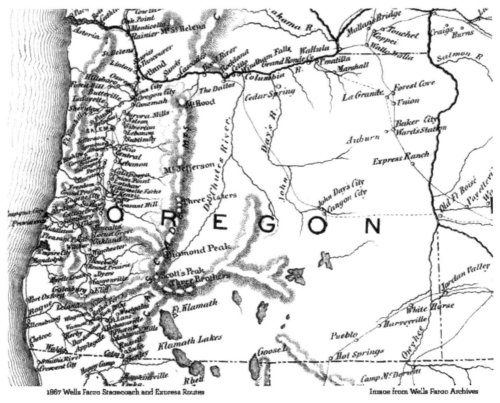

An 1867 Wells Fargo map of the stage and express routes through Oregon.
Courtesy of the Wells Fargo archives

Eli Bangs Livery was one of the larger ones. Headquartered in Eugene, it provided stagecoach service to outlying areas.

In 1903, Charles P. Barnard sold out his Empire Livery, Feed & Sale Stable and his stage line which served Roseburg-to-Marshfield and bought the Bangs Livery. It was considered the largest and most complete livery establishment south of Portland.

Stage travelers heading north from California into Oregon, usually entered Oregon on the Applegate Trail section of the California Trail from Yreka, California, 25 miles south of the Oregon border.

An 1866 Overland Mail poster from the Wells Fargo archives listed the main Oregon

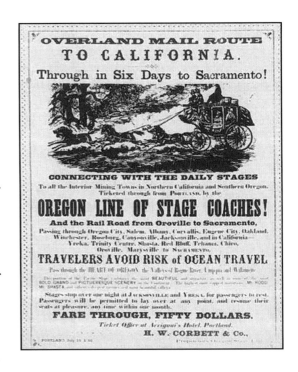

stops (going south to north) as Jacksonville, Canyonville, Roseburg, Winchester, Oakland, Eugene City, Corvallis, Albany, Salem, Oregon City and Portland... It boasted, "Six Days from Portland to Sacramento!" but there were many more small stage stops along the way.

The Impact of the Railroad on the Eventual Route of Pacific Highway/ U.S. Highway 99

As part of the Pacific Railway Act of 1862 that was later modified in 1866, the federal government began to offer land grants to the California and Oregon Railroad of California and a company to be designated by the Oregon Legislature to build a railroad line connecting California and Oregon.

According to information derived from a Bureau of Land Management report entitled, "O&C Sustained Yield Act: the Law, the Land, the Legacy, 1937-1987":

"As part of the U.S. government's desire to foster settlement and economic development in the western states, in July 1866, Congress passed the Oregon and California Railroad Act, which made 3,700,000 acres (1,500,000 ha) of land available for a company to build a railroad from Portland, Oregon to San Francisco, distributed by the State of Oregon in 12,800-acre (5,200 ha) land grants for each mile of track completed..."

The Oregon Central Railroad was soon organized to begin building from Portland southward on the west side of the Willamette River, while the California and Oregon Railroad of California was to begin in California, working northward. The Oregon contingent received the land grants on November 25, 1866 to move forward. However, because the California company had not obtained control of the Oregon Central Railroad, it decided in July 1865 to incorporate a second and competing OCR company referred to as the Oregon Central Railroad, East Side. Thus began a competition between the East Side company and the West Side company supported by the City of Portland.

The West Side Company broke ground in Portland on April 15, 1868, and the East Side Company began its construction in East Portland the very next day, claiming that the land grants that were awarded belonged to them.

Unfortunately for the West Side Company, Portland's guarantee on its bond interest was declared in violation of the city charter and their efforts got no further than McMinnville. The East Side Company lost no time in gaining the support of local businessmen, including Ben Holladay of Salem, who had created the Overland Stage Company of California, and state legislators. Together, they succeeded in having the land grants reassigned to the East Side Company.

In 1869, the Oregon Central Railroad, East Side, ran a 20-mile stretch of line south of Portland to New Era. Ben Holladay, who by then owned the railroad, changed its name to the Oregon and California Railroad.

By 1872, the California line was extended as far north as Redding, California and the Oregon line, begun in Portland, reached as far south as Roseburg.

The project was delayed for several years at that point, and stage service was continued between Redding and Roseburg until the lines met.

1905 "Old Betsy" Oregon & California Railroad engine. *Courtesy of Wikimedia Commons* (Oregon BLM)

The BLM report continues:

"...In 1869, Congress changed how the grants were to be distributed, requiring the railroads to sell land along the line to settlers in 160-acre parcels at $2.50 per acre. The purpose of these restrictions was to encourage settlement and economic development, while compensating the O&C Railroad for its costs of construction.

"...The land was distributed in a checkerboard pattern, with sections laid out for 20 miles (32 km) on either side of the rail corridor with the government retaining the alternate sections for future growth.

"By 1872, the railroad had extended from Portland to Roseburg. Along the way, it created growth in Willamette Valley towns such as Canby, Aurora, and Harrisburg, which emerged as freight and passenger stations, and provided a commercial lifeline to the part of the river valley above Harrisburg where steamships were rarely able to travel. As the railroad made its way into the Umpqua Valley, new townsites such as Drain, Oakland, and Yoncalla were laid out... Construction efforts were sporadic, finally reaching completion in 1887."

The railroad line was eventually completed over the Siskiyou Mountains, connecting with the California and Oregon Railroad at the border between the two states in 1887. Southern Pacific Railroad assumed control over the financially-troubled O&C Railroad soon after the completion, although it was not officially sold to SP until January 3, 1927.

The Pacific Highway through Oregon

In 1860, the first legislature under state government decreed that "every male between the ages of twenty one and fifty years of age, except persons who are public charges or too infirm to perform labor" was required to do two days' work on the public roads of the county in which they lived, or pay $2 for every $2,000 of taxable property they owned or go to jail and serve it out. That was the system until 1899, when the legislature also provided that "all able-bodied persons" sentenced to the county jail should be liable to work on the public roads, under the full power of the county court.

This legislation became vital to this story as it was entirely the responsibility of the counties for road construction except for one notable piece of legislation... In 1901, the legislature passed a law providing for the construction of *"bicycle paths on either or both sides of all public highways of the state for use of pedestrians and bicycles."*

To finance the construction, every rider was required to pay an annual tax of $1 to the county clerk and receive a tag which, the law decreed, *"must be securely fastened to the seat post of each and every bicycle."*

That statute was the precedent for the present system of automotive licenses, gasoline taxes, fines and penalties which were established a decade later and dedicated to the task of constructing the state highway system.

Apparently, when discussion on building a major north/south highway connecting British Columbia and the Pacific states to the Mexican border first began, there was a movement, led in part by Samuel Hill, to run the route through Central Oregon instead of through the Willamette, Umpqua and Rogue River valleys. The proposed route was to go (from south to north) through *"Klamath Falls, Central Oregon, The Dalles and Portland."*

Sam Hill was a businessman, lawyer, railroad executive and advocate of good roads in the Pacific Northwest. His Good Roads group also failed in their attempt to convince the State of Washington to build the Columbia River Highway on the north (Washington) shore of the river, but once that was rejected, he was instrumental in getting the State of Oregon to build it on the south shore. He also advocated the use of convict labor to build roads.

According to the Good Roads campaign in 1910:

"There could be no greater godsend to the people of this state or to the convicts themselves than to employ at least one-half of them out-of-doors in the construction of state highways. Those men would be better off and would be returning to the people of the whole state something for their custody and in return for the laws they have violated and costs they have heaped upon the taxpayer. The present system of employing them in the manufacture of stoves on the contract plan is unjust to the convicts themselves. The state should not sell their labor for a mere pittance..."

Sam Hill's mansion is now the Maryhill Museum on the banks of the Columbia River.

After his proposed route for the Pacific Highway was rejected, it was the same Sam Hill who, in the company of Oregon Governor Oswald West, turned the first spadeful of dirt to begin the Jackson County section of the Pacific Highway over the Siskiyou Pass. It was done at 3:00 p.m. on November 28, 1913, near the Barron Ranch, seven miles south of Ashland.

Sam Hill and Governor Oswald West, turning the first spadeful of dirt to begin the Jackson County section of the Pacific Highway over the Siskiyou Pass. *Courtesy of Oregon Department of Transportation (ODOT) History Center*

Section 1

U.S. HIGHWAY 99 - OVER THE SISKIYOUS AND THROUGH ASHLAND

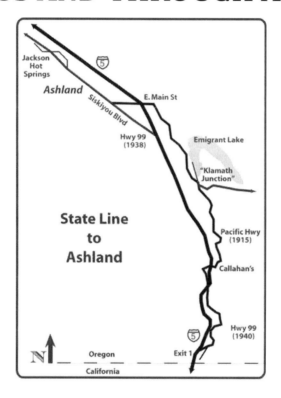

THE SISKIYOU PASS

The historic Siskiyou Pass, located in Jackson County near the Oregon-California border, is considered the "most-used mountain pass" in the State of Oregon. Used originally as a trail by animals and native tribes, it became the main route for the Hudson's Bay Company to haul goods between the two territories. The name "Siskiyou" is believed to be derived from the Cree language meaning "bob-tailed horse." It set the stage for later development by the California & Oregon Stage Company routes as well as railroad lines and, eventually, the Pacific Highway – U.S. Highway 99.

"Early Travel Through the Siskiyous" by Sue Waldron, local historian for the *Table Rock Sentinel* and *Southern Oregon Historical Society*, September/October, 1991:

"Where some sixty million years ago, the growing Cascade Mountains bumped into the older Siskiyous, a pass formed. Animals and then Native Americans used the gap. In 1838, Peter Skene Ogden used it for a north bound cattle drive and then a U.S. government expedition in 1841. A few others passed, single file, through the narrow, and often snowbound, route to hunt gold or fur.

"In 1858, the Territorial Legislature passed an act to incorporate the "Siskiyou Mountain Wagon Company" with a twenty-year franchise for the construction and maintenance of a road over the Siskiyou Mountains." Michael Thomas, a builder from Ashland was awarded the franchise. Construction of a road began. Lindsay Applegate and some of his grown sons came south to work for Thomas. Thomas ran into financial difficulties in 1859 and Lindsay purchased the franchise.

"The Siskiyou Mountain Wagon Road climbed the foothills south of Ashland, passed in front of the Barron Family ranch house, twisting and turning through rocks and scrub oak southwest over the top of the mountain and down to the canyon floor, turning south again to the California border, connecting to Cole's Station. The toll road was completed on August 29, 1859 and opened for business. Two horseback riders paid $.25 a piece. First by a steep, narrow trail, then by a road just wide enough for a wagon, California and Oregon were connected.

"The road suffered mudslides and washouts in the spring and packed snow in the winter, demanding constant attention. In 1860, Lindsay moved his family from Douglas County to the log cabin at the tollgate.

"In 1860 the California Stage Company received a government contract to carry the mail between Sacramento and Portland, proving to be the toll road's most dependable source of income. The Applegate family operated the toll road for nine years, building a new large tollhouse made of cut lumber. They also developed an interest in the Klamath Lake area. In 1864, Lindsay became the agent for the new Klamath Indian Reservation and sold the toll road in 1871, James Laughlin and his two foster sons bought the franchise for $10,000. During the four years they had ownership, the road was regraded and graveled. In 1875, the corporation was sold to a corporation headed by Jesse Dollarhide who owned several hundred acres on the side of the mountain through which the toll road passed. Since he made much of his income from cutting wood and had teams hauling the wood to town, rather than pay the toll, he bought the road.

"The road stayed in use until the construction of the Pacific Highway was begun in 1913, following almost the exact route of the old toll road. A rocky culvert and a faint clearing through the brush are all that remain of the old link to California."

A more modern account of traveling on the Old Siskiyous Highway was related by Jeff Jensen, author of *Drive the Broadway of America: U.S. 80*, on his website blog, "Bygone Byways":

"The Siskyous. These lovely mountains in Southern Oregon once posed quite the challenge to the early automobiles. Treacherous curves and steep grades were the norm, not the exception. Today's I-5

just blasted right through and left many wonderful stretches of 99 intact for us to explore today. For example, I took the Oregon 66 exit, and turned off on the twisty (and I mean twisty) Old Siskyou Highway. It ended up being a real treat. At first, I was engulfed by trees and endless curves, but the road eventually opened up a little and I approached the old summit.

"Along the way, I came across an intriguing bridge, the railing type unfamiliar to me. It seemed vaguely familiar somehow, so I took a photo and continued on. Imagine my surprise when I got home, and sure enough, I had a postcard of the same location! The railings are different and the trees larger, but it's the same place!

"From the bridge, the summit's not far. Under I-5, and a left turn, follow the unmarked (at least on my two maps) old highway to the original summit. I got to the summit just as the sun was about to set. You could see Mt. Shasta off to the south, and a beautiful view of the valleys and sunset off to the west. I soaked up the solitude for a few minutes, but decided to head on before it got too dark.

"Continuing on down towards California on this unmarked highway, I found the road to be in fine shape and no problem at all. There were a couple of gravel-filled washouts, but they were easy to traverse. Any car could do it. I did come across one large rockslide a mile or two beyond the summit, but the makeshift road was easily passable. I would say that this whole area could easily be explored with the family sedan except perhaps right after a rain/snow shower.

"On we descended. Eventually, the old highway rather rudely spit us out onto I-5. At this point, we had no choice but to continue on into the golden state of California!"

Editors' note: In a visit to the summit in 2013, the road was blocked and marked as private property beyond that point.

The last stage stop in California before the Wells Fargo stages entered Oregon was Cole's Station. It was located one mile south of the California/Oregon border in the community of Cottonwood in Siskiyou County and was run by Rufus C. Cole on his 612-acre property.

A stagecoach stopped at the Mountain House, with Martha Barron, the proprietor, on the front porch in the 1880s. *Courtesy of the Southern Oregon Historical Society*

After leaving Cole's, the teams of horses pulled the heavy stages over the Siskiyou Mountains for eight miles before stopping at Barron's Station, also known as the "Mountain House." It was owned and run by Major Hugh F. Barron from 1859 until it closed in 1884, except for sporadic years when it did not contract with the stage lines as a stage stop. These included 1867, 1873, 1876 and 1877.

The Barron's Station inn is still standing and was renovated and served as a beautiful and popular inn called the Mountain House until it closed in November 2013. Listed on the National Registry of Historic Places, it is now being used by its former innkeepers, John and Kathy Loram, as a private residence. Kathy provided the following history:

"The Mountain House was located at the foot of the Siskiyou range, right along the California-Oregon Trail that evolved into the stagecoach route. Not surprisingly, the inn became a 'home stop,' a way-station, where stagecoach passengers and drivers were fed and teams of horses were switched out and stabled.

"The original building was designed to serve as an inn and was completed in 1852. Shortly after, gold was discovered in nearby Jacksonville, attracting a flood of miners up the California-Oregon Trail. Wagon trains also began arriving over the Applegate Trail, and the steady stream of customers brought prosperity to the travelers' accommodation and tavern.

"A few years later, the Mountain House became a stagecoach stop and a post office was opened there. And for almost the next 30 years, stagecoach passengers tumbled out of the coach to eat huge, hurried meals before being rushed back onboard for the next leg of the trip across the mountains.

"For 25 years, the stagecoach stopped here, for exactly half an hour. According to a winter schedule from 1878, when the stage arrived at the Mountain House on

Waiting for the train at the Siskiyou settlement. *From the collection of Jerry McGrew*

its way north, it did so at 2:15 am, meaning that it made the perilous trip over the Siskiyou Mountains in the dead of night.

"...The oldest building in Southern Oregon, the Mountain House was initially an outpost in the wilderness. It grew into the heart of a thriving, 8,000-acre ranch that remained in the hands of the Barron family for over a century. A part of Oregon history lives on in the remarkable continuity of this place."

In the years when Barron's was not operating, the stages stopped at Henry and Elizabeth Casey's, one-half mile to the north of Barron's.

After Barron's was closed in 1884, the next stop on the stage route was Kingsbury's Soda Springs, about one mile north of Barron's. It was owned by Charles B. Kingsbury and was located at the junction of the California-Oregon stage road and the old Greensprings Road. The property that it sat on is now covered by 35-feet of water, in the middle of Emigrant Lake.

The Early Railroad Through the Siskiyous

In 1887, Southern Pacific Railroad, the former Oregon & California Railroad Company, completed a rail line between the two states. It's interesting to note that the railroad line, once completed, had to cross the Dollarhide toll road seven times due to all the curves in the road.

While the line and a tunnel through the mountain were being constructed, a small settlement called Siskiyou grew up on the northeast end of the tunnel above the entrance to the toll road.

Railroad workers and miners were the main occupants of the settlement, and it had its own post office for a while. It also served as a stop where passengers could be picked-up. It included a small station and a turntable to turn around the helper-engines for the run back down to the headquarters in Ashland. After the main railroad line that transported passengers was moved to Linkville, later renamed Klamath Falls, the number of people in the settlement decreased. Eventually, the post office was eliminated and much of the town disappeared.

Before 1887, as the Oregon and California Railroad built south from Portland, its steam engines were fueled by wood harvested from nearby forests, and kept cut and stacked at stations along the line. East of the Cascades, coal ran most of the engines, but a good coal source wasn't available in Oregon.

In the meantime, the railroads of Southern California were beginning tentative trials of oil as fuel, sometimes switching back to coal if prices fluctuated. In the mid-1890s the Southern Pacific began searching for oil and found important fields on their original land grants. As the transition from coal to oil slowly made progress, so did the construction of the infrastructure including fueling stations, updated locomotives and tank cars.

Excerpt from "The Great Transfomation: Coal to Oil on the Southern Pacific" Volume 85 by Larry Mullaly and Arnold S. Menke in *SP Trainline Magazine*, 2005:

"When a 50,000-gallon tank was installed in Ashland, Oregon in 1904, a reporter was amazed to discover after 36 oil cars had been unloaded, the depth of oil in the 30-ft. high tank still stood at only five feet." Finding enough oil to fill the tanks and run the whole system would be awhile.

"The transformation from coal to oil fuel was considerably delayed in Oregon and Nevada. SP's Oregon Lines were most unusual because of their long-time reliance on cordwood. Although passenger trains running between Ashland and Portland began using coal in 1900, as late as 1905 many of the division's engines were still fueled by wood. Once the decision had been made to switch to oil fuel, however, the changeover was rapid. In 1906, oil fuel stations were established along the main line at Grants Pass, Glendale, Roseburg, Junction City, Albany and East Portland. By the end of that year, the Woodburn-Springfield Branch was also equipped for oil. But cordwood was used as late as 1910 on the Newberg branch.

"The fueling infrastructure, designed in 1900, supported the railroad for the next half-century. Until the advent of dieselization, no other technological advance had such a profound an impact on the West's greatest railroad."

Wobblies on the Rails - 1911

In 1905, a new international labor union, the Industrial Workers of the World (IWW) was formed. It differed from others primarily in that it wasn't limited to a particular trade or trade group and it promoted activism. It was most prevalent in the areas where there were large groups of hired workers. Other labor groups, industrial employers, and even the government were opposed to the organization as being radical, or worse.

Jay Mullen, a history professor at Southern Oregon University, researched the event that has been nearly forgotten in the 100+ years since it took place.

In an interview with Jay Mullen by Paul Fattig of the *Medford Mail Tribune*, June 13, 2010:

"They were advocating the replacement of the existing economic system. They believed that working people were the producers. But they weren't Marxists

Fresno-bound Wobblies being removed from freight train cars in Ashland. *Courtesy of Southern Oregon Historical Society*

who advocated violent revolution. They thought that if you could organize all the workers, you could stop the economy, and once it stopped, the whole system would collapse and they would step in and take over."

It was with that background that, on February 16, 1911, 112 members of the IWW, who called themselves the "Wobblies," left Portland on freight trains heading for Fresno, California in support of fellow IWW strikers there who had been jailed for asserting their right to speak freely and organize during the infamous Fresno Free Speech Fight of 1910-1911.

Branded as an "army of hoboes" by the press, each Oregon city with a newspaper warned that the radical "Wobblies" were on their way south. The group rode the rails in the freight cars heading south. However, they caused the townspeople no problems and were not bothered themselves. They were, for the most part, young, single working men – loggers, miners, immigrants, day-laborers and agricultural workers – many of Scandinavian descent, who wanted to improve life for "common people" and their right to free speech. It was in Ashland where they were greeted by a police force hired by the railroad to remove them from the freight cars. IWW organization rules called for peaceful resistance, so they disembarked in Ashland and began walking. They camped south of the city limits and then walked along the railroad tracks to Steinman, a railroad watering site about ten miles south of Ashland. There was snow on the ground even at that elevation. They got wood for fires and a small amount of food from the railroad section boss – but not enough for the 102 men. From there they hiked along the tracks, ascending the Siskiyous, to Tunnel 13, hoping to board another southbound train. They bought food to make a stew at the Siskiyou store while they waited. Railroad detectives arrived to prevent a boarding of another freight train south, but offered them a ride back to Portland. They turned the offer down.

Through one of the coldest winters on record in the Siskiyou Mountains, they kept fighting their way through three feet of snow. On the California side, most of the small towns along the way offered some sort of support – a place to camp, firewood, an open tavern – even beds and hot meals. One of the Wobblies dropped out of the trek after suffering frostbite and two more left before reaching their goal. But, by the time the remaining 98 Wobblies were leaving Red Bluff, the situation in Fresno had ended and so had their mission. By then, they had walked almost 150 miles past Ashland through the Siskiyou winter for a cause that they passionately believed in.

Train Robbery on Siskiyou Mountain – October 11, 1923:

Left behind by a restless father and always searching for an easier life, three young Deautremont men sought a way to strike it rich in one lucrative event. Two of the brothers were Ray, impatient with education and hard work, and his twin, Roy, who went to Chicago in an attempt to join big-time gangsters. When those ventures proved unsuccessful, Ray and Roy decided to return to Oregon where their father was living with his new family. They looked for get-rich-quick possibilities and finally decided on robbing the Southern Pacific train nicknamed the 'Gold Special' during the years when it did, indeed, carry gold from the mines. They heard rumors it would be carrying a shipment of cash as well as gold, and began plotting an elaborate plan which would include an escape on the Pacific Highway. To make their plan work, they recruited their younger brother, Hugh, to the scheme.

The brothers knew the train would need to slow in order to complete a brake test shortly after it came out of Tunnel 13, below the Siskiyou Summit, so it would be easy to get on board. They sought out nearby hiding places in the woods, scouted the area, stole dynamite at a construction site, purchased a car and finally settled on the date of October 11, 1923, for the robbery.

On that date, just past the railroad community of Siskiyou on the Oregon side, Roy and Hugh jumped on the train. Ray waited at the south end of the tunnel with the dynamite. Roy and Hugh climbed from the baggage car, over the tender, and dropped into the engine cab. Hugh ordered the engineer, Sidney Bates, to stop the train near the tunnel exit. The twins, knowing little about dynamite, packed all the dynamite against the mail car with the mail clerk, Elvyn Dougherty, inside. The explosion blew away much of the car, set it on fire and killed the mail clerk. The twins couldn't see into the car and they couldn't get the train moved out of the tunnel because of the damaged car. The brakeman who walked through the thick smoke was shot by Ray and Hugh and then they shot the fireman, Marvin Seng, and Bates, the engineer.

The four murders outraged the railroad, the town, the state and the federal government. The brothers had planned to use the paved Pacific Highway to escape in a car they had purchased and later hidden. The robbery went so badly and the manhunt was so large, however, they didn't dare use the highway. The three killers found their way to one of their temporary hideouts under a fallen tree and hid for several days while a huge manhunt was conducted by the federal government, Oregon National Guard troops, railroad workers and a local posse. Hiking through the forest and over the mountains to California, they nearly starved to death in their escape. They then divided up, agreeing not to contact each other for a year so as to avoid being caught. The brothers then slipped away with no supplies or money.

It was four years before Hugh was located. He had joined the military and was serving in the Far East. Hugh's trial, held in Jacksonville, was underway by the time the twins were arrested in Ohio a short time later. They were all found guilty.

Roy had a mental breakdown and died in the State Hospital in Salem. Hugh was paroled in 1958, but died of cancer soon af-

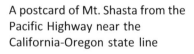

A postcard of Mt. Shasta from the Pacific Highway near the California-Oregon state line

ter. Oregon Governor Tom McCall commuted Ray's sentence in 1972 and Ray died in 1984.

The tunnel involved is still visible and frequently visited by hikers and sightseers."

PACIFIC HIGHWAY - A DREAM COME TRUE

In 1905, the first vehicle registrations were due and payable at the rate of $3 for a one-time charge.

In 1910, California, Oregon and Washington agreed on the need for a road connecting the three states. Oregon formed the State Highway Commission at the state level, but provided no state money. Each county was to do its own financing.

In 1911, the first annual vehicle license renewal began. The revenue that it generated was to be placed in the General Fund and dedicated to road-building and maintenance.

On October 17, 1911, *The Oregonian* newspaper reported a meeting of some fifty people, primarily from the California State Highway Commission and Siskiyou County Good Roads advocates from Ashland and Medford. The group, including the mayors of each city and members of the Jackson County Court, met at the historic old Cole's Station, just over the California state line. A banquet was spread under the trees. Speeches were made promoting the building of a road following the old pioneer highway linking the two states. In that article, it states,

"The Jackson County officials promised the Californians to begin the building of a permanent highway across the Siskiyous from the California line through

---

"Definite word has been received that the survey of the Pacific Highway connecting with the new Jackson County road at the state line had been accepted by the California State Highway Commission and that work would begin at once so that both roads can be opened simultaneously. It is planned to have the Tri-State Good Roads Association meet in Medford at this time. The Governors of California, Washington and Oregon will be invited and a banquet will be given on the crest of the Siskiyou at midday.

"For many years, the present toll road over the Siskiyou, rough-surfaced, with a maximum grade of from 25 to 30 per cent, with many dangerous curves and chuck holes, has been an effective barrier against tourist travel by auto between the two states. The new road will let down the gates. It is estimated the tourist travel in 1916 alone will repay the people of Jackson County for voting the $500,000 bonds.

"The maximum grade on the new road will be but 6 per cent, open curves will have a radius of 100 feet and closed or blind curves 200 feet, so that at no point in the road will an approaching team or auto be hidden from sight at a dangerous proximity..." **The Sunday Oregonian, Portland, November 30, 1913.**

The construction of Pacific Highway through the Siskiyous. *From the collection of Ben Truwe*

the Rogue River Valley to the county boundary on the north not later than June of the next year. This announcement was met by cheers from the Californians."

In 1913, the Oregon State Highway Department was created by the State Legislature to "bring Oregon out of the mud." At the time, there were only 25 miles of paved roads in the entire state.

In 1919, the first gas tax of one-cent per gallon was levied against Oregon drivers.

Jackson County, including Ashland and Medford, was the most eager of the Oregon counties for the highway connection south. They needed to end their isolation from markets in California. Landowners were required to donate one day in labor for each $1,000 in property value. In addition, day-labor from prison inmates was also added. To accomplish their goals, they finally passed the first bond issue in Oregon to raise money for road construction. Since the funds statewide were

Pacific Highway at the Oregon-California line, 1932. *Courtesy of Gerald W. Williams Collections, Special Collections & Archives Research Center, Oregon State University Libraries*

The maintenance shops on the Siskiyou Pass. *Courtesy of Arlene Poole Cox*

raised county by county, the progress was uneven.

The first stretch, over the Siskiyous, was prepared and graveled as a fifteen-foot-wide road in 1915, then paved over with concrete during the next two years. It generally followed the route of the Southern Pacific Railroad, which had been finished in 1887, and crossed it twice, over two viaducts. That early road connected Oregon to California and was part of the Pacific Highway, heavily promoted by millionaire Sam Hill, an important enthusiast of good roads.

By 1920, the Pacific Highway through Oregon had 327 paved miles, 18 under contract to be paved, 51 being planned and 14 miles of short gaps where grading changes needed to be done or where bridges were needed. It was also decided that enforcement was needed to ensure weight limits were met, to close the road if there was a need and ensure the driving rules were obeyed.

Also in 1920, driver's licenses were required. In order to qualify, the driver had to be at least 16 years of age, have five days experience operating a motor vehicle. The license cost 25 cents and was valid for life.

That same year, the first Department of Motor Vehicles branch office opened in Portland.

The State Traffic Force, the forerunner of the Oregon State Police agency, was created in 1920 and enlarged in 1921. In that year, the officers helped drivers in 715 wrecked vehicles statewide, but no accident reports were required.

In 1923, the Pacific Highway over the Siskiyou Pass was kept open during snowy winters by a crew of two men operating a 10-ton tractor equipped with a 12-foot moldboard snowplow.

By 1926, the state had decided that having its own equipment on-site and doing its own maintenance was practical. Six maintenance patrols with equipment and sheds were provided and houses for a foreman and helper and their families were provided in isolated areas. They were rented to the workers at a reasonable rate in order to cover the expense to the state.

By 1926, the eleven miles of the Pacific Highway over the Siskiyou Mountains were being kept open with a truck plow and a five-ton tractor with a rotary plow.

In 1926, the road went from being state-funded Pacific Highway to U.S. Highway 99 with a promised infusion of federal money.

The Siskiyou Summit with the former Richfield station at left. Elevation 4,522 ft., 1932. *Courtesy of Gerald W. Williams Collections, Special Collections & Archives Research Center, Oregon State University Libraries*

However, all the Federal highway road work was to be under the supervision of the state. Plans could be made for a much-needed major repair and realignment. The decision was made to abandon the old route (Old Highway 99S) and build a new road a little higher on the mountain.

Automobiles were not the only means of transportation gaining in popularity in the early part of the 1900s. After World War I helped to define the airplane's advantages in not only warfare, but as a means of travel, its many uses began to catch on in the private sector. World War I aces returned to the U.S., inspired with a love of flight, and their visions for the uses of the airplane soon caught on with investors and others who could see its potential.

The Richfield station and the Tower of Lights at the Siskiyou Summit Lodge. *From the collection of Ben Truwe*

Inspection of aircraft was added to the duties of the newly-formed Oregon State Traffic Force, the forerunner of the Oregon State Police, in about 1921.

During the mid-1920s and 1930s, when the airplane first became an obsession with the public; when distance and endurance records were constantly being reset and Charles Lindberg was the national hero, the Richfield Oil Company of California came up with an advertising scheme called the "Lane of Light." It not only provided a valuable service to automobile drivers, but to private pilots, as well. At that time, it was common practice for pilots of those early planes to follow highways and railroad lines, using them as their main means of navigation. The noses of the early planes were so long, however, the pilots could not see over them, so it was necessary to look down over the side door. Radar and guidance systems were a thing of the future, so they had to "fly by the seat of their pants." It was during this time that U.S. Highway 99 became the main aviation flyway in Oregon.

The Richfield gas stations were spaced less than 100 miles apart along U.S. Highway 99, so automobile drivers would be approaching the next station when their fuel gauges were nearing empty.

The stations were comfortable, almost luxurious, and the service was exceptional.

Near each of the buildings, a 125-foot steel tower was assembled. Each individual tower had a blinking beacon on top that spelled out the name of its location in Morse code. In addition, neon letters were placed on one side of the tower spelling "Richfield," and on the opposite side was the name of the town nearest to its location. Some of the properties had airfields for small planes to land and hotels were planned for others... some had both. The company's plan was to make these sites a small community in themselves. Richfield owned them, but generally, they did not operate them. In most cases, they were leased to local businessmen.

In California, most of the stations were built in the Mexican stucco style, but from Mt. Shasta north, they were of the Norman-style with a tower and peaked roofs.

"Huge Beacon to Be Constructed." *Ashland Daily Tidings,* **June 20, 1929:**

"Mr. and Mrs. W.B. Norris, proprietors of the Summit Ranch Lodge and Service Station, located on the Pacific Highway on the summit of the Siskiyou mountains, have lately leased the service station and garage to the Richfield Oil company of California. The company will install attractive improvements at once, and a force of workmen has already commenced work upon them. A steel tower, 125-feet high, will be erected, electrically lighted, displaying a huge beacon on its top and illuminations on the sides and will advertise the company. The old service station and garage will be torn down and in their stead, attractive up-to-date buildings will be erected, displaying for sale all types of

The Summit Ranch Lodge on the Siskiyou Pass. The sign at the right says, *"Highest Point on Pacific Highway. Shell Gasoline & Motor Oil" Courtesy of the Peter Britt Photograph Collection, Hannon Library Special Collections, Southern Oregon University*

The Summit Ranch Service Station. *From the collection of Ben Truwe*

Richfield products. When completed and ready for business, the new station will be one of the finest and best equipped on the Pacific Highway between Canada and Mexico.

"Across the highway from the station, Mr. Norris will operate a confectionary store, lunch counter, and tea room for the accommodation of tourists."

That Summit Ranch Lodge station was the first Richfield to be built at the top of the Siskiyou Summit after U.S. Highway 99 crossed into Oregon, but it was not the first built in Oregon. Both Grants Pass and Roseburg stations preceded it.

With construction on the Summit beginning in 1929, and completed in early 1930, the station featured elaborate restrooms with a lounge, a well-equipped salesroom and a large and well-landscaped parking area.

Unfortunately, the Depression sent that division of the company into receivership and many of the stations that were already built went into other uses. The one at the Siskiyou summit closed after a relatively short time.

Farther down the mountain, close to where the Dollarhide Toll Road had been, Dudley Dollarhide opened a service station that did a good business for twenty years.

The first unit of the new road being built to replace the old Pacific Highway route, Wall Creek to Torrent Creek, was started on October 1933. Seven years and fourteen separate contracts later, a sixteen-mile stretch of the highway was finished between the California border and Ashland.

The original Summit Ranch Lodge Richfield Station was one of the buildings lost to a major rebuilding of the road that took place in 1940. The construction made a deep cut in the roadbed in order to realign the highway. So much dirt and rock were removed at the summit that the road was lowered by 47 feet and the new high point of the summit was a short distance to the south of the re-aligned highway.

The Summit Ranch Lodge itself was rebuilt, more in the style of the Richfield Stations, and it included a gas station on the new, lower summit. It offered comfortable beds and good meals and operated successfully until Interstate 5 was being constructed in the late 1950s.

One of the popular truck stops/cafés along the old Pacific Highway was Ruby's Kitchen. The first realignment of the highway caused Ruby's Kitchen to be moved from the summit closer to where the exit to Mt. Ashland is now located.

Called "a greasy spoon" in a 2009 *Medford Mail Tribune* article, the restaurant burned to the ground on August 13, 1955. Guy Parker was one of the wildlands' firefighters for the Oregon Department of Forestry at its Table Rock Road station at the time. He told about being the only responder to the fire call. After receiving the call, a crew of three headed out in their early-1950s pumper truck with a heavy load of water. They had to travel from Medford to the scene of the fire on the Siskiyou Pass. It was slow-going and by the time they arrived, *"Ruby's Kitchen was history."*

Another popular stop for some refreshments over the years was, and is, Callahan's, an historic restaurant and lounge.

Callahan's Siskiyou Lodge was built by Don Callahan in 1947.

According to the Callahan website:

"In April 1964, the original Callahan site was condemned for the new Interstate 5 right-of-way. Not wanting to be out of business, Don bought a larger piece of land a short distance up the highway below the

summit of the Siskiyous and reopened in July 1965. The site is actually a part of the old village of Siskiyou."

That building was destroyed by fire in August 2006, and a new lodge was built on the site at Exit 6 from Interstate 5.

Much of the original Pacific Highway/ U.S. Highway 99, going north into Ashland, has been buried under Interstate 5, but there are a few remnants. For those interested in history, beautiful forest scenery or the way the road was constructed, a six-mile section of the original road, used as a stage road from 1857 to 1915, is still in use by private residents and tourists.

From Interstate 5, take the Mt. Ashland exit, cross under the freeway to the east side and you will be driving on "Old Highway 99S" also known as "Old Siskiyou Highway," (Oregon 273). The sometimes curvy drive includes peeks into the entrance to the Dollarhide Ranch, where the Dollarhide toll road, bought from the Applegate family, originated. The road then takes you over the Steinman Bridge where the road loops back over itself, along the old stagecoach road and past the former Barron's Stage Stop, where the Applegate wagon train came off of the mountain.

"End of the Road" at Emigrant Lake. *Courtesy of Tim McCartney*

The "Loop the Loop" of the Pacific Highway through the Siskiyous known as the Steinman Bridge, 1932. *Courtesy of Gerald W. Williams Collections, Special Collections & Archives Research Center, Oregon State University Libraries*

The road eventually ends at Emigrant Lake, southeast of Ashland, where it now connects with Highway 66 (Green Springs Highway), the early route to Klamath Falls. The original roadbed of Old Highway 99S, however, continues straight into Emigrant Lake and now lies at the bottom of the man-made body of water.

Emigrant Lake itself was created in 1926, by the building of a federally-approved earthen dam by the Talent Irrigation District and others. Some landowners were forced to relocate at that time and then again when the lake was enlarged in 1960. The second time, many of the old pioneer gravesites also needed to be moved.

At the junction of Old Highway 99S and Highway 66 was the Junction Service Station and Garage belonging to Clyde Caton. He also owned the biggest and best wrecker anywhere closer than San Francisco. It was sent for anytime there were serious problems on the Siskiyou Pass. A small community of businesses was close by, including, at different time periods, a fruit packing shed, an apple press and a roadhouse known as Klamath Junction Café, later known as the Dutch Mill. It was a dance hall and a Shell gas station. Beyond, there were apple orchards, a small air field leased by the city of Ashland and a lot of empty land and rolling hills.

The combined road, at the outskirts on the south end of Ashland, passed farms, a dairy, the Oak Knoll Golf Course and small rural properties including the old Mountain View Cemetery. Closer to town there were a few small businesses, and later, a small mall with a grocery store that was frequented by college students as well as locals.

Today, Old Highway 99S, joined with Highway 66, enters Ashland on Siskiyou Boulevard, in front of the Southern Oregon University Campus.

The New U.S. Highway 99 Route

The 1940s alignment of U.S. Highway 99 came down by Callahan's new location and to the west with fewer curves. That road to the summit is still accessible if you take Exit 1 to Mt. Ashland, but it does not go through into California. Going down toward Ashland, from Callahan's and the maintenance shed, much of Highway 99 is now buried by Interstate 5. It passes forested mountain slopes and scattered residences until the south Exit 11 into Ashland.

From that point, Highway 99 reappears as it approaches the more level suburb of Bellview on the outskirts of town.

ASHLAND MILLS / ASHLAND

In the days before the highway, after leaving Kingsbury's Soda Springs, the stagecoaches headed for the Ashland Mills Station, aka the Ashland House. There was neither a stage facility or barns, but it provided an overnight rest stop for the passengers. It was the earliest hotel built on the route and was owned and operated by Eber Emery.

Ashland, at the base of the Siskiyou Mountain and on the California-Oregon Trail, began as an agricultural settlement. The early emigrants found the primary requirement of water for power and irrigation made the location desirable. The settlement was first named Ashland Mills for its grist, wool and sawmills powered by Ashland Creek. The mills and the crops planted by the early settlers supplied the necessities for the gold miners who had flooded into nearby Talent and Jacksonville in the 1850s.

Those settlers brought with them knowledge and cultural beliefs from the areas they left behind. That knowledge and the experiences they brought with them allowed them to make new homes and create livelihoods as well as build a new society, often very different from what they had left. None of it was begun or left behind without strife.

During the Civil War, when the regular army was pulled away from duty protecting the Oregon settlers from the natives, the governor of Oregon, John Whiteaker, raised a cavalry to escort emigrants on the Oregon Trail and protect miners in Eastern Oregon. The men were paid wages and, in addition, received 160 acres of land at the end of their three years of service. Many of the men deserted to become rich in the mine fields. The only soldier whose desertion wasn't later pardoned was the one who also took his government-issued mount with him.

John Marshall McCall, a captain in the Oregon cavalry was an Oregon pioneer of 1851. After the war, McCall founded Ashland Woolen Mills and the Bank of Ashland. He was later appointed brigadier general of the Oregon Militia, and is buried in the Ashland Cemetery.

The settlement grew and the "Mills" was dropped from the name in 1871, when the Ashland Post Office was established. More businesses were developed to meet the needs of the settlers and the town was incorporated in 1874. Ashland became a stopping point on the California & Oregon Stage Co. route when it opened, so a small hotel was built to give respite to the stage passengers.

In 1883, passengers could cross the country from the East Coast to San Francisco, California, by rail, but still had to transfer to a stagecoach to come north into Oregon. The new Southern Pacific Railroad line connected in Ashland with a golden spike ceremony in December 1887.

The railroad in Ashland became a major employer and a whole new neighborhood developed near the track, station and roundhouse. In Ashland, the railroad district ran almost parallel to Siskiyou Blvd./U.S. Highway 99, covering several blocks north between the tracks and the highway. It included housing for employees and businesses needing to be near the tracks.

"Early Ashland Railroad Story" by Jo-Brew:

"During my research of the Ashland area, I was told the following story, but I was never able to document it, so it's being used here as an 'It was told to me' story and can hopefully be verified by other researchers...

"The Southern Pacific Railroad built a large dining room in Ashland for riders on its new passenger trains. At the stop in Ashland, before the long ride through the Siskiyous, the passengers disembarked and went to the dining room for a very formal, but quick, dinner. The pictures that I have seen show that all of the waiters and helpers were black. I know this had to be before 1926, because the regular passenger trains no longer went through Ashland after that, but I was confused because Ashland had a strict 'Sundowner law,' even in 1950. Finally, an acquaintance told me that the railroad brought the help in daily, but they stayed overnight in a railroad car parked on a spur just outside of town."

Ashland Academy, Ashland College and Normal School, Southern Oregon Normal School, Southern Oregon College of Education, Southern Oregon College, et al.

Vitally important to Ashland and Southern Oregon is the college that, with many names, has traversed a rocky road through its history since it was established in 1872. Originally the Ashland Academy, founded by Rev. Henry Skidmore of the Methodist Episcopal Church, it was renamed the Ashland College and then, by 1879, the Ashland College and Normal School.

The State of Oregon, however, did not provide any funding for it despite its being named as an official normal school under the system. Without funding, it closed in 1890. The school was moved to a new site under the sponsorship of a Methodist group in Portland and by 1892, it became the Ashland Collegiate Institute.

In 1895, the school once again changed its name to the Southern Oregon Normal School and was awarded full state funding in 1899 until the funding was pulled in 1901 and the school once again was closed. During this period, the editor and driving force of the Portland *Oregonian* newspaper, conservative Harvey Scott (brother of Abigail Scott Duniway,), was one of the most influential leaders in the state. He opposed public high schools in Oregon, particularly in Portland, women's suffrage, the labor movement and publicly-funded schools.

In 1926, the state reestablished South-

Stan Smith's Hamburger Stand - Ashland, across from SOU on the easement of highway. *Courtesy of the Smith family.*

ern Oregon State Normal School in Ashland at a new location on land donated by the city, where the university is currently located.

In 1932, the Oregon State Board of Education renamed the institute Southern Oregon Normal School.

In 1939, under the influence of Harvey Scott, the state board eliminated normal schools in Oregon and funding was cut. The university then received full accreditation from the American Association of Teachers Colleges. With the accreditation, Governor Charles A. Sprague signed into law the bill changing the institution's name to Southern Oregon College of Education. Because the college curriculum expanded beyond a

U.S. Highway 99, a popular route to Southern California, with Southern Oregon State College in background, 1954. *From the Smith/Edwards family collection*

teacher's college, the name was once again changed, in 1956, to Southern Oregon College (SOC) to reflect the institute's diverse degree options. In 1975, SOC was renamed Southern Oregon State College (SOSC) and finally in 1997, SOSC became Southern Oregon University.

With the arrival of the railroad, the activity in the mills and a highway in Ashland, a new prosperity led to many of the brick commercial buildings on the plaza, the development of Lithia Park and the building of the Chautauqua Hall to house summer activities.

The first grand hotel, Hotel Oregon, was three stories high and later renamed Ashland Hotel. It was built in 1888 and went through several renovations, housing taxi offices, beauty shops and other small businesses on the bottom floor, before it was demolished in 1961.

The Chautauqua revivals like those held in Ashland during the late 1800s and the early part of the 20th century, were extremely popular all over the U.S. Chautauqua was a nationwide traveling program of lectures, seminars and entertainment that originated in New York and brought the first education, entertainment and, sometimes, revivalist meetings, to rural Oregon. They existed as a way of coming together as a community. The summer encampments combined the entertainment of vaudeville with the inspired education of the Lyceum lectures for the purpose of improving the social, intellectual and moral fabric of society. Different areas hosted various offerings including lectures, vaudeville, music, drama, and even opera. They had the sociability of a county fair and the down-to-earth feel of rural environments.

The first Chautauqua meeting was in Central Point, but the next was scheduled for Ashland. A building designed to hold 1,000 people was needed. In 1893, a big beehive-shaped dome, designed without any interior

The Chautauqua camp in Lithia Park in Ashland. *From the collection of Ben Truwe*

posts or pillars was built and shingled from base to cupola. It was built in a location slightly above and bordering the undeveloped park and was connected to it by a walkway. The building was soon called the "Chautauqua Tabernacle."

According to the Oregon Shakespearean Festival website:

"Families traveled from all over Southern Oregon and Northern California to see such performers as John Phillip Sousa and William Jennings Bryan during the Ashland Chautauqua's 10-day seasons."

In 1916, it was decided the Chautauqua would make more money if the building were larger, so the original was demolished and townspeople carted it away in pieces. It was replaced in 1917 with circular concrete walls that were topped with two wooden domes – one over the stage.

When the Chautauqua movement died out in the early 1920s, the structure fell into disuse. The dome was eventually torn down in 1933, but the concrete walls now enclose the current Oregon Shakespearean Festival's outdoor Elizabethan theater.

The Oregon Shakespearean Festival

In 1935, a young English composition and speech instructor at Southern Oregon Normal School had a vision. Angus Bowmer convinced the city to include a three-day festival of Shakespearean plays as part of the annual 4th of July celebration. Using some of his students, volunteers from the town and ten men from the Public Works Administration's road crew, a stage was built in the remains of the old Chautauqua Hall. Afraid that the plays would not be successful, the celebration committee scheduled prize-fights ahead of the Shakespearean production, bringing in young men from the Civilian Conservation Corps (CCC) camp. Not surprisingly, the plays did better than the prize-fights.

Today, the non-profit Oregon Shakespearean Festival has three theatres including two indoor stages – the Angus Bowmer Theatre and the Thomas Theatre – and the famous outdoor Allen Elizabethan Theatre, which opens in early June and runs through mid-October. Each year, the organizers offer eleven different plays that include four by Shakespeare and seven by other classic writers, as well as modern and contemporary work and world premieres.

Those attending can now see up to nine plays in one week!

In 1912, businessman, Henry Enders, decided to meet all the business needs of the town in one building. He built a block-long structure with arches connecting businesses including a bank, grocery store and clothing store on the first floor with apartments on the second. It was known as the Enders Block. All of the original businesses were owned by him, but that gradually changed over time.

When Dr. Francis G. Swedenburg moved to Ashland in 1909, he sought a location for a community hospital. A private residence on Main Street was at first used, but the roof burned in 1909. It was decided to build a new structure rather than repair it. Granite Hospital, located on Siskiyou Boulevard (Pacific Highway) opened its doors in 1910, but struggled financially. In 1921, a very well-to-do businessman, Jesse Winburn, decided to retire to Ashland. He built a home for himself at the far end of Lithia Park and formed a friendship with Dr. Swedenburg. The friendship led him to purchase Granite Hospital, remodel it and give it to the city. That

The Enders Block, downtown Ashland, Oregon. *From the collection of Ben Truwe.*

hospital, located on Pacific Highway between Southern Oregon College and the Swedenburg home, was a fixture of the town. It was often in disrepair and outdated until the new Ashland Hospital was built in another location during 1960s. Both the older Pacific Highway hospital site and the Swedenburg home are now part of the Southern Oregon University Campus.

Although Jesse Winburn, "an eccentric millionaire philanthropist," contributed much to the city including a hospital, a women's center, swans for Lithia Park and numerous small projects, he continuously fought the rules pertaining to his own behavior. He owned an upscale cabin behind Lithia Park on Ashland Creek which happened to be the source of Ashland's water supply. He was constantly cited for fouling the water with garbage, allowing his livestock free access to the stream and fishing in the town's water supply. After about two years' of conflict with the city leaders and becoming disenchanted with the way that the Ashland Development Commission, which he founded, was being run, he sold his house and property on Ashland Creek and moved from the area.

Bert Greer came to Ashland in 1912, bought the newspaper, *The Tidings,* changed its name to the *Ashland Weekly Tidings* in 1919, and immediately expanded it to a daily which was then called the *Ashland Daily Tidings*.

Upper intake for Ashland water works, 1915. *Courtesy of Gerald W. Williams Collections, OSU Special Collections & Archives; Rogue River Valley album*

Ashland had a natural asset not common in many early settlements – it was rich in mineral waters, both sulfur and lithia.

Bert Greer began promoting the idea of turning the town into a commercial health spa like ones in New York and Carlsbad, Germany. The idea caught hold. The lithia-laden water was there and could be piped to town if the voters would pass a bond issue. Voters agreed and taxed themselves to pipe the water to covered gazebos in the undeveloped park in 1914.

In addition, the Ashland Springs Commission paid $250 to secure the title from a Mr. Berkley for the Berkley Hot Sulphur Springs property located south of town.

Lithia Park

A ninety-two-acre, free auto camp was opened in 1915 for people attending Chautauqua revivals or other activities in hopes of attracting tourists from the new Pacific Highway on their way to the Panama Pacific Exposition in San Francisco.

John McLaren, superintendent of San Francisco's Golden Gate Park, was retained to develop landscape plans, and two local men, Gwin Butler and Domingo Perozzi, added additional land, funds, a statue of Lincoln and a fountain that were dedicated to the park in 1916.

In the 1920s, the plans for the development of a hot spring resort to be built in Lithia Park with private money had waned, but there remained places to walk, picnic, and even a camp. It also had a community store and activity rooms, and as many as 16 cabins were eventually built with common restrooms.

During the Great Depression, Chester Corey, a young graduate of the Oregon State College Landscape Architect program was desperately looking for steady work. He'd worked at Lambert Garden in Portland, but

Lithia Park, Ashland, 1923. *Courtesy of Gerald W. Williams Collections, OSU Special Collections & Archives Commons*

Lithia Park, Ashland, 1944. *Courtesy of Gerald W. Williams Collections, Special Collections & Archives Research Center, Oregon State University Libraries*

Downtown Ashland.
Courtesy of Tim McCartney

was laid off when they were out of money. He had been working at the Mt. Lasson National Park in California, planting annuals on a temporary basis, but his wife was living with her parents in Oregon. On his way for a weekend visit with his wife, he stopped in Ashland to check on an opening for an assistant park supervisor's job. He was immediately hired. His job was to enlarge Lithia Park, building it into a mostly-undeveloped canyon, using John McLaren's original plans.

Corey had no money and no staff. He began by doing everything including cleaning restrooms. His main equipment was an old truck. He scouted the watershed for trees three feet tall that he could move in and plant, adding whatever he could find. Somehow, he held the old dump truck and the park together. He eventually got some help from a few Works Progress Administration (WPA) workers so they could add a water system, build bridges, waterfalls and rapids, plant roses, create a nursery, a playground and even a zoo. He and Ashland developed one of the most beautiful parks in Oregon.

"Living in Lithia Park" by Jo-Brew:

"In 1959, my husband, Ken, needed to attend summer school in order to finish his Masters program. We would not be going back to Grants Pass in the fall, so we needed summer housing. A posting at Southern Oregon College led us to an opening in Lithia Park. Way at the back end of the park, past the zoo and tennis courts, where a free campground had once been, there were still two or three small cabins and an office/store combination. In addition, a good-sized mobile home had been brought in and was for rent.

"We stored our belongings in my parents' garage and moved in, much as if we'd been staying in a motel. Ken drove to the other end of town for his classes, I typed his thesis and spent most of my time with the children.

"With a seven-year-old boy and a girl, twenty-two months younger, it seemed ideal for us. We had a park to live and play in. There was a creek just feet away from our door, a small zoo a little farther away, a duck pond and a playground within walking distance. The children seldom actually walked anyplace, but there were hills to climb and paths to run on. Very few other people walked through the open space, but friends and my family came up to visit once in awhile.

"One day, after we'd been there awhile, my son came in from his first outside visit of the day and said there was another boy staying in one of the cabins. The next information that I got was from the boy who said his mother was ill and needed a glass of water. I was hesitant, but went to check. From the open door, I could tell he was right – more than right – she was delirious and bent backward on the bed.. I went to the office and assured them a doctor was needed in a hurry. The family had come in during the night as the father had a job and was to report in the early morning.

"We watched the doctor come and then the ambulance which took her to that old and 1920s Granite Hospital. It wasn't long before there were other people there to see us, including the Public Health Department. I had suspected that she might have the dreaded polio, but I was wrong. It was meningitis, I was told, as they posted quarantined signs on our door and gave us the sulfa medication and instructions. The next two weeks weren't so much fun, particularly as our little Melissa had a low-grade temperature and a slight rash for a few days. It cleared up on its own since no medical personnel were eager to break quarantine. We had friends who came to celebrate when the quarantine ended and we were able to go back to our normal routine.

"Living in Lithia Park was an adventure worth having even with a time period of being confined in the middle."

The Pacific Highway had been widened to 16 feet and paved by the 1920s as automobile traffic increased. For the City of Ashland, 1926 brought several major changes. The Pacific Highway became U.S. Highway 99 and brought an infusion of federal money for needed upgrading.

About this time, the Southern Pacific Company also opened a new main railroad line, called the Natron Cutoff, from Eugene to Oakridge and then through Klamath Falls (then called Linkville) to California. That moved many of the railroad activities and eliminated many Ashland jobs. It also eliminated much of the business from tourists heading to California. Many of the railroad families were forced to leave to find work and the empty homes and businesses in that area increased.

Passenger and freight trains continued to run up and down the line between Portland and Ashland to serve the needs of Oregon

Ashland Railroad Yard. *Courtesy of Tim McCartney*

Roy Frazier, standing next to the Ashland school buses, was the owner/bus driver for the school district for many years. *Courtesy of Arlene Poole Cox*

until 1955. The trip took 14 hours, stopping at every small town along the way. As one train went north, the other came south. Each was composed of a combination of a mail car, baggage cars, coaches, a dining car and a Pullman sleeper. The engine required a turn-around in Ashland and in Portland. As the train moved south, freight cars were left at Salem, Albany, Eugene, Roseburg, Grants Pass and Medford. These would be picked up the next day. One crew would work from Portland to Roseburg and another crew, from Roseburg to Ashland. With increased automobile and truck travel, however, the Southern Pacific discontinued that service in 1955.

Over time, the railroad yards and most of the track have been removed, but many of the historic buildings remain.

In the 1930s, U.S. Highway 99 was widened to 22 feet as automobiles got larger and traffic increased.

"Faith Healer" by Jo-Brew:

"Many towns and cities have people who quietly have an effect without attracting a lot of publicity. Ashland was one.

"In the days before World War II, in 1932, Susie Jessel, her husband and family arrived in Ashland. She was 'the lady with the healing hands,' a faith healer. She quietly gave treatments; in time, more than a hundred a day. She never promised a cure and she did not charge, but she did wear an apron with an available pocket. People came from all over, some staying for weeks or months if they had time. They were sometimes referred by doctors when nothing more medically could be done and sometimes by word of mouth. Some were wealthy, but many were not. She evidently brought some measure of comfort and maybe acceptance and believed that 'With God, all things are possible.' When she died in 1966, her son carried on her work. When he too passed, her daughter, Alma Jefferson carried on.

"Among the permanent residents of the area, it is not uncommon to meet someone who originally arrived with family seeking Susie Jessel and any of us who settled in Ashland knew of her and her work even if we didn't understand it."

War-Time Ashland

The beginning of World War II changed life in Ashland as it did for every town and city in the country. All the available young men were mobilized. The schools made plans to care for children in the event of an air raid. Oregon Governor Charles Sprague announced plans for an enlarged Home Guard. Civil Defense workers were drilled. Auxiliary emergency responders simulated activities that would be likely during an attack. Aircraft Observation Stations were set up and manned by volunteers on a round-the-clock basis. Local ration boards were formed and ration books issued. Sugar, shoes and gasoline were rationed. Many common items suddenly became scarce – clothing, liquor, beef, coffee and cigarettes. Most production of household appliances and farm equipment was stopped and the manufacturing firms were converted to the war industry. Victory Gardens were planted. Scrap iron, fat, tin cans and waste paper were collected. Buses were crowded, passenger trains were discontinued. People bought war bonds, children saved dimes and quarters for saving stamps, and everyone paid higher taxes.

In Ashland, the golf course was closed and cattle moved on to graze the course to help the effort; the Shakespearean Festival was shut down. Many of the popular dance halls and dinner clubs were closed. Women were asked to take jobs vacated by men.

One Ashland High School graduate remembers that some of the women formed baseball teams for social contact, often taking the children along while they played.

"World War II" by Marge O'Harra, *Ashland Daily Tidings*:

"*In 1944, during the height of World War II, I was the* Ashland Daily Tidings *'star reporter... or, at least, I thought I was. Actually, I was a junior at Ashland High School who aspired to be a journalist...*

"*The Tidings' news staff during these war years was composed of the managing editor, the society editor, and the sports editor... his name was "Speed" and he was also the pressman. These three wrote all the local stories the newspaper carried... except, that is, for the 'locals,' the short paragraphs that appeared daily on the back page. This was my job.*

"*I would report to the office every afternoon after school... and take the paper and pencil to the street. I'd loop up one side of Main Street and down the other... stopping at the barbershop, the bakery and the hotel lobby where the guest register was always good for an item or two. On to Short's Drug Store, the dime store, the jewelry store, Elhart's Music store, the Second Hand Store, and work my way back down to the Plaza where Mrs. Madden, in the tire shop, usually had an item or two for me, as did Glen Simpson in Simpson's Hardware Store and Cash Perrine, proprietor of Perrine's Department Store.*

"*Locals were well-read because, as I came to realize in later years, they were just short of gossip... who had been visiting in Yreka, shopping in Medford, on a business trip to Grants Pass; who had out-of-town relatives as house guests, who was ill, who was recuperating... This was the stuff of the locals. They were AWFUL, but I didn't think so at the time. My goal was to get as many locals every day as I possibly could.*

"*The Tidings' building was on Main Street... the building now occupied by Ashland Homes Real Estate and Shakespeare Book Store.*

"*In the* Tidings' *lobby, just inside the front door, stood the teletype machine. It clattered from early morning until late afternoon as it spewed out wire service stories on long continuous rolls of yellow paper. Bells on the teletype would ring at an excitable pitch when a breaking story started to move over the wire. Television hadn't reached the Rogue Valley yet and local radio was limited to one station in Medford. The Tidings' office on Main Street was the news center for wartime Ashland.*

"*Once the editor cut a 'News Flash' off the teletype, he would post the story in a window-box fronting the street... 'Twelve U.S. Warships Sunk in Java Sea'; 'General MacArthur Flings Defiant Challenge'; 'Planes Hammer German Troops near Cassio.' It was here that people would stand in tight little knots trying to match the locale of the news with the last letter they received from a son or grandson... relative... neighbor... or friend... serving overseas.*"

"This Was Wartime Ashland" by Marge O'Harra. *Ashland Daily Tidings*:

"*The story of a small town, population 5,000, caught up in the events of a* world it scarcely knew, was a story chronicled by the Tidings during the 1940s.

"Let's go back to Sunday, December 7, 1941, the day the residents of Ashland listened in stunned disbelief to the radio announcements. On Monday, they gathered in front of the Tidings' window-box to read the headline... 'Pearl Harbor Attacked by the Japanese; U.S. Declares War.'

"Congress declared war on Japan and Japan's allies; Germany and Italy declared war on the United States. Before World War II was over, the names of more than 1,200 Ashland men and women serving in the Armed Forces would be recorded on a huge 'Role of Honor' board that stood in a vacant lot on East Main Street. Gold stars signified death; there were more than twenty. Gold stars were painted after the names of the three sons of one family. I will never forget standing on the sidewalk and watching Mr. De Mille, the sign painter, as he climbed the ladder and began to paint a gold star after the name of his own son.

"Sons, brothers, uncles, cousins began to leave Ashland as full-scale mobilization of the Armed Forces was ordered. Teachers, doctors, dentists, friends and neighbors suddenly were gone. The headlines posted in the window-box told the story: 'AHS Athlete Now Leatherneck.' 'City Recorder Takes Army Physical.' 'Minister Becomes Chaplain.' 'High School Coach Leaves.'

"Ashland made plans to care for children in the event of an air raid. It was reported that an Ashland man employed on Wake Island was a prisoner of the Japanese as the result of capture of the island. His wife and sons were in Ashland.

"On February 9, a United Press dispatch read: 'Almost every inch of the Oregon and Washington coast is defended against surprise attack Beaches, ports, river mouths, strategic military highways and airports all bloom with soldiers. Machine gun nests lurk behind innocent looking piles of driftwood. Big, nearly camouflaged, coastal defense guns are backed up by speedy mobile artillery that could rush to defend any threatened area of the coast.'

"Ten days later, a California senator said the coastal states were practically defenseless. He warned of the possibility of another Pearl Harbor on the West Coast...

"A government official predicted Japan would stage an all-out-attack on Hawaii, Alaska, the West Coast and the Panama Canal in April. Residents of a small town in California thought the Japanese were blitzing their town with poison gas when a valve broke on a chemical machine, releasing a yellow cloud.

"Oregon Governor Charles Sprague enlarged the Home Guard with units trained in blocking roads, destroying bridges and combating paratroopers.

"Ashland began to have 'war jitters.'

"Civil Defense workers mobilized. Auxiliary police, firemen, demolition squads, utilities guards, air raid wardens and other voluntary workers simulated activities that would be likely during a real attack on Ashland.

"The headlines were frightening: 'Japs Strike Hard Blow, Head For New Invasion.' 'Twelve U.S. Warships Sunk by Japs in Battle of Java Sea.'

"In an editorial, the Tidings questioned – and I paraphrase – We are losing the war. Our continent is in danger, but do we admit the possibility that one dark night a bomb may drop on our children as they sleep?... that one fine day the enemy may come marching or filtering down the street of our town?

"Shortly after the war started, the Office of Civilian Defense was created to coordinate federal, state and local civilian defense, and to train volunteers. Before the end of 1941, more than a million volunteers were enrolled nationwide.

"In Ashland, a Civilian Defense Board was set up on the second floor of City Hall. Ashland was divided into 18 zones, each organized with fire watches and wardens.

"Volunteers were trained in first aid, fire defense, gas defense and general preparedness. Several buildings were equipped as emergency hospitals. An air raid warning system of sirens was established. Specific buildings were designated as air raid shelters. In the Tidings' building, it was the newsprint storage room.

"Police organized an auxiliary force to help during a blackout or air raid emergency. School children built scale model airplanes to use in identifying various types of airplanes.

"Aircraft observer stations were set up and manned by volunteers on a round-the-clock basis. Incidentally, it was necessary to remind observers at the Hargadine Street station that freight trucks, not airplanes, shift gears on the Plaza hill.

"However, after all this 'preparedness,' the Tidings' editor was aghast when a plane hedgehopped over Ashland, skimming 50 feet over the Elks Building. Everyone did EXACTLY the wrong thing, he said. They ran out and stood in groups in the middle of the street to see what was going on. 'Had this been an enemy ship, machine guns could have filled every hospital in this area in a few seconds, or a few bombs could have blasted a toll of casualties.'

"Ration books were issued. Sugar was rationed, as was meat, canned food and butter. Automobiles were not available. Tires, tubes and gasoline were rationed. Clothing, liquor, coffee, cigarettes were scarce or not to be had. Shoes were rationed. Girdles, made of rubber, were scarce and silk stockings were not available. The raw material was used for parachute lines. One woman had her girdle patched at a tire repair shop, and fashion conscious women wore leg makeup. Ashland bloomed with Victory Gardens.

"Scrap iron, tin cans, and waste paper were collected. Passenger trains were discontinued; buses were crowded. Transportation was a problem. People bought war bonds and paid higher taxes. It was an all-out effort. 'Remember Pearl Harbor!' was the cry.

"'We shall win,' said General MacArthur, 'or we shall die.'

"Sabotage, espionage and 'fifth column' (terrorist) attacks were feared. Railroad bridges and tunnels were guarded. You couldn't go into the forest unless you had legitimate business there.

"Aliens were registered. Ashland had no Japanese residents, but feelings ran high in areas with large populations of Japanese. Before the war was over, more than 33,000 Japanese-Americans were confined to segregation centers; 17,000 were at the center in Tulelake, California.

"The Ashland Elks took part in a national inventory of manpower drive by having people fill out questionnaires that included information on their physical *condition, possession of automobiles and firearms.*

"Women were mobilized to fill positions left vacant by men who were in the military. During a house-to-house campaign, 2,000 Ashland women said they were willing to work in the fields, the orchards, packing houses, canneries. Some said they could drive trucks, operate heavy machinery, handle saw and hammer. One 92-year-old woman wrote, 'There must be something I can do.'

"On January 7, 1942, it was announced that Army construction of a camp near Medford had been authorized. Construction was estimated to employ 4,000 to 8,000 and to take from three to six months.

"The entire Rogue Valley went into a dither. Skilled workers would be needed. Housing would be needed. What about schools? Transportation? Food? Recreation?

"Ashland schools organized classes in carpentry and practical electricity. The Chamber of Commerce drew up a list of housing and organized a Fair Rent group.

"Before the rush of newcomers started, an announcement said that all residence and apartment vacancies were filled in Medford, and that only rental rooms were available. Everything that could be papered, painted, and rented was – not only in Medford, but in every community in the valley. Sheds and garages became studio apartments; spare bedrooms were listed for rent.

"Army officials said the entire valley would be declared off-limits if prices got too far out of line, citing instances of rents being boosted from $30 to $60 a month. Profiteering would not be allowed.

"Ashland, along with the other towns in the county, tried to accommodate the influx of people – first the construction workers, then the servicemen. USOs and church recreation centers fought what, at times, seemed like a losing battle as streets were filled with throngs of young men looking for something to do on a weekend pass. In Ashland, the Civic Club House across from Lithia Park served as a sort of make-shift USO.

"In June, 1944, the Second Front opened in Europe under the leadership of General Dwight D. Eisenhower. The war ended in Europe in May 1945. The Tidings printed an Extra – the 4-inch-high headline, 'VICTORY...Germany Quits' was posted in the window-box on Main Street. 'This is VE Day, the day for which the world has waited so long,' the editor wrote. 'But, VE Day will not bring loved ones home. Most will be sent to the Pacific region.'

"The Pacific war ended in August, 1945, with the bombing of Hiroshima and Nagasaki. 'The Japanese Have Surrendered!' The headline was posted in the window-box on Main Street. Tears mingled with laughter and the streets are filled with crowds as friends rejoiced with friends at the news,' the Tidings reported. 'As crowds gather, there is the noise of horns, whistles and sirens.'

"Thanksgiving services were held at the churches.

"The sons, brothers, uncles, cousins... teachers, doctors, friends and neighbors, began to return home. Life in Ashland began to return to normal.

"Vet's Village and Susanne Homes Hall were built on Southern Oregon State College campus to accommodate return-

Ashland Plaza with the "Iron Mike" or "Pioneer Mike" statue and Carter Memorial Fountain in downtown Ashland. *Courtesy of Tim McCartney*

Lithia Springs Fountain, Ashland, 1923. *Courtesy of Gerald W. Williams Collections, OSU Special Collections & Archives Commons*

"Iron Mike" in downtown Ashland, 1910. *Courtesy of Tim McCartney*

ing veterans, many of whom were going to school on the G.I. Bill. This, plus the boom in the lumber industry, was primarily responsible for a sixty-three percent population increase in Ashland. Because of the demand for lumber, more than a dozen mills operated in Ashland during the early 1950s, many of them running three shifts a day.

"World War II was not forgotten as Ashland went on to other things. The Tidings now had a city editor on staff and a reporter... and, someone else was writing the locals."

Although the Southern Oregon campus continued to grow slowly, World War II caused its attendance to drop to mostly a few women, as the men were either in the service or in wartime work, as were many of the women who normally would have gone on to college. After the war, as soon as the recipients of the G.I. Bill were able to enroll, the spread of the campus began. Some buildings were added across the highway, athletics and housing, and many more were moved up the hill behind the original campus.

According to Jo-Brew, *"The pond my family shared with the college is gone; so is the house I called home."*

Omar's Restaurant

From the south, past the Bellview neighborhood, Highway 99 passes through residences, motels, restaurants, a strip mall and then in front of Southern Oregon University campus on Siskiyou Boulevard. In 1945, Omer and Hazel Hill constructed Omar's Steak & Chicken House on the south side of the college campus on the former Berkley Hot Sulphur Springs site. They ordered the large neon sign and patiently waited for its arrival to open. It came misspelled with Omar's instead of Omer's, but they decided to go ahead and open it under that name. It became a favorite eating place for the town as well as a party place for the college. It is currently the oldest restaurant in Ashland.

A few of the Ashland men from diverse occupations and training – none of it musical – formed the Southern Oregon Scottish bagpipe band. The bagpipes and kilts were authentic, from Scotland. Before World War II, an occasional negative comment about the bagpipe band would show up in the paper, but it did get better. After the war, when some veterans were attending school and took an interest in joining, it improved rapidly. Once a few women dancers began performing with the band, the performances took on a professional quality and the band's popularity began to grow. It became famous in the northwest for its colorful performances and entertainment appeal.

Omar's Restaurant on Siskiyou Blvd. in Ashland. *Courtesy of Tim McCartney*

Even before the streets were paved, with only a few exceptions, Ashland celebrated the 4th of July with a parade on Siskiyou Blvd./ U.S. Highway 99 to begin the festivities. During the time the highway ran through the center of town, the local business people, lodge members, clubs and associations planned and prepared entries and people came from all over the area. Some were there every year and others came and went. A Grand Marshall and color guard led the parade as the entries passed by the crowds. An antique fire engine carried the Firehouse Five, local businessmen-musicians. There were floats created by local businesses and clubs, sleek horses, fire trucks, classic cars, Blue Birds, Cub Scouts, 4-H, marching groups, the

Ashland Community Marching Band, 1940s. *Courtesy of Tim (aka "Tim-bone") McCartney*

Ralph and Nureen Leach walking down old U.S. Highway 99, north towards Talent. *Courtesy of the Leach family*

Leach's Myrtlewood Manor. *Courtesy of the Leach family*

city band, the high school band and a kilted band of bagpipers, among others.

Following the parade, many of the watchers moved into Lithia Park to visit the food booths, picnic and listen to the band concert. Once or twice, a few carnival rides were set up in the parking lot across from the park. A fireworks' display in the evening was popular, but the locations changed in different years and included at Emigrant Lake, the college campus and the high school.

"The Ashland Mine" by Jo-Brew:

"Farther west than even Lithia Park there is another part of Ashland's history. In 1891, a discovery of gold was made in the hills west of Ashland, the same rich mineral belt that once ran from Yreka, California to Cottage Grove, Oregon. Both of those other cities have historic displays to show the importance of gold in their development, but Ashland was focused, very early on, in other directions. In the ten or so years I lived in Ashland, I never heard of the gold mine. One reason was probably that the mine suffered from legal problems with neighboring property owners who claimed the mine was trespassing on underground rights of their properties. Stop-work orders were issued and it was only worked in spurts as the ownership changed hands a number of times. It was still in operation when all the West Coast mines were ordered closed in 1942 as a wartime measure. One source indicates $565,000 worth of gold was taken from the mine. It never reopened."

Section 2

U.S. HIGHWAY 99 - TALENT TO GRANTS PASS

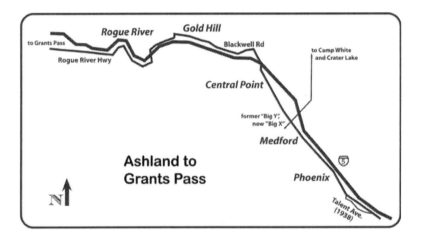

EDEN / WAGNER CREEK/ TALENT

By the time that early settlers arrived in Ashland, another settlement to the north called Talent, also called Wagner Creek, had already been established in the Bear Creek Valley. It had replaced two native villages along Wagner and Anderson Creeks.

Miners were the first whites to come to this area in their search for gold, but they didn't settle. In 1852, emigrant farmer, Jacob Wagner, was considered the first settler. He arrived from the east and filed a 100-acre donation land claim in the area called Wagner Creek, which was also known as Eden. It was Joseph Wagner who filed for the first water rights in Oregon and built the first irrigation ditch in the state at the junction of Bear Creek and Wagner Creek.

In 1853, Fort Wagner, a picket stockade, was built around Jacob Wagner's log cabin to provide protection for not only himself, but for other settlers living nearby during the Indian Wars of 1853–1856. Settlers took shelter there and sometimes wounded soldiers were carried there to be cared for. Later, when it fell into disuse, the stockade was taken down.

The supplies and mail for the miners who worked the mountainside, and later, the settlers and the stores that began to open along the route, were all brought by packers. The goods were delivered to Scottsburg by an ocean-going ship traveling up the Umpqua River and were then picked up by a packer with a string of wagons, mules or horses and taken east and as far south as Yreka.

Building the Pacific Highway with teams of horses and mules near Talent. *Courtesy of the Talent Historical Society.*

By 1856, The Oregon-California Stage Company was passing over the route from Jacksonville to Yreka three times a week on the Dollarhide Toll Road through the Siskiyous.

In the 1870s, Aaron Patton Talent bought over 100 acres of the old Wagner land and divided it into sections, creating a town site. He opened a general store on one of the plots. Eventually, other businesses opened and a small community began to take shape. For a time, the town was alternately called Wagner or Talent, but the town was officially named Talent when the post office opened in 1883.

The area was primarily agricultural and early farmers supplied the miners from Jacksonville with vegetables, wheat for flour and livestock. The Stearns family planted peach seeds which grew readily, but the fruit did not ship well. Pears and apples proved to be better for shipping, and orchards of them began to flourish. The area itself began to grow faster than even Ashland or Medford.

In 1883, the Oregon & California Railroad, which had been stalled in Roseburg for ten years, was routed through the Bear Creek Valley, but there was no siding or depot for Talent. For the first several years, the train bringing the mail would slow and a railroader would stand in the open door of the box car, call out, "Talent!" and toss the bag of mail onto a wagon waiting to deliver it to the post office.

It has been said that it was the railroad that created the town. The community leaders wanted a train stop, so they put together a plan to entice the railroad to put in a sidetrack so the train would stop for passengers. When that was accomplished, they began trying for a depot. Unlike the other communities along the main line, Talent was not an established commercial locale nor were its citizens willing to "buy a depot with grants of land."

A road crew upgrading the Pacific Highway near Talent, Oregon. *Courtesy of the Talent Historical Society.*

It was not until June 15, 1900, that Talent was provided a railroad depot when the old Medford depot was shipped south on the tracks and put in place in Talent by the Southern Pacific Railroad. A lightweight passenger car, powered by gasoline, ran on the tracks between Ashland and Grants Pass from 1903 to about 1907, providing minimal, but much-needed, service to Talent.

By 1903, as orchards in the area flourished, a packing house was operating in Talent, shipping out both pears and apples. By 1910, the *Ashland Tidings* reported that *"...the Talent berries and peaches bring the highest market prices in Portland; the apples and pears bring fancy prices in New*

A motor bus on the Pacific Highway between Ashland and Medford in 1915. *Courtesy of the Talent Historical Society.*

York and London. Talent took the prize at the World's Fair in Seattle last year..." (*Ashland Tidings*, June 23, 1910).

In 1910, Talent finally incorporated as a city and became a self-governing community. In January 1911, a major fire broke out, destroying much of the town's commercial area. With the orchard business doing well, many of the replacement buildings were constructed with brick or concrete when feasible. These included the Talent State Bank, churches and the massive brick high school which had a separate gymnasium added later. Residences and small businesses were built better. The town embarked on a path of civic improvement, contracting and selling bonds to provide for a municipal water supply and the mains to deliver it. With private enterprise, new distribution systems for both gas and electricity were arranged; sixteen street lights were installed, sidewalks were built and selected streets were paved.

Universal Mental Liberty Hall

Convention, common in many early Oregon small towns, was often ignored in Talent.

Jan Wright, former Director of the Talent Historical Society shares the following in the extensive on-line Oregon Encyclopedia Project:

"*In the 1880s, a Universal Mental Liberty Hall was built to provide a place for debate and social gatherings. Schoolteachers Willis J. Dean, Rosa Waters, and others were intent on teaching Wagner Creek students to think for themselves and to challenge traditional notions with scientific methods.*

"*Many Talent residents practiced spiritualism, were skeptical toward conventional religions, and supported Free Thought. Spurred on by the* Talent News *in the 1890s and through the 1910s, many residents had populist and even socialist leanings. The citizens of Talent elected William Breese, by all but one of the votes cast, as the first Socialist mayor in Oregon. Shortly after women got the vote, Talent elected Leta Luke to serve as the first female city recorder. Two socially and politically savvy women, Mae Lowe and Alice Burnette, typed, mimeographed, and delivered their own publication, the* Talent News Flashes, *from 1934 to 1989. The* Talent News and Review *continues that tradition.*"

Kay Attwood, author of *Jackson County Conversations*, interviewed historian, Lewis Beeson, about the Universal Mental Liberty Hall:

The Universal Mental Liberty Hall located near Talent, Oregon. *From the collection of Ben Truwe*

"Anyone could talk on any subject they wanted provided that, after they got through, they would answer, without getting mad, any questions put to them. The audience would get the man's reply. They were probing his mind; they were learning. There was only one time the rule was ever violated.

"There was some sort of a preacher that got up there and they put the questions to him and he got mad. He walked out."

Going against convention was also illustrated by Welborn Beeson who elected to build the only octagon house ever constructed in Southern Oregon. He promoted the advantages of the shape, adding to the understanding that Talent residents didn't always follow the norm.

In 1911, the brick school building on Wagner Street was built. The present Community Hall, which had been the Talent school, became city property. The Talent Community Club was formed and, in 1918, created the beginnings of the Talent Public Library.

Commercial development continued. By 1911, the Wagner Creek Nursery Company, the Suncrest Orchards east of town, and mining and lumber projects were all underway. The Talent Coal Company was incorporated in 1913, but never developed into a major industry. The town grew with the establishment of a quality hotel, a cooperative creamery and the continued operation of the box factory and sawmill. In the summer of 1912, Dr. W.R. Bagley, formerly of Duluth, Minnesota, built the Bagley Canning Company that was financed by and on land donated by the citizens of Talent.

The Bagley Cannery dominated the commercial scene until Dr. Bagley moved the entire operation to Ashland in 1924, and left the building empty. Another blow occurred in 1927 when the assets of the Talent State Bank were purchased by the First National Bank of Ashland. Talent's only bank closed its doors.

Excerpt from the City of Talent webpage:

"The Talent area was created by floods! Talent is located on an alluvial plain, created by the deposition of soil and rock carried by meandering streams from area hillsides into the Wagner Creek valley. The result is a large area of streambed soils, wetlands, riparian woodlands, and broad floodplains. The Talent area also has high water tables that limit the soil's ability to absorb rainwater, so areas outside of floodplains are also subject to water damage from heavy rains."

The up-and-down fluctuation of the orchard industry convinced many in agricultural pursuits of the need for stable water for irrigation. The early settlers handled the collecting and saving of water on their own, but the increasing amount of agriculture in the area required more. Groups of farmers planned for an extensive irrigation system to supply their farms and orchards, but the cost was more than the farmers could afford and it was never built.

Finally, in May 1916, local landowners voted 105 to 11 to form the Talent Irrigation District. In 1917, land owners voted for a $600,000 bond to finance the project. The Talent Irrigation District began construction of dams on Emigrant Creek, Hyatt Creek and Howard Prairie Creek, creating two reservoirs, Hyatt and Howard Prairie, that are now used for recreation and stable water for irrigation. An extensive system of laterals and canals was developed. Although the District

Talent Avenue. *Courtesy of the Talent Historical Society.*

struggled financially through its early years and it later needed reorganization, the availability of a water supply still remains a major factor in the role of agriculture in the region. Today, the Talent Irrigation District supplies needed water to Ashland, Talent and surrounding areas, having created and tapped into Emigrant, Hyatt and Howard Prairie reservoirs. It should be mentioned that dry years can still create problems whenever there are drought conditions in the area.

When, in 1927, the Southern Pacific Railroad shifted its main route to Klamath Falls to avoid the steep grade of the Siskiyous, the change impacted all the trains in the southern part of the state. Talent no longer needed its depot and the building was razed.

When Oregon joined with California and Washington to plan a highway connecting the three states in 1913, it was the wagon trail and the railroad tracks that became the basis of the route through Southern Oregon. Since most of the communities and towns along the proposed route of the Pacific Highway were beginning to be settled before the road was constructed, not all "Main Streets" were on the new highway. In fact, many of the original business establishments were not. That made a significant difference. In Talent's case, the original road placement put the highway through a residential area and then into downtown.

The original Pacific Highway route as it left Ashland, heading north, continued past the turn-off to the Ashland Mine Road and Jackson Hot Springs. It then made a left turn onto Talent Avenue, only four miles from Ashland.

Older businesses along the route gradually shifted their emphasis toward automobile traffic. Blacksmiths added the repair of the new automobiles to their offerings; one church altered the way it faced; motels and auto camps were built; and restaurants opened to feed the travelers. Gasoline pumps were added to grocery stores, feed and seed businesses, and anywhere an automobile could stop. Talent Avenue was then able to service both the traveling public as well as its local customers.

In June 1936, for the second time, the question was raised of relocating U.S. Highway 99 outside the central Talent business district to avoid the steep hill into Talent. This time, in spite of support from Ashland and protests by local merchants and commissioners, the State Highway Commission made the decision to proceed, based on the advantages to the general public. The highway was moved about a block west of Talent Avenue.

Much of the downtown business was

Hotel Ames, Talent Mercantile Co. and the business block in Talent. *From the collection of Ben Truwe*

lost. Building the community once again was a slow process. Some new businesses, tourist cabins and motels, auto repair shops and used car lots developed along the new corridor, but many of the old businesses struggled. The negative impact it had on the downtown business district caused many families to leave to find work wherever they could.

With World War II looming on the horizon, more families left to find work at the Portland shipyards, leaving many vacant homes and a dwindling economy.

In 1941, the decision to build Camp White, east of Medford, resulted in a huge influx of temporary residents who managed to fill many of those vacancies, but the shift in the economy still impacted the daily life of the community.

In 1943, the Talent School District put out a desperate plea for teachers. There was a shortage because of the exodus of women, especially those whose husbands were looking for opportunities and work elsewhere.

One local woman, in particular, wasn't a teacher, but her husband was away fighting in the war, so she decided to help out. She began teaching fourth grade, but transferred to the high school in mid-year. There she taught geography, home economics and U.S. history. She also supervised a study hall and tutored students.

In times of need, communities all over the state and nation were having to "make do," as best as they could.

As the war drew to a close, Talent citizens looked toward the town's future. Plans were made for construction of a water storage system. New housing developments and other additions brought in more residents. There was a departure from the agricultural environment. Patio Village Retirement

The Talent Hardware Store. *Courtesy of the Talent Historical Society.*

Hills Mercantile and Talent Service Station in Talent. *Courtesy of the Talent Historical Society.*

Homes, built on a former orchard, was the first subsidized retirement center for low-income seniors in the State of Oregon. Mobile home parks grew in popularity, eventually providing several hundred spaces. But, there was still more to come.

"Talent Train Depot" by Jo-Brew:

"In Talent now, near the railroad tracks, an exact replica of the original train depot has been constructed. A cozy coffee shop occupies one end of the building where I stopped before visiting the Talent Historical Society Museum. While I was there, I discovered the painting by Pam Sessions that I used for the cover of my book, OREGON'S MAIN STREET: U.S. Highway 99. 'The Stories.'*"*

That area includes the Talent City Hall, the old Community Hall, built as a school in 1899, and the Talent Historical Society Museum. The old Community Hall served as a school house until 1911. It has also been used as a meeting site for groups, a city hall, a fire house, a police station, a library, a dance hall, a movie house, a place for church meetings, entertainment for the Federal Relief Camp and almost anything else the public needed it for.

On Talent Avenue, which is also the original Pacific Highway, the old Talent Feed Store has become the Camelot Theater, bringing live theater into town, and in 1945, Skeeters and Skeeters Sawmill was built on the corner of Valley View and U.S. Highway 99.

In 1956, Bear Creek flooded and washed away part of the new U.S. Highway 99 that didn't go right through the business district of town.

Driving on the current U.S. Highway 99 through Talent, one icon still remains. Jim's Better Buys; Used Cars and Wrecking Yard, owned by Jim Walker, has a 1959 Fiat 500 mounted atop a column of old steel wheels.

Another Talent icon from the past was Tig Dunham. He was a believer in the First Amendment rights of free speech and practiced his beliefs by posting large signs indicating his opinions – often both insulting and profane. Pictures of his signs often show up in stories about Southern Oregon or Talent.

On Columbus Day, October 12, 1962, many of the valley women were at their annual jobs in the packing houses. Suddenly, the power flickered and then went out. They were given instructions to close up for the day and go home. It wasn't until they stepped outside that they realized a terrific windstorm had come up. As they ran to their cars, they dodged flying debris. Signs from buildings, trees and power lines were blowing down, making the drive dangerous. Many of the mothers needed to get to neighboring communities to check on their children and most found the schools closing and parents arriving for pick-up.

In some areas, heavy hailstorms began with marble-size hail pounding down and for many of the women, the drive home itself was dangerous, weaving around trees and debris in the road. Not many had power when they finally reached home, but shelter of any kind was welcome.

The historic storm affected all parts of Oregon along the Highway 99 route that year and other local stories are scattered throughout this book.

On U.S. Highway 99 Toward Phoenix

In 1858, James V. Amerman purchased 320 acres of prime farm property, just south of Gasburg (Phoenix) from the original donation land claim owner. When the daily Oregon-California Stage began running in 1860, James opened for business as a contracted stage stop. Amerman's had no accommodations for overnight stays, however. Those travelers who were wanting to spend a night on the route had to travel another mile north to Oatman's Hotel in the town of Phoenix. It was owned by Harvey Oatman and operated during the 1860s.

James Amerman died in the 1870s, and his widow later married the Yreka-based superintendent of the stage company, Colonel William S. Stone. They raised fine horses on the farm and kept the stage station going.

At the end of the staging time in 1887, the Stones sold their property to Jackson County.

Jackson County Poor Farm

The original Amerman property later became the Government Extension Station and housed the buildings of the Jackson County Poor Farm. Many of the county's "down-and-outs" lived there, beginning in 1907, and into the early 1950s.

Like many poor farms in the country, it was a working farm. Many, but not all, of those who lived there were in their 70s or older. A lot of them had been miners or common laborers; some were just alone in life regardless of their former occupation; some were widows or widowers with no other place to go. They had no family to live with and no other place to live.

Pacific Highway between Talent and Medford. *Courtesy of the Oregon Department of Transportation (ODOT) archives*

The Jackson County Poor Farm was a self-sustaining farm where they raised all their own fruit and vegetables, eggs and meat – beef, sheep, pigs and chickens. They butchered what they needed and nearly everything was produced on the farm. It offered a healthy environment in more ways than one. The residents contributed work to the extent of their abilities – whether it was in the garden, in the maintenance shop or in food preparation. The big two-story house where they lived had rooms upstairs and a big lobby. It provided them with socialization as they shared meals at the big dining table or gathered on the wrap-around front porch. There was also a small hospital for the residents who were bedridden. A small cabin from the stagecoach days stood on the property for much of the time that the County Poor Farm was in operation.

The residents could come and go as they chose or find activities that interested them. One went down to Bear Creek to pan for gold every day, others whittled or went into Medford.

Gold Mining in the Area

Excerpt from "The Gold Dividing Line" by Carol Barnett for the Jefferson Public Radio (JPR) series:

"The idea of panning gold in Bear Creek wasn't far-fetched. There was a basis for believing in the possibility.

"The old Southern Pacific Railroad line coming over the Siskiyous from Redding to Roseburg is roughly the same as the dividing line between the old and the new mountain formations. All the land to the west of the rails belongs to the 'old formation.' The land to the east has been covered and disturbed by volcanic action.

"It is in the old formation that gold is found. Intelligent miners caught onto this and began to search along this division. Gold was found as far north as the Umpqua River. The rivers themselves carried particles of gold that had been washed from the gold-bearing quartz rock at higher elevations.

"Other things were found at this joining of the old and new mountains including fossilized mastodon bones, elephant fossils and fossils of sea life. This proved that there was an ocean shore in this area long before the mountains were formed."

GASBURG / PHOENIX

In the early 1850s, Samuel Colver settled a donation land claim on the site where the present town of Phoenix is located and in 1854, laid out a townsite, which was at first named Gasburg. Samuel's brother, Hiram, took out an adjacent claim, as well. The curious name of the town had tongue-in-cheek origins and was only in formal use for a short time until the establishment of the post office in 1857 which was named Phoenix.

An excerpt of a book entitled, *The Phoenix Centennial History* published in 1952 that is posted on the City of Phoenix website:

The *"most credible and accepted story"* about how the town that is now known as Phoenix originally was called Gasburg: *"In the town, among a considerable number of young bachelors, there was just one young marriageable woman. Her name was Kate Clayton, who was employed by Mrs. Waite to help her cook for the men who were employed at the Lumber Mill. She was a girl about* twenty, and one of the most fluent talkers I ever met.

"As every young girl fourteen years of age and above was considered a young lady of marriageable age, and usually had a dozen or more admirers, Miss Kate, as the sole attraction of the community, was pursued by almost every single male of any age in the community. She was well able to carry on more than a dozen conversations with her admirers at once, and to put any of them in their place with fast and fiery repartee. She did all of this while continuing to cook as well as serve them meals without missing an order or step. She was given the nickname of 'Gassy Kate' because of her skill at conversation.

"When the subject of giving the town a name came up, the unanimous verdict among Kate's many admirers was to call it 'Gasburg.'"

However, another much less detailed and interesting account was published in *Oregon Geographic Names:* "It was initially known as Gasburg, allegedly for a chatty young woman who worked in the kitchen at a flour mill there."

Samuel Colver built a large plantation-style house on his donation land claim, first of logs, later adding sheathing to it with sawed lumber. It served as a refuge for his own and neighboring families from the native tribes during the Rogue River Indian Wars. The house also served as a meeting place, sometimes as a lecture hall, as a rooming house and occasionally as a stage stop.

It later served as the centerpiece of the town until it burned in September 2008. The Phoenix Museum managed to save one log from the house after the burn for display. It is much larger around than those used in most log houses built in the last century.

In 1855, a blockhouse, called Camp Baker, was erected and served to protect the settlers during uprisings by the Rogue River Indians. Nearby, during the Civil War, the U.S. government built Fort Grant which housed the Southern Oregon volunteer military recruits needed to protect the miners and settlers.

A much-repeated story that we believe had its roots in one of the 1930s *Oregon Oddity* issues tells about the paymaster at the fort who set up a side-business as a banker. Since there were no banks close by, the local prospectors, settlers and ranchers would "deposit" their gold dust and coins with him until he could take it to the bank on his next trip to town. In between trips, he kept the money and gold securely in a large iron pot that he kept buried somewhere nearby.

Unfortunately, as the story goes, he suffered a massive stroke that silenced his speech and while trying to draw a map to show where the pot was buried, he died. After his death, the camp was searched – holes were dug and the ground was probed with rods in an effort to locate the treasure-trove.

The Samuel Colver house in Phoenix, Oregon.
From the collection of Ben Truwe

The Phoenix School in about 1910. *From the collection of Ben Truwe*

If it was ever found, no one was talking and the legend is still alive and well today.

With its gristmill and wheat crops, Phoenix prospered in the 1860s. In 1884, it was connected to Portland and Ashland by railroad, and in 1910, Phoenix was incorporated as a city when apples and pears were replacing the wheat as the main crops.

As Phoenix grew, community members began to form social organizations. In 1900, the Woodmen of the World, a social and insurance organization, built a two-story building for its use. In 1931, a group of 52 charter members organized the local Grange. They met in the upstairs of the Woodmen of the World building, using an outside stairway. The lower floor was used for basketball and skating. The Grange eventually bought the building and the Phoenix Grange Hall was used by several social organizations for dinners and meetings, as well as Saturday night dances.

Like Talent, its neighbor to the south, the community of Phoenix proved to be a bit more broad-minded than some of its neighbors. In 1912, Abigail Duniway, from the Portland area, had been working with the suffrage movement for over 41 years as a publisher and writer for her own *New Northwest* weekly journal. During the course of her statewide campaign to gain women's right to vote, Abigail traveled around the state, speaking to groups – in many cases hostile ones – both men and women.

From *The Gasburg Gazette*, Spring 1914:

"During the summer of 1879, Abigail Scott Duniway, publisher of the New

The Phoenix Drug Store - Soda fountain, Ice cream and confec-tionary. *From the collection of Ben Truwe*

4th Street, Phoenix in the 1960s. *Courtesy of the Oregon Department of Transportation (ODOT)*

Northwest, *a Portland newspaper and leader in the movement for Women's voting rights made a visit to Southern Oregon, In Phoenix she was welcomed into the home of Sam and Hulda Colver, a leader in the town noted as being more liberal than many of the day. She reported her lectures there were well attended and received. Her earlier visit to Jacksonville was not so well received, eggs were thrown at her and outside the crowd burned her in effigy. She later wrote, in The New Northwest, 'Only one egg hit us, and that was fresh and sweet as it struck us square on the scalp and saved a shampooing bill.' She did go on to comment on the manners and morals of that town. She also pointed out that patience was needed, as, in her words, 'there's no form of tyranny that dies so hard as man's right.'"*

JACKSONVILLE

For the purposes of this book, we are including Jacksonville in the line-up even though U.S. Highway 99 bypassed it. Because it was such an important segment of the history of Southern Oregon – history that is very well-documented elsewhere – and because of its connection to Medford, we felt it was necessary to include it for those who wish to plan a trip along the highway. It's a town that should definitely not be missed for those who want to steep themselves in the history of the area.

The California & Oregon stage office was situated in a variety of locations in Jacksonville over the years. It was owned by the California Stage Company for overnight guests and was Western and Southern Oregon's center for staging.

In an interview for the WPA's *American Life Histories Collection: Manuscripts from the Federal Writer's Project, 1936-1940*, Benjamin Beekman told about the Jacksonville Station. He was interviewed by Manly M. Banister on July 11, 1939:

"My father, C[ornelius] C. Beekman, came west in 1850, landing in San Francisco. His father had been a contractor and he had taught his boys the trade. He found plenty of work in San Francisco and went to work at once. He came to Jacksonville in 1852, mining for a while nearby. He made quite a bit of money and sold out and commenced buying gold, which was the start of his banking business.

"Later, when the Wells Fargo express-company put in its appearance, he was appointed agent. The stage stopped at his door where all goods and passengers had to be loaded, so he worked under an advantage so far as robbers were concerned. No one knew when he was going to make a shipment of gold. Another thing to his advantage was that he never shipped gold

in the iron-bound express box. When bandits hold up the stage, it was customary for them to ask for the registered mail and the express box. My father would take an ordinary candle box, put in fifteen hundred or three thousand dollars' worth of gold, and fill up the remaining space with paper, straw, or excelsior, so that the weight of the loaded box was about equal to what it would be if it were loaded candles. This he would ship, confident in the knowledge that no highwayman would rummage around among the baggage, looking for gold in an old tallow box.

"The only time there was any danger of a hold-up was along in 1910 when the Pinkerton agency, under whose protection he had placed his bank, unearthed a plot in Portland to rob the bank. Officers stayed around across the street for several days with pistols and rifles, waiting for the would-be hold-ups to arrive, but they must have got wind the bank was being watched, for none of them ever came."

Jacksonville was the site of one of the first placer gold claims in the early 1850s. The thriving town was Jackson County's first county seat and the major financial center of Southern Oregon until the railroad chose to locate its tracks about six miles to the east, closer to where the town of Medford currently sits. Many of the original buildings in town have been preserved and in 1966, the town of Jacksonville was one of the few towns that have earned a designation as a National Historic District. The designation includes over 100 buildings.

In 2004, while roadwork was being done in the community, Chinese artifacts dating from the 1850s and 1860s were discovered, leading archeologists to believe that Oregon's first Chinatown was located there. After a 4-day dig, the scientists found broken dishes, Chinese coins, handmade bottles and pieces of opium paraphernalia there.Medford's Connection to Jacksonville: How the Railroad Defined the Area

The government agreement with the railroad stated that the railroad would be granted enough land to lay their tracks and to sell the additional for enough money to pay for materials and labor. However, the land the government owned was not in the right places to put the tracks, so it was up to the railroad to locate the land and negotiate a donation with enough extra to sell to recover the labor and material costs.

In Southern Oregon, the Oregon & California Railroad, which later was taken over by Southern Pacific, was expected to go through Jacksonville as the most settled area at the time, but the route through Jacksonville was almost nine miles farther west and would cost the railroad more to move closer to the hills rather than straight through the Bear Creek Valley. When the O&C Railroad asked Jacksonville for a bonus to cover the longer route, the request was refused, but according to Benjamin Beekman, the son of C.C. Beekman, Wells Fargo agent and banker of early historic days of Jacksonville, Oregon, there was a good reason for the refusal.

Benjamin Beekman continues his story:

"If you go into a newspaper office or pick up the usual history book, you will find that the usual reason for the railroad's passing through Medford instead of through Jacksonville is that the citizens of Jacksonville failed to gather in a bonus required by the railroad; but this is not

true at all. The railroad made two surveys, one passing through the present site of Medford (which was not in existence then), and another that passed within two and a half miles of Jacksonville. Medford is five miles distant. The present route is the longer, while the other ran along the base of the foothills It all depended on Ashland. If the closer survey was more adhered to, the line would wind up into the hills above Ashland; otherwise, on the flats below. It so happened that Ashland was placed in a strategic position to be a division point of the railroad, and this determined the survey as the one in present use. The other would not have permitted the building of roundhouses, workshops, and necessary appurtenances of a railroad division. Considering these things the citizens of Jacksonville saw it was useless to raise the money required, for the difference in a distance of two-and-a-half miles from town to the railroad, and the present distance of five miles was not enough to get fractious about. Either would have spelled doom to the town of Jacksonville, either by creating a new town (viz. Medford), or by moving the business district of the old, two-and-a-half miles to the railroad. This is the real reason why the railroad now runs through Medford instead of Jacksonville."

Deciding to bypass Jacksonville, the railroad then looked at Central Point which was a small settlement to the north where two main trails crossed, but the local farmers weren't willing to give up the particular land the railroad wanted.

Hearing this, four property owners south of Central Point got together and made an offer to give the railroad twenty acres for a depot and other railroad purposes and alternate blocks in the new 80-acre townsite to sell in exchange for the tracks and a depot. The O&C Railroad agreed and several businesses were started before the railroad actually arrived. In short order, two hotels, a few saloons, a livery stable and a dozen businesses dotted the muddy streets. The first business district grew on Front Street facing the depot. During that first year, the first church was organized, a schoolhouse was built and more. At that point, a community had been created and the railroad had potentially saleable land in the newly-platted townsite of Medford.

Even though the stage routes went through Jacksonville, a major stop for the California Stage Company and the Western and Southern Oregon's center for staging for many years, the decision made by the railroad to bypass it in favor of the Bear Creek Valley, sealed the eventual routing of the Pacific Highway through the commercial center of Medford.

MEDFORD

The early settlers in the area that eventually became Medford grew products for themselves and to satisfy the needs of miners and others in the near vicinity. Fruit, and particularly pears and apples, did very well in the sticky mud of the Medford area and could be shipped by pack train for short distances. Three months of the year, the mud roads in many areas couldn't be used at all.

Joseph Stewart

The soil of the Rogue Valley and the prospect of the completion of the Southern Pacific Railroad through Oregon and into California drew the attention of Joseph Stewart. Stewart was a fruit grower of stature and a

Four mule team on harrow on Hillcrest Orchards, Medford, 1910. *Courtesy of the OSU Special Collections & Archives Commons*

former legislator in Illinois. In 1885, the Stewart family arrived in Oregon with fruit trees and settled on 160 acres south of what is now Medford, in close proximity to the newly-laid railroad tracks and established one of the early orchards planted in the area as a commercial venture.

By 1887, the Southern Pacific Railroad had linked the Rogue Valley to the markets of San Francisco as well as Portland. Stewart named his orchard "Eden Valley" and added 100 more acres. His trees served as the budwood for the establishment of other large orchards across the Rogue Valley. By 1896, he was able to ship out 95 carloads of pears and apples.

He went on to other ventures and left such a mark on the community and the area that he has a street in Medford and an Oregon State Park near Prospect, named after him.

Harry and David

Of all the businesses that grew up near Medford, particularly along U.S. Highway 99, the one that has been a lasting presence and long-term influence on both the city and the state is Harry and David.

From the Harry and David Website:

"Samuel Rosenberg, father of Harry and David, was a successful hotel owner in Seattle, Washington, but his true love was agriculture. In 1910, he traded the luxurious Hotel Sorrento for 240 prime acres of pears in Southern Oregon's valley and named them Bear Creek Orchards after the nearby waterway.

"Following Sam's death in 1914, his two sons, Harry and David, took over the family orchard business. The brothers were schooled in agriculture at Cornell University and they put their agricultural training to good use. Harry and David decided early-on to specialize in the Comice pear for which there was a good export market to the grand hotels and restaurants of Europe. The Rogue Valley proved even better suited to the Comice pear than its birthplace in France. Harry and David named their luxurious pears "Royal Riviera" to set them apart from varieties grown elsewhere. Throughout the Roaring 20s, the fame of the Royal Riviera pears spread and business boomed.

"Then came 'the Crash' and the Great Depression, and Harry and David's affluent market vanished. There was no question that the Royal Riviera pears were unsurpassed in quality, but how would Harry and David find new buyers? Always innovating, the brothers came up with the idea of selling their pears by mail. In 1934, they made their famous sales trips to San Francisco and New York to visit the captains of industry and pitch their pears as ideal business gifts. Soon orders were rolling in. It was the beginning of Harry and David as America's premier direct marketer of fruit and food gifts."

Scattered throughout the newspapers of the period, the two names of Harry and David consistently appeared. In 1924, Harry and David Rosenberg invented a metal and canvas picking pail for pears and later became involved in some real estate development. In 1937, they announced their plan to build a plant emulating the architecture of the Chicago World's Fair. In 1938, they came up with the idea of the Fruit of the Month Club. In 1939, Harry and David launched a basket-making enterprise, and that same year, they changed their name to Holmes – that of their stepfather. In 1947, the "Tower of Treats" was introduced. Their innovations and expansions have continued and touched many in Medford and other parts of the state and they have become one of the nation's oldest catalog mail order companies.

Now the company, which is no longer owned by the Rosenberg/Holmes family, is an important and visible entity in all parts of Oregon and throughout the country. There are call centers for holiday ordering, retail outlets, and connections to international centers. The corporate headquarters and much of the production remains on Highway 99 on the southern end of Medford with a particularly nice retail outlet nearby where tours can be arranged.

In the early days, many of the orchardists in the area came together and formed the Associated Fruit organization to consolidate their interests as a group. When, during World War II, and for some time after, there were not enough local workers to harvest the fruit, they worked to bring pickers, or braceros, from Mexico. The braceros were often housed in bunkhouses or barracks at Camp White.

As discussed previously, the planned construction of the railroad through the Bear Creek Valley caused the city of Medford to

A group of Mexican braceros brought in to harvest fruit, 1945 © Thomas Robinson

The Hillcrest Orchard, 1935. *Courtesy of the OSU Special Collections & Archives Commons*

Transporting fruit in Medford's Hillcrest Orchard in 1910. *Courtesy of the OSU Special Collections & Archives Commons*

be created and platted in 1883. The town was named Medford by David Loring, the railroad's right-of-way agent. One story is that he took the "Med" from the site's location in the middle of the valley and combined it with the "Ford" derived from the nearby McAndrews Ford auto business, a half-mile north of the town. Another theory is that the "ford" part of the name was inspired by a city near Loring's home town of Concord, Massachusetts.

In was not until 1901, that the state authorized the counties to levy, annually, *"not to exceed ten mills on each $1 of assessed values on real property within the county with which to finance county road construction."*

Jackson County was the first to use the financing opportunity, as the area around Medford had the biggest need for roads. That area was mostly isolated before the railroad came through and lacked the alternatives available in other places. Portland had ocean and river ports; Roseburg could get goods in and out by connecting with the ocean-going vessels from Reedsport at Scottsburg using the old military road; Oregon City and Salem had river transport on the Willamette.

It was Medford and the area around it with its adobe, or "sticky soil," which was so good for the growth of fruit trees, but which also made transport difficult for three months a year. Raised roads were the best solution, but even those didn't make local transport possible after the rainy season started.

Just as Ashland, early on, envisioned itself as becoming a cultural center and tourist attraction, Medford turned its interest toward business and commerce. As early as 1885, the city offered incentives to businesses willing to set up there – a grist mill, a planing mill and others. It also invested in services to make it easier for the businesses to survive. Their investments included roads, a telegraph, irrigation systems, a fairgrounds and eventually the Jackson County Seat.

The first dozen businesses were set up in three months' time. It had a post office by1884, and was first incorporated as a town in 1885. It quickly became the chief trading center for the region and through an election in 1927, took the county seat of Jackson County away from Jacksonville.

When the railroad began bringing passengers into Medford, the Commercial Club, a forerunner of the Chamber of Commerce, built a special building adjacent to the depot for the display of products, investment opportunities and interesting activities in the area. Another opportunity to display the attributes of the area came up again at the Panama Pacific International Exposition, a World's Fair held in San Francisco in 1915 to celebrate the opening of the Panama Canal.

In a departure from the ordinary of the time, the County Court, aka "County Commissioners," endorsed the idea of making a silent movie – a motion picture – and appropriated $600 to make a promotional film that would show the wonders of Southern Oregon.

A local orchardist, A.C. Allen, with an interest in photography and a hand-operated Ememann 35 movie camera, became the cameraman. Attorney Holbrook Withington, who had a love for theater, was selected to direct the movie. The two prepared a screenplay that highlighted the region's resources, especially the orchard industry and the glamour and excitement of social life in the area.

The local Andrews family had operated an opera company before retirement and their daughter, Grace, a successful Broadway actress, was visiting at the time. During her visit, she met Conro Fiero who was a recent arrival and investor in nearby Central Point. Grace agreed to play the part of a visitor learning about the area, touring some of the interesting sights. During the tour, she and Conro Fiero's character, would begin a courtship. Of course, there was a rival suitor role played in slapstick style by Fletcher Fish, well known in regional theatrical circles. All of those involved were familiar with motion pictures, but none were experienced in the production of movies.

Filming began on April 3, 1915. The old Medford Golf Club was featured, as was the beautiful hillside home of George Carpenter. Some early pioneers shared their stories, schoolgirl dancers performed in butterfly costumes, a boat ride was filmed around Crater Lake, and a train robbery was staged.

The movie was a hit at the Panama-Pacific International Exposition. With the closing of the Expositon in December 1915, the movie returned home to Medford. *Grace's Visit to the Rogue River Valley* was shown in local theaters in Ashland at the Vining, in Medford at the Page and the Star. It then went home with Allen where it languished for nearly fifty years. In 1960, the film was restored and is in the collection of the Southern Oregon Historical Society.

In a WPA's *American Life Histories Collection: Manuscripts from the Federal Writer's Project, 1936-1940* interview done on February 13, 1939, Rev. W.C. Driver tells his story. His interviewer was William C. Haight:

"The early days of preaching in Oregon have been filled with pleasant memories for my devoted wife and myself. In our evangelistic work we had to travel from house to house, staying wherever we could. These visits in other homes were most trying. The usual house had about one-half dozen people in three or four rooms.

"When my wife and I would visit with the people they would have to bed-down the children on the floor. Most often my wife and I would have preferred the floor to the torturous mattresses we have had to sleep on. We were subjected to every inconvenience humanly imaginable. The food, though usually plentiful, ranged from the ghastly to the less horrible. Often I have wondered how man could live on the food I have had to eat.

"These homes we visited in were primitive in conveniences. Most of the people had a well quite a distance from the house, where they obtained water. These wells often were most unsanitary. The distance of the wells from the houses was probably responsible for the usual amount of filth that we found. Sanitation and domestic science were unheard of in those days. Most everything was accomplished in as simple and direct a manner as possible.

"Obtaining a bath was perhaps one of the hardest things to do. We usually had little privacy in these homes. Our room, when not utilized for sleeping was used, in many cases, for other things during the day. This added to the precarious task of bathing. It was a great task to bring the water from the well, find space on the stove to take the chill off the water, and then find a tub large enough to bathe in. Then barring the people from the room was the problem. Either my wife, or myself, would take refuge in the tub while the other stood guard at the door to bar the family from entering. Many, many times we mere embarrassed by interruptions – although there was little attention paid to such interruptions. To survive these ordeals of inconvenience a sense of humor was a necessity.

"Interesting in comparison to modern methods was the handling of dairy products. They would milk the cow, bring the milk in and separate the cream from the milk. The milk and cream were handled with little thought of sanitation. The products would be put in a pail and set down by a gate near the road until the mailman would pick it up.

"A modern mother would be horror-stricken if she thought her child would have to drink unsanitary milk. Then, milk was milk and sanitation was skimming the dirt off the top.

"Transportation presented a difficult problem. Particularly so during bad weather. Many, many times the mud was hub-deep on the wagon wheels, necessitating the driver and quite often the passengers got out and help the horses lift the wagon out of the mire.

"The church was usually several miles from the homes we had to stay in. This was bad because the people we were staying with would have to get up much earlier in order to get us to church. They were kind and agreeable, though, most of the time.

"Later we were rewarded for our sacrifice by an appointment as pastor in one of the railway cars operating in Oregon.

"These cars were given thrilling (sic) names: Evangel (Poetic and thrilling);

Emmanuel (God With Us); Message of Peace; Glad Tidings; Good Will; Grace (An all steel car commemorating the memory of a girl that died. Her family were extremely wealthy – to perpetuate her memory they presented the Baptist Church with this lovely car).

"The name of our car was Good Will. It was fitted out so we could seat about 100 people in it. The opposite end from the church part, was fitted up as our living quarters. This car was most convenient in living arrangements.

"These cars aided us in performing a valuable service to the isolated people of Oregon.

"In the southern part of the state there were children as old as 20 that had never heard a Christian service. They would walk miles to hear the preacher in the railway car. The novelty of the car probably attracted them as much as the religious side. Children generally, were delighted with the idea of going to church in a railway car.

"My wife and I lived in this car for 12 years. Here we developed the habit of eating only two meals a day, which is still our routine. We have breakfast at nine in the morning and our other meal at 4:30."

One of the early businessmen coming to Medford looking for opportunity was John Lawrence, a watchmaker. He and his family came by train in 1908, with all their belongings, including his tools and work bench. He opened a store on South Central Street, sharing space with the Southern Oregon Electric Company. He purchased the inventory of a local jeweler who wanted to move on for $500. That building burned, so in 1916, he opened the John H. Lawrence Emporium at another location, sharing space with a milliner. He kept building the business, offering good service and honesty.

In 1909, Medford led the world in autos per capita – one for every 30 residents. Jackson County definitely needed roads. The stretches of road between Medford and Central Point, Ashland and Medford, were the first links of the great Pacific Highway laid in the State of Oregon.

Vern Gorst

In 1910, a young man and his wife, Vern and Julia Gorst, arrived in Jacksonville with the intention of developing a gold mine. Deciding the venture was too risky, Vern withdrew from the project.

"Passenger Automobile Pays: Medford-Jacksonville Service Is Heavily Patronized." *Sunday Oregonian*, **July 2, 1911**

"An automobile passenger service has been established between here and Jacksonville by V. C. Gorst, who formerly ran a passenger launch between Port Orchard and Seattle. A round trip is made at present every hour, but so well is he patronized that Mr. Gorst says he intends to put on another machine and a truck to haul freight.

"The new passenger and freight service is in direct competition with the Rogue River Valley Railway, which for years has made only three round trips a day between the two cities. Petitions have been circulated and presented to the railway management requesting better service. When no improvement was made Mr. Gorst was invited to put on an automobile service, which he did. Since that the railway company has put on 18 trains a day."

According to Ron Bartley in his book, *Vern Gorst and The Pacific Air Transport Air Mail*:

"While living in Jacksonville, Vern recognized the need for a better transportation service from Jacksonville to Medford, a distance of about five miles. In the fall of 1910, Vern bought a new Cadillac and started a stage-line between Jacksonville and Medford. In 1911, he bought a second Cadillac and also took in Charles O. King as a partner. The new Oregon Stage Line was successful."

"Auto Stage Line to Jacksonville is Discontinued" *Medford Mail Tribune*, **May 11, 1912:**

"The Gorst auto stage line to Jacksonville has been abandoned, Messrs. Gorst and King going to Marshfield, where they will put on a similar stage line between Marshfield and North Bend. Whether someone else will put on a car or not is not known.

"The auto stage line was instituted by Gorst over a year ago and has definitely shown what an auto will do to a railroad where they are brought into competition. Gorst instituted the line with one machine, which cost him $700. Later he was forced to increase the number of machines to three, and he forced the railroad to hourly trips at half the old fare.

"When Gorst started the auto stage line the train service on the Barnum line was very unsatisfactory. Very few trips were run, the round trip fare being 50 cents. Later Barnum was forced to put his train on an hourly service and reduced the round trip fare to 25 cents. Barnum attempted at one time to run an auto stage line in competition with Gorst but failed after a month or two at it.

"It will be interesting to note whether Barnum, now that competition has been done away with, will drop back into his old habit of charging 50 cents with a service which runs according to inclination.

"Gorst in stopping says that he has a better route at Marshfield. He wishes to thank the many friends who patronized him during his operation on the local line."

An excerpt from the *Medford Mail Tribune*, August 12, 1919:

"The paving began in November 1915, and ever since its completion has been a source of delight alike to tourists and home autoists and made a vast improvement in the quality of travel and transport. Building the road over the Siskiyous brought to the state thousands of people from all parts of the nation and world whose auto tours heretofore had ended in California."

With the new road in, the city business leaders began thinking about ways to bring in new people – those with money to spend other than just after harvest time. They built a permanent display of products near the new Southern Pacific railroad depot, but the increasing interest in automobiles could do more. The 1915 International Exposition in San Francisco, with its ties to the National Park Service, would encourage people to travel on the new road right through their city and the forward-thinkers wished to capitalize on it.

The road to Crater Lake wasn't paved, but it was useable. Slogans were developed – "Gateway to Crater Lake" – and the promotion began. Banners were made and displayed and a large sign to span the road hung over Riverside Dr. (Pacific Highway) proclaiming "MEDFORD" in large lighted letters and "GATEWAY TO CRATER LAKE" in smaller letters below.

With that promotion, tourism was added to agriculture to draw in other visitors and businesses.

The forests on the western crest of the Cascades, generally as far north as the Union Creek area and west along the ridge, and draining into the Rogue River, became the Crater National Forest. It was established by Theodore Roosevelt in 1908, and renamed the Rogue National Forest in 1932. The Rogue River National Forest encompassed the forest land to the west until it met the Siskiyou Forest Reserve. (The Siskiyou Forest Reserve was established by Roosevelt in 1905, and renamed the Siskiyou National Forest in 1907.) The headquarters were in Medford.

Troubling Times

After World War I, the country went through a period of what many historians call "discontent." Workers, descendants of early emigrants, were dissatisfied. They weren't able to get ahead and frequently worked long hours for low wages in often unsafe and unpleasant conditions. Some began to harbor socialist ideas and many harbored anger at other races or religions. Oregon was no different. It had primarily been settled by white Protestants, and during this period, many feared and disliked any who were different. It was a time when labor unions formed all over the country, some more radical than others and some even organized by the government in order to achieve some control.

The Oregon Blue Book of 2011 describes it this way:

"Wartime stress, emphasis on patriotism, distrust of German Americans, eugenics campaigns championed by Dr. Bethenia Owens-Adair, and anti-Catholic bigotry created fertile ground in Oregon for the rise of the American Protective Association, Federation of Patriotic Societies and the Ku Klux Klan."

According to a segment in the on-line *Oregon Encyclopedia Project*, written by Eckhard Toy, Jr.:

"The first Klan organizers (Kleagles) arrived in Oregon from California and the South in early 1921. Maj. Luther I. Powell, a gregarious Louisianan, swore in the first Oregon Klansmen in Medford while his fellow Kleagles recruited in Portland, Eugene, Salem, Astoria, Hood River,

A Ku Klux Klan contingent marching in an Ashland parade. *From the collection of Ben Truwe*

Pendleton, and other communities. Historians estimate that the national Klan attracted more than two million members during the 1920s, and by 1923 Oregon Klan leaders claimed 35,000 members in more than sixty local chapters and provisional Klans. Hundreds of other Oregonians joined the Women of the Ku Klux Klan, the Junior Order of Klansmen for teenagers, and the Royal Riders of the Red Robe for foreign-born Protestants."

As the recruiters moved through the state, tens of thousands of Oregonians paid their $10 membership fee and had their white robes hanging in the closet.

"...The overwhelming majority of members were ordinary Oregonians who represented a cross-section of their communities. Few members engaged in violence. Many local Klans strengthened fraternal bonds by organizing bands, baseball teams, family picnics and charitable activities. But members also used the Klan to impose their moral and cultural beliefs on other Oregonians, often splintering communities, churches and social organizations. Numerous Protestant ministers, largely fundamentalist and evangelical, joined or supported the Klan, and several became prominent spokesmen for its anti-Catholic crusade. With few black people in the state, they concentrated on Catholic and Jewish residents."

In Medford, however, a black man was chosen by Powell and a few of his Keagles for an example. He was subjected to what they called a "neck-tie hanging" where a rope was placed around his neck and he was lifted off of his feet only long enough to absorb the terrifying message that he was not welcome in Oregon. When his feet returned to the ground, he was told to leave town.

There were other reports of burning crosses on hilltops, and possible horrendous acts of brandings in Southern Oregon, but fortunately the movement was never implicated in murder that was documented.

With the aid of the KKK newspaper, *The Western American*, and the leadership of Grand Dragon Fred L. Gifford, the organization became a potent and controversial political machine during the elections of 1922 and 1924. The KKK managed to get an initiative measure passed requiring all children eight to sixteen years of age to attend public schools. The law faced numerous legal challenges and was never implemented. Other bills resurrecting controversial racial and religious issues that had been rejected previously were passed. One of them was a bill prohibiting the ownership of land by foreign immigrants, aimed primarily at those of Japanese descent. However, they also supported bills to improve state roads and public education.

The *Medford Tribune*, the *Salem Capital Journal* and the *Portland Telegram* were among the newspapers who editorialized against the Klan.

Scandals and corruption at the national level as well as internal strife and Gifford's dictatorial style alienated members and by 1924 many Oregonians had quit the organization. Later attempts to revive the state organization failed.

Medford Aviation

As World War I ended and the veterans returned home, interest began to grow in the fascinating vehicle with wings... the airplane. At first, the interest was not as something practical, but as a curiosity. When an occasional pilot appeared to "barnstorm" communities and rural areas by doing stunts or offering rides for a fee, he drew crowds of interested spectators. Some were willing to pay for rides.

In Medford, one of the most interesting of the barnstomers was Seely Hall, who had been an early recruit into the U.S. Army Air Corps and spent the whole war overhauling aircraft and engines. He and Floyd Hart, who had been a pilot, got together and decided to buy an airplane and start barnstorming. They wanted to fuel their love for flying and make a little money, too. They canvassed the town, going up and down the streets in 1919, and sold stock at $100 a share in their venture to about 30 people. They formed the Medford Aircraft Operation and went to Sacramento to buy a plane for $2,850. They flew it to a wheat field about halfway between Jacksonville and Medford, and began taking up passengers, charging them $5 to $10 dollars per person.

In 1920, the City of Medford established Oregon's first publicly-owned airfield. The purpose was to provide a location for the U.S. Army Air Corps and the U.S. Forest Service to operate forest fire air patrols over the forests of Southern Oregon. It was named Newell Barber Field, for a Medford pilot shot down and killed on his first trip across the line during the war.

The racetrack at the fairgrounds encircled the airfield. Noted pilots landed there, airplanes were fueled there and Harold Sander set up the Sander Aeronautical School there and began giving flying lessons.

That same year, Vern Gorst, the young entrepreneur who first saw the need for public transportation between Medford and Jacksonville years before, also had an interest in flying. He bought an airplane in 1912, learned to fly it and began to put together a plan for a new business idea that would revolutionize local transportation needs.

With Seely Hall, the barnstormer and owner of a Medford transportation business, the two men talked over the idea that airmail delivery would someday grow into passenger service and it would be good to bid on the government airmail contract. They set an estimated cost of $68,000 to purchase enough airplanes to set up one trip each way from Los Angeles to San Francisco to Vancouver and on to Seattle. At the time, there was no place to land in Portland.

Gorst began selling stock in Jacksonville, and even had his taxi drivers promote it. He called Seely Hall and asked him to sell stock in Medford. Seely did. Gorst finally went to Julius Meier of Meier and Frank to obtain a loan of about $25,000. They raised enough capital to order eight Ryan monoplanes, and Gorst persuaded Standard Oil Company to paint the names of towns on the roofs of its buildings.

In 1926, Gorst formed the Pacific Air Transport Company to deliver mail by air from Los Angeles to Seattle, using the highway as a flying guide. That air transport company needed air fields built in between the major stops for the scheduled planes to land in order to the pick up and deliver the mail. They also needed some landing fields constructed that could be used for emergencies.

A Boeing 40A airmail plane. *From the collection of Ben Truwe*

The first Oregon field for scheduled landings of the northbound mail planes was Medford's Newell Barber Field.

Pacific Air Transport obtained a four-year lease, built a hanger and a small office on the east side of the Jackson County Fairgrounds. The graveled portion of the runway was 25 feet wide and 1,500 feet long with a 300-foot overrun. If Medford was fogged in or the weather was severe, the mail was unloaded and put on a train passing through, as there were no navigational instruments on the planes yet. The early planes did not even have an enclosed cockpit, although some planes could carry a passenger, in a separate, enclosed compartment. Each airfield along the way had an emergency backup. Twenty miles south and east of Medford, the Barron Ranch had a large field that could be used for that purpose when needed.

Since the airway was not lighted, the airplanes needed to follow U.S. Highway 99. The first leg left Los Angeles at midnight and flew to San Francisco. Big Ford headlights were placed on the water towers in different towns along the road and the pilots flew from one light to the other. They always made sure that they could see lights behind them as well as in front of them. Coming over the Siskiyous, there was often bad weather in winter and the Medford area struggled with fog. From there, the pilot could take the mail by car over to Montague, California. Montague didn't have much fog, so the mail could be flown from there to San Francisco. Pacific Air Transport also had the authority to stop a train anywhere to provide emergency transport of the airmail. Many of the winter trips went out of Medford by car.

The one-way flights took 18-hours with stops for fuel and mail at Bakersfield, Fresno, San Francisco, Medford and Vancouver. The route was begun September 15, 1926, and operated daily in each direction. Seely Hall became the first field manager of Pacific Air Transport at the Medford Newell Barber Field, the only scheduled landing site in Oregon. Six airplanes were lost the first year of operation.

B.F. Irvine, editor of the *Portland Oregon Journal*, was quoted by the *Medford Mail Tribune*:

"Medford is one of the main stations on the new air mail line from Seattle to San Francisco and Los Angeles, and has the distinction of being the only city in Oregon to have an airport.

"The Medford Chamber of Commerce put over a novel idea of advertising the first air mail flight. They issued 2,000 'Greetings From Medford' cards sent by the people of Medford to every part of the globe. This greeting contained a four color picture of Crater Lake. The envelope carrying the greeting had special advertising for Medford and the Rogue River Valley and was arranged in color to attract attention."

Pacific Air Transport pilots weren't the only people using U.S. Highway 99 as an airway. As airplane travel became popular, many pilots, and people learning to be pilots, were in the air. Small air strips, many only grass strips, were located near towns all along the highway. It's still not uncommon to see buildings with the town name and sometimes an arrow pointing to an airfield painted on the roof. Tangent, Oregon, toward the north, is one of the most noticeable.

By 1927, Vern Gorst saw the need for newer airplanes that could go faster, higher, and carry passengers. That was the same year that the airmail route was lighted with beacons along the way with Richfield's "Lane of Lights."

By 1929, airplanes that could carry passengers were available, but the Newell Barber Field was not big enough to handle the larger planes. To make the transition, Pacific Air Transport and Medford needed a larger airport. It was put to a vote at the cost of $120,000 – one of the first bond issues in the country for an airport. After the new field was acquired and built, the Civilian Workers Administration hired local labor to build roads designed to decrease flooding. Some of those workers lined trenches with tile to drain the new airfield.

In the transition process, Vern Gorst needed an influx of money to move toward a passenger line. He went to Boeing for the needed funding, but had to give up much of his control. Pacific Air Transport became a subsidiary of Boeing, and both eventually became part of United Air Lines.

In the early 1930s, the whole country was in financial trouble and the government had begun to put in programs to put people to work. From this environment, a movement called the "Jackson County Rebellion" took place.

From Ben Truwe's *Capsule Histories* on his website:

"Long-simmering political tensions surfaced under the pressures of the Depression. As banks closed, businesses failed and workers lost jobs, orchardist and newspaperman, Llewellyn Banks, capitalized on this unrest and formed a movement called the Good Government Congress."

Banks, the "demagogic" publisher of the *Medford Daily News*, and Earl Fehl, a "perennially unsuccessful political candidate," joined together in promoting the GGC.

Their message appealed to the people who resented the political order and joined the Good Government Congress. The movement then quickly turned toward insurgency, intimidation and violence. The theft of 10,000 ballots from the Jackson County Courthouse vault to prevent a recount brought the situation to a head. The authorities suspected Llewellyn Banks and issued an arrest warrant. On March 16, 1933, Constable George Prescott went to the Banks' home to serve the warrant, but was shot by Banks and died instantly. After Banks was jailed, his followers rushed to alienate themselves from him and the GGC, and the insurgency faded away.

While Banks and his followers had been promoting their dislike of the political order, Robert Ruhl, publisher and editor of the *Medford Mail Tribune* consistently condemned the methods of the Good Government Congress and urged citizens to stand by their government and remain calm.

"...In 1934, when it came time to award the Pulitzer Prize for 'meritorious public service,' the judges selected the Medford Mail Tribune for its campaign against unscrupulous politicians in Jackson County Oregon."

As the country began to shake off the effects of the Great Depression, the local economy gradually got better, Medford continued to grow, and "normal" family life resumed.

Possibly after watching Medford High School manhandle Benson Tech 39-0 in the 1928 state championship game, an *Oregonian* sports editor, L.H. Gregor, wrote: *"From out of the south, Medford swept over the field like a Black Tornado."*

The unofficial name stuck for football as Medford High School dominated the Southern Oregon football scene and it was officially voted the mascot by the student body in 1953.

A newcomer to the Medford area was movie star Ginger Rogers. Her ranch was outside of town, but close enough that she hired and utilized local workers. She was a welcome addition to the community during the times she was there.

Probably like many other places, local opinions in Medford seemed to change over time. As the length of the Depression stretched on during 1911, the *Medford Mail Tribune* stories reported police raids on homeless camps, and another reported that the police escorted 35 homeless to the north city limits and told them to leave. Another of the officers met a freight train to keep the hoboes from getting off. Another 21 were rounded up, taken to court, and then escorted by police for a cup of coffee, a little bread, and then told to get out of town.

By the 1930s, the attitude of the town had changed to some degree.

"Local Jail is Haven to Bedless Men," *Medford Daily News*, December 14, 1930:

"The rush of hungry, homeless men to the police station in quest of a place to sleep continues night after night. As many as twenty indigents, and always at least eight, are allowed to sleep in the city jail, police say. In the jail, the unfortunates at least find warmth, blankets and a place out of the rain.

"Police believe that it is wiser to permit the down-and-outers to slumber in the jail, rather than have them wander about the streets of the city all night.

"Most of the men are not criminals in any sense of the word, just hungry, dirty, unfortunate men in search of a place to earn a living. As it is, they get little out of life, and suffer the utmost in misery, in so-called prosperous America.

"It is said that Medford sees little of the vast number of unemployed throughout the nation, as most of the unfortunates travel by the other railway line through Klamath Falls and into California.

"Last night, an aged married couple entered the police station in search of something to eat and a place to sleep. They had walked the streets for hours and found no aid. Finally, as a last resort, they went to the police station. They were traveling from California to the home of a relative at Burns, where they expected to be allowed to pass the winter. Hitchhiking along the Pacific Highway had proven a slow mode of travel for the unfortunates."

The Civilian Conservation Corps (CCC)

In 1933, President Franklin D. Roosevelt was granted emergency powers allowing him to recruit thousands of unemployed young men, enroll them in a peace-time army, and send them into battle against destruction and erosion of our natural resources. By the end of July of that year, 250,000 men had signed up and were in camps across the country. Before the CCC ended in 1942, over three million young men had engaged in a massive salvage operation described as the most popular experiment of the New Deal.

Logistics was an immediate problem. The bulk of young unemployed youth was concentrated in the East while most of the work projects were in the West. The U.S. Army was the only department capable of merging the two and they quickly developed new plans to meet the challenge of managing this peacetime mission. The Army mobilized the nation's transportation system, and moved thousands of enrollees from induction centers to working camps. It used regular and reserve officers, together with regulars of the Coast Guard, Marine Corps and Navy to command companies temporarily.

The Army was not the only organization to evoke extraordinary efforts to meet the demands of this movement. The Departments of Agriculture and Interior were responsible for planning and organizing work to be performed in every state of the union. The Department of Labor was responsible for the selection and enrollment through state and local relief offices.

Some basics were required at each camp – shelter, healthy food, medical care and meaningful work. The young men were required to be single and physically able. Each man was paid $30 a month, of which $25 was to go to his family at home. As the program got underway, education was added on a voluntary basis and dependent on the abilities of the officers and staff at the particular camp. It's estimated that 40,000 illiterate young men learned to read and write. Many learned skills to enable them to make a living from leatherwork, typing, driving equipment and woodworking, among others.

Although the main transportation for arrival and departure was the railroad, these men had to be transported by other means to different areas to work. Most of the camps in Oregon were located in forested areas, seldom close to U.S. Highway 99. However, the young men occasionally spent time-off in towns along the highway, some even helped with construction on the road itself or on a project for the public-good in a nearby city.

Some helped with the building of a stage for the first Shakespearean Festival in Ashland and took part in a city-sponsored prize-fight on the Fourth of July. Accounts told of them watching movies in the Community Building in Talent and finding entertainment and "R&R" in the communities all along U.S. Highway 99.

The CCC headquarters for Southern Oregon was in Medford and there were 44 camps managed from there. The list of camps in Oregon doesn't include any in Medford itself, but they were located at Union Creek, Ruch, Rogue River, Prescott, Butte Falls, Crater Lake, Ashland, Trail, Evans Creek, Diamond Lake and others in all directions. The Civilian Conservation Corps, camps and workers, show up in stories all through the state, so they too are part of the web that was U.S. Highway 99.

In 1933, the Riverside section of the U.S. Highway 99 in Medford was widened. After the improvement was completed, trucks began to replace the rails in bringing logs to the mills and business continued to grow. At one time, a 110 lumber mills were working in the immediate area.

The beginnings of World War II brought more changes to Medford than just the increased demand for lumber. The cantonment, Camp White, was built north and east of Medford.

In answer to the increased traffic to the airport and Camp White, the part of U.S. Highway 99 that went through the city was divided into one-way streets – Riverside to the north and Central to the south.

Camp White was filled with young men being trained for war and they visited Medford and nearby towns during their time off. New business developed to provide entertainment and activities geared for them. Available nearby housing filled with families, and activity on that end of town increased.

After the troops were gone, some of the

facilities at Camp White were used to house German prisoners-of-war. The camp was selected as a site to experiment with the concept of changing the "attitudes" of the prisoners, but instead of using harsh methods, the prisoners were treated courteously. They had the use of a library, classes in English, and in some cases were taken in groups to help in the orchards, receiving some slight payment for their labor. When they too were gone, the camp hospital was still in use for returning veterans and still serves some of that purpose today, although many of the other buildings and housing are gone.

During the War, the entire airport facility was leased to the U.S. Army for the "duration of the war plus six months." A control tower was added to the airport building. Commercial traffic was relocated to the United Airlines building which added a new passenger and ticketing facility.

A volunteer group established the Wing-In Canteen to serve the air crews and soldiers passing through. By the end of the War, they were serving 400 meals a day. As time went on, the U.S. Army purchased more land and put up temporary buildings. This, in turn, caused some delay in returning the airport to the city after the war.

Some of the young men who trained in construction at Camp White became the contractors who built or added on to the schools – both at nearby high schools and several at Southern Oregon College as well as other major local projects.

In 1949, George Millican was an air traffic controller at the Medford airport. That year, the scourge of polio struck his good friend, Art Winetrout, who was unable to survive the long drive to Portland for treatment. This loss galvanized Milligan's resolve to establish Mercy Flights, the nation's first nonprofit air ambulance run entirely by volunteers.

Mercy Flights' first aircraft was a surplus Cessna T-50 Bobcat, commonly referred to as the "Bamboo Bomber." It transported its first patient on February 28, 1950. Mercy Flights still provides air and ground ambulance service to the entire Rogue Valley.

Oregon streetcar archivist, Richard Thompson, shares his considerable knowledge about the Medford-Jacksonville streetcar system as part of the extensive on-line Oregon Encyclopedia Project:

"Spencer S. Bullis organized the Southern Oregon Traction Company (SOTC) on July 15, 1913, to operate streetcars in the city of Medford. Three years later, the SOTC incorporated the Rogue River Valley Railway's (RRVR) line (founded in 1891) between Medford and Jacksonville. Though even the expanded SOTC did not achieve the same status as the larger streetcar systems in the Willamette Valley, it was an important regional transit option until 1920.

"The SOTC's first trolley, a single-truck Birney, arrived on March 16, 1914. Tracks ran east on Main Street from the Southern Pacific Railroad (SP) mainline to Eastwood Drive. After a crossing of the SP tracks was completed, the line was extended west through downtown to a terminus at Oakdale Avenue. A line was also built eastward to Siskiyou Heights, but it was removed when that development proved slow, and its rails were used to extend the Main Street tracks to a connection with the RVRR at Eighth and Elm Streets. A planned line to Ashland was never built.

Southern Oregon Traction Company Birney car No. 1, East Main Line run through downtown Medford, about 1915. *Courtesy of Richard Thompson*

"In 1915, Bullis obtained control of the RVRR, which ran six miles between Medford and Jacksonville. It was electrified and merged with the two-and-a-half-mile SOTC system in January 1916. Both systems used standard-gauge track (4' 8½" wide).

"The Rogue River Valley Railway, which began operations on February 12, 1891, started as a steam short line. For most of its life, both before and after Bullis, the RRVR was operated by William S. Barnum. Barnum had pioneered modern passenger service with the RVRR by introducing an eight-passenger Fairbanks auto car in 1905. He had followed this in 1909 with a twenty-eight-seat Black Crow, gasoline-engine-powered, combination freight and passenger car of his own design. The SOTC improved passenger comfort further by adding another lightweight streetcar and a double-truck car bought used from the Cleveland, Ohio, system.

"In 1918, bankruptcy returned control of the company to Barnum. He abandoned passenger service in 1920, and so ended the streetcar era in Southern Oregon."

Much attention was given to William S. Barnum's son, John Corbin Barnum, who, at the age of 13, became the youngest conductor in America when he joined the family business in 1893. He later became the General Manager of the Rogue River Valley Railway.

As traffic increased, now on two streets, U.S. Highway 99 businesses tried creative ways to get the attention of tourists and townspeople, often in the buildings themselves, as well as with signs and other attention-getting devices.

Roadside drive-in restaurants were very popular with young people in the 1950s. Pizza parlors were just coming in and families seemed to prefer sit-down restaurants, but, in 1959, another type of eating establishment opened in Medford on U.S. Highway 99. North's Chuck Wagon offered a buffet where each person was charged a flat price and could serve himself anything he wanted from their well-filled food tables. The food included many standard favorites and the business became so successful that the founding brothers, Jim and John North were able to build a chain of 24 restaurants. Others followed the model throughout Oregon, but, after the freeway moved the traffic faster and shopping trends changed, most of the buffet restaurants that remain are located in malls under a wide variety of names.

CENTRAL POINT

Central Point grew from a small post office established in 1872, at a place where two stage routes crossed, a few miles northeast of Jacksonville. It was incorporated in 1889. By 1915, it had long been established in an agricultural area with crops of peaches, apples, pears, apricots, berries, grapes, alfalfa, potatoes, onions, melons and all varieties of garden truck.

Central Point, Rogue River and Grants Pass were some of the Southern Oregon towns connected by the Pacific Highway where the highway itself did not go through the main business districts – it only intersected them.

For this reason, many of the towns' businesses grew and developed to serve the residents. Travelers and tourists passing by sel-

Lumberjack billboard ad in Medford. *From the Brew family collection*

The Coffeepot Drive-In. Note that part of the building was shaped as a coffeepot. *From the collection of Ben Truwe*

dom came into the towns themselves, although some businesses – motels, gas stations, restaurants, farmstands and grocery stores – developed along the highway.

One of the places where Highway 99 has been altered is the stretch between Medford and Central Point, so the division between the two cities is not as clearly defined as during the time when the main connector was the highway.

In Central Point, U.S. Highway 99 was named Front Street and its route parallels the railroad tracks. Approaching the center of Central Point, the change is more defined when the Grange Co-Op tower comes in view.

In 1934, a group of Rogue Valley farmers invested $10 each in the Grange Co-op. In 1941, the co-op decided to begin buying local grains and a warehouse was built just off U.S. Highway 99. In 1947, the elevator was built and the co-op began mixing local feeds for farmers in Southern Oregon and Northern California.

The elevator tower on Front Street has been an icon of the town for more than half a century in spite of fire damage, remodeling and enlarging. As of 2013, the co-op was still a growing and successful business. It employs many local workers, has seven retail outlets, more than 2,000 members and mixes more than 50 kinds of natural feed.

On the south end of the city, where it borders Medford, is the Jackson County Fairgrounds. Central Point not only hosts the Jackson County Fair, but other large events including the Holiday Market, concerts, and many others.

The nearby Crater Rock Museum is a popular attraction that has many beautiful rocks, minerals and gems found in the area on display as well as many other artifacts that reflect the life of the Native Americans.

In Central Point, like in other cities in Oregon, the lumber industry came and went. Nearby mills closed and eventually the old metal wigwam burners disappeared. Wigwams were a common site during the glory days of the timber industry along U.S. Highway 99 and throughout the Pacific Northwest. Almost every mill had one. They were conical in shape with a domed mesh screening at the top. Waste wood, sawdust and other wood products were dumped into them, usually by conveyor belt, and burned for disposal. The mesh domes kept the sparks from the fires from flying out and possibly, in the dry months, igniting grass or forest fires

Recent photo of the Central Point Grange Co-op tower. *From the Brew family collection*

U.S. Highway 99 through Central Point. *Courtesy of the Oregon Department of Transportation (ODOT)*

The converted wigwam burner in Central Point. *From the Brew family collection.*

nearby. Because the screens did not prevent the smoke and ash from polluting the air, however, they were phased out in the 1970s and actually banned in Oregon as part of the Federal Clean Air Act by the mid-1980s. Most were torn down and removed as were many of the mills that once operated them, but there are still a few of the iconic reminders of the once-prominent timber industry in Oregon up and down the Highway 99 corridor.

Currently, one such burner is located in Central Point, just off Highway 99, although it fills a different need than what it had been designed for. No fire burns in it, and the top screen that covers it appears to be in use to collect sawdust from a furniture-making operation. Another that can be seen from the highway is located in Drain, Oregon.

The Rogue Creamery

The Rogue Creamery, located not far north of downtown Central Point, right on Highway 99, was founded in 1935 by Tom Vella, a cheesemaker from Sonoma, California. It produced butter and cheddar, colby and jack cheeses. During the Depression and World War II, the creamery saved many local dairy farmers, purchasing their milk and producing the cheese to be sold to the government. In later years, the factory moved away from the standard cheeses into bleus and other artisan cheeses. They are now marketed in specialty stores and often served in the best restaurants.

GOLD HILL

Located about eight miles north of Central Point, Gold Hill was founded in the mid-1800s by miners along the Rogue River who stayed and homesteaded. In the 1850s, some began discovering gold in the creeks that fed into the Rogue – Galls, Sardine, Foots and Kane. All the area creeks and watershed in both Jackson and Josephine Counties produced gold, some richer than others. Here, in 1860, the first steam quartz mill in Jackson County was established to crush the gold-bearing rock.

In an interview done on January 23, 1939 as part of the *WPA's American Life Histories Collection: Manuscripts from the Federal Writer's Project, 1936-1940*, Carl Hentz, tells his story. His interviewer was William C. Haight:

"I came out west to mine. It seemed to me that the best money could be made

Extension demonstration train at Central Point, Oregon. Crowd gathers with Rogue River Valley Band, 1918. *Courtesy of the OSU Special Collections & Archives Commons*

in mines in Oregon. I have been here in Oregon looking for my bucket of gold for quite a spell.

"You know, every miner feels that the next day will bring the answer to all of his prayers. You learn to be optimistic when you are mining. You have to be. Hell, a pessimist for a miner is unheard of. At least, I have never met such a critter..."

As more miners and settlers moved in, the conflict between them and the Native Americans grew more intense, with violent brutality, skirmishes and major battles. The U.S. Army was brought in and Fort Lane was established. In 1856, the Native American non-combatants, led by Chief Sam of the Rogue River Indians were removed to southeastern Oregon for their safety.

Discovery at Gold Hill – 1860

An Irish emigrant, Thomas Chavner, arrived in the Rogue Valley in 1856. He acquired land directly across the Rogue River from where the town of Gold Hill was sited, near Dardanelles. It was on his land that one of his employees, James Hayes, and a friend were searching for stray horses on January 8, 1860. The friend found an interesting piece of quartz and put it in his pocket. That incident later led to the first major gold strike in the area with Chavner as a partner.

In time, Chavner bought out one of his partners for $5,000. The vein, which they called the "Gold Hill Pocket," was two-feet wide and twenty-feet long, It went fifteen-feet deep and produced over $100,000 in gold. Other gold discoveries in the area followed, but none were as productive.

Chavner, a good business manager, prospered, using the gold to acquire more land, sometimes acting as a money-lender and always working long hours on his property.

Gold Hill was named after the hill located on the Chavner property northeast of the present townsite, With his share of the profits, Thomas Chavner acquired nearly 2,000 acres of prime land along the Rogue River. In 1876, he had the Centennial Toll Bridge built to cross the river and later sold it to the county. Its replacement was built as part of the U.S. Highway 99 in 1927, and was still in use in 2013. He also sold the right-of-way through his property to the Oregon & California Railroad in 1883.

In January 1884, Chavner and his wife, Rosa, filed the plat for the town of Gold Hill and donated streets and alleys to the public.

The Oregon & California Railroad arrived in 1883, the post office in 1884, and the town was incorporated in 1895.

With the arrival of the railroad and the building of the depot, the town had a community center. The trains hauled lumber, gold, quartz, fruit, grains, livestock and passengers. The town had a hotel and a grocery store. The bars and taverns had busy Saturday nights as the miners came in for supplies and refreshments. The town built a large pavilion where basketball games were played and county fairs were held. By 1915, Gold Hill had two lumber mills, a box factory, a machine shop, a cement factory and five gold mines with mills.

A Southern Pacific gas-powered, rail-mounted passenger bus operated through town until the 1950s. The depot was then shut down and later removed.

The Rogue River Telephone Company built telephone lines in 1895; the *Gold Hill News* was established in 1897; and a fire department formed in 1898. The next decade brought schools, a sewer system, electric lights, a city waterworks project and Gold Ray Dam.

Some of the mines were promising enough to bring in investors able to provide funds for equipment to make the mines a profitable business.

One of those large mining operations led to a major change in the whole county and beyond. In 1900, a pair of investors from the east, Dr. Charles Ray and Colonel Frank Ray, brothers who had money in the Braden mine, got the idea of building a dam across the Rogue to provide energy for an electric plant. They sold bonds on the New York Stock Exchange and the Condor Water and Power Company was incorporated in 1902.

Construction of the original log crib dam, four miles above the city, ran into one obstacle after another, but the first electricity was generated by rope-driven turbines on December 7, 1904. The first unit was later replaced by two 750kw generators. The original goal of the project was to supply the nearby mines with electricity, but Gold Ray went on to supply Ashland, Medford, Gold Hill, Jacksonville and Grants Pass with domestic power, as well. It lit the entire Rogue River Valley for nearly 70 years. The original dam was replaced by a concrete structure in 1941. The power plant went out of use in 1971 when the cement plant in Gold Hill closed.

When the Pacific Highway was built, it crossed the Rogue River several times, once at each end of Gold Hill, giving the town two beautiful bridges.

U.S. Highway 99 from Central Point to Gold Hill was called Blackwell Road

The Cement Factory

By the mid-1920s, most of the area gold mines had played out, but the employment slack was taken up by Del Rio Orchards at Rock Point and the operations of a large cement plant, constructed in 1915 by the Beaver Portland Cement Company.

In 1913, the Beaver Portland Cement Company established a cement plant on 18-acres of city property. Making cement basically requires mixing crushed limestone with shale, adding water to form a slurry and then firing the mixture in a huge kiln. After cooling, gypsum is mixed in, and this is then ground to a fine powder.

The lime for the cement was first quarried at Zacher Crossing where the Bristol Silica Plant is located. The quality and quantity of the limestone from there was not satisfactory for long, so the limestone was later brought by railroad from Marble Mountain several miles out of Grants Pass. The cement plant leased the railroad cars and maintained the lines. Ten rail cars of limestone were shipped daily except on weekends.

About 25 percent of the material needed was mined from the shale pit at Gold Hill after it was loosened with dynamite. The plant employed between 100 and 150 people for 60 years, first as the Beaver Portland Cement Plant, then as The Pacific Portland Cement Plant and finally as the Ideal Cement Plant.

The use of "Portland" in the names did not refer to Portland, Oregon, but to the type of cement that was being made. The name is derived from Portland stone, a type of building stone that was quarried on the Isle of Portland in Dorset, England and used in the making of cement in the early part of the 19th century.

Although, by the mid-1900s, the big mining boom had essentially ended, there was still gold in the creeks feeding the river. Several of the families farmed part of the year and worked the creeks for gold the rest of the time. Eventually, dredges were brought in, cleaning the gold off the creek bottoms and leaving an ugly landscape behind.

In the 1950s, three brothers from Germany with the name, Jeddeloh, operated a sawmill on Galls Creek near Gold Hill and then, in 1955, because they were dissatisfied with the quality of the saws available for their mill, they decided they could build better saws not only for their own use, but for other mills, too. They named the new business the Jeddeloh Brothers Sweed Mill. Eventually, they branched into manufacturing other custom mill equipment and sold the business to Cascade Wood Products in 1986. It is now called Sweed Machinery, Inc. the largest business in Gold Hill.

The House of Mystery or The Oregon Vortex

One of the mills near Gold Hill, the Old Grey Eagle Mining Company, on Sardine Creek, was developed as a successful roadside attraction in the early 1930s and still draws and fascinates visitors during the summer months.

The House of Mystery, also known as "The Oregon Vortex" has been a Gold Hill attraction longer than the gold mines lasted.

John Lister, a reputed geologist, mining engineer, and physicist, acquired the property in the 1920s and, in the abandoned and tilting structures, he apparently noticed visual and phenomenal oddities, tall people seemed

Gold mining at the Foots Creek Dredge near Rogue River. *From the collection of Ben Truwe*

to shrink, water appeared to run uphill and so on. He developed the area and opened it to the public in 1930. He and his wife served as promoters.

According to a promotional brochure:

"The House of Mystery itself was originally an assay office and later used for tool storage, built by the Old Grey Eagle Mining Company in 1904. In the history of the surrounding area, The Oregon Vortex, goes way back to the time of the Native Americans. Their horses would not come into the affected area, so they wouldn't either. The Native Americans called the area the Forbidden Ground, a place to be shunned."

The Flood of 1964

Even though Shady Cove is quite a distance to the east from the route taken by U.S. Highway 99, the story about it and the horrific flood of 1964 will illustrate the conditions that many of the communities along the Rogue River faced that year.

The '64 Flood" by Paul Fattig, *Medford Mail Tribune*, December 22, 1964:

"Shady Cove logger Bill Littlefield figured it was time to skedaddle to high ground when floodwaters started shoving his D-8 Caterpillar around.

"After all, the bulldozer the catskinner had been using to haul Shady Cove residents to safety was no pushover, weighing in at roughly 50,000 pounds.

"And darkness was settling on Dec. 22, 1964, when the Rogue River roared over its banks.

"The last time I went through there, the water was moving the cat sideways, he said. I'm guessing the water was three or four feet high and real swift. We got that big surge right after it got dark.

"— There we were on pavement (Highway 62), sliding sideways in the current, he added. I probably had eight to 10 people on that cat.

"The 60-year resident of the river community nosed the big cat onto dry land and parked it for the night.

"A portion of the bridge over the Rogue at Shady Cove washed away at about 8 p.m. Logs from a local mill rushed past, en route to the ocean. The power was already out, leaving the town in the dark.

"What experts would call a 100-year flood had arrived.

"Littlefield, now 69 and still working in the woods, had never seen the like.

"We had hard rain for, gosh, I don't know how many days, he said. That river kept coming up and coming up. Some people lost everything.

The mysterious Oregon Vortex. *From the collection of Ben Truwe*

"Fellow Shady Cove resident Virginia Rasmussen, 78, can attest to that: She and her late husband, Charles Mathis, and their seven children lost their home near Trail to the river earlier that day.

"'When the river started coming up, we got out with just the clothes on our back. We put all our Christmas stuff upstairs and left.

"'The two-story house along Meadow Lane had survived the 1955 flood. But logs from a holding pond in Prospect floated down, lodged in the gorge to dam up the water, then broke loose. That's what tore out everything.

"'The flood took the Mathises' house, barn, garage, even many of the trees. Like most residents, they didn't have flood insurance. But good Samaritans in a boat were able to reach the house to rescue the family pet, a three-legged pooch named King.

"'Someone told me later they saw our house float down under the Shady Cove bridge, she said. They said it went around the corner, hit a rock pile down there and just blew up.'"

ROCK POINT

After leaving Gold Hill, Highway 99 (Sams Valley Highway) turns onto the Rock Point Bridge at Rock Point west of Gold Hill in southwestern Oregon. Once known as the Old Pacific Highway Bridge, it spans the Rogue River. In 1859, a covered bridge spanned the site and a toll was charged to cross. Later, a concrete arch span replaced it. It was operated by the Rock Point Bridge Company, but the span was later purchased by Jackson County and made into a free crossing. The present Rock Point Bridge opened to traffic in 1920.

Rock Point was an official stage stop on the route heading north.

In *Knights of the Whip*, the history of stagecoaches in Oregon, Gary and Gloria Meier describe the Rock Point Station:

"In 1859, Lytte J. White and his family settled on the Rogue River at what was known as Rock Point... The wagon road or trail passed through Lytte's property on the north bank of the river. When the daily stages began running through from Sacramento to Portland, White established a hotel to provide services for the stage company and travelers, as well as local people Construction began in 1864.

"The house was elegant and large. There were thirty rooms for guests, a bar, a second floor ballroom, a finely appointed dining room and large kitchen where Mrs. White prepared sumptuous meals for stage passengers and friends. A parlor for the use of women travelers was located on the first floor, and a men's parlor was across the hall...

"...After the stage station was established, the small community of Rock Point began to grow. In addition to the hotel, there were homes, a post office, store, school, saloon and a blacksmith shop. The trail crossed Rogue River at Rock Point on an open wooden bridge built by L.J. White in 1863. In 1878, it was replaced by a long covered bridge..."

The Rock Point station supposedly had one of the first telegraph stations in Oregon, too.

The community of Rock Point began to grow around the station during that time. Besides homes, it soon had a post office, a general store, a school, a blacksmith's shop and, of course, a saloon.

The Rock Point Tavern, 1934. *From the collection of Ben Truwe*

The Rock Point Bridge, 1923. *From the collection of Ben Truwe*

The town was believed to have been one of the casualties when the railroad bypassed it in favor of a route through Gold Hill. While the town of Rock Point no longer exists, a cemetery remains with over 900 documented graves.

After the staging days, Rock Point and Miller's Gulch area was planted in pear trees and became an orchard with its own packing plant. The property now belongs to the Del Rio Wine Company with the tasting room in the large barn that was the pear packing plant.

"What Is That Mining Operation in Gold Hill?" by Jim Craven. Medford Mail *Tribune*, **Sunday, April 22, 2007 Our Valley:**

"Since its discovery in 1938, the quartz mine at Miller's Gulch along North River Road outside of Gold Hill has yielded more than five million tons of ore, including 3 million tons of silica."

"Historical information about the 160-acre, aggregate-zoned site is patchy, but the longest-running operators were the Bristol family of Grants Pass, who ran the mine for decades beginning in 1938."

Although no longer in operation, *"the mine's high purity quartz in crystal bulk form is a rare find in the Pacific*

Northwest. It is often used in the making of glass and, in smaller amounts as nursery and landscape material. ...In addition, the mines dolomite limestone can be crushed and sold for use as agricultural fertilizer."

GOLD RIVER / TAILHOLT / WOODVILLE / ROGUE RIVER

In the 1850s, an influx of whites – miners, settlers and others – began taking over and destroying the hunting and fishing grounds of the Native Americans. Not just from the town we call Rogue River, but those from all over the valley of the Rogue. Hydraulic gold mining destroyed fisheries; farmers and miners removed game habitat. The Donation Land Act permitted settlers to claim land and establish farms, although the Indian ownership of the land had not been relinquished. Skirmishes became common and Indian Agent, Joel Palmer, established three reservations in an attempt to calm the problems. However, an incident in 1855 near the Table Rock reservation set off a battle that left several hundred Indians and about a fifty miners and settlers dead. Palmer decided the Indians needed to be removed for their short-term safety. Beginning in January 1857, the Indians were forcibly taken to the Coast Reservation, relocating an estimated 4,000 people to situations where they were unable to make a living.

It was during this period of time, the Gold Rush days of the 1850s, that the Jackson County town of Rogue River had its beginning at a crossing of the river known as Evan's Ferry, along the route of the California-Oregon Trail. There was a post office nearby from 1855 to 1859 with the name of Gold River. Next came an unofficial stage stop and the name Tailholt in 1872. Then a rural post office was opened in 1876 with the name Woodville, probably named for the first postmaster, John Woods. The Oregon & California Railroad came through in 1884 and in 1912, Woodville changed it's name to Rogue River when it incorporated into a municipality.

Rogue River has been primarily a lumbering and farming town with other, occasionally interesting, enterprises trying to achieve success. One that has now disappeared was a rattlesnake farm or garden, directly across the river from the town.

In the Works Progress Administration (WPA) book, *Oregon, End of the Trail*, published in 1940, and revised in 1951, the business was described:

"Eight-thousand rattlesnakes are being fed and fattened to provide rattlesnake meat and venom, which is used medicinally. A Los Angeles packing company purchases the meat and a drug company, the poison, which is often prescribed in epileptic cases and in the preparations of anti-toxins. The public is invited to visit the rattler farm, and if any person will bring a live native rattler with him, the standing price is one dollar each. To keep the serpents at home, there is an inner wall of masonry, four-feet high and three-feet below the surface of the ground, and an outer wall eight-feet high and three-feet below the surface."

Camp Wimer CCC Camp

In 1938, the 5453rd company of the Civilian Conservation Corps was stationed at Camp Wimer, a state forest camp located on Pleasant Creek, 11 miles north of Rogue River. The camp was first constructed in

Fishing has always been a favorite pastime on the Rogue River, 1922. *From the collection of Ben Truwe*

1934, and the 5453rd was the third company to occupy it. Work projects included truck-trail, telephone line and lookout tower construction and maintenance and fire hazard reduction. During the summer, fire-fighting took precedence over everything. In 1936, the men of Camp Wimer put in 7,266 man-days of work on the fire line. Members of the local area attended camp activities including educational motion pictures, athletic contests, camp theatricals and a weekly talking motion picture show.

The natural attributes on the Rogue River often contributed to commerical enterprises. Fishing, white water rafting, boating and tourism services have all done their share over the years. Motels, resorts, boat landings, highway farm stands and restaurants all have contributed to the local economy.

U.S. Highway 99 followed the Rogue River, where it ran east and west between the bridge at Gold Hill and Grants Pass,

One of the more well-known resorts along that stretch was the Weasku Inn, located right on the river. Built in 1924 as a log fishing lodge with stone fireplaces, it was popular with movie stars. Clark Gable, Carol Lombard and Walt Disney were among the guests. It has recently been restored and updated into a luxurious resort again.

Historic Weasku Inn Resort, Rogue River, Oregon. *From the Brew family collection*

Section 3

U.S. HIGHWAY 99 - GRANTS PASS TO WOLF CREEK

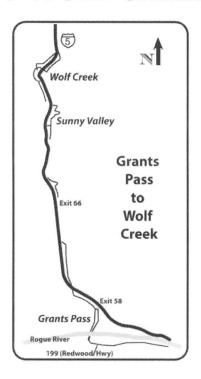

PERKINSVILLE / GRANT'S PASS / GRANTS PASS

By the 1820s, Hudson's Bay Company trappers and hunters following the Siskiyou Trail passed through what became the site of Grant's Pass.

In 1850, the United States Congress passed the Donation Land Claim Act to encourage settlers to move to the Oregon and Washington Territories. The law granted 320 acres of designated areas free of charge to every unmarried white male citizen 18 or older, and 640 acres to every married couple arriving in the Oregon Territory before December 1, 1850. The husband and wife would each own half of the total grant in their own name. It was an extremely unusual provision at the time and was one of the first laws in the country allowing a woman to own land.

Half-blood Native Americans were also eligible. Claimants were required to live on the land and improve it for four years in order to own it outright.

Those arriving after the 1850 deadline,

but before 1854, could claim half the amount. Claims under the law were granted at the federal land office in Oregon City and surveyed by the Surveyor General of Oregon.

After 1854, land was no longer free but was available for sale at $1.25 an acre with a limit of 320 acres in any one claim. The law expired on December 1, 1855.

This offer brought a flood of emigrants into the valleys of the Rogue, Umpqua and Willamette Rivers, taking the land from the Native Americans, not always peacefully, and changing the environment and culture forever.

Gold prospectors on the hunt began showing up to search the area creeks and many found it.

One of the first settlers in the area was Joel Perkins. He moved with his family from Lafayette, Oregon in Yamhill County, which he had founded. He built a log home with a strong stockade around it on the eastern side of what is now Grants Pass. He built the first ferry crossing on the Rogue called Perkins Ferry, and the area became known as Perkinsville.

"Joel Perkins" by Joan Momsen. *Grants Pass Daily Courier*, January 3, 2012:

"In and around the vicinity of Grants Pass, Oregon, the story of Joel Perkins is told, but the facts always seem limited. From old newspaper accounts and assorted old documents and information from the Yamhill Historical Society, this is the tale of the founder of what eventually became the town of Grants Pass.

"...In 1851, Joel Perkins operated a ferry across the South Umpqua River in Kenyonville, with Joseph Knott. According to the State of Washington and Oregon Territorial Map compiled by the Bureau of Topography in 1859, the main trail going south crossed the South Umpqua River approximately four miles south of present day Roseburg. There is no notation of a community named Kenyonville, but it's possibly an unconfirmed misspelling of nearby Canyonville.

"In the same year of 1851, Joel and Laura Perkins built the first house and general store in the Rogue River Valley. In 1852, 17-year-old Laura gave birth to their first child, Harriet. Technically and geographically speaking, Grants Pass is in the Rogue River Valley and Medford is in the Bear Creek Drainage area, so the house was the log cabin built near Grants Pass. In 1851-52, Jacksonville was established in the southeastern portion of Jackson County. There was no Josephine County. What eventually became Josephine County in 1856 was still Jackson County when Perkins opened his store

Joel Perkins' cabin. *Courtesy of OSU Special Collections & Archives Commons*

and ferry business. In 1852, the Perkinsville Election Precinct was created in Jackson County. In 1868, the precinct was renamed the Grants Pass Precinct, but it was still in Jackson County. It was not until 1885 that the eastern county line of Josephine County was adjusted and Grants Pass became part of Josephine County.

"In 1854, the Perkins were living in Southern California in El Monte, just 12 miles east of Los Angeles. They planted a vineyard and had their second child, a son named Dan Hawn Perkins. Laura Perkins was a mother for the second time and just 19 years old herself.

"In 1856, when Joel Perkins was in his 35th year, he was murdered by his hired hand and supposed friend, John Malone, who had become romantically involved with Laura Perkins. Joel Perkins, Laura, their son and daughter and John Malone were heading from California back to Lafayette with 49 head of mules and horses and trade goods to be sold when they arrived in the Willamette Valley. They stopped to visit friends and camped along the border where Joel discovered the romance between his wife and his friend. This happened near the Samuel Hughes' ranch along Cottonwood Creek which is a tributary of the Klamath River on the south side of the Siskiyous.

"On the morning of July 24, 1856, Malone and Perkins went out to round up the horses so they could continue the trip. Malone came back alone and when asked, said Perkins would be coming directly. When Perkins did not come back, as expected, Samuel Hughes initiated a search party. The neighbors were rallied and they took Malone with them. Malone began to protest and said that Perkins had probably been killed by Indians. Nothing was found.

"John Malone, Laura and her kids continued on to Jackson County where the authorities became suspicious. After being detained by the Jackson County Sheriff, John Malone confessed to the murder, claiming Laura had urged him to kill her husband. He said he shot Perkins in the head and then beat in his head with the gun and buried the body. He led them to the grave all the time saying he was under the spell of Laura. The details in the Jacksonville newspaper were very detailed and those specifics are not included here, but it reads like something from a 2010 news article, not 1856. Laura was also arrested as an accessory to murder.

"While incarcerated in the Jacksonville jail, John Malone committed suicide by hanging himself with the chain used to subdue him. He pried the ring loose from the jail floor and used it as a noose and in a matter of moments, on July 27, 1856, when the sheriff stepped outside for a brief time, John Malone killed himself. He slipped the chain over a joist at one end and through the ring at the other, making a noose, and jumped off the bedstead with about a three foot fall, and broke his neck. The sheriff returned to find Malone, 'yet swinging, and his heart had not ceased beating, but the deed was done.'

"Laura was questioned, but eventually was released. The judge said that what Malone had confessed and the story he told of Laura's involvement was basically hearsay and not enough to hold her for trial. There was no other testimony against her and the confession of Malone was not sufficient to hold her.

The Perkinsville Ferry plaque dedicated to Joel Perkins. *Grants Pass Park & Recreation Department*

"...A plaque has been recently located near Taprock at the north end of Caveman Bridge. Perkins' Ferry was upstream from the bridge just past where the new firehouse stands. The site is not accessible to the general public."

(**Authors' note:** More of the Perkins story can be found in the Lafayette, Oregon segment in Section 12)

Josephine Rollins Ort was the daughter of Floyd Rollins, the man who first discovered gold in the area. It has been said that in 1851, Josephine was the first white woman living in that part of the state. Her father named a nearby creek, "Josephine Creek," after her. Later, on January 22, 1856, a new county split off from Jackson County and was named "Josephine" after Josephine Creek. By that time, Josephine Rollins had married and gone on to California, but her name remained.

The county boundary change shifted Perkinsville from Jackson County to Josephine County and the town later known as Grant's Pass became the county seat of the newly-formed county.

In 1859, Oregon became a state and the next year a stage station called the Louse Creek Station, began operating. It was located near Louse Creek on what is now Granite Hill Road, about three miles north of Grants Pass.

Jacob Wagner was the owner/operator beginning in 1853 until he and his family were killed by Indians and the house was burned down. James McDonaugh built another station in the same location and ran it until 1864 when the road was moved to an easier grade over Merlin Hill, and the station was bypassed.

The easier grade that later bypassed the Louse Creek Station next took the stages to Thomas Croxton's station, referred to as both Croxton's and the Grants Pass Station. It was located over Merlin Hill several miles north of Louse Creek in the area of today's 7th Street (Highway 99), just north of Savage Street.

It was also a hotel and post office and Thomas Croxton was the postmaster. He submitted the name "Grant" for the post office, but it was denied because there was already a post office by that name in Oregon. So, he resubmitted the name "Grant's Pass" in honor of the new route over Merlin Hill and that name was accepted without the apostrophe in the early 1900s.

Thomas Croxton also purchased an interest in a gold mining operation which he worked during the winter months. In addition, he was a circuit-riding Methodist preacher, traveling all through Southwest Oregon and Northern California.

Croxton ran the station and post office from 1864 until about 1866 when his son-in-law, Eb Dimmick, took over. Dimmick operated the stage station until the railroad came through and ended the need for stages. Today, nothing remains of the old station.

The community moved down into the valley and closer to the river after C.J. Howard surveyed a new site, but it remained small until the Oregon & California Railroad constructed a terminus in 1883. A railroad depot was built along the tracks right in the center of what is now 6th Street. It was the first of three stations. There was also a roundhouse and later a warehouse. People from Medford and Jacksonville had to come to Grant's Pass to catch the train or ship goods until the railroad pushed farther south.

In 1885, the *Grants Pass Courier* was established, the city was incorporated and the county borders adjusted.

In 1886, the first bridge across the Rogue River was built at Grant's Pass while there was still essentially a wagon road, and in 1908, a steel bridge was built across the Rogue River to replace the older single-span one built in 1886. Connections to the rest of the world were growing and Grant's Pass was building its identity.

The Louse Creek Stage Robbery from "Oregon Back Country Is Rich in Legends of Buried Treasure" by Finn J.D. John in *Offbeat Oregon History* - January 16, 2011

"In 1890, a group of robbers held up a stagecoach near Louse Creek in Josephine County, north of Grants Pass.

"According to this legend, the robbers were chased down and killed in classic 1890s Oregon gold-field style; but one of them, with his dying breath, said the loot had been stashed a few hundred yards from the crime scene, in a hole in the ground.

"For years, treasure seekers scrounged around the area, looking under every leaf. As far as anyone knows, they found nothing.

"Then, in 1933, a gold prospector named C.L. Eubanks, beating the bushes along the creek, came across a manzanita tree with some peculiar carvings on the trunk. The date 1890 was there, along with the initials MLP and LPM (the robbers' names, perhaps?) and, below that, a message. Eubanks could just make out the words "Go to" — beyond that, the tree's healing powers in the previous 35 years had made the carving unreadable.

"That summer, Eubanks devoted himself to the hunt for the missing loot. But, so far as anyone knows, he never did find it."

In a interview done in 1938 for the *WPA's American Life Histories Collection: Manuscripts from the Federal Writer's Project, 1936-1940*, William Huntley Hampton, a mining engineer, Professor of Chemistry at Willamette University (1885-1886), and representative of the U.S. Bureau of Mines, tells his story. His interviewer was Walker Winslow:

"...I discovered a new mineral on Josephine creek – Josephinite – an alloy. It doesn't amount to much but it sounds good. Iron and nickel. There is a good deal of quicksilver in that country and it will be worked some day. Gold is all right as an incentive for discovery, but it is the other metals that have the true economic value. You are learning to get along without gold aren't you? Try to get along without steel, etc..."

"Female Miners in Southern Oregon?" Southern Oregon mining historian and author, Kerby Jackson, mentions some interesting aspects of the history of gold mining in Southern Oregon on the Oregon Gold website:

"When one thinks of the old timers who worked the rivers, creeks, gulches and hills of Oregon in search of illusive riches, we think of the iconic old grizzled pros-

pector. Red-shirted and bearded, with a pick over his shoulder, a .45 slung low on his hip and accompanied only by his trusty mule whose back is heaped high with gear, he is the traditional icon of the gold rush era. That image is so powerful and so well known that today, it adorns anything having to do with the word 'gold' and like his cousin the cowboy, everyone recognizes him just by his outline. Yet contrary to that traditional image, he wasn't the only fella who was out there breaking his back for a few bits of color. The patience and hard work of the Chinese and their contribution to the Southern Oregon Gold Rush are legendary, but even lesser known today were the efforts of Pacific Islanders (so-called 'Kanakas'), Mexicans, Free Blacks and other groups of men who came to toil in Oregon's creeks and gulches hoping to strike it rich. And as the following article, originally published over a century ago attests, not every person working in the gold fields of Oregon was necessarily 'one of the boys.'"

Article in *The Mining Review*, Grants Pass, Oregon, May 18, 1904:

"The gold fields of Southern Oregon mineral zone appear to be particularly attractive to women; at least this section has its fair share of women miners, and there is no gainsaying that it has profited thereby. A visitor to the Forest Queen hydraulic mine, near Grants Pass, will find a handsome woman busily engaged about the diggings, operating a giant, retorting gold or even 'bucking' the boulders on the bedrock. This woman is Mrs. Wisenbacher, but she was formerly Miss Pipes and was one of the stunning 'Sadie Girls' with the popular Anna Held company in 'The Little Duchess.' Last year, Mrs. Wisenbacher quit the stage and became a full 'partner' with her father and brother in the operation of the Forest Queen Mine. With a woman about to assist, the season has been a successful one at the Forest Queen.

"'Though I had become fascinated with the life behind the footlights,' said Mrs. Wisenbacher to a Mining Review correspondent, 'I am equally so with the life of a gold digger in Southern Oregon. There are few spots anywhere prettier than that where the Forest Queen is located.'

"Mrs. Wisenbacher, being a 'Sadie Girl' is, of course, handsome. She would have this season been a 'La Mode' girl in the same popular company, but she was induced by her father, who is a prominent Colorado and Idaho miner, to give up the stage and live a life of greater ease and freedom in the Southern Oregon Mountains.

"The Mining Review correspondent also came unexpectedly upon another woman miner, a woman 'piper,' if you please, in a Southern Oregon mine. She is Mrs. M.E. Moore, and this lady, like the other mentioned is a full 'partner' in a placer mine. Mrs. Moore is a piper, an expert piper – not the kind the Scotch Highlanders know so much about – but a hydraulic mining piper – the operator of a hydraulic 'giant.' Every day this woman is at her post beside the giant, long before the sun is up, and she remains there throughout her shift. None know better than she how best to swerve the big nozzle to drive an avalanche of boulders down the gulch ahead of the giant's stream, scattering them like a handfull of bullets shot from a catapult, or how to bring that long and deep growl to the monster as its cuts and gnaws deep at the base of the tower-

ing red clay bank till a great slab of a thousand tons topples and falls with a crash from the mountainside.

"Mrs. Moore has been a 'partner' of her husband in the mining business for nearly twenty years. She has followed the trails through the mining regions of Colorado, Montana, Arizona, California and Oregon, prospecting, pocket-hunting, digging, always on the lookout for a color, a strike, a bonanza. She has traveled hundreds of miles on pack pony and burro, through the snow and over the burning sands. Those twenty years, spent altogether out of doors, have been days of perfect health for her. 'Yes,' said she, 'mining is the life for me. I love it. I love the freedom of the mountains and the ozone of the pines. There is no other life like it; none as enjoyable for me, at least.'

Kerby Jackson continues...

"The Forest Queen Placer, mentioned in this article, was located on Louse Creek, a few miles east of Merlin, Oregon. At the time, it was owned by J.P. Pipes and T. Weisenbacher (or Wisenbacher). The property was originally known as the Lance Placer and at the time of this article it consisted of 212 acres of ground that was worked with the assistance of two miles worth of ditch, 2500 feet of pipe with a pressure of 200 feet, three giants and a Ruble Rock Elevator."

It was fortunate that gold mining lasted longer in the Grants Pass area than in Jackson County, because the granite soil in the Applegate Valley, Illinois Valley and some areas west of Grants Pass, was less tillable and not as conducive to agriculture. The dry summers caused a different native vegetation than most of Western Oregon. The trees were mostly madrone, deciduous oak and other species that are not common farther north. The conditions also limited the crops that could be successfully grown there. With a couple of exceptions, farming was not generally a paying industry and only provided for the needs of most settlers.

For many years, however, the growing of hops, used in the brewing process of beer and ale, was a major industry in the Medford/Grants Pass area and in the Willamette Valley.

Albert J. Walcott was the first grower on record in the Rogue Valley. He began in 1855. Since most farmers could manage to feed themselves and their families, they survived, but they needed a way to bring in cash. After the railroad came through, a market opened up for the product in U.S. and European cities. By the late 1880s, there was considerable hops' acreage being grown west of Grants Pass, and by 1910, Oregon was the largest grower of hops in the country.

For a time, hops-growing in the valley provided the highest yield in the state, but it was a labor-intensive crop. The plant is a perennial, replenishing itself from its roots, year after year. Farming hops required the plants to be staked on trellises up to 18 feet in height, in regular intervals of 3-7 feet along each row of plants. Then, wires to support the vines were run between the posts. The vines grow and produce cone-like blossoms on long stringers. For years, these were picked by hand, then cleaned and dried in a drying shed.

In September, at harvest time, many families from around the area came to help with the harvesting. They set up camps and stayed for several weeks while the whole family picked. When the number of nearby families weren't enough to complete the harvest, special trains brought hops-pickers in from other areas. The farmer usually arranged some kind of food and shelter for them.

Although it was hard work, it was also a time when people socialized together. Most accounts tell of some pleasant memories despite the hard work and sore hands from the abrasive vines.

In Southern Oregon, Prohibition in the 1920s and the lure of big money being made in fruit orchards brought the large hops' production to a halt. Suddenly, everyone was growing fruit – so many that the orchardists began harvesting more fruit than could be sold. As this became more evident, many of the orchardists began pulling up their fruit trees and going back to hops. As late as 1958, it was still considered a major crop.

In addition to its orchards and hops farming, Grants Pass also developed as a center of the timber industry in the area. It began shipping untold millions of board feet of lumber over the years.

Right across from the railroad depot on Sixth Street, an open area was called Railroad Park. People gathered there after parades on Sixth Street, to listen to speakers, band performances or even watch a fireworks display. It may have hosted a hot-air balloon event at one time or other, too.

Most of the downtown businesses were built on G Street, close to the intersection with Sixth Street.

Pacific Highway into Grants Pass

In 1910, Sixth Street, the future highway through the center of downtown was paved, although the rest of the highway into or out of town wasn't. By the early 1920s, the Pacific Highway was paved and completed as it made its way into Grants Pass. It was used by many as a means to travel for recreation, vacations and to see the sights in the area – the Oregon Caves, the Rogue River Wilderness area and popular areas for fishing and hunting among them.

Riverside Park, the first Southern Oregon free municipal auto camp, was located north of town and almost under the bridge as visitors entered on U.S. Highway 99. The Riverside Motel began as a few cabins along the river called Riverside Best Camp. Later, Scully's Landing, which served meals and drinks, was located next to the bridge on the west side and the Bridge Motel was built along the river to the left of the restaurant.

In 1916, a group of Mormon families

"Womens' First Vote." *Rogue River Courier*, **December 2, 1912**

"Two days after Oregon women were given the vote in 1912, an important city election took place in Grants Pass. A new mayor and city council were to be elected. The state took intense interest. Everyone wondered how many women would register and how they would vote.

"During the fight for women's suffrage, one of the arguments used in opposing its passage was that women didn't want the vote. The Grants Pass election decisively proved this wrong. The ladies were there early and late and they were ALL there. They cast a full half of the 1,600 ballots that were recorded.

"The administration of Robert Smith, as mayor, was given a strong endorsement. He was returned to office having received almost as many votes as his two opponents combined."

The steel bridge over the Rogue River in Grants Pass. *Courtesy of Gerald W. Williams Collections, OSU Special Collections & Archives Commons*

came to Grants Pass to build and work in the Oregon-Utah Sugar Company factory built south of the river. However, the area was lacking a good irrigation system and couldn't grow large enough crops to keep the factory open. The factory lasted two seasons and then was torn down and moved to Washington State. Some of the families stayed on.

The Grants Pass Irrigation District was formed because of that need for an irrigation system, and its formation led to the eventual construction of the Savage Rapids Dam in 1921 on the Savage Rapids area of the Rogue River. The dam was named for early settlers in the area.

The Josephine County Carnegie Library

Andrew Carnegie, immigrated with his family to the United States from Scotland when he was 13 years old. Surrounded by poverty, he needed to work to survive. From bobbin boy, then telegraph messenger, on to

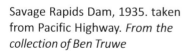

Savage Rapids Dam, 1935. taken from Pacific Highway. *From the collection of Ben Truwe*

operator, he built his skills. In 1853, Thomas Scott, superintendent of the Pennsylvania Railroad, hired Carnegie as his personal secretary. By 1859, Carnegie had become the railroad's superintendent. He invested his earnings and eventually entered the steel manufacturing business. When he sold his company and retired, he was the richest man in the world. However, his company had been associated with poor working conditions, low wages and child labor. He did little to better the life of his laborers and he came to be considered by many to be a "robber baron." While in his 30s, Carnegie publicly announced that it was his responsibility to use his wealth for the betterment of others. In 1881, he built his first library, in his hometown of Dunfermline, Scotland.

His foundation offered to build libraries in more than a thousand cities and colleges in the United States, but the city, county or college also needed to make a commitment. Oregon built more of these libraries than any other state. Besides the Southern Oregon towns of Ashland, Medford and Grants Pass, other Oregon towns along the U.S. Highway 99 route with Carnegie Libraries include: Albany, Dallas, Eugene, McMinnville, Newberg, Oregon City, Portland, Salem and Woodburn.

The Carnegie Foundation offered to build each library at a cost of $12,500 if the county would furnish the site and provide $1,200 annually toward operations.

Josephine County held special elections in 1917, 1918 and 1919 in which the measure was voted down. In 1920, Mayor Denaray received notification that the offer was about to expire. Not wanting to lose out on the opportunity, he signed the letter of acceptance himself and worked with the county court to make it happen. The library opened on April 6, 1922, under the joint management of the city and the Josephine County Court. The city and county shared the benefits of the large new library for 57 years, but it was eventually razed and replaced in 1975.

Oregon Caves

As roads improved, Grant Pass, sited on U.S. Highway 99, was in a prime location to promote tourism. As Medford began promoting itself as the "Gateway to Crater Lake," Grants Pass claimed the Oregon Caves. The establishment of the Oregon Caves National Monument in 1909 helped stimulate tourism as an economic force for the city with its access to the Rogue River, the Oregon Caves and as a junction with Highway 199 which crossed the coast range to the Pacific Ocean.

On the south side of Caveman Bridge, the road split into three highways. U.S. Highway 99 went east, Highway 238 (Williams Highway) went south and Highway 199 went west. In the mid-1920s, a small service station, with two pumps and a white uniformed attendant was located at the intersection of the highways next to an information center for travelers.

Also in the 1920s, a group of businessmen formed a service organization, calling themselves "Cavemen." Promoting the Oregon Cave connection, they dressed in pelts, carried clubs and began taking part in city parades and other events. Even the high school mascot became a Caveman. At the 1931 dedication of the Caveman Bridge, the Grants Pass Cavemen helped in the celebration.

A famous visitor to the area was Zane Grey. Grey was a passionate, but not very skillful, fisherman. He made many fishing visits on the Rogue River. His greatest thrill was to

The Caveman Bridge. *Courtesy of the Josephine County Historical Society*

ride downriver through the wild whitewater rapids. This persuaded him to buy property at Winkle Bar, upstream from Marial, where he built a fishing cabin. It was accessible only by trail or river boat. Nevertheless, Grey always arrived with family and friends plus secretaries, a cook and a cameraman.

He was born in 1872 and received a degree in dentistry from the University of Pennsylvania and practiced for several years. He was thirty and newly-married before he became a serious writer. His first stories were historical novels. It was the fishing that got him started writing westerns. He traveled from one fishing spot to another and would write a story with the local history as a background.

Grey was already well-established as a major writer when he built his Winkle Bar cabin. He wrote a number of stories centered on the Rogue Valley and describes the area in detail. His love of the wild country rings true.

When Savage Rapids Dam was built in 1921, Grey became disillusioned with the Rogue River. He later fished the North Umpqua River, but never publicized it as he had the Rogue.

"Zane Grey, the Rogue and Me" by Michael J. "Hoss" Barker, author of *Out of Oregon; Logging, Lies and Poetry* and the soon-to-be published, *My Time in Paradise*:

"When asked to write a few paragraphs about the Rogue River, I was at first pleased and eager to start my chore until it dawned on me – how do you write just a few paragraphs about arguably one of the most famous waterways in the nation?

"I make no claims as an authority on the Rogue, but the old girl and I do have a history together, albeit a far too brief one. It was in September 2001, about two

Oregon Caves Chateau, 1936. *From the collection of Ben Truwe*

weeks or so after 9-11, and I had just secured a job as a handyman at Paradise Lodge, right smack in the middle of the famed 'Wild and Scenic Section.' It was no accident I wound up on the Rogue – I was on a mission to write a book of poetry and short stories about my career as an Oregon logger and Alaska timber tramp. I was bound and determined to do it where my favorite childhood author, Zane Grey, had a cabin and plied his trade.

"*Getting on at Paradise was fate or providence – however one looks at things like that – as it lies about three or four miles downriver from Zane Grey's historically-preserved cabin on the Rogue. I would be there – literally in Paradise – for almost six years, two or three weeks on and then one week off. There are no roads in the canyon, no phone or power lines; everything comes up on a jet boat and it will forever be that way.*

"*I wasn't long in discovering the allure and majesty of the canyon from the sleepy tidewater with its bucolic and pastoral homesites on the Gold Beach end of the Rogue. There are remarkable geographical similarities as well on the upper stretch in the Medford, Grants Pass area before it enters the Wild and Scenic section.*

"*At Grave Creek, the river loses its homey rock-a-bye baby innocence of the 'old sway-back cow chewing her cud by the sagging gate,' and becomes what could be said as 'schizophrenic,' for lack of a better term.*

"*For first-timers, the river is awe-inspiring, if not terrifying, as you go shooting through boulder-strewn stretches of whitewater with the slate and granite canyon walls towering 1,500 to 2,000 feet on either side. Few places offer such a testament to the power of time, water and gravity as the mighty Rogue carves its way through the Coast Range to seek its end at the Pacific Ocean.*

"*Intermittently, the gauntlet of boulders and whitewater gives way to brief respites of calm, and one can take in the rugged beauty of spartan patches of firs and cedars mingled amongst the dogwoods and madrones, all of them clinging for dear life on the steep, craggy canyon sides. They stand over their fallen forebearers, lying strewn about as nature saw fit to place them, on the hillsides or in the water or piled up in bunches where the angry torrents of winter deluges threw them. There's no rhyme or reason to any of it, as it should be in wild places. They* lie among the thousands of silver-gray snags, already dead, that await the day they too will fall.

"There are the scars of the Silver, Biscuit, and Blossom Complex fires that ravaged the canyon, over the years. I was there for the Biscuit and Blossom fires, ready to don a life jacket and head for Gold Beach if the need arose!

"Here and there are a few isolated lodges for river-weary travelers. They are havens where they can actually have a little time to reflect on what they are experiencing and to wonder what the next day will offer.

"The seasons provide entirely different experiences for folks. Obviously, summer is the biggest draw and the critters aren't the least bit shy. The old doe and her bouncing fawns will pay you no mind and the big sow bear and her cubs could care less who you are as they tear apart a salmon and bawl like the babies they are. The otters will put on a show for you like

Rogue Awakening

Holed up in a cabin on the banks of the Rogue,
I wrote verse and I pondered and I sighed.
I was ambling through canyons rugged and steep,
As deep into the wilds I plied.

I could feel the stare of someone not there,
As wearily onward I trod.
'Twas adventure I sought, but instead what I got,
Was a glimpse of the wonders of God.

Oh Lord what a sight, in the summer's twilight,
Watching the bats try to chase down the stars.
Those planes are so rude, how dare they intrude,
I wish they'd all fly off to Mars.

I never would care, to bring grief to a bear,
That never did nothin' to me.
They rumble and tumble, then fumble and stumble,
In a race to the top of the honey tree.

Up high in the skies, what a treat for sore eyes,
Like puppets on angels' strings,
Bald eagles soar, above the din and the roar,
Waving at all with their wings.

Held captive I stare, through the river's bright glare,
At the salmon coursing below.
The wonders won't cease, and offer a peace,
That only one humbled may know.

Through oak groves galore, madrones by score,
Through fir stands tall and great.
She's carved canyon walls, like cathedral halls,
Through miles of real estate.

Further I trekked, yet onward I pressed,
Crazed for the next mountain's crest.
Through silver gray snags, over mossy backed crags,
Undaunted, I harried my quest.

Razor-backed mountains, too many for countin',
Leap skyward and stand in defiance.
I'm so far from home, and I'm so all alone,
As the solitude shattered the silence.

Then once she's got ya, she's always got ya,
She'll lure you, you'll rant and you'll rave.
Was this happenstance, my river romance?
Who knows, but we're kin 'till the grave.

~ *Michael J. Barker 2001*

they're on the payroll, and if you keep your eyes peeled, you'll see turtles sunning themselves on the rocks and the bald and golden eagles can't help but show off... you would too if you looked that good!

"Winter was my favorite time. I had the whole canyon to myself; very rarely do people venture there in the winter. Paradise, at that time, was the only lodge that kept a staff on through the winter. When the rain is persistent and they dump water from Lost Creek Dam into the river, the water can rise 10-feet overnight. It's unsafe to boat on for weeks at a time, as I found out on a few occasions.

"Amid all the splendor and beauty, one must always keep in mind that it is the wilderness, and it can be very unforgiving of your mistakes as a few unfortunate folks find out every year the hard way. Sadly, I was privy to six deaths in my tenure – every one of them a 'freak' incident.

"There are a few ways to treat yourself to the Rogue's wild and scenic wilderness area. You can either enter from Grants Pass by taking the Hellsgate jet boat trips or from Gold Beach using Jerry's Rogue Jets or the Mail Boats... I hear they merged a few years back.

"For a more peaceful, laid-back trip, there are many experienced river guides to choose from; rafting and fishing trips abound. Go for it! But be careful so that you can live to tell others about it! You'll never forget the experience."

By 1923, airplanes began taking off and landing from the American Legion Air Field just off the highway, headed north from Grants Pass. Charles Augustus Lindbergh was 25 years old when he barnstormed in the Rogue River Valley in September 1927. He had made his historic non-stop flight across the Atlantic on May 21 of that same year. He returned to the area shortly after for his first week of fishing on the Upper Rogue. Even there, he was not able to entirely get away from the public eye.

Business in Grants Pass grew along with the increase in population, first with hotels, and then motels and auto camps. Some of the big chains moved in – J.C. Penney, Montgomery Ward, Sprouse-Reitz, The Golden Rule, Piggly Wiggly Grocery and U.S. National Bank. The major gasoline companies set up service stations – Shell, Flying A and Richfield. Local businesses developed and some, including the Club Café with its Caveman theme, Nandie's Steakhouse, Zottola's Ice Cream, operated for a long time. Drug stores, hardware stores, dress shops and real estate agencies sprung up, as well as Ford, Studebaker, Huppmobile and Kaiser-Frazer car dealerships.

During the 1920s and 1930s, a hamburger stand near Railroad Park became Grants Pass' first "fast food" restaurant.

Hotels, cafes, clothing stores, grocery stores, car dealerships, auto repair shops, movie theaters, shoe stores, drug stores, sporting goods stores, hardware stores and all manner of other businesses came and sometimes left, moved, enlarged or decreased over time. Some were burned in uncontrolled fires; a brewery was closed when the city passed a local prohibition ordinance; and a family-owned cigar factory morphed into the Pastime Tavern over a period of 99 years before closing.

The Golden Rule was a well-stocked department store, part of a chain of 21 stores founded by C.C. Anderson of Colorado that included stores in Washington, Oregon, Idaho and Colorado. It operated in Grants Pass for more than 25 years and left a lot of unhappy Oregon customers when the whole chain was finally sold.

Like most other communities of the time, organizations and lodges grew and flourished. Early on, the Klu Klux Klan was active, at least in parades and gatherings. The Grange, Knights Templar and I.O.O.F. were some that were active as well as the Woodmen of the World which held log-rolling contests on a street in town.

"Lane of Lights." *Grants Pass Courier*, July 22, 1929

"Begun in May 1929, the Richfield Oil Corporation of California came to Grants Pass with their 'Lane of Lights,' a 125-foot, three-sided, neon-lit, steel tower built on land leased from the Josephine County Airport north of the city. It sat just across from where the Caveman is now. The neon lettering spelled 'Richfield' on two sides and a 15-foot tall 'G.P.' on the third. It was topped with a powerful beacon light. By July, the tower was joined by a $35,000 service station. This station and one at Roseburg were built simultaneously.

"The new station is of Norman design and measures 35 feet by 70 feet, with a central tower, 45 feet. Salesrooms comprise the central part of the building with a canopy extending over the pump toward the highway.

"Lounging rooms for men form the south wing, ending in a covered porch. Ladies' rooms form the north wing. Both wings incline toward the highway at a slight angle from the central tower, making better use of a semicircular paved driveway surrounding the building and beacon tower. Beamed ceilings will mark the interior and walls will be of rough plaster. Six such stations are planned and are in different stages of completion permitting crews skilled in different construction to move from station to station, specializing in their work. The station paving will be of rock and asphalt and 2,000 yards of fill will be required.

"About the station will be a complete semi-circle on a seventy-five-foot radius carrying six clusters of flood lights and air and water connections. The site will be planted to grass and flowers. A concrete retaining wall around the tower base will enclose other plants."

The Jackson County Commissioner's court provided more information:

"At the urging of the Richfield Oil company, several buildings were moved off the county property adjacent to the airport to give room for a prospective hotel and other concessions."

In the 1930s, the Western Express Air was advertising flights from San Diego to Seattle and Catalina by air out of the Grants Pass airfield. In 1936, air races were also held there.

After the Richfield Oil Company went into receivership before being rescued by

The restored Richfield "Lane of Lights" station located at the north end of 6th Street in Grants Pass. *From the Brew family collection*

Sinclair Oil in 1936, the stations were sold and the Grants Pass building became a tavern called the Lantern. It was successful for quite a long time. In 2011, it had been updated and enlarged and was the Beacon Bar and Grill until it closed in June 2012.

At the north end of town, on the edge of the early Grants Pass Air Field, a huge Caveman statue stands in front of the Chamber of Commerce building on Vine Street. Across the street is the preserved-but-remodeled, former Richfield Beacon station.

In the mid-1930s, under the New Deal and Works Progress Administration, a Roosevelt plan to help pull the country out of the Depression put unemployed men to work on projects for the public good. One such project was a large new post office built on 6th Street which managed to leave some of the trees which had been planted along the road around 1908. Briefly the city had two post office buildings.

In 1927, Josephine County had 43 acres of gladiolus bulbs. The next year there were an estimated 350 acres. The flower bulb industry peaked at a total of over 1,200 acres. For a time, it was an important part of the agricultural economy.

In 1936, a Gladiolus Show was proposed to celebrate the flower's success in the area. The whole Grants Pass district got behind the idea and made it a huge affair. Prizes were given for the best new variety, the tallest spike and for artistic displays.

It just so happened that famed child-actress, Shirley Temple, and her family were on a vacation trip in Josephine County during that time and came to the Gladiola Show. Shirley became the main attraction. The *Grants Pass Courier* kindly posed her pictures so as to hide the fact that she had just lost her first tooth. One of the loveliest pink gladiolus that year was named the "Shirley Temple."

The Gladiola Show was interrupted by the war, but revived again in 1947. In 1953, the show was combined with the Josephine County Fair and the gladiolus lost importance. Gradually the event passed into history.

When World War II ended, the high demand for new housing drove the demand for more lumber. California wartime employees from other parts of the country who were now without jobs, came to settle in the area.

The new one-person chainsaw and more efficient ways of getting the logs out of the forest changed the nature of logging. Highway construction cut new routes and many road workers settled down in the area when the roads were completed. Logging and lumber mills absorbed the migration.

"Oregon Trails: The Tragic Grants Pass High School Bus Crash" by Red Shannon. *The Bleacher Report***, Gonzaga University Newsletter, 2009:**

"In 1948, the Grants Pass football team defeated mighty Medford's Black Tornado and then Albany to battle against Portland powerhouse Jefferson High in Multnomah Stadium for the state championship. Grants Pass won. The follow-

The Grants Pass' mascot, "The Caveman." *From the Brew family collection*

Grants Pass High School, about 1910. *From the collection of Ben Truwe*

ing morning, the coaches, players and family began the long journey back on the twisty narrow two-lane U.S. Highway 99 over the mountains into Grants Pass. A few players were riding with family, but most chose to ride in the older Greyhound bus that had been chartered especially for the championship trip to Portland.

"The team made a lunch stop in Eugene before proceeding south through the hilly Umpqua region, stopping once more in Roseburg for gas. Coach Ingram decided to switch from the bus to ride in the car with his wife for the final stretch of the trip.

"From Roseburg south, U.S. Highway 99 crossed a series of mountain passes with steep inclines and wooden guardrails. At the foot of one of the passes, near Sunny Valley, several riders on the bus noticed a "rocking" or "swaying" as the bus passed a large truck. The darkness of early December was beginning to fall and the driver had been asked not to make unnecessary stops as a celebration would be waiting for the team.

"At 5:15, the bus crested the summit of Sexton Pass and was making its final descent into the valley and Grants Pass.

Team members had been passing the championship trophy back and forth – admiring it.

"The assistant coach, Jess Loffer noticed the driver suddenly having trouble controlling the bus steering. The front tires caught the loose gravel on the road's shoulder. The bus skidded sideways and rolled onto its top, breaking through the guardrail, eventually coming to rest with its rear section hanging over the 80-foot embankment. The full gas tank exploded and the rear section broke loose and plummeted in a ball of fire to the base of the cliff.

"Players who were not stunned or knocked cold by the initial impact forced their way through the window, rammed out by the championship trophy. Those exiting the rear of the bus tumbled down the steep embankment. Passing motorists picked up the injured and rushed them down the highway toward the hospital.

"When details of the tragedy were finally available, the toll was two dead and 25 injured. The charred remains of Sterling Heater and Al Newman were found in two separate pieces of the bus.

"The huge funeral was attended by

high school football players, coaches, students, and athletes from all over the state and the students who died are remembered in special ways at their high school. The beat up trophy is also in the trophy case.

During the 1960s, as the energy to the Civil Rights and Anti-War movements dissipated, some of the protest generation activists turned their thoughts toward environmental issues, wanting to live lightly upon the land, usually together in rural communes. This part of the Rogue Valley hosted one of the largest concentrations of back-to-the-land migrants in the United States.

In her book, *In Timber Country*, Beverly Brown describes a new population surge in the Grants Pass area:

"Land was cheap enough for local working people to acquire homesites that were widely disbursed throughout the forested area. Local people could balance their own interests with a boom-and-bust timber and mining economy by depending upon the mountains, rivers and gardens – or stubbornness and simple living – to get by during the hard times. Few people were wealthy, but few were destitute."

Some of the homesites were on logged and abused land and some on old mining claims which could be leased cheaply from the government with stipulations that some mining was to be done. At one time it was estimated that more than fifty communes were in the area.

Like other stressful times in the past, there was a lot of dissension. Some of those living in the communes disregarded the rights and safety of others which, in turn, caused tension and conflicts with long-time residents who had an established lifestyle and were opposed to the communes.

The 1964 Christmas Flood

The Caveman Bridge withstood the terrible Rogue River Flood of December 1964 in good shape. In what was termed, the "Flood of the Century" the Rogue River rose 35 feet, 15 feet over flood stage in Grants Pass. It came nine years after the previous big flood in 1955 that was the impetus for the building of the Lost Creek and Applegate Dams in the area for flood control.

In the 1920s the highway numbering system was developed. Before the roads were numbered throughout the United States, they were given colors or old trail names, once in awhile just a description – i.e. "...the road just past the Thomas barn..." When U.S. Highway 99 was decommissioned in favor of the freeway, it left an odd situation in Grants Pass. U.S. Highway 199, the branch-off highway to the coast, kept its U.S. Highway designation while the main highway didn't.

Early town development was in the G Street area which has been restored as an historic area where some of the early churches, lodges and public buildings were located.

Like many other communities along U.S. Highway 99, Grants Pass has survived through the ups and downs of resource and market changes. The move to restore its historic downtown created a pleasant area for local residents to meet their needs just as the building of the freeway took away much of the tourist traffic that supported business built along the highway.

Leaving Grants Pass, the highway joins, or is buried by, the Interstate 5 freeway to climb Mt. Sexton.

Pacific Highway on Mt. Sexton, about 1932. *Courtesy of Gerald W. Williams Collections, Special Collections & Archives Research Center, Oregon State University Libraries*

GRAVE CREEK / LELAND / SUNNY VALLEY

After descending the Sexton Pass, 13-miles north of Grants Pass, Highway 99 passes through a small valley where the town of Grave Creek was sited. The curious name has a story attached to it...

Martha Leland Crowley, a young pioneer girl with the Applegate wagon train died in 1846 of typhoid fever and was buried near a creek. Sometime later, when James W. Nesmith (eventually a U.S. Senator) was passing through the area on his way to the California gold fields, he and his party found Martha's grave, apparently desecrated by Indians. They reburied her remains and called the nearby creek, "Grave Creek."

The town that grew near there was named after the creek, but the name was legally changed to Leland after a small community began to form in 1855. The railroad called the stop "Leland," but the local residents persisted in the old name. During the 1940s, the community changed its name once again to the more appealing, Sunny Valley.

During the staging days, the stagecoaches traveled thirteen miles north of Croxton's, to Grave Creek to the donation land claim of James H. Twogood and his partner, McDonough Harkness. Both men worked pack lines from Scottsburg, Oregon to Yreka, California.

By 1853, they built a large log house, a wayside inn which included a tavern, on the same site.

McDonough Harkness became its first postmaster, but when he was killed by Indians while riding dispatch for the U.S. Army, his brother, Samuel Harkness, took over his interests and became Twogood's partner.

During the Indian battles of 1855-56, their house was commandeered by the U.S. Army. A stockade was erected and a hospital was installed in parts of the house. It became a refuge known as Fort Leland. After the Indians retreated, Fort Leland became a gathering point of a large force of regular army and volunteers.

A major encounter of the war took place some eight miles west of the fort and resulted in 37 dead, wounded or missing. Some were buried north of Fort Leland at the corner of the present Leland Road and U.S. Highway 99.

Twogood sold out his interest in the hotel in 1866 when he moved out of Oregon, and Harkness continued to operate it until 1879 when the California & Oregon Stage Company built their own stage house and barn one half-mile south of Grave Creek House. It became a home station for the stage drivers and was the only station facility in Oregon actually owned and operated by the stage company. It effectively put the Grave Creek House out of business.

The building of the Pacific Highway brought other settlers and businesses into the area. The Grave Creek Store sometimes included a restaurant; the Radio Park Auto Court had a gas station, cabins and a dance hall; Shady Nook store, restaurant and campground also welcomed visitors.

In 1939, The Tillicum Hotel, or Tillicum Tavern, boasted a café and Standard Oil products and was in business next to the store.

The privately-owned Applegate Trail Interpretive Center Museum has recently been developed to create a historic representation of the area and its earliest settlement period. Extremely well done as a tourist draw, it shares worthy artifacts and history of the emigrant travelers on the southern route to Oregon led by Levi Scott and Jesse Applegate.

In 1917, Julian Elmer Nelson, the son of Swedish emigrants, was a resident engineer with the newly-formed Oregon State Highway Commission. About a year later, he was sent to Josephine County to work on a road project. He settled in Glendale with his wife and three children. It took nearly a year for the five-mile road-grading project to eliminate four steep grades on what would become the Pacific Highway between Grave Creek and Wolf Creek. When the project ended in 1918, Nelson quit the highway commission and took a job as superintendent of construction with a Grants Pass company

Leland School (above) and Leland Store (below).
From the collection of Ben Truwe

Restored Grave Creek covered bridge, 1954. *From the collection of Ben Truwe*

that was contracted to grade an additional five miles of the highway and then pave both sections.

In 1920, Nelson bid on the contract to replace a timber bridge over Grave Creek while the covered bridge was still in use. Painted bright white, it is one of the few covered bridges that remain in Southern Oregon. It took him four months to complete it.

Nelson also built a simple concrete span over Wolf Creek near the Wolf Creek Inn for the State Highway Commission. Once a vital bridge on the Pacific Highway, it was bypassed in favor of U.S. Highway 99 and, eventually, Interstate 5.

From a 1918 newspaper article:

"At a meeting of the State Highway Commission held at Salem Tuesday, three post road projects were authorized. They will probably be paid out of the first $400,000 worth of Bean-Barrett bonds which were sold yesterday by the State Board of Control.

"The first three post road projects include what is known as the Wolf Creek and Grave Creek projects of nearly five miles on the Pacific Highway just south of the Douglas County line to be constructed for $83,606.50.

"Another of the three projects is from Canyon Creek Canyon, south of Canyonville, to the Johns ranch. This is a distance of about two and one-half miles, and will cost $23,680.60.

"The third project is from Myrtle Creek to Dillard, a trifle over 10 miles distance. This improvement will cost $173,648.50.

"These projects represent a total estimate of $280,935.60, of which the state pays half, the Federal Government standing the balance."

Throughout the years, the Grave Creek watershed was home to hundreds of gold miners. Many millions of dollars' worth of gold came out of the area. The community of Golden and other settlements formed when miners and their families arrived, but they all but died out when the easy gold ran out and the miners left to seek it elsewhere. Golden, located about 4 miles east of Interstate 5, is easily accessed from the Wolf Creek Tavern and is an interesting place to visit. The little church there has been preserved.

Grave Creek and its tributaries have produced quantities of placer gold.

According to the Oregon Gold website:

"The largest dredging operation in Josephine County was conducted between 1935 and 1938 on the south side of Grave Creek east of Leland. Bedrock became too deep for the dredge to clean and operations terminated. An undisclosed, but significant amount of gold was recovered."

An interesting notice appeared in the November 21, 1901 edition of the *Rogue River Courier*:

"We have a miner who stands 7 feet 8 inches in his stocking feet. If anybody in the country can beat that we will look over our miners again and perhaps we can find a bigger one. Grave Creek is noted for its big men, also big women."

The Rand National Historic Site

The Rand National Historic Site is about 20-miles west of Sunny Valley and is on a terrace on the west side of the Rogue National Wild and Scenic River. The gold found there drew miners to the area in the 1850s. Rich gold veins were discovered in 1874. In 1906, the Rand Mining Company and the Almeda Mining Company joined and constructed several dwellings and a school on the terrace. After President Theodore Roosevelt created the Siskiyou National Forest in 1906, Rand became home to the first Forest Service rangers serving the Siskiyou National Forest.

From 1933 to 1941, 200 Civilian Conservation Corps (CCC) workers made Rand Camp No. 1650 their home. The Forest Service managed most of the area projects and CCC enrollees assisted forest managers with fire suppression, road construction, communication development and recreation site construction. They remodeled the ranger's residence, the protective assistant's residence and the Rand Ranger Station. A garage, woodshed, fire warehouse, barn, blacksmith shop, gas and oil house and extensive masonry walls were also constructed. The barracks and supporting structures that housed the CCC are no longer standing, although all other structures are still on site today.

The CCC work was not limited to improvements at Rand. The CCC built sections of the first truck roads in the canyon and a 344-foot-long cable suspension bridge over the Rogue River at Grave Creek. It was replaced in the 1960s by the existing bridge. The Corps also battled fire on the rugged canyon slopes and collected wood ticks for the Rocky Mountain Laboratory to help with the study of Spotted Fever.

In 1963, the Siskiyou National Forest moved the Galice Ranger District headquarters into Grants Pass. After the passage of the Wild and Scenic River Act of 1968, designating the Rogue River as "wild and scenic," the Bureau of Land Management acquired the Rand site. In 1999, Rand was listed on the National Register of Historic Places and essentially remains the same as when the structures were first built.

ALMADEN / WOLF CREEK

Not actually one of the official stage stops, the historic Wolf Creek Tavern, four miles north of Grave Creek, was used for a rest stop for weary travelers who wanted a good meal and to spend the night in a comfortable setting before continuing their journey. The original hotel/inn was known as "The Six Bit House" and it stood about a mile northeast of the Wolf Creek Community Center.

Folklore has it that it was given the name

The historic Wolf Creek Tavern, now on the National Register of Historic Places, 1948. *From the collection of Ben Truwe*

when the owner interrupted the hanging of an Indian near the ranch by some of his customers. The owner demanded that the hanging be temporarily delayed until the Indian paid six bits – 75 cents – that the owner was owed. It's not a funny story, but it was indicative of the times.

Regular California & Oregon stagecoach service began in 1860, but the current Wolf Creek Tavern was not built until about 1883, just as the railroad came through and replaced the stagecoaches. It was built for Henry Smith, a local merchant-entrepreneur, and was well-crafted by local sawyers and skilled workers in the building trades. The inn served local traffic and travelers to area mines and other places along the road. It was never a stagecoach station of the California & Oregon Stage Line, although it looked the part and occasionally some stagecoach passengers were discharged and picked up there. The timing was off and it was too close to the contracted stations, both north and south to be official. However, the Greenback Mining Company ran a stagecoach between the hotel and the mine for a short time.

During the 1920s, under the ownership of John and Dinky Dougall, more rooms were added. Located halfway between Sacramento and Portland, it was a good place to take a break in travel. Overnight accommodations, meals and a friendly welcome brought guests back more than once, and some were famous – President Rutherford B. Hayes, Jack London, Sinclair Lewis and Clark Gable were among celebrities who stayed there.

The Dougalls owned it from 1922-1935 and John compiled a photographic history.

Their daughter, Martha, was born in Room 4. She told stories of wolves that gathered around the house, within their sight, when food was being cooked and how she and her brother were sometimes tied with a rope during outside play in the rose garden to keep the wolves from getting them.

When U.S. Highway 99 was replaced by the freeway in the 1960s, the building was slightly off the main travel route and tourists did not stop as frequently. The Oregon State Parks and Recreation Division acquired the Wolf Creek Tavern in 1975 and designated it as a State Park. The building was restored as an inn and restaurant and is now on the

National Register of Historic Places. It is the oldest continuously-operating hotel in the state.

The town of Wolf Creek, Oregon is located about 8 miles north of Sunny Valley, about a mile off of I-5 Exit 76.

The early residents of Wolf Creek grew some fruit, farmed and raised poultry, but like other communities in the area, the biggest draw was gold mining.

The Wolf Creek post office was established in 1882, and a railroad station called "Almaden" was located in the same area in 1883. The station was renamed to match the post office in 1888. At one time there were two lodges, a mercantile, a garage, a train station, the Triangle Motor Court, two hotels and a school with 122 pupils in grades 1-12 in Wolf Creek.

Several small communities in the area developed around working mines, but most of the supplies came from the Wolf Creek settlement, often packed out to the mines by horses or mules. As the mines petered out, the hard-core miners moved on, selling their claims if they could.

In *First There Was Twogood; A History of North Josephine County* by Larry L. McLane tells the story of proposed community developer and minister, W.G. Smith:

"The Reverend W.G. Smith had big dreams for Wolf Creek, Oregon. He envisioned a sober, happy, industrious community whose vast fruit orchards would make the area self-sustaining. To make his dream come true, he purchased over 2,700 acres of land which he subdivided and sold through brochures mailed back East. Many came.

Miners working at Leland. *Courtesy of the Josephine County Historical Society*

A ranch scene near Wolf Creek. *Courtesy of Gerald W. Williams Collections, OSU Special Collections & Archives Commons*

Pacific Highway as it climbs Wolf Creek Hill, 1920. *Courtesy of the OSU Special Collections & Archives Commons*

A load of logs on the way to the mill going over Wolf Creek Hill in 1951. *Courtesy of the Oregon Department of Transportation (ODOT)*

"There were flaws in Rev. Smith's vision. It takes years for an orchard to produce sufficient fruit to be marketable. Even more important, Wolf Creek was in the mountains where fruit developed weeks later than in the valleys. By harvest, the valley orchards had cornered the fruit market. The vision began to fall apart.

"Adversity brought bickering and name-calling. Smith became the most un-

popular man in town. The plan that had so hopefully started in 1908, floundered and finally died in the 1920s."

There is still an occasional old fruit tree around Wolf Creek that dates from that almost-forgotten era.

Logging also enhanced the local economy until that, too, peaked and began its decline. As late as 1953, there were two lumber mills in Wolf Creek with a wigwam burner still smoking. One was a planing mill called Trufir Lumber and the second was the sawmill, Tunnel Creek Lumber Company. It and the Schmitt and Crews Lumber Company sawmill at nearby Fortune Branch furnished rough lumber for finishing at Trufir.

The Tunnel Creek Lumber Company may have derived at least part of its name from the tunnel the railroad put through the mountain between Wolf Creek and Glendale. One tale mentioned that a young woman from Glendale worked at Wolf Creek and walked through the tunnel daily to get to work.

In her book, *As It Was,* Carol Barrett writes that well-known author, Jack London, was a superstar in the early 1900s. His name was often in the papers for barroom fights, notorious love affairs and an adventurous past.

"He loved the wild outdoors and hated the destruction of the land that he saw in his native California. He bought some misused, over-grazed land in Sonoma Valley, California and tried to reclaim it. The story of this project and his belief in man's relationship with the land was used in his book The Valley of the Moon. *While he was writing the book, he lived in Wolf Creek, Oregon. One of his favorite spots was a mountain peak nearby which was named London Peak. This was only one of several summers London spent in the Rogue River Valley."*

Section 4

U.S. HIGHWAY 99 - WOLF CREEK TO WINCHESTER

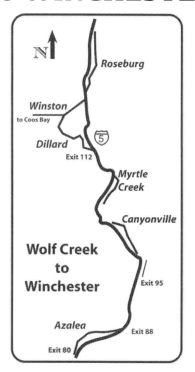

On Highway 99, as it leaves Wolf Creek behind and just before the turn-off to Glendale, is a road sign that says "Stage Road Pass, 1,916 altitude." At this point, the highway is going through the Umpqua Mountains and descending into the Cow Creek Valley.

Cow Creek makes a large circling route through the valley and is crossed by Highway 99 twice – once as it enters the community of Glendale and again, farther north as it reaches the Umpqua River.

The general topography of the Cow Creek area is one of ridges and valleys. The surrounding mountains reach altitudes as high as 5,000 feet, according to the early railroad surveys, and the Cow Creek Valley itself extends some 10 miles in length and lies in a north-to-south direction.

There are very few places in this valley that have large flat, open spaces and because dense forests cover a large part of this section, communities are somewhat isolated from each other and from industrial centers by the terrain. The railroad created some connection, but it was the highway that brought about the most important changes.

The Cow Creek Valley was part of the traditional hunting, fishing and gathering grounds of the Cow Creek band of the Umpqua tribe of Indians for many generations. The Umpqua tribe was made up of bands living in independent villages, each made up of several families. Each village had its own headman and some had a war leader or medicine man, sometimes a woman healer. Since they were situated away from most other Northwest groups, they developed their own culture and dialect. They were semi-nomadic part of the year, hunting, fishing, gathering berries, acorns, seeds and the camas bulbs which supplied their food needs.

By 1852, the Cow Creek Band was decimated to half its original number by epidemics thought to be brought into the area by the miners, trappers and white settlers. In 1853, the remaining survivors ceded 800-square miles of the land to the United States government for the promised sum of $12,000 and a small reservation to be sited in the general region. The treaty was never fulfilled and the tribe was never officially recognized by the U.S. Government until a full century later.

"The Cow Creek Indian Story" from the Cow Creek website:

"The Cow Creek Band of Umpqua Tribe of Indians is one of nine federally recognized Indian Tribal Governments in the State of Oregon. The Cow Creek Tribal Nation, located in Southwestern Oregon, has nearly 1,594 members who are governed by an elected eleven member council known as the Tribal Board of Directors. The Cow Creek Tribe has a rich history in southern Oregon that reflects hard work, perseverance and the desire to be self-reliant.

"The Cow Creek Tribe is unique in that they, on September 19, 1853, were one of the first two tribes in Oregon to secure a Treaty with the United States of America. This Treaty, ratified by the U.S. Senate on April 12, 1854, established the Government-to-Government relationship between two sovereign governments. As a result of the Treaty, the Cow Creek Tribe became a landless tribe, ceding more than 800 square miles of Southwestern Oregon to the United States. The Tribe was promised 2.3 cents an acre for their land. The U.S. Government was selling that same land, through the Donation Land Claims Act, for $1.25 an acre to pioneer settlers. This Treaty between the United States Indian agent, General Joel Palmer, and the Cow Creek Indian people, had many deficiencies. Specifically, there was no understanding by the Indians of the language or the concept of signing (making their mark on) the Treaty document and further, there was no understanding by the Indians of land ownership, let alone land boundaries (hunting, fishing and gathering sites, as well as tribal composites, were well established)."

This area has its share of stories about the persecution of the Natives by the early settlers. The persecution included requiring the native children to attend the mission school in Umatilla where an attempt was made to cure their Indian ways; later, it included the tribe's near-starvation. The legends also tell about some of the people from the desperate Cow Creek Band who joined the warring Rogue River Indian tribe.

Efforts were made to remove the tribe to the Coast Reservation at the Siletz agency near present-day Newport or to the Grand Ronde agency further north. Both reserva-

Lithograph of Leven's Station from A.G. Walling's *History of Southern Oregon*, 1884

tions were on land west of the Willamette Valley and totally foreign to them. Many of the Cow Creeks resisted relocation efforts. They remained in seclusion while trying to maintain their way of life. Eventually many of them married pioneers, miners and fur traders in the area. However, they continued to meet and hold council as their ancestors had always done. A century later, the historical tribal documents from these meetings were instrumental in providing proof of the Cow Creek tribal ways.

The rest of their story is continued in the Canyonville segment later in this chapter...

GALESVILLE

After leaving the Grave Creek station, the stagecoaches traveled 13 miles farther north to the next stage stop.

In 1854, Daniel Levens had a 320-acre donation land claim which was the fifth DLC awarded in the Cow Creek Valley. When the stagecoaches began making runs up and down the wagon track, passing right at his door, Levens decided to open his house as a stopping place for the stages. It became famous, known as Levens Station, and was an important stop for the California & Oregon Stage Company. The home had a stockade built around it during the Rogue River Indian War of 1855 and 1856, and it became known as Galesville when the post office was established there.

Located about 2½ miles from present-day Azalea, Oregon, it was the California Stage Company contract station for the Cow Creek Valley. It provided comfortable accommodations and excellent meals for the weary travelers during the whole period of time that the stages ran. Daniel Levens, the owner of the stage stop was also the postmaster of Galesville for many years and owned property – a hotel and store – in nearby Canyonville.

The Levens' stage stop also served as a "home station" for drivers. They used it as a layover on their runs and provided lodging for the passengers, as well. The hotel was known as both the Galesville Hotel and the Dew Drop Hotel. It burned to the ground in 1931, but portions of the barn were still standing as of 1987.

A birdseye view of Glendale, Oregon, 1915. *Courtesy of Gerald W. Williams Collections, OSU Special Collections & Archives Commons*

STUMP TOWN / JULIA / GLENDALE

A log flume at work - *Courtesy of Gerald W. Williams Collections, Special Collections & Archives Research Center, Oregon State University Libraries*

Although the builders of the Pacific Highway followed the route laid out by the Oregon & California Railway much of the time, it didn't always. Glendale, north of Grants Pass and located on Cow Creek, is the southernmost community in Douglas County. It had an economy based on logging and mills and was a helper-station along the Oregon & California Railroad. The railroad came through the logging settlement first called "Stump Town," and even put a station there in 1881. When the highway was finally built, it passed several miles east of the town. That left the small unincorporated city, first named Julia, and then renamed Glendale, mostly isolated. Still, the population depended on the highway for transport to any place out of their own town, particularly after the passenger trains quit running.

Loggers in the Cow Creek drainage and many other places where the forests were in terrain too rugged to run a railroad, built huge log flumes to transport logs. The earliest were square chutes of wood raised above the terrain on scaffolding. Water was diverted from a river or lake and the logs were washed down the flume to the mills, sometimes for many miles.

Glendale was an area where a large flume was built. Occasionally, "flume-herders" would ride small boats or craft down the flumes in order to check them for needed repairs and maintenance. They were the actual precursor for the log rides that are so popular in many amusement parks today.

A fire in the early 1900s and then a second major one in 1928, burned out much of the Glendale business district. This was a very common occurrence in communities where there was no ready-access to water or a way to deliver it, particularly when many, or all, of the buildings were constructed of wood. The business district was rebuilt, but today there are few historic buildings left in the town.

The area around Glendale was not an easy place to live, but when Mother Nature conspired to make matters worse, it became much harder.

In 1890, Glendale had seven feet of snow. The town became isolated when train service came to a halt. Cattle and wildlife died, and in the spring, melting snow brought floods and landslides.

Glendale resident, Julian Elmer Nelson, an Oregon State Highway Commission civil engineer who designed major improvements of Pacific Highway during the 1920s in Josephine County, was also responsible for improving Glendale's water system, expanding the local cemetery and platting subdivisions nearby.

One of Glendale's claims to fame was the fact that resident, Kathryn Clarke, whose family owned and operated a hotel in town, was elected as Oregon's first female senator.

NEW ODESSA

In 1882, an early Russian Jewish commune with about 35 members called New Odessa was established on heavily-wooded land near Glendale. Only a small portion of the land was tillable. They purchased the property, which contained two homes, with a down payment of $2,000. The remaining $2,800 was due in installments over the next few years. The group lacked agricultural experience and relied heavily on borrowed equipment and advice given by those already settled in the area.

From "New Odessa Colony" by Joshua Binus in Oregon Historical Society's online *Oregon History Project*:

"In 1881, the assassination of Czar Alexander II led to a renewed wave of pograms against Jewish communities across the Russian Empire. Many Jews responded to the rise in anti-Semitic violence by emigrating. In the Ukraine, one of the emigration organizations formed to assist refugees was called Am Olam ('the eternal people'), which encouraged Jews to resettle in Palestine and in the United States as agriculturalists. Am Olam's leaders urged Jews should abandon their business-oriented lifestyles, which they believed provided a basis for degrading Jewish stereotypes and conspiracy theories, and return to the age-old agricultural traditions documented in the Torah.

"The first group of 'Am Olamniks' arrived in New York in January 1882 and made plans to form a socialist agricultural commune. They sent scouting parties to Texas, Oregon and Washington before deciding to locate their community in

Oregon's Douglas County. In September 1882, thirty-four Am Olamniks arrived in Portland, and after negotiating the purchase of 760 acres from Hyman and Julia Wollenberg in March 1883, many relocated to the heavily-wooded land between Wolf and Cow creeks in the upper Umpqua River Valley. According to the Articles of Incorporation for New Odessa, the community was created for 'mutual assistance in perfecting and development of physical, mental, and moral capacities of its members.'

"By 1884, the population of New Odessa had grown to sixty-five but the community was marked by a disproportionately high number of single men compared to a small number of families and single women. For its income, the community cut and sold timber to the Oregon and California Railroad for use as railroad ties and fuel. For food they planted vegetables and wheat on more than 100 acres of land and hunted and foraged food from their surrounding environment. Where the colonists found themselves short on agricultural experience and supplies, the surrounding community lent tools and expertise to help them.

"Political divisions within New Odessa ultimately led to the community's demise. William Frey, a charismatic, but uncompromising Russian atheist who had been asked to join the community in 1882, believed that the entire community should adhere to a 'religion of humanity' with philosophical roots in the positivism preached by Auguste Comte. Not everyone was willing to adhere to Frey's communal ideology, and by 1885 the community had fractured beyond repair. During the next two years, the population of New Odessa abandoned the community, most returned to New York, and in 1888 the land was returned to its previous owners."

Past the Glendale turnoff on U.S. Highway 99, an early automobile driver would come to one of the many auto camps which developed to meet the needs of both the automobile and travelers. The Fortune Branch Auto Camp had gasoline and cabins to rent and was purported as a good place to stay.

STARVOUT / BOOTH / AZALEA

***Oregon, End Of The Trail* by the Workers of the Writers' Program of the Work Projects Administration in the State of Oregon, 1940:**

"Azalea, in a little open valley surrounded by forests of fir, yellow pine, oak and alder, was named because of the abundance of this plant with it's beautiful tinted blossoms in the vicinity."

Azalea is an unincorporated community in Douglas County – about 10 miles northeast of Glendale in the Cow Creek Valley. A post office named "Starvout" was established in 1888. The name was changed to "Booth" in 1907 and, finally, Azalea in 1914.

"The History of the Cow Creek Valley" and "The Johns' Family" by Jennene Johns, *Pioneer Days in the South Umpqua Valley*, Vol. 29, p 17-32.

"The first store in Azalea was built in 1917 by Thomas and Winifred Townes. The lumber was cut in the Pickett Mill. The store opened before anything was finished inside. Originally the store

building was a long building with only one room across the south end, both upstairs and downstairs. The downstairs room was their living quarters. They started having Saturday night dances on the upper floor right away. Winnie Townes served supper at 12 o'clock sharp on a long table set up in the store downstairs. Everything shut down for at least an hour so everyone could eat. The neighborhood gatherings were very popular, but as more people got cars, the crowds became too large to handle.

"Several years later, the room on the north side was built for a dining room. Winnie cooked and served chicken dinner on Sunday, only for awhile, then turned it into a general restaurant. The upstairs was later converted to a hotel, known as the Canyon Pass Hotel that accommodated many travelers, including a number of celebrities. The store was later sold and a service station added. By 1928, it also housed the Azalea Post Office...

"...Eighty years ago, how very different the road from Azalea to Canyonville was than it is now. Sometimes when I get in the car and run over to Canyonville, which is only about a ten-minute ride, I think about what it must have been like for our ancestors, really such a short time ago. Clara Johns, who lived on the hill over what is now the southbound lane of the freeway at Azalea, wrote in her calendar diary on August 11, 1916, '83 motors and one cycle went past today;' and on July 3, 1917, '120 autos passed today.' Can't you imagine how many go by on the freeway on a July 3rd now?

"...I was asked to write something about the highway, the way it was in comparison to the way it is now. I thought about it and decided the best way was to write about some of the things family members have told us and about some of the notes from Grandma Johns' calendar diary. Ed Johns told of furnishing material and labor for building 1500 feet of corduroy road between Azalea and Canyonville in 1920. Corduroy road was built by placing logs one after another across the road. This type of road was especially useful in wet spots. Can't you imagine how rough that would have been to drive over?

"...In the late 1930s and early 1940s, before the new highway went in, about 200 yards north of the Cow Creek Road intersection and just below the Johns' ranch house, there was a very sharp curve. At that time, during one of those years, there was, on the average, one head-on collision a month on that curve, quite a few fatalities, and lots of people badly injured.

"...There was a Greyhound bus wreck about a mile north of the Azalea interchange in about that time period. The bus went over the bank and turned upside-down. There were people pinned in it with gas dripping down on them for hours. For fear of it catching on fire, the police had Ed Johns, who had a cat working up Cow Creek Road about a mile, walk his cat down Cow Creek Road and up the highway to where the bus was. He then had to pull the bus off of the people who were pinned in. There was not a wrecker around big enough to remove it. The people were pinned in for several hours before they could get them out. I believe there were several fatalities in that accident."

"The T.B. Johns Place" by Jennene Johns:

"After coming to Azalea, and for years while the horse and buggy were the only means of travel by road, the home of the Johns' family became known as a good place to stop and the hosts' kindness was long remembered. Clara Johns would cook for guests nearly every night and then give them a bed to sleep in. Of course, there would also then be breakfast in the morning to fix. There was always a place in the barn for a guest's team of horses. They had their meals at the dinner table with the family and one bedroom upstairs was reserved for overnight guests. It had the best homemade comforter on the bed and a beautiful set consisting of a china wash bowl, pitcher for water and a chamber pot. The wash bowl and pitcher sat on a marble-topped wash stand and the chamber pot on a shelf below.

"Heavy freight wagons pulled by teams of six to eight horses and mules hauled mining equipment to the mines at Grants Pass and Jacksonville. These freight drivers often stopped at the Johns' place overnight and Shorty and Ed would have to give up their beds and sleep on the floor if the guest room was already occupied.

"Also, during the summer, there were a lot of 'hobos' walking through the country. They would all stop at the ranch looking for work or a hand-out. Clara would have them split wood for her. When she thought they had enough to pay for their food, she would call to them, hand their meal out the kitchen window and they would eat it at the table in the woodshed. Usually, they would then go back and cut more wood so she would give them cake or something to take with them.

The Canyon Creek / Pioneer / Cow Creek Bridge south of Canyonville, Oregon, 1915. *Courtesy of Gerald W. Williams Collections, OSU Special Collections & Archives Commons*

"Clara Johns was deaf in her later years, so she recruited her granddaughter, Bernice Johns, starting when she was very young, to stay with her if she had to be alone. People startled her if they suddenly appeared near her and she hadn't seen them."

Heading north on Highway 99, the mountainous 1.2 million acres of the Umpqua National Forest to the east were closer to the road and for the communities and towns along the road, they were an integral part of the area's development.

"Canyon Creek Arch Bridge" from an article written by Bill Miller for the *Medford Mail Tribune* 10/02/11

"In 1920, about six miles south of Canyonville, at the spot where the pioneers traveling north on the Applegate Trail were nearly defeated by the steep canyon walls, the Pioneer Bridge was completed. It was 118 feet long, with a narrow 19-foot-wide roadbed between curbs. It was supported by a 20-foot-wide reinforced concrete arch. It was funded by the United States Bureau of Public Roads, designed by an unknown architect, and built by Stebinger Brothers, contractors from Portland..."

Plans to widen the highway began just before World War II, and by 1951, the road had been reconstructed and relocated. The bridge was gone. By the end of the next decade, even the relocated highway would disappear under Interstate 5.

"Mail Plane Crash" by Ron Bartley, *Pioneer Days in the South Umpqua Valley*, Vol. 25, p.18

"On Tuesday morning, October 2, 1928, airmail pilot for Pacific Air Transport, Grant Donaldson, was flying the route between Portland and Oakland-San Francisco. He ran into low clouds hanging over the mountains north of Canyon Creek Pass. The passenger with the mail in the enclosed cabin behind him in the Boeing 40c eliminated the possibility of parachuting to safety, so he entered the canyon at the pass, flying the big biplane in the narrow space between the tree tops below and the low clouds and fog above. As he flew, he looked down to keep the Pacific Highway in sight. As he approached the Pioneer Bridge, two and a half miles from the pass, it happened... The plane went down."

"Mail Plane Crashes at Canyonville," the *Roseburg News Review.*

"A Pacific Air Transport company plane flying from Medford to Portland crashed this morning on the summit of Canyon Mountain, 9 miles south of Canyonville, seriously injuring H.G. Donaldson, the pilot. A passenger, said to be B.P. Donovan of Los Angeles, was reported to be missing. Donaldson was brought to Roseburg in a semiconscious condition, suffering from bruises, concussion and burns. He was taken to Mercy Hospital.

"The accident occurred about 10 o'clock this morning when the plane, flying at a small elevation because of low-hanging clouds, was caught in shifting fog in the canyon south of Canyonville and crashed.

"Despite his serious injuries, the pilot made his way to the highway, about a hundred yards away, where he was picked up in a semiconscious condition. He

gasped about incoherent details of the wreck before lapsing into an unconscious state. Men were immediately sent out to the scene to look for the passenger who was supposed to have been in the ship at the time of the wreck..."

Roseburg News-Review, October 3, 1928:

"The body of D.P. Donovan of Los Angeles, passenger in the ill-fated Pacific Air Transport mail plane wrecked yesterday south of Canyonville, was found late yesterday afternoon in the cabin of the burned plane. The body was charred beyond all recognition, the extremities being completely burned away. Searchers were greatly handicapped by brush and fog, and did not find the plane until several hours after the accident. Pilot Grant Donaldson who was terribly burned about the face and hands was taken to Portland yesterday evening in a plane piloted by Lt. J.R. Cunningham.

"Donovan apparently was killed by the impact when the plane struck the mountainside. The plane was finally located because it had mowed the tops from several large trees before it crashed on the hillside..."

According to local resident, Ernie Shippen of Canyonville, following the crash, a few older pilots and several local residents told of rumors that the plane's passenger, Mr. Donovon, had been transporting diamonds. Apparently, the area has been well-searched by treasure-seekers in hopes of recovering some of the missing diamonds, but so far their searches have been in vain.

Like other Northwest mountains, Canyon Mountain, where the plane crash occurred, could be dangerous in more ways than one. On January 16, 1974, nine employees were working inside a Pacific Northwest Bell structure at the base of the mountain when a 125-foot-wide, 400-foot-long mudslide slammed into the 15' x 20' concrete building and pushed it into the nearby creek. It buried the structure and all nine men inside under a vast amount of mud and debris, killing them instantly. The slide came in the wake of heavy rains and snow melt-off that caused the streams throughout the Northwest to reach record highs. It was considered one of the deadliest single landslides of the 20th century in the U.S. There is a memorial to those men at Stanton Park in North Canyonville.

"Alpine Lodge" no author named, *Pioneer Days in the South Umpqua Valley*, Vol. 25, p. 23:

"Two miles south of Canyonville, the Alpine Lodge Resort, cottages, coffee shop and gas station were nestled in a deep canyon just off Highway 99. The large log lodge was originally built as the home of Leander and Loulla Converse and their ten children in 1932. It offered an old-fashioned fireplace, a radio and plenty of books for a chilly, rainy day.

"Dee Humbracht, the owner from 1935 until 1944, established a trout farm where a visitor could catch their own mountain trout for dinner. There was a small lake within a stone's throw of the cottages for a swim, and a wide scenic creek ran within 20 feet of the backs of the cottages. Tame ducks and geese were always on hand for treats. Nearby were tame deer, native pheasants, golden pheasants and imported geese. The lodge had its own cows and chickens providing fresh food to the coffee shop.

"After Dee Humbracht married, she sold the lodge and several other families later owned it. The coffee shop and gas stations were managed by different local people. The lodge burned and Interstate 5 took the spot, leaving the location barely visible. A long list of local people were involved over the time the popular resort was a special stopover on Highway 99."

"Mexia's" by Jo-Brew:

"For years, a famous stop for travelers on U.S. Highway 99 was at Mexia's Pies, a tiny little isolated house nestled in the trees and topped by a big sign visible from the road. The pies were so good, the stop became legendary. Although I had many testimonies to her pies, particularly apple, and some physical description of the couple who ran the pie shop, there wasn't much else on record about them.

"I knew he was tall and quite aristocratic in appearance and she seemed small and plump with black hair.

"I did know that it was an old cook stove with a large oven that the pies came out of, that the four or five tables with white covers were in their living room, and I knew that he served customers in a white dish towel apron. His wife usually stayed in the kitchen, often on a stool with a bowl of pie dough on her lap to work, but she was alert and inquisitive, and kept an eye on customers through a partially-open door. I didn't know they also served sandwiches and occasionally hired a girl to help. It was during my interview with Verna Forncrook Wilson that more pieces fell into place. Their names were Mr. and Mrs. Loson Winn and he had grown up in Canyonville."

Loson and his wife Mexia began serving their famous pies north of Canyonville in 1927 from their Fountain Service Station. When Interstate 5 was built, replacing U.S. Highway 99, the house was put on wheels and pulled across the canyon onto a frontage road where Mrs. Winn continued to bake.

Mexia was quoted in the article as saying that they didn't plan on quitting any time soon, even though Loson was 81 years old at the time.

CANYONVILLE

Located on the California-Oregon Trail, Canyonville, sits at the northern end of Canyon Creek Gorge, at the confluence of the South Umpqua River, Canyon Creek and Cow Creek. It is a trade town that developed as a station on the California-Oregon Stage route. That route, traveled by Hudson's Bay Co. trappers and early settlers and later followed by the Pacific Highway in many places, goes along Canyon Creek. The original travelers found the passage at the southern end of the state, crossed into California, back around the southern end of Klamath

"Bridge to Nowhere." The old entrance of U.S. Highway 99 into Canyonville from the south. The road dead ends on the other side of the bridge. *From the Brew family collection*

Lake and up to Fort Hall. There they managed to induce some members of the 1846 migration to follow their lead over the new trail. The immigrants with loaded wagons, animals and families were harassed by Indians, struggled to get through the mountains to the Rogue River Valley, then the mountains of the Umpqua chain, facing starvation and barely surviving the steep descent of some 1,300 feet, strewn with fallen trees and washouts. The trail they blazed became a road as its use increased, heading in both directions.

Jackson Reynolds settled the initial donation land claim where the town was sited in 1851, and later sold the land to Jesse Roberts. Roberts platted the site and named the town Canyonville. He built a grist mill and the Roberts Hotel.

As the next stop on the northward journey for the stagecoaches, Canyonville was thirteen miles north of Levens' Station. The Overland Hotel (aka Canyonville Hotel) served the weary travelers. The owner, David C. McClallan and his wife Electa were *"...paid $110 a month by the stage company for providing services such as hay and grain for stage horses, keeping the horses and boarding the hostlers and drivers,"* according to *Knights of the Whip*.

In the 1870s, the McClallans sold the hotel to William and Christina Spicer. After William's death, Christina married John Beverly and the Beverlys continued as proprietors. In 1880, the Beverlys provided a presidential luncheon there for President Rutherford B. Hayes as he passed through the area.

The bridge on Canyon Creek was a toll bridge, but having to pay to use it angered some of the road users. A lawsuit was filed by the Douglas County Road Company against all who were involved in charging tolls.

The suit went all the way to the Oregon Supreme Court. The court ruled for the plaintiff and the tolls ended.

A post office was established in 1852 as well as a small store, and the Roberts' hotel and grist mill. The discovery of gold brought an influx of miners and settlers for whom Canyonville became an important way station. The builders of the California & Oregon Railroad avoided the canyon, but pack train wagons, stagecoaches and later, the Pacific Highway/U.S. Highway 99 wound through it. Canyonville was incorporated in 1901.

At the present time, a visitor, walking down Main Street, can not only see many of the historic buildings of the old town but, on the south end, can walk across the old concrete bridge built when U.S. Highway 99 was paved during the 1920s. The road dead ends at the bridge, but gives evidence of the construction and width of the highway.

The Cow Creek Tribe history continues...

The 1853 treaty that was offered to the Cow Creek Tribe in the area was never acted upon and the tribe was never officially recognized by the U.S. Government. A century later, in 1954, the government issued the Western Oregon Indian Termination Act which was supposed to "set the Indians free" for the purpose of terminating treaties and relations with over 60 tribes in Western Oregon. The Cow Creek tribe, however, had never received any benefits from the broken treaty of 1853, and were not considered to be a "recognized" tribe.

According to the history recorded on their website:

"...Ironically, however, they were 'recognized' for the purpose of their involun-

tary termination in 1954. Since the Cow Creeks received no prior notification of the Termination Act, as required by law, they were able to take a land claims case to the U.S. Court of Claims..."

The settlement of the lawsuit was an award to the tribe of $1.5 million in a negotiated settlement.

The tribe, under the leadership of Sue Shaffer as its long-time chief, vested the whole sum into an endowment from which they draw only the earned interest. From that interest, they have built a strong base towards economic development, education and housing that benefits all Cow Creek tribal members as well as Douglas County.

Some of their accomplishments since the award in the 1980s is the successful Seven Feathers Hotel and Casino, the Creekside Restaurant, a Career and Development Program, the Cow Creek Health and Wellness Center and the Cow Creek Foundation which awards grants to give back to the communities where they live and work.

"...The mission of the Cow Creek Umpqua Indian Foundation is to offer assistance in youth education, to strengthen the home and family, to provide positive youth development, and to add to the quality of life for people in the community. The Foundation awards up to $15,000 per grant and prefers to make small grants that will make a real impact on the project or for the sponsoring program.

"Each year the Cow Creek Umpqua Indian Foundation awards nearly one million dollars in grants to community non-profit organizations in Douglas, Coos, Lane, Deschutes, Klamath, Jackson and Josephine counties."

These businesses and programs have, in turn, provided much-needed jobs and economic support in not only the Canyonville area, but throughout a large part of Oregon.

"Canyonville Christian Academy" by George Shaffer, *Pioneer Days In The South Umpqua Valley*

"In 1923, Rev. A. M. Shaffer, his wife Adele, daughters, Helen and Ruth, and son, Robert, were on their way from Lafayette, Colorado to Los Angeles. Their 1918 Willys Knight Touring car broke down in Canyonville. They stayed. Adele sold her heirloom diamond ring to buy the property where the academy (they established) is still located. Within a year,

The Canyonville Christian Academy. *Courtesy of Visitor 7 at Wikimedia Commons*

Rev. Shaffer had built the little wood Gospel Mission that stood where Canyon Chapel is now, and had begun excavation to build the three-dormer building that served as the girls' dorm. Bible-teaching classes were started in the church under the name Canyonville Bible School, but the need and emphasis soon changed. It became a coed boarding high school with the emphasis on sound teaching and Christian living.

"To reflect the change, the name was changed to Canyonville Bible Academy. In the 1940s, during WWII, the enrollment reached over 160. Several years ago the Academy changed its name to Canyonville Christian Academy and is an accredited college-prep Christian high school. Some of the original family members are still active in the affairs of the academy."

"Dodge Inn/Stanton Park" from a conversation with Lillian Stevenson who serves on the board of the South Umpqua Historical Society

"Dodge Inn was located on U.S. Highway 99 on the north end of Canyonville. It was owned by Mr. and Mrs. Glen Dodge who had come to the area from Chicago, probably in the mid-1930s. Their youngest daughter, Jeanette, was the same age as my sister, who was born in 1922. They were in school together and good friends. Dodge Inn consisted of a campground where there were several little log cabins to stay in. The house where the Dodges lived was also made of logs, and there was a main building, along the highway and a rather small building where they may have had a café at one time. After the county bought the property, most of the buildings were removed except for the 'main' building and the Dodge's second house. The original log house had been torn down. The newer Dodge house is still there. It is where the caretakers live, I think, but the main building was finally torn down about 10 years ago since it was on the verge of collapse from dry rot, etc. The Historical Society toyed with the idea of trying to save it, but it was past saving.

"One of the nice things about Dodge Inn besides its picturesque buildings, was the access to the river where we all went to swim. The Dodges didn't seem to mind having people traipse through the property to reach the river, and I sort of remember a small bath house where one could change into one's bathing suit. And, there was a diving board. After Mr. Dodge died, his wife finally moved away, I think this may have been in the 1950s when I wasn't around, and the property was sold to the county."

The South Umpqua River, slow-flowing and about 95 miles long, drains the uplands at the north end of the Canyonville area and flows through the valley bottoms. It is surrounded by oak-dotted savannas and open meadows. Trappers and traders of the Hudson's Bay Company used the river valley to move along Indian paths to link with the central valley of California. It was also an area vital to the food sources for the Indians. Gold was discovered in the river bed in 1848, causing an influx of miners which, in turn, increased the tension with the Indians.

DAYS CREEK AND TILLER

At this point, we are going to take a bit of a detour off of U.S. Highway 99. Entering the forested area along the Tiller Trail Highway, seven miles northeast of Canyonville, the settlement of Days Creek developed, primarily inhabited by families involved in forest-based jobs, but close enough to Canyonville to participate in life and business there.

Fifteen miles southeast of Days Creek and nearly directly east of Canyonville, Tiller was another settlement tied closely to the forest.

Even though these two communities did not lie right along the route of U.S. Highway 99, they contributed to a large part of the area's history. They hosted the first ranger station in the Umpqua National Forest and an important CCC camp that served much of the area.

Forestry and forest management was a big part of the economy in the Cow Creek Valley. The U.S. Forest Service set up ranger stations and lookout towers in strategic locations throughout the area where the forests could be properly managed.

Tiller is one of the areas where the giant sugar pines that David Douglas searched for in the 1820s were located, and the Umpqua Forest still hosts the largest in the world. During the 1940s, Douglas fir and sugar pine were cut for use in the war effort and logging was intensified drastically after the war due to the increased demand for housing. With pressure for better forest management, in the late 1940s, the requirements for District Ranger positions were changed, requiring a college degree.

Tiller Ranger Station, 1936. *Courtesy of Gerald W. Williams Collections, OSU Special Collections & Archives Commons*

"Days Creek" by Susan Waddle, Director of the Canyonville Museum, *Pioneer Days in the South Umpqua Valley*, Vol 42, p. 24

"The United States Forest Service was created on July 4, 1905, and the Tiller Ranger District in 1906, with Clarence Jackson as Ranger. The first Ranger Station was called Summit. Clarence was the only year-round employee. He was charged with maintaining the land within the district. In the beginning, there was no access into the interior. Fire control was necessary and seasonal employees were hired to develop trails for transportation, to build lookouts for fire watch and gradually develop roads to allow access for the developing timber needs of the country. Trails were built by hand by crews with horses and mules. The first headquarters was located four miles north of Drew at Summit Guard Station. Administrative headquarters of the District was moved to Tiller in 1914. The District's first ranger was charged with building the transportation and communication network, plus protecting the forests against fire and erosion. Dwelling construction, surveying of property lines, packing and woods skills were requirements."

Coyote Point Lookout tower, Tiller Ranger District, 1942.

U.S. Forest Fire Lookout Towers

The U.S. Forest Service, with the aid of the Civilian Conservation Corps (CCC), built and set up tall, long-legged lookout towers throughout national forest land all over the Pacific Northwest and the Nation. Their purpose was to provide a means to spot, locate and deal with potential forest fires. In the beginning, most were only accessible by horseback or hiking into the area on foot. Later, rough, winding roads were built back into the wilderness area where many of the lookouts were located. Some are still only accessible by helicopter or pack animal.

According to the U.S. Forest Service website:

"Following the devastating fires of 1910, early fire detection became a priority within the Forest Service. To help aid detection, lookout towers began to be built on national forests throughout the country. These building efforts were further aided during the 1930s by the Civilian Conservation Corps, who worked on numerous lookout building projects across the nation.

"The fire detection process was also aided over the years by an invention de-

veloped by USFS forester William Bushnell Osborne, Jr. Osborne first invented a 'firefinder' in Oregon in 1911 using a rotating steel disc with attached sighting mechanisms. This instrument allowed lookouts to accurately pinpoint the geographic location of forest fires by sighting distant smoke through the device. Further modifications and technological developments were made by Osborne to the firefinder over the next 30 years. The Osborne Firefinder was widely used by Forest Service lookouts throughout the 20th century, and production of the devices by various companies continues."

Lookout towers are still in use today, although other technologies have limited the numbers and the way that they are managed. The heyday of their use was in the 1930s, 1940s and 1950s. During World War II, the men and women who manned them along the West Coast also served as enemy aircraft spotters for the Aircraft Warning Service. The lookouts were also used to provide weather readings for the U.S. Weather Bureau /National Weather Service.

Many of the people who manned the lookouts were college students who chose the work for summer employment since they were normally manned during the hot summer months when fire danger is the highest. Most worked alone, unsupervised, and had little human contact during their stays. Supplies were frequently packed in by mules or horses and it was a spartan existence.

Very seldom was there electricity or running water in the lookout towers. Most water had to be packed in or hauled from a nearby stream or other water source.

Today, many of the no-longer-used towers are being preserved by volunteer non-profit groups. Some are made available to hikers and campers to rent as a unique wilderness experience... and some are still being used by fire spotters each summer.

"Stone Johnny" by Teresa L. Anderson

(**Author's note:** The following story took place in Idaho, but it will give our readers a good insight into what living in a lookout tower in the middle of a U.S. National Forest wilderness area was like.)

"One thing I never imagined experiencing in life was to live on a lookout tower in Northern Idaho. It happened in June, July and August of 1962.

"I was newly married (December 27, 1961) to a college student who was majoring in forestry at Michigan State University in E. Lansing, Michigan. I had already graduated with a professional degree in nursing from Mercy School of Nursing in Grand Rapids, Michigan. My husband, Francis "Frank" thought the experience would be a great combination adventure and honeymoon since we hadn't had time for a trip when we got married between college terms. I thought it might be an opportunity to travel and see some of the country. I did not know what I was getting into. I also was about four months pregnant and just beyond the nausea stage.

"In early June, we drove by car across the country from E. Lansing, Michigan to Priest Lake Ranger Station in Priest River, Idaho. The drive must have been more than 2,000 miles. There, my husband and I were given instructions, equipment and directions to take to the Stone Johnny Lookout Tower. The area was beautiful.

"As we traveled up the mountain, we drove up a road which at first was paved and then became gravel, very rugged,

curvy and narrow with hairpin turns and switchback curves. We finally reached our destination and got our first view of what would be our full-time home for the next three months. It was a very small cabin with surrounding railing, standing on a tower of tall stilts, affording a panoramic view of the surrounding wilderness. We got out of the car and started climbing the 60+ steps up the tower. When we opened the door, we were immediately struck by the dark, dirty, musty interior. It was covered with spider webs and who knows what else. I heard mice scurrying around. There were two small bunk beds, a table, two chairs and a wood stove. In the middle of the cabin was the 'fire-finder,' the device we were to use to chart locations of possible forest fires. It included a map and an arrow in the middle that could turn and be pointed to the desired area to indicate where there might be a forest fire. There was also a two-way radio in one corner of the tower. It was our only link with the outside world and was used to contact the local ranger station.

"The view was outstanding. You could see many mountains, valleys and rivers and all the different colors of the sky as the day wore on. You could even see north into Canada and the lights of Spokane, Washington at night.

"Once our eyes became used to the dimness in the cabin, it was time to go to work. We began by lifting up the shutters that were covering the windows surrounding the cabin. We made trips up and down, carrying heavy burlap bags of water, wood, cleaning supplies, linens, clothes, food – everything we would need to survive the next three months. And then the work really began! I cleaned, washed windows, mopped the floor and organized our possessions. Those first few days were spent figuring out how to work the wood stove and... how to survive.

"Frank was 27 years old at the time. He had been in the Navy for four years and was to start his fourth year of college in September. In other words, he was older and had 'seen the world.' He had also been raised on a farm and was more than familiar with camping, fishing, hunting and sports. He was also very strong and was the 'go to' guy when it came to moving a piano. I was just the opposite. I felt completely out of my element and quite the 'pansy.'

"I was small-boned, weak, had never been camping and didn't have a clue of what I was getting into. I had never been out of the State of Michigan. Being a nurse, my world was one of being sterility-conscious, organized, clean and having everything handy and convenient. True, I was raised on a farm, but my brother claims I never set foot in the barn.

"We eventually got it all together – I set up a routine of meals made on a wood stove and tried very hard not to use any water since it all had to be hauled up by hand. Our refrigeration was a screened container that hung from the bottom of the tower. The breeze was supposed to keep things cool. Needless to say, it didn't work, so we had to eat many meals of ham since it had some preservative properties. An accomplishment I remember was making pumpkin pies in the oven of the wood stove. Other than that, I did a lot of hand-wringing when it came to cooking.

"To maintain my sanity, I started reading books that we had brought along and started a craft project of painting pictures on 1" slabs of wood. Of course, this was not dried wood, so after a couple of weeks, there were huge cracks in my 'works of art.' After a while, my artwork was put into the wood stove to burn for cooking. I definitely had to find another craft.

"I suppose I should mention something about the real reason we were on the lookout tower. It was to watch for forest fires. I was supposed to be my husband's helper in spotting them and I could have cared less. Survival was my main goal. There must have been about five or six fires that Frank zeroed in on with the fire-finder and radioed in. Maybe, if he were still alive, he would tell you differently. In fact, if he told you this story, I'm sure he would have given a totally contrasting version of it.

"On Sundays, either Frank or I would drive down the mountain, go to church and get groceries in Priest River. There was one Sunday that Frank went down into town. The radio crackled on from the ranger station and mentioned that there might be a fire that would be visible from our lookout position. I was supposed to use the fire-finder to see if I could locate it, but I never did.

"About this time, there was a huge swarm of bugs – thousands of them – that descended on and in the tower. They were everywhere, crawling on everything including me, and I was in a panic. Frantically, I called on the radio and reported the invasion. They told me to get a pole and hang a wet towel on it. This was supposed to attract the bugs. Of course, it didn't do any good and they stayed around. Then, just as quickly as they came, they left. I have never seen anything like that before or since. Nobody could give me a name for them, except I remember them as large, winged bugs.

"Monday was wash day. We had one large wash tub and a clothesline below the tower. One time, I remember carefully washing a huge load of clothes, rinsing and hanging all this laundry on the clothesline. It was hard work and after finishing the job, the whole clothesline came down and fell into the dirt. I can remember screaming and trying to hold the lines up, but to no avail. I had to start the whole job again.

"Saturday night was bath night. I remember Frank hauling all this water up so we could take a bath in a couple of inches of heated water in the round, galvanized container that we also used as the laundry tub. Well, I got in the tub and took my bath and then thought Frank would throw the water out and get some fresh. But, he didn't. He took a bath in the same water that I had just taken my bath in.

"One of our 'neighbors' was a man who was stationed on one of the more desolate and higher-up lookout towers by himself. He was always very cheerful and chatty on the radio. One day, he came on the radio and we heard him singing and then he started cursing, swearing and carrying on. After a while, I finally heard someone else's voice say, 'Somebody better go get that guy off the lookout tower.' Yes, the guy had cracked up. Somehow, I could sympathize with him. Needless to say, that tower was shut down.

"One problem with being pregnant is you have to go to the bathroom frequently. Our bathroom was way down the many steps of the tower and further down a couple of hills. It could have been a mile away as far as I was concerned. So, necessity was the mother of invention. I found a small pan that I started using as my personal chamber pot in the lookout tower. (Yes, finally the last of my dignity was gone.) I then poured the contents over the railing of the tower. One day, the wind was quite strong and as I was pouring it over the railing, it all came flying back at me. Frank was watching when I got the urine shower and he thought it was the funniest thing he had ever seen.

"The weather was incredible. We experienced quite a few lightning and windstorms. When a lightning storm went through, we were instructed to sit on special stools which were supposed to absorb any electrical strikes that might hit the tower. The windstorms at night bothered me the most. When it was really blowing, the tower creaked and swayed. Frank asked the forest ranger to come and test the tower's wood poles for rotten areas or other problems. None were found, but there were times I just wanted to get off the tower and sit in the car located below the tower when the wind blew at night. According to historical accounts, Stone Johnny Lookout was destroyed in 1969 – seven years after we left – most likely by a windstorm.

"As I said, I was pregnant at the time with our first child, Julie. I have since told her if she ever has any problems with anxiety in life, it must have all started when we went to live on the lookout tower. She must have been swimming in amniotic fluid loaded with adrenaline. My stress level was – well, it was off the charts.

"About the 4th week in August, my husband was below the tower hacking down 5' tall weeds. All of a sudden, I heard a scream. When I looked down, I found Frank lying on the ground writhing with severe back pain. The hard work and the loads of water he had hauled up the tower had taken their toll. I called the ranger station and a couple of hours later, the forest ranger came, loaded him into his truck and took him to the emergency room. He was admitted to the hospital, put into traction and was to stay there about a week.

"Meanwhile, I was to remain on the tower by myself and continue to look for forest fires. At that time, the weather had begun to change. There were about three or four days of constant thick fog. On about the fourth day, I was going "stir crazy" being alone. I contacted the forest ranger and said that since it was 'socked in' with fog, there wasn't any way I could see forest fires and I was not going to stay on the tower any longer. I was about seven-months pregnant and getting quite large. Also, there was less than a week left that the towers were supposed to be manned for the summer. So, a couple of hours later, the forest ranger drove up the mountain to pick me up. I stayed with his family for about three days until Frank got out of the hospital. I was so grateful to that kind family for taking me in at that time and it was such a relief to leave the lookout tower.

"Finally, Frank was ready to be discharged from the hospital. He was still having quite a bit of pain. He refused any medication for the pain which didn't help his disposition, but that was his choice. I picked him up at the hospital and he managed to crawl into the back seat of the car with some pillows. I was not accustomed to driving outside of Michigan, but I got behind the wheel and we started our *journey back home. I had survived and, just maybe, I was the strongest one after all..."*

Camp South Umpqua Falls, 1934

The Civilian Conservation Corps (CCC) camp at South Umpqua Falls, east of Tiller, was a typical camp set up to house between 150 and 200 men. The camps consisted of barracks, a mess hall, school – complete with library, infirmary and shower facilities – officers' quarters and electrical plants powered by large diesel generators. The camps provided educational opportunities to any of the men who wanted to participate. The most popular programs were learning to read and write, auto mechanics and leather working.

"Many Stars in His Crown; A Tribute to Dr. Robert S. Kinoshita" by Laura Hartley for *Pioneer Days in the South Umpqua Valley*, Vol. 35, p. 25

"Dr. Robert Kinoshita was born to Japanese parents in Honolulu, Hawaii. He graduated from the University of Nebraska Medical School and served his internship at Emanuel Hospital in Portland. There he met Evelyn, not Japanese, a nurse at the hospital and they married, in spite of objections from their families.

"He was an Army Reserve doctor from 1936 until 1942, serving with the Southern Oregon District Civilian Conservation Corps, the CCCs. He arrived in Tiller, Oregon, near Canyonville, in 1937, with his wife and son Bobby. The South Umpqua Falls CCC camp, Co. 2904, was located about three miles farther up. He and his wife took care of the boys of Co. 2904; their first priority, taking care of their medical needs and listening to their problems. Evelyn created a warm and caring home and welcomed the young men, even serving chocolate birthday cake for young visitors. The doctor found one of the young men with an interest to serve as a First Aide Attendant for the doctor's hospital in Co. 2904.

"He also took care of anyone who fell ill in the Umpqua Valley and needed his care, often making house calls. This was not his duty and he was not paid in cash, but by venison, hams, strings of trout, fresh salmon, garden vegetables and fruit.

"As time went on, he was moved to the Medford headquarters where he managed the medical care for all the camps in Southern Oregon.

"With the closing of the CCC camps in 1942, Dr. Kinoshita was put on active duty and received orders to report to Fort Omaha. The family stopped in Portland to visit relatives. While there, the Executive Order No. 9066 came out. That order declared that people of Japanese ancestry, living on the West Coast must report to a collection point for removal to Relocation Camps further inland. The collection point in Portland was the Portland Livestock Pavilion.

"Dr, Kinoshita and his son reported. Evelyn, pregnant at the time, signed away her civil rights and went with them. They were confined at the concentration camp at Heart Mountain, Wyoming. When word got back to Canyonville, many people wrote to the government, probably with no effect. When Mrs. Kinosita's child was ready to deliver, she demanded to be allowed to go to a regular hospital and succeeded. They were released in March 1943 when the doctor was called to active duty. Dr. Kinoshita served in the European theater, at one point behind the German lines in Holland.

"In the battlefields, he crawled on his belly, dragging his medical kit to any of our soldiers that were still alive, and dragging them back to safety to give them first aid until they could be picked up by the Red Cross men. He was honored with many medals and recognition from his government.

"When the war was over, the family was reunited and decided to settle in Portland, Oregon, and started up a successful family medical practice there. The couple passed away, a few days apart, in 2001."

"Reminiscing" by Robert H. Weich for *Pioneer Days in the South Umpqua Valley*, Vol 27, p. 28-31

"My letter of acceptance told me to report to Vancouver Barracks, Washington – an Army post. Ten of us found our names on a list for assignment to Camp South Umpqua Falls at a place called Tiller, Oregon. We were soon assembled, roll-call taken, and transported by military truck to the Union Station in Portland where we boarded a Southern Pacific train coach to Roseburg. We were met there by two enrollees from camp. We climbed into the rear of a forestry truck, and the 58-mile ride to camp went through Myrtle Creek, leaving Highway 99 at Canyonville and proceeded by Days Creek, Tiller, past the ranger station and to the camp some five miles along the South Umpqua River.

"We spent the first few days in orientation and indoctrination – getting acquainted with the various camp activities and scheduled meetings with supervisory personnel, both military and forestry relative to the mission and functions. We became acquainted with the Company Duty Roster, the various additional duty details we would be expected to perform on a rotating basis.

"Company 2904 had a winning basketball team in 1938. I requested an opportunity to try out. I first played against the Days Creek High School team for about two quarters. Coach Willis decided to accept me as a team member. He generally used me against the opposing team's smaller, faster players, man to man; a great way to stay in shape.

"As we progressed with clearing the trail, there were several trees that had fallen across the trail some time since the previous fire season; some were quite large. The largest one, I remember, was approximately four feet in diameter. We sawed out an eight-foot chunk, and rolling it off the trail, I slipped and something gave way in my right inguinal area. When we got to the Divide Lookout, our leader cranked the phone to reach Dr. Kinoshita at the company dispensary for medical advice. I was to be placed on light duty status.

"The first sergeant gave me a few days off until an assignment could be found to work for Mr. Claude Baker, the Camp Education Advisor. Initially, the job only entailed maintaining the classroom area. After finishing my chores, I began to practice my typing skills, and when Mr. Baker discovered I could type, my job included typing his correspondence, schedules, etc. Eventually, I became editor of the camp newspaper. Evenings I was asked to teach a typing class and began to accept students.

"Not long after, First Sergeant Ray Rife, suggested I try out for clerical duties in the orderly room. In addition to learning to become a Company Clerk, Kenneth King was kind enough to give me advance driver training in the operation of forestry and military vehicles, which allowed me to pass the licensing exam on the first try.

"My first long trip was to Coquille, Ore. The trip combined both driving and clerical duties. Mainly the trips were to Roseburg, Medford, Diamond Lake and, on occasion, driving Dr. Kinoshita to other camps when the assigned physician was absent. On a few occasions it was necessary to transport emergency surgical patients from camp to Mercy Hospital in Roseburg using his personal 1938 Pontiac. He was a fine physician and surgeon, not only highly-regarded by all members at Camp South Umpqua Falls, but also by families from the surrounding community where he responded to emergency medical needs on a voluntary basis.

"I was discharged from Company 2904 CCC and obtained a driving job in Portland in February 1940."

"A Tiller-area Plane Crash" by Ron Bartley, *Pioneer Days in the South Umpqua Valley*, Vol. 37, p. 9

"On July 7, 1944, Paula Loop, a Women's Air Force Service Pilot (WASP), was ferrying a Vultee BT-13 northward to Seattle. She landed at the Medford Army Air Field for fuel, and took off a short time later. That same afternoon, a U.S. Forest Service employee, Lowell Ash, noticed a fire in the Richter Mountain area, and promptly headed for the fire with a small crew. He discovered Paula Loop's burning aircraft at the site of the fire, and the deceased pilot. Army Air Force personnel were notified, and they arrived to investigate, but were unable to determine the cause of the crash, although down-slope winds were suspected as a factor. The aircraft had hit several tall trees, a wing had been sheared off, and the gas tank still contained fuel.

"Paula Loop was born at her parents' family farm near Manchester, Grant County, Oklahoma. The eldest of four children, she attended a rural one-room school and later graduated from the Women's College in Chickasha, Oklahoma. She was an accomplished musician and taught several subjects in the Arnett Public Schools.

"In 1939, Paula worked as a secretary in Ponca City, Oklahoma. She took flying lessons there, and soloed on September 22, 1940. By 1942, she was a Link Trainer instructor for British Cadets. Paula enrolled in the WASP program in December 1942, and received her silver wings at Avenger Field, Texas, on May 28, 1943. During April and May 1944, Paula attended the WASP Training course at Orlando, Florida and was then transferred to the 33rd Ferry Group in Kansas. By the time she died at age 27, she had approximately 1,000 hours of solo time and had flown in every state, and part of Canada.

"The WASP pilots performed flight duties, many of which were dangerous, such as target-towing, ferrying, training, flight testing and flew all types of military aircraft.

"More than 1,000 WASPs earned their wings before the organization was disbanded in December 1944. Thirty-eight WASPS lost their lives performing flight duties in a vital part of the war effort at that time. When the WASPs returned to civilian life, they did not receive veterans' military status or compensatory benefits."

By 2012, some of that stigma is being rectified. The remaining WASP members have received special governmental medals, some veteran benefits and now are able to be buried in Arlington Cemetery, although as of 2012, it is still without the 21-gun salute.

RIDDLEBURG / RIDDLE

"Riddle, Oregon: Founding to Boom Days" by Elaine M. Strobridge, *Pioneer Days in the South Umpqua Valley*, Vol. 26

"The first white settlers in the Cow Creek Valley were William H. and Maxamilia Bouseman Riddle in February 1851. They constructed their two-story log home at the foot of Old Piney (Nickel Mountain) Other pioneer families arrived and found land that suited them. Later in the year, Thomas Smith came from the mines in California and joined with Clement Glasgow to run a ferry and a 'sort of store and liquors' in the Golden Frontier. Smith later became one of the first Douglas County Commissioners in 1852. If settlers wanted to go from Riddle to Myrtle Creek and points north, they had to ford the South Umpqua or cross on a ferry.

"The Riddle family came to know the nearby bands of Cow Creek Indians and lived in peace with them. The mild climate and abundance of fish, game and plants assured an abundance of food for the Indian families.

"Twelve years later, their grown son, John, bought a donation land claim for $800. That land claim was bisected by the Oregon & California Railroad. The railroad provided the impetus for John to plat the townsite of Riddle in 1882, naming the streets for his wife and daughters. Riddle was the railhead for Canyonville, Days Creek, Perdue (Milo), Tiller and Drew. The mail for the area came to Riddle, all the products in and out were from Riddle, as were all the passengers. A depot was constructed, as was the hotel, a saloon and a livery stable. The farms were productive, a school was built, and a church shared by Baptist and Methodists.

"The town flourished and incorporated in 1893. Nickel was being mined and 100 Cow Creek Valley citizens were employed. Riddle had a bank, a Masonic Temple, a lumber company, a doctor and a dentist. Claud Riddle published the weekly Riddle Tribune which predicted a glowing future for the city. The Riddle Concert Band played weekly summer concerts and in the Fourth of July Parade. The Rod and Gun Club boasted 1,000 members and held free venison barbecues. By 1912, a steel bridge replaced the old covered bridge on South Main Street, as the new Pacific Highway was engineered to go through Riddle. By 1916, the Highway was redesigned to follow the South Umpqua River and bypass Riddle. Riddle fought to keep the original route and won in the lower courts, but the fight lasted until 1920 when the Supreme Court overturned the ruling.

"The city population dropped to 195 during the Depression. The bank failed and prune production was the largest business. In 1935-1936, the Works Project Administration provided major funding for the present high school building to supply local employment.

"When the Depression was ended by the advent of World War II, and then the war ended, lumber mills sprouted all over the valley. Many failed in the 1955 recession, but three expanded and grew. The mining and smelting operation of nickel added another expansion. The city government stretched to meet the needs *of the rapidly growing population.*

"Mobile home parks, rooming houses, motels and gas stations proliferated, and a few new businesses built and several small businesses opened in vacated buildings.

"The commercial area didn't expand to its full potential, but Riddle has excellent schools, an impressive city hall-park complex, and close proximity to mountains or beaches, hunting or fishing, It's a good place to live."

Early-day Riddle boasted a "magnificent" hotel that became a popular destination for honeymooners. It was built in 1886, replacing the first hotel, the Riddle Hotel, which burned in 1885. Soon a large saloon was built next to the hotel and it became the social center for the whole valley.

The town of Riddle was incorporated on January 30, 1893, and became the southern operating terminus for the railroad. It was considered a rough and rowdy town in those days.

Relatively successful gold and nickel mines were developed in the area, but it was the railroad that provided the economic means for the community to survive through hard times. As the terminus for Southern Pacific Railroad, products and incoming freight arrived on daily runs and were utilized by the whole area. Passenger service became quite popular, too. People could leave Riddle at noon for Roseburg, do their shopping, and return on the 6:00 p.m. train.

The long Cow Creek Valley, also referred to as the Missouri Bottom, was 4-miles long and 2-miles wide. While most of the farms there produced the provisions needed to keep a family going, ways to bring in cash were in short supply in the period before refrigeration and fast transportation. The solution came in the form of prunes and walnuts. These cash crops could be harvested, dried and shipped all over the world and they provided the main economy for the area for many years. They were both popular and profitable crops grown from the southern communities of Azalea north through the Willamette Valley. Local farms with large harvests built dryers and dried for those who didn't.

The Rosenberg Brothers prune-packing plant was Riddle's only industry during the Great Depression. Orchardists from all over Douglas County sent their prune crops to the dryer in Riddle to be processed and shipped by rail.

By 1932, 10,000 acres of prunes were

Gold panning lessons in Cow Creek near Riddle. *Courtesy of Joe Ross, Bureau of Land Management (BLM) Roseburg District*

in production along the path of the railroad and many went to other countries. Germany was one of the important buyers. The industry peaked in the 1920s, but was still active until about 2000.

The economy of the town boomed until the Pacific Highway was built east of town, bypassing the community. Trucks began hauling the freight and cars provided the transportation to other areas once served by the passenger trains.

After World War II, logging and lumber mills became the main economic staple of the community of Riddle, and in 1954, Hanna Nickel once again opened the once profitable nickel mine and smelter begun by Will Q. Brown, on Nickel Mountain, also referred to as 'Old Piney.'

In the 1990s, the Nickel Mountain Mine, most recently operated as the Glenbrook Nickel Company, closed because of the decreased value of nickel ore. Glenbrook operated its smelter in Riddle at full capacity during 1997, processing mostly garneritic laterite ore from New Caledonia, but closed in 1998. The closure of the complex left almost 300 employees without jobs.

The last official passenger train went through Riddle on May 16, 1956, and the last freight train stopped at the Riddle Depot in the summer of 1978.

TRI-CITY

"Tri-City" by Lillian Stevenson

"Tri-City is the area a few miles south of Myrtle Creek on Old Highway 99. It really isn't a town, but is called Tri-City because it is between Riddle, Myrtle Creek and Canyonville. It has grown a lot since the 'old days.' The South Umpqua High School is in Tri-City now, plus other businesses, and homes.

"The unincorporated community of Tri-City is equal in size to Myrtle Creek. The grouping of those together for the South Umpqua School District, the Tri-City Water & Sewer District and the Myrtle Creek Municipal Airport all support and serve the larger area."

"Stories of the old Tri-City Airport" by Ron Bartley, *Pioneer Days in the South Umpqua Valley*, Vol. 34, p.19 with information furnished by the Oregon Aviation Historical Society, Roy V. Hatfield and others on the Tri-City Airport pilots.

"The Tri-City Airport was created late in 1944 or early 1945 when Larry Womack cleared a path through a prune orchard located in Missouri Bottom, several miles south of Myrtle Creek. The dirt landing strip, which was about 1,800 feet long, was located between U.S. Highway 99 and the Civil Aeronautics Administration Emergency Field, just west of the strip. The present day Myrtle Creek Airport is about one mile northeast of the old Tri-City Airport site.

"Larry Womack was well-known locally as the owner and cook of the Airport Café in Canyonville, that was identified by its wind-sock. He had learned to fly at Roseburg, probably during the late 1930s, and soon became a flying instructor in the Civilian Pilot Training Program, going to Washington State, where he trained future military pilots. After establishing the Tri-City landing field, he acquired an aircraft, an open-cockpit Timm2SA that had been used in a Civil Pilot Training program. At the landing field, aviation gas was hand-

pumped from 50-gallon barrels. Carl Glanville of Riddle, was the part-time mechanic.

"In the mid-1940s, Bill Cox of Canyonville, became a partner in the Tri-City Airport operation which now included flight instruction, charters and scenic flights. The Tri-City Flying Club was founded in 1946 and purchased both a Taylorcraft cabin plane and a Piper PA11.

"Early in 1947, Larry Womack sold his interest to Roy Hatfield Jr., an ex-Navy pilot who also bought the interest of Bill Cox. The Tri-City Flying Service was established, hangars built, and a Flight School was started under the GI Bill for teaching veterans to fly. Additional aircraft were purchased, surplus military planes were now cheap and several were acquired by local pilots. In 1952, the airport was sold, and a drive-in theater was built on the south end of the property."

"Twentieth Century Man...Oregon Style: Tri-City Drive-in" by Bob and Virginia Proctor for *Pioneer Days in the South Umpqua Valley*, Vol. 30, p 25-31.

"Elmer Love was a man of many skills – truck driver, ran a cat for a lumber company in the upper Cow Creek area, a millwright and road builder as well as an interim police chief for Riddle. Elmer Love, Jack Markham, Marion Kusler and Bill Markham formed a corporation, bought the old airport at Tri-City, and opened their Tri-City movie drive-in on August 27, 1952 with a Randolph Scott film, 'Tall in the Saddle.' Later, they built and opened the Starlight Drive-In near Roseburg and added Paul Frentress to the corporation. They were in that business until September 3, 1979 – 27 years and 7 days.

"The Tri-City Drive-In was an instant success as there wasn't much entertainment for a family, and the drive-in was no competition for the movie theaters in the town. They stocked a bounteous snack bar – families would load the kids in the cars and have supper, too. As winter came on, they installed heaters and that, too, was a success. Elmer said it was partially due to an influx of workers at Harbor Plywood which had just put on another shift. Families were living in temporary cabins at the mill and would come in every night because their houses were cold. At the drive-in, they could buy their suppers, keep warm and entertained. The drive-in business was peaceful for ten years or so until people started bringing in liquor and dope."

MYRTLE CREEK

It was gold that brought minors and settlers north from California to the rivers and creeks of Southern Oregon on the California-Oregon Trail. Settlers first came to the valley of the South Umpqua and the forks of Myrtle Creek in 1837.

On January 24, 1851, a large area along the Umpqua River of Southern Oregon was designated by the Territorial government as Umpqua County, but it was to be a short-lived arrangement. By January 7, 1852, the Oregon Territorial Legislature had created another new county – Douglas County – from the eastern portion of Umpqua County. Another chunk to the west was taken into newly-formed Coos County on December 22, 1853, leaving only a small portion that was

Myrtle Creek School built about 1890. *Douglas County Historical Society*

east and northeast were settled. The settlers began growing fruit, dairying and raising poultry. By 1915, they had a prune packing plant, poultry-raising business and lumber mills.

Eventually, as the local farmers moved away from growing prunes, many began raising turkeys. Many of the fields were planted with sunflowers used for turkey feed and nearby Oakland had a processing plant.

The area's greatest wealth, however, was in its forests which continue to provide rich harvests.

Myrtle Creek" by Dora Dyer, *Pioneer Days In The South Umpqua Valley*, Vol. 42, p. 46-65

"During the 1850s, Moses True Dyer was one of the first settlers in the Umpqua region and one of the earliest sawmill operators. Dyer built the first water-powered sawmill on South Myrtle Creek where he and his wife, Sarah, took up a 320-acre donation land claim. Lumber from the Dyer sawmill was in great demand and used in the construction of many houses of the time.

eventually taken over by Douglas County on October 16, 1862.

James B. Weaver settled at the site of Myrtle Creek in 1851. By the 1850s, farmlands and homesteads were established in the area. A post office opened in 1854. By the 1850s, farmlands and homesteads were established in the area. A post office opened in 1854.

In 1862, John Hall bought Weaver's property, had it surveyed, platted and subdivided to lay out a townsite.

The Oregon & California Railroad came through in 1882 and connected to California in 1887.

Myrtle Creek, named for the presence of myrtle trees, incorporated in 1891, but ran out of money and closed down in March 1901. It then re-incorporated on February 5, 1903. Soon, the outlying rural areas to the

"The first grist mill followed soon after to supply all the settlers of the area with their cereal products. The stones for the grist mill were brought around the Horn in a sailing vessel to Scottsburg, a tidewater landing on the Umpqua River, and freighted to Myrtle Creek. The mill was torn down in August 1930 to make room for the Highway 99 bridge over Myrtle Creek.

"During the time when goods had to be brought by ship to Scottsburg and then packed to nearby settlements and as far south as Yreka in California, Congress authorized the U.S. Army engineers to survey and construct military wagon roads

from Scottsburg to Myrtle Creek and then south to carry freight and travelers from the head of the tidewater on the Umpqua River to the mining districts in the Rogue Valley and Northern California. This was the first government money spent on Oregon roads, and it caused the building of a basic road that an army, a wagon, or stagecoach could travel over.

"The 1860 census recorded 38 families and 213 people in the Myrtle Creek area. In 1862, telegraph service began and, in 1864, a school house was erected, serving four students. In the early 1870s, the Myrtle Creek Christian Church began on the third Sunday of each month. They held their gatherings in the school house. In 1878, the very first prune orchards in Douglas County were planted in Myrtle Creek by John Hall and Jake Chadwick. The railroad and all its benefits were also welcomed into Myrtle Creek.

"In 1886, the Citizen State Bank was founded by John Hall. It was one of the first banks in Douglas County.

"In 1890, the Myrtle Creek Consolidated Hydraulic Gold Mining Company excited the interest of local residents who took their savings and invested in the China Ditch project. It employed many men and Chinese laborers and was 27 miles long; however, it was never finished. It ran four oversize water hoses often used hydraulic mining called 'giants,' but never did supply the dreamed-of energy for mills and factories.

"1898 - The tributaries of Myrtle Creek gave up $150,000 worth of gold.

"1902 - Johnson Lumber Company constructed a sawmill on the same site where Moses True Dyer had his mill in the 1850s.

"On March 3, 1903, Johnson Lumber started building the 'Johnson Flume' at a cost of $25,000. This project required 3-million-feet of lumber. It was completed on October 5, 1903, and was used to float

Building the Pacific Highway near Myrtle Creek, 1918. *Courtesy of the OSU Special Collections & Archives Commons*

The McCullough-built Myrtle Creek Bridge. *Douglas County Historical Society*

lumber six miles from the mill to the Southern Pacific Railroad spur where a planing mill and dry kiln were located. The flume's highest level was 50-feet above ground. The waterway had three-foot sides and was four-feet, three-inches across the top.

"1904 - The Mason's Maple Lodge #127 was started July 17, 1904, and constituted July 17, 1905, with Ben Hunsaker as the first Master.

"1906 - High school education began in Myrtle Creek with the construction of a new school at the corner of Pleasant and Second Street.

"1910 - Census records show the population was 419. The Chieftain and the Continental Mines, located out South Myrtle Creek, began operation.

"1912 - Myrtle Creek's first theater was in the back of C.J. Ritchie's carpenter shop.

"1914 - Fred Johnson constructed sawmills on Boomer Hill.

"1922 - Pacific Highway comes through Myrtle Creek.

"1923 - Stelzier's Box and Woodworking Factory opened.

"1930 - The Myrtle Creek Bridge over the South Umpqua River was constructed. The bridge was designed by Conde McCullough, with three arches and 547 feet to cross the river.

"1931 - A new business enterprise, Oregon Dehydrating Equipment Company, Inc., was established. The purpose of the company was the manufacture and sale of the prune-grader which was recently perfected and patented.

"1931 - The Wollenberg Ranch in Missouri Bottom, announced that they had some 25,000 pounds of dried prunes from the 1930 crop, which they fed to the hogs. At the prevailing price of 1 cent per pound, it is more profitable to feed the prunes to the hogs than to sell them."

The China Ditch Project

In 1890, the "China Ditch Project" was initiated by the Consolidated Gold Mining and Manufacturing Company to provide a means of bringing sufficient water to the gold-mining sites near Myrtle Creek to operate their two large mining machines called "Giants." These Giants used high-pressure jets to blast away rock and sediments in order to expose deposits of gold. Because they could only be used in the winter when the waters of North Myrtle Creek were sufficient to

Downtown Myrtle Creek. *Douglas County Historical Society*

Downtown Myrtle Creek in the 1940s. *Douglas County Historical Society*

power them, the China Ditch Project was proposed to carry water from the East Umpqua "Little River" to North Myrtle Creek so they could be used year-round in the higher elevations.

It took 80 men and about one year to complete the first seven miles of the V-shaped ditch. It was 5-feet wide at the top, 3-feet at the bottom and 5-feet deep. They envisioned that the ditch would also provide irrigation water to the local prune orchards and a means of transporting logs to sawmills in Myrtle Creek, as well.

For the remaining 26 miles, 200 Chinese laborers were hired to complete the project. In addition to bringing water from the East Umpqua, the plans were to include four other streams along the way. However, when they reached the property of R.L. Cavitt on which Cavitt Creek was located, he would not allow them to put the ditch through his land and insisted that they redirect the ditch around the creek. Apparently, he was mining the creek, himself, and did not want water taken from it.

The construction included building a 400-foot tunnel through a mountainside using three of the Giants to drill out the hole and with three miles to go, it was decided to divert the water around the rocky hillsides by building a wooden flume system. A sawmill was built and, in 1893, a fourth Giant was brought in. By this time, and with all of the expenses of the new equipment and labor costs, the Consolidated Gold Mining and Manufacturing Company had fallen on hard times.

The *Roseburg Review* newspaper reported that several attachments had been filed against it including $6,000 in unpaid wages. The owner, Dr. L.W. Brown had been accused of salting his mines to accrue more investors and hiring more men than he could afford to pay. The company was decreed to be sold at a Sheriff's Auction on October 18, 1895, to recover 1894 delinquent taxes.

Few of the Chinese laborers who worked on the China Ditch remained in the area, but artifacts of their culture have been found over the years along the ditch.

Dr. Brown, the owner of the mining company, later moved to Eugene where he practiced medicine and invested in the Bohemia Mines and the Eugene Theater Company.

The China Ditch has formally been registered with the National Register of Historic Places and is still accessible on a driving loop and walking trail, although it has suffered from landslides and erosion.

Like other settlements, most public services in Myrtle Creek needed to be undertaken by volunteers. Many even provided their own tools until their communities were incorporated and city funds used for that support.

"Myrtle Creek Fire Department" by Frank W. Starr, *Pioneer Days In The South Umpqua Valley*, Vol. 26, p. 32

"The Myrtle Creek Fire Department was originally organized at a public meeting held at the Hotel Johnson, Second & Oak Streets on October 3, 1903.

"At that time, the organization was called the Myrtle Creek Volunteer Fire Brigade. Their first order of business was

J.N. Sharpe Union Station in Myrtle Creek. *Douglas County Historical Society*

The Myrtle Creek Standard Station. *Douglas County Historical Society*

Umpqua Auto Camp near Myrtle Creek. *Douglas County Historical Society*

to write the constitution and bylaws and set a regular meeting time.

"As with any emergency-response team, basic equipment was needed. The early fire equipment included a fire bell and tower, hose cart and hose and water supply, as well as protective shields for protection from heat while fighting fires. Throughout the years, enthusiasm was high for awhile, and then, with no major fires, the volunteers gradually lost interest in the service. It was necessary to reorganize the department every few years, probably after each major fire occurred."

Myrtle Creek had been on the transportation route through the mountains beginning with the Applegate Trail, and later the stage and railroad line that brought people, supplies and products to the town. The automobile made changes to Myrtle Creek and other small towns more than any of the other forms of transportation.

With the increased use of automobiles, the need for places to get gasoline increased as did the competition among different suppliers. First several businesses along Main Street put in pumps, but it wasn't long before special stations were built that supplied other needs for the driver – oil, tire patches, and sometimes tools.

As the number of vehicles increased, other businesses, geared for gas-powered vehicles, began to open. These included auto repair shops, auto camps and motels which soon replaced hotels.

Interview with Glyn Petty and Dianne Foster by telephone in December 2013:

Glyn Petty: *"Our family – my husband, my little girl, Marlana and me – came from Texas in 1969. Highway 99 was crooked and scary all the way. We rented a place in Myrtle Creek for awhile and then bought our place on Highway 99, thirteen acres where I stayed for thirty years. My husband had a small disability pension, but I was trying to think of a way to earn some money. I have been legally blind since birth – cataracts over both eyes – but I have some very limited vision.*

"Myrtle Creek was a small town with not many opportunities for me to work. There weren't even many places to shop. Our shopping and any business was done in Roseburg."

Dianne Foster had gone to elementary school in Grants Pass, where she lived on

Myrtle Grove Motel near Myrtle Creek. *Douglas County Historical Society*

S.W "H" Street. Her parents decided to move to California, but she promised herself she would move back to Oregon some day. In 1969, Dianne and her husband finally did. Her husband worked at the Nickel Mine in Riddle, and their new home was close to Glyn's.

The women became friends and had a mutual love for animals. They decided to raise Cocker Spaniel dogs and put a big "Dogs For Sale" sign out by the highway. Glyn bought a trailer and put it on her property where the dogs could be housed. The two worked on training and showing the dogs and selling puppies. Over time, they traveled to shows from Ashland to Portland. Handlers would do some of the showing, but Glyn and Dianne always did the obedience work themselves. Over time, they had six champions and sold the purebred puppies all over the country. One pair even went to Denmark.

At times, Glyn also had a guide dog, which proved very helpful, allowing her to get around. While her daughter Marlana, also blind from birth, was attending the School For The Blind in Salem, the guide dog helped Glyn meet her at the Greyhound Bus Depot in Roseburg when Marlana came home for visits or a school break.

The neighbors in that area were all friendly and visited back and forth. They also helped each other when it was needed. One time when Myrtle Creek flooded and the water was up to their knees, a neighbor with lower ground was worried and asked if he could move his horses to her field. Glyn agreed.

After that, Glyn began taking in rescue horses. She wanted to bring them home to heal. She went through the Commission for the Blind to obtain funding for a horse trailer. Marlana was afraid of horses, so Glyn became a 4-H leader, working with both the horses and her daughter. Caring for horses that needed extra attention and Glyn's interest drew Marlana in and eventually she reached the place where she was also riding and later competing in horse shows.

At that point, Glyn and Dianne groomed dogs, boarded horses and took part in the local trail riding program. When the horses' health allowed it, the two women often went riding. There was an abandoned prune orchard nearby where they could ride and even stop for a horseback snack of prunes. Today, that orchard is a Ray's Market, a parking lot and some low-income housing. There were also trails leading up to abandoned cabins and to covered bridges where they could immerse themselves in a bit of local history.

When Glyn's marriage failed, she went

to live in Texas for awhile, but returned to her home property and went to work at the Veterans Hospital in Roseburg as a transcriptionist. During the time Glyn was gone, Dianne was working at a motel in Roseburg as a night clerk and there were times when she got off work and went right out to load dogs to take to a show.

When Glyn returned, she added miniature horses and later llamas and pigmy goats to the animal family.

About five years ago, she sold the property and moved into town on a smaller, 5-acre place. Dianne also moved nearby and the two women have remained close friends although they no longer ride horses or show dogs.

OAK GROVE / DOLE / RUCKLES

When the stages left Canyonville in the early 1860s, they progressed 14 miles north to the community of Oak Grove where the horses were changed. The station sat on the east bank of the South Umpqua River and was owned and operated by Samuel Stevenson on his donation land claim until he was accidently killed in 1864. His son George inherited and managed the ranch and stage station. In later years, Matt Ruckles took over and the town was called both Dole and then Ruckles after the railroad came through the area in 1882.

The area, situated north of Myrtle Creek, is now considered a ghost town.

DILLARD / WILLIS CREEK

From the Winston, Oregon website:

"Although today the Winston-Dillard-Willis Creek area is often regarded as a single entity, the Umpqua River separates Winston from Dillard and Dillard from Willis Creek. Therefore, before 1900 the three communities developed independently...

"The early history of the entire area, then, centers on Dillard. One of the first settlers, the Reverend John Dillard, arrived in 1851 and bought the valley for $800.00. In 1854 he established the first Presbyterian Church in Douglas County at the foot of Bragg Mountain.

"The town developed slowly, in part because it lies almost entirely in the floodplain. Severe winter flooding was an annual event. In 1880 the first store was opened, but real growth began in 1883 with the completion of the Oregon and California Railroad as far south as Glendale, Oregon. That same year the first train arrived at the Dillard Depot. Within two years, a hotel was built, a blacksmith shop was opened, and the Dillard Post Office was established (June 16, 1884). In 1895 Mr. and Mrs. George Leonard opened Dillard's second store.

"Throughout the early years, most people in the area made their living by farming and raising livestock. Agriculture expanded in the early 1900's when the commercial berry and melon growing, that still exists in the Dillard area, began to develop.

"A turning point in the history of both Dillard and Winston occurred in 1900 when a swing bridge across the Umpqua, linking Dillard and the Willis Creek area, was constructed. This bridge indirectly linked Dillard and Winston, though by a seemingly circuitous route. Later washed out by winter floods, it was replaced in 1903.

"Another step toward tying the area

together came in 1913, when a farmer's petition to the county prompted the construction of a wagon bridge between Dillard and Willis Creek. Finally, Dillard and Winston were directly linked with the completion of the U.S. Highway 99 in 1920. Dillard continued to be the more important of the two towns, however. Electrical service became available there in 1927."

Dillard continued to dominate the area's economy until the close of World War II when lumber mills began to be built to process the timber that was being harvested in the area.

Kenneth Ford founded Roseburg Lumber Company in Dillard in 1936. It produced quality wood products for customers throughout North America and was one of the largest private lumber companies in the United States.

CIVIL BEND / BROCKWAY / COOS JUNCTION / WINSTON

Development in Winston had been much slower than in either Dillard or Willis Creek. The town, also called Civil Bend and Brockway in earlier times, remained relatively undeveloped throughout the 1800s and early 1900s. One of its attractions, however, was a nice fairgrounds that was popular for horseracing.

"According to local legend, because of the crowd's raucous behavior at the track, the area was called Civil Bend as a sarcastic gibe," according to the history website. The fairgrounds eventually closed in 1875.

After the Civil Bend Post Office closed in 1888, a new post office was established in 1893 and was named Winston after W.C. Winston, a well-known horticulturist who settled in the area from New York. That post office was short-lived, however, closing in 1903.

The mill workers who were actively recruited from other states began settling in Winston because many of the large holdings were being subdivided to attract new homes. Because of the sudden growth in population in Winston, the post office was reopened and businesses began to be built to accommodate the new residents. Soon a restaurant, store and service station were established.

In the 1950s, more growth began to take place. A water district was formed and water lines were laid to bring water from the South Umpqua River, necessitating a water treatment plant and later, Winston's own fire district.

In 1953, it was decided to incorporate the town under the name of Coos Junction and the first City Recorder was hired and a City Council formed. The next year, Paul Bender was appointed its first mayor and Harrison Winston, its first City Attorney.

In 1955, a new City Charter was formed and approved which reinstated the town's name of Winston.

Wildlife Safari

One of Winston's most notable "claims to fame" is Wildlife Safari, a 600-acre drive-through game preserve which opened in 1972. Right from the beginning, its purpose was dedicated to the study of the animals that it showcases and the preservation of endangered species. Its focus centered on the cheetah, and the cheetah breeding program has been its most successful accomplishment. Since the park opened and the cheetah breeding program began, over 170 cheetahs have been born at the park, giving it the distinction of being one of the top breeders of the beautiful animals in the U.S. and the West-

A couple of cheetah cubs getting socialized at Wildlife Safari in Winston. *Courtesy of the Edwards family*

ern Hemisphere. The offspring are used to populate zoos all over the United States and, in turn, provide education to the general public and research that will aid in bringing up the population of the cheetah both in captivity and in the wild.

Educating the public is another primary goal of Wildlife Safari. They conduct field trips through the park for school, scouting and youth groups and their outreach programs take their ambassadors, both human and animals, out on the road to visit schools and community groups for hands-on educational experiences to teach about the animals and their environments.

DEER CREEK / ROSEBURG

Native Americans had settled in the Umpqua Valley thousands of years before the first Europeans arrived. The first explorer was Jedidiah Smith who reported on the abundance of fur-bearing animals to the Hudson's Bay Company in 1828. In 1836, the Hudson's Bay Company built Fort Umpqua on the main Umpqua River, a mile upstream from Elkton. Before it burned in 1851, Fort Umpqua served as a trading post for Native Americans and white settlers coming into the valley. It also had a combination hospital/billiards hall for soldiers stationed there.

Joseph Lane

Joseph Lane, the Oregon Territory's first governor, was appointed by President Polk in 1848. Although he had been a successful flatboat operator and articulate legislator in Indiana, it was his battlefield successes during the Mexican-American War that won attention.

After two years as governor, he resigned the position and was elected as the Territory's delegate to Congress in 1851.

On January 29, 1851, Lane County, Oregon was newly-formed and named in his honor.

That same year, he took out a donation land claim of one square mile just north of Roseburg and also purchased 2,000 acres east of Roseburg and built a home overlooking the South Umpqua River.

In 1853, while still a territorial delegate to Congress, Lane was appointed as a brigadier general and put in charge of a group of volunteers who were to deal with and suppress the Indian uprisings in Southern Oregon. He was wounded at a fight at Table Rock in Sams Valley near Medford and Central Point.

As a territorial delegate, he persuaded Congress to appropriate funds for the initial Umpqua River Lighthouse, the first on the Oregon Coast. It was very important to the ships heading up the Umpqua to Scottsburg where the goods were transported in and out of Southern Oregon.

When Oregon was admitted as a state in 1859, Lane was elected as one of Oregon's first two U.S. Senators.

In 1860, when Breckenridge ran as a pro-slavery Democrat for President, Lane ran for Vice President. They were defeated and with the beginning of the Civil War, Lane's political career ended. He was so pro-slavery and pro-secessionist that he continued to keep his personal slave in defiance to Oregon law. In a public argument with Andrew Johnson on the Senate floor during his last day of office, Lane accused Johnson of selling his birthright as a Southerner, but Johnson's rebuttal was that Lane was a hypocrite for blatantly supporting an act of treason against the United States.

After his retirement, Joseph Lane spent much of his time at his daughter's home in Roseburg, although he never lived there. Her house has been preserved and is known by various names – the Creed Floed House, the Floed-Lane House or the Joseph Lane House. It is now a museum maintained by the Douglas County Historical Society.

Joseph Lane died at home on April 19, 1881.

In 1852, the Oregon Territorial Legislature created Douglas County and named the community of Winchester as the county seat. Settler, Aaron Rose, traveling north over the Applegate-Scott Trail, settled with his family about four miles south on the east bank of the South Umpqua River. He purchased land and also filed for a donation land claim of 640 acres at the confluence of Deer Creek and the South Umpqua River. He had it surveyed and platted, naming it Deer Creek.

He immediately built his home which also served as a tavern, a stable, a store and a

An old stagecoach road near Roseburg, 1915. *Courtesy of Gerald W. Williams Collections, OSU Special Collections & Archives Commons*

South Umpqua River going through Roseburg. *From the collection of Ben Truwe*

butcher shop. With promotion by Rose, the site was selected as the Douglas County Seat over Winchester.

Rose donated the land for the courthouse. Rose Academy was the first school and in 1857, it too, was built on land donated by Aaron Rose. That first school was later demolished and the Rose Public School was built on the same site in 1887.

The Deer Creek Post Office opened in 1851, but it was platted and renamed Roseburgh in 1857. Roseburgh was incorporated as a city in 1868, and the "h" was dropped on March 7, 1894.

Buildings from the town of Winchester, including the U.S. Land Office were physically moved four miles south to Roseburg. A ferry was built to carry passengers across the river and a sawmill was constructed and a store opened. Soon, it also had a newspaper, physician, pharmacy and a jail. Roseburg also became the headquarters for the Northern Battalion of the Oregon Volunteers during the Indian Wars of 1855. Providing supplies for the U.S. Army gave another boost to the economy of the town.

The Eagle Hotel, the first large hotel built in Roseburg, opened for business in 1857 and became a stage stop along the Wells Fargo route. It catered to stagecoach passengers traveling between Portland and San Francisco. Later becoming the Metropolitan Hotel, it was an attractive wooden two-story structure with a second-story balcony that sat on the southwest corner of Jackson and Washington Streets.

In 1880, the hotel hosted a reception for Rutherford Hayes, the 19th President of the United States, who had come from the south by Concord Stage after a lunch stop in Canyonville.

The Metropolitan Hotel burned in 1884, taking a good portion of downtown Roseburg with it. Fortunately, the staging barn, located a few blocks away, was not damaged and continued to service the stage company until the end of staging days. It was torn down in 1909.

The Oregon & California Railroad's push southward from Portland reached Roseburg in 1873. By the time the railroad arrived, the town was already established as the most important Southern Oregon city north of Jacksonville and had become a busy, growing center for sheep and cattle ranchers, but the O&C Railroad was out of money. Its progress stalled in Roseburg for a decade before the southward expansion resumed.

Despite its money problems, when the railroad came to Roseburg, it made big changes to the downtown area of the young city. Since the line ended in downtown Roseburg, a roundhouse and yard were built to store and turn the engine back north.

The Southern Pacific Railroad took over the building of the railroad and in 1912, the second Southern Pacific Railroad depot was built in a new location,. It included warehouses, an office and repair shop.

In February 1939, Mrs. Hortense Applegate was interviewed by Sara B. Wrenn, for the *WPA's American Life Histories Collection: Manuscripts from the Federal Writers' Project, 1936-1940* in the home of Mrs. Applegates' daughter. (This is a part of the interview that is also being used in other parts of this book.)

"...Going back to my schooling, Mr. Clark Smith, former assistant under Professor Royal, succeeded to the principalship for 1867-68. He taught one year and was succeeded by Prof. J. H. Herron. I, with a number of other students,

applied for a certificate to teach, as many districts were calling for school teachers.

"John Booth was county school superintendent. I applied for the Ten Mile Valley school, south of Roseburg. School teachers at the time received only $30 a month and boarded with the scholars.

"I was young and just out of school, and was sure at home among my scholars, though I had several girls in the school of my own age. The three months went by quickly. There were two schools in the valley, North and South Ten Mile. A Miss Vandeburg taught the south school. Returning home to Wilbur, after the close of school I visited a sister, Mrs. John Imbler, living near Roseburg. While there I met Mrs. Tom Brown. Her husband ran a ferry across the South Umpqua, near Roseburg. Both she and her husband were pioneers of 1847. Mrs. Brown was a woman of intellect and fair education, and wanted a school in the neighborhood for her four children. She asked if I would teach a three months' school there, if she could get enough scholars at $5.00 each to pay me for the period. I took up her proposition.

"The first day she harnessed up her horses to the light spring wagon, and started out, taking the prospective teacher... Some were pleased; others wanted to think it over. Some of them appeared to think we were trying to 'put something over' on them. Mrs. [??] a big, red-haired woman, was eating her dinner. As Mrs. Brown talked, this woman bit viciously at her knife as she ate. I thought to myself, 'She is opposed to school; she will never send her children.' And she never did... Finally, Mrs. Brown had twelve on the list, with others promising to send their children. She felt they would be true to their word, and I commenced the school.

Roseburg in 1913. *Courtesy of Gerald W. Williams Collections, OSU Special Collections & Archives Commons*

The Pacific Highway approaching Roseburg from the south. *From the collection of Ben Truwe*

I taught six weeks. No more scholars came. One morning Mrs. Brown told me that if I didn't feel like continuing to teach so small a number, to discontinue and she would pay me for my time, telling me to advise the children that day, and she would take me to the bank at Roseburg, the next day. She was true to her word. She was the mother of George M. Brown, who was elected to Oregon's Supreme Court bench in 1920..."

The Umpqua Valley has been a fertile agricultural area with fruit orchards, poultry and dairy farms. Lumber mills added to the economy. When the railroad construction began again in 1884, Roseburg was finally better-connected to the southern part of the state and, eventually, to California where they were able to ship many of their products all over the nation and world.

Telephone lines were connected to California in 1889, and by 1890, Portland Telephone and Telegraph Company began installing telephones in private homes for $20 and a $5 monthly service fee.

Businesses opened and developed to meet the needs of the residents. Soon, there were bakeries, butcher shops, grocery stores, general merchandise stores, breweries, ice companies, dressmakers, millinery shops, cabinet makers, funeral parlors, saloons, barber shops, banks, bicycle and motorcycle repair shops, photographic studios, hotels and boarding houses.

In more recent years, the economic agricultural boost includes vineyards and Oregon wines.

Community activities flourished and organizations formed and grew. Roseburg participated in the Chautauqua Circuit in addition to festivals and other local celebrations. A strawberry festival became a tradition as well as the Douglas County Fair and in 1925, a rodeo. Booster clubs, lodges and other organizations became part of the local life.

Oregon State Soldier's Home / National Soldiers' Home for the Pacific Northwest / Veteran's Hospital

In 1893, an act of the Oregon Legislature established the Oregon State Soldier's Home, allocated funds and appointed a board of trustees. In May 1893, the trustees were to select the location, but a bitter altercation developed and much of the 1893 appropriation was lost. They finally chose Roseburg as the site of the facility. It offered forty acres of river bottom land that had an abundance of pure water. With General James Varney supervising, a two-story home with a basement and attic, a garden, a barn and shed for farm animals were built.

Fifty-four "non-Indian" veterans were the first residents to move in. Three of these had served in the Rogue Indian War; others had served in the Mexican War and the Civil War,

In 1917, a larger and nicer home was built. It had an administration building, two barracks, a hospital, central heating plant, kitchen and mess hall, laundry, garage and barns. The male residents were all needy with incomes of under $50 a month. At that time, the Oregon service pensions were $12 a month. The amount increased over time until it reached nearly $200.

Boredom became a problem for the men, so volunteers from the town helped with entertainment, books and visits. Crops were planted using the labor of the able-bodied residents, and they provided much of the food that was served. Soon the 25-acres surrounding the home were a showcase of the successful agricultural project. Surplus crops were sold to help fund the home.

During this time, Roseburg suffered a crisis. In 1926, the Southern Pacific Railroad completed a new line crossing the Cascades south of Eugene and from there into California on the east side of the mountains through Klamath Falls to avoid the Siskiyous. That change cut off most of the rail traffic through Roseburg, the South Umpqua Valley and the communities farther south. Douglas County lost jobs and payroll. In addition, local farmers and merchants lost reasonable shipping on a frequent schedule. The area was severely hurt.

With the onset of the Depression in 1929, Roseburg civic leaders sought ways to stimulate the local economy and cooperated to put in a bid for the location of a new federally-funded hospital for veterans. The promoters, working with their congressional delegations, met with other Oregon cities and veterans organizations asking for their endorsement. In September 1931, the decision was made to build the new branch of the National Soldiers' Home for the Pacific Northwest in Roseburg.

According to the Umpqua Valley Arts Association website:

"Excitement mounted in Douglas County when the local newspaper reported that the government would spend an estimated $2.5 million for three general hospitals, three convalescent buildings, service structures, and residences for the

Oregon State Soldiers' Home, Roseburg, 1929. *Courtesy of Gerald W. Williams Collections, Special Collections & Archives Research Center, Oregon State University Libraries*

The campus of the Oregon State Soldiers' Home in Roseburg, 1930. *Courtesy of Gerald W. Williams Collections, Special Collections & Archives Research Center, Oregon State University Libraries*

manager, nurses, and officers. In addition, the project included a bridge across the South Umpqua to the site of the old State Soldiers Home which was to find new use for administrative offices..."

On February 16, 1932, the state legislature ratified the transfer of the 40-acre property from state to federal control. A committee of Roseburg citizens negotiated the purchase of 410 acres on the west side of Roseburg, fronting the South Umpqua River. Work commenced in April 1932 on the new veterans' complex. Local workers were given priority for jobs and the project did much to help Roseburg survive the Depression and has given employment opportunities since.

On May 8, 1933, the first 69 veterans moved into the new facilities. The peak in veteran patients reached 670 with 370 full-time employees.

In 1957, Virginia P. Dixon in her research paper on the History of the Roseburg Veterans Hospital for her Social Science program at Southern Oregon College wrote:

" The buildings are red brick and stone, the grounds have well-kept paths and roadways and green lawns speaking to orderliness and restfulness."

By the 1970s, the Veterans Administration was operating a psychiatric ward, a center for alcoholic rehabilitation and 218 beds for medical patients at the Roseburg facility.

The hospital helped the town survive the Depression, but it was the construction of the

Roseburg-Eugene Stage Bus. *Courtesy of the Oregon Department of Transportation (ODOT) History Center*

"All aboard!" Courtesy of the Oregon Department of Transportation (ODOT) History Center

A food stop at the Kozy Korners Cafe for the passengers of the Roseburg State Bus. *Courtesy of the Oregon Department of Transportation (ODOT) History Center*

Pacific Highway, and then the improvements made by the creation of U.S. Highway 99, that caused a growth spurt. The highway passed through the center of the city, originally on Main Street, but later, after major fill-work was done, on Stephens Street which carried the northbound traffic and Jackson Street, the southbound.

With automobiles increasing in popularity and a useable road to bring tourists through the state, new opportunities came into being. Buses began taking the place of passenger trains, carrying passengers to points all over Oregon and beyond. Until air travel became more affordable and during the days when families only had one car to share, buses were a popular means of travel for those who did not have access to cars.

The Pacific Greyhound lines, owned primarily by the Southern Pacific Co. was formed in 1929, and despite the depressed economy, it earned enormous profits during the mid-1930s. It not only brought tourists to communities all over the western states, but it was well-used by students, commuting home from college and by family members who wanted to visit Grandma and Grandpa or to help bring their grandchildren into the world. Others, who were just beginning their adult life's journey and could not yet afford a car, traveled by bus to seek new jobs. They used the buses to travel to nearby communities, across the state or journey across the nation for many and varied reasons.

Bus stations were built in almost every community along U.S. Highway 99. They frequently provided a place to rest and get a meal while the buses were being serviced and new passengers were dropped off and picked up along the way. They also began being used to ship packages to sites along its routes.

Roseburg's Greyhound station is still located on its original site on southeast Stephens.

Pacific Greyhound was not the only bus line operating up and down the U.S. Highway 99 corridor. West Coast Trailways also served the area on a limited basis in the 1950s, but it had a troubled history.

As told by the late Jon Hobijn on his West Coast Trailways website:

"In the fall of 1946, disaster struck the fledgling West Coast operation when one of the Aerocoaches was involved in a horrendous accident on US 99 in Southern Oregon, resulting in a huge story in the newspapers with much bad publicity along with Car Leasing recalling their remaining four buses. West Coast was forced to cut back to two rounds per day.

"It was tough going for the new company. Besides the bad publicity from the accident, West Coast was operating through territory long cherished by Pacific Greyhound as their own. In addition, West Coast only held interstate authority and had no local rights within the states of California, Oregon and Washington. Intrastate rights within California were granted in May 1948, but only from Sacramento north, San Francisco to Sacramento, a prime local market, remained restricted against local traffic. Oregon intrastate authority would come in the early 1950s. Another problem for West Coast was as a result of an error in their original ICC application... They forgot to ask for authority to handle package express! Package Express authority was finally obtained; however, intrastate authority in the State of

The West Coast Trailways Bus Depot in Roseburg, 1945. *Courtesy of Jon's (Hobijn) History Corner website.*

Washington was never obtained due to Washington's one-route, one-carrier law and West Coast, and later Continental, refused to challenge the law in court. This made West Coast operations between Portland and Seattle very weak. In essence, when a West Coast schedule left Portland for the last five and a half hours of its 907-mile trek north, it could only drop passengers, no one could get on, 190 miles with closed doors, coupled with the first 100 miles restricted against local passengers leaving San Francisco."

Those who did have access to cars for their travel were treated to luxurious new service stations along U.S. Highway 99.

"Richfield Beacon Tower," *Roseburg News Review*, **July 17, 1929:**

"Construction of the service station in connection with the Richfield beacon, located north of Roseburg on the Pacific Highway, was started this morning, in line with The Lane of Lights plan.

"The company has acquired a four-acre tract north of Roseburg, and has already erected the beacon tower on which the huge neon sign is now operating. The buildings will be constructed in a semi-circle, with the exception of the service station, which will occupy a space 35 by 70 feet in the center. The building is being constructed on a very substantial plan, using heavy concrete base with a steel skeleton, covered with stucco.

"The service station, which is to cost approximately $35,000 will be one of the most elaborate on the Pacific Coast. Those in the Pacific Northwest are to be of the rugged Norman-type with high-sloping roofs, gabled wings and wide porches. The central portion of the building will contain the supply room, and in front will be the canopy over the gasoline pumps. In each side-wing will be located restrooms, which will be fitted with lounging chairs, dressing tables, smoking stands, etc. with toilets and washrooms adjoining. These lounge rooms will be attractively furnished."

As noted in the Ashland segment of this book, the Depression sent the Oregon division of Richfield into receivership; the Roseburg station closed and the building was demolished during the widening of Stephens Street in the 1940s.

"Richfield Beacon Tower Will Be Moved to Lookout." *Roseburg News Review*, **April 20, 1942**

"April 20, 1942. A crew of workmen from the Douglas Forest Protective Association, under the direction of Ira Mann, foreman, is engaged in razing the Richfield beacon tower, located four miles north of Roseburg and will relocate the tower at Bell Lookout, near Elkton."

Recovering from the Depression, the Roseburg area began to see increased growth in the 1930s. It resumed building its economy and bringing in more people to fill the jobs that these new businesses offered. Umpqua Dairy was one of the highly successful ones.

From the Umpqua Dairy website:

"Umpqua Dairy Products Company was founded in 1931 by Ormond Feldkamp and Herb Sullivan with $500, a 1929 Hudson delivery truck and a little wooden ice house next to the railroad tracks on Sykes Street in Roseburg,

Oregon. The pair began bottling milk, churning butter and making ice cream to sell to railroad passengers as they stopped at the train station in Roseburg. Soon they began delivery routes throughout the county. In 1936, the wooden building housing the original Umpqua Dairy was torn down and a new brick building was built in its place. A portion of ths building still stands today, incorporated into the still-newer facility.

"Umpqua Dairy has continued to grow and prosper through the years, being the first in the Northwest to introduce the half-gallon round ice cream container in the late 1940s, commonly referred to as our 'red round.' The original logo design, created in the early 1930s, was inspired by the Native American culture in the area. The now famous Indian-head logo design is still reminiscent today in all of our packaging. In 1946, Umpqua Dairy became the first dairy in Oregon to put milk in paper quarts, pints and half pints.

"The family tradition continues today, as third-generation Feldkamps, Doug and Steve, guide Umpqua Dairy by the same principles as their father and grandfather."

During the early 1940s, the war-born need for lumber became a boon for the Roseburg area's economy and by 1943, the city found itself referred to as the "Lumber Capital of the World." Centered in Oregon's greatest stand of untouched timber, the Umpqua National Forest, the town became the focal point for vast undertakings in logging and lumber processing, an industry which continued to grow in volume under peacetime demands. Where, in 1939, there were only 37 mills in all of Douglas County, by 1947 there were 278 mills. Following the war, wood utilization industries were built, including two plywood plants. Four concerns had million-dollar-a-year payrolls. In 1950, Douglas County's standing timber, most of it virgin growth, was estimated at 65,000,000,000 board feet. Lumber mills still provide jobs for hundreds of people in the area although forest management is a top concern for all.

Ken Dare of Lorane, Oregon remembers a memorable trip his family took on their move to Oregon from California on U.S. Highway 99:

"When I was about nine, my mom, dad, sisters Judie, Nancy and Trisha, and Uncle Oris, Aunt Lu, and their two children, took a trip from California to Oregon on U.S. Highway 99. This was about 1956, and much of the highway was two-lane. Our first stop along the way was a side trip to camp overnight at Crater Lake. Trisha and I slept in the car, and that night it froze; not a comfortable night. We then continued north toward Eugene. My cousin John was a baby, and Aunt Lu washed his diapers and hung them on their car antenna to dry as we drove along. We camped at Heritage Park in Eugene and I remember swimming in the river. We got a bunch of the other campers together and had a big potluck that evening."

The once small community of Roseburg continued to grow and prosper during the 1950s, but a devastating event took place at the end of the decade that would necessitate the rebuilding of almost its entire city center.

The Roseburg Explosion

At the end of the day, on August 6, 1959, a truck driver for the Pacific Powder Company found that Gerretsen Building Supply Company, where the delivery was headed, had already closed. He parked his explosives-filled truck on a downtown street, near Oak and Pine streets and checked into a hotel for the night. The truck was loaded with two tons of dynamite and four-and-a-half tons of the blasting agent, nitro carbo-nitrate. In a weird coincidence, the Gerretsen building caught fire at about 1:00 a.m. Firefighters arrived to extinguish the fire. The parked truck went unnoticed until shortly before it exploded at around 5:00 a.m. in a blast that demolished buildings in an eight-block radius and severely damaged 30 more blocks.

The explosion left a crater 60-feet wide and 20-feet deep, leveled all the buildings for blocks around and took the glass out of windows nine miles away. Fourteen people died and 125 were injured. Damage was estimated at ten to twelve million dollars. The downtown retail core of Roseburg was literally destroyed.

The slow process of rebuilding began to take place as soon as the debris had been cleared. Two factors – the explosion and the construction of Interstate 5 which bypassed the city in the 1960s – influenced the rebuilding of the retail business district further to the north of town and closer to a freeway entrance. Many businesses rebuilt by using money collected from insurance claims and a new bridge was built and relocated over the South Umpqua River on parcels of land that had been affected by "The Blast."

Today, Roseburg is once again a vital,

The Roseburg Blast which took place on August 7, 1959, destroying a large part of the Roseburg downtown area. *Courtesy of the City of Roseburg*

Devastation everywhere. *Courtesy of the City of Roseburg*

prosperous city. It's the largest in Douglas County at over 21,000 population. Besides the Veteran's Hospital, it is also the home of Umpqua Community College and the Ford Family Foundation, a large charitable organization founded by Kenneth W. and Hallie Ford, the owners of Roseburg Forest Products Company.

The Ford Family Foundation

"The Ford Family Foundation is unique in its commitment to small rural communities in Oregon and Siskiyou County, California, and in its commitment to investing in the capacities of individuals and communities through scholarships, grants and the Ford Institute of Community Building."

WINCHESTER

The town of Winchester was laid out in 1850 by Addison R. Flint, who was the land surveyor for Winchester, Payne & Co. of San Francisco. It was also known as the Umpqua Exploring Expedition. The town was named for one of two brothers named Winchester who took part in the expedition. Flint first settled in Winchester where he was instrumental in helping to establish its first schools and churches. The Winchester Post Office was established in 1851, and Flint served as the first postmaster.

The community, six miles north of Roseburg, was the largest settlement in the Umpqua Valley for several years and it was the county seat until 1854 when voters chose Roseburg instead. When the county seat was moved to Roseburg, the community dwindled in size and served for a number of years as a supply center for the surrounding farms in the area which raised cattle, sheep and grain.

The community was incorporated as a city by the Oregon Legislative Assembly on February 20, 1891, but is now listed as unincorporated.

In spite of the fact that Winchester is now treated much as a suburb of Roseburg, a trip north on U.S. Highway 99 through the area provides business signs that let passersby know it is Winchester and many of the old businesses, including the Del Ray restaurant are still there.

Section 5

U.S. HIGHWAY 99 - WINCHESTER TO CURTIN

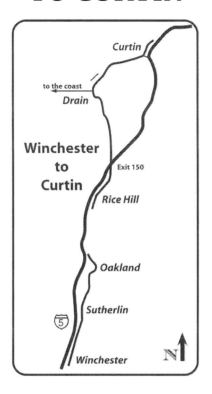

BUNTON'S GAP / WILBUR

Before the days of the stage lines and railroads through the area, the community of Bunton's Gap was the terminus for the main military road leading from Scottsburg that carried freight wagons full of supplies to the early settlers. Scottsburg, located some 20 miles from the Pacific Ocean in western Douglas County, was a freshwater seaport servicing the interior of Southern Oregon in the 1850s and 1860s.

Bunton's Gap was settled by Elijah Bunton, a farmer and minister, and his second wife Keziah, sometime before 1854 when they were shown on the tax rolls of Douglas County, Oregon. They were members of the Immigration to the Oregon Territory of 1844. Before that, in 1849, they were living in Clackamas County where they returned by 1856.

The book, *Vigilante Victims: Montana's 1864 Hanging Spree*, tells of the hanging of Elijah's son, Bill Bunton, who apparently had killed a man in self-defense in the State of Washington. Followers of the man who was killed began searching for Bill Bunton, and years later, they found him and hung him in Montana. In Bill's story, a bit more is told about Elijah Bunton and his reasons for making the trek to Oregon.

"During Bill's early years, the family enjoyed prosperity, but when he was four, a severe depression swept the countryside. Though the Panic of 1837 left Elijah with a crop of corn and wheat that he literally could not give away, at least the farmers did not go hungry the way city dwellers did. Dissatisfied with his inability to get ahead in the world, Elijah cast about for new directions. By 1843 the entire county was abuzz with the wondrous beauty and great opportunity in a distant land called Oregon. Returning travelers ecstatically related tales of majestic mountain ranges covered with evergreens, a mighty river teeming with salmon, and undisturbed valleys waist high in red clover. The pure air would prevent fever and ague, and the soil was so fertile that a man could generate a fortune in wheat, fruit and cattle.

"Taken with Oregon fever, Elijah and his nephew signed a circulating agreement to depart for the Pacific coast the following spring. It was to be no mere migration to obtain free land in an area shared with a detested foreign power and occupied by Indians. Instead, the would-be colonists viewed themselves as the rightful heirs to the founding fathers of the Massachusetts Bay settlement. Theirs was a daring, high-minded experiment in forming an 'independent colony,' conceived to best suit the temper of the founders.

"The momentousness of the upcoming migration was not wasted on eleven-year-old Bill and his siblings, who recognized that their devout father was a leader in the movement..."

After their arrival in Oregon, a notice by Elijah Bunton was published in the May 27, 1847 edition of the *Oregon Spectator*:

"I hereby caution all persons (particularly General Alanson Husted) against trespassing in any manner whatever upon my Land Claim situated on the bank of the Clackamas River, opposite to the Indian village, and which was recorded by me on the 18th day of January, 1847 – on which I am now residing. And I also caution all persons from purchasing any part or parcel of the same from said Husted, as he has no lawful title to any of said premises. Elijah Bunton."

Apparently, not satisfied to stay in one place very long, in 1860, Elijah is reported to have bought a hotel in Umatilla County, Oregon on what was then known as "Cole's Crossing" near Milton (now Milton-Freewater), Oregon.

Elijah Bunton died in 1861 *"on the Walla Walla River, during the gold excitement."*

According to *Oregon 1859; A Snapshot in Time* written by Janice Marschner in 2008:

"Fleming R. Hill built a home along the Applegate Trail in 1851 and provided a bed and board to passing travelers. Known as the Wilbur Tavern today, it is one of the oldest standing buildings in Douglas County and Southern Oregon."

The Wilbur House is believed to have been the next horse-changing station on the Wells Fargo route, heading north. The distance between Roseburg and Oakland, the

> "In many ways the Willamette Valley is very different from Southern Oregon. The valley lies between two parallel ranges of mountains that feed the many streams that flow from east to west into the Willamette River. The river flows gently northward and very naturally the travel and trade did and does follow it. But the Umpqua and Rogue River valleys tip westward and their splendid rivers with a mighty rush, characteristic of no other Oregon streams, go by leaps and bounds to the Pacific cutting in their way mighty gashes in the Coast Range for their channels. Futhermore, these southern valleys are separated from the Willamette by the Calapooia Mountains, a short range extending east and west at the head of the Willamette Valley and connecting the Cascade and Coast Range of mountains." R.A. Booth, *History of Umpqua Academy*, 1918

next major stop, was 19 miles and company policy was that the horses should be changed every 12 miles or so, with 19 miles being the maximum. The community of Wilbur was 10 miles north of Roseburg and the Wilbur House was well-used by travelers, but it has never been documented as one of the authorized stage stops along the route. We were able, however, to find the following recollection recorded for the *WPA's American Life Histories Collection: Manuscripts from the Federal Writer's Project, 1936-1940*.

This interview of Hortense Applegate, conducted by Sara B. Wrenn on February 22, 1939 provided the following:

> "...I recall many recollections as a little girl of the old stagecoach when I lived at my sister's home on the main county road. This was a stopping place, the post office being at this point, in the small town of Wilbur. I remember watching the big stage come in, its four horses plunging under the driver's lash, as they pulled the coach through mud and slush sometimes up to the hubs in winter. The stage driver would snatch a bite to eat and a cup of hot coffee, and then on to the next stop, ten miles distant, where horses and drivers changed."

"History of Umpqua Academy" by R.A. Booth, *Oregon Historical Quarterly*, March 1918:

> "It's a bit difficult to write the last word, for there is more than a suspicion that Wilbur town may not seem as important to those who now hurriedly pass by in autos or Pullmans as it did to those students of early times. The location will seem more definite to say that it is at the junction of the 'Old Scottsburg Military Road' with the main state thoroughfare, 8 miles north of Roseburg. This place was known by early travelers as Bunton's Gap, named for Elijah Bunton, who settled there in 1850. He sold his claim to B.J. Grubbe,

A portrait of James H. Wilbur included in the Booth article in the 1918 *Oregon Historical Quarterly*

frequently mentioned in this article. A considerable portion of the town of Wilbur was built on the claim of James L. Clinkinbeard, but no town plat was filed.

Rev. James H. Wilbur, the founder of the Portland Academy under the auspices of the Methodist Church, was sent in 1853 by the church to organize a mission in the Umpqua Valley as a "feeder" for Willamette University.

"History of Umpqua Academy" by R.A. Booth, *Oregon Historical Quarterly*, March 1918 continues:

"Willamette University at Salem, the oldest educational institution west of the Rocky Mountains, had been organized for some years and was well calculated as the center of a school system as well as to serve a local need. It was Wilbur's idea that academies, correlated to Willamette University, should be established at different points that reasonable facilities might be thus offered for a liberal education to the pioneer families. How natural to his thought, then, that in this 'Umpqua Mission,' comprising the entire Umpqua basin, the Umpqua Academy should be established!

"Among the early farmers, stockmen and miners of Southern Oregon, this messenger of the gospel and apostle of education [James H. Wilbur] moved freely and found a welcome wherever there was a hungry soul and a task wherever he could plant ambition in a boy or girl. The admiration and high regard in which Mr. Wilbur was uniformly held by all who came under his benediction, mellowed into an affection that compelled the title 'Father Wilbur' and ever afterward it clung to him. He seemed an essential part of the early growth and development of the Umpqua country, as he formerly had been in each western community where his lot had been cast. It was but natural that the seat of the Umpqua Academy should be named for him and thus the village that grew about the school that he established, took its name from his. Formerly the locality had been known as Bunton's Gap..."

Upon arriving in Douglas County, Oregon, James Wilbur, fondly known as "Father Wilbur," took out a donation land claim in 1853 near Bunton's Gap, and by 1854, the Umpqua Academy was a reality.

"... Mr. [James L.] Clinkinbeard gave a few acres of his claim to the academy trustees, but the tract upon which the academy buildings stood, the old playground and all that pertained, were the gift of Father Wilbur, a total of 58.43 acres. This is the same tract that was sold at auction in 1877 to James T. Cooper."

On his property, Father Wilbur built a small log cabin to temporarily house the new school. By 1857, he built a permanent school, a large white, 2-story building located on Lincoln Mountain, overlooking the newly-renamed town of Wilbur, Oregon. By 1858, there were 46 students enrolled at the school and the following school year, *"41 female and 52 male"* students were in attendance. It graduated its first class in 1864.

In the *Oregon Historical Quarterly* article written by R.A. Booth, he included some reminiscences of former students. One of them, by George B. Kuykendall, M.D., expresses his many good memories of the Academy:

"Reminiscences of Early Days at the Old Umpqua\Academy," 1918, By George B. Kuykendall, M.D.:

"With recollections of the Umpqua Academy fifty-five to sixty-four years ago, what a panorama of memory pictures come trooping up.

"What a throng of faces young and fair, of forms youthful and strong, what a chorus of voices joyous in song, sport, laughter or screams of delight. What pictures of school days and social life; the old time school exhibitions, Saturday fishing excursions, with the inevitable swim in the Umpqua river, the Christmas anniversaries, Fourth of July celebrations, strawberry parties, rambles over the hill back of the academy, and rolling those great stones of conglomerate that went bounding and thundering down among the oaks, laurels and brush, and broke into thousands of pebbles that went sprawling everywhere, to the terror of chipmunks and cottontails.

"Then their pensive strollings, books-in-hand, among the trees, or sitting in the shade, conning over amo-amas-amat, or trying to conjugate some tough Greek verb or figure out a problem in logarithms, while robins sang in the boughs above, or saucy little chipmunks with striped backs, and with tails erect and bright inquisitive eyes crept over logs and stumps about you. Those were halcyon days. Ah, the soft, balmy, dreamy atmosphere, the deep blue sky, the beautiful oak and laurel crowned hills and the enchanting valley spread out between!

"Such are the memory pictures that come to me like a dream of a lone: vast, far away fairyland."

In February 1939, Mrs. Hortense Applegate was interviewed by Sara B. Wrenn, for the *WPA's American Life Histories Collection: Manuscripts from the Federal Writers' Project, 1936-1940* in the home of Mrs. Applegate's daughter:

"My father, Dr. Calvin Reed, with his family, left the State of Iowa, crossing the plains in Oregon, in 1850. His train of immigrants included a hundred families, together with a number of single men. He first settled in the Willamette Valley, spending the winter of 1850-'51, at Clackamas, near Oswego, and from there moving to Milwaukie. Later, finding the climate of Southern Oregon more congenial, he moved to the small town of Winchester, on the North Umpqua River. That was where I was born, as I have already told you.

"Father bought an old grist mill from a man by the name of Nelson Brebant, together with 320 acres of land, and in addition filed on a donation land claim of 320 acres, so that he had in all 640 acres. He repaired the mill with burrs he brought across the Plains. All the furniture was of his handiwork. The bedsteads, tables and chairs he made were in use long after I was grown. They were nice enough for any ordinary home and, but for a fire in which they were destroyed, would probably still be in use.

"After the death of my father, mother bought a small farm near the town of Wilbur and, with her family, moved there, so that my older brothers and sisters might be educated. My memory holds a beautiful picture from the long ago. The home, not a mansion, was a plain one-story house, of kitchen, bedroom and living room, with a porch facing the northeast, so that we could see the sunrise. The house stood on a knoll, surrounded by fields.

Below the house, to the east, was the barn and cow shed, with just a short distance away a grove of poplar trees, the leaves of which – all the colors of the rainbow at times – quivered and seemed to sing with every wind that blew. Those poplar trees gave me my first impression of the loveliness of autumn, a loveliness that still charms me and takes me back in memory to that simple home and my mother.

"I don't remember that my mother was ever cross. There was a cut-off over the hill and through the woods that we called the Gap. My mother used to take me by the hand and lead me through the Gap to church on Sunday. It was a path I loved. I thrilled to the trees and flowers along the way. I used to play alone, picking buttercups and little toadstools, and setting them up – making little men and women out of them.

"In 1862 the picture changed. Our mother was taken and the family separated, no more to gather around the home fireside. A guardian was appointed over the four youngest children, one sister, two brothers and myself. We went to our older sister's home, a public place known as the Wilbur House. We were all sent to school, but in a few years were scattered. My brothers drifted off first. My sisters married. I was the last to stay. I never knew my oldest brothers, Oscar, Nelson and Madison, until after middle life.

"I was reared and educated at the Umpqua Academy, under the Methodist missionaries and pioneers by whom it was inaugurated. The Umpqua Academy was located at Wilbur, Douglas County, Oregon. It was chartered by the Oregon Territorial legislature on January 15, 1857, but a school, bearing the same name, was previously taught in the same locality, a shadow of coming events. The Reverend James H. Wilbur was the founder and author of the events that led to the establishment and splendid career of the school, and Father Wilbur, as he was called, had active supporters in men of ability to help put his plan into operation.

"The first teacher, I remember was James Stork. According to the records, he taught the primary department, under Professor Arnold. The Reverend T. F. Royal was the succeeding principal, from 1859 to 1867...He watched over his flock as the proverbial hen 'gathers her brood under her wing.' ...Every morning our school opened with prayer and singing.

"The memory of those school days brings to mind the bell that through the years rang out its clarion call... It talked morning, noon and night, as it hung in the open space at the top of the building. It could be heard throughout the whole village, calling us to our tasks. On Sunday it reminded us to respect this as a day of rest, calling us to the chapel to worship. In sadness it told us of some sorrow in our midst, tolling out the number of years of the departed, a custom at that time, but now long since discarded...

"The last of the Academy teachers was Professor A. J. Garland, in 1887. The work heretofore done by the academies of the State was superseded by the public schools. The church had fulfilled its mission in educational work of that nature. In 1888, on June 30th, it was voted to lease the Umpqua Academy premises to the public school district for ten years, for $500, the rental to be applied to improvement of the building and grounds. In 1900 a resolution was adopted to sell the pre-

mises to the district for $400. There, the records of the old academy close...

"Of the years of the Civil War there is much that I recall, though I was a little girl, too small to take part in the exhibitions, as they were called. But how excited I would be when they put them on... We were for the Union. The songs we sang were all patriotic. My niece Mary Hill, or Mollie, as we called her, but two years younger than I, was a little songbird. She learned all the popular songs of the day and was ready to sing on any occasion. Dixie Land was one of her favorites. She earned the pet name of 'Dixie' by this song. Other songs that were sung in school entertainments were 'When Johnny Comes Marching Home Again,' 'On the Field of Battle, Mother.'

"The assassination of President Lincoln was a great sorrow. I was too young to understand its meaning, but years after, when I met my schoolmates we talked of how deeply the students of all ages were impressed. The news came in the afternoon. It spread like fire, and in a short time everybody knew. The students held a memorial meeting that evening, for which preparations were hurriedly made. George Kuykendall, one of the older students, concluded to write something in the same meter and style as a dirge the students had been singing. I remember only the first verse:

> *"'Murdered by a southern traitor*
> *While his friends were near his side.*
> *Asking God to save his country,*
> *Lincoln for the Union died.*
> *Rest! Lincoln, Rest!'*

"As they sang there was sobbing all over the room... Such was the love and reverence for our president.

"My brother-in-law, F. R. Hill, was an enthusiastic supporter of the Union, as was my sister, Delinda. They were both anxious for news, as the war progressed, news that was carried over the telegraph. My brother-in-law had a bulletin board in front of his hotel, upon which he printed the news with chalk as it came in. To make good news more impressive, he, with others, took a piece of iron piping, carried it to a hill, set it on a foundation, filled it with powder, and fired it off. The report could be heard miles away. As far distant as Roseburg, eight miles, the people would yell, 'Hurrah for Flem Hill!!!' I cannot recall just what the news was about, but anyway they filled their pipe too full of powder, and it burst..."

CAMAS SWALE / SUTHERLIN

John and Sarah Carmichael Sutherlin came to Oregon from South Carolina in 1850 and settled in Douglas County in 1851 on land on which an abundance of camas, also known as wild hyacinth or Indian hyacinth plants, grew wild. The plant tends to grow in great numbers in moist meadows. It grew well in the area which eventually became Sutherlin, and it covered the meadows with its blue floral blooms.

The local Indian tribes came to the area each year once the flowers had died down to harvest their winter's supply of the camas bulbs or "roots." They camped in the area for weeks at a time while they dug and dried the camas roots. When pit-cooked, the camas bulbs look and taste sweet – similar to a baked sweet potato, but even sweeter. When dried, the bulbs could be pounded into flour which was a main staple for the local tribes' winter-time diet.

The earliest settlers, including the Sutherlin family, called the area "Camas Swale" for this reason.

The Sutherlin family prospered in their new home. They broke ground, built their home and began ranching, raising cattle and operating a sawmill.

In 1858, John Sutherlin wrote:

"I never injoyed health so well as I have while in Oregon. I weigh upwards of 180 lbs... I have 8 or $9000 thousand dollars mostly at twenty five per cent per annum, about 90 or 100 head of cattle & 12 or 15 head of horses, last Spring I sold three mares for $600.00, a short time sence I sold thirty five cows and calves for Seventeen hundred and fifty dollars on twelve months credit... I have rented my saw mill after being idle 2 years for one dollar a day for twelve months, and (it) to be repeared and put in good order. I have ten acres of land set out in orchard, five hundred apple trees, two hundred peach trees... 25 pears, 25 Cherry, & 30 plum trees, set out last fall looks well, with bloom on some of them."

The Oregon & California Railroad came through the valley in 1872, and a post office was established in 1909.

One of the Sutherlin's sons, Fendal, became known as the "Father of Sutherlin." He had an extensive fruit orchard and practiced irrigation. He also began raising turkeys and other poultry and had both a grist mill and a lumber mill.

By 1883, Fendal was Douglas County's wealthiest landowner and after his death in 1901, his daughter, Annie and her husband, Frank Waite, took up the reins and subdivided some of the property and developed the town of Sutherlin, Oregon.

According to Stephen Dow Beckham's book, *Land of the Umpquas; A History of Douglas County, Oregon*:

"The Waites joined Henry Luce to advertise 'orchard homes,' small acreages for sale on generous terms. They erected homes, secured a railroad siding, and built a depot, hotel and planing mill. Sutherlin incorporated in 1911 and continued development by the Luce Lane and Development Company until Luce's eventual bankrupcy."

The town of Sutherlin was sited along the Pacific Highway.

In the 1870s, there were 12 grist mills operating in Douglas County, one of which was owned by the Sutherlin family. A grist mill was used to process grains and corn into

Sutherlin's Main Street, U.S. Highway 99. *Courtesy of Dot Dotson Photography*

flour and other foodstuffs. They generally used a waterwheel to power the grinding stones, or millstones, inside a wooden building, but in some areas, wind or livestock provided the power. After the grain was ground, it was put through a series of sieves to remove larger pieces and the final product was sewed into cloth sacks and sold as flour or cornmeal.

The flour sacks were made of closely-woven cotton muslin in order to keep the flour from escaping, and when washed, bleached, and sometimes dyed, they were frequently put to good use by area housewives as clothing after the flour had been used. The cloth continued to be used as sacking for many years, even by the large companies such as General Mills, until eventually, paper came into prominence and became the sacking of choice for flour products.

Even though the following story took place in the Lane County community of Lorane, it seems to be a good fit for this segment...

"A Story from Wayne and Maybell Robinson's, *Two Teachers Wore a Dozen Hats* manuscript" in *From Sawdust and Cider to Wine* by Pat Edwards:

"...In the ensuing years, it became the policy of the (Lorane, Oregon) school board to try and hire a married couple to serve as the high school's principal, teachers, coaches, janitors and bus drivers. Wayne and Maybell Dey Robinson fit the bill and were hired in 1930. They remember their experiences in this capacity very well and wrote about them in an unpublished manuscript entitled Two Teachers Wore a Dozen Hats*... Both lived and worked at the high school from 1930 until 1933.*

"...Most of their laundry had to be sent out to a local lady, as the Robinsons found there was too little time for that chore. They were amused to learn, however, that their laundress felt that Maybell's underclothes were more fashionable than those being worn by other ladies in Lorane at the time, so she cut a pattern from them. A couple of her friends were so impressed with them that they, too, cut their own patterns. Because the Depression was closing in on the families in the area about that time, many of the "dainties" were made from flour sacks. It was said that one particular lady in Lorane was quite fashionable in her muslin underdrawers with 'Pillsbury's Best' written across her bottom."

The Sutherlin area has been a popular destination for fisherman and sportsman since the Cooper Creek Reservoir, a 140-acre lake with an earthen dam was built in the late 1960s by the U.S. Soil Conservation Service. It is located two miles east of Sutherlin,

Fishermen find a wide variety of wild and stocked fish there that they try to woo with their favorite baits. They include large-mouthed bass, bluegill, crappie and stocked trout. The panfish and bass grow to large sizes, but the public has been cautioned to eat them at their own risk because of the mercury pollution from old mine tailings that has been discovered upstream.

According to an Oregon Department of Human Services' report, "Elevated Levels of Mercury in Sport-Caught Fish from Cooper Creek Reservoir, Douglas County":

"In 2001, the Oregon Department of Human Services issued a mercury-related health advisory for fish caught in the reservoir. However, municipal water from the reservoir was deemed safe to drink, and

the mercury posed no threat to recreational activities in the lake."

The Bonanza Mine, the nation's sixth-largest operating mercury mine, is thought to be the source of the contamination. It is situated eight miles east of Sutherlin.

Despite the warning, Cooper Creek Reservoir remains a popular recreation area which also offers two boat launches, a swimming area, a pavilion and picnic area, restrooms and a hiking trail that circles the reservoir. Many use it for not only fishing, but also for waterskiing and jetskiing.

OAKLAND

Oakland, located on Calapooia Creek, was named for the groves of Oregon white oak and Garry oak that dot the valley. They bear great clumps of the broad-leaved mistletoe in their branches which is harvested for Christmas decorations. Oakland is surrounded by rich rolling farmland, ideal for cattle, sheep, horses, agriculture and, in more recent years, for vineyards and wineries.

The original town of Oakland was the second oldest incorporated city in Oregon before it relocated. It was a stopping point for the old California & Oregon Stage Company's coaches. Nine miles north of Wilbur, the stages stopped at the Pacific Hotel which fed and lodged travelers. It was also where the horses were changed again.

Oakland was the center of three diverging mail routes leading to points south, north and west. These routes wended their way south over the old California-Oregon Trail to the bustling mining region of Jacksonville; north to Eugene and Corvallis; and west to

Downtown Oakland. *Courtesy of Dot Dotson Photography*

Downtown Oakland, Oregon... Marshall-Wells with Shell gas pump. *Courtesy of Dot Dotson Photography*

Oakland sawmill next to the railroad tracks.
Courtesy of Dot Dotson Photography

Scottsburg on the lower Umpqua where a connection to a sea-going vessel could be made.

In 1872, when word was received that the railroad would be bypassing the Douglas County settlement, A.F. Brown purchased parcels of land three miles south of Oakland, and the merchants in the town literally moved their businesses to the new site in order to be on the direct railroad line. Some buildings were dismantled and moved, some were pulled on rollers or logs.

The town, in its new location, was incorporated in 1878. It had a sawmill, a planing mill and a creamery, and with the addition of a turkey processing plant, it became the largest turkey shipping center on the Pacific Coast. In 1929, Oakland sponsored the first Northwestern Turkey Show, which came to be noted as the largest in the world. Competition was intense among those who raised and showed their various breeds and the recognition of having your turkey named "The Finest Bird in the Show" was truly coveted. In addition to turkeys, sheep and fruit also contributed to the local agricultural economy.

After a fire in the 1890s destroyed the majority of its wooden buildings, the town rebuilt with brick and stone. The economy of Oakland declined some in the 1920s and 1930s, but rebounded after World War II. U.S. Highway 99 brought in new businesses where there was empty space, but it didn't change the downtown area.

Following World War II, logging and lumber production became important to this town

A wooden logging road similar to those found near Oakland and other parts of Oregon.
Courtesy of the Sawdust and Cider collection.

as they did to many others in the Pacific Northwest. Log ponds and lumber mills became part of nearly every community with access to trees. Getting the logs into the ponds changed as new equipment became available. The logs were first transported by being pulled along the ground by horse or oxen teams, then by water, in flumes. Some were hauled out by train and eventually by truck when a road was available. Some of those early roads were built with logs and lumber over marshy areas.

In May 1968, Oakland was the first city to be placed on Oregon's historic register and in 1979, the Oakland Historic District was listed on the National Register of Historic Places.

RICE VALLEY / RICEHILL / RICE HILL

Rice Hill is an unincorporated community in Douglas County. It is located less than 10 miles north of Oakland and sits at the summit that divides the watersheds of Elk Creek and the Umpqua River. The two-mile-long Rice Valley below it stretches south from the community of Rice Hill where the Southern Pacific Railroad had a station.

In the town of Rice Hill, itself, a granite monument commemorates the Reverend Josephus A. Cornwall. The Rev. Cornwall was a Cumberland Presbyterian minister and was said to hold radically pro-slavery beliefs. He and his family were traveling through the Oregon Territory for his church in the winter of 1846-1847, when he lost his oxen. In order to save his wagons and their contents, he constructed what has been recognized as the first cabin built by a white man in Douglas County near the site of the current monument. The following spring, he contin-

Construction on the Anlauf-to-Rice Hill section of the Pacific Highway. *Courtesy of the Oregon Department of Transportation (ODOT)*

ued his journey north and eventually founded churches in several communities including Marysville, now named Corvallis, in 1849.

The steep grade of Rice Hill, elevation 710 feet, was an obstacle for pioneer travelers and also created problems with the construction of the railroad, as it rises 325 feet in three miles.

There were major conflicts with the improvement of U.S. Highway 99 in this area that involved condemnation proceedings. They created some long-seated antagonism towards the building of the highway as the changes weren't always welcomed by the residents.

A.G. Walling in his 1884 book, *History of Southern Oregon: Comprising Jackson, Josephine, Douglas, Curry and Coos Counties***, included a section on Rice Valley:**

"Four miles north of Oakland is Rice Valley, named in honor of W.S. Rice, who settled there in 1852, and is still one of its most prominent citizens. The valley is five miles long and one mile in width, and is drained by Cabin Creek, a tributary of the

Calapooia. It is under a high state of cultivation, producing a superior quality of grain, fruit and berries and is well-stocked with sheep and cattle. The earliest settler was A.J. Knowles in 1851, followed by W.S., Ira and Isadore Rice, Wesley Allen, Frederick Thieler, W.S. Tower and John Canaday, who are still its principle owners. The Oregon & California Railroad traverses the valley, at the head of which is Rice Station, the general shipping point. The population of seventy-five maintain a good school. A little trouble was experienced with the Indians by some of the settlers who located claims upon tracts of land the natives desired to keep and cultivate for themselves. This culminated after the War of 1856 in an attack by two of the whites upon an Indian house in which two of the inmates were killed. Serious trouble came near resulting from this, and mob violence was threatened. The men were tried for the act, but were not convicted."

Rice Valley, as noted by Walling, was named for William Street Rice, who had a donation land claim at the north end of the Rice Valley, but some historical sources show that it's uncertain whether the town of Rice Hill was named for him or for Isadore F. Rice, who was also in the area in the 1850s. It's very possible that the two were related since W.S. Rice had a son named Isadore Edwin Rice.

The Rice Hill post office was established in 1892 and was later renamed Ricehill. Its tenure was short-lived, however. It closed in 1908.

Today, Rice Hill's major draw is as a rest stop for truckers and tourists. There is a large truck stop, motels and restaurants on the east side of the Interstate 5 freeway, but its biggest claim to fame is the low-profile ice cream concession stand that sits on the west side. Over several decades during the summer, the parking lot is filled with cars driven by travelers who have made the current K & R Drive-In a special stop whenever they go through the area.

YONCALLA

Located in Douglas County, 28-miles north of Roseburg, the community of Yoncalla was first home to the Kalupuyan Indians and later to white settlers with the desire to farm. Among those were the Charles, Jesse and Lindsay Applegate families who arrived in the 1840s.

A post office was established in 1851 and the railroad came through in the 1880s. In 1872, George Burt gave the Oregon & California Railroad 48 acres of his donation land claim on the condition that a depot would be erected on his farm. Businesses were established and the town of Yoncalla began to form on the Burt property to the west of the railroad right-of-way. Robert A. Booth and Caleb E. Tracy were two of the early merchants. The Tracy store handled dry goods and became the Wells, Fargo & Company agent in the 1880s.

Robert Booth was the Yoncalla postmaster, merchant and sawmill owner. He built his Yoncalla sawmill in 1882 and gained a contract with the O&C Railroad to cut ties and timbers for bridges and tunnel shoring along much of the rail route south of Roseburg. In 1886, he moved to Grants Pass where he continued his lumber business and became a banker. In 1899, the same Robert Booth organized the Booth-Kelly Lumber Company of Springfield, Oregon. He also secured control of tens of thousands of acres of O&C grant lands, and became president of the

The Lower Yoncalla Valley, 1907. Courtesy of the OSU Special Collections & Archives Commons

Douglas County National Bank in Roseburg.

Traveling north from Oakland, the Ambrose Stage Station was located 11 miles north of Oakland and one mile southeast of Yoncalla. It not only supplied the meat, vegetables and fruit for the guests, but also provided boarding and feed for the stage horses and accommodated the overnight stays of the drivers.

According to the Meier's *Knights of the Whip*:

"...Ambrose's was a gathering place for social events and celebrations. Twice-daily visits by a wide variety of interesting stage passengers, going north and south, added to the liveliness of the house on the knoll, and it remained a place of interest and note."

The Applegate Family

Yoncalla became home to the Applegate family who were leaders of the migration to Oregon in 1843. The three brothers first settled in Polk County before Lindsay and Jesse led an expedition, in 1846, to blaze a new trail into California. Charles stayed home on Salt Creek while the others scouted the Applegate Trail. The three brothers were so taken with the beauty of the area which would later become Northern Douglas County, that they brought their families there to live.

Jesse Applegate was the first to settle in the area. He filed a donation land claim where he built a log cabin for his family. Charles and Lindsay soon settled nearby.

Jesse is said to have given the valley the name "Yoncalla," and he served as postmaster for a number of years. In 1858, he built a large two-story home.

Jesse became politically active with the Republican Party and in 1857, he was elected as a delegate to Oregon's constitutional convention. He recommended a friend and colleague, Samuel E. May, as Secretary of State, and when May was elected, Jesse signed a performance bond underwriting his honesty. Unfortunately, May was found to have embezzled $12,000 during his two terms as Secretary of State. May was tried in criminal court and found not guilty. Civil action was brought against him, but by then he had left the state and was declared insolvent. After lengthy court proceedings, Applegate, as the bond signer, was found liable for a large portion of the defaulted debt. He owed the state $5,793, and in the fall of 1874, all of Applegate's land and his home were confiscated to cover the loss.

He moved his family to 40-acres of property owned by Jesse's wife, Cynthia, and built a small cabin. He eventually paid off the deficit created by his former friend and, after Cynthia's death in 1881, moved several more times. The original homesite where his family lived is now noted by a marker which proclaims

Jesse's brother, Lindsay Applegate, who

> **JESSE APPLEGATE, 1811-1888**
>
> Pioneer, statesman, philosopher.
> Leader of migration to Oregon in 1843.
> Leader of Provisional Government of Oregon in 1844-49.
> First Surveyor General in 1844.
> Trail blazer, Fort Hall, Idaho to Willamette Valley in 1846.
> Member of Oregon Territory Legislature in 1849.
> Member of Constitutional Convention for State of Oregon in 1857.
>
> Settled here in 1849, ½ mile west of this spot.
>
> His house was the scene of first court of the Provisional Government, Southern District, 1852."

settled for a year or so in the Yoncalla Valley, became part of the California Gold Rush. He explored the Rogue River area on his way south and returned to Southern Oregon in 1849 where he settled and operated the toll road from Ashland, Oregon over the Siskiyou Mountains.

From *The Centennial History of Oregon*, Volume 4:

"CHARLES APPLEGATE, a prominent representative of a family whose history is closely interwoven with that of Douglas county and the state of Oregon, took up a donation claim of six hundred and forty acres adjoining the present site of the town of Yoncalla, in the spring of 1850. There he continued to reside until called to his final rest in 1879, when in the seventy-fourth year of his age.

"...It was in 1851, that Charles Applegate and his brothers built the first schoolhouse in Douglas County, installing James Applegate as teacher and conducting the institution independent of outside aid. At the cost of one thousand dollars they purchased from Harper's Publishing Company of New York City, a library which was shipped by water around Cape Horn. James Applegate, the first teacher of Douglas County and the son of Charles, was later chosen Douglas County judge and subsequently served as County Commissioner. For several years he was a member of the state legislature.

"In 1864, he enlisted for service in the Civil War and was made sergeant major of his regiment, acting in that capacity for one year, or until the close of hostilities.

"Charles Applegate, who passed away in 1879, was survived by his wife until 1888. The latter reaching the age of seventy-six years. Thus the community lost two of its 'most highly respected and valued' pioneer settlers. They are buried together in what was once the family's cemetery."

The original home of Charles Applegate and his family, built in 1852, has been pre-

The Charles Applegate Home in Yoncalla. *Courtesy of the Applegate Family*

served along with 100 acres of the original property, and is used as an educational resource. The National Register of Historic Places landmark recognizes it as the oldest known residence in Oregon that has remained in continuous family ownership since its construction.

The Applegate family was large in number by today's standards, and many family members stayed in the area, often maintaining close ties to each other. They also developed close ties to the local tribes in the area and were especially close to Chief Halo of the "Komemma people" – the Yoncalla Kalapuya tribe.

Authors' note: It should be noted that the tribal name of the Native Americans in the Umpqua Valley northward has various spellings, depending on the region and the time period. The most commonly used and accepted spelling is "Kalapuya," but landmarks and earlier references to the tribe are frequently spelled "Calapooia," "Calapooya," and even "Calapuya." Instances of these different spellings are the Calapooya Mountains and Calapooia Creek in the Lane and Douglas County region.

The Applegate Family Cemetery is located in Yoncalla and is managed by Shannon Applegate, a descendent of the family and an author with an interest in preserving the family's history. Other descendants are also authors, so there is much information about the family members and the Applegate family's participation in the early Oregon development.

In 1920, after the passage of the Women's Suffrage Law of 1912, there was a list of complaints against the city of Yoncalla that included sidewalks in disrepair, poorly lit streets, motorists speeding through town, the stench of the local outhouses and countless dogs running at large. The residents of Yoncalla met to discuss their grievances and two ladies filed for council seats. All of the incumbent males resigned their unpaid positions. The women then swept the entire ticket and became the first all-female city government in America. The mayor was Mary Burt and her council members were Nettie Hannan, Jennie D. Lasswell, Edith B. Thompson and Bernice Wilson. The news made national headlines and the story put the women in several magazines.

Yoncalla was one of the towns along U.S. Highway 99 that was bypassed by Interstate 5. Lying about 2.5 miles west of the freeway, it has had minimal growth since the construction.

As with other areas of northern Douglas County, agriculture and logging were the economic mainstays.

Today, Yoncalla is home to the largest apple orchard, in terms of variety, in the United States. It's said to be the largest private collection in the world. The 10-acre orchard, owned by Nick Botner, has over 6,000 trees bearing over 4,500 different varieties of apples.

Not only does Mr. Botner have apples, but there are also 500 pear trees, 170 plum trees, 150 cherry trees, about 475 grape cultivars plus other fruits and berries. Nick does not spray for plant pest or disease problems and his orchard is tilled each spring to keep the weeds down.

Unfortunately, according to an Oregon Public Broadcasting special produced on November 7, 2013, because of health issues, Nick was no longer able to care for it the way he felt it needed to be and he put the unique property and collection up for sale.

Fearing that the collection would be lost when new owners took over, the Home Orchard Society has launched a program to obtain cuttings from all 4,500 varieties in the collection. They have recruited volunteers to take scions, or cuttings, and splice them on to new roots.

A non-profit organization called the Temperate Orchard Conservancy, was formed to preserve the valuable genetic diversity represented in the Botner collection. Members of the organization will also collect scions from other collections across the U.S. to preserve as many varieties as can be found.

The organization, with a permanent home near Molalla, Oregon called Almaty Farm, will ultimately have a laboratory and will do DNA fingerprinting of the collection for the use of farmers who want to determine the source of their fruits for the local food banks.

The name "Almaty," appropriately, comes from the Kazak language meaning "place of apples" or "full of apples," according to Joanie Cooper of the Temperate Orchard Conservancy.

In her interview for the *WPA's American Life Histories Collection: Manuscripts from the Federal Writer's Project, 1936-1940*, Mrs. Hortense Applegate told about her childhood years in Wilbur in the Wilbur, Oregon segment. Her story now takes us off of the U.S. Highway 99 corridor for a short while, but returns to Scotts Valley and Yoncalla:

"My next school was in Coos County, at Myrtle Point, in 1870... Coos County was my first and only school out of Douglas County. Coos County seemed a long way off and quite an adventure. The roads we had were bad...

"In the spring of 1870, I started on horseback with my brother Dwight, to

Myrtle Point, in Coos County. Leaving the village of Wilbur early in the morning, we travelled as far as Camas Prairie, where we stopped for the night. This was the end of what could be called a road, and thence we took the mountain trail to the coast. My brother was in the lead. The trail was narrow, and in places rocky and steep. I kept my saddle, though at times it seemed straight up and down. A more tired girl could hardly be found when we arrived at Myrtle Point the next forenoon. Why the name Myrtle Point I soon learned. We approached through a grove of dark green trees, so dense the way grew dark. Such magnificent trees and sweet odors from the heavy, leafy foliage I can never forget.

"The next business was to prepare for the opening of school. First I had to take my examination, and to do that I was obliged to go to Empire City, down the Coquille River and across Coos Bay. My brother Oscar's farm was on the river. He had his own boat, as he frequently made trips for trading purposes. Arriving at Coos Bay Landing, which took most all day, we boarded the steamer and went across to Empire City. There I had the examination, received my certificate, and returned to my work.

"The schoolhouse stood on a raise in wooded surroundings. The many beautiful shrubs and flowers presenting a rural attractiveness. Monday morning found me at my post of duty, with almost every pupil of school age in the district, promptly an hand... [After?] two weeks of school I came down with the measles... I had taught two days, feeling badly and not knowing the trouble. It was customary in those times for the teachers to board with the scholars. As I kept getting worse, I sent for my brother, Oscar. He took a good look at me and remarked, 'Why, Tensa, you have the measles.' The eruptions were plain to be seen on my chest, but I could not be convinced that was what I had. My brother asked if I could ride, proposing to take me home with him.

"'But what about you and the family, taking me there with measles?' I asked.

"'We'll have to take our chances,' he replied, as he wrapped me in a big overcoat, after I'd put on my warmest outfit. Then he put me on a horse, while he took the lead on another. In many places of the narrow trail the overhanging limbs had to be dodged. My back and neck ached with pain when I went to bed at his home. In a week or ten days I was back at school, and nothing further interrupted...

"Returning from the three months' school at Myrtle Point, I applied for the primary department in the public school at Roseburg, and that winter taught under Professor Rice. The next spring I taught at Scotts Valley, Douglas County.

"A Miss Harrar, from Portland, had applied for the school. She was a niece of Mrs. Letsom. J.H. Todd was the school superintendent at Wilbur, where she went to get her certificate. She failed to pass and came back quite [crest-fallen?]. A young man of Yoncalla met her, to take her to Scotts Valley. It seems the superintendent, to whom she applied for her certificate, was a red-haired man. Irked and disappointed, she blamed the red-headed superintendent for her failure. 'I always did hate red-headed men' she told the young man, who, unfortunately, was red-headed too. He took the thrust good-naturedly, with the private decision, 'I'll take no more schoolmarms home, if that's their opinion of red-headed men.' When I arrived at Yoncalla, who should meet me at the depot but this same young man. I thought him nice and gentlemanly, and I always thought myself a good judge of gentlemen.

"I had never visited this part of the county (Douglas) before. It was a beautiful valley, surrounded by low, undulating hills, covered by pine, maple, cedar, and dogwood, with various other kinds of trees and shurbs of many blooming varieties. There were fine farms and fertile fields. In the four busy months of my school, from April 1st to and including July, I met many fine people, among them pioneers of 1843. The first settlers in the valley were the Cowan brothers, Robert and Tom. Robert had a family. The brother was single. Shortly after came the three Applegate brothers, Jesse, Charles and Lindsay. Their names have gone down in Oregon history for their statesmanship, and their unbounded hospitality and helpfulness to the early missionaries and immigrants to the State.

"In all localities you find odd and rather eccentric people. A few cases of smallpox had broken out at Oakland, some ten miles away. The next morning after the news, a number of the scholars came to school with Asafoetida tied around their necks. Occasionally they chewed it, making the atmosphere of the room very unpleasant. I proceeded to remove the wads from their necks. Ella Adams, quite a large girl, objected strenuously, but I succeeded, with the promise to return it after school.

"This school ended my days of teaching... I married the young man of red hair, who had met me at the depot three years before. Forty-six years we travelled down life's trail together. The call came to him at 74 years of age, in 1921."

In an interview for the *WPA's American Life Histories Collection: Manuscripts from the Federal Writer's Project, 1936-1940*, Mrs. Ella Burt told of her life in the Yoncalla area. She was interviewed by Manly M. Banister on March 13, 1939:

"I was born in Oregon eighty years ago, near Yoncalla. My first husband was the son of Charles Applegate. My father was W.H. Wilson. He came to Oregon with Jesse Applegate.

"We had lots of venison and wild game. There were a lot of deer and wild animals then. My father was an awfully

Yoncalla, Oregon (date unknown).
Courtesy of the Oregon Department of Transportation (ODOT)

good shot and kept his gun handy.

"We had lots of old-fashioned spelling schools. We'd go horseback – that was the only way to get around in those days.

"For supplies, they drove ox-teams into Eugene or Oregon City, where we'd load up with supplies and bring them home. There were flour, bacon and things like that. Didn't need to buy fresh meat because we had plenty of beeves; and it was awfully good beef, I can remember that.

"Cattle-raising is mostly what went on down there (Southern Oregon). Soon they went into farming and raising grain. They got sheep and sold the wool at Scottsburg which was the nearest port where the wool could be shipped.

"There wasn't any school house, so school was kept first at one house and then at another. The scholars paid so much apiece to the owner of the household for the privilege of coming there, and they had a teacher. But he wasn't paid much – usually about eight or ten dollars a month. But those conditions didn't last; they got better and better all the time. There weren't any churches either, and the preacher did his preaching at somebody's home; first at one place then at another, and everybody would come horseback.

"Uncle Jesse was the first person to have a little store at his home about a mile this side of Yoncalla. He sold things to people there. Uncle Charlie Applegate raised lots of sheep. He had a great mess of boys, seven or eight of them; and they worked hard at raising sheep and got wealthy at it. They would haul their wool, six or eight wagonloads at a time, in shearing season to Scottsburg for shipment. They was a very industrious lot of people, my goodness!

"Wheat was flailed out with a flail [illustrative motions], or tramped out by horses. We always came down to Portland to get flour. Whenever they traded in their wool, they always brought enough supplies at once to last a whole year. They laid in supplies of sugar, syrup, coffee, and things like that."

Boswell Springs

Located between Yoncalla and Drain, Oregon, was a mineral spring resort alternately called Snowden Springs, Payton Springs and finally, Boswell Springs after various owners. Conrad Snowden originally bought and developed the site in 1874 when he noticed that the local wildlife, especially deer, came to the area regularly to lick the minerals in the earth. The water in the springs that went through the property was later determined to be rich in potassium, sodium, magnesium, calcium, and iron compounds. Snowden saw the possibility of developing a resort that would draw people who wanted to cure various ailments including "rheumatism, catarrh, stomach, kidney and liver troubles," as reported later in an advertisement in the Roseburg *Plaindealer* newspaper.

With his partner, Dr. Daniel Payton, Snowden built a large, three-story hotel, right along the Oregon & California Railroad tracks and made it into a popular tourist attraction in the area. If the healing waters weren't enough, they also offered putting greens, swimming, fishing and cabins. Guests could hike in the hills or relax in natural beauty.

In the 1880s, Payton and Snowden sold the property to George W. Cartwright.

After the property was purchased by Benjamin Boswell in the 1890s, he developed it even more. It not only offered possible restorative cures, but elegant surroundings featuring art displays, fine dining and recreation – a swimming pool, horseback riding trails, croquet, tennis courts, as well as hunting and fishing.

The hotel burned in 1901, and another building on the site that had been used as a dormitory and ballroom was redesigned and used as a hotel until the 1950s when the spring was abandoned.

The Booher Family

In addition to being the home of the Applegate family, Yoncalla and, most specifically, Scotts Valley, is home to another large well-known family.

The Booher Family is known internationally for its music, beginning with old-time fiddling, classic western and gospel and expanding into country-western and popular.

Mike and Dolores Booher started it all. Theirs became a true musical family, performing with the Oregon Old Time Fiddlers Association beginning in 1983 and at other local events individually. Their lively, foot-stomping music became more and more popular and they were asked to appear in shows all over Oregon and beyond. From 1993 to1998, they toured with their only daughter, Meriwyn and the three youngest boys, Ben, Brendan and Gabe, performing in Canada, and five seasons at Silver Dollar City, Branson, MO.

The family's website gives a bit more information:

"In 1996 and 1997 they were invited to take part in the International Folk Festivals in Poland, where they performed several weeks at a time. Their travels ended when they opened up the Diamond B Chuckwagon in Tumalo near Bend, and for six years, they served up delicious cow-

Pacific Highway / U.S. Highway 99 between Yoncalla and Drain (1/4 mile south of Drain looking north), 1923. *Courtesy of the Oregon Department of Transportation (ODOT)*

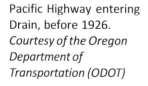

Pacific Highway entering Drain, before 1926. *Courtesy of the Oregon Department of Transportation (ODOT)*

boy suppers and fun family entertainment to folks from around the world!"

DRAIN

Drain was originally settled in 1847 by Warren Goodell. He filed for and received a donation land claim in 1850. In 1858, Jesse Applegate bought the property and in 1861, it was purchased by Charles C. and Anna Drain. Charles was the last president of the Oregon Territorial Council and he and his son, John, were both members of the State Legislature.

The Estes Ranch stage stop, also known as the Calapooya or "Stri-ped Horse" Station was about 12 miles north of the Ambrose Station and located in the Drain area. The California-Oregon Trail ran through the Estes Ranch. It had a large log hotel and was a major stopping point along the stage line.

In an interview with George Estes, conducted on November 28, 1938, as part of the *WPA's American Life Histories Collection: Manuscripts from the Federal Writer's Project, 1936-1940* project Mr. Estes tells about the station. His interview was conducted by Andrew C. Sherbert:

"My parents, Elijah T. and Susan Estes, emigrated from Iowa by ox-team, Oregon bound. They left Iowa in 1850 and arrived in the Willamette Valley in 1852, after nearly two years enroute. They remained a short time in the Willamette Valley, later moving south to a point near the foot of the Calapooia Mountains. The old homestead, near the town of Drain, is still known as the Elijah T. Estes Donation Land Claim.

"In the early fifties, there were no such things as stage lines, and, of course, there were no railroads either in Oregon. In the later fifties, however, a stage line was projected and established between Portland and San Francisco. As fortune would have it, the stage line's proposed route bisected my father's land claim. When the line opened for business, my father set up a stage station on his place and did a thriving business. The station was a sort of division point, much as a railroad division is designated today. Here the stages changed horses and drivers – the coaches themselves remaining but a few moments before they once more sped forward. As many as fifty horses were kept at this point. Drivers and hostlers of course made it their headquarters. It became a very busy place. The stages in use were known as Thoroughbrace Coaches, the name no doubt indicating the staunchness and sturdy construction of the coaches.

"...To my way of thinking, no more colorful or picturesque character ever crossed the horizon of pioneer times than the stagecoach driver. In my book, The Stagecoach, *I have tried to make him live again, with debatable success."*

Today, nothing remains of the old Calapooya Station hotel and Estes ranch except for some fruit trees.

Until 1865, Estes Station was the last chance to change horses before the grueling trip over the Calapooya Mountain on its way to the Cartwright House (aka Mountain House Hotel) near Lorane. After 1865, however, the route was changed to provide an easier trip for the teams of horses and it went over the mountain via Pass Creek Canyon which is the route later taken by U.S. Highway 99.

The Central Oregon Normal School, aka The Drain Academy, in Drain, Oregon was located where the North Douglas Middle and Elementary Schools now sit, 1902. *Courtesy of North Douglas School District.*

The construction of the Oregon & California Railroad through the area prompted the Drain family to sell 60 acres of land to the railroad for $1.00. In exchange, the railroad surveyed and platted the townsite in 1872, and added a station and yards. It was named Drain after the family.

By 1883, Charles Drain had built a large brick mercantile and other businesses, including a hotel, a livery stable and a drug store, began to spring up in the small town.

Also in 1883, the Methodist Church established a school called the Drain Academy to train teachers. Two years later, the state legislature named it Central Oregon Normal School. It was funded by the church and operated without state funding until it was eventually closed in 1908 and moved to Monmouth, Oregon.

Drain was officially incorporated in 1887, and John Drain was the first mayor.

The building of the elaborate Queen Anne-style residence of Charles and Anna Drain, began in 1893 and was completed in 1895. It is listed on the 1976 Statewide Inventory of Historic Sites and the National Register of Historic Places. The design of the Victorian house is attributed to George Barber of Tennessee and was said to cost $2,600 to build. The Drain home, referred to as "The Castle," is currently owned by the North Douglas School District. Between 1995-1997, a citizens' committee raised $80,000 to restore the house and that restoration has been on-going since.

Another classic Victorian home in Drain that is also listed with the Statewide Inventory of Historic Sites is the Charles Hasard house. Charles Hasard moved to Oregon in 1880 and was employed as a carpenter for the Oregon & California Railroad. He arrived in Drain in 1892 and began work as a hotel

The Charles & Anna Drain home today. *Courtesy of Wikimedia Commons*

The Charles Hasard house today. *Courtesy of Wikimedia Commons*

Professor Van Scoy's home today. *Courtesy of Wikimedia Commons*

keeper. Later he became a farmer and merchant. Hasard was appointed a U.S. Land Commissioner in 1902, and it was that year when his family home was completed. It has a similar design to the Fullerton House in Roseburg, Oregon, which also happened to be owned by the family attorney of Charles and Anna Drain.

The Hasard house has a variety of features and exterior textures with multiple ornamented gables and a tower rising above the main entrance. The home is currently a private residence and is not open to the public.

A third historic home in the town is the Van Scoy House. Professor Van Scoy was the last administrator of the Central Oregon Normal School.

In its Special Collections and University Archives, the University of Oregon has a letter dated December 8, 1904 from W.T. Van Scoy, of Ashland, Oregon, written to Charles Drain of Drain, Oregon. In the letter, Scoy writes that his wages at the Southern Oregon State Normal School were so terrible he could not eat and pay his bills, and he apologized that he couldn't pay Drain the insurance money he owed him.

In 1906, the Southern Pacific Railroad began construction of a route from Drain to the coast, but after spending an estimated $1.5 million on the project, it was abandoned and a line from Eugene to Coos Bay was built, instead.

Fires swept through the downtown district of Drain in 1903, and again in 1914, destroying many of the commercial buildings. Adding the commercial devastation of the fires of downtown Drain to the losses of the railroad line to Eugene, the Normal School to Monmouth, and a telegraph plan that never materialized, the economy of the area declined and people moved away. Drain had a population of 500 in 1881, but it took another 40 years to recover to the point where it was at that time.

This picture is believed to be a rock crusher at or near Drain, circa 1920, where Scott Mangold's grandfather, Martin Prather, worked on the construction of Pacific Highway / U.S. Highway 99. *Courtesy of Scott Mangold*

Grandpa Prather's dump truck. *Courtesy of Scott Mangold*

Memories from Scott Mangold:

"By the time I got interested in family history, all the old folks were gone and no one told significant stories through the years. About all I remember of Grandpa Prather (Martin Lair Prather) was his telling me that when WWI ended, he bought a war surplus dump truck and contracted to move dirt and asphalt around the Drain area. He married Grandma (Alma Howard of the Lebanon area) and they rented a room from an elderly lady who had a big rooming house in Drain. She had a parrot which spent time with Grandma while Grandpa worked on Highway 99."

The George Estes' story continues:

"...In the year 1867, the first telegraph line was put through from San Francisco to Portland. It was called, The Union Telegraph Company. This amazing boom to the spread of intelligence, consisted of a single wire suspended precariously from tree to tree through the wilderness. The line followed the route of the stage line to facilitate reaching the source of trouble when the wire broke – which occurred frequently – because of wind or weather.

"Upon establishing a telegraph station at Eugene and another at Oakland, Oregon, these two towns being 60 miles apart, the telegraph company decided that a station was needed somewhere between these two points. A station was then established on my father's place, where it continued until the stagecoach era ended.

"As a very small youngster I was initiated into knowledge of the intricacies of that marvelous instrument, the telegraph. I was fascinated with contemplation of the thought that by merely tapping a series of unintelligible sounds on the telegraph key, a person's express words could be conveyed by that slender strand of wire with the speed of light to Eugene (I had been there, and it seemed a long way off) and that they would arrive right side up, sensible and understandable. But the unintelligible sounds did not long remain unintelligible to me. I soon learned to read the Morse Code and the messages which clicked through our station kept me informed of the happenings of the outside world, almost, if not quite as well as today's radio news flashes came to the ear of the modern boy. Telegraphy grasped firm hold of me at that early age and occupied my constant thoughts and activities for a great deal of my life."

Drain, Oregon train depot (date unknown). *From the Curtis Irish Collection*

Interviewer's comment: *"Mr. Estes is an accomplished writer, author of seven published volumes. Skilled linguist, fluent in Scandinavian languages, Chinese, and several Indian tongues, notably Chinook and Calapooia. Keenly interested in natural sciences."*

In the 1930s, Southern Pacific rerouted its main line from California through Klamath Falls to Eugene and traffic through Drain decreased markedly.

Books, diaries and letters written about the Great Depression years in Oregon frequently describe the effects it had on settlers and those who came later to farm. They struggled as surely as those who worked in other jobs in town. In fact, many farmers needed to find other work in order to keep the farm. Large gardens and hard work might feed the family, but cash was needed to pay taxes, medical care, equipment, feed and sometimes seasonal help.

In one family, the farmer-father made the trip from Cottage Grove to the Booth Kelly Logging Camp out of Springfield where he worked for low wages and lived at the camp. Another worked on road construction and some followed the crops doing seasonal farm work on other farms.

It was often the women, left to run the farm, tend the garden and preserve the products, as well as care for the children, who found another way to bring in some of the needed cash. In several rural parts of the state, chickens and turkeys were the answer.

Ada Van Prooyan of the Cottage Grove area, whose diary entries appear later in this book, and Anna McKirdy Lovelace of Drain in her book, *Annie's Story*, are two of the women who wrote about the process. Information from the two stories are combined here to make a more complete picture.

The turkey pullets were ordered in the early spring and arrived nearly helpless. They would need to be confined and kept warm until they were old enough to survive outside. The first week, the temperature would need to be 95 degrees, not easy to maintain safely before electricity. Each week the temperature could go down five degrees. By two weeks, they would begin to make feathers, and by six, they could go outside to range. They had to be dewormed – one pill for each turkey for round worms and one for tape worms before they were turned out.

At market time, the hens would be processed first. If the husband was working away from home and none of the children were old enough to help, the farmwife would probably need to hire a picking crew to achieve a fast kill and clean pick. Preparing the meals

Myra Hedrick and her turkeys in Drain, Oregon. *Courtesy of the Letsom Letters Collection - Jody Johnson and Kathy Matthews*

Sawmill at Drain, 1911. *Courtesy of Gerald W. Williams Collections, OSU Special Collections & Archives Commons*

Griswold Lumber Mill in Drain. *Courtesy of Dot Dotson Photography*

for the crew would be part of her job, but she usually helped with the work, too. When the turkeys were gone, the brooder pens, or houses, would be disinfected and baby chicks brought in to provide fryers and layers for the next cash crop.

Drain became a shipping point for the fruit, vegetable and turkey-growing operations. Logging and agriculture supported the town, and by 1940, the population reached 637.

After World War II, lumber became a major contributor to the town's stability. The E.G. Whipple Mill and the Drain Plywood Company were built and became prosperous. Lumber mill activity boosted the population total to 1,204 in 1970.

In 1952, timber mill owner, Harold Woolley, brought jobs and more to the community. He and his wife Donna loved baseball, so he began sponsoring an amateur baseball team called the Drain Black Sox. Amateur and semipro teams were very popular at the time. The Woolleys built a nice ballpark and bought the finest equipment. Players were paid wages to work for the Woolley Logging Company, but they spent most of their time playing baseball. The roster included mostly college-age players.

The team was successful and, in 1958, earned a spot in a field of 31 teams at the

One of the few remaining wigwam burners left in Oregon at Drain. Wigwams are no longer legal to burn wood waste in Oregon. *Courtesy of Wikimedia Commons*

National Baseball Congress Tournament in Wichita, Kansas. The National Baseball Congress, comprised of fifteen semipro and amateur leagues, was founded in 1934. Featuring the best teams from around the country, the tournament was known as the NBC World Series. Many NBC players have gone on to succeed in the professional ranks of major league baseball.

With grit and the determination to win, the Black Sox defeated all the odds and won the National Championship in the 1958 NBC World Series.

LEONA

Leona was a logging community north of Drain near the current Pass Creek Nursery. There was a large mill in the area and two railroads. The Southern Pacific Railroad line passed through it in a north-south alignment and there was also a spur line which passed under Sand Creek Bridge that brought logs to the mill pond for processing into lumber.

The town was named for Leona Perkins, and its post office was established on February 14, 1901. Thomas E. Bledsoe was its first postmaster.

ANLAUF

Anlauf, now considered a ghost town, was located just off of the original route of Pacific Highway on Buck Creek Road. Its recorded history is sparse, but it is said to have been named after either Frank Anlauf, who started one of the first sawmills in the area, or his son, Robert, on whose land the first post office sat.

In 1872, Frank Anlauf and his sons, Frank, Pius, Otto and Robert, settled on a 240-acre donation land claim in the commu-

The Ward's Butte lookout was located near Anlauf, east of Highway 99. It was built in 1934 and destroyed in the 1962 Columbus Day Storm. It was rebuilt in 1963, but was removed in 1975. *Courtesy of the on-line Lookout Sites Registry*

nity of Comstock and in 1888, they built a mill on Pheasant Creek near the site of the town of Anlauf. They "splash-dammed" the logs down Pheasant Creek to the mill for processing.

A splash dam was a temporary wooden dam built in rivers and streams to raise the water level ahead of logs that were being floated to local mills.

The January 21, 1897 edition of the Roseburg *Plaindealer* newspaper lists Otto Anlauf (wife, Robertina) of Comstock as one of the road supervisors, who was reported as having been killed in a boiler explosion at the Booth-Kelly Mill near Saginaw in May 1900.

The Anlauf Post Office was established in 1901 and later discontinued in 1946. Jimmy Sterling was the first postmaster. The town had a train depot hosting the Oregon & California and later, the Southern Pacific

Railroad lines.

Robert Anlauf and his brother – either Frank or Pius – were carpenters and built many houses in Drain and other areas. Many of the homes built by the Anlauf brothers are still in use today.

Letter to the Editor from Jas. A. Sterling, Anlauf postmaster, to *The Plaindealer*, Anlauf, Oregon, August 27, 1903:

"Either by jest or meanness, I notice that someone has given you the item that the telephone was open to Elkton to Drain. The same is false. The wire was shipped August 7th from Kokomo, Ind., some 3000 pounds, and ought to be here in a few days, freight and goods paid. J.E. Baker is getting out poles near Elkton and E.I. Lane near Drain. I shall soon peg where post holes are to be dug, and I am glad of rain as I can get along faster. I have material of all kinds on hand to run to Scottsburg except wire, and I have made preliminary arrangements with the Pacific States Telephone Co. to exchange and lease their phones. I will as soon as the coast line is finished build a private line from the Drain depot to the residence of J.O. Johnson near Leona, for his own use and for his railroad business; and may, if encouraged to run a phone to Leona, Chas. M. Henderer's, Anlauf, and Perkins and Mires saw mill."

Many who moved to Anlauf were those who came to work in the mills. One of the larger early mills was the Perkins and Mires sawmill that Sterling mentioned in his letter. It was owned by W.A. Perkins of Drain and Benton Mires.

In 1904, there was a rock crusher called Shadybrook in the area, and Anlauf was prominent enough to have its own column in the *Plaindealer*. An April 1904 entry mentioned that Mr. Robert Anlauf was having mechanical problems with his woodmill; Miss Lonny Woody had a birthday party with 25 people in attendance and that *"Miss Lura Heftly received the piece of cake with the ring, which was to indicate good luck."* It also mentioned the Anlauf baseball team – *"The baseball team at Anlauf have their supplies with which to commence business and are ready to give or accept a challenge, and will be hard to catch"* – that Mr. Hill, the Anlauf merchant, was doing a good business, and *"Mr. Joe Ritchey has just received a new road plow and will soon be seen repairing the roads."*

Lumber was definitely the main industry in Anlauf over the years. In 1923-1934, there was the Anlauf Lumber Company, owned by C.W. Cone. It sat on the east side of the railroad tracks where, in later years, the South Fork Lumber Company was located. South Fork, which was moved from its original Smith River location to Anlauf, was the major mill in the area for many years, employing men from all over North Douglas and South Lane counties.

According to Gary Thompson of Lorane, Oregon:

"Anlauf was located right across the highway from Buck Creek Road. My father, Eldon Thompson, was one of the first fallers to use a chainsaw in the Drain area when he worked for George Churchill Logging Company in the 1940s."

In 1972, probably due to the decline in the timber industry, South Fork was closed and torn down.

The Southern Pacific train that passed through Curtin and Anlauf daily. *Courtesy of Chuck Booher*

Jim Suiter of Eugene told his story:

"Just east of the intersection was a lodge – Anlauf Lodge – along with several cabins for rent. My mother Vera "Babe" Suiter worked at the lodge after graduating from high school in Drain."

Before 1924, Anlauf had a store and post office owned by a Mr. Roberts who was also the postmaster.

CURTIN

An unincorporated community in Douglas County, seven miles northeast of Drain, Curtin was named for Daniel Curtin, a sawmill owner during the 1890s. The Southern Pacific line had a station there at one time.

When U.S. Highway 99 passed through the community, the Stardust Motel and a general store, first opened in 1911, were avail-

Early-day Curtin. U.S. Highway 99 was in the foreground at that time before the I-5 Freeway was built. *Courtesy of Chuck Booher*

able to service motorists driving by. A post office was established in 1908, but has been closed for several years.

The highway passed through Curtin on what is now Pass Creek Road, but it was destroyed when Interstate 5 was built. Pass Creek Road now deadends just north of the small community of Comstock, but Highway 99 can be rejoined from the freeway at Divide where an exit leads back to it.

Today, Pass Creek Park, a very nice reststop for travelers, sits on the west side of the freeway and can easily be accessed by both north- and southbound traffic.

"An Interview with Chuck Booher" by Pat Edwards, on March 17, 2014:

"Charles "Chuck" Booher was gracious enough to grant me an interview when I was seeking someone who could tell us a bit about Curtin. He showed few signs of his advancing years – 95 of them – and he was excited and eager to share some of his memories of the communities of Curtin, Comstock and Anlauf near which his family settled in the early 1900s.

"His maternal grandparents, Charley and Alice Turpin, settled in the area in about 1915. His paternal grandparents, George Washington and Sarah Booher, were early settlers in the Yoncalla area.

"According to Chuck, the road that eventually became the Pacific Highway/U.S. Highway 99, once ran along the hillsides north of Curtin. Without the paving that we know today, it was too muddy in the winters to traverse the lower levels where the highway was later built.

"There were two daily Southern Pacific passenger trains that passed through the area – one from the north at 1:00 p.m. and the other from the south at 2:30 p.m.

The fossil found by Charley Turpin north of Curtin remains in the family and is treated with a great deal of respect. *Courtesy of Chuck Booher*

Most of the residents in the community rode the trains to run their errands and pick up supplies from Cottage Grove. The trains also delivered the mail. If there weren't any passengers waiting to be picked up, however, the trains didn't stop. The train was rigged with a hook that would grab the bags of mail hanging from the station as it went by. Mail to be delivered was thrown off the train in canvas bags as the train passed through. There was also a freight house in Curtin where the mail was left when the train stopped to let passengers off.

"In 1930, Chuck's Grandpa Turpin was working for the State Highway Department one day per week to help supplement his income leading up to the Depression. While he and the road crew were digging out an area at the base of the wooden pilings supporting the bridge that went over the railroad tracks near Comstock, his shovel brought up a unique find. He thought at first that it was a large rock, but on closer examination, it was obviously a perfectly-preserved fossil from the sea. Chuck carefully took the beautiful piece of antiquity out of a box to show my husband and I. It was amazing to see, hold and instantly know its history, and we felt

The wreckage of a circus wagon on the Booher property near Curtin on June 30, 1942. *Courtesy of Chuck Booher*

a special connection to the past in just viewing it.

"Chuck attended the Curtin School in the 1920s and 1930s. One of his classmates, Isabelle Cline, used to walk to school and back home every day from the Cline home at the base of the Lorane Hill, about four miles away. That was how many of the children made their way to class in those days.

"The Curtin School, located on Curtin Road (U.S. Highway 99) was closed by the North Douglas School District quite a few years ago, and has since been converted into apartments and an RV park called the Lucky Duck Campground and RV Park.

"The Boohers lived on Curtin Road, north of Curtin in the early 1940s. One day, Chuck was outside in their front yard watching a circus caravan passing by on the road. Chuck thinks that the driver must have fallen asleep. The load shifted in the large semi-truck, causing it to roll over onto its top. He soon had several horses, llamas, a couple of camels and two or three zebras lounging in his nearby pasture while they waited for the trailer to be put back on its wheels to continue its journey towards Cottage Grove.

"In 1942, Chuck and his wife Dorothy leased the Curtin Store and the home behind it from her parents and ran it until 1946. The store was originally owned by Wilbur Hill who was also the postmaster. He sold it in 1935 to Dorothy's parents, Albert L. and Flora Holt. Their son, Harry, and his wife Bertha, later founded the Holt International Adoption Agency.

"Dorothy served as postmistress for several years at the Curtin Store during

Chuck Booher in front of the old gas pumps at the Curtin Store in the early 1940s. *Courtesy of Chuck Booher*

The Curtin Store in later days. *Courtesy of Wikimedia Commons*

the time her parents owned it and, in 1938 or 1939, Albert dammed the creek on the property, put in a water wheel and generated his own electricity for the store and their home. He also installed a water pump to bring water from the creek to the store. The rest of the Curtin community had to wait until 1940 to get their electricity by the more conventional means.

"While they had the store and gas station, Chuck pumped the Texaco gas to customers for 16-to-18 cents a gallon from its two 4,000 gallon tanks. They also sold groceries which he obtained from Pacific Wholesale in Eugene.

"In the early 1950s, Chuck bought three houses at an auction. They were located on what is now the east side of the I-5 freeway across Bear Creek Road from the old boarded-up gas station. He had them moved west and placed on property that he owned across Bear Creek Road from the Curtin Store. Another house, which Chuck had built in 1943 was already located on the property. He also built three other houses in the Curtin area. When asked if he was a building contractor, he said that, 'No... it was just a hobby.' He worked for years at Drain Plywood.

"Chuck and Dorothy Booher had six children – 3 girls and 3 boys. After 68 years of marriage, Dorothy passed away in 2009.

"One of their daughters, Debbie Davis, formerly of Lorane, has been a good friend over the years to my husband and I, and was the person who put me in touch with her father for this book.

"The oldest of the Booher's sons, Mike and his wife Dolores, are the architects of the well-known musical Booher family from the Yoncalla area and all of the Boohers and Holts seem to have built their own legacies in the Lane and Douglas County areas.

"Chuck now counts his great-grandchildren at 48, so there won't be a scarcity of Boohers or Booher descendants any time soon."

COMSTOCK

James J. Comstock built the Comstock Lumbering and Manufacturing Company, one

Comstock, Oregon. The school was located at the far right. *Courtesy of Joe Griggs*

of the first mills in the area that was operating as early as 1875.

"The Death of a Community: Griggs Family History - Comstock, Oregon" by Pat Edwards:

"On April 21, 2014, I met with Joe Griggs, the great-grandson of John Allen and Sarah Griggs who settled in the Comstock area in 1873 or 1874. Joe believes that they chose the location because John was hired by the Oregon & California Railroad to be the area's Section Foreman.

"Comstock, Oregon became the main refueling stop between Drain and Cottage Grove. In the late 1870s, it's believed that the Griggs bought a large 2-story home sitting on a hill above the railroad tracks from James Comstock and made it into an inn. Sarah cooked and served meals to train crews at all hours. The inn also served as their family home and they built a cottage on the property in which other family members lived. They added on to the inn and remodeled it in the early 1900s. There was a bunkhouse called "The Men's Room" that accommodated the crewmen who laid over in Comstock.

"At our interview, Joe Griggs shared a family history that was written by Grace Griggs Blackford, granddaughter of John and Sarah Griggs, in 1976 or 1977. According to Grace, 'The bunkhouse opened off the side porch and was a large, sparsely furnished room – only a large table and

The Griggs' home and Comstock Hotel. *Courtesy of Joe Griggs*

The Comstock Store, 1928, with *Pete Marchetti* in front. The tracks ran behind the store. *Courtesy of Chuck Booher*

old captain-style chairs. It had a large fireplace and was a comfortable place for men to sit in the evening and play cards or just talk. My father and brothers were never allowed to sit there in the evenings – one of my grandmother's rules.'

"Over the years, the Griggs added on to their holdings and investments. By 1885, the family owned almost 1,000 acres covering a good portion of the northern end of the Pass Creek Canyon.

"In 1899, the Griggs family agreed to lease from Henry M. Stewart the property known as the 'Old Depot Building ground' according to an indenture agreement. Included with the property, was 'the said building and ten feet around the same except what faced the railroad track for 5 years for a monthly rent of $2 for a store to keep all merchandise except liquor.'

"The old Comstock store sat across the tracks from the hotel. It housed the Comstock Post Office and both were run by Pete Marchetti for many years.

The Comstock School. *Courtesy of Carol Chapman*

"As can be seen in the picture, the railroad had a large refueling tank located along the tracks and the trains would stop there for water and fuel. There was also a station house and a large railroad siding on which cars not in service were kept.

"The community built a one-room schoolhouse where the local kids went until they were old enough to attend the Drain Normal School.

"According to Grace Blackford, 'The first Comstock school house was in a draw just north of the Comstock Cemetery and it was my understanding that Grandpa Griggs gave the land. I do not know when the first building was erected, but some of the residents in the area whose names appear on an old abstract map were Ward, Hall, Moore, Hedrick, Watkins, Clark, Anlauf, Griggs, Laurence, Mooney, O'Neil, Alden, Schaffer, Hinman, Stewart, Marchetta, Jackson, Allen, Skidmore, Hills, Oleson, Delauney, Wolford, Walkley and Tucker. My father and his two brothers attended this school and I remember well some of his stories about the early teachers.

"'It was moved, burned, rebuilt and at last, with the coming of the district

John Allen and Sarah Griggs. *Courtesy of Joe Griggs*

schools and buses, was no longer needed and has disappeared, leaving no trace except in the memories of those who attended, among whom were my brother Allan and myself.'

"The schoolhouse was not the only thing that disappeared in Comstock over the years. In 1926, when the main railroad line was moved through Eugene, Springfield and Oakridge, passenger service halted and few freight trains came through the Willamette Valley south of Cottage Grove, eliminating the need for ticket and freight agents. All of the rail-

The Southern Pacific train making a stop at Comstock. *Courtesy of Joe Griggs*

road buildings, including the station house and water tank, were soon torn down.

"After Sarah Griggs' passing in 1917, the inn became the home to a succession of family members. Once the railroad vacated the community, about the only buildings left were the 'big house,' as the former inn was called, and the small cottage.

"After Joe's father, Lloyd Griggs, graduated from Oregon State Agricultural School in 1932, he lived in Eugene where he worked for Shell Oil Company. That's where he met his future wife, Jeane, who was a secretary there. In 1935, they moved to the old hotel in Comstock for two years before once again moving their family to Cottage Grove where he took over his father's job at Pacific Bell Telephone Company where he was in charge of the outside plant. Later, in 1952 or 1953, Lloyd bought into the Pioneer Hardware store where he worked until 1964. It was in 1964 when Lloyd was named Cottage Grove Chamber of Commerce's "First Citizen."

"By 1939, the cottage on the Comstock property had been torn down. The last family tenants in the former hotel were Chauncey and Helen Blosser who lived there between 1938 and 1953.

"With big plans for a major interstate freeway, the Oregon Highway Department bought a right-of-way through the farm from the Griggs family. The planned route included most of the land where the house stood and later, in 1953, they began construction on the freeway.

"According to Grace Griggs Blackford, 'They tore down the old house and the front yard disappeared under tons of earth.'

"About the only remnants of the community of Comstock today is the old barn."

As mentioned, before 1865, the stagecoaches navigated the mountainous curves of the old Territorial Road to the next stop on their journey north after leaving the Estes Station near Drain. The Cartwright House, also known as the Mountain House Hotel, was located three miles south of the community of Lorane in Lane County, Oregon. Even though U.S. Highway 99 followed the newer route through Pass Creek Canyon, we are taking you on a detour of the older road to give you an idea of the earlier stage route.

Serving the California & Oregon Stage Company until 1865, the Cartwright House or Mountain House Hotel was considered the best official stage stop on the route between Portland and San Francisco.

After the northbound stages left the Mountain House Hotel, they journeyed approximately 12 miles farther to the next horse-changing station.

Pat Edwards recounts new information on what we'll refer to as the "Welsh Changing Station."

"Gary and Gloria Meier mentioned in their book, Knights of the Whip, that they had not been able to determine where the next stop was after leaving the Cartwright House, but after reading their book and researching the area, I discovered that I think I know.

"When we bought our home place on Lorane Highway in 1966, it was referred to in the area as the 'Old Runk Place.' We had always heard that the big old barn that was on the property had once been a stagecoach stop, but had never tried to run down its history. After reading the Meier's statement about not being able to locate it, I decided to do some of my own investigating.

Jacob Runk and friends in front of the Welsh Changing Station stage barn. *Courtesy of the Runk family*

family in my books (Sawdust and Cider; A History of Lorane, Oregon and the Siuslaw Valley, *1987; and* From Sawdust and Cider to Wine, *2006) and even had a picture of Jacob Runk in front of the old barn. So I immediately asked Jacob's grandson, Ellis, if he remembered his family talking about the place as being a stage stop. He told me that his family referred to it as the old stage barn, although later, his grandparents had added milking stanchions on to it and sold milk to the local dairies."*

"The property was originally part of the donation land claims of Jeremiah and John P. Welsh who settled two 160-acre parcels, adjacent to one another, in 1853. It's not known if the Welsh's were actually the ones who ran the changing station, but members of the Jacob Runk family, who bought the property in 1884, confirm that they had always believed the big old barn on the property had been a stage stop.

"I had included a history of the Runk

From the Welsh changing station, the pre-1865 stages could very possibly have continued their northbound routes by connecting with the Old Territorial Road, going through Franklin, Cheshire and on to Milliorn's near Junction City, bypassing Eugene City entirely. But, we cannot be sure. After the route was changed to go through Pass Creek in 1865 – the same year that the Milliorn stop was moved to Lancaster – it would have gone through Eugene City and on to Lancaster.

Section 6

U.S. HIGHWAY 99 - DIVIDE TO JUNCTION CITY

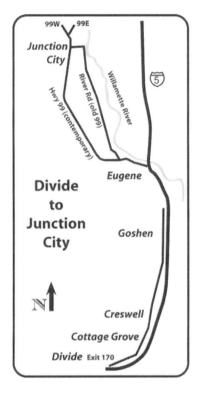

DIVIDE

The Divide landmark is located at the I-5 exit 170. It marks the little-noticed pass that divides the Umpqua River watershed from the Willamette River watershed – Southern Oregon from Northern Oregon. It is here where a traveler can return to U.S. Highway 99, now called the Goshen-Divide Highway, to visit the towns where the highway once brought prosperity.

At one time, there was a post office called Divide that was established on May 31, 1900 and closed on January 15, 1921. It may have been moved across county borders, or its county designation may have changed in a boundary shift between Lane and Douglas counties.

After 1865, the stagecoaches no longer used the steep Territorial Road to cross the Calapooya Mountains, past the Cartwright House/Mountain House Hotel and Lorane on

1916 pictures of the Divide School that sat on Hawley property. The two pictures on this page are actually one long picture that was scanned twice. We are leaving it this way for more detail. The baseball group of kids on the left above are the same as those on the right side of the picture below. Children who attended that year included Clare, Sherman and Leslie Chapman and their cousins, Charles, Nefa and Nancy Chapman; Norby, Clovy, Lillian, Milan (?), Peachy and Roxie Seward; Charles Byrd; Kathleen and George McReynolds; John and Amerigo Mostachotti; Mac and Toni (not in picture) Tonole; Wilbur and Wayne McCue; Cleal Mackay (the one lying down); Beth (and her sister) Bailey; and the teacher, Zora Gridley. *Courtesy of Mike Chapman of the Two-Bit Ranch*

NOTE: Looking south, the Pacific Highway ran along the fenceline to the left of the picture below. Across the road from it is a steam train.

Playground at the Divide School, 1916. *Courtesy of Mike Chapman of the Two-Bit Ranch*

their way north. Instead, they were rerouted by way of an old road which wound through Pass Creek Canyon. The road was poor, soft and muddy along the creek bottom and the canyon passage was narrow.

Robert H. Ward, who lived at the southern end of the new route, built a corduroy road by laying 8-foot cedar logs side by side across the road through the pass. This road became known as Ward's Toll Road, with Ward collecting a toll from northbound travelers and Ira Hawley collecting the southbound tolls.

On the later stage route, Hawley's Station was located 10 miles north of Estes Ranch on the Ira B. Hawley donation land claim. It provided a rest stop and a horse-changing station there.

The passengers found food and overnight accommodations at the house and a big barn sheltered the team of horses on the large 4,000 acre cattle and sheep ranch. The small Divide school that served the surrounding area sat on the property.

Today, Highway 99, south of Cottage Grove passes the red ranch buildings and barns which belong to the present Hawley Land and Cattle Company on the site of Ira Hawley's Stage Station.

Hawley Ranch History by Bill Hoyt, descendant of Ira Hawley:

"Hawley Ranch is owned and operated by 5th generation family members, Bill and Sharon Hoyt. In 2002, the family celebrated 150 years of ranching on the same ground as their Hawley ancestors have since 1852... In 1848, Ira was farming with his wife, Elvira Riley Hawley, in Rome, Illinois when gold was discovered in California. Gold fever struck Ira; in 1849, he and a friend headed for California to claim their fortune. He did not return to his family until January of 1852...

"...After months of travel and hardship, Ira set down 'stakes' in our present location some 6 miles south of what is now the town of Cottage Grove...

"...The land that Ira secured and where our ranch is now located is the spot which marks the division between the waters of the Umpqua and Willamette Rivers. Over the generations, old time residents have referred to us as the "ranch at divide" where Ira Hawley found good water, good grass and what would become a crossroad for progress.

"True to his generation, Ira had great vision for the future: he predicted the value of timber, mining, roads and the judicial use of Oregon's natural resources. Among his many accomplishments, Ira is credited with building roads, providing a stage stop between Portland and Sacramento, hosting a community school and starting the first cattle drive up the Willamette Valley to markets in Oregon City which fed the expanding Oregon population.

"Ira's wife Elvira served as the midwife for our area of Oregon for many years and there are countless stories of her heroic exploits. Ira and Elvira welcomed 12 children of their own, including 5 boys and 1 girl who lived to adulthood. I am proud to say that I am a direct descendant of their only surviving daughter, Medora Ann Hawley Stockwell."

From the *Cottage Grove Sentinel*, June 3, 1921:

"Pacific Highway has been completed between Walker and Saginaw north of here and has been open to traffic for sev-

The Hawley ranch house.
Courtesy of the Hawley family

eral days. Operations were moved by the Blake-Compton company to the other end of the job at Divide and work will progress towards the paving plant at Saginaw."

"Farming Practices" by Ada Van Prooyan:

Ada Van Prooyan and her husband Abe built and ran a small store and gas station on U.S. Highway 99 south of Cottage Grove until they decided to sell it and become farmers. Ada left a summary of her life for her family – written in her own hand. This part of their story begins when they bought the farm in the fall of 1929.

"Moved to the farm today – June 1930. Took Philip's sheep on shares, about 5 cents a head. Traded our Ford Sedan for cattle! Traded our electric washing machine for a cow that was no good. Kept a milk cow and some chickens – raised a hog or two for meat. Had some fruit and berries and raised a big garden. In those days that was called 'subsistence farming.' We tried to produce as much of our own food as possible and raised hay and grain for our livestock and some to sell.

"We had three children when we moved to the farm: Clifford almost 6 years old, Claudia, 3, and Marvin just 1 year old. The huge old house had 21 rooms and lots of porches – five of which were off the upstairs rooms for sleeping porches. The porches downstairs went nearly around the house and were a great playground and race track for the kids and their little red wagon.

"We had no electricity. A pitcher pump on the back porch supplied water for the house. Some garden was irrigated by water carried from the creek. Kerosene lamps lighted the house and lanterns were carried to the barn and hung on hooks and slid along a wire as we worked from place to place. We did have a country line telephone with fourteen parties – a real 'gossip column.'

"Mail came to the end of the county road, but was delivered to our door when the road was finished later that year.

"The first year was a tough one. In August, I had surgery – first an appendectomy, then they removed my gall bladder also – so the family had to have a niece to help because it was harvest time for our first crops of oats and wheat and Abe was a busy man. Before that year was out, Abe was laid up for several weeks with a bad spell with his back. In the spring, we lost our small boy to leukemia. He was just two-and-a-half. We were very discouraged. The Depression was at its worst and I guess we would have given up except that we were both too stubborn to admit failure and the farm did supply most of our needs. Being 'poor' on a farm isn't real poverty.

"Then things began to look better. We picked fir cones to sell for the seeds, picked wild blackberries for the cannery and Abe cut and sold firewood and some fir poles and stakes. In the fall of 1932, right after Franklin Roosevelt was elected president, Abe was able to find a job at his old trade, donkey engineer, for Booth Kelley at Wendling. The pay was very low and he had to live at the logging camp all week so he could only 'farm' on Saturdays and would have to lay off at harvest time. Clifford was now big enough to help with chores, so we managed OK.

"The farm still made most of our living and Abe's wages helped us acquire some more cattle, sheep of our own, a herd of angora goats, much-needed fencing and a team of horses. As he continued to work when he could, we acquired an old Ford tractor and several pieces of machinery. We still kept a team until 1937 when we finally got a new rubber-tired tractor and some better haying and harvest equipment.

"About 1933, we 'eased' into the turkey business by buying six turkey hens and a tom. They ranged all over – stole their nests out and had to be put in cages to raise the poults they hatched. We now raised more grain and some corn for the hogs and turkeys.

"We kept several milk cows and separated the milk and sold cream. Then we fed the skim milk to the hogs and turkeys. Now we had better gardens, berries and fruit, chickens and eggs, milk, cream and cottage cheese, our own pork and lard, our own beef to butcher and can, an occasional fat lamb, turkeys and chickens for meat. So we really lived abundantly with little cash. The sale of surplus grain or hay, fat lambs and hogs, wool and mohair and some cattle took care of our needs for cash for taxes, etc.

"In the summer of 1936, while Abe was away at work, a flue fire caught our roof on fire. Neighbors and nearby millworkers got it out with no great loss except to the roof itself, but we couldn't live in it. We tore down some of the parts of the big house that we weren't using and built us a 'shelter,' just two rooms but enough. We had already poured the foundation for the new house near the old one, so we began at once to have construction of the building started. We had planned the 'shelter' to be a chicken house after we finished the new house, but I think we lived in it two winters before we could move, carrying water from the old well, some distance away.

"Time was slipping by. Before we could get the inside of the house finished, World War II had begun and some building supplies were scarce. Electric wire was unattainable, plumbing supplies and pipe were hard to find. We finally moved into the new house with it very incomplete except for the kitchen. Nearly all interior walls were finished only on one side so wiring could be done later. R.E.A. electric lines had not been built yet, anyway. We finally were able to get pipe to bring water to the house from a good spring on the hill above. Running water, both piped in and out, was a real luxury. Only after the war was over in 1946 did we finally get supplies to finish the electricity and the inside of the house.

"Abe, having been in France in the U.S. Army in World War I, felt that he must do something now. He worked 24 months in the shipyards in Portland, just coming home weekends. We stayed on the farm.

"During these busy years, the kids grew to teenagers. They had finished at our local grade school and were being bused to high school in Cottage Grove. They had been active in 4-H clubs for years. In high school, Clifford also began classes and projects with Future Farmers, and he had a nice small flock of registered Suffolk sheep of his own. Claudia was good to help on the farm, too, but domestic things such as sewing, cooking, and gardening were her choices.

"We tried a new crop venture, alfalfa. We limed, fertilized and planted ten acres and raised a beautiful crop of hay. Our Willamette Valley climate wasn't ideal, though, and it was difficult to harvest the first cutting because of wet weather at haying time. One year we cut, raked and shocked the hay, then continued rain made it impossible to cure. We had to remove it from the field because the second crop was coming. All the other fields were in grain crops, so Abe had to haul it off and just stack it. After it rotted, he had to haul it out and spread it on the grain fields where it made excellent fertilizer. We kept the one field in alfalfa for about four years, but never did plant more because of the difficulty of harvesting a hay crop. The second crop was wonderful pasture for fattening our lambs for market, so we never cut a second crop of hay.

"In the meantime, we'd decided to use the 'shelter' we'd built and meant to use as a chicken house. We decided to use it as a brooder house and raise day-old baby chicks and poults. We built a hen house for 300 layers and raised 600 baby chicks. We sold the roosters as fryers at about three to four pounds and raised the pullets for layers for the new house. We got the baby chicks quite early, raised them, then cleaned and disinfected everything. We then put in 500 baby turkey poults which we raised to market age, then killed and dressed most for market. Those were very busy years, and Abe worked away from home less and less as our projects at home were making good profits.

"After we started raising turkeys in large numbers, we planted more corn for feed. It too was a difficult crop to harvest if we got real fall rains, so we only planned to raise enough for our own stock. For turkeys, it had to be shelled.

"After we got our first radio, we would bring in the ear corn and all sit and shell corn while we listened to the radio in the evenings, a tiresome chore was soon done as our fingers flew in time with music, or as we laughed at 'Amos and Andy.' We also learned to make hominy from the corn so it made family food, too.

"Food from our own produce was a major necessity, and it really was quite interesting as I reminisce. In the early years we didn't have electricity or a freezer so we canned or dried fruit, vegetables, meat, poultry, etc. We smoked our own bacon and ham and made lard. Made pickles and sauerkraut. Our 'fruit closet' in the new house was carefully planned and insulated to store some 700 to 800 quarts of canned produce and had storage places for such things as apples and potatoes for winter use and stoneware crocks for pickles, sauerkraut, homemade mince meat, etc.

"Since the place was joined to federal timber land and deer were plentiful, Abe hunted and always brought home venison which we canned.

"Both children finished high school and started to college, so our new house was pretty empty. But, everything was going well for us and we kept improving the place, getting better equipment and better livestock. Over the years, we also sold some timber and put that money into improvements. We acquired a bigger tractor and a combine and Abe did harvesting for all the neighbors who raised grain.

"We finally sold the Angora goats when Mohair prices went too low to be profitable. Mohair was the major fiber in automobile upholstery until after World War II when plastics and new synthetics replaced it. Goats helped in clearing land of brush and weeds so they were a part of our improvement plans for the farm, but then became too unprofitable.

"Our best money makers were still our turkeys, the laying hens and the fryers we raised, dressed and sold. One of Cliff's 4-H projects was a beautiful brood sow, so we raised more hogs for market and also sold 'weaner pigs' to people who just wanted some to raise for their own use. We continued to milk cows and sell cream, but gradually built up a nice beef herd, too.

"We kept improving our pastures by clearing, liming and using commercial fertilizer so that we could now raise more livestock. Even so, at times our improved fields produced more stock feed than we could use and we sold grain and hay. By this time custom balers were available, so our surplus hay was baled and sold.

"By 1944-1945, we were able to pay off the Federal Land Bank loan on the place and it was all ours and clear of debt. We now had a better home and a more productive farm. We would never get rich farming, but it was a good way of life that we both liked. As we improved our own property, the phone company, the electric co-op, the schools and their buses and the road department also kept making improvements. Life became easier and more interesting. Radio, then television, and better cars gave us most of the advantages of city people, and we liked our way of life better.

"After the kids left home and after we got electricity, we bought a freezer and then had ideal storage for our meats, fish from our own creek, and some of our vegetables and fruits. Strawberries and raspberries, for instance, are much better frozen than canned. Perhaps I put too much emphasis on food for family use. It was a major part of our living and perhaps a major reason we made a financial success of our farming project. I well remember the Depression years where we not only ate well but also gave fruits and vegetables to less industrious neighbors who just went on 'relief.'"

After the children were both married and Abe and Ada were alone on the farm, they decided to sell the major part of the place and just keep the house and 31 acres. They also quit raising chickens, tore down the hen house and built a small barn to be used for sheep, cattle or hay storage since they bought their hay and grain. They also quit raising hogs and turkeys. When Abe decided to retire at 80, they again downsized to a small parcel with a double-wide mobile home. In 1976, Ada needed emergency surgery, and they realized they needed to be closer to medical care, so they sold the last little piece of the old farm and moved again, this time into Cottage Grove, leaving behind 47 years of memories.

LATHAM

Latham, situated about three miles south of Cottage Grove on Highway 99, is a small milltown-community that was named for Milton Slocum Latham, a former California governor and senator. He was a Democrat and a good friend of Abraham Lincoln who, throughout the late 1860s and into the 1870s, helped finance the California Pacific and the North Pacific Coast Railroad. Because of his involvement, he earned recognition as one of California's major rail barons. Latham was also a strong supporter of the 1862 Pacific Railroad Bill which was being proposed to fund an inter-oceanic railway that would connect the Pacific with the Atlantic Oceans. Milton Latham later became the president of the New York Mining and Stock Exchange.

With a big name to live up to, the community of Latham at one time had a post office, established on September 16, 1878, that was in operation for ten years, closing on February 14, 1888. James J. Comstock was its first, and possibly only, postmaster.

Two of the first settlers in the Latham area were Henry Wells Taylor and Charlotte Taylor who arrived in about 1852.

In 1853, a log schoolhouse was built in Latham, and beginning in 1857, it was used for church meetings and services every Sunday.

The current Latham Elementary School, which is considerably larger than the original little one-room log schoolhouse, is the oldest public school in South Lane School District. The current building was erected in 1922, but was moved in 1942 to its present location on Latham Road. Even though many small rural schools are being closed, Latham Elementary is still operating.

The community is the home of the large Weyerhaeuser plywood mill at the intersection of Highway 99 and Latham Road which makes good use of the adjacent railroad tracks for shipping its products.

SLAB TOWN / LEMATI / COTTAGE GROVE

The town of Cottage Grove is at the confluence of the Coast Fork of the Willamette and Row Rivers. The first white settlers came to the area in 1848 over the Oregon Trail, and later, on the southern Applegate route. Until that time, only the Kalapuya tribe occupied the southern part of the Willamette Valley.

The name Cottage Grove was given to it in 1855 by the first postmaster, Greenberry C. Pearce. His home, located near Creswell, housed the post office, as well. Over the years, the post office moved into the home of each new postmaster until the late 1860s when it settled into its final location near the Oregon & California Railroad station in 1872.

Before the railroad came through, the settlers depended on riverboats to bring supplies from Portland to Eugene. They didn't come on a regular schedule since the boats could only get through during high water. When one did arrive, the settlers would make the difficult two-day wagon trip to bring the supplies back.

The nickname, "Slab Town," came into use because in the winter the streets were so muddy, they were nearly impassable by wagon. Wooden slabs were laid to facilitate crossing – a very bumpy ride. In 1902, money from Lane County and the residents of Cottage Grove was provided to gravel the highway that passed through the town. That section was called Main Street.

Gold was discovered in approximately 1864 about thirty miles east of the settlement in a mountainous area on the north slope of the Calapooya Mountains which became known as the Bohemia Mining District. It was over 2,000 acres in size and produced a considerable amount of gold.

The first major find had to be dug out of the sides of the mountains or sometimes blasted loose. Mining companies were formed and miners were employed to work the mines all year round, sometimes in deep snow. "Bohemia City" was the first mining

Mining in the Bohemia Mining District in 1904. *Courtesy of Gerald W. Williams Collections, OSU Special Collections & Archives Commons*

settlement to be established with a number of cabins and several other buildings. In 1868, a road was built in the area.

Cottage Grove became the outfitting and supply point for the miners. Everything had to be transported by wagon to Bohemia City, in some places over a toll road. In the early 1900s, a privately-owned short-line railroad was built up the Row River to the base of the mountainous mining area to bring the ore down and to take supplies up. Called the "Old Slow and Easy," the train soon added a passenger car to serve the public, and the miners and their families were able to make the run to Cottage Grove for medical treatment or extra supplies.

Riding down the hill on the Bohemia Mine tramway, 1909. *Courtesy of Gerald W. Williams Collections, OSU Special Collections & Archives Commons*

The stagecoach road that went through Cottage Grove after 1865 followed the river along the west side and a settlement of scattered residences and businesses began to grow along it. The route later was the one used in the building of the original Pacific Highway in 1923.

When, in 1926, Pacific Highway became U.S. Highway 99, several places along the route, including the Cottage Grove area, were realigned by the influx of federal money. The changes were made to better serve the traveling public, but the realignments often bypassed local businesses that had serviced travelers, forcing them out of business. In Cottage Grove, that realignment happened twice.

When the Oregon and California Railroad built through the town in 1879, the depot was on the east side of the river and a few businesses began to build up there. As more people came to "Slab Town," the South Fork of the Willamette River divided the newer east side and the older, more settled, west side. The west side of town included established businesses – retail stores and the offices of some progressive developers and farsighted, upstart businessmen.

As the east side developed, its taverns and 'bawdy' houses became popular and catered to the miners, giving them plenty of options for how they could spend their money.

From a historical summary by the Cottage Grove Historical Society for their web page:

"At one time, there were seven saloons on the north side of Main Street. Those who didn't have anything to do with cards,

Cottage Grove as it looked in 1908. *Courtesy of Gerald W. Williams Collections, OSU Special Collections & Archives Commons*

Main Street, Cottage Grove, 1908. *Courtesy of Gerald W. Williams Collections, OSU Special Collections & Archives Commons*

Doing business in downtown Cottage Grove. *From the George Lancaster Collection.*

The old Cottage Grove Grist Mill from a 1918 postcard. *From the Woodard Family Collection.*

dancing or alcohol, walked on the other side. The ladies and children had small park areas and inside reading rooms to rest while waiting for their men to take the family home."

A feud developed between the east side "rabble rousers" and the well-established businessmen of the west side. By 1893, the feud had escalated to the point where the east side petitioned the State Legislature to be incorporated as a separate town. Even with the west side fighting the petition, east Cottage Grove was granted a township. It became known as Lemati and the feuding continued. Lemati dominated, developing its own improvement plans for water and sewage, which did not include the properties on the west side of the river. In spite of the hard feelings and disagreements, however, many realized that the two towns needed each other. The west side had the wagon road and the east side, the railroad.

In February 1899, Lemati and Cottage Grove were again incorporated into one town and the name Lemati was soon abandoned, but not entirely forgotten in the history of the town.

The production of the Bohemia mines slowed in the 1920s, although some were still operating into the 1940s.

Southern Pacific log trains through Cottage Grove, 1909. *Courtesy of Gerald W. Williams Collections, OSU Special Collections & Archives Commons*

According to the Bohemia Mine Owners Association, Inc.:

"World War II and the issuance of order L-208 closed down all but strategic metal mines of which the Bohemia Mining District was considered to have none. It led to scavenging and salvaging of equipment in the district for scrap metal.

"The years since the war have seen some production, a fair amount of exploration work and some changing of claim ownership. Roads into the area have vastly improved and there are still claims with current mining activity on them. A paper sponsored by the Bohemia Mine Owner's Association in conjunction with the Northwest Regional Conference of the Western Mining Council entitled 'A Reconnaissance of the Bohemia Mining District' states that sufficient bodies of high grade mineralized ore remain throughout the Bohemia Mining District, which is over 2,000 acres in size, to provide a basis for profitable mining operations in the future. The only formula for success is a combination of men and women with courage, the proper equipment for mining financial resources, luck and hard work."

Once the mining activity slowed, logging in the area increased and more sawmills were built. At one time, there were up to 25 mills in the area. The Bohemia Mining District train, "Old Slow and Easy," became the means to bring the logs and lumber down the mountain.

One of the prominent logging families was

Bohemia Railroad car, Cottage Grove, 1915. *Courtesy of Gerald W. Williams Collections, OSU Special Collections & Archives Commons*

Corrected Page

The Woodard Logging Crew near Cottage Grove. *From the Woodard Family Collection.*

The Woodard Logging Crew near Cottage Grove. *From the Woodard Family Collection.*

the Woodard family which has left its imprint as benefactors in the Cottage Grove area for the past several generations. Dee Malchow of Shoreline, Washington, a great-granddaughter of Ambrose and Ella J. Woodard, shared her family's history:

"*My great grandparents, Ambrose & Ella J. Woodard, settled in Cottage Grove in 1900. He was involved in the timber industry and his son, Walter A. Woodard, made the business quite successful.*"

Ambrose Woodard was credited with donating a library to the city and the land on which to build its first junior high school.

According to his great-grandson, Kris Woodard in a 1985 *Register-Guard* article:

"*He had a strong place in his heart for the people of Cottage Grove. He was a very generous person and he liked to do nice things for the community.*"

Ambrose's son, Walter A. Woodard, built and successfully operated the W.A. Woodard Lumber Company's mill which was located south of Cottage Grove. In 1957, the family sold it to Weyerhaeuser Company for $15 - $17 million dollars. Another mill south of Divide was sold to Bohemia Lumber Company. Afterwards, Walter Woodard and his son Cart invested the money in the building of a luxury resort motel that helped to put Cottage Grove on the map. They named it the Village Green and its dining room was soon given one of the few 5-star ratings in the Northwest. Even though the freeway to replace U.S. Highway 99 was still in the planning stages, the Woodard family had a

Corrected Page

A Woodard log flume. *From the Woodard Family Collection.*

long-term vision to promote tourism to the area.

In 1952, Walter A. Woodard created the Woodard Family Foundation. For many years, it provided grants to social service and arts projects throughout the Lane County area.

Walter's grandson, Casey Woodard, continued his family's heritage of generosity by working to raise funds for a new hospital in Cottage Grove and he helped to raise $30 million towards the construction of the Sacred Heart Medical Center at RiverBend in Springfield.

In 1973, the Woodard family built the Valley River Inn in Eugene which Casey Woodard later worked at in sales and marketing as a part-owner.

He and his brothers, Kim and Kris, built the Middlefield Village golf course and residential area in Cottage Grove.

Excerpts from the autobiography that Ambrose Woodard wrote for his 80th birthday, on December 22, 1937:

"...We came to Salem, Oregon, in 1900 by train and stayed with relatives for two weeks. Then we moved to 5 miles south of Cottage Grove and for the next twenty six years, I logged or operated a sawmill in and around south Lane County.

"I bought up some houses to rent when I saw a good buy and if I could get timber acreage at a good price, I would also buy that. I would buy and sell as prices changed. After Walter took over the mill, I bought a truck and sold wood fuel."

The following information was taken from notes of Ambrose's daughter, M.B. Horton, and from interviews with several other of his close relatives:

"...In 1900, Ambrose brought his family west and bought land on the Coast Fork River south of Cottage Grove, Oregon. Here he cut and sold stove wood and piling, with his boys working hard to help him.

The Woodard Logging Crew near Cottage Grove. *From the Woodard Family Collection.*

The Woodard Logging Crew near Cottage Grove. *From the Woodard Family Collection.*

the Woodard family which has left its imprint as benefactors in the Cottage Grove area for the past several generations. Dee Malchow of Shoreline, Washington, a great-granddaughter of Ambrose and Ella J. Woodard, shared her family's history:

"*My great grandparents, Ambrose & Ella J. Woodard, settled in Cottage Grove in 1900. He was involved in the timber industry and his son, Walter A. Woodard, made the business quite successful.*"

Ambrose Woodard was credited with donating a library to the city and the land on which to build its first junior high school.

According to his great-grandson, Kris Woodard in a 1985 *Register-Guard* article: \

"*He had a strong place in his heart for the people of Cottage Grove. He was a very generous person and he liked to do nice things for the community.*"

Ambrose's son, Walter A. Woodard, built and successfully operated the W.A. Woodard Lumber Company's mill which was located south of Cottage Grove. In the 1950s, the family sold it to Loran LaSells "Stub" Stewart, owner of Bohemia Lumber Company, one of their fiercest competitors. Afterwards, Walter Woodard and his son Cart invested the money in the building of a luxury resort motel that helped to put Cottage Grove on the map. They named it the Village Green and its dining room was soon given one of the few 5-star ratings in the Northwest. Even though the freeway to replace U.S. Highway 99 was still in the planning stages, the Woodard family had a

A Woodard log flume. *From the Woodard Family Collection.*

long-term vision to promote tourism to the area.

In 1952, Casey Woodard, grandson of Walter A. Woodard, created the Woodard Family Foundation. For many years, they provided grants to social service and arts projects throughout the Lane County area.

Casey Woodard continued his family's heritage of generosity by working to raise funds for a new hospital in Cottage Grove and he helped to raise $30 million towards the construction of the Sacred Heart Medical Center at RiverBend in Springfield.

In 1973, the Woodard family built the Valley River Inn in Eugene which Casey Woodard later worked at in sales and marketing as a part-owner.

He and his brothers, Kim and Kris, built the Middlefield Village golf course and residential area in Cottage Grove.

Excerpts from the autobiography that Ambrose Woodard wrote for his 80th birthday, on December 22, 1937:

"...We came to Salem, Oregon, in 1900 by train and stayed with relatives for two weeks. Then we moved to 5 miles south of Cottage Grove and for the next twenty six years, I logged or operated a sawmill in and around south Lane County.

"I bought up some houses to rent when I saw a good buy and if I could get timber acreage at a good price, I would also buy that. I would buy and sell as prices changed. After Walter took over the mill, I bought a truck and sold wood fuel."

The following information was taken from notes of Ambrose's daughter, M.B. Horton, and from interviews with several other of his close relatives:

"...In 1900, Ambrose brought his family west and bought land on the Coast Fork River south of Cottage Grove, Oregon. Here he cut and sold stove wood and piling, with his boys working hard to help him.

"A.L. was in the shingle business prior to 1906 when he bought the first Woodard mill and later he purchased the Shortridge mill. In 1920, he sold the Woodard mill to his son, Walter, who later, in 1957, sold it to Weyerhauser for $15-$17 million dollars. Ambrose also purchased a third mill south of Divide which he operated for two years and then sold to the Bohemia Lumber Co. From this he went into the wood business for the next 20 years and built over 15 homes in Cottage Grove.

"One of the most impressive things about Ambrose is that he remained active and productive even as he aged. At age 87, he was still running a wood business and making good money out of houses he had bought.

"When 91, he finished building his 15th residence and started another. He still drove his own car and transacted all his own business. At age 99, he said he was building what he said was his last house – and he was right.

"A.L. was a good napper and would take a nap whenever he tired. While working on his 'last house,' one day in winter, he chose to take a nap on the cold framework. He developed pneumonia from which he never recovered. He was apparently upset when he realized he wasn't going to make it to 100.

"Ambrose claimed the ownership of the first car in Cottage Grove. People thought he should dispose of it as it scared all the horses. He also boasted of owning the first truck. He is credited with the first improvements on 9th Street (now Highway 99) and the opening up of Taylor and Fourth streets. When the present school was built, he was director of the school district.

The A.L. Woodard Lumber and Dry Wood company float in the Cottage Grove 4th of July parade, July 13, 1908. A.L. Woodard is standing at the side of the wagon. *From the Woodard Family Collection.*

"He told Ed McCall that he could float down the Row River from Hebron to Latham (4 or 5 miles) standing on two railroad ties. Apparently he picked up that skill in his sawmill days.

"At age 91, A.L. skated across Cottage Grove Lake on homemade skates made by Frank White. Those skates with photos, are now on display at the Cottage Grove Museum.

"...His daughter, Ruth, had many good things to say about her 'Papa.' 'I really loved Papa a lot. Sunday afternoons, if it was good weather, he would sit in a big rocker on the porch and Juliet and I would sit on his lap. Neither Papa nor I could sing, but we made a joyful noise anyway. 'When the Roll is Called up Yonder I'll be There,' 'At the Feast of Belshazar,' or 'The Handwriting on The Wall,' were favorites he wanted every time. We had a little songbook and would just sit and sing for a long time.

"'He was converted when he was young at a Free Methodist Camp meeting. We had Bible reading and prayer every morning after breakfast as long as most of us were home. As I got older, maybe 12, it seemed to me Papa was always reading something from Proverbs about 'training up children in the way they should go.' We always went to church. Mama went in the morning after we moved to town, but Papa and Juliet and I went evenings together.

"'His word was law! We children soon learned we had to obey. He had a bad temper and as the boys grew older, he was cross with them. He was very fond of little children and never minded how much noise we made unless we were quarreling, which we did not do when he was in the house. If he got mad at us he would 'box our ears.' He was always fond of us four girls.'

"His granddaughter, Lillian, shared some stories she heard from her mother, Juliet. 'Grandpa would go build a fire in the mornings and then holler up the stairs – 'Johnnie, Oscar, Walter and Albert, Mattie Belle, Susan, Ruth and Pet – Get up!' Lillian and the other grandkids thought that sounded so funny that they made a little jingle out of it to play and jump rope to.

"Lillian said that once when they still lived at the Snyder place, about 5 miles south of Cottage Grove, the boys rigged up a cable between the house and the barn (after A.L. told them not to). One of the boys (Walter or Oscar) got hurt on it and had to stay in bed a few days. Ella J. said nothing about it and Ambrose didn't even notice that one of the kids was missing from the dinner table!

"'...He was a small man and developed into a leader. He was always ready for an argument. He kept one or more hired men all the time after we moved out to Oregon. He just had to have someone to 'boss.' They used to call him 'Little Imp' when young.'

"'...He saw President Lincoln's funeral train in Illinois. He was about 5 and remembered it going very slow so that one could walk along side of it. It was draped in black crepe-like material. The whistle blew often.

"'...Once he had gone down to Mrs. Foster's house south of Cottage Grove. They had an old delivery truck with no fenders on the front. The wheel went over a 'cow pie' there which ended up on top of the tire. The boys watched as A.L. was talking casually to the lady, he leaned back against the tire and put his hand right in the cow pie. He pulled his hand off, looked at it and smelled it, and said, as he shook it off, 'I do believe that's shit!' That is said to be the closest thing to swearing he ever did.'

"...Ambrose told Ed, if he ever got some money ahead, he should invest it in land. Ed felt that was good advice and, indeed, made some good profit on such an investment. He felt it was that mindset that caused Ed to be practical and only buy a basic truck with no chrome. Only pay for what you can really use. A.L. taught Ed to always pay his bills on time and to pay cash whenever possible.

"During his years of building houses, A.L. was known to paint them odd colors. He would go to the paint store and pick the leftover paint on sale and then mix it all together. That became the color for the current house!

"Once he bought a small wedge of leftover land along the highway for $275. A fellow wanted to buy it from him, but kept dickering on the price and leaving. Every time he came back Ambrose raised the price. He ended up selling it to the guy for $3,500!! He claimed he probably would have sold it for $280 if the guy hadn't been so ornery.

"...Ambrose boasted 111 descendants at age 99. The following are a few things to which he attributed his longevity:

"His ancestors lived to ripe old ages but he outlived them all. He worked hard all his life – all outside work. He vowed at age 12 that he would never touch liquor or smoke. This vow he has kept..."

Dee Malchow shared more of the family memories:

"My great-granddad, A.L. Woodard, had a habit of giving timber land to each of his kids as a wedding gift when they married. I have a tattered copy of a deed that my grandmother, Martha, received in 1907, for 160 acres. The family story is that she sold it for a down-payment on a very modest house in Seattle in 1909 or so. I'd love to find where that land is today. I expect it's all 'developed.'

"My dad's cousin, Steve Woodard, is 85 and lives in Cottage Grove. He has been in the forestry business all his life and has two daughters, who are also 'into it.'

"He is very pleased with the achievement of obtaining the original land that his own father, Oscar Woodard, was given by A.L.

In an additional excerpt from M.B. Horton's family history, she states, *"In 1922, Ella J. and Ambrose went on a trip across the country in his Model T Ford. It took nine months and they saw many relatives, from New England through the Southwest. They separated not long after that, but lived next door and ate most of their meals together.*

Dee Malchow added, *"Ambrose and Ella J. Woodard left Cottage Grove on April 22, 1920, for an auto trip across the country. Their trip began through Oregon on the Pacific Highway. Ella documented the trip in the many letters she sent back to her grown children.*

A.L. and Ella Woodard's 1920 Auto Trip on the Pacific Highway as Written by Ella J. Woodard in Letters to her Daughters:

"We started from home then went to bid the girls good bye. Stopped at Juliet's. They came out and picked up the baby without dressing. They phoned to Ruth &

they met us at the road. Then we started on our journey.

"It was fairly good till we reached Drain. There the State had a man to pull through. There was about 80 yards of steady mud cut up with ruts. We waded in and another fellow from Albany followed. He had a large car. Papa looked back and there he was stuck in mud. Well, Papa put on his rubber boots & went to help and the State man went too. They have you put on steers and the team goes slowly on, resting at times. In the meantime Papa had returned.

As they passed, Papa called out, 'When do you think we will get through?'

"'You will be there a good while,' was the reply. Well we started and went through all right.

"The other fellow was in front and got stuck on the next hill. We waited for him to be pulled through and his wife, a jaunty young woman dressed in pants, coat & cap, actually got out with a camera and took their pictures. I bet she did not do that every time. We went by. This man was thin with a red neck and squeaky voice. He was dressed like his wife except her pants were large across the seat & hips. We only saw him once more. Papa looked back and there he was being pulled, I guess, all the way.

"Well, we got on till we reached Yoncholly (do not know if that was spelled right). Well we reached a place there in town. Papa stopped and went ahead to look and get his bearings. All the chuk holes were full of water. This he did all the way. He wore the boots to Oakland. When he came back he said we could not get through that or the next hill. So he backed slowly the rest of the block and off a small bridge. The hind wheels & one front one were all right. One front wheel dropped, Papa said, about two feet. I thought four. We got out and he got some men to lift us out. Four kind old ladies ran out to see how I got on.

"One said, 'Why didn't you scream? I would have screamed!'

"The men looked over the machine and said it was not broken. Also that people got stuck every day & had to be pulled out at a cost of $6 or $8 dollars.

"Mountain Roads in July" A vintage postcard that apparently wasn't used for promotional purposes

They said some one backed off the other side a week ago.

"Papa went down a couple of blocks and came to a short place where we stuck (we got ourselves out of that). Then as we were nearly to the top of the hill we had to be pulled a short way. Some road men were going by and gave us a lift. We went – slowly on about half a mile & had to be pulled up a hill. This cost $2.50. Then we went on awhile slow and came to another big bad place (the way was all bad). There was a very large farm house and a very large barn. George will know the place. Here was a long stretch of very bad road. Then in a mile or so we came to a frightful place. Papa did not venture in. He got pulled through – cost $3.50 – then went another short way and got pulled again - $1.75. Then we made it through to Oakland where we struck good road. Then at Sutherland, more good road.

"Here we missed the road and went to north Umpqua. Here is a fine prosperous country – stock dairying & fruit. The hills were green with oak trees scattered over them. Here we camped and went on the next day & enjoyed every bit of the way. People were cutting cord wood along the way. There is a fine country around Roseburg and the city itself, from where we saw it is beautiful. Then after leaving there we missed the road again and went through one of the finest countries I ever saw. Here it was – stock and fruit. A man told us land was from $8 to $700 per acre. The hills were cheap. It was near Dillard a man told us he raised & cut fine crops of alfalfa off one piece of ground and he raised watermelons, musk melons, & tomatoes without a bit of rain from June till November. That he sold tomatoes to Brurud (?) and two other merchants in Cottage Grove. Said it cost 10 cents for the box and 14 to ship. Said rent of such land was $30 an acre and 5 acres was enough.

"After leaving Myrtle Creek, the country grows poorer. There is no underbrush after Drain and no fir timber to speak of then as we went farther south. We went near the hill on the [word unreadable] and followed the stream. The hills coming closer together at Canionville. We got where the hills came close together there. The fire has been through years ago. There is no grass or moss on the ground, only little green patches in the valley. All along the way there were men crushing rock and working on the road.

"...At Canionville we began to climb- it is 14 miles over the hill. (At Canionville is where they catch the fellows carrying liquor over the border. They get them at the bridge.) We hug close to the hills 8 miles then bend after getting 8 miles. Papa's car stopped and a couple of boys from Eugene came from the other way and stopped to help. He was out of gasoline and on a road away above the foot of the hill. They let him have 1 ½ gal. and went on. His car would not go so all we could do was to get back. Here we backed carefully and a curve where we came to a place where we could turn at a house built for the construction men. I got out and walked beside the car to help him slowly back around the bend. It was some scary. Well we went back, got the gasoline and came on again. Got a little farther than the last time and the machine stood still so we had it to do over again. The spark plugs were dirty. Well we got them cleaned and had the machine looked over. The garage man looked it over and ran it some.

"We started back and in a mile or so, camped for the night, and started early. We got a little farther than the other times when we stopped again. This time a traveling man came along. He said the trouble was the cilender oil was not good and not enough for a new car. That on a steep grade the oil did not get to the front of the engine. He stayed right with us to the top of the hill. Papa said we were going up on a 20 per cent grade. The road was cut up in deep ruts. You would get out of one and into another where it was hard to pull out. After reaching the top we went over a corduroy road, a piece which had been very bad but was fixed. This man told us he went over it a week ago and every little ways some of the corduroy had been pulled up. He was supposed to help out some one who was stuck in these places. You would drop to the hub then climb on again.

"From here we got along fine to Glendale. After passing this we had another mountain to climb. We got on all right. Papa said this was a 20 per cent – this was higher than the last. In these climbs we had to stop every once in awhile and let the engine cool.

"When we got pretty well up – what should we meet but two women with a horse & buggy going down where there were ruts and only a little more than enough room for one rig. Here we stopped and blocked the wheels. One woman coolly got out and helped to push our car nearer the edge and went on as if nothing was the matter.

"When on top we stopped and cooled the engine. I climbed the bank and there was a grand view. The mountains came around a basin. Here was a sign, "Dangerous grade – go slow and toot your horn." At every bend here we curved around, went down a little ways and then around a curve, then drop, and so on to the bottom. Papa said it was 25 per cent grade and only room for one rig, then fine roads all the way.

"Grants Pass is a fine town with cement streets and fine stores and residences. Oh, I forgot something before we reached the last hill I spoke of. We had to cross Smith hill. Well we had heard all along the way of this place. Before coming to this place we came to a good ranch with a sign, Dead Creek Ranch, then Dead Creek itself. Here the soil was red. The most so I ever saw and the water in the creek was orange. Well we went on a little farther and we came to something sure. Papa went ahead to see and he stayed a good while. A boy came along and I said, "Is this the Pacific High Way." He said, "Yes and we have a car hung up thar."

"After awhile here came a car groaning along with a team hitched to it. Then another team and car and papa. We had seen bad roads before but nothing like this. It took two teams for a large car and all the power you could put on and one for a Ford. I walked up the hill - $5.00 for the pull. It all made us nervous and we were very tired.

"We were leaving Grants Pass when I saw a sign, 'This way to the Oregon Caves 37 miles.' So we have started that way and are camped for Sunday. We will have to go 9 miles on pack horses and strike the snow line.

"We hear the apple trees were nearly in bloom at Drain. The lilacs were nearly in bloom in Roseburg and pears & apple trees here. The country around here does not look good.

"The lunch Juliet fixed and the cheese you made were nice. It lasted us to Oakland where we bought more."

April 28, 1920:

"We went to see the caves. Got near enough to see the mountains. Were told that there was no chance to see them as the snow was 50 ft. deep on the top & 7 to 9 ft. in the trails. So we'll have to see them another time. They said they were a wonderful sight. Had been explored ¾ of a mile and the government was going to put in electric lights & iron ladders this summer.

"We then went to Medford and stayed at the camping ground. When we got there Papa said, 'We have run into a pack of Gipsies.' I do not know if they were. We went a short way further up and camped.

"The next day we went over the Siskiues. Had a good trip. Made about a hundred miles to Weed. The roads were pretty good. We got some snow balls to eat. Found a new plant, yellow and a kind of stunted cedar. The hills got bare there. We came to where people had mined then to a town where we got more oil. Papa was telling how bad the roads were and ran about a gallon on the ground. Then we went on. Got to Weed. Found Ralph Wills and stayed all night. They made us welcome. Delbert & his wife came over and visited. Then in the morning Papa went over to the Weed Mill. They are working 1500 men there. Papa saw them saw two logs at once. This morning, about 10 o'clock we left.

"We reached Redding before night beside stopping at the state fish hatchery. Saw a man shoot a fish eagle. This was a large bird, about 3 ft. spread of wings. He fell in the water and floated on his out spread wings. They drew him in with a net and killed him with a stick. The young fish are in long tanks. Saw some hatching. The egg sticks to him till he lives on it. When about three months old, they are about (draws about 1½ inch thin fish) so big. They are fed on sour milk and ground liver. The larger ones are in tanks outside. They are fed ground fish. A man takes a bucket full and with a dipper he dips up a dipper full and throws it in the water and they scramble for it & eat it all before it slowly ebbs to the bottom. They keep them in running water all the time. Some die. They have a brush like a paint brush and go carefully around the edges and pick out the dead ones. Then a man has a screen like a fly flip. He shoves it in carefully and scoops up the fish. He then turns it and the sick and dead ones stick and are thrown out. Another man had a glass tube & bulb – picking out sick ones one at a time.

"We then came on to Redding and stayed with Cousin John Woodard. Found them fine people but not well off. He works in an abstract office.

"We started and got a nail in the front. We had to put in a new tube then in leaving the garage, the machine stuck. Had to be brought in and have it fixed so here I am writing while they are at it. It was not broken, only bent. Papa left the spark or something too far down. Papa says we can make 20 or 30 miles on a gal. of gasolene.

"We came over mountain roads yesterday. It bent and turned around the one place. [She has a drawing of a

Ambrose and Ella J. Woodard finally made it to some warmer climes on their road trip. *From the Woodard Family Collection.*

switchback type road – DM] *The road came around below the bridge then turned and went over it."*

Ambrose Woodard passed away before his 100th birthday on February 8, 1957.

His wife, Ella, was known for her volunteer work in administering aid and comfort to the sick and distressed whenever it was possible. She died on February 20, 1937 and her obituary stated that, *"In early womanhood, Mrs. Woodard taught school and was particularly interested in art. She had attended Wheaton college in Illinois where she studied art. She had many paintings to her credit and did a number of water color sketches from still life and copy."*

Another large mill owner in the area was J.H. Chambers.

An article printed in the July 15, 1981, *Cottage Grove Sentinel*, and written by Margaret Lamster, tells about the experiences of Kermit Sams of Cottage Grove when he worked at the Chambers Mill. It is typical of the large lumber mills of the early 1900s.

"Sams remembers timbers 12" by 30" that were 60' long. 'I remember sawing a 50- or 60-foot timber in two,' Sams writes. 'This had a very horrendous effect on the mill boss who almost went crazy. But he considered I was about 16 years old and just took off and imbibed in some nerve tonic.'"

"He also describes the dangers of mill work in those early days. *'Those mills and logging operations had their fair share of accidents... Logging and lumbering was a dangerous occupation at its best. Any carelessness was usually fatal and paid for with terrible results.'*

"...The average pay for mill workers in the early 1900s was $3 to $4 a day for working in the mills and up to $6 a day for working in the woods. But once the Depression hit, wages plummeted. Workers then were lucky to make 'two bits' (25 cents) *an hour.*

"Some of Sams' fondest memories of those early days center around the horses used in the woods and in the mills. '...In the early days all things were moved by horses. Usually these horses had as much character faults and virtues as most of the men. Some of them weighed a ton and only certain men could drive them. Working around planers and resaws and other machinery, almost rubbing the machines, was quite a skilled and touchy

job [for the horses]. *Each horse had his own special personality. Some could be worked by only one man and drivers were as temperamental as the horses. Sometimes if a driver was ill, the horse was idle and just waited until his driver returned.'"*

Logging practices began to expand and change as modern technology and invention took over. No longer were horses used to pull the logs out of the woods to the sites where they were loaded aboard log trucks. Machinery and equipment not only took over that chore, but also cutting and stripping the trees in preparation to haul them out to the mills.

In recent years, creative, but not necessarily safe, methods were tried and some are still being experimented with in the woods. Hoss Barker, a former logger in one life and the maintenance supervisor for Paradise Lodge in the Rogue River Wilderness Area of Southern Oregon in another, told of his experiences with balloon logging. This particular story took place in the Sweet Home area, east of U.S. Highway 99, but the logging company was Cottage Grove-based:

"Balloons Ain't for Kids" Excerpts from *Out of Oregon; Logging, Lies and Poetry* and the soon-to-be-published, *My Time in Paradise* by Michael J. "Hoss" Barker:

"The fall of 2002 was getting underway at Paradise Lodge. The fishing for half-pounders was picking up and we were starting to get the fishing groups coming in. One day, The Boss told me that he wanted the place shining like a new nickel, as there was a group of VIPs coming up in a few days on a guided float with the Helfrich Boys.

"'Who is it, Boss?' I nagged over and over, but he held off telling me for a while. He finally succumbed to my persistent nagging.

"'You ever hear of Stub Stewart?' he asked.

"'Shit ya! Who hasn't?' I assured him. I'd worked for his brother, Faye H. Stewart back in 1979, at an outfit called, Flyin' Scotsman...

"...We were in the Cascade Mountain range above the beautiful little town of Sweet Home, Oregon. It was on Gold Creek, a small tributary of Quartzville Creek, it was very rugged and beautiful country.

"The yarder engineer and I lived in a 1950-something, single-axle camp trailer on the banks of Quartzville Creek. The living conditions were spartan at best, but the ambience was unrivaled and remains with me to this day.

"We shared our stretch of the river bank with a couple of retired guys who didn't seem to know much about retiring. They were up there gold mining. I'm not talking about a placer mine either, they were hard-rock mining with powder and heavy equipment. Carl and Sam, were their names, if memory serves me correct. They were pretty well-off, I gathered from all of the equipment they were running. Their claim was a patented claim, and they would take off some timber from time to time.

"I'll always treasure those nights that we sat around the camp fire passing the jug around. When we ran out of stories and lies to tell, we would just listen to the night sounds and the creek. It was one of those nights after everyone had passed out and went on to bed that I had the fire and the night to myself.

"I was working for Flying Scotsman Inc. This was a balloon site and turned out to be every bit the adventure I had hoped for... and then some!

"Balloon logging is a very expensive and dangerous method of getting logs out. It's usually used on very steep ground that has sensitive environmental issues. Things can go bad very quickly and be costly and sometimes fatal.

"When a conventional tower lands a turn of logs, a man runs out and unbells the chokers and the rigging is sent back out to the brush. If you have 'tight uns' [1] (which you always will) you can kick 'em, roll 'em, or whatever you need to do via hand signals to the engineer; no big deal for a good chaser.

"Enter the balloons... When a balloon lands a turn of logs, the chaser has to hide under the landing yarder to avoid being hit by all the debris falling out of the sky from the turn. If he survives that, then he can work on getting the chokers unbelled. The yarder engineer literally has to 'land' the load of logs. He pulls 'em right out of the sky – damndest thing you ever saw!

"The Chaser's job is hard and dangerous. When the logs touch down, they don't stay still for very long, as the balloon is always bobbing around and so are the logs. You watch your tago line when it gets some slack in it; then you go in and unbell the chokers. When it starts back up, you get out of the way and wait for slack again, so you can get the rest of your chokers undone. Invariably, under pressure for production, a man will push his luck from time to time. This is usually when fate will send you little warnings that you aren't Superman and to slow down a little ... or else. I was to get such a warning one sunny summer day.

"The rigging crew had been cutting a fat hog in the ass all day long and the landing was in shambles. I was a pretty good chaser, but still pretty green to balloon logging. The time when the balloon takes the rigging up and back out to the brush is when the fun starts on the landing. The chaser (me) must limb the logs, buck any and all broken ends and brand each log at both ends. He then bunches them all up with a grapple skidder and run them a quarter-mile down the road to a 'safe' landing where the trucks are loaded out and sent to town. That's a lot of work for one man!

"...We had gotten a heads-up from the side rod, Vic, that Faye Stewart – 'The Old Man,' as we called him – was going up in the Bohemia helicopter some time that day to see how we were doing. We were making a concerted effort to have everything looking ship-shape for his arrival, but we were losing ground as the day wore on, and not having a concrete arrival time had us all on edge.

"When we landed a turn of logs with the balloon, the logs were literally pulled in from the sky, hundreds of feet above our heads and it was very dangerous for the chaser who just happened to be me. I had to hide under the yarder to avoid all the debris falling from the turn of logs. Once they were landed, I would have to unset the chokers in a tangled mess of wire rope and wood. They were never still for long, either, as the wind would catch the balloon and move it around, making things real dicey for me at times. This particular 'turn' or group of logs, was the

---

[1] A "tight-un" is a log lying so tight on the ground the choker-setters had to dig choker holes under them.

Balloon logging. *Courtesy of the Forest History Society, Flickr Commons*

biggest mess I'd ever seen. I had stray logs scattered all up and down the whole road leading to the 'safe landing.'

"I was 15 feet or so up in the air on an unstable mass of logs, being jerked around by a wind-buffeted balloon while trying to unset the chokers. I was scared shitless and mad as Hell! Right when I knew things couldn't get worse, they did. We heard the 'whop-whop-whop' sound of the helicopter, in-bound with the fire-brand 'logger's logger,' Faye Stewart, to inspect a crew that was one log away from being 'fly-blowed' to a standstill.

"I had lost my footing and grip, and I was back on the ground faster than I would have preferred. As his chopper touched down, I wasn't in the mood for any bullshit from anyone, Faye Stewart included. I momentarily lost my awareness of where the 'tag line' was when I looked over at the helicopter. It had dropped down behind me and, as the balloon dipped down with a wind-gust, it came up with my right leg snared in a loose choker. It thrashed me around the landing a little bit and then somehow miraculously turned me loose, just as fast. I lay on the ground stunned. I was afraid to look at my legs, so I put my hand down to feel for blood.

Fortunately, there was none. I moved my leg slowly and was relieved to find out that it still worked, so I slowly stood up and tried it out. I was a little sore, but otherwise intact, aside from being really pissed off.

"I turned and cast a dirty look towards the menacing machine that had distracted, and damn near caused me to get maimed or killed and saw Mr. Stewart standing there, summoning me over with his index finger to have a chat. Like a bolt of lightning, I formed a plan of action. If he started in on me with a raft of shit, I was going to chew him up one side and down the other, repeat it a second time, and head for Sweet Home and a barstool at my old watering hole. Back in the day, I had my own parking space at the Skyline Inn and it's where I cashed my paycheck – I had to, to pay off my bar tab.

"Obediently, I limped over to the chopper as it shut down and approached Mr. Stewart.

"'Young man do you know how much money it would cost me if you were to get hurt or killed up here?' he asked me.

"That did it! I glanced up at the cab of the yarder where my pal Lonnie was to make sure that he saw my performance. I was shocked to see him with his fist

> ## The Logger
>
> Born in the high country, wild and steep,
> Spry and nimble as a mountain goat,;
> At home in canyons wide and deep,
> Works in the woods, far away and remote.
>
> Beasts of the timber, rugged and lean,
> Downright hard to the core
> A full head of steam that's seldom seen,
> Never leaves them asking for more.
>
> Cut up, scraped up, battered and bruised,
> Yet still he just won't quit.
> It's in your blood, not something you choose,
> Tempered in the furnace spit.
>
> He plays in the fog, rain, snow or heat,
> It's all just part of his day.
> Men strong of back, and tough to beat,
> Wade headlong into the fray.
>
> A breed all their own, they go it alone,
> They're seldom found in the crowd.
> A will of cast iron, a jaw made of stone,
> they're men born fierce and proud.
>
> Tight logs and hang-ups all day long,
> Lines, see-saw, high overhead.
> It's Murphy's law, when things go wrong,
> One little slip, you could be dead.
>
> Stove up and wore out, by age forty-five,
>
> He's lost count of all his stitches;
> He's glad as hell to still be alive,
> But it's rags 'n more rags;
> to Hell with the riches!
>
> ~ *Michael J. Barker*
> Author of *Out of Oregon; Logging, Lies and Poetry*

doubled up shaking his head back and forth saying, 'Don't you do it! Don't do it!'

"What's a guy to do? I quickly assessed the situation, recalling Lonnie's penchant and passion for punching people out and quickly retorted 'Don't worry, Boss, we do this all the time,' and limped back to work.

"Mr. Stewart didn't hang around long before he was back in the wild blue yonder in his chopper with the venerable Joe Murphy at the stick. (Joe tragically died in a 'copter crash in the coast range in the early 90's, trying to fly out an injured logger. He was well-known in the timber industry as an 'angel of mercy' for anyone, anywhere at no charge.)"

Opal Whiteley, a young woman from Walden, a small lumber camp community located southeast of Cottage Grove, has become both revered and a mystical legend over the years. Opal Whiteley was born in 1897 and raised in the logging camp by Ed and Lizzie Whiteley who, she later claimed, had adopted her in 1904. A very unusual child, she told others that she was the daughter of an unmarried French prince – Henri, Prince of Orléans. By the age of 13, she was accepted into the University of Oregon as a student and became a noted amateur naturalist and nature writer... knowledge that she obtained during her childhood in the woods around the Walden logging camp. She became a world-traveler and was considered a genius, although she lived in poverty much of her life and she was institutionalized at the end of it. She had unusual abilities and insights that still draw attention, and her experience has led to various theories on multiple personalities.

The publication of her diary in *Atlantic Monthly* and as a book called *The Story of*

Opal: The Journal of an Understanding Heart in 1920, and the strangeness of her life's story, have formed a cloud of mystery surrounding her life. A mural in downtown Cottage Grove has been painted on one of the buildings to commemorate her life as the "princess" from Walden.

Like many of the other towns along the U.S. Highway 99, the downtown area of Cottage Grove was developed in an east and west direction, at a right angle to both the railroad and the highway, so the historic downtown in Cottage Grove remained almost intact. During the time of heavy U.S. Highway 99 use, tourist businesses grew up on the edges and along the highway. Many of the well-built historic buildings are still in use.

From the *Cottage Grove Sentinel*, October 1, 1920:

"When the Pacific Highway was rebuilt through Cottage Grove, beginning in 1918, the highway was rerouted up 5th Street to Main, and two new bridges were built across the Coast Fork to the north and south of town, alongside the existing railroad bridges. A short stretch of new highway was built at the south end of town from its intersection with River Road, across the new south bridge and beside the rails up to the south end of 5th Street. The highway was then routed north up 5th, turned east along Main Street to the intersection of Main and Lane Streets near the depot, where it proceeded north along Lane Street adjacent to the railroad tracks across the new north bridge and the road again connected with the older Pacific Highway route to Creswell and Eugene."

A few years later, about 1924, a new section was built that rerouted the Pacific Highway north from Main Street up 9th. At the north end of 9th, a curving section was added that connected with the bridge and North Lane County.

In 1926, the same year the Pacific Highway became U.S. Highway 99 through town, Hollywood paid a visit. Silent film comedian, Buster Keaton and a crew arrived to film a Civil War comedy based on the famous chase of the locomotive called *The General*. The railroad line up the Row River played the major role in the movie as the spectacular ending involved tumbling the locomotive into the river from a flaming trestle. The wrecked train became a minor tourist attraction until it was dismantled for scrap during World War II.

Highway 99 / Main Street of Cottage Grove. *From the Woodard Family Collection*

The movie set for the 1926 Buster Keaton movie, "The General" filmed in Cottage Grove. *From the Curtis Irish Collection*

Like the other settlements and cities along the Willamette, Cottage Grove was frequently subject to flooding. During the 1940s, the Cottage Grove and Dorena Reservoir dams were built to reduce the amount of flooding, but there continued to be occasions when the local residents had to deal with it. Fortunately, the flooding no longer occurs yearly and never up to the former levels.

"The Durbin Line - A Memoir" by Mary L. Alexander

"My family migrated north from Los Angeles in one the last years of the Great Depression, 1939. That summer my Dad was 33 years old, Mama, 30, my brother Maurice was 12, sister Peggy June, 10 and yours truly, Mary Louise, 4. I deeply admire the courage it took for my folks to journey north, not knowing a soul in Oregon and having only their own determination as their strongest resource.

"By the spring of 1940 Dad proposed that they purchase a ten-acre plot of ground in the Silk Creek area a few miles east of Cottage Grove.

"To persuade Mama, Dad said, 'Berenice, the house is kinda rough, but it has water inside and a good cook stove. There's plenty of firewood to be cut right on the property. The barn can keep more than one cow. It's got a large field that's been cleared to grow hay and alfalfa, and there's a good garden plot. We'll be able to grow everything we eat.'

"Mama, ever pragmatic, countered, 'Bill, it may be the best we can do right now, but I won't be without electricity. This is the 20th century, and I've put up with kerosene lamps as long as I'm going to. If you promise to get electricity for us, I'll go along.'

So electricity became Daddy's first priority. It was not a small challenge for him.

"Meantime, Mama scrubbed, polished, and painted every surface in the house, in addition to setting up a chicken coop, inhabiting it with a fearless rooster and a harem of Rhode Island Reds. Every morning and evening Mama milked our cow, Tilly. Peggy was assigned the job of cleaning the cream separator Mama acquired so she could sell the excess cream that we didn't consume ourselves.

"Marty set about building a pig pen and installing a young boar. That boar stayed in the pen at night or while Marty was in school. The rest of the time he followed Marty at his chores all around our little farm. We knew when Marty was in the out house; there would be Sam, patiently waiting outside the door. Dad bought a plow horse, Nelly, to turn the soil for the alfalfa field. Marty was expected to feed and care for Nelly.

"As the youngest, and probably the most inept, my chores were pretty modest. Until we got electricity, I had to clean the kerosene lamp chimneys. My hands were small enough to fit inside these easily. I was supposed to dry the evening's dinner dishes, but I often escaped that task by falling asleep by the heating stove in the living room. At this late date I'm willing to admit, I sometimes faked it, and I would hear Mama say, "Let her sleep. She helped me by picking and cleaning the berries we had for supper."

"I took care of our dog Corky, as he was my special companion while I roamed the ten acres. He was a beautiful canine cross between an Irish setter and golden cocker spaniel, and I loved him dearly.

"Dad was up before daylight and off to his paying job for the Oregon, Pacific, and Eastern Railroad. The long hours made it hard for him to make good on his promise to Mama that he would get electricity to our house. Our mail address was a box on Lorane Route. The highway from Cottage Grove to Lorane had power lines running beside it, but they did not extend to our little Silk Creek road. What Dad had to do was poll everyone who lived along our road from the highway to the last house up the mountain, and get them to sign his petition to bring the power all the way up. He didn't expect it to be a problem. Surely everybody wants electricity, he thought.

"The old couple who lived just a little down the hill from us, the Overholsers, were in their 80's, still living on their own, and had done very well, thank you, without any new-fangled electricity. They liked Mama and Daddy, but didn't see the need for making a change.

"Across the road, and up a bit was the home of young folks, Clara and Clarence Duncan. Clara was the oldest sister of my best friend, Joyce Allen. The Duncans were thrilled with the prospect of getting the power. Clara declared, "The first thing I'm going to get is a radio. It gets so darned lonesome here all day when Clarence is at work."

"Clara's family, the Allens, had their farm up at the end of the road. Mr. Allen had cleared the land himself and raised his family there. He came down the road every Sunday to lead the services at the little church that served the whole community of the area. The church yard and cemetery were adjacent to the one room school grounds.

"Mrs. Allen had a pump organ in their living room. She also played the church's pump organ for services. They had a large comfortable home, but with few modern conveniences.

"Like our elderly neighbors, Mr. Allen had trouble seeing any need to spend money for electric power when he had managed well without it. Dad tried to help him see things from his perspective. Daddy had great plans for improving his own property once he had the advantage of electricity. He spoke of powering the well to pump water for a duck pond, and to replace the old hand pump in our kitchen, so all we would have to do is turn on a tap. He mentioned the pleasure of having *a radio to keep in touch with what was going on in the country and the world. Perhaps it was Mr. Allen's own daughter, Clara, whose voice made the difference in his final decision to sign on.*

I don't remember clearly, but I think the Hanks family lived downhill and across the road from us. Rosemary and Billy Hanks attended the same one-room school that we did. Billy Hanks was in my 1st grade. At any rate, Daddy needed Mr. Hanks' signature, too, on his petition, and was glad when he signed on.

"My sister, Peggy June, would visit the Overholser's with occasional gifts of Mama's cooking or baked goods. She would do a little housecleaning for Mrs. Overholser. In appreciation, they would pay her in coins for her efforts. Once I was allowed to accompany her. Mrs. Overholser showed me how to use their stereopticon. I thought it was magic. I had never seen one before, and only in museums since. It made the first 3D pictures. Peggy was very respectful toward these old folks.

I don't know if her kindnesses influenced Mr. Overholser to finally agree to Mr. Edison's invention of electricity in his home. I do know that years later, Joyce Ann Allen married the Overholser's grandson, Connely Overholser, who was my playmate when he visited his grandparents.

"Dad ultimately secured all the signatures required. Credit is due to his persuasive skills and determined persistence. The power poles were set in place and lines strung the full length of our road up the hill.

"The day the power was turned on was a day for real celebration. Daddy had already set the lines to the house and wired the rooms with sockets and light bulbs. He made good on his promise to Mama. The power company named the tangent from the highway up our road The Durbin Line."

According to an article that appeared in the May 27, 1926 *Cottage Grove Sentinel***:**

"The Cottage Grove Golf Club, although not yet completely organized has been declared by experts to be what can be made (into) one of the finest nine-hole courses in the northwest. It is the David G. McFarland property of 74 acres located on land bordering the north city limits and is but a block from the Pacific Highway, just across the bridge from Woodson's Auto Camp. Purchased from the David G. McFarland estate, it is unencumbered."

The golf club is now called Hidden Valley Golf Course. The Woodson Auto Camp in Cottage Grove was similar to the free auto camp in Ashland's Lithia Park. There were four cabins with lean-to-carports for cars that served motorists during the 1920s and 1930s. A mobile home park now occupies the old auto camp site.

Another long-time icon of the Cottage Grove area is the Cottage Grove Speedway. It is still located along U.S. Highway 99, just north of Cottage Grove.

The Cottage Grove Jaycees envisioned *"a place for family entertainment in a park-like atmosphere,"* **according to Curt Deatherage in an article written for the** *Cottage Grove Sentinel***:**

"...The Jaycees planned to use proceeds from conducting auto races to fund other civic improvement projects.

"...The speedway was built on property obtained and donated by local

The Golden Rule Auto Camp, Cottage Grove, Oregon. *From the Woodard Family Collection.*

businessman Stan Daugherty. Another local businessman, Gene Cutts, was the 'Race Track Chairman' for the Jaycees. Frank Williams, the first President of the Cottage Grove Jalopy Racing Association, was another of the driving forces behind the construction. Thanks to donations of material from local businesses and hundreds of hours of volunteer labor, Cottage Gove Speedway was ready for its first race.

"July 4, 1956 was the inaugural race for Cottage Grove Speedway. Jalopy racing caught on quickly in the local area. Drivers like Wally Morelock, Jim Mathews, Bob Mc Coy, Frank Williams, Russ Denker, West Peterson, Vern Coop, Don Hill, Don Wilson and Darryl Jossart became local heroes to adoring race fans.

"By the end of the 1960 racing season, some of the Jaycee volunteers were tired of spending their spare time conducting auto races, so the racing was discontinued for a short time.

In 1961, Archie and Dot Radonski moved to Cottage Grove, and within a week were the new owners and promoters of Cottage Grove Speedway. The Radonskis installed a lighting system which allowed for racing on Saturday nights, a major improvement over Sunday afternoon racing.

"Throughout the sixties, more kinds of races were held, the speedway became more well-known and drew more special races and more of the best West Coast drivers. Over the next several years, the speedway changed hands several times and numerous traveling tours made appearances at the speedway..."

Gradually, the speedway began experiencing dissent from disgruntled neighbors who did not like the noise and dust. The family, park-like, atmosphere that the Jaycees originally envisioned seemed to have been lost. In recent years, the speedway continues to have a large following and a group of dedicated volunteers have set up work parties to clean up the area and prepare it for each season's race schedule.

SAGINAW

From "Public School Compositions," *Oregon Teachers Monthly*, Volume 16 #9, May 1912, a composition by Jennie Sharon, Sixth Grade, Saginaw, Oregon:

"Saginaw was named in 1896. The man that founded it was J.I. Jones, now of Cottage Grove. He first built a sawmill in the mountains about six miles away and then a flume to carry the lumber to Saginaw. He built the store about a year later. He then sold it to Booth-Kelly Lumber Co. of Eugene. Booth-Kelly built all the houses in Saginaw except the one which J.F. Neat and family live in. The big school room was built in 1898. The school was divided into two rooms, the primary department being taught in what is now used as a wood house. The present school house was finished in 1901. The first two teachers were Mr. James Abbott and Miss Gardner. Mr. E.P. Redford is one of the oldest residents and one of the first settlers in the vicinity of Saginaw. At one time, he owned the land where the school house now stands, and all the land on which Saginaw stands. He also owned much land on the east side of the river from Saginaw."

U.S. Highway 99 still runs through the small unincorporated community of Saginaw. The only thing that remains of the once-thriving little mill town, however, are two stores. The big Westwood Lumber

Saginaw, Oregon looking toward the south, 1912. *From the Curtis Irish Collection*

The Booth Kelly Lumber Company Store in Saginaw, 1911. *From the Curtis Irish Collection*

An aerial view of the Rickini Lumber Company in Saginaw, Oregon, ca 1955. *From the Curt Deatherage Collection*

Company kiln-drying and planing mill that once produced many board feet of alder lumber is now standing empty on the north side of Saginaw Road, although there are still some lumber stacks on the south side. The former grange hall is empty and boarded up, but a new economy is evolving. The Saginaw Winery on the north Delight Valley School Road is breathing new life into the area.

The Delight Valley School which served the area's children for many years was closed down by the Cottage Grove School District in 2010, but was reopened as a Head Start Program Center the next year.

WALKERS / WALKER

In 1881, the Southern Pacific Railroad put in a station along its route between Creswell and Cottage Grove and called it "Walkers." The community of Walker became official in 1891, however, when Francis Smith established a post office. He had purchased some property from Mrs. J.F. Walker, an area pioneer, and named it for her, although the area had been known as Walker for at least a decade. The name of the railroad station was changed in 1898 and the post office stayed open until 1925.

The community also had a small schoolhouse and the Walker Union Church was built in 1895, but now it has neither.

There was a Farmers' Club in Walker, Oregon during the turn of the 20th century. The purpose of the club was to allow local farmers to advertise their products and merchandise as a group. G.O. Walker was the spokesman for it. He offered to list the farmers and the items they had to sell and distribute it on bulletin boards throughout the area. One news article in 1903 mentioned that the Southern Pacific Railroad Company displayed the farmers' advertising lists at various points along their line "gratis," including at Walker Station.

In an ad published in multiple issues of the *Bohemia Nugget* in 1901 for the Farmers' Merchant at Walker, Oregon, Walker listed not only farm products, but "*dry goods, groceries, bluestone, lime, the best Northern-grown seeds in bulk and a complete line of patent medicines; Oregon product paint, and the celebrate wood preserver, Avenarius Carbolineum. Come Once and we will make you our Friends.*"

Today, Walker has no general store or

post office, but it does have its own air and hobby field. It was built on 20-acres of land on August 1, 1946 and is privately-owned. The 1,200 foot grass runway is well-groomed for about 400 feet on the south end, but there are no real obstructions on either end of it, according to experienced pilots who have landed there.

In 1948, W.W. Hileman purchased 50 acres south of Creswell in the Walker area on U.S. Highway 99 as the new home of the former Cottage Grove Rod and Gun Club which had previously operated off of South 6th Street in Cottage Grove, on property which later became the local drive-in theater. He gave the club over 20 acres with the proviso that they construct proper facilities for a gun club "free of debt."

A large club house was built and four traps installed. Most of the materials and labor were donated with the remainder purchased by the club. The caretakers's house was completed in 1953. The traps were changed from mechanical to electric in 1955. Additions and improvements were made to the clubhouse; dining room, kitchen, restrooms and a storage building.

When the clubhouse of the Eugene Gun Club burned in 1967, the clubs merged and the name changed to the Cottage Grove-Eugene Sportsman Club. With additions and improvements, the facility is one of the best and largest in the state.

CRESWELL

Thirteen miles beyond Hawley's Stage Station was the Robinett Station, which was located 12 miles south of Eugene City. When the stage route was changed in 1865, the Robinett's property, which was already hosting stage travelers, was located in an ideal location and was the proper distance to change horses and provide travelers a rest stop. James Robinett was contacted by the stage company and asked to provide services.

From the *Blue Valley - A History of Creswell* by George W. Ross, Joan Campbell and Sandra Wilson, 1993:

The James J. Robinett homestead near Creswell. *Courtesy of the U.S. Forest Service and OSU Special Collections & Archives Commons*

"In 1845, James Clyman led an emigrant party south from Rickreall, down the west side of the Willamette Valley and over the Calapooya Mountains into the Umpqua and Rogue River Valleys, as they followed the Indian trails. It came to be known as the west winter stage road and was traveled by the Oregon and California (O&C) stagecoach line. James and Jemima Robinett had the stage stop at Creswell located on property where Sherman Morse, descendant of Benjamin Morse built his house in 1905. Today it houses Creswell Faith Center on Pacific Highway."

In 1871, James Robinett, the owner of the Robinett stage stop, and Alvin Hughes donated ten acres of land, five acres each, to plat the town of Creswell. The plat specified that on the boundary line of their two properties was to run an 80-foot avenue. The street, Oregon Avenue, is almost at a right angle to the the route that U.S. Highway 99 would later take as it passed through the area heading north and south.

The Oregon and California Railroad built through the site of Creswell in 1871, about 10 miles south of Eugene in Lane County. The promoter of the railroad, Ben Holladay, gave the name to the station, which was also applied to the post office the same year. The name was chosen to honor the U.S. Postmaster General at the time, John A. Creswell.

The railroad built a depot and in the winter of 1871, it brought both passengers and goods from Portland as far as Creswell. The passengers who wished to go farther south, however, had to go by stage. Because there was no roundhouse or switch yard, the train then had to back all the way to Portland. Work began again in the spring of 1872, and the railroad pushed through to Roseburg.

In the Creswell area, early farmers grew hops as a cash-crop in addition to their own provisions. Hop-picking was often a family project, as was fruit-picking. The Kalapuya natives in the area often joined other pickers. In time, the land surrounding the town produced fruit of various kinds – prunes, apples, pears, cherries, walnuts and filberts. There were cattle and sheep ranches, dairy farms and, in the 1940s, turkey farms.

In 1913, the Creswell Cannery was begun along the Southern Pacific tracks just north of Creswell. It canned apples, pears, cherries, blackberries, loganberries and loganberry juice. Many of the local women took seasonal jobs in the cannery. The building is still there and has at least one portion occupied by a barber shop.

When Blue Lake pole beans became big business in the 1940s, young people in Creswell, like those in Eugene, Junction City, Harrisburg and other towns in the area, earned money for school clothes by picking in the bean fields. In many families, the whole family worked in the fields for extra cash until timber jobs offered the men better pay.

The settlement of Creswell grew into a small agricultural trading center and timber

Old Creswell schoolhouse, ca 1874. *Courtesy of the Creswell Area Historical Museum*

mill town. It was incorporated in 1909. Like many other early settlements, telephone connections began with a telephone line between two families in 1894, then grew to 14 rural lines that serviced 28 families. In 1909, a switching station was put in the general store. In 1927, Creswell Consolidated Telephone Company was organized and offices established with new switching equipment. In 1955, members of Creswell Consolidated Telephone Company approved, by a vote of 290 to 5, to transfer the local phone service to a company of stockholders. Today, the telephone company is one of the most modern independent exchanges in the state and it would be very difficult to find any difference in the service between that city and any others nearby.

The community of Creswell took its civic responsibilities seriously over the years. Creswell had a local militia or "Home Guard" made up of men who were not in the military, but were organized and available to defend their homes if need be.

There was also an aircraft observation post manned 24-hours-a-day that was organized by Captain Joe Richards of the Air Force Reserve. The tower was first located behind Leslie Goheen's house on North Sixth Street with Edna Goheen as chief observer. It was later moved to North Fifth Street where Vivian Ross acted as chief observer.

The observation tower was equipped with a telephone and a special number to call whenever information needed to be reported. Some of the observers who manned the tower were members of the Rebekah Lodge or other area organizations and worked in shifts. Air raid wardens for each area of town were appointed with a staff of men to carry out their orders in the event of an air attack.

The town honored its military heroes, as well. Dale Kuni, Creswell's only fatality of World War II, died in the Philippine Islands in 1944 and a road has been named for him northeast of town.

Helen Hollyer of the *Creswell Chronicle* reported on July 21, 2011:

"Private Dale M. Kuni (U.S. Army), was killed in action in 1941 during World War II; Corporal John Raymond Lee (U.S. Marine Corps) was killed in action on October 12, 1967 during the Vietnam conflict; Seaman Duane D. Hodges (U.S. Navy) was killed in action on January 23, 1968 at sea during the seizure of the U.S.S. Pueblo off North Korea; and Naval Aviation Crewman Ray D. Becker (U.S. Navy) was killed on March 21, 1991 when his aircraft collided with another submarine aircraft off the California coast."

On Wednesday, February 7, 1968, a Salem *Capital Journal* article told about the death of Duane D. Hodges...

"CRESWELL OR (UPI) - A young Navy man from this small Willamette Valley community, Duane D. Hodges, 21, was identified today as the crewman fatally injured when North Korea hijacked the U.S.S. Pueblo.

"His parents, Mr. and Mrs. Jesse Hodges, were notified of their son's death early today by a Navy commander and a Marine captain.

"'It's terrible, the suspense has been so long,' said Duane's brother, Marion Hodges, 33, a Eugene contractor.

"The parents were not accepting telephone calls.

"The original report from the Pueblo following its seizure by North Korean

patrol boats was that four men had been injured, one critically. The United States learned later that the critically-injured sailor had died.

"It was speculated at the time of the seizure 23 Jan (1968) the men might have been injured while destroying secret electronics gear aboard the intelligence ship. The Pueblo carried a crew of 23.

"Hodges was in fire control on the Pueblo, which he joined when the vessel came out of mothballs at Bremerton WA last fall.

"He was one of two Oregonians aboard. The other is Michael O'Bannon, 21, Beaverton.

"The Defense Department said fireman apprentice Steven Woelk was 'seriously injured' and radioman 3C Charles H. Crandell and Marine Sgt. Robert J. Chicca were 'slightly injured.' It declined to disclose the home towns of the three injured men.

"Creswell was the home of the late Harry Holt who transported thousands of Korean orphans to new homes in this country flowing the Korean War."

Harry and Bertha Holt

Bertha Holt was born in Des Moines and received a degree in nursing in 1926. In 1927, she married a cousin, Harry Holt. Newly-married, Harry and Bertha moved to South Dakota where they rented farm land until they could afford to buy their own. Drought and poor farming conditions during the Depression caused the couple to lose their farm for taxes. They then made the move to the Willamette Valley. Harry worked as a lumberjack and eventually had his own lumber company and farm, becoming quite wealthy.

Harry and Bertha, were Evangelical Christians, raising their family of six children in Creswell. A documentary showing the plight of unaccepted children fathered by American troops in Korea caught their attention and sympathy in 1954. First they thought about making financial contributions and then about the possibility of bringing some of the children into their home.

They looked at ways to house more. They decided to bring eight children to the U.S. to live with their family, dividing some rooms and changing the use of others in their big, comfortable two-story farmhouse on Howe Lane.

The project had to be approved first by both houses of the United States Congress. After they got approval, in 1955, Harry Holt flew to Korea and brought back eight children. The event received a lot of publicity – both praise and condemnation. The standard adoption procedures of the time were to try

Harry and Bertha Holt with three of the children who found new homes in the U.S. The photo is one displayed at their memorial building in Ilsan, Korea. *Photo courtesy of Anita J. Miles*

to match the backgrounds and race between the adoptive parents and children as closely as possible. In spite of the charitable nature of the program, the idea of creating mixed-race families was not universally popular in much of the country.

Nevertheless, the Holts set about helping others to adopt, using unconventional, but legal methods to get through restrictions; they soon formed the Holt Adoption Agency. Harry would sometimes fly a large number of babies in on private airplanes to waiting parents, popularly called a "baby-lift flight."

The organization continued to grow, later becoming the Holt International Children's Services and, although both Harry and Bertha have passed on, it still is active. The headquarters is now located in Eugene and the adoption procedures have been modified to fit with current standards for the welfare of the children.

After Harry died in 1964, Bertha continued their work with the orphans and soon began to expand and improve the programs to include children with special needs, first in Korea and eventually in other countries. She was energetic and active and was named American Mother of the Year in 1966. She was presented with a Civil Merit Award from Korea, and several honorary doctorate degrees. She is included in the National Women's Hall of Fame.

An interesting additional achievement occurred in 1996 when she set the world record for the 400-meter race in the over-90 age group at the Hayward Classic at the University of Oregon in Eugene. She passed away on July 24, 2008 in her Creswell home following a stroke.

A two-acre park and playground in Creswell is named in honor of Harry Holt.

"A Tribute to Harry and Bertha Holt" by Anita J. Miles:

"I was adopted in 1963 at the age of six months from Seoul, Korea through the Holt International Adoption Agency.

"I recently had the opportunity to visit Korea with the Holt Gift Team in December 2013. We were able to see the facilities that Holt International has sponsored and developed. We visited the Jeonju Baby Home, the Unwed Mothers home, Ilsan orphanage and the memorial building of Harry and Bertha Holt. I also got to see the grave sites and beautiful headstones of the founders who chose to be buried there.

"The thing that stood out to me the most was the unselfishness of these won-

Anita Miles sitting at the gravesites of Harry and Bertha Holt in Ilsan, Korea.
Photo courtesy of Anita J. Miles

derful people, Mr. and Mrs. Holt, who initially adopted nine babies after the war. They had a vision that has benefited so many children and parents since inception. Unfortunately, in 1964 Harry passed away and wasn't able to continue his vision, but his wonderful wife, Bertha, carried it on. A quote from Harry says it all: 'Every child deserves a home of his own.'

"I am forever grateful to these people. I was very ill and dying when I was adopted. Harry personally saw that I made the trip to America safely, because of my condition. The grace of God, the love of my adoptive parents, Lyle and Hazel Conrad of Lorane, and Holt's vision, saved my life. Now, Holt International is helping children from many different countries.

"I was recently involved in the making of a short documentary film about what it was like growing up as an adoptee. It wasn't easy growing up in a small rural town, but I was given a chance at life and the opportunity to succeed, and for that, I am very blessed."

On Columbus Day, October 12, 1962, rain-soaked Oregon was hit with the leftover force of Typhoon Freda, a low pressure ridge meeting warm humid air with gusting winds formed in the Pacific Ocean. By 1:00 p.m., skies in Creswell had darkened and sheets of corrugated roofing were sailing off the school and landing a block away. Buses were being loaded with winds already at fifty miles per hour. The chimney on the school tumbled. Power and telephone lines, tree branches and trees were all brought down. The town and outlying areas were without heat, lights and communication with each other or the rest of the world. By the time the buses had finished their runs, most roads were blocked by downed trees. Six hours later, it was over, but the results weren't. Barns, sheds and trees were blown down all over the area. Farmers lost animals and orchardist lost trees that had taken years to grow. Homes were damaged and sometimes destroyed.

GOSHEN

Slightly farther north from Creswell, the Goshen area was settled in the 1870s and the Goshen Post Office was established in September 1874. The name "Goshen," was taken from the Bible. That Goshen was the pastoral land in lower Egypt occupied by the Israelites before the Exodus.

In 1884, Goshen, Oregon was a station on the Oregon and California Railroad line, and the town had a store, blacksmith shop and a school. In 1957, the post office was discontinued when it became an Independent Rural Station of Eugene.

Later, it was also the site of the large Cone Lumber Company, which is still operating, and it had a tavern, a truck stop and a café. The Goshen School is now part of the Springfield School District and serves as a rural alternative school.

Lane County's Howard Buford Recreation Area, a 2,363-acre site at Mt. Pisgah, is located north of Goshen. Much of it is at the base of the mountain, but the recreation area includes the summit. The park includes trails through natural wetland area, open country and the summit, as well as an arboretum, historical buildings and special trails for equestrian visitors.

The area was settled in the 1850s by homesteaders who grew wheat and raised cattle. Hop farming became a major crop by the 1890s and early 1900s. By 1915, Oregon was the leading hop producer in the United

States with some 200 hop farms in the Eugene-Springfield region.

Harvesting hops was done in August or September and, in that time period, was labor-intensive. Farmers employed local townspeople to travel to the fields and camp for the harvest season. Whole families came because cash was welcome and because they also had social contact. Often Native Americans came to work the harvest – members of the Warm Springs tribe worked the lands around the Buford Recreation areas, sometimes arriving by special trains.

One of the largest and most prosperous farms was owned by Alexander Seavey. Three of his sons founded Seavey Hops Company and were successful until the 1920s when World War I, Prohibition and a disease that killed the plants contributed to the decision to diversify. One of the Seavey hops barns is still located on Seavey Loop Road and the Howard Buford Recreation land.

Also on Seavey Loop Road, near Franklin Blvd., which was the old U.S. Highway 99 before it was rerouted, there is what is believed to be about the only U.S. Highway 99 cement marker left standing.

Ron Rogers of Eugene provided a picture of it, with the following information:

"I lived in Goshen for 15 years and was on the Fire Department there for just as long. In front of my old house, there is an original mile marker made out of concrete from where Highway 99 used to be. It's about 4 feet tall and has the numbers on the top. There is probably not another one in existence anywhere in the state. The Highway Department tore them all out back in the 1960s and 1970s. Its location is approximately across from mile marker 189 on I-5."

Dan Warnock, author of *You Can't Borrow Yourself Rich; Warnock Ranching History*, spent several years of his childhood in the late 1930s, living next to U.S. Highway 99, between Goshen and Glenwood. He offered some memories of that time:

"I remember the county mowing the grass along the right-of-way with a very large, beautiful span of mules, all trimmed and shod, clipping along very quickly. We lived in the house on Franklin Blvd., still there, with sale junk inside and in the yard, just north of the S-curve underpass – maybe 2 miles north of Goshen. Harpole's chicken farm was next door to the north and was a pretty big deal at that time.

"The S-curve underpass with concrete abutments was a magnet for Saturday night wrecks.

"The 'Dollar Line' bus line furnished service both ways if you stood out along the road and waved at it.

"Glenwood was my school with Jay F. Oldham as chairman of the school board – he even had his picture on the wall."

Excerpts from *You Can't Borrow Yourself Rich; Warnock Ranching History* by Dan Warnock:

"Living on old Highway 99 south was interesting and educational. Travelers coming west during the Depression created quite a sight. Many were also escaping the dust bowl.. Rattletrap cars piled high with belongings and family members were a common sight. Running gear of trucks or autos without cabs, but piled high was also used. Any conveyance including

wagons pulled by various livestock were often observed. One traveling family was using a thin milk cow and a donkey hitched together to pull their wagon with another cow tied behind, for moving west. Foot traffic was also prevalent. Hobos stopped to ask for food and often Alice [Dan's mother] would fix them a sandwich or dish up a bowl of soup. One fellow only wanted a cup of hot water. She gave him a sandwich also, but he just sat and held the hot cup with both hands for a long time. Mostly, Alice asked them to work for the food. She would have them split wood or spade the garden plot while she fixed something to eat. No one seemed to fear any of these folks, but Alice confined them to the porch rather than inviting any inside. Empty boxcars going by on the railroad across the highway very often had men standing or sitting in the open doorways..."

"...I also walked home from school part of the time and by spring of the third grade, I was walking home almost all the time. Usually, another schoolmate or two was along, at least part way. Sometimes a neighbor driving by gave us a ride. I was admonished to always go by way of the highway instead of the railroad to get home. Obviously, my parents assumed the hobos that frequented the railroad would be a bad influence. Rules were made to be broken and the railroad route was much more interesting, so I walked the railroad when I thought I could get away with it. Sometimes, there was a hobo camp underneath the highway overpass and visiting with those guys around their campfire was a hoot for me. My parents never found out about that. All of this took place prior to any diesel locomotives, just the good old steam and occasionally a speeder.

"Before starting to school, there were no other kids to play with except the little sister to the one-legged boy across the highway, Paula Lyons. She was my age and we got along reasonably well. Our mothers took turns letting us play at each other's house. Our house sat back some distance from the highway and was a fairly nice house for the times. Their house was a really small cracker-box that sat midway between the highway and the railroad, which wasn't very far. We mostly played on the floor, stacking blocks or with cars and trucks and similar games. When the train went by her house, the whole place shook. It would knock over our stacks of blocks; you couldn't hear and all activity was stopped until the train had passed. She said, 'You get used to it and it doesn't wake you up at night.'"

SPRINGFIELD

U.S. Highway 99 only skirted the west edges of Springfield, but it deserves recognition as a major city in the area. Eugene and Springfield are physically separated by a river – Eugene on the west side of the Willamette and Springfield on the east – but the difference between the two is much greater than can be measured by distance.

While there are people who might consider Eugene and Springfield "sister cities" because of their proximity to each other, they are more like fraternal twins or stepsisters borne of two mothers. In their infancies, while Eugene suckled at the breast of the mighty Willamette River, the city of Springfield was obviously the product of the wild, rough-and-tumble, but vastly beautiful McKenzie. It has a strong history of its own – one firmly rooted in the richness of the forests and mountains

The Springfield bridges over the Willamette River, connecting Springfield, to the left (east) to Glenwood, to the right (west). *From the Woodard Family Collection*

Miller Gas Lumber Carrier at Booth Kelly mill in Springfield. *Courtesy of the Harold Frodsham Photographic Collection, OSU Archives Commons*

to the east. Its economy has long been based on its timber resources and the famed recreation areas to which it is a gateway.

While Eugene has long prided itself on its art, culture and education, Springfield has proudly embraced its blue-collar heritage. Their relationship has not always been loving, but both bring their own special qualities and assets to the residents of Lane County.

GLENWOOD

The unincorporated community of Glenwood, now annexed to Springfield, but bearing a Eugene address, has long served as the umbilical cord of the two cities, joining them via U.S. Highway 99. It lies along the Willamette River between Springfield and Eugene on the former route of the Pacific Highway.

According to John Tamulonis from Springfield, Franklin Blvd. from Goshen to where it comes in west of the Springfield Bridge, was the old route of U.S. Highway 99.

The small Glenwood School sat back from the highway on the west side, south of the railroad bridge that crossed the Willamette River.

South of the school, according to both John Tamulonis and Dan Warnock, was a skating rink that Dan believes was called "Evergreen." It was owned by the Christner family in the mid-to-late 1930s.

Both men also remembered the Willamette Park and a rather rowdy dance hall.

According to Dan, it was located *"maybe a mile south along the river and railroad tracks. That was a big deal on week-ends. My family never went, but I could see the leftovers from it, walking the railroad home from school."*

In 1938-1939, the Federal Government, facing the possibility of a war, legislated four million dollars to improve the north-south corridor of U.S. Highway 99, one million of that to be spent on the road from Eugene south. The construction didn't happen before World War II, but soon after, and the road became four lanes through Eugene. In 1955, the cut-off that took U.S. Highway 99 away from Glenwood effectively killed the growth of the town.

Despite the slowdown, Glenwood is host to the BRING Recycling's Planet Improvement Center as well as the Lane Transit District's transportation headquarters. It has a Dari Mart, an army surplus store, a Cash King discount liquidation store, an auto parts store, a bar and several restaurants, including the Roaring Rapids Pizza Company which has an indoor carousel and riverfront dining.

Heading into Eugene from Glenwood, U.S. Highway 99 once shared pavement with U.S. Highway 126. The two highways overlapped along Franklin Boulevard west to Broadway, Mill Street, and the one-way street couplet of 6th and 7th Avenues. U.S. Highway 126 was relocated as a freeway in 1971, and decommissioned in 1972 as Oregon 126.

The Oregon 126 business route was commissioned along the former surface street alignment through both downtown Eugene and Springfield and Oregon 99 and 126 business routes maintain an overlap.

SKINNER'S / EUGENE CITY / EUGENE

Named for its founder, Eugene Franklin Skinner, Eugene, Oregon is located near the confluence of the Coast and Middle Forks of the Willamette River and the McKenzie River. The Willamette River is one of the relatively rare rivers that turns north after it

Pacific Highway along the Willamette River near Eugene, 1928. Postcard

comes out of the mountains. It eventually joins the Columbia near Portland to reach the ocean. The Willamette Valley in which Eugene lies, is bounded on the east by the Cascade Mountains and on the west by the Coast Range.

Dick Pintarich, in his *Great and Minor Moments in Oregon History,* paints a different picture of this period in the Willamette Valley than we usually envision:

"The Willamette Valley was deserted. Crops rotted in unattended fields as once-productive farms surrendered to weed. The legislature had to postpone the 1848 session because only nine representatives were left in the territory. No one remained who could set type or run presses, causing two newspapers to fold and the Oregon City Spectator *to suspend operation for nine months. A visitor to Oregon City in 1848 said its population appeared to consist of 'only a few women and children and some Indians.'*

"Gold had been found in California, and many believed the sudden exodus of two-thirds of Oregon's male population spelled doom for settlement in the Willamette Valley. It was, in fact, the best thing that ever happened to Oregon.

"Oregon had practically no trade, no market for what they raised and no money to buy what they needed. The legislature made wheat legal tender, IOUs against future harvests were common and a service might be paid by a note that was good for brown sugar at 12 cents a pound or anything along those lines. The territorial legislature voted to make wheat, beef, or almost any product legal payment for taxes.

"Territorial Governor George Abernethy vetoed the measure as inconvenient, but didn't supply an alternative. Willamette Valley farmers mining in California before the big rush often came back bringing gold with them... $2 million dollars. It turned the future of the state around.

"They brought more than gold, they returned knowing there was a market for Oregon products. The warehouses packed with surplus wheat, the lumber and produce, were all needed and Oregon's future turned around. The gold rush also opened the more remote Southern Oregon valleys for gold discoveries and development there."

Eugene Skinner arrived in 1846 and erected a rough cabin west of what is now Skinner's Butte. A small settlement grew up around it and eventually, the town of Skinner's was platted. It was bordered by Water Street to the north along the river, and Seventy to the south. There were also High, Mill and Ferry streets.

As other settlers arrived, Skinner operated a ferry near the location of the current Ferry Street Bridge that spans the Willamette River. Heavy winter rains turned the site into a mud hole, so higher ground was sought. Skinner and Charnel Mulligan each donated forty acres and helped plat the new townsite, called Eugene City, in 1852 in an area farther south, away from the Willamette River.

A post office for Eugene City was established in 1853 with Eugene Skinner as postmaster.

Eugene City was located 12 miles north of Creswell and was the next stage stop on the route. The stages took the passengers through the Camas Swale area which was marshy and hard to maintain and stopped at the St. Charles Hotel in Eugene City. The hotel was located on the corner of Broadway and Willamette Streets and the barn was around the corner at Broadway and Charnelton.

The hotel was owned by Dr. A. Renfrew. He built it in 1855 and managed it until 1874, when he rented it to others to manage before he sold it to Charles Baker in about 1876 or 1877.

Large maples shaded the front of the hotel. Mrs. Tirildy Renfrew's good meals could be enjoyed inside for twenty-five cents, but by 1877, the price for a meal had gone up to thirty-five cents.

As part of the *WPA's American Life Histories Collection: Manuscripts from the Federal Writer's Project, 1936-1940*, Mrs. J.R. Bean shared a story from the reminiscences of James Meikle Sharp, who, at the age of eight, crossed the plains with his father and mother in 1852. Her interview was conducted by Sara B. Wrenn on January 31, 1939:

"Once, when it rained for seven days and nights continuously, I made a raft and traveled on it from Eugene to our ranch, a distance of seven miles.

"During this time when I was clerking in Eugene, I was standing in front of the stage depot one day when the stage came in from the south, and the driver threw down his reins, and told us of a most unusual experience. Down on the Umpqua, the water was up two or three feet around the houses, and in one yard he saw a woman with a long pole fishing around.

"'Anything I can do for you?' the driver, asked the woman.

"'No, I guess not,' the woman replied, "The children are crying for a drink, and I'm just trying to find the well.'"

Douglas Card, local historian and author of *From Camas to Courthouse: Early Lane County History*, explained how the city was incorporated twice in a Letter to the Editor published in the *Register-Guard* on June 23, 2014:

"Bravo to those who rescued part of the Eugene Celebration, for we have something extra to celebrate this year. Thanks to Eugene's quirky history, there's a second city incorporation sesquicentennial to recognize.

"It seems the first one in 1862 didn't quite take, as local media blasted the thought of new laws and new taxes in terms that would have delighted today's tea party (disagreements started early here).

"So on October 22, 1864, the Legislature passed a new incorporation law that repealed Eugene's first charter and required a vote of the people.

"The second charter changed the name from "Eugene City" to "City of Eugene," altered the city's boundaries and included multiple ordinances, license fees and a 1 percent property tax. It also designated the new city's officials, including J. B. Underwood as 'president of the board' (mayor) and Eugene Skinner as one of six 'trustees' (city councilors).

The second time around there seems to have been little opposition — but little interest as well. On Nov. 14, 1864, residents voted 27-1 for the new charter, therefore establishing Eugene's first functioning city government 150 years ago."

At the time of Eugene's second incorporation, like the rest of the nation, the local citizens were very involved in the growing furor over the question of slavery. People who had emigrated brought with them the beliefs and customs they had grown up with, which were not always the same as their neighbors.

According to the on-line *Oregon Blue Book*:

"Secessionist sympathizers surfaced in Oregon. The Knights of the Golden Circle, an anti-Union group, reportedly plotted the seizure of Fort Vancouver, military headquarters on the Columbia River. They did not act. When pro-Confederate partisans raised their flag in Jacksonville, they faced opposition and backed down."

As discussed earlier in the Roseburg segment, the namesake of Lane County, Joseph Lane, was pro-slavery and brought with him a personal slave when he settled in Oregon. There were many tensions between neighbors who disagreed on the question and sometimes these tensions divided cities. Eugene had its share. The most notable was in a skirmish known as "The Long Tom Rebellion."

Philip Mulkey crossed the country by covered wagon from Kentucky with his family in 1853. He was a pioneer Gospel preacher and took out a donation land claim in the Monroe area. On May 6, 1865, only three weeks after President Lincoln had been assassinated, Mulkey took to the streets of Eugene City hollering hurrahs for Jefferson Davis and celebrating Lincoln's death. It was suggested he might have been drunk. He was arrested and put in the Lane County jail.

A pro-Union lynch mob was ready to take matters another step. In response, pro-Confederate sympathizers from the area along the Long Tom River were arming themselves and preparing a rescue. Guards were shoved aside as the Union rioters kicked through the jail door. Mulkey pulled a knife from his coat and slashed the first man through the door. The mob paused just long enough for the Oregon Infantry to arrive and surround the jail. The crowd dispersed. Late at night, Mulkey was slipped out of the jail by the soldiers, marched to Harrisburg under guard, and put on a steamboat for the stockade at Fort Vancouver. The Long Tom men went home. Four days after Mulkey's arrest, Jefferson Davis was captured and the Confederate States of America was dissolved.

Mulkey spent three months in prison and was then released without trial. When paroled, he filed suit against the government for false arrest and violation of his free speech rights. He asked for $10,000 in compensation. Two years and 14 court hearings later, he settled for $200. He then returned to his calling as a circuit-riding minister. The officer who had arrested him ended up stuck with about $1,200 in attorney fees and other costs for his defense.

Eugene City continued to grow, annexing local neighborhoods and communities that had begun to form. The "City" was dropped from its name in 1889.

One of those neighborhoods which eventually became part of the city was located on the higher ground that we now call the Friendly Street Neighborhood. During the 1840s, the donation land claims of Daniel Christian, Charnel Mulligan and William Breeding covered College Hill. Residential development was limited by the lack of a transportation route. An electric streetcar system which ran from 1907 to 1927 caused an increase in development.

Some significant early developments took place in this part of the young city. The first college in Eugene, Pacific College, later named Columbia College, was built in 1856 at the corner of 19th and Olive Streets. It was created by the members of the Presbyterian Church which was looking to found schools to educate ministers for future service in the church. A minister, Enoch Pratt Henderson, was selected to serve as the first college president. The school opened on November 1, 1856, classes started on November 17, and on November 20, it caught fire and burned. The fire was believed to have been arson. Classes resumed in a nearby rented home, and when the new building, meant to be temporary, was completed in November 1857, 150 students enrolled. Unfortunately, the second structure also burned in February 1858. A third building, faced with sandstone, was then built, but before it was completed, Columbia College closed – due, partially, to turmoil in the denominations making up the Cumberland Presbyterian Church over slavery issues preceding the Civil War. Their funding was pulled and, in 1867, the unfinished sandstone building was torn down.

The College Hill section of Eugene was named for Columbia College.

The Friendly Street neighborhood is also the home of three Eugene water reservoirs, the oldest of which was built in about 1915. Another was built in 1939.

Civic Stadium, constructed in 1938, became home to Eugene's own minor league baseball team, the Emeralds in 1969. A popular part of Eugene culture for many years, it is now vacant and was purchased from the Eugene School District by the City of Eugene. As of this writing, the intent is to refurbish the old wooden stadium and use the fields for soccer games and other community-related recreation.

Across from Civic Stadium on south Willamette Street is the former site of the Eugene General Hospital. It was build in 1906, renamed Mercy Hospital in 1912, and closed about 1928. It sat empty from then until it was razed in 1940.

The area once was the home to the Eugene Airpark, a municipal airport established in 1919. The size and location changed as the city grew and additional property was needed, but it is often described as having been between Polk and Chambers Streets, an area mostly occupied by Westmoreland Park today.

Eugene's early industry centered on milling and agriculture. The shipping to other markets was greatly speeded by the coming of steamboats, but Eugene could only be reached by navigation when rains were sufficient to increase the depth of the water. During the 1850s and 1860s, steamboats only occasionally served Eugene during high waters, bringing a few staples from Portland and heading back with full loads from both Springfield and Eugene. The irregular water transportation on the upper Willamette was practically abandoned when the railroad arrived in 1871.

The railroad was built from Portland, only as far as Eugene in 1871, but it wasn't without considerable effort on the part of the city fathers. Eugene was near the California-Oregon Trail, as was Springfield. The Oregon-California Railroad under construction from Portland south, roughly followed the trail, but it took a cash payment from the citizens of Eugene to put its tracks through Eugene instead of Springfield.

The deal was supposedly made over a lavish dinner put on by the city fathers for Ben Holladay, the rumored unscrupulous builder of the Oregon and California Railroad. Since that route involved building a steel swing bridge over the Willamette River at Harrisburg, it was the more expensive route and Holladay demanded $60,000 to build it. Eugene raised the funds and became the shipping center for everything north.

The yards in Eugene also provided work for some men and gave the city a big boost, although it didn't connect it to California until 1887. The construction bogged down at Roseburg during which time the railroad went through a bankruptcy, eventually becoming the Southern Pacific Railroad.

In an interview on December 8, 1938 for the Works Progress Administration (WPA) Folklore Studies, Mrs. Hortense Watkins told her story:

"I am hardly what you would call a pioneer, since it was only as far back as 1883 that I came to Oregon, and not in a covered wagon. But even the way I came with my four children is something of a day that is no more. We came from Kansas to Oregon by way of California, in what was known as a family tourist coach. It took ten days at that time from Kansas to California. I have forgotten just what the railway fare was, but I do remember that children under twelve were half fare, and in some manner I had an extra half. So when a fellow passenger who had six children and not tickets enough to go around found herself in a quandary after boarding the train, I took the surplus youngster on with my extra half. Every time we had a new conductor he would say something about how little that child resembled the rest of my brood, for he was tow-headed and all of mine were dark. We had quite a time, but finally got through all right, and I breathed a sigh of relief when the poor woman and all her six reached their destination.

"Those tourist cars weren't very pleasant traveling, but I guess they were a lot better than six months of oxen and wagon at that. We had to furnish our own bedding, even the mattresses, which were made of ticking filled with straw, so they could be thrown away at the end. We had to furnish our own food too.

"There was a stove in the corner of one end, where we women cooked. I have forgotten just how many were in the car, but I do remember there were sixteen children, so you can imagine the hubbub. This sounds like an old fashioned funny story, but it's true. That train went so slowly in places that once when one of the men had his hat blow off, he jumped off, caught his hat and got on the train again without stopping. There were two old men that I cooked for. One of them, who wore a tall, silk, stovepipe hat, had his overcoat stolen just before he got on the train, so I loaned him a shawl, which he wore all the time. We had our own brooms, with which we had to sweep the car too. I don't think Heaven can look more beautiful to me than Southern California, when we finally got there. We were there just a few weeks and then came up to Eugene, which then had a population of about 2,000.

"The only building of the Oregon University in 1883 was Deady Hall. Villard Hall was then under construction, if I recollect. My husband, who was a lawyer, had come to the Coast ahead of me. Later my mother, who was known all over the country subsequently as 'Grandma Munra', through her operation of famous Oregon Railway & Navigation eating houses, the first one at Bonneville and the last one at Meacham, up in the Blue Mountains. After mother joined me we took charge of the old St. Charles Hotel

at Eugene, a two-story, wooden, rambling affair, with a veranda all around two sides. There were chairs on the veranda in the summer time and the hotel guests would line up out there, especially the traveling men. Down in front were watering troughs and hitching rails, where the country people tied their horses when they came to town.

"We entertained Bob Ingersoll, his wife and two daughters, on one of his lecturing trips through the country. They were all charming people. It rained all the time they were here, and he worried a lot, fearing no one would come to his lecture because of the rain. I told him rain made no difference to people in 'Oregon.' His hall was crowded. Henry Villard stopped there too. Another person who used to come often was a well-known circuit rider by the name of I.D. Driver. He was unlucky with his wives. They all died. I think he had six in all. He always spoke of the latest deceased as 'my angel wife.'

"When I first came to Oregon, we seemed to have just two big holidays, Christmas and Fourth of July. I believe there was more excitement at our house on the Fourth than at Christmas, because one and sometimes two of my daughters rode on the liberty car, and there was an uproar for days before. Liberty cars are something we don't hear anything of nowadays, but they were mighty pretty. And instead of queens and princesses as they have for everything today, there was Columbia. She sat up on top of the [Liberty] car, and all the little States were grouped in tiers about her, each little girl in white, with a big sash down over her shoulder, showing the name of the State she represented. Columbia always had to have fair or golden hair. It didn't matter so much about the States, only they had to be pretty. The car was a big dray, all painted and draped with bunting and decorated with flowers and greens, with the seats arranged in rows one above the other. The car was drawn by four white horses, with lots of tassels and netting to set them off. The [Liberty] car was the most important part of the parade, but the 'plug uglies' – young blades about town all rigged out in masks and fantastic costumes – excited a lot of interest, everybody guessing who they were. Once in a while they would get a little hoodlumish. I think that is why they were eventually ruled out. Anyway, we mothers were always rather relieved when the parade was over and our little States returned safely to us. There was always the fear of a runaway, what with the firecrackers and everything to scare a horse. We usually had some dignitary from elsewhere to deliver the oration, and at night everybody turned out to see the fireworks – Roman candles and set pieces like the flag, George Washington, etc.

"Those were great days all right. I think everybody was happier then."

The University of Oregon

The Oregon Legislature established the University of Oregon in 1872. Eugene residents struggled to help finance the institution. They raised $27,000 through strawberry festivals, church socials and produce sales to buy 17 acres of land for $2,500 and to build the university's first building, Deady Hall, named for Matthew Deady, Oregon's first federal judge. It wasn't until 1876 that it opened. Five faculty members taught 155 students. The first graduating class in 1878 had just five students. In 1881, the school, which was $8,000 in debt, nearly closed. Railroad magnate, Henry Villard donated $7,000 to pay down the debt and the faculty took a 25% salary cut. In 1885, the University received its first appropriation from the Legislature for $30,000 and the funding had been increased to $47,500 by 1901.

During Prince Lucien Campbell's tenure as president, from 1902 to 1925, the university experienced increasing growth. The budget, enrollment, facilities and faculty members all expanded greatly. Numerous schools were established – the School of Music in 1902, the School of Education in 1910, the School of Architecture and the College of Busines in 1914, the School of Law in 1915, the School of Journalism in 1916, and the School of Health and Physical Education in 1920. It lost the School of Engineering, however, to Oregon Agricultural College which later became Oregon State College and now Oregon State University.

In 1913, and again in 1932, there were proposals that the University of Oregon and Oregon State College be merged into one university, but both proposals were defeated.

After World War II, the University of Oregon continued to grow and spread. As

Cruisin' on campus; University of Oregon, Eugene, 1908. *Courtesy of Gerald W. Williams Collections, OSU Special Collections & Archives Commons*

Gerlinger Hall, University of Oregon. *Courtesy of Dot Dotson Photography*

The Stage Terminal Hotel in Eugene, ca 1915. *Courtesy of Gerald W. Williams Collections, OSU Special Collections & Archives Commons*

returning veterans entered school, some 100 surplus housing units from Camp Adair and other places were brought in on railroad flatcars to house students with families. The Amazon Married Student Housing units were established in this way and remained in use for almost five decades.

Eugene's Early African-American Population

Eugene, as well as all of Lane County, was not known for a large population of African-Americans. A few, after the Civil War ended, found their way west, but for the most part, the area was inhabited by whites and some Native Americans.

The Oregon Territory had laws passed forbidding slavery in the new state of Oregon, but there were also laws excluding free black people from living here. If found, they faced the penalty of whipping, but there is no evidence that the penalty was ever applied in the area.

In 1890, a Mr. Holden from Texas visited Eugene and saw potential for a new business. He bought a block of real estate, made arrangements with the city to construct a railway, and imported two streetcars and three brindle mules from Texas to pull them.

In 1890, a black man, Wiley Griffon, came to Eugene, possibly under the sponsorship of Holden. He was well-known and popular as the operator of one of the small, mule-drawn streetcars. His route ran along narrow-gauge tracks from the train station in downtown Eugene, south on Willamette Street, and then east along 11th Avenue to the University of Oregon. Holden was absent for much of the time, so Wiley was left completely in charge of the operation.

Holden was said to have developed City View Park, "a pleasure park" on the lower east slope of College Hill.

The streetcar venture was evidently unprofitable because Holden disappeared along with everything but the rails. Those rails were said to have later been taken up by a miner for use in his mine.

However, in a recent repaving project on Willamette and 11th Street in Eugene, the construction crew uncovered some of the old trolley tracks – probably those same ones used by Wiley and his mule-drawn streetcar.

On June 17, 2014, the *Register-Guard* published a picture showing where the city decided to *"place pavers around a section of the metal rail in the middle of Willamette Street as part of a larger crosswalk installation between 11th and 13th avenues in front of the Capstone apartment complex. The decorative addition to the pedestrian right of way is designed to pay tribute to the trolley line that ran down the middle of Willamette Street in the early 1900s."*

According to Josephine Woolington in a *Register-Guard* article published on June 8, 2013, called "Celebrating a Pioneer," Wiley Griffon didn't disappear with Mr. Holden. He remained in Eugene, working as a waiter and as a janitor at a university dormitory. He owned a home in a predominantly black community along the Willamette River near what is now the Ferry Street Bridge.

The Ferry Street Bridge community was a cluster of tents and makeshift homes that whites called "Tent City." It developed on a flood-prone area of county land that is now Alton Baker Park. The village-within-a-town, was made up of much of Eugene's black population. It developed in the 1940s, probably partially due to the end of shipbuilding and other war-time jobs in the Portland area. The residents were tight-knit and supported each other in times when they did not feel welcome among the whites. They were extremely unhappy when they were evicted to allow for the reconstruction of the Ferry Street Bridge in 1949.

A second small black community was established off of West 11th Avenue on what is now the short Sam Reynolds Street, possibly about that time. In that location a small white church and a cluster of small neat homes and businesses were built.

Wiley Griffon died at his home with flu-like symptoms in 1913. He is one of only two known black people buried in the Eugene Masonic Cemetery and a monument to Wiley was recently placed at his grave to honor him, thanks to the efforts of local residents Mark Harris, his wife Cheri Turpin, the Lane Community College Black Student Union and private donors.

The following two letters were written by Jost Petrie to his son, Channing, in Wisconsin in 1882. Jost and his wife Jerusha were living with their oldest daughter and son-in-law at their home in Eugene while Jost was searching for the perfect property to buy. He and Jerusha had moved from their farm in Wisconsin which was still being managed by Channing in hopes that he could find a buyer for it. In the letters, Jost describes the merits and deficiencies of farming in Lane County and tells about the topography of the region around Eugene. The letters are transcribed as written.

"Eugene City Aug 24th 1882.

"Dear Channing, ...I have not made up my mind when or what or where I shall buy yet but intend to invest somewhere before long – I find everything pretty much as I expected except that the Willamette Valley is rather too flat for good drainage and consequently apt to be worked when it is too wet, to the injury of the Spring crops especially – Last winter and Spring (they say) was excessively wet and since the 4th of July there has been no rain in the upper part of this vally. Consequently all late crops are rather poor – I have looked over considerable of the country between here and Portland and also about Siuslaw and examined several places ranging from 200 to 1700 acres with Buildings orchards etc ranging in price from 2 to 10 thousand dollars. These places are all among the foothills and better drained naturally with plenty of Springs and living water and wood conveniently near large towns or Depots and I cannot decide which I ought to buy

provided I should buy either of them. I don't wish to get a place in the flatest part of the vally because it is too wet much of the time and the ballance of the time too dry and destitute of Wood and living water except on the margin of the Streams.

"We are all as well as usual – Ma is gaining in flesh a little we think. She would like to see the Children very much, as well as myself – There is no perceptible difference in my health or appetite – <u>all the rest of the friends are hearty</u>, working at Harvesting & threshing - I think I shall soon take another prospecting trip and see if I can decide what to do about locating – I don't want to give you all my particular impressions about his country Just yet as I may change them Slightly. Love to you and Mary and little Winnie. Affectionately, Your Father"

Eugene Nov 18th 1882

"Dear Chan, and Mary, and Winnie, This being my 60th Birth day I thought I would write a few lines to you . You must not think I am very proud of our home here because I have taken so much pains to represent it to you. I done it because I thought you would feel a little curious about it and no one else would do it – If the old place is really sold I am willing to sell this also if I can to advantage – I presume I got this place pretty cheap – the owner was badly in debt and was obliged to sell. I suppose the buildings are worth nearly or quite half what I paid for the farm – There is about 220 acres of good land, the river Spoiling the rest for tilling purposes. I think the time will come when it will be worth double what I paid for it. I don't intend to decide as to how I like this country until I have been here one year at least. – I knew before I came here that it was a good country everything considered and think So still although in some respects it is not quite as I expected. This farm like nearly all the lands in the McKensie and Willamette River Vallies is <u>very level</u> and in this rainy climate is apt to be too wet rather too much – If you do not come out here and see for yourself I shall probably sometime sum up the advantages and disadvantages in living on this coast and strike a ballance. I think I know on which side the ballance will be but I don't know how large it will be – I enclose for you a fair sample of the Wheat raised on this farm last year. It is either Winter or spring wheat – I wish you would send me a Sample of the winter and Spring wheat raised on the old place last season... I will tell you a little more about the House. The rooms are all ceiled overhead. The siting room and dining room, are both Wainscotted and nicely grained. Also the doors in imitation of White ash, the doors in dining room have fruit painted on them Such as apples, Pears, Plumbs Peaches Cherries and Grapes. The Kitchen is all ceiled above the mop Boards and the siting room is ceiled. The Parlor is a very nice room nicely papered – The rooms upstairs are all papered except the drying room which is all ceiled and now if you want to know any more about it you must come and see it – There is no Stone on the place except the gravel. I spoke of in a former letter neither is there any needed of any except to underpin buildings. No Stoning wells, and no cellars to be stoned – About 1½ miles east there is a Spur of a mountain about 2500 feet high jutting into the valley like a Promontory into the sea, and 4 miles south there is an isolated and very Sharp Peak about the Same height *called Spencer Butte and away to the East & south much higher mountains can be seen. One of them always covered with snow which looks very beautiful – From the windows of the house we can probably see south and east from 10 to 125 miles and by going on to the mountains near the house we can see up and down the Willamette Valley and looking east can see much of the Cascade range – Its Spurs – The Calopooia Mountains and Several Peaks covered with perpetual snow. I think one can look over ¼ of Oregon. Last night there was a very beautiful display of Boreaallis. I will not say Northern lights because the greatest and prettyest part appeared in the east – Did you see it in Concord? We are having rather pleasant wether here – Occasionally a frosty night – a Sunny day or two or warmish rainy wether...*

"Ma wants to know if you gathered any Hickory Nuts Etc – We sometimes have very good Music with Organs accompaniment dispensed by Petrie's Band.

"And now a Little Letter to Little Winnie. I gave all my (Children and Grand Children who are out here) some candy on my Birth day. I wished very much that you were here to have some too – Tel your Pa to take some of GrandPa's money and buy some candy for all of you. Grand Pa"

In 1883, the Petries found the property they had been looking for south of Lorane, Oregon. It was a 1,200 to 1,800 acre ranch that had once been part of the Cartwright property near where the Cartwright House stage stop was located. Sadly, Jost's beloved little granddaughter, Winnie, that he wrote to above, died before they were able to see her again.

During the mid-1890s, the Eugene city fathers decided to make one more attempt to use the river for transportation, despite the problems in the past. They believed that river travel would be relatively inexpensive, pleasant and often romantic. They built the steamboat, the *City of Eugene*, and it was launched with a big celebration. On that first cruise, it headed downstream, going safely over the rapids, but at the bend in the river, out of sight of those watching, the *City of Eugene* slid gently onto a gravel bar and became stuck. All the while, the onboard guests ate their picnic lunches, danced on the deck and sang in the moonlight. Somehow, after dark, it was able to make its way back to the dock. The *City of Eugene* was later sold and used on the upper part of the Willamette River between Oregon City and Harrisburg and ended the short duration of riverboats in the immediate area.

Living along the Willamette River was like living on other rivers. Floods were possible when heavy rain saturated the soil and snowmelt sent more water downriver. The banks didn't always contain the additional water. The flood of 1881 was so bad that it was said to have floated wooden sidewalks in downtown Eugene.

The flood of 1890 took out every major bridge in Lane County and virtually isolated Eugene with no mail service for ten days and no train service for two weeks.

The 1943 flood spread across the old flood plain where the Willamette and McKenzie Rivers join. By New Years Day of 1943, hundreds of homes in Glenwood and River Road districts near Eugene stood in four feet of water. And those were only the floods that were considered to be at the 100-year level.

The construction of area dams eased the extreme flooding conditions. They provided flood control and created energy and recreational sites.

The "Grey Eagle" & "City of Eugene" sternwheelers at Salem, Oregon, about 1915. They were both owned by the Charles K. Spaulding Logging Company in Salem and were used for towing lografts to Salem. The "Grey Eagle" was built in Portland in 1907 and abandoned in 1930, the "City of Eugene" was built in Eugene in 1894 and was no longer in operation by 1918. The latter was the larger of the two at 130 feet and carried 339 tons whereas the other was only 110 feet and carried 151 tons. *From the Ben Maxwell Collection, Salem Public Library Historic Photograph Collections, Salem Public Library, Salem, Oregon*

Eugene City originally began as a trading center for agriculture, but industry increased in the early 1900s, too. A millrace, brought together from two sloughs, created the energy to feed industry. Lumber mills, planing mills, woolen mills, a grist mill, a creamery, a vegetable cannery, a box factory, an excelsior factory, poultry and livestock processing, fruits, filberts and walnuts all contributed to the livelihood of the residents.

After the Oregon and California Railroad failed and was taken over by the Southern Pacific Railway Company, that company was preparing to establish a terminal in Eugene in about the early 1930s for its expansion. The city fathers of Eugene were interested and came together with a scheme to arrange a deal.

According to *The Story of Eugene* by Moore, McCornack and McCready:

"They paid $250,000 for acreage to the west of town and offered it to the railroad for one dollar. The Southern Pacific was delighted, Eugene was bonded to the amount paid. The bonds were to carry 5.5% interest and would mature in 1962-1963."

The Southern Pacific yards have been a steady source of employment in the area ever since, although not always at the same level over the years.

In September 1907, electric streetcars began running from the train depot to the university. The 18-miles of streetcar lines included the Blair, College Crest, Fairmont and Springfield lines. The longest was the 4.8-mile route between Eugene and Springfield. The last addition was the two-mile-long line along Eighth, Blair and River Road. The

Street scene at 8th and Willamette in Eugene. Early 1900s. *From the archives of the Eugene Register-Guard*

planned extension to Santa Clara was not built.

"At its peak, a crew of 27 conductors, motormen, and shop workers kept a fleet of nine cars running from six a.m. until midnight each day. Twenty-minute headways were maintained during peak hours."

In 1926, the Springfield line was the first to be converted to a bus operation. The last trolley in Eugene ran on October 15, 1927.

The Oregon Railway opened a line from Portland to Eugene in October 1912. Two years later, the Oregon Electric Railway had its own station in Eugene.

The Oregon Electric Railway was built to link together the urban areas from Portland to Eugene with stops and branch lines along the way. The first leg of service from Portland to Salem began in 1907. It was purchased by Jim Hill, the owner of the Spokane, Portland and Seattle Railway in 1910 and, by 1912, it was extended to Eugene with connections to Albany and Corvallis. In its heyday, the OER ran five daily runs each way between Portland and Eugene. The basic fare was six dollars. The runs included two limited trains that served meals and provided lounge cars with observation decks, locals and night trains equipped with sleeping cars. There were also special-event trips, a train to bring hop-pickers into the valley or for an activity at the University.

In 1914, Southern Pacific began the Red Electric trolley service in Portland to compete with Oregon Electric Railway. They featured mahogany interiors and plush seats. The Red Electrics connected to both Salem and Corvallis, but never made it as far as Eugene. The Red Electrics survived until 1929, when Southern Pacific stopped running them. They had become unprofitable, so Southern Pacific sold its rolling-stock, widened the tracks and began using the lines for freight.

The widening of the track necessitated changes to the depots. Several, such as the

Oregon Electric Railway train at the Eugene Station (above). *Courtesy of Dot Dotson Photography*

Depot Park, looking east, 1910, and (inset above), the Eugene Depot with a fountain in front, 1911. *Courtesy of Gerald W. Williams Collections, OSU Special Collections & Archives Commons*

Eugene City Hall. *Courtesy of Dot Dotson Photography*

Meadowview station between Eugene and Junction City, had overhanging roofs that sheltered waiting passengers and freight. They were cut back in size to accommodate the wider cars when the line was switched from narrow gauge to standard.

By 1930, as the popularity of buses and automobiles grew, passenger service on the electric lines decreased and the OER reduced its service, as well. There were only two daily runs scheduled out of the Portland metro area and by 1933, regular passenger service to the Willamette Valley and Eugene had been discontinued. Oregon Electric freight service continued until 1945. The tracks are still in use. Some stretches between Tigard and Salem are now owned and maintained by Portland and Western Railroad.

Beginning in 1977, the Eugene OER station, along with a couple of converted dining cars, were operated as the Oregon Electric Station restaurant for many years. It was known for its fine prime rib, seafood and steaks. In 2014, however, it was purchased by sister and brother team, Rossella and Raffaele Ruggeri who will convert the menu to Italian cuisine.

With better transportation bringing travelers and visitors in, hotels and even livery stables developed on Willamette Street, forming the basis of the town's shopping area. The shops run by locals began to open in buildings built to house several tenants, so jewelers, shoe stores, piano stores, cafes, banks, general merchandise shops, and even a saloon or two, flourished.

However, in 1908, before the days of Prohibition, Eugene voted itself "dry," which made the streetcar runs to neighboring "wet" Springfield popular and crowded. Luckey's Club Cigar Store, the oldest bar still operating in Eugene, boasts a sign saying, *"Serving the gentlemen of Eugene since 1911."* Even in the days without liquor, Luckey's continued to have card games and cigars, and was the first to acquire a liquor license at the end of Prohibition.

Overlooking the developing city was the Shelton McMurphey Johnson house, partway up Skinners Butte.

People gathered for concerts in the park blocks and formed parades for special occasions. More streets were paved and more businesses opened including a public market, a movie house, a bowling alley and a Carnegie Library which had the backing of the Fortnightly Club and the city.

In 1913, the Oregon Legislature established the State Highway system, proposing the route of the Pacific Highway

Eugene Carnegie Library. *Courtesy of Dot Dotson Photography*

from Portland to the California state line, but the funding was left up to the counties. Lane County was in no hurry to raise the money. The City of Eugene, however, had tackled some paving efforts. In 1908, the two-block business district on Willamette Street in front of the train station was paved and a few streetlights that required a lamplighter were added later in the same area.

Eugene was one of the early cities of Oregon with a downtown or business district that was established before Pacific Highway was built, so rather than passing through downtown Eugene, the highway was at a right angle to it. The early businesses that developed in the downtown area primarily served the residents of the city rather than travelers or tourists. Even now, Willamette Street serves much of the same need. Later, gas stations, restaurants, taverns, auto courts and other businesses to meet the needs of visitors developed along the highway where space was available.

Between all of this activity and the river, Franklin Boulevard (U.S. Highway 99) coming into or leaving Eugene from the south, snakes along almost parallel to the Willamette River. It winds around Judkins Point, named for Edward F. Judkins, who owned quite a bit of land in the area. It then went through a business corridor before passing in front of the University of Oregon, jogging to East Broadway which quickly becomes 6th Avenue.

The southbound route of the highway is

University High School, Eugene. *Courtesy of Dot Dotson Photography*

U.S. Highway 99, Judkins Point, Eugene, 1948. *Courtesy of the Oregon State Highway Department, Construction Division.*

U.S. Highway 99, Judkins Point, Eugene, 1953. *Courtesy of the Oregon State Highway Department, Construction Division.*

on 7th Avenue. It funnels briefly onto Mill Street before joining Franklin Blvd., heading in the reverse direction. One of the businesses that grew on the edges of the University district along the highway was Williams Bakery. The aroma of freshly baked bread permeated the air each morning and remains a pleasant memory to the students who attended the University of Oregon and lived on campus.

Franklin Blvd. (U.S. Highway 99) was divided into north and south lanes by a long island of planted grass as it passed the University. The island provided the bed where the original train rails were laid. The Southern Pacific trains once traveled between the two lanes of automobile traffic. The tracks were later moved closer to the Willamette River.

Before the highway was paved, the downtown area was centered near the railroad station at the end of Willamette Street or at the Oregon Electric Station on 5th Street. Hotels and businesses were built along the streets leading from the stations. Those streets eventually became the early downtown shopping and business area.

Newman's Fish Market

One of the earliest and longest-running businesses in the Eugene area was started in 1890 by John Henry Newman. When he was 13 years old, he began working at a downtown market to supplement the family income after his father had been injured on the farm. At 16, he worked for a man who had a small fish market and he carried fish in a basket, selling them to hotels and restaurants. For the next 20 years, John Newman peddled fish from a horse-drawn

The Greyhound Bus Depot in Eugene at 10th and Pearl Streets. Courtesy of The Bean Team, Waymarking

cart along the dirt roads of Eugene and Springfield, often with his brother, Frank.

By 1911, he also owned his first store on 6th Avenue; other locations followed. In 1913, John gave up the horse and wagon for a 1912 Model T Ford and continued making deliveries. In addition, he and his family were active in Eugene civic affairs and were prominent members of the community.

In 1963, after 73 years in the fish business, the Newman brothers, John and Frank, sold Newman's Fish Market and the business has continued under different ownership.

Pacific Greyhound Lines

During 1921, several small bus companies consolidated and began serving the towns along U.S. Highway 99. In 1930, the Southern Pacific bought one company and changed the name to Pacific Greyhound Lines. The popularity of the bus line grew and reached its high point in the 1940s when travel was an important part of life and passenger cars scarce during the war and after. Eugene was an important hub in the center of the state, so the bus station that was built was large. It also served as a post house, having a café on the station premises. It had a separate package shipping department that was well-used by many businesses as well as residents needing speedy deliveries. Frequently, films going from one movie theater to another, automobile and other mechanical parts, shipments between stores, Christmas gifts and many other items traveled to their destinations in the bellies of the large buses.

The bus station was large enough to shelter several buses at one time and often did. The passengers had some time for restroom and food breaks before the buses pulled out on 10th to resume their journeys. The Greyhound building is still in use on the corner of 10th and Pearl in downtown Eugene, although its once very visible neon sign, and even the restaurant, are now gone.

Taxis were always available to transport disembarking passengers from either the train or bus station, as well.

J.W. Quackenbush & Sons

By the 1940s, the big chain stores were coming to Eugene – Montgomery Wards, J.C. Penneys, Bon Marche, Woolworths and Newberry's in addition to favorite local stores such as Quackenbushes, the Broadway and Kauffmans. The competition was fierce.

Even as late as the 1960s, J.C. Penneys and the J.W. Quackenbush & Sons Hardware store were still using the old

10th & Willamette, Eugene. *Courtesy of Dot Dotson Photography*

The corner of Broadway & Willamette. (Calkins Finance is where co-author, Pat Edwards, worked for several years in the early 1960s). *Courtesy of Dot Dotson Photography*

vacuum tubes to transfer extra money and invoices upstairs to the office. Quackenbush's was in business from 1903 to 1980 and the red-brick building still stands at 160 E. Broadway and is listed on the National Register of Historic Places.

In a *Eugene Register-Guard* newspaper article on December 2, 1953, Arthur Quackenbush reminisced about Eugene in 1903 when he opened his store:

"... The family store was surrounded on all sides by dwellings when it opened for business in 1903. The larger part of Eugene's business district was on Willamette Street between 7th and 9th Avenues, and few stores and offices extended up 9th Avenue (Broadway today) from Willamette to Oak Street.

"'Those were days,' Arthur Quackenbush recalls, 'when Willamette Street itself could become a muddy bog during heavy rains. Sidewalks and crosswalks were wooden, and the street was kept in tolerable condition only by shoveling excess mud into wagons and hauling it away...'"

"The Bon Marche in Eugene" by Jo-Brew:

"In 1958, the year that my husband and I lived in Grants Pass, we were told by other teachers that the Bon Marche in Eugene had a very special annual

Christmas toyland event for children. There was nothing like that in Southern Oregon and, most years, the Medford Christmas Parade was both foggy and cold. We decided to take the children to Eugene the weekend after Thanksgiving and do a little Christmas shopping while we were there.

"It turned out to be a very exciting experience with escalators, decorations and lots of bright lights. There was a whole basement set up with a log cabin scene and a Santa. Since it was evening, there weren't many people and our children, who were in awe, got friendly attention from one lady who had been a part of the event for a long time. There were also some very impressive toys.

"Other store windows had displays with motorized animals and toys to look at. While we were at the Bon Marche, I managed to buy Melissa a special Christmas dress in secret. We stayed in a motel on Highway 99 close to downtown. That was also a new experience and exciting.

"The Bon played an important role in our family while it was there. Over the years Melissa had two special dresses from the Bon Marche. Her first formal also came from there some ten or eleven years later."

Like other communities in the Willamette Valley, the Eugene area was devastated by the Columbus Day Storm on October 12, 1962. The storm was created by two typhoons that joined forces off the Northern California coast and then turned north along the coastline. The tremendous force of the wind destroyed property and killed two dozen people in the Willamette Valley.

In Eugene, Larry Johnson and his wife were living in the Amazon Housing Units while he finished his degree at the University of Oregon. They were awaiting for the arrival of their baby.

The windows were always drafty, but when the wind outside was screaming and peeling tiles off the roof of the school down the street, Larry leaned out the window, trying to tape cardboard over the glass. One of the flying roof tiles sailed through the open window and sliced into Larry's chest. His wife called an ambulance and they rode to the hospital together. He didn't make it. He was only one of the five who died in the Eugene-Springfield area because of the storm.

Trees crushed cars and blocked streets; structures collapsed; signs flew past, slicing through the air; store windows downtown were shattered.

The wind flattened burning wigwam burners in Eugene and Junction City, and Eugene firefighters battled seventy five fires that night.

River Road, as U.S. Highway 99, Towards Junction City

In Eugene, from the south, the new Pacific Highway originally followed the current Franklin Boulevard. It became Sixth Avenue, made a right at Blair Avenue, took another right on Van Buren and went over the tracks to go west on Railroad Boulevard. From there it went north on River Road. Although River Road was designated as the Pacific Highway in 1913, it wasn't paved until 1920, and then only as two narrow lanes.

Some of the houses and businesses established on Blair reflect the period when it was part of the highway as do some on Railroad Boulevard and River Road.

On Blair, the owners of Tiny Tavern took over the Spencer family home in 1945 and it retains some of the appearance of a home of the earlier period.

Sam Bonds Garage actually was a garage and had a gravity flow gasoline pump. There are others if you study the area.

When Pacific Highway/River Road was paved in 1920, its first service station was built to service the expected increase in automobile traffic. It was a Richfield station and it sat next to the railroad tracks.

The designation of River Road as a state, and later, a federal highway, began to change the area's agrarian landscape. Before the change in the land-use laws that were created to preserve farm and forest property, many owners of the donation land claims subdivided their properties, allowing business and services catering to the automobile to be established.

Automobile camps developed. These camps generally consisted of a gas station, a communal restroom and small, detached cabins. On River Road, there was Cabin City, Green Gables and Fir Grove auto courts. By 1948, an appliance store, department store, dry cleaners, a manufacturing plant, grocery stores and small offices sat amidst the six filling stations lining the road.

Today on River Road, several groups of small apartments reflect their history as auto courts, and many of the homes reflect the time period before the highway with large yards and there are even a few buildings that reflect their past as gas stations.

One long-time business that was established along River Road to serve the local farmers who raised fruits, filbert/hazelnuts and walnuts, was Brunner Dryer.

Brunner Commercial Dryer

The Brunner Commercial Dryer and the large, charming home next to it were a familiar sight along River Road. Frank Brunner and his wife Bertha purchased the property in 1920 after their arrival in Eugene from Iowa where he had raised grain and cattle.

Once in Eugene, he took a job at Eugene Fruit Growers while he decided where to invest in another farm. On the advice of fellow workers, he purchased 24 acres on River Road and an additional 54 acres nearby. He put all of his land in fruit, mostly prunes, cherries and walnuts. Shortly after buying the land, he began construction of that large two-story farmhouse and moved his family into it in 1924. He also built a small commercial dryer to process his own crops as well as those of others. That dryer burned in the early 1930s and he soon built a larger one.

During that time, Helen Brunner, Frank and Bertha's daughter, invited a friend, Marie Darrington, to a social gathering at the Brunner home where she introduced Marie to her brother Ernest and his good friend Peter Schmitz. In 1937, Ernest and Marie were married and after Frank and Bertha moved to a newer home nearby, the couple moved into the Brunner farmhouse and managed the Brunner Dryer. Tragically, in March 1939, Ernest was killed in a tractor accident, so Frank and Bertha moved back into the farm home to be with Marie and her six-month-old son, Joe.

A little over a year later, Marie married Peter Schmitz. Peter and Marie then purchased the Brunner's house and ten acres of surrounding land from Frank and Bertha.

Through the Schmitz' efforts, the dryer business grew, and they maintained the Brunner Commercial Dryer name. During World War II, the Schmitzs were awarded a government contract to provide dried fruit for the troops. The income that they received from the contract enabled them to pay off the house and land in a matter of a few years.

The operation was expanded to include

strawberries, sweet and sour cherries, a variety of nuts including filberts from the George Dorris orchards in Springfield. They also became an agent for the wholesale distributor, Hudson House, in Portland. The fruit and nuts dried at the Brunner Commercial Dryer were shipped to bakeries across the country.

Over the years, Brunner Dryer provided employment for many area boys and girls during the summer months when school was out.

Peter Schmitz kept the plant running during its peak years in the 1950s and 1960s and remained in charge until his death in 1989. Joe Brunner, Marie and Ernest's son, took over the management of the business until 2003 when he passed away.

Marie had the dryer torn down to prepare the property for development before she passed away in 2006.

Today, the only thing that remains of Brunner Commercial Dryer is the wonderful old Brunner-Schmitz house at 1410 River Road, now a City of Eugene landmark that bore witness, for so many years, to the successes of an extended Eugene farm family.

The Richfield Beacon Station on River Road was a part of the whole string of stations built by the Highway Community Corporation, a department of Richfield Oil that went bankrupt in 1939.

"Site Acquired for Big Highway Hotel;" *Eugene Register-Guard*, **April 3, 1929:**

"...The Highway Community Corporation of Los Angeles, a division of the Richfield Oil company, acquired five acres of the old Spencer place on the west side of the highway, about two and one-half miles north of Santa Clara. The property provides the community corporation a frontage of 450 feet on the highway. An engineer will be making surveys and other preparations looking toward erection of the hotel and service station. There will be a steel beacon tower about 125 feet tall with a revolving beacon light near the entrance from the highway. The plans call for shops of various types to be provided in the hotel building, the whole establishment making up a community center for the higher class of automobile tourist. It is reported that the project contemplates eventual development of an airport in addition to the automobile service facilities."

"Richfield Beacon to Have Opening;" *Eugene Register-Guard*, **March 8, 1930:**

"The $35,000 neon-lighted air beacon and service station, seven miles north of Eugene on the Pacific Highway is now completed and the opening, to which the public is invited, will be at 8 p.m. Monday evening. The Eugene beacon, located on the airline, is the twenty-first beacon to be completed by the Richfield Oil Company of the 35 scheduled to be installed from Mexico to Canada.

"The service station unit at the foot of the tower is constructed with Norman architecture, and will operate on a 24-hour basis. The station has been leased and will be operated by the T.A. Winter Company."

Two communities formed in the area, neither of them currently inside the Eugene city limits or receiving city service. The first is the River Road district which extends north to Randy Pape Belt Line Road and the next is Santa Clara which extends from Randy Papé Belt Line north to Beacon Drive.

Randy Papé Belt Line is the east-west connection between Springfield on the east and the western development of Eugene that was built in the early 1960s. It is an important and heavily-used link. Where Randy Papé Belt Line Road crosses River Road, in both north and south directions, for a couple of blocks, there is increased business development with strip malls, grocery stores and both small and large businesses.

The line between city and county in those areas is becoming increasingly blurred. It occasionally makes for odd neighbors – a Eugene Fire Station located less than a block from the Santa Clara Volunteer Fire Department is but one example.

Beyond Santa Clara to the north, both sides of the road have been developed generally for housing until River Road comes to Beacon Drive which, early-on, was designated as the dividing line between Eugene's growth boundary and Junction City by the U.S. Postal Service.

As U.S. Highway 99's route continued north of Beacon Drive the scenery increasingly became rural.

The American Legion developed a site and the Harwood family subdivided a part of their land and turned it into a space rental for residential trailers. Located farther out, Shadow Hills Country Club and golf course is another business that found the rural setting and developed road appealing.

The short drive between this point and the entrance to Junction City allows a visual history of rural life as time went on. Along this road are reminders of the past – a school house remodeled into a home, a few old barns, a prune shed, some very old homes, equipment sheds and even a water tower.

A few of the old donation land claims are still being farmed, but not always in the same way. One, along the former route of U.S. Highway 99, has become a Christmas tree farm; another sells seasonal garden starts; two or three are nurseries.

The newest trend in farming in the area is showcased in the large commercial farms that specialize in Fall Harvest events. They not only raise fruits, vegetables and flowers that they sell at their large farmstands during the fall harvest, but they also host u-pick pumpkin patches, horse-drawn hayrides, corn mazes, petting zoos, performing animals and playgrounds.

The newest, Lone Pine Farm, was begun in 1985 and has been a popular destination with many of these family activities planned around the harvest season and Halloween.

Just down the road, a bit further to the north, is a neighbor with a past... Thistledown Farms.

An early pioneer, Gay Masterson, came by wagon train on the Oregon Trail and lived her life raising a family and settling the northwest. She spent the last years of her life living with her daughter and her son-in-law, Louis Vitus, on River Road, north of Eugene, on the donation land claim farm called Thistledown.

Gay's diary in *One Woman's West* by Lois Barton, includes:

"...a very quiet Sunday. Very little travel, only 2 or 3 automobiles passed. A few buggies and other vehicles.

Pacific Highway / River Road north of Eugene, 1920. *Courtesy of the Oregon Department of Transportation (ODOT) History Center*

"Monday, June 5, 1911. Automobile procession passed this morning on the way to Portland to attend the Rose Carnival, decorated with Pennants and streamers."

"April 2, 1916. Clear and bright. A fine day for automobiles and they were on the go early. Hundreds of autos passed and not one stopped...Our mail comes now in an automobile... quite an improvement on an Ox wagon of 65 years ago.

"June 3, 1915. I am now getting ready to go to Eugene on the Jitney bus to stay a few hours. Yes, we are off for a ride. We got home at half past 4 p.m. Had a fine sunny day for our ride. Saw several friends and also saw the new summer goods. Everything was just grand along the way to Eugene, orchards, gardens and flowers."

Entrance to the Hentze Family Farm off of Lovelake Road, the former route of Pacific Highway. *From the Brew family collection*

Thistledown Farm, with its large red and white barn and beautiful landscaping has gone through several owners since the Mastersons first filed their donation land claim. Since 1972, it offers a farmer's market/retail store where fresh homemade pies, jams, jellies and other products are also sold. Their greenhouses are stocked with hanging baskets and, like Lone Pine Farms, they offer horse-drawn wagon rides to their own pumpkin patch.

As it nears Junction City, the original Pacific Highway appears on an early map to make the turn toward Junction City to Fifth Street instead of going straight onto Lovelake Road, formerly Dane Lane.

In those early days, Lovelake Road was a wagon road that passed in front of the Hentze Family Farm, coming out on the current Highway 99, a little south of Lancaster.

The historic Hentze Family Farm, established in 1902, is still operated by the members of the Hentze family who have participated and supported community events through several generations, celebrating "end-of-harvest" picnics in the last century to the current activities surrounding the Scandinavian Festival. Like the other larger commercial farms in the area, they, too, provide their guests with wagon rides to their pumpkin patch.

With the problems presented by both the railroad crossing the River Road route of U.S. Highway 99 and frequent winter flooding, it was agreed that the highway needed to be moved. It was temporarily moved west to Prairie Road which solved part of the problem, but the highway needed a clear entry into Eugene. In 1936, the new road was built to the west of the railroad yards, giving the highway an entrance without interference. These changes left River Road somewhat orphaned, once again, serving mainly local traffic. The old auto courts disappeared or were converted into apartments. Most of the gas stations were removed or converted to other uses.

Sixth and Seventh Streets, as Highway 99, toward Junction City (1936 on):

The new U.S. Highway 99 became an extension of 6th and 7th Streets to the north of Eugene. At the Big Y site, the two streets merged as they headed north out of town and the new route took traffic over an overpass of warehouses and commercial businesses, avoiding the railroad yards and railroad crossings as it headed for Junction City. This eliminated both the wait for trains and the possibility of having to navigate flooded roads for the highway travelers. It also opened up a new area for increased business development with easier access than what was available on River Road.

A major industrial area grew along this edge of the city. As this new route toward Junction City became U.S. Highway 99, more motels, auto repair shops, gas stations and taverns filled in the empty spaces that had once been farm fields.

The area closest to Eugene became known as the Bethel district and it has its own school district, but was, and still is, part of the City of Eugene.

After World War II, the need for housing increased and contractors began to purchase large plots or land to build affordable homes based on similar floor plans. The process was slower and involved fewer workers than it would today, but the homes filled rapidly. The subdivisions were mostly scattered in the outlying areas of the city. One of those was on land west of Highway 99 as it passed north from Eugene. Royal Gilbert began building many single story basic homes and, as time went on, he was building some that were more elaborate. By the time he was finishing his work, he added a handy shopping center and a nearby apartment building where a 1950s North End Drive-in theater had been on the corner of Highway 99 and Barger Drive.

His Gilbert Shopping Center was one of the first in a trend that would locate retail centers away from the downtown area near residential developments.

During the 1950s, drive-in movie theaters were very popular family entertainment. Besides the North End Drive-in along Highway 99, there was the West 11th Drive-in and the Eugene Drive-in, located at 28th and Willamette Street. At that one, the screen faced the nearby hills, so residents who lived there could watch the movie from home. Knowing this, the owners of the drive-in offered them the rental of a speaker that could be connected in their homes.

Both Junction City and Springfield had their own drive-in theaters as well.

Lou and Ev's

Across the road from the Gilbert Shopping Center, a small, unassuming building once housed Lou and Ev's, one of Eugene's favorite restaurants for down-home fried chicken dinners. It was purchased from Lou and Ev Franssen in 1946 by Will and Flo Hein who retained the name. It is remembered by many for its large, multi-colored neon sign with a rooster on it.

It was so popular that the Heins weren't even able to upgrade their plywood booths because of the uproar the suggestion caused

with their regular customers. One man had proposed to his wife in one, and another said that he had made a million-dollar deal in another. So, very little changed over the years including the excellence of the food they served.

Unfortunately, after 45 years in business, Lou and Ev's closed its doors on New Years Eve in 1991. Several other eateries have tried to make a go of the site, but none have succeeded for more than a few months.

Jerry's Home Center

Eugene kept growing until it was soon the second largest city in Oregon. In the 1980s, with big box stores and national chains crowding out many family-owned businesses, the Orem family took a gamble. For many years, after owning and running their small "hole-in-the-wall" building material and hardware store just off of U.S. Highway 99, north of Eugene, the Orems built a large new store that offered lower prices, more selection and a focus on do-it-yourself shoppers. With a building to rival the biggest of the home improvement chain stores, a convenient location on Highway 99, and later a second store in Springfield, smart marketing and creative advertising, Jerry's Home Center celebrated its 50 years in business in 2011.

Beyond Jerry's Home Center on the north end of town and near the railroad tracks, lumber mills and other industrial business ventures flourished. Gas stations and truck stops serviced large trucks which, in turn, served the industrial development in the area.

Eugene Airport / Mahlon Sweet Field

Still farther north, but just a short distance off of U.S. Highway 99, the municipal airport, now called the Eugene Airport/Mahlon Sweet Field, was established.

Only a short time after the highway relocated, a major event was underway. Mahlon Sweet, a local Studebaker dealer and the head of the Eugene Chamber of Commerce's Aviation Committee, launched a campaign to get a new – a "real" – airport for Eugene. Mahlon Sweet had been interested in aviation since a pilot ran out of fuel and made an emergency landing in a cow pasture near Friendly Street in 1918. The air park in use around that time was in the Chambers Street area, but Sweet helped get the first dirt strip airfield out on West 11th built in 1919.

For the new airport, the city and the federal government purchased 900 acres west of the new location of U.S. Highway 99. The airport, opened in 1943, was christened Mahlon Sweet Airport. The first commercial flight, a United Airlines DC-3 prop-liner, landed there on May 1, 1943. United was formed in a merger of Boeing Air Transport, National Air Transport, Varney Airlines and Pacific Air Transport in 1928, so it was fitting that the airline with partial Oregon roots landed that day in 1943 with more than 8,000 spectators gathered to mark the occasion.

One of the activities planned for the opening of Mahlon Sweet Airport was a recruiting session put on by UAL's Chief Stewardess, Vera Smith. She set up a recruiting session at the Eugene Hotel to enlist young women to become stewardesses. The candidates had to be 21 to 25 years old, attractive, weigh less than 120 pounds and possess a pleasing personality. They also were required to have at least two years' college education.

The first year that Mahlon Sweet was opened, 913 passengers flew in and out of the airport.

David Joyce's "Flight Patterns." Eugene Airport artwork. *Photos by Pat Edwards*

Mahlon Sweet Airport underwent major reconstruction in 1964 and again in 1988 when it was renamed the Eugene Airport. To honor the past, the landing field was to be called Mahlon Sweet Field.

The last project increased the square footage to 86,000 square feet. In 2012, the number of passengers totaled 809,457. It now has a 6,000-foot runway and an 8,009-foot runway which can accommodate most commercial aircraft.

One of the most popular and much-loved decorating schemes in the terminal is the 235-foot "Flight Patterns" artwork project done by photographer, David Joyce, which entertains and delights passengers walking along the concourse to their flights. In 1988, local dignitaries and celebrities, as well as others of all ages from the Eugene community, were invited to be photographed in Joyce's studio in all manner of dress and lifestyles. They were positioned, lying down on a plush mat, with arms extended like they were flying while Joyce stood on a tall ladder and photographed them from above. Some had umbrellas, some had briefcases hanging from their wrists; others flew tandem, some held hands with a child. When completed, over 170, 2/3-lifesize cutout prints of people and clouds depicting the exhilaration of flying, were mounted on the walls of the A-concourse leading to the loading gates. After hanging for 23 years, the exhibit was looking a bit shabby, so it was taken down and refurbished. The project was a joint effort of the Public Art Committee, David Joyce's widow, Kacey Joyce, and the staff at the Eugene Airport. On February 2, 2012, the 178 people and cloud photographic cutouts were rehung to the delight of travelers and community alike.

The businesses and residences along the highway continue all the way north until they meet those on the outskirts of Junction City. That whole length of U.S. Highway 99 parallels the railroad tracks running along the east side of the road.

The dividing line between Eugene and Junction City along the current Highway 99 route has now been established as Meadowview Road.

LUPER

Marked only by a cemetery and a nearby restored train depot, Luper, Oregon is now a ghost town. Once a train station belonging to the Oregon and California Railroad now referred to as the Meadowview Station, the

The Meadowview Oregon Electric Railway Station between Eugene and Junction City. *Courtesy of the Lane County Historical Society*

community was located between Junction City and Eugene near Meadowview Road between Highway 99 and Prairie Road, south of Junction City.

According to Lane Historical Society records, the community was named for James N. Luper, a pioneer born in 1852 in Illinois.

An excerpt from McArthur's *Oregon Geographical Names,* included in a Wikipedia entry gives us a little more detail: *"James Luper's daughter, Oregon State Engineer Rhea Luper, recalled in 1927 that her father had purchased the Luper-area property around 1870, and thereafter constructed a warehouse and railroad spur. The area became a shipping point for wheat."*

The Luper Cemetery, located off West Beacon Drive, is known to have approximately 160 graves. It was established in 1857 on land donated by Thomas and Elizabeth Baker.

More Memories by Jo-Brew:

"For years, I watched the prairie land on the corner of Meadoview Road and U.S. Highway 99 as I drove past. My attention was not drawn to the old Oregon Electric train station that was gradually disintegrating on the east side of the road, but in some years, to the big flock of Tundra Swans that would land there to spend a few days. The swans haven't been there for the last four or five years, however. Construction of a new State Mental Hospital and other industrial uses on the site is underway and they've left. Just as I thought that the old station had seen its last days, it has been moved about 100 feet, rebuilt and is ready to be used again, not as a passenger station, but as a storage facility on a nearby farm."

JUNCTION CITY

Fur trappers were the first to visit this prime agricultural area, but most continued on. Eventually, a few settled to begin farming. In 1847, one of the first settlers, Lester Hulin took up a claim along the Long Tom River. After he left that claim for the mine fields in California, in 1850, he filed for a donation land claim about three miles southeast of what is now Junction City, becoming the first settler in the area. He formed ties with the community as it grew, although he also invested in farms in other areas of the county.

Gil Hulin, former newspaper reporter and descendent of multiple early area settlers, shares the story of his family:

"My great-grandfather, Lester Hulin, helped lead an 1847 wagon train to the Willamette Valley by way of the Applegate Trail. He had previously explored the Great Plains as far west as Colorado with John C. Fremont before returning to St. Joseph, Missouri, to join with other settlers moving west. Lester Hulin's diary has been reprinted by the Lane County Historical Society, complete with a pencil sketch of Chimney Rock, Nebraska, The volume ends with his arrival at Eugene Skinner's cabin in a very wet November 1847.

"He filed a land claim in the Long Tom area. Following the discovery of gold in California in 1848, Lester made two horseback trips to Central California, returning north both times by ship. The first trip, his ship was wrecked at the mouth of the Rogue River and Lester crossed the Coast Range on foot in returning to Eugene. The second trip, his ship made it to Astoria where it was to spend several days unloading provisions, and Lester, impatient to keep moving, hired a rowboat to take him to Portland.

"Lester farmed in the Veneta, Junction City and Monroe areas, eventually marrying Abigail Craig, who had come to Oregon by ship around Cape Horn. Unfortunately, she did not keep a diary. Their son was Lester Gilbert Hulin, who married Damaris Schofield, and their son was Wilbur Schofield Hulin, born in 1899.

"Gilbert's father, Wilbur, liked to tell of childhood horse-and-buggy trips to Newport, where he was always seated at his parents' feet, right behind the horse. Later, as a teenager, Wilbur worked on the day trains between Albany, Corvallis and the coast. He would board the westbound train at an isolated station high in the Coast Range mountains, probably Nashville or Summit, offer to deliver passengers' luggage to their Newport hotels that evening, and issue claim checks. The railroad went no farther than Yaquina, between Toledo and Newport, so the journey required a train-to-boat transfer for the final leg of the journey, and then the long hikes to the numerous Nye Beach hotels. In the morning, the process was reversed, thus placing young Wilbur back in the mountains for a few hours of reading.

"Wilbur's many years in higher education began with a freshman year in Southern California at Occidental College, followed by a bachelor's degree from the University of Oregon, a master's degree from Princeton University and a Ph.D. from Harvard University. He remained in the East for seven years of teaching at Princeton before returning to Eugene in 1937.

"Meanwhile, the woman Wilbur would marry in 1940 was born to Warren Melvin Marshall and Nora Day Marshall in Eugene in 1907. She was also named Nora Day Marshall, but to avoid confusion, never was called Nora and went by Day, later 'Daye,' all her life. She went through school in Eugene, graduating from the University of Oregon with an art education degree in 1930. Daye felt very fortunate to get a teaching job at Eugene's Roosevelt Junior High School directly out of college and at the start of the Great Depression. Roosevelt was then located directly opposite the U of O campus at East 18th Avenue and Agate Street in what later became Condon Elementary School.

"Daye's own pioneer ancestry goes

back to her great-grandfather, Mahlon Hall Harlow, born in 1811, died in 1895. He traveled the Oregon Trail to Eugene in 1852. Eugene's First Baptist Church was organized in the Harlow living room and it was at the Baptist Church where Daye Marshall and Wilbur Hulin first met in 1937. They were married at the pastor's cabin on the upper McKenzie River in 1940. That winter, after ending 10 years teaching at Roosevelt, Daye spent one year as Superintendent of Art Instruction for the Corvallis School District while Wilbur finished up research and teaching projects in both Eugene and Portland. Then they saw the country for three years while Wilbur continued his education and taught at University of Chicago, Harvard and Stanford University. They were living in Chicago at the time of the attack on Pearl Harbor and Daye vividly remembered taking the elevated train downtown the following day as clerks were removing all Japanese merchandise from the shelves at Marshall Field's department store.

"In 1944, Wilbur and Daye Hulin settled in Forest Grove, Oregon, where he had been hired as a psychology professor by Pacific University. When the administration learned of Daye's art background, a spare classroom was cleaned out to become the newly-established art department. Daye was also named Dean of Women, a job that was simplified by the fact that only four male students were on campus during the height of World War II.

"Wilbur and Daye's only child – me – was born at the end of 1945 and I was named to recognize both sides of the family, Gilbert Marshall Hulin. I spent my first three-and-a-half years in Forest Grove before moving in 1949 to Eugene where both sets of grandparents still lived.

"The family's new home at West 18th Avenue and Lawrence Street would not be vacated for three weeks, so we stayed on a 16-acre farm that my grandfather, Lester Hulin, owned near Veneta. I remember the hand-pumped water-well delivering such rusty water that drinking water had to be imported from Eugene each day.

"It was during the three weeks staying in Veneta that Southern Pacific Railway's Shasta Daylight streamliner was inaugurated. At three-and-a-half, I vividly remember touring the train during its exhibition stop in Eugene prior to starting regular service which cemented a love affair with every phase of railroading that has existed to this day."

The original Pacific Highway/U.S. Highway 99 followed parts of the northern stagecoach route once it left Eugene City, probably using an old wagon road following the River Road route which was later used by U.S. Highway 99. Before 1865, the stage route appears to have come from the Cartwright House in Lorane, directly up the Old Territorial Road to Milliorn Station. Early pioneer, Thomas Milliorn, took out a donation land claim in 1853 in the Junction City area and became quite prominent in its history.

Milliorn Station appears to have been in an area just south and east of Oaklea Road where it connects to Highway 99W, on the east side of the current highway.

The *Portrait and Biographical Record of the Willamette Valley, Oregon* book tells about the Milliorn family:

"Thomas A. Milliorn, now one of the oldest citizens of Junction City, which is built upon a part of the land which formed his donation land claim, taken up in 1853, and for many years where his activities have been given for the advancement of the welfare of the city and community. An evidence of the prosperity which has followed the efforts of Mr. Milliorn since coming to Oregon lies in the property which he has accumulated, he having built the finest residence in the city, is a stockholder and director and one of the incorporators of the Farmers & Merchants Bank, owns twenty acres adjoining the town and one hundred and six included in a farm on the banks of the Willamette River.

"...Mr. [James] Hoffman married, in Lane County, Eugenia Milliorn, who was born in Missouri, and came with her parents to this county in 1853, locating on the present site of Junction City. Her father kept Milliorn Station, on the overland stage route, for twenty or more years, it being a celebrated stopping place for travelers in pioneer days."

In his book, *Early Days of Junction City, Oregon*, Chris T. Wilde, talks a bit about the Milliorn (which he spells "Milliron") Cemetery near where the stage stop was located:

"That tract also contained the one-half acre known as The Milliron Cemetery, which is about one-half mile west of town on the north side of the High Pass Road.

"...This place was a stage coach stopover for years. We are told that a stage coach fare from San Francisco to Portland, was fifty dollars and could be completed in around five days. The horses and drivers must have been changed every so many hours apart. The roads were very rough, muddy, with the riders often expected to get out and help repair the narrow ten-foot-wide roads, before continuing on their journey."

After the Civil War, the government offered generous land grants to railway companies that would build tracks into the interior of Oregon, with stipulations on how much profit the railway could make on the sale of the land they were granted. There were two competitors for the land grants to build from Portland south. As noted previously, the Oregon Central was begun on the west side of the Willamette River and the Oregon & California on the east side. A contest was set up between the two to build a short stretch in a limited period of time. One way or another, Ben Holladay with the proposed Oregon & California line won the contest as well as the land grants.

The distance a wood-burning steam engine could go in a day from the Oregon City area before refueling was where the site of what became Junction City is located. The Oregon & California Railway purchased 90 acres from T.A. Milliorn, L.D. Gilbert and G.H. McQueen there. They made plans for a refueling station that would service two railroads. A roundhouse was built as well as warehouses. Wood was cut for ties and more was cut and stacked to burn.

A city began to grow and its residents expected it to be a junction of the two railroads. Some railroad workers built homes there for their families; farmers brought their products there for shipping, and business developed to service the railroad workers, keep the trains running and meet the needs of the farmers.

The post office opened and Junction City incorporated in 1872, but there was no junction at the time. The town developed as an agricultural supply and shipping center.

With the shift in the course of the Willamette River that left the community of Lancaster, to the north, high and dry, and the arrival of the railroad, river transport was no longer viable. Five or six Lancaster buildings that were no longer being used were put on rollers and moved to Junction City.

One of those buildings was the home and office of Lancaster physician, Dr. N.L. Lee. He was one of the first graduates of Willamette University and the first physician to set up a practice in the area. He added on to his original Lancaster cabin to house his family as well as treat his patients. This house now belongs to the Junction City Historic Society and is often open for tours.

With the addition of the Lancaster buildings, other businesses began to open – a blacksmith shop, a general store, a boarding house and a saloon.

The expected second railroad line got as far as McMinnville before the construction began to stall. It eventually reached Corvallis. Years later, the line was extended, but not into Junction City. Instead, it passed through Monroe and connected with the Eugene line to the coast.

Like in many other fledgling settlements in Oregon, fire was a potent enemy, particularly because there were so few ways to fight it once it started. In 1882, the large three-story J.H. Berry Hotel on the corner of Sixth Avenue and Front Street burned to the ground. The fire moved on and took out two saloons and a saddle and harness shop. A little over a month later, a mill and grain elevator and its contents in the north part of town went up in flames.

Another fire in July 1910 took the Bushnell Warehouse. This one was caused by hobos who had been smoking in the building. The sparks spread and six buildings were ignited. The Eugene Fire Department responded to a call for help, sending fire hose and 200 railroad and fire volunteeers on a flat car and one box car that was pulled by the engine.

The list of fires goes on. Without a delivery system for water, and no fire department, the town of Junction City had no defense against the flames. Over and over,

View of Junction City in 1908. *From the Gregory Schultz Collection*

Junction City Hotel block, 1908. *Courtesy of Gerald W. Williams Collections, OSU Special Collections & Archives Commons*

the residents voted down the expense of fire equipment. After insurance companies refused to write policies on local properties, though, a volunteer fire department was finally formed and a fire engine purchased.

In 1902, A.C. Nielsen of Minnesota bought 1,600 acres of land east of Junction City and advertised in a Danish-language, Midwestern newspaper for Danish people to come and make a new life in Lane County. Some 40 families of Danish heritage responded to the call, bought small farming parcels and established a Lutheran Church, bringing about 200 more residents to the city.

By 1910, Junction City had a fruit cannery and two grain elevators, a flour mill and two creameries.

The building of the Pacific Highway in the 1910s and 1920s gave Junction City access to the main road which continued north to Albany, Oregon City and Portland. It also brought automobiles traveling through Junction City, opening the small city to more visitors.

In the 1930s, an alternate highway route from Junction City was built along the west side of the Willamette River through Corvallis to Portland and designated U.S. Highway 99W. The original highway became U.S. Highway 99E. Finally, Junction City had a junction.

In addition to the usual fruit trees and produce that were grown in the mid-Willamette Valley, the rich river bottom land around Junction City was found to be ideal in raising peppermint. At harvest time, the fragrant plants were cut and the oil was distilled in nearby Harrisburg, making it a practical crop for both shipping and storing.

From *Junction City to Denmark* by Visti Favrholdt, a son of a Danish Lutheran minister writing about his memories of life in Junction City during 1933:

"During the Depression years in the 1930s, there was a great number of unemployed men traveling all over the United States in search of work. They rode the rails free of charge, not by permission, but by toleration on the part of the railroads. The freight trains on the Southern Pacific line, passing through our town had their share of passengers, who were called hobos. There could be as many as three or four hundred on one train, many of them sitting at the sliding door openings of the box cars, but most of them on the roof. They looked dirty and tired. Many were unshaven with scruffy-looking clothes. We saw them every day. Freight

Main Street, Junction City, ca 1948. *Courtesy of Dot Dotson Photography*

Driving through Junction City. *Courtesy of Gerald W. Williams Collections, OSU Special Collections & Archives Commons*

trains only stopped in Junction City to shunt box cars. Nonstop daytime trains passing through town would slow down to allow hobos to jump off or on the trains. Not many got off in our town. They seemed to know that Junction City was not a place to look for work.

"...Right in the middle of summer, when we least wanted it, came the call for bean field pickers. Lots and lots of kids used to pile into trucks early every morning to be driven out to the bean fields down near the river, myself included. When we spilled out of the truck, it was all there – the weigh scales, the checkers, the empty sacks, the countless number of endless rows and the foreman shouting about what rows were to be picked. Five o'clock was the time to report to the weigh scale checker. Payment was one cent per pound of beans, payable once a week."

"...We used to roller skate all the way from Junction to Harrisburg on the concrete highway. One year, the Willamette River overflowed its banks and part of the roadway became flooded, including Junction City itself east of the Southern Pacific tracks.

"...My friend Harold and I used to walk to Benton Lane Park outside of town and swim in the outdoor pool which was the only one in the whole Lane County as far as we knew. We paid five cents for one hour and twenty-five cents for a whole day. We could only afford one hour."

McEldowny Bros. Appliance Store at night. *From the Gregory Schultz Collection, F.R. Schultz, photographer*

Bugsy's Fine Food and Spirits, Junction City. *Courtesy of Joe Kunkle*

train to slow down and pick up the mail. The mailbag would be hanging from an arm at the station right at the track and another projecting in the door opening of the train's mail car would grab it as the train passed by. The sound of exploding detonation caps, triggered by the train wheels, could be heard all over town. We always knew when there was mail to go."

Like Eugene and other larger cities, Junction City had its own drive-in theater. The Vista Drive-In Movie Theater was on First Street, behind where the Guaranty car lots were located.

In 1941, Gladys and Howard Gibson established Lochmead Farms, one of the largest independent dairy farms in the Pacific Northwest. In 1965, they opened the first DariMart convenience store as a way to market the farm's dairy products. DariMart remains unique among convenience stores for featuring high quality fresh, local dairy products. Although the chain of 43 stores was begun after U.S. Highway 99 was decommissioned, many, but not all, of those stores are located along the Highway 99 route from Albany to Cottage Grove. The dairy farm and stores are a family-owned-and-operated business employing approximately 450 people throughout the area.

Visti left the United States with his family and returned to Junction City as an adult with his wife and children. His story continues:

"...The train station was still there. I told the kids how they used to place two detonation caps on the track rails just outside of town when they wanted the

One of the long-time popular businesses on Highway 99 as it passed through Junction City was Ralph's Drugs and Gifts owned by Ralph and Orine Bruncheon.

Part of their marriage agreement included a proviso that he would go deer hunting every year. It happened that, in 1962, his deer hunting trip near Burns, Oregon was during the same time when the Columbus Day Storm hit the area, so he missed it.

It was a memorable time for Orine. She hired a pharmacist from Eugene to come in and run the pharmacy. She ran the store and kept it open during the storm and the days that followed. There was no electricity, so the electric cash register would not work and she carried the money home with her at night. The pharmacist couldn't get back to Eugene, so he stayed in town. Orine and their children ate a lot of cold food and hot dogs cooked over the fire in a neighbor's fireplace until the electricity was restored.

One former resident of Junction City, Chris Wilde wrote:

"During The Columbus Day storm of 1962, winds were so violent they flattened a wigwam burner in Junction City scattering sparks and starting a blaze that destroyed two blocks of downtown. Winds from the southwest attained gusts over 90 miles an hour. Fire engines, trucks and men came from all the neighboring fire stations to help contain the flames. The wind was so terrifically strong that the flames flew northward horizontally. A wind change, blowing the flames toward the east, saved the city from a terrible holocaust."

Like many of the towns located along Highway 99, the building of the Interstate 5 freeway several miles to the east, isolated Junction City. Travelers seldom traveled through the town to get to their destinations. There were few casual visitors who would stop for a meal, overnight or for gasoline.

Scandinavian Festival

In order to find new ways to support local businesses and bring in money from outside, Dr. Gale Fletchall, began discussing the possibility of a festival to celebrate the city's very real, but dormant, Scandinavian heritage. With encouragement from older Danish residents and financial support from the Chamber of Commerce, the four-day celebration of Scandinavian heritage began in 1961 and has been held in the second week in August each year since.

Each of the four days of the festival celebrates a different culture – Norwegian Day, Swedish Day, Danish Day and Finnish Day. There is no admission charge and the only costs are at the food and crafts booths. There are three stages presenting music, dance and informational entertainment and demonstrations. Visitors can find unusual handcrafts such as Hardanger Embroidery, bobbin lace, and Rosemaling displayed and sold among the paintings, woodcrafts and jewelry. The food booths offer a wide variety of cuisine including authentic Scandinavian treats. The longest line is frequently at the aebelskiver booth.

"The Scandinavian Festival" by G.F. Fletchall, M.D., Lane County Historian, Lane County Historical Society, Vol. XIV, No. 2, Summer 1969, pgs 25-26

"...A few days before the first Festival, the flower boxes in full bloom were transported downtown, the streets were closed, a dance platform was erected in

Scandinavian Festival's Viking wannabes. *From the Rick Obst Collection*

the center of the mall, and the Scandinavian buildings were erected on both sides of the street. Colored lights draped the streets at night, and the flags made a colorful canopy over the streets in the daytime. During that first four-day Festival, over 25,000 people visited the city. Representatives from 28 states and many foreign countries registered. At the registration booth, each person was allowed to choose the Scandinavian nationality he desired, and he was given souvenir citizenship papers. Various groups, churches, lodges, service clubs and individuals prepared and sold Scandinavian food and souvenirs. These items were kept at a very nominal fee and there was no charge made for entertainment. In a true Festival atmosphere, everyone entered the spirit of the thing, dressed in Scandinavian costumes and participated in games and folk dancing. It was apparent that our desire to avoid a formal show was successful for young and old came to participate and many expressed their appreciation for something so spontaneous, noncommercial, and different.

"Many interesting guests appear at each Festival. One year, a young foreign exchange student had just arrived from Norway. The atmosphere of the Festival was reminiscent of her home country causing her to feel welcome. Her adjustment that year was easy. Another, a lady from Latvia wore her national costume which she had fashioned from articles collected during her internment in a Nazi prison camp. Her story and the explanation of her costume brought to mind the sacrifices these countries have paid for freedom.

"Prior to the first Festival, few individuals had costumes of any sort. It was necessary to spend much time in research collecting data, pictures and descriptions, fashioning patterns and sewing costumes to be worn at Festival time. By opening day, fully a third of the townspeople had their own costumes which added to the color and pageantry of the occasion.

"Many mistakes were made in the first Festival. Perhaps the greatest mistake was the underestimation of the crowd which would attend. A

Smorgasbord had been scheduled for Saturday evening at which 3,000 were served and at least another thousand turned away. Other groups, too, failed to have enough food prepared and spent nights preparing Danish pastries to supply their shops during the daytime..."

After passing through the main part of Junction City on Highway 99, a noted landmark was the jug-shaped building on the west side of Main Street. Formerly a gas station, the Brown Jug, it now is a retailer for windows.

At one time, in the triangular piece of land at the junction of Highway 99W and Highway 99E, there was a popular restaurant called the Junction House. It had two front doors, one for 99E and the other for 99W. The parking lot handled cars from both sides. It was a convenient stop for travelers headed north on either road and it was a popular nightspot for locals.

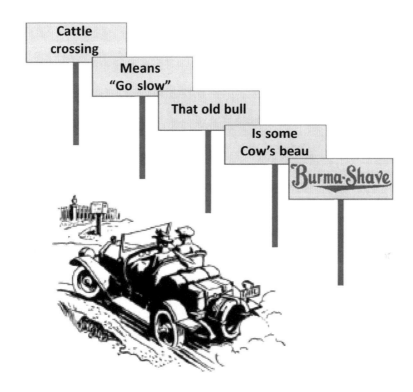

Section 7

U.S. HIGHWAY 99E - JUNCTION CITY TO ALBANY

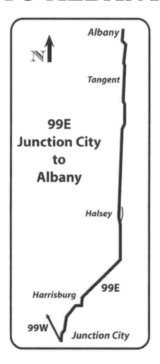

WOODY'S LANDING / WOODYVILLE / FREEDOM / LANCASTER

Heading north from Junction City towards Harrisburg, the original eastern route of U.S. Highway 99 takes travelers past large farms on both sides of the road. Two miles on the left, a sign and an old gas station converted to an antique store marks the community of Lancaster, formerly known as Woody's Landing or Woodyville. At one time, it was situated on the banks of the Willamette River and, during high water, boats from the north tied up at its docks to load and unload goods. Families began to settle around the landing since most of the farmers in the area used it to ship their products to market.

According to Howard McKinley Corning, in his book, *Willamette Landings: Ghost Towns of the River*:

"The California & Oregon Stage Company moved its stand from here [Milliorn] to Woody's Landing [Lancaster] in about 1865."

1964 flood; looking south from Lancaster to Harrisburg. *Courtesy of the Oregon Department of Transportation (ODOT) History Center*

1964 flood; looking south from Lancaster to Junction City. *Courtesy of the Oregon Department of Transportation (ODOT) History Center*

That means that if the stage stop was moved to Woody's Landing in 1865, the route from Eugene City changed somewhat. It then must have traveled north on the old River Road route and connected with the current Lovelake Road to Lancaster where the Woody's Landing stage stop was located on the present-day Highway 99E.

Near the unincorporated community of Lancaster, Oregon, Woody's Landing was located 1½ miles due east of Milliorn and sat along the route of the current Highway 99E north of where Ayres Lane connects with 99E.

Lancaster was described as the "Fightingest Town on the River" by Ralph Friedman in his book, *In Search of Western Oregon*:

"*In its prime, Lancaster was the fightingest town on the river because of bullying, obstructionist tactics to make the landing the head of navigation on the river. In 1852, a burly fellow named Woody opened a roadhouse and soon the locale was known as Woody's Landing, or Woodyville, with the most prominent building being Woody's crude, candle-lighted saloon. It thrived on rivermen who wanted to look down on something stronger than water and on road travelers who were inclined to wipe off – or wash down – the dust. Woody had a lot of kinfolk with the manners of the Dead-End Kids and the scruples of the 40 Thieves, and cargo unloaded here at twilight was mysteriously missing at dawn. Anyone even hinting that the Woody Bunch might be responsible was inviting mass attack. In 1858, the post office of Freedom opened. About then, Woody sold out to another gang of toughs and crooks, Mulkey & Co., and a warehouse was built and the settlement grew. A few years later – probably 1864 – the town took its place on "the big road" from Corvallis to Oakland by way of Eugene, when the California & Oregon Stage Company moved its station here from Milliorn, 1.5 miles to the west. By then, however, the town had been severely damaged by the 1861 flood and separated from the stream when the Willamette changed course. In 1866, the post office changed to Lancaster. The coming of the railroad to Junction City performed last rites on Lancaster as a viable community and in 1872, the post office moved to Junction City."*

When Woody established his "house of entertainment," wharves and storehouses there, he also made and sold a popular local distilled beverage called Blue Ruin. Later, an island in the Willamette River was also named Blue Ruin, attesting to its popularity.

Woodyville became the trade center for the whole area. Competitors were not welcome and disagreements were not always peaceful, nor was the travel on the river.

Woody had a strangle-hold on the landing while it was in operation. When the California and Oregon Stage Company moved its stage stop from Milliorns (misspelled in the Friedman book), one-and-a-half miles west, to Woodyville, Woody received additional funding for the stage stop and post office, extending his power. With no other access to markets, the area was increasingly dependent on Woody and his family.

When a competitive steamboat company tried to make it past Woody's to a new landing, the waterway was blocked by newly-cut trees. Neighbors helped clear the channel and the steamship got through only to face the same problem the next time it came.

John Mulkey, who bought the property from Woody, built a sawmill there and renamed it Lancaster. He and his family also fought to maintain the monopoly on the river landing, even filing a legal complaint after attempting to block the passage.

The floods of the 1860s took their toll on the farmers and businesses. The greatest calamity for the community was the altered course of the river. The newly-grooved channel was to the east and the water no longer washed against the docks. There was no longer a landing.

Through the 1850s, more settlers arrived, many on the wagon trains of the "Great Migration," and began establishing farms, growing sheep, cattle and grain. After the Lancaster landing was lost, the Long Tom River was thought to be a possibility for navigation, but boats couldn't make it through. The nearest good steamboat landing was at Harrisburg. A ferry was available to cross the

Willamette at Harrisburg and that made it possible to ship to Albany, Salem or Portland, but not easily. Wagons also brought goods in and out, but both means were subject to unreliable weather conditions. The wagon tracks were often muddy or marshy and slow – the Willamette River was subject to flooding and had a tendency to meander – and there was a constant shifting of gravel bars.

For years, a farm sat on the right-hand side of Highway 99 as you approach the bridge crossing over the Willamette River from the south. For years, it was owned by the Gavatte family who farmed it, raising mainly Blue Lake pole beans each summer.

As was common on some of the farms, the Gavatte farm had migrant cabins that provided temporary housing for itinerant workers to supplement the labor force during harvest season.

Our first book, *OREGON'S MAIN STREET: U.S. Highway 99 "The Stories,"* included a story of life on the farm, told by Jane Gavatte. We mention it again here so that we can include a few more pictures supplied by the Gavatte family to show what life was like on the family farm during the mid-1900s.

CROW'S NEST / PRAIRIE CITY / THURSTON / HARRISBURG

Harrisburg, located on the Willamette River in an area settled by farming families in the 1850s, is in Linn County. It was briefly called Crow's Nest, Prairie City and Thurston before the name Harrisburg, after the capital city of Pennsylvania, was adopted in 1866. The town is located in a fertile valley chosen by many pioneer farmers in the 1840s and 1850s. In 1848, the settlers established a primitive ferry, two boats lashed together with a platform for carrying a wagon.

The Gavatte farm when the Willamette River went over flood stage. *From the Jane Gavatte Collection*

The Gavatte farmhouse. *From the Jane Gavatte Collection*

Migrant cabins on the Gavatte farm. *From the Jane Gavatte Collection*

The horses or oxen swam behind. Later a scow was built to carry both wagon and team. When the community was incorporated in 1852, it was called Prairie City, and the name was changed to Thurston in 1853. The post office opened in 1855 and was located in David McCully's store, the first store in town.

Early on, the river channel was located a mile away, but, as mentioned earlier, the course of the river was changed during the flood of 1861 and is now, and continues to be, right at the edge of the town. From the north, in times of high water, riverboats could reach upriver as far as Harrisburg and sometimes beyond, so it became a supply center for area settlers. Large warehouses and wharves were built along the waterfront and the steamboats anchored at the foot of Smith Street.

The Harrisburg community was incorporated in 1866. The Oregon & California Railroad passed through the town in 1871, crossing the river on a swing bridge designed to allow river traffic. This route was not on the original plans the railroad presented to the government or the state. The road was planned to go down on the east side of the river to Springfield.

During those early high-water years, if the Willamette was cleared of gravel bars, debris and snags, an occasional steamboat could make the trip all the way to Eugene. Because for many years it was the furthest point south that a steamship could navigate on the Willamette from Portland, Eugene was called the "headwater." During much of the 1850s, however, the trip to Eugene had not been possible because of low-water conditions, but the headwater designation had not been changed.

When discussion began on designating Harrisburg as the headwater and plans were being made to build new turnstile or "lift" bridges across the Willamette in that location, it met opposition from the railroad and the City of Eugene.

The city fathers of Eugene wanted the railroad to build through Eugene badly enough to approach Ben Holladay to try to negotiate a way to change the route. There was some merit to the idea because Eugene had more business potential, but the cost of a bridge to let ships go through was significant.

1910 Ferry crossing the Willamette River at Harrisburg. *From the Tri-County Chamber of Commerce website.*

Pacific Highway looking south from Harrisburg to Junction City. *Courtesy of the Oregon Department of Transportation (ODOT) History Center*

Holladay, agreed to change the route if Eugene could cover the cost of the bridge and make it worthwhile for the railroad. Eugene came up with the money and land to bring the railroad in. By 1912 an Oregon Electric train also ran daily from Portland to Eugene, on its own drawbridge between two towers, with a stop at the depot in Harrisburg, but automobiles still had to cross on a ferry.

Over the years, the ferry had a litany of problems – horses or mules pulling the wagon into the water; the ferry stranded in the middle of the river; the landing collapsing – to name a few. The addition of automobiles for transport didn't decrease the problems. They only made the rescues more complicated. The horses and mules that didn't drown could help themselves out – but that wasn't true for an automobile.

When the new Pacific Highway was coming through Harrisburg, the ruling that required a lift or turnstile bridge again became important. It had been a long time since riverboat traffic to Eugene had been possible, but there was continued opposition from the railroad to changing the headwater designation.

During the early part of the century, and for a long time after, the network of granges, or "Patrons of Husbandry," were bonded together for the betterment of farm commu-

The Pacific Highway leading up to the Willamette River Bridge at Harrisburg. *Courtesy of the Oregon Department of Transportation (ODOT) History Center*

Coming out on the other side into Harrisburg, Oregon. *Courtesy of Joe Kunkle*

nities and they had a strong political voice. It was the Charity Grange of Harrisburg that recognized the expenses involved in keeping the Oregon Electric Railway bridge functioning when there were no steamships able to go farther upriver. By that time, it was already working to promote the change.

Southern Pacific continued to be a major proponent of keeping Eugene as the headwater of the Willamette River and it was in favor of stalling competition from the proposed highway. Harrisburg had a ferry for a longer time than most other cities in the state. When Pacific Highway/U.S. Highway 99 connected the towns along the river, a ferry was used there until nearly the end of the construction.

With political support, the headwater designation was finally moved to Harrisburg. The bridge at Harrisburg – a truss bridge, the last one constructed in the project – finally spanned the river in 1926.

In an interview with Jo-Brew for her *"The Stories"* segment of this series, Margaret Hayworth Huston remembered the ferry that crossed the Willamette River at Harrisburg as well as the construction of the bridge over it. A gala parade was held when the bridge opened in 1926. Her father, Joe Hayworth, had a Ford truck which carried the band across the bridge for the first time.

In an interview on January 31, 1939 for the Works Progress Administration (WPA) Folklore Studies, Mrs. J. R. Bean told her story:

"I'm afraid I can't tell you much. If only my mother were living, she could tell you everything about early days in Oregon: but I was the youngest of the family, and in some way I have never been interested, until now it is too late.

"Yes, of course, I went to camp and revival meetings when I was a girl. They used to have great times down at what was known as Harrisburg Bridge. The people would come from all over the country and camp for days at a time. The Methodists had it in charge. There would be services both in the afternoon and at night. The night services were the ones we young folks, who were not Methodists, would attend, for that was when there was excitement and halleluiahs and amens. Those converting and those being converted would get in a high state of emotion, and we youngsters would go home half scared to death, thinking the world was coming to an end without delay.

"I went to camp meetings and picnics in the summer, and to dances and spelling schools in the winter. Then there were church and other socials, with lunch baskets, where the gentlemen bought or drew chances by some device for a basket, and the lady who brought it would be his partner when it came to eating.

"I was pretty small when I went to these, going with my father and mother, and I don't remember very much about them, but I do remember one. I was sitting with my mother on the stage or rostrum of the hall where the party was, when suddenly a bullet whizzed over our heads. A man there stole somebody else's girl, by getting her basket through some unfair means, and that led to further trouble between the men, which ended in the shooting of the man whose girl was stolen from him. I don't think he was killed, but his assailant, if I recall correctly, was imprisoned for life."

In another of the stories, Mr. Thomas Sommerville of Harrisburg, was inter-

viewed on February 17, 1939 for the Linn County *WPA's American Life Histories Collection: Manuscripts from the Federal Writer's Project, 1936-1940* project:

"My name is Thomas Sommerville. I was born on the Sommerville donation land claim about six miles due east of Harrisburg, Linn County, Oregon, in the year 1881. My father's name was John Sommerville and he was born Feb. 26, 1841 and came to Oregon with his parents in 1853 at the age of twelve years. He was really the cause of his parents coming to Oregon for he had been suffering from Asthma for some time and it was finally decided to bring him to the Pacific Coast in the hopes that the change of climate might be beneficial. This hope proved justified, for after the very first day on the cross-continental trip his asthma left him and never bothered him again during his life...

"...When my grandfather reached Oregon, he found the land where he wished to settle pretty well taken so he bought out another settler who was about ready to prove up on his claim. The man whose name I never heard was sick and sold his rights for $80.00. Dad's uncle also bought a claim just south of Grandfather's place but later sold it out to the Grimes family. This uncle was named Alex(ander) Sommerville. The early neighbors in this region were Paul Belts, Paul Clover, the Rampeys, the Wigles, the Whites, the Waggoners, and others. It was in school district No. 47, known then as Sommerville district.

"When the first settlers came, they took up their claims hit-and miss. When the land was finally surveyed there were some bad jogs and crooks revealed in the joining claim lines. In the Sommerville neighborhood there was found to be one strip unclaimed which was only two rods wide and nearly two miles long. Another unclaimed bit was only a few rods wide at one end and tapered down to nothing at the other and over a mile long. The early settlers, with neighbors few and far between often resorted to various schemes to live close together. One house built in the early days stood with its four corners on four different land sections. The house was divided into four rooms and four different men lived in it, each upon his own land. Two of the men were Paul Belts and Bob Rampy, but I have forgotten who the others were...

"...The town of Halsey where we did our trading in early days was quite a steamboat center at one time. The McCully family who lived here were pioneers in upper-river steamboating.

"Harrisburg was first called 'Crows Nest' and later Thurston. I can remember when the steamboats were running and at times there would be three commercial boats and a government snag boat tied up here all at one time. In the early days the boats coming to this part of the river did not usually stop at Harrisburg proper but at the old town of Lancaster just across on the Lane County side.

"Some of the boats which used to come to the upper river were the Elmore, Hogue, Gypsy, Isabell, and City of Eugene. One of the last boats to come up the river was the Mathaloma with Captain Hatch in command.

"In early days there was a flour mill on a slough near the Willamette about one and one half mile south of Harrisburg. Jim Brasfield, Cal Briggs and a man named Waters worked there at different times.

Some of the millstones were still on the ground there until recent years. The millers kept a great many hogs to feed and the place was called 'Hogem.' Some of the old waterwheels were moved from that old mill to McCreadie Springs. There was also another flour mill in Harrisburg. Part of that mill still stands. It was remodeled into a dwelling house by Art Tandy. It stood north of the present schoolhouse.

"The town of Irving formerly went under the name of 'Wellow Dog,' and the McCreadie Springs under the unsavory name of 'La Biche.'

"A small place which used to be quite a center of commerce was the town of Liverpool. It stood north of the town of Monroe in Benton County just where the road turns towards Alpine. At one time there was a grist mill at that place also. When it was dismantled, a part of the mill was brought to build the mill in Harrisburg."

"Harrisburg's Early Years" by Jo-Brew:

Taking snippets from the book, *Historic Harrisburg – A Little Town on the Willamette River*, written by Bess Tweedt, helps to paint the picture of Harrisburg's early years. The book, recently retrieved and now available through the Harrisburg Historical Museum, was written in 1994, and although the words below are my own, the information was gathered from Bess' work.

"In 1917, when war was declared with Germany, armed guards arrived to guard the railroad bridges and a call was sent out for volunteers to join the service. A draft was begun to call men to serve in the armed forces and to produce lumber for ships and planes. Women stepped up to provide some of the at-home labor, in the fields and other places they were needed. Then, the disease they called influenza spread through the troops; three of the young Harrisburg men were among the soldiers who died. A local chapter of the Red Cross was formed after a visit from national spokeswoman.

"The Harrisburg quota for war bond sales was reached and passed. Troop trains were passing through almost every day. The army was a major purchaser of potatoes that were grown in the area. Chautauqua programs in September 1918 included Red Cross presentations, and a special food conservation program as well as several musical programs. The Armistice was celebrated November 11, 1918, and veterans began returning home.

"January 1919 set a record-breaking cold snap. It was the same year the influenza epidemic hit Harrisburg the hardest. There was no snow, but it was so cold that glass windows broke. The ferry couldn't run because of ice floes in the Willamette River. North of town, it was frozen over

Irrigating pole beans. *From the collection of Jane Gavatte*

with ice so thick and strong that a horse with a wagonload of wood could be driven over it. This was proven repeatedly because some of the people had used up their winter's supply of wood in the severe cold. Business was at a standstill with the cold, and the school was closed. Teachers and pupils were ill with influenza. The school building was set up as an infirmary to take care of people with influenza. Whole families were sick, and in many homes, no one was able to keep the fires going or take care of the ill. Six members of one family died as well as a doctor, a popular contractor and others. Fifteen awaited burial at one time with no one well enough to dig the graves.

"The rich soil in the area led to diversified agricultural production over the years – beans, corn, berries, potatoes, ryegrass for seed, sheep, horses and cattle. In 1917 the Mint Growers Association was formed and mint is still a major crop in the area. Before Prohibition, the area was also a major producer of hops, but the market changed and powdery mildew had become a serious problem. That crop has never come back in a significant way.

"During World War I and after, wheat, flour, bales of hops and bags of wool were shipped north by sternwheelers from the Harrisburg landing. That mostly ended after about 1920 and the boats moved to the lower Willamette."

Detering Orchards

In 1934, Gerald and Marie Detering, started a small, 40-acre truck farm on rich river-bottom land near Harrisburg. It was right in the midst of the Great Depression and Gerald was a bookkeeper in a jewelry store, but it was a dream of both to have their own farm.

They began raising a large variety of fruits and vegetables including asparagus, blackberries, cabbages, carrots, muskmelons, rutabagas, rhubarb, turnips and peaches. Most of the crops were sold in nearby Eugene.

According to the Detering family, *"Gerald and Marie had four children and the Deterings increased the size of their farm with each birth. Gerald became involved in public service and was serving his fifth term in the Oregon House of Representatives when he died in 1970. Marie eventually handed the management of the farm over to her eldest son, Roger, but she continued to do the books for the farm until her death in the late 1980s."*

The size of the farm has increased to over 200 acres and it continues to be family-owned and operated by Roger's daughter, Becky, and son, Greig Detering. With the addition of its famous orchards, *"it is considered to be one of the largest diversified pre-pick/u-pick fresh fruit and vegetable farms in the Willamette Valley."*

Through World War II, Harrisburg remained a supply center for the war effort. For a time before the war and in the early war years, flax was in short supply and needed. The farmers were encouraged to grow and process flax to make linen. The processing was slow and labor intensive, so it wasn't a crop that grew to prominence, although ten drying operations were built in the area. Harrisburg had one and so did Monroe.

When the Japanese bombed Pearl Harbor and the United States declared war, the Harrisburg area was considered an important military route. The railroad and highway bridges over the Willamette were vital in getting troops and supplies from the north to Southern California where they could be shipped overseas. Protecting it was a top priority. On December 8, 1941, the soldiers from Company D of the 162nd Infantry were sent to Harrisburg to guard the bridges.

Morse Bros.

In the mid-1930s, Clinton and Lydia Morse bought a farm off of U.S. Highway 99 near Harrisburg. It bordered the Willamette River, but before they could move onto the property, the old farmhouse caught fire and burned down.

At the time, the family was living in Tangent, Oregon at the tail-end of the Depression. Clinton and their oldest son, Joe, operated a feed warehouse called C.F. Morse and Son. Using the already meager income from the business to rebuild the house that burned on their property in Harrisburg, the business, without any infusion of profits, failed. Father and son worked together to get some money coming in. By 1936, 24-year-old Joe took out a $1,000 loan, with some help from a family co-signer, and invested in an old 2½-yard dump truck. He spent his days hauling gravel for Linn County. His nights and weekends were spent digging shovelsful of gravel by hand out of the Willamette River next to their farm, filling the truck as best he could and selling the gravel to local farmers and contractors. Joe gathered discarded equipment from salvage yards wherever he could, and his efforts kept the family going through the Depression until the economy improved.

Both Clinton and Joe learned a hard lesson from their experience – one that has been retold over and over within the family – always reinvest into your business to allow it to grow.

By 1940, the local farmers had turned to growing flax because there was a immediate market for its use to produce parachutes for the impending war. Joe saw it as an opportunity to expand his gravel operation. Flax production plants had been proposed to be built in Harrisburg and gravel and concrete would be needed to build them.

He asked his brother Forrest, who was driving truck for the Linn County Road Department, to join him in establishing the Harrisburg Sand and Gravel Co. By early 1941, it was a reality.

Their younger brother, Bill, was a student at Oregon State College at the time, but he worked for the family business part-time on weekends and summer vacations. He then took a position at the Kaiser Shipyards on Swan Island in Portland and the Oregon State Highway Department for awhile, but joined his brothers in the sand and gravel business as a full partner in January 1943.

In 1945, a large project to rebuild U.S. Highway 99E as a military highway from Tangent to Harrisburg was proposed. This was the opportunity that the brothers had been waiting for. They were awarded the contract.

Clinton & Lydia Morse. *Courtesy of Pat Edwards*

The Linn County crushing pad near Lebanon, Oregon in 1917 before the Elmer Fitzgerald's Sand & Gravel bought it. It was then purchased by the Morse brothers in 1946. *Courtesy of the* Lebanon Express, *Russell C. Rose Collection*

In a December 15, 2013 *Albany Democrat Herald* article by Alex Paul, Joe's son, Frank Morse told how they did it:

"Dad haggled the contract down to the half-cent. He was proud of that. They sold 42,000 cubic yards of gravel at $1.12½ per yard."

To fulfill the contract, the Harrisburg Sand & Gravel Co. plant ran around the clock. Joe and Forrest ran the day shift and Bill oversaw the night-time crew.

By 1946, following the family's mantra of "reinvest in your business," Joe, Forrest and Bill decided it was time to expand. They bought Elmer Fitzgerald's Sand and Gravel in Lebanon that had been in business since 1917. The rock crusher was located on the Santiam River near the old Grove Street bridge. They repaired and rebuilt the old equipment themselves.

Bill was the engineer of the family who figured out how to keep old machinery running and how to build a new piece of equipment to meet any need.

Joe had a business acumen borne of his experiences during the Depression, and Forrest was the outgoing, social personality of the family. Together, their business grew.

In the *Albany Democrat-Herald* article, Frank Morse is quoted as saying, *"Instead of letting their differences pull them apart, they used their individual talents to become stronger. They settled disagreements by consensus, but they never voted two against one. They would continue talking about an issue until they reached an agreement they all could live with."*

After the purchase of the Lebanon business, Joe and Forrest moved there and Bill stayed in Harrisburg to oversee the home site.

In 1950, they changed the name of the business to Morse Bros., Inc.

According to their niece, Sandy Pierce, whose mother, Shirley, was one of the Morse sisters:

"Morse Bros. moved the rock crusher to the other side of the Santiam River in 1946. We had a farm house there by that time. The Strawberry Festival held some of its events on the old site after all the gravel plant and shop had been removed."

The business kept expanding and a good reason for that was the help and influx of other Morse family members into it. The Morse wives, Marjorie, Laura and Lois, took on bookkeeping duties; sons, daughters, nephews and nieces began working and filling many needed positions. Some originally hired on as part-time help ended up staying years with the company.

In 1958, the company branched out into developing and making prestressed concrete and it continued to open up new plants – Corvallis, 1961; Sweet Home, 1970; Eugene, 1976; Salem, 1986; and Beaverton in 1987.

The second generation of Morses, Mike, Greg and Frank, were working full time in the business by the late 1960s and eventually took over the reins from their fathers, Frank becoming chairman of the Board of Directors.

A hard decision was reached by the Morse family when, in 1998, it merged the business with Knife River. At the time of the merger, the company employed 550 people and owned more than 400 pieces of heavy equipment. It was the state's largest construction materials company.

In 2011, Morse Bros., Inc. was inducted into the Oregon State University's Engineering Hall of Fame.

After the war, Harrisburg and other communities in the flatlands of the valley along that stretch of Highway 99, developed a new

Bill, Joe and Forrest Morse standing next to their first 1942 cement mixer, 1987. *Courtesy of the Morse family*

and very profitable crop, grass seed. New homebuilding and landscaping, housing developments and remodeling projects have caused a high demand for quality grass seed all over the United States and the dominance of the crop – mainly varieties of ryegrass and fescue – has made the Willamette Valley the "Grass Seed Capital of the World."

According to Oregon State University statistics:

"Today, seed crops of over 950 varieties from eight grass species are grown on over 375,000 acres statewide. Of these, 347,000 acres are located in the Willamette Valley."

Another successful crop in the surrounding area is mint. Harrisburg's Lochmead Farm Peppermint Distillery is the largest of the five distilleries located in the Junction City/Harrisburg area. It processes the peppermint oil from the local harvests. For the two weeks of the mint harvest, the strong, pungent odor of peppermint permeates the air. The Lochmead family from Junction City, which also owns a large dairy and a chain of DariMart convenience stores, produces, in the Harrisburg facility, thousands of gallons of pure peppermint oil for use, not only in the popular ice cream it sells through DariMart, but much of it is sold and shipped out by the barrel for use in Colgate toothpaste and other mint-flavored products.

HALSEY

The Halsey area has been settled since the 1840s, before the Oregon & California Railroad was built through the town in 1871. The town took its name from William T. Halsey, who was, at the time, vice-president of the Oregon & California Railroad. The town plat was filed by Halsey and incorporation followed in 1876. The town became the shipping point for agricultural produce, replacing the steamboat landing at Peoria, some six miles west. Much of the farming in the area centered around wheat and, later, grass seed.

In the late 1800s, Halsey had a planing mill, a grange warehouse and a general store. Halsey State Bank was formed in 1910. It was later bought out by the Citizen's Valley Bank which eventually became part of Key Bank. The Halsey branch was eventually closed in 1997.

In 1936, the town built a new school which served as both high school and grade

Halsey's Main Street / U.S. Highway 99. *Courtesy of the Oregon Department of Transportation (ODOT) History Center*

Halsey, Oregon. *Courtesy of the Oregon Department of Transportation (ODOT) History Center*

school for many years until it consolidated with the Brownsville and Shedd school districts, forming the Central Linn School District in 1957. A new Central Linn High School was built about a mile east of Halsey in 1958, and the old Halsey school is now a middle school.

BOSTON / BOSTON MILLS / SHEDD'S STATION / SHEDD

In 1858, Richard Finley bought the water rights to the Calapooia River for $75. He and his associates then constructed a grist mill and laid plans for a flourishing community that they named Boston. They platted the town in 1861 with a New England-style town square. The town became a stagecoach stop and the Boston Mills post office was established in 1869. Other businesses were established and people came from other areas to settle in the village. But, efforts to get the Oregon & California Railroad, which was under construction south from Albany, to come through Boston Mills were unsuccessful.

Instead, in 1871, the railroad built through neighboring Shedd's Station, named after Captain Frank Shedd, the owner of the donation land claim where the community was sited. For this reason, the Boston Mills post office was moved to the Shedd site and renamed "Shedd's." Soon, all of Boston's other buildings except for the grist mill,

Downtown Shedd. *Courtesy of the Oregon Department of Transportation (ODOT) History Center*

were also moved west to be near the railroad. In 1899, the railroad changed the name of the station to Shedd, but the name of the post office didn't drop the "'s" until 1915.

Boston Flour Mill, on the Calapooia River, is Oregon's oldest continuously-operating water-powered mill and is now part of Thompson's Mills State Heritage Site and it welcomes visitors to tour the facility.

TANGENT

From the City of Tangent website:

"It is believed that the first people to inhabit the Tangent area were the Calapooia tribe of mound builders whose earthen mounds line the Calapooia River from Albany to Brownsville. When the first settlers arrived in the area, the Calapooia people used canoes as the primary means of transport and thrived on the rich natural abundance of the area as a fishing, hunting and gathering people."

"Tangent was established in 1871, when the railroad was built through the valley. The name 'Tangent' refers to the twenty miles of straight track north and south of town. The town was a gathering place for local farmers and a train stop. The first Grange hall in Oregon was completed in Tangent in July 1873. In 1886, Tangent acquired a post office. By 1891, William Felzer of Tangent acquired a small amount of grass seed. This may have been the actual beginning of the present-day rye-grass industry. Forest Jenks may have been the first commercial producer of rye-grass, when he began growing seed in 1922. The seed grown by Jenks was later cleaned at W.A. Vollstedt's seed-cleaning plant in Tangent. The seed was bought by Jenks White Seed Company that was instrumental in opening the eastern market for grass seed."

An old building with the name of the town on the roof. *From the Brew family collection*

Tangent, Oregon. *Courtesy of the Oregon Department of Transportation (ODOT) History Center*

Kitty Kat's red barn next to Tangent City Hall at the Bass Farm prepared to move to its new site. Courtesy of the City of Tangent

Tangent was incorporated in 1973 and the City Hall first located at the Community Center, but it later moved to a house on the John Bass Estate. When John Bass, a prominent grass seed grower, died, he bequeathed his estate to his cat named Kitty Kat. In his will, he left $70,000 for maintenance for not only Kitty Kat, but for the house and the big red barn, as well. A man who lived on the estate in a mobile home was given the job of staying on the property and taking care of the cat. The Tangent City Hall was then moved into the house where meetings were held once a month on Monday nights. The will also stated that when Kitty Kat died, the estate would be given to the city. Kitty Kat passed away at the age of 19 in 1993.

The $70,000 maintenance bequest eventually was used up and the large red barn on the property began to deteriorate. A proposed levy to repair and maintain it was defeated and no one wanted to buy it. Even the estimated $15,000 cost of tearing it down was more than the city could afford.

When it was decided that the only thing to do was to demolish the beautiful old red barn, Tangent resident, Beth Timmons, offered to buy it and move it to her property even though she already had three barns on it. She just could not allow it to be destroyed.

Kitty Kat and her caretaker in the 1980s. Courtesy of the City of Tangent

The City of Tangent sold it to her for $1 and helped her to obtain the permits needed to move it to her Circle of Life Farm. With her father's help, they hired a firm to prepare it for the move, jack it up on wheels and tow it across fields to her nearby property.

In its new home, Timmons plans to make it available to the people of Tangent as a community center. Their previous one which had, at one time been used as the Tangent City Hall, had been destroyed in a windstorm when a large tree fell on it.

The Jenks Century Farm

The Jenks family of Tangent, Oregon has owned the same land since 1866 when James Benton Jenks bought the 139-acre homestead from Charles and Lucy Ann Williams. In the past, wheat, oats, cheat, barley, cattle, hogs, horses, fruits and vegetables were raised there, but in 1910, Enoch Jenks established Jenks Hatchery, and it is now considered the oldest hatchery in the Pacific Northwest.

The farm has been increased in size to its present 215 acres and is run by Enoch's grandsons – cousins John and Larry Jenks. One of his great grandsons Aaron Jenks is joining the business, as well.

In 1969, the Jenks' farm was awarded Century Farm status and will soon qualify for Sesquicentennial status.

The Century Farm & Farm Ranch Program began honoring families with long connections to the land in 1958, the year before Oregon observed its own centennial. CF&R confers its coveted distinction in conjunction with the Agricultural Education Foundation, the Oregon Farm Bureau, the Oregon State Historic Preservation Office, the Oregon Travel Information Council, OSU Libraries and the Oregon Department of Agriculture.

To qualify for the award and certification, someone from the family has to have lived on the farm or managed it for the entire 100 years. It isn't easy to qualify. The applicant needs to have all of the documentation – photographs, deeds, etc. – showing residence and possession of the property to prove his/her claim.

To date, 1,117 Oregon families have formally received the "Century" designation and 22 families have received the "Sesquicentennial" award.

TAKENAH / NEW ALBANY / ALBANY

In 1845, Abner Hackleman filed the first donation land claim in the area of present-day Albany, Oregon, and asked an associate, Hiram N. Smead, to hold another claim for Hackleman's son who was scheduled to arrive the following year. Unfortunately, when Hackleman left for the family home in Iowa to bring back his family, he died, and Smead retained the claim in his own name. Hackleman's son, Abram, traveled to Oregon and took over his father's original claim and built a log cabin and eventually a large house. The community surrounding the property was known as Takenah which is a Calapooian word meaning "deep pool." It was well-sited at the confluence of the Calapooia and Willamette Rivers and was surrounded by rich valley farmlands.

In 1847, brothers Thomas and Walter Monteith from New York, arrived and acquired Smead's claim for $400 and a horse. In 1848, the Monteith's laid out the townsite which they named Albany after their hometown in New York instead of adopting the name Takenah that was being used on the neighboring Hackleman claim. The Monteith's section was later called New Albany, but was changed back to just Albany in 1855. In 1855, the rival communities of Takenah and Albany were combined by an act of the Territorial Legislature in spite of their different political philosophies.

According to the City of Albany's website on the history of the area:

"During this early period in Albany's history, the Monteith family and the

Hackleman family were literally and politically on opposite sides of the fence. Residents in the Monteith's portion of town were mainly merchants and professionals, consisting mostly of Republicans. They tended to sympathize with the Union during the Civil War. The residents from Hackleman's portion of town to the east were made up mostly of working class Democrats who sided with the Confederacy. The two sides even went so far as to plant a hedge separating the sides of town near Baker Street."

An excerpt from the book, *Oregon's End of the Trail, 1940*:

"Early Albany was the scene of many hard-fought political battles and was noted as the birthplace of the Republican Party in Oregon. On August 20, 1856, Free State men held a meeting and adopted a platform that included the bold declaration, 'Resolved, that we fling our banner to the breeze, inscribed, free speech, free labor, a free press, and Fremont.' February 11, 1857, delegates from eight counties assembled in Albany at a territorial convention and selected a committee to prepare an address on the slavery question which placed the issue squarely before the people for the first time. In the sixties, Southern sympathizers were numerous in the city and made themselves known vocally, and fistically, if occasion presented. During the stormy period of 1861, a cannon, mounted on the bank of the Willamette and used for local celebrations, was stolen and sunk in the river by "Joe Lane Democrats" to prevent the victorious 'Cayuse Republicans' from firing it as a triumphal gesture. The old howitzer lay in the river for almost 70 years, when it was dredged from the bottom and placed on exhibition by a local sand and gravel company."

The territorial convention held in Albany succeeded in introducing an anti-slavery bill to the people of Oregon, and at the beginning of World War II, the cannon was donated to the scrap-metal drive for the war effort.

In 1851, a gristmill was built, and in 1852, the steamship "Multnomah" first nosed into the muddy landing. Linked to markets by an Albany-based steamship service, Albany soon became a shipping center for grain, flour, woolen goods and pottery on the Willamette River. The steamships brought in sheep, cattle, kerosene and other needed supplies.

A post office was established in 1850. Albany was named the Linn County Seat in 1851, and a courthouse was built in 1853. The first schoolhouse was built in 1855, and the first church, in 1857. The first newspaper in the region, the *Oregon Democrat*, was established in November 1859.

The California & Oregon Stage Company made a stopover in Albany. The line also became the delivery system for Wells Fargo Bank.

The City of Albany was incorporated in 1863, and in 1867, Albany Collegiate Institute was founded and developed into the small Albany College. It moved to the Portland area in 1938 and became Lewis & Clark College in 1941. Lewis & Clark has since become the largest private college in Oregon.

After a $50,000 payment to bring the railroad to town rather than have it pass by a short distance away, Albany was connected to Portland by the Oregon & California Railroad in 1870 and developed as a minor railroad and industrial center along the route.

In 1880, the completion of a canal bringing drinking water and hydropower eighteen

The "Albany", a sternwheeler, on the Willamette River between 1896 (date the vessel was built) and 1906 (date the vessel was reconstructed and renamed Georgie Burton); 1910 postcard.
Courtesy of Wikimedia Commons

miles from the Santiam River to the growing city increased the city's growth. The canal was hand-dug and crossed through Lebanon, to the east, and across farmland to Albany. Once in Albany, the water flowed to the Water Treatment Plant at 3rd and Vine. Originally, the canal was planned for transporting goods to the Willamette River, but the current proved too swift for barges. The canal has been in continuous use since it was completed in 1912.

The railroad and the canal project brought 70-80 Chinese-born residents to the area. They occupied a one-block section of downtown during the construction.

Albany became a city of industry with foundries, blacksmith shops, furniture factories, tanneries, a bag factory, carriage factory, flour and flax mills, a twine factory, creameries and sawmills.

C&E Bridge across the Willamette at Albany.
Courtesy of Gerald W. Williams Collections, OSU Special Collections & Archives Commons

The city also became a connection center to other places. By 1910, 28 passenger trains departed from Albany daily, going in five different directions. The world's longest wooden railroad drawbridge was built in 1888 for the Albany-to-Corvallis run.

A woolen mill opened in 1889. Albany became a center for sheep raising, prune, hops and walnut growing and later, food processing plants.

Albany's first streetcar. Today's city buses have nothng over the early-day streetcars. Note the advertising on the side. *Courtesy of the Albany Regional Museum*

Congestion in Albany, Oregon ca 1910... a streetcar, bicycles, pedestrians, horses and buggies, cars, dogs... *Courtesy of the on-line Oregon Encyclopedia*

J.C. Banks 2nd Hand Store, Albany Oregon. Now, those were antiques! *Courtesy of the Albany Regional Museum*

Trains passing at the Albany railroad yard (date unknown). *Courtesy of the Albany Regional Museum*

World War II brought new growth to Albany when military contracts for lumber products added jobs, a trend that would continue during the post-war housing boom. The city also provided off-base housing for nearby Camp Adair, and became a center of shopping and entertainment for the camp personnel.

In the 1940s, the city started the Albany World Championship Timber Carnival which drew in competitors from all over the world to participate in logging skills contests. For many years, the Timber Carnival took place over the Fourth of July with men and women competing in climbing, chopping, bucking, and burling contests for four days. The declining timber economy and lower attendance caused the event to be discontinued after 2000.

In 1942, the U.S. Bureau of Mines established a research center on the old Albany College campus, focusing on the development of new metallurgical processes. First known as the Northwest Electro-Development Facility, the site produced titanium, hafnium and zirconium and fostered the growth of a new rare metals industry in Albany. That brought in internationally recognized companies like the Oregon Metallurgical Company and Wah Chang.

Albany has been a leader in the historic preservation movement in Oregon. A visitor can find excellent examples of small-town commercial and residential architecture in the 350 historic homes from the 1880s into the 1910s. Historic districts include the Thomas and Walter Monteith house, built in 1849 and the Hackleman house that still stands on the

The very popular Timber Carnival parade through downtown Albany. *Courtesy of the Albany Regional Museum*

The Calapooia River through Albany. Postcard. *Courtesy of OSU Archives Commons*

More advertising on an automotive service van, Albany. *Courtesy of the Albany Regional Museum*

The Albany Magnolia Laundry with their workers lined up outside. *Courtesy of the Albany Regional Museum*

corner of 5th and Jackson Streets. Albany also has the oldest Carnegie Library still being used.

The Amtrak Station was built of masonry in 1909 for the Southern Pacific Railroad and is one of the oldest, continuously-operating passenger stations in the country. It also has one of the best-equipped engine shops in the northwest and routinely has other historically important locomotives visit for repairs and restoration.

In 2004, the station and surrounding area underwent a restoration and now serves the Amtrak long-haul train, Coast Starlight, route from Los Angeles to Seattle and the Amtrack commuter trains between Vancouver, British Columbia and Eugene, Oregon several times daily in each direction. The proposed Pacific Northwest high-speed rail line would also use the Albany station.

In 1920, a privately-owned airport was opened and then purchased by the City of Albany. It is the oldest-known operating general aviation airfield in Oregon and has a single asphalt runway. There are 58 aircraft based at the airport and an average of 62 aircraft operations a day. It has also been the site of air shows through the years and annually hosts the Northwest Art and Air Festival.

Albany also became known for its Veterans Day parade each November. It's the largest and most well-known Veterans Day parade in the state. It honors military veterans from all over the nation with a deep reverence and respect and is always well-attended.

BUSINESS BLOCKS, ALBANY, OREGON.

Section 8

U.S. HIGHWAY 99E - ALBANY TO SALEM

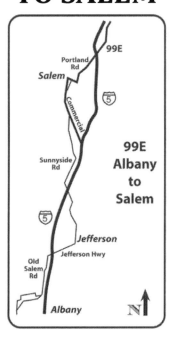

From Albany toward Salem on Highway 99E, the road heads north on Salem Avenue which becomes Old Salem Road. The route takes a left turn where the sign says "To Millersburg," and crosses the tracks through the Murder Creek Underpass.

MILLERSBURG

One of Oregon's newer towns, Millersburg was incorporated in 1974, apparently as a means to prevent the City of Albany from adding Teledyne Wah Chang, the community's largest employer, to its tax roles.

For many years, approaching travelers closely identified the Millersburg area, north of Albany, by its unique sulphurous odor – some called it a "stench;" others referred to it as the "smell of money" – associated with the Western Kraft paper mill. It was owned by Weyerhaeuser Corporation and it sat along U.S. Highway 99E and later, Interstate 5. Much of the blame for the odor was incorrectly attributed to the nearby Teledyne Wah Chang zirconium processing plant operated by the Bureau of Mines, but it was, in fact, Western Kraft.

In 2008, after 55 years of operation, Western Kraft, was purchased by International Paper Company as part of a $6 billion deal for several of its container-board and box plants. The Millersburg mill was closed down in 2009 due to a downturn in the demand for office paper, consumer packaging and cardboard boxes. In addition, the Millersburg facility had aging equipment that would have had to be replaced. At the time of the closure, 270 employees were laid off. The closure made a huge impact on the whole area's economy.

According to a December 16, 2009 KATU television news report:

"The final day of production for the International Paper plant signaled the end of a way of life for generations of families."

The mill stood idle for a couple of years, and in July 2012, International Paper arranged to have the mill's iconic boiler tower that sat along I-5, imploded. The event was scheduled for 8:00 a.m. on a Sunday morning and traffic on Interstate 5 was halted for the 10 minutes that it took for the building to come down.

JEFFERSON

Mrs. Elma West Blanchard, interviewed in the late 1930s for the Benton County, Oregon *WPA's American Life Histories Collection: Manuscripts from the Federal Writer's Project, 1936-1940* project:

"My parents were both born in England. My father, Ashby West, came to Oregon first about 1850. Then he returned and brought his parents over in 1852. It is my understanding that they came to Oregon by water, but I do not know whether they came around the Horn, or by way of the Isthmus of Panama.

"At that time in England, children of the poorer people were often bound out at a very tender age. My mother, Anna Scott, was bound to her future mother-in-law as a traveling companion. She was nine years old at the time. Later she grew up and married the son of her mistress.

"With my father came his brother William West who was a preacher and doctor. He rode on horseback and preached all over Marion County. Later he had a drug store at Jefferson. The site of the town then was a mile or so below the present location. Because the old townsite was on the lower river bottoms and overflowed frequently, the new location was chosen on higher ground.

"Father took a claim about one mile north of Jefferson. This was covered by timber and brush and had to be cleared. Father raised grain on this farm.

"My parents had five children: Albert, Edna, myself, Homer and Alice. Edna is dead but the others are all living within forty miles of the old home place.

"I went to school at Jefferson and remember among the teachers there, Mrs. Peel and Mr. Barzee. I studied only reading, arithmetic, writing and geography. I did not get much education.

"I married [Mr.] Blanchard and we lived on farms in different parts of the upper Willamette Valley. My husband died a few years ago. Our children were Gilbert, Elma (Mrs. York) and Warren."

Emigrant settlers arrived in the Jefferson area by 1840. In 1851, Jacob Conser established a ferry on the north bank of the Santiam River near the site of the future town of Jefferson. The residents of the area established a private academy they called Jefferson Institute in 1856 as the first school. The Jefferson Post Office, located in Marion County, was established in 1861.

In an interview for the *WPA's American Life Histories Collection: Manuscripts*

from the Federal Writer's Project, 1936-1940 project, Mrs. Frances Cornell, daughter of Jesse Looney, told about the staging business at Looney Station. Her interviewer was Sara B. Wrenn and it took place on January 24, 1939:

"When the mail route was established between Portland and San Francisco by the California Stage Company, my father's farm was used as the first stage station south of Salem. It took seven days to go from Sacramento to Portland, with the stages travelling continuously day and night, the relay stations, where they changed their horses being about fifteen miles apart. First, after Portland, was Oregon City, then Aurora ("Dutch Town"), Salem, Looney's, Albany and two farmhouses between there and Eugene. Some of the relay points farther south were farmhouses near the present Grants Pass, Grave Creek, Phoenix ("Gasburg"), Jacksonville, Ashland. The stages used were of the heavy Concord type, with four to six horses being necessary where the road was hard-pulling – as most of the roads were in those days... Sometimes at the relay stations it became necessary to use unbroken horses, and that was exciting for everybody, most of all the passengers... The horses were tied, blindfolded and harnessed. The driver clutched the lines as the passengers scrambled willy nilly into the swaying vehicle, the blindfolds were snatched off, and away they

Jefferson's Conser Bridge built by Conde McCullough. *From the Brew family collection*

Southern Pacific and wagon bridge over the Willamette River in Jefferson, Oregon. *Courtesy of the Gerald W. Willaims Collection, OSU Archives Commons*

went, the stage swaying from side to side, the horses plunging, until the driver finally wore them down.

"As the incoming stage drove down the hill to the Looney station, the driver blew his horn once for each passenger on board. The number of toots indicated the number of eggs to fry and biscuits to bake. There is a marker now at the old farm, on the highway now known as Route 99E, showing where the stage horses used to drink."

According to *Emigrants to Oregon in 1843*, Jesse Looney and his wife, Ruby Crawford Bond, had 15 children. He was the first cousin to President Andrew Johnson and was raised on a plantation in Tennessee.

"In the 1850s, his farm was an official stop for the California & Oregon stage coach line. He developed one of the largest orchards in his part of the territory, was active in helping to build churches and schools, was a member of the Cumberland Presbyterian Church, and served as a member of the Provisional Legislature."

In 1870, the Oregon & California Railroad built southward through Jefferson toward Roseburg and the town was incorporated in the same year. The Jefferson Institute was used until a public school was established in Jefferson in the 1890s.

By 1915, a creamery, a flour mill and two sawmills were operating and the farmers grew wheat, hops, potatoes and fruit.

The beautiful 1933-era, concrete Jacob Conser arch bridge over the Santiam River, designed by famed bridge architect, Conde McCullough, drops the traveler into downtown Jefferson with a stoplight and left turn onto Main Street.

Jefferson Highway was the U.S. Highway 99E routing until 1946, and paralleled the Oregon Electric Railway tracks, which were built in 1912, for several miles.

Among businesses listed in an old directory were the Miller & Caldwell Hop Yards, a prune dryer, a turkey ranch and, during World War II, the Jefferson Flax Plant.

Jefferson seems to be a city that loved parades. A 1883 parade featured a horse-drawn wagon called the Victory Car. In 1915, the town had its own Rose Festival Parade with the city band participating. In 1949, there was a May Day parade, but many of the celebrations centered around its famous mint-production by the mid-1950s. Jefferson is also the self-proclaimed "Mint Capital of the World" as well as the "Frog Jumping Capital of Oregon."

During the 1970s, a pizza parlor that featured Dixieland Music by popular bands drew followers from all over the state.

On Main Street, Jacob Conser's 1854-vintage Greek Revival-style house is a landmark listed on the National Register of Historic Places. It now houses the Jefferson Public Library and City Hall.

The original Pacific Highway bridge over the Santiam River was replaced in 1933 although remnants of the road leading to the old bridge are visible on both sides of the river. Also on Main Street with other businesses is a restaurant now called the 99 Café. It was once the Greyhound bus terminal and had a motel attached to it. It was referred to as "The Terminal."

Gene Jones tells of his own recollections of "The Terminal"... the Jefferson Greyhound Bus Depot:

"Of all the memories that I have of The Terminal, two stand in the forefront. For two years I delivered The Oregonian

The Terminal, Jefferson, Oregon. *Courtesy of Mike Barnes & Ellis Hamby on Gene Jones' Jefferson Chronicles website*

to customers from one end of Jefferson to the other. I picked up my papers at The Terminal about 5:00 am every morning. As long as my bicycle was functioning, I could finish my rounds in a little less than two hours. I covered a lot of territory. My route took me through town via Main Street, across the railroad tracks and out a few blocks past Callihan's Corner. On the return route I delivered papers to customers on the north side of Jefferson-Scio Road. The Terminal was a very convenient place to take a break before heading for the north end of town. But it was also my dietary downfall. Most people might not relish a pineapple sundae at 6:30 am. And not just one, but often two; and on very special occasions, I inserted a strawberry sundae between the two pineapple sundaes. My favorite drink at the time was Grapette and, on occasion, Lemonette. At twenty or twenty-five cents a sundae and five cents for the Grapette, I spent half of my daily paper route earnings at The Terminal before I even finished my deliveries.

"During the summer of 1948, I became a short-term run-away. I purchased a ticket to Doris, California from the agent at The Terminal. I'll bet you have no idea where Doris, California is located. I didn't either with one important exception; I knew that it was the first Greyhound bus stop on the south side of the Oregon-California border. To make my run-away authentic, I reasoned, I had to travel beyond the Oregon border. A week later, having slept on park benches too many nights in the interim, I stepped off of a Greyhound bus at The Terminal, a few pounds lighter and much more appreciative of the support provided by my parents and family."

Heading north from Jefferson, Highway 99E and the railroad part company. The tracks swing northeast and find a nearly level grade into Salem. The highway takes to the hills and winds and climbs over several ridges before reaching the more level Salem plain, a route more difficult on which to build, but some three miles shorter.

The shorter passage may have been the reason for selecting the hilly route, but another might be because of Jesse Looney.

Looney, a member of the Provisional Legislature, was appointed in 1848 to be one of the Commissioners in charge of selecting the official stage route south from Salem. He arranged to have the wagon road run through his land claim on Looney Butte.

Looney developed a stagecoach stop with facilities where he and his family, with thirteen children, could provide lodging, food,

Main Street, Jefferson, Oregon looking north. *Courtesy of Mike Barnes & Ellis Hamby on Gene Jones' Jefferson Chronicles website*

Jefferson Ferry crossing the Santiam River. *Courtesy of Mike Barnes & Ellis Hamby on Gene Jones' Jefferson Chronicles website*

Another view of the Jefferson Ferry crossing the Santiam River. *Courtesy of Mike Barnes & Ellis Hamby on Gene Jones' Jefferson Chronicles website*

hay for horses and fruit for travelers. His family had planted one of the first large orchards in the valley, as well. In 1856, he also helped to organize Jefferson Institute, a public school that any child could attend, but it was officially a private school since it was supported only by tuition and donations.

In an interview on January 18, 1939 for the Works Progress Administration (WPA) Folklore Studies, Mrs. Frances Cornell told her story:

Mrs. Cornell was born the daughter of the early pioneer Jesse Looney near Jefferson, Oregon in 1864. She attended public schools in Jefferson and Willamette University in Salem. For a number of years she was a Matron at the Oregon State Hospital for the Insane.

"...As I have already said, I was born here in Marion County. My father and mother, came to Oregon from Alabama in 1843. They came in the same train with the Applegates, the Waldos, Nesmiths, Smiths, Fords, Kaisers, Delaneys, Lovejoy, and many others who became prominent in Oregon history. My people were opposed to slavery. They had six children when they left Alabama. Six more children were born to them in Oregon, of which I am one. They objected to bringing up their children where slavery existed. Their wagon train left Independence, Missouri, on May 22, 1843, and they arrived in the Walla Walla Valley in October of that year. Indian troubles were threatening when they reached the Whitman Mission, and they left hastily for Fort Vancouver, where Doctor McLoughlin extended his usual gracious hospitality. From there, on specially constructed rafts, they left for up the Willamette River, and father eventually selected his claim of 640 acres in the Chepulcum valley, 12 miles south of Salem, known generally as Santiam Valley. Chepulcum, in the Indian language means 'Beautiful Valley.' Father's 640 acres embraced what has long been known as Looney Butte, where his family was brought up and four of his sons maintained their homes until death came.

"My mother was the first white woman in Chepulcum Valley. Shortly after settlement in Oregon, mother was invited by the Waldos to a wedding at their place over in the Waldo Hills, as they came to be called. Mother went, expecting to enjoy quite a gala affair. She was out in the kitchen with Mrs. Waldo, when the young people's arrival was announced. Mother was a little disappointed in the lack of preparation, but still looked forward to something of what she had always associated with a wedding. When somebody called 'Come quick, they're getting married,' she got into the front room just in time to hear Mr. Waldo say, 'I pronounce you man and wife, by God.' Mr. Waldo had the authority through some source to perform marriage ceremonies, but he hadn't had much experience, and those few words were all he could think to say. Mother never did get over that."

"We used to have a lot of fun up here, around Salem, when I was a girl. Nobody was extremely rich, but nobody seemed very poor either. We all seemed to have comfortable homes, with plenty of room for entertaining, and there was much hospitality. Perhaps because we were a big family of young people, our home was always open house for everybody, and the young folks of Salem thought nothing of the twelve-mile drive out home, even

though the roads were a far cry from what they are now.

"There was a time in the [18]70s, I think it was, when what might be called the society of the capital and countryside went in strong for masquerade parties. There was one, I recall, given by the Werner Breymans, in their big house on State [street?]. There were over a hundred masquers at that affair, and the costumes covered everything from kings, cardinals and dukes to jockeys, among the men, and from Dianas to Bopeeps among the women and girls. If I remember correctly, I represented Phantasia.

"Along about this time we had a fancy-dress party at Jefferson, the town adjoining us, which we Looneys rather felt we owned, there were so many of us living thereabout. We had a band out from Salem to furnish the music, and everything was done up in grand style. Here's a clipping from some paper, that I have saved all these years, about that party, part of which you might like to copy:

"'The party broke up shortly after one o'clock, and the Band was invited to partake of refreshments and spend the balance of the night at Mr. Thompson's, the mayor of the city. The proceeds more than paid all expenses, and the ladies went home happy. 'A word to the wise is sufficient', and I trust that the following criticism will be taken and appreciated by those to whom it is due:

"'The ladies have been very justly offended at the conduct of two or three young men at the parties this season, who make a practice of going out into the entry during the intervals of dancing, and smoking cigars, until the air coming through two open doors is thick with tobacco smoke, which is not only disgusting, but sickening, to some of the ladies, and the wraps hanging in the entry do not lose the offensive odor for days afterward. Now, the ladies think and say that if any gentlemen is so wedded to his cigar that it is impossible for him to spend a few hours in their society without smoking, that he would better stay at home altogether, or at least take a walk in the open while he indulges in the deadly narcotic. Mr. Editor, I desire to ask you a question for information. Is it considered just the thing in the best society of Oregon, for a

A bus traveling on Pacific Highway north of Jefferson, Oregon. *Courtesy of the Oregon Department of Transportation (ODOT) History Center*

Jefferson, Oregon train station. *Courtesy of Mike Barnes & Ellis Hamby on Gene Jones' Jefferson Chronicles website*

Sunnyside Grade School, 1925. UO Libraries Archives Commons

gentleman to catch a lady around the waist and hug her while he swings her in a quadrille, and is it tolerated by the ladies of Salem?'

"I forgot to say that this party was one given by the ladies, so it must have been in a leap year."

The old Highway 99E winds through the rural countryside, coming out at Interstate 5's Exit 244. The earliest highway is found by crossing the freeway to Sunnyside Road turning north toward Salem, but that route was changed in approximately 1938.

SUNNYSIDE

Sunnyside, now part of Salem, Oregon, was once a small, independent, unincorporated community. It was an agricultural area where prune orchards were first planted in 1890. They were developed by the Oregon Land Company sometime before 1900.

"John Minto Was a Pioneer Who Knew How to Cultivate the Land" by Scott Bassett. Special to the *Statesman Journal*, April 2, 1911:

"John Minto was a pioneer who arrived in Oregon by wagon in 1844 and the acres he planted in orchard gave him a deep sense of satisfaction during his lifetime.

"He and his family initially homesteaded in the Sunnyside/Battle Creek area outside Salem, and he, along with many other Willamette Valley men, spent time in the California gold fields in 1849.

"Upon his return to Salem, he became a successful apple grower and merchant, selling apples in Portland and as far away as the California mining camps. In 1867 he bought property along the Willamette River near town, where he planted fruit trees and raised Merino sheep. Eventually he served four terms in the Oregon Legislature and is credited with being key in bringing the state fair to Salem."

SALEM / CHEMEKETA

Sunnyside Road merges with Commercial Street upon entering the Salem. The most commonly-used route now, however, is to enter the freeway at Exit 244 and exit at Commercial Street, Exit 249. This was the entrance to Salem until the early 1950s when the Salem Bypass, now Highway 99E / I-5, was completed.

To follow the earlier route, stay on Commercial Street until it becomes one-way, then continue north on Liberty, turn right on Court, and then left on Capital to Portland Road.

Salem is the Oregon State Capital as well as the Marion County Seat. It is situated along the Willamette River which runs north through the city and is the dividing line between Polk County on the west and Marion on the east. The city neighborhood of West Salem is actually in Polk County.

Our research wasn't able to locate a stage stop in the Salem area, but the obituary of one of the stage line's first drivers, L.C. Scovell, published in 1905, tells an interesting story.

"In 1856, while driving the stage on the Oregon City-Corvallis line, he had a thrilling adventure with highwaymen. He was driving from Jefferson to Salem at night, and had a number of passengers, who as was the custom, carried considerable sums of money. The robbers had planned to hold up the stage at the top of Jackson's hill, the summit of the range of hills south of Salem, on the Jefferson road. From the top of the hill there is a long, steep grade toward Salem. Just as the horses turned around a curve in the road at the crest of the hill, two masked men sprang into the road on either side of the stage. "Hold up!" was the command, but taking in the situation at a glance, Scovell swung his great whip back, cutting one robber across the face, and the next instant had cracked the lash over his leaders. The four horses dashed at a breakneck speed down that mile of heavy grade and did not stop their gallop until they neared the city. The passengers guessed the cause of the mad race and patiently endured such a shaking up and they never had before or since. But for Scovell's prompt and daring action all would have been relieved of their money. Had the robbers chosen a spot at the beginning of the ascent the stage could not have escaped."

The Scovell obituary included two other stories about his adventures with driving stages in this area.

"...Scovell related two stories of hard drives made at the request of men who were of no small importance in Oregon affairs at the time. In 1868 ... trains ran only as far as Lake Labish, five miles north of Salem. Ben Holladay was the owner of the road. He had important interests awaiting the action of the legislative assembly of that year, and came up to Salem to see that the members of that august body were fully advised upon questions of public moment. It happened that a number of his opponents came up on the same train with Holladay and his friends, and the opposing faction had each a desire to be the first to reach Salem. As soon as the train stopped at Labish, both parties alighted and Old Ben sought out Scovell with the request that his party be driven to Salem in time to beat the other crowd.

"Scovell undertook the task, and started on the drive with Holladay on the seat beside him. Scovell said: 'Holladay patted me on the back and told me to put the horses through if every one of them dropped in his tracks. He said we must beat the other fellows, and he would pay for any injury to the horses. When we got nearly up to Salem he kept urging me on, and said if I beat the other fellows I should have a free pass over that railroad as long as there should be a rail left of it. My horses came in ahead, and it didn't kill them either.'

"'Ben gave me the pass as he agreed, but I never got a chance to use it until the road got down as far as Salem in 1870. After I had been driving here in Salem about six months I took a day off and went down to Portland. When the conductor came around I gave him the pass. He looked at it pretty closely, punched it and gave it back. On the trip back, the conductor took my pass and said that it had expired and that he would keep it. I told him: 'No, you don't! That is my pass, and you give it back.' He would not, and I made for him in a hurry. I would have killed that conductor if some of the passengers hadn't held me. He kept the pass and the next time I saw Ben Holladay I told him I wanted him to keep his promise. He laughed and said he would fix it after the next legislature, but he never did. That's the kind of man he was.'

The newspaper article went on with the story:

"Old Cal's eyes snap when he tells of that conductor who took away the testimonial of his efficient service, and though the conductor probably obeyed his instructions, he may be thankful he did not have his battle to fight alone on that eventful day 21 years ago. Old Cal did not like the treatment he received and has not been over the road since.

"But fond recollection presents to Old Cal's view pleasanter incidents than his experience with Ben Holladay. During one session of the Legislature a messenger was sent to H.W. Corbett, at Portland, requesting that he come immediately to the capital. The message was delivered late in the evening. Mr. Corbett, then a storekeeper, hunted up Cal Scovel, and inquired whether the drive to Salem could be made that night. Cal says: 'I told him If he wanted to go to Salem I would take him there. It was a dark, stormy night, but we started and drove into Salem before the Legislature met next morning. Corbett told me during our ride that if I got him through all right he would pay me $15 a month extra as long as I drove on the stage. And he did it. I drew my salary every pay day with the rest of the boys, and then I went down to the store and got my $15 extra. Corbett treated me white, he did, just as he always does everybody.'"

The open landscape, fertile soil and Mill Creek, a source of water power, were all reasons why the site was chosen for the location of Jason Lee's Methodist Mission in 1834. The goal of the mission, sponsored by the Methodist Episcopal Church, under Jason Lee's leadership, was to convert the Native Americans in the area to Christianity. It was first located in Mission Bottom, about 10 miles north of Salem, but illness and deaths among the Native Americans became a tragic consequence.

According to *Chronicles of Willamette* by Gatke and Gregg, 1943:

"In the first year, there were fourteen Indian students in the mission school. Seven of these students died and five ran away. In 1836, there were twenty-five Indian students and sixteen died. One of the surviving Indians converted to Christianity. Indians in the Willamette Valley were dying at a horrendous rate. Retrospectively, it appears that this might have been due to new diseases unwarily brought to the area by the new immigrants. In 1841, serious flooding resulted in relocation of

Jason Lee's Methodist Mission, ca 1834. *Courtesy of Gaston's "The Centennial History of Oregon."*

the community and the Manual Labor School from Mission Bottom to the Chemeketa site within present day Salem."

Among his other interests, Jason Lee built a sawmill. His house and several other buildings are now open to the public on the grounds of the Willamette Heritage Center, near the corner of 14th and Ferry Streets.

By 1843, the Rev. George Gary replaced Jason Lee and he soon closed most of the Mission branches. After the mission failed, the Methodists decided to lay out a town and sell lots to establish the Oregon Institute, a literary and religious institution of learning. It was to emphasize the schooling of white children emigrating to the area and was the forerunner of Willamette University, chartered in 1845.

Excerpts from the Biography of J. Henry Brown obtained for the Works Progress Administration (WPA) Folklore Studies with permission to copy granted by Miss Nettie Spencer, 1938:

"*About the middle of October 1847, we arrived in Salem, thus finishing our long-journey of over 2000 miles across the American continent. Salem at that time was a missionary town, that is, had been laid out a short time previously by the missionary Board, and was the seat of protestant education, and only contained three or four houses. My grandfather opened his store, the first ever there and soon had a thriving business, taking for pay goods, the currency of the inhabitants – wheat at the value of one dollar per bushel. For groceries he went to Oregon City, the then emporium of Oregon, making most of his purchases of Dr. John McLoughlin, and when that good old man was told that he had brought his store across the plains, his astonishment knew no bounds, it seemed so incredible that for a time he was inclined to doubt the statement.*

"*...I will now revert to a subject that should have been mentioned before. When I came to Oregon, there were no mail facilities whatever. We only received newspapers by the Missionary ships once a year, and letters from friends by emigrants* across the plains, and the war with Mexico had been closed some six months before we heard of it. It generally required two years to write and receive a letter and then we paid 50 cents to have the letter carried to the first postoffice in Missouri by persons returning to the States. When the P.M.S.S. Co. established their line and crossed the Isthmus, we hailed it as one of the remarkable achievements of the day; we were then able to hear from our friends once every three months. The next great step was the overland mail and telegraph, and finally the completion of the continental railroad, the acme probably of human progress, and now if there should be a delay of a few days of a severe blockade, what a howl is set up, conclusively showing the perverseness of human character at a momentary delay. The first U.S. Mail that was ever received in Salem was three days coming from Oregon City on a keel boat, and the day it left that place a gentleman came through on horseback and told the good news, consequently we were all excitement until it arrived."

From *Salem Directory for 1871* by J. Henry Brown:

"In the summer of 1848, Thomas Cox, an immigrant of 1847, who came by the Barlow route, brought in a small stock of drygoods, and engaged in merchandizing, the first in Salem, Oregon during the winter of (1847-8). He selected the northeast corner of Commercial and Ferry streets in Salem and built a two-story house upon it, which was used by him as a store and a dwelling during the time of his residence in Salem. His was the first building put up in Salem after the town was surveyed. Afterward a two-story house built by Thomas Powell, blacksmith, about one block west from Commercial street was removed and placed in the rear of the one built by Thomas Cox. These two were united and formed the Union Hotel which was burned with nearly all the buildings in that block. A few years since J. B. McClane had goods brought from California gold mines in May 1849, goods from San Francisco costing about $2,500 which in a few months sold for $6000 cash in hand still leaving a considerable portion of them on hand. This was the second stock of goods opened in Salem."

In an interview on January 12, 1939 for the Works Progress Administration (WPA) Folklore Studies, Mr. Harvey Gordon Starkweather told his story:

"...Now, as to the story of the State Seal. It was designed by my uncle, Harvey Gordon... Harvey Gordon was eighteen when he set forth for Oregon in '46. Young as he was, he was well educated, considered a master mathematician. He had been sent to private schools, and had had special training as a surveyor and draughtsman. Big and husky, he was studious and serious, and very determined. Careful of his cattle, all the way across the plains, he was never known to ride the wagon-tongue, but grim, grimy and dirty, he strode in the dust at his oxen's side, his whip in his hand.

"When the party left Missouri, Oregon's boundary line was still in dispute. The treaty was signed on June 15th, 1846, and none of them knew as they plodded along whether their journey's end would be in America or British territory. It must have given them considerable food for thought.

"I have reviewed all this so as to show something of the trend of thought of the young man, possibly, when at the age of 29, he was commissioned to draw the first seal of the State of Oregon – caused him to give thought, and place in his drawing the departing sailing vessel of the English, as England's dominion withdrew from Oregon's shores, while America's arriving steamship symbolized the new, and imme-

The Oregon State Seal

diately after there must have sprung to mind the picture of the covered wagon, with that long trudge beside it in his memory. The elk, with its 'haunching' antlers, was a noble example of our then-abundant game, and what could be more typical, by 1857, of Oregon's agricultural possibilities than the plow and the rake and sheaf of wheat. As to the pick-axe, I am inclined to think that was added because it was close to Harvey Gordon's heart. In '48 he went to California and dug out a fortune, and a second time he went there and picked out a fortune in the gold mines. Gold hadn't yet been discovered in Oregon. The thirty-three stars, of course, represent the thirty-three states, Oregon making the thirty-third. The ordinary bearing across its face. 'The Union,' as Oregon's motto ('She flies with her own wings' being the territorial rather than the State motto) reveals Harvey Gordon's strong feeling on the question of slavery and sedition, growing of more and more paramount national interest. Though his ancestry was southern, both he and his people were all for an undivided country.

"The seal as designed was adopted by the Oregon Constitutional Convention, at 2 p.m., of the afternoon session, September 18, 1857 (see page 99 of that year's Journal), and the story I have given you as to the motivating influences of Harvey Gordon in creating the design, is the story as known to his family and descendants, of which I am a member..."

When Oregon became a territory in 1849, Salem got a post office and was selected as the territorial capital which had previously been in Oregon City.

However, a conflict between the Democrats and Republicans and dissatisfaction with the accommodations for legislators caused a delay in the changeover involving one legislative session where the governor and several of his party refused to leave Oregon City for Salem. Another session was held in Corvallis before the Comptroller of the U.S. Treasury settled the conflict by refusing to release funds for the Capitol building or other public buildings to be located anywhere but Salem. When Oregon was admitted to the union as a state in 1859, Salem continued as the State Capital.

The townsite was platted in 1850 and 1851. It's believed that it was named for the city in Massachusetts. The name, "Salem," is derived from the Semitic word for peace.

The first Capitol building, a wooden frame structure, was built in 1855 and burned to the ground after it had been occupied for only two months. Arson was suspected. The members of the state government met in various buildings around town for several years.

The Oregon State Capitol, ca 1920. Postcard. *Courtesy of the OSU Special Collections & Archives Commons*

The first stage of a permanent State Capitol building was erected in 1876, and finished in 1893. This second Capitol also burned in 1935, and was replaced by the current Capitol building with its barrel rotunda and Pioneer statue in 1938. Several surrounding homes were moved to give more space for other state buildings.

In an interview on March 27, 1939 for the Works Progress Administration (WPA) Folklore Studies, Frank E. Coulter told his story:

Mr. Coulter was described by his interviewer, Sara Wrenn, as a minister of the United Brethern Church and the maker of stringed instruments. She said that he was *"especially interested in political and economic questions dealing with humanitarianism."*

[Frank Coulter] *"Now, I'm going to tell you some stories of Oregon laws. This one is about the Initiative and Referendum. Away back in 1885, there was a man running a newspaper in Albany, Oregon, named John W. Roark. He was a strong believer in real democracy; that the people of a democracy should do things directly. He had a good, strong voice and was a pretty good orator. So he sold his paper, bought a wagon and a pair of cayuses, and with his wife and two children started out to convert the State. For the next four years he visited every section of Oregon, preaching the gospel of direct primaries, and for the peoples' control. It was a political question for both parties. Then a man named Nelson, a painter in Portland, became a zealot in behalf of the measure. Once when the two political parties each had their convention in Salem at the same* time, he played one against the other. He made them believe that each had to beat the other to it. Finally Roark, Nelson and Mrs. (Henderson) Lewelling, got together and formulated a law that they introduced to the legislature. That was when U'ren stepped into the picture. Later, when submitted to the people, the measure carried and became a law. But it was Roark, who died in 1891, who may truthfully be said to be the father of Oregon's Initiative and Referendum Act.

"Now as to the Parole Law. Judge Henry McGinn (on the circuit bench of Oregon from 1910 to 1916), was a warm personal friend of mine. Whenever he was disturbed over some question he would come in here and talk it over. Sometimes he would get so excited he would jump up, prance around the room and shed half his clothes; while he cussed and slapped his hands together. He had a great habit of slapping his hands. In 1909 there was an old gentleman and his wife in Portland, named Henderson. They had two sons in Alaska, and one of the boys came home, bringing gold dust to the amount of $700.00, which he turned over to his father to pay off a mortgage for that sum on their home. As the old man was going down town to pay the mortgage he was robbed by a young fellow with a gun. Well, the money was gone, he couldn't get in touch with his sons, and it looked like the old folks were going to lose their home after all. But the very next day, after the robbery, a prostitute in the old Paris House, at 4th and Couch streets, called the Police Department and reported that a young fellow, drunk and with a lot of money was at her place, and for the police to come and get him. The police got him all right, but he only had a little of the money left. Three weeks later the young robber went to trial. When Henry came in then he had the worst spasm of all. He raved and swore. The boy was going to prove guilty and there was nothing to do but send him to the penitentiary. But what good was that going to do anybody? It wouldn't save the old people's home, and it would probably mean the boy's eternal ruination. I took my apron off and sat down facing the judge.

"'Now, Judge,' I said, 'haven't I read somewhere that a circuit judge can make the law? If that's the case, if I were you, I'd make a little law. Give the boy the limit, and hold the commitment over him till he pays that money back; and then tear the commitment up.'

"The Judge cussed something awful. 'There ain't no law for that,' he yelled.

"'To hell with the law,' [sez?] I.

"'Yes,' sez he, 'You'd have the guts to do it, law or no law.'

"Well, the case went before the judge; the prosecuting attorney did his stunt, and the lawyer for the defense put in a plea of guilty.

"I can hear McGinn snort now, as he delivered sentence, which in effect was: 'You can't escape that way. That was a cold-blooded robbery that deserves the limit of a 25-year sentence to the penitentiary.'

"The court was aghast. Then the Judge continued, "Your going to the penitentiary won't help these old people to keep their home. But with that sentence hanging over you, you can undertake payments on the mortgage so as to stop foreclosure proceedings, and you can keep on doing that until the mortgage release is in my hands.'

"At that, the father of the boy spoke

up and said he could raise the money right away if they'd let his boy off. But the Judge held that by doing that the boy wasn't being punished at all; his father was. Finally he made the decision that if the boy would make restitution to his father, it could be managed that way. So the father paid the mortgage, and the boy paid his father a little at a time, and when he got it all paid, the judge tore the commitment up. That started the parole law, the passage of which was forced through the very next session of the state legislature..."

Lane County Grange Display at the 1915 Oregon State Fair. *Courtesy of the Lane County Historical Society*

Sawmills, paper mills, machinery, equipment and furniture manufacturers, and other businesses developed along the waterfront in order to connect to the river steamers which shipped their products to other parts of the territory.

The flood of the Willamette River in 1861 set the progress back for another decade, only to be restored with the arrival of the first railroad in 1870.

Not long after the first railroad came through the area, a streetcar system came into use and continued to transport the people of Salem around the city until 1927.

The city became the permanent home of the Oregon State Fair in 1861.

Wastewater and sewage systems were installed and streets improved. After the first automobile arrived in 1902, the city began paving a few of the streets and the first project involved five blocks of Court Street. By 1927, the city had more than 35 miles of paved streets.

By the early 1900s, Salem had a high school downtown.

After the passage of women's right to vote in 1912, many of the women became involved in the political and cultural life of the city. The Salem Woman's Club was instrumental in securing funds for a Carnegie Library. Salem's women also helped establish Deaconess Hospital, a forerunner to Salem Hospital.

Two radio stations were broadcasting during the 1920s.

The Elsinore Theater

Downtown, the Elsinore Theatre opened in 1926 on the site of what had been a livery stable. George Guthrie, a lover of art, commissioned the building of a splendid theater designed to resemble the castle in Shakespeare's *Hamlet*. The theater quickly became recognized as the finest theater between Portland and San Francisco. For several years, audiences enjoyed silent movies accompanied by a mighty Wurlitzer, 900-pipe, 13-rank organ. They also enjoyed performances of "Fanchon & Marco," a vaudeville circuit that brought in many promising new performers including the John Phillip Sousa Marine Band and Clark Gable.

In 1929, the theater was converted to accommodate talking movies. Then, the Elsinore was leased to Warner Brothers The-

Early Salem horse-drawn streetcar. *Courtesy of the Lane County Historical Society*

Ouch! *Courtesy of the OSU Special Collections & Archives Commons*

Roy V. Ohmart's Liberty Store -- groceries, drugs and merchandise, Liberty Road, Salem, 1916. *Courtesy of* Salem Public Library Historic Photograph Collections, Salem Public Library, Salem, Oregon

Logging with oxen in the Salem area. *Courtesy of the Lane County Historical Society*

The tower of the Elsinore Theater collapsed during the 1962 Columbus Day Storm. *Photos courtesy of the Salem Public Library Historic Photograph Database, Salem Public Library, Salem, Oregon*

aters who ran it as a movie house until 1951.

In addition, during the 1930s, on Thursdays, talented young people would audition for Zollie's Mickey Mouse Club Matinee. The best would be selected to perform the following Saturday afternoon. Created and hosted by teenage Zollie Volchok, a group of regulars included pianist Donnie Edwards and young trumpeter, Doc Severinsen, later of Johnny Carson fame. The talented guests would perform a 45-minute live stage show. There would also be cartoons, movies and pipe organ music.

One truly marvelous feature of the theater was its acoustical design. A speaker on the stage could be heard throughout the theater without the assistance of a microphone.

By 1954, the theater was sold, and again, twice more. Neglect and audience-abuse caused it to lose the last of its audience appeal. In 1962, the Wurlitzer organ was dismantled and sold for parts. By 1980, plans were being made to demolish the Elsinore and replace it with a parking lot. A grassroots organization called the "Save the Elsinore Committee" formed, stepped in to save the treasure and, by 2004, with support from talented people and loving donations, had restored it to a magnificent theater with one of the finest Wurlitzer pipe organs in the country.

In 1931, Salem's first dial telephone was installed and the police radio in 1933. The *Oregon Statesman* publisher, Charles Sprague, served as Oregon Governor from 1939 to 1943.

Salem was also home to many of the state institutions – the Oregon State Penitentiary, Hillcrest Youth Correctional Facility and the Oregon State Mental Hospital.

Two of those Oregon State facilities, the Oregon State Penitentiary and the Oregon State Hospital, were said to have brought more people and business into Salem than all the other government businesses. They both have long and complicated histories which will barely be introduced in this book, but more information is easily available to complete the picture.

The Oregon State Penitentiary

The Oregon State Penitentiary, Oregon's first state prison, was originally located in Portland in 1851. In 1866, it was moved to a 26-acre site in Salem. It is the state's only maximum security prison accommodating up to 2,150 inmates and now occupies 194 acres. It includes a disciplinary segregation unit, a mental health infirmary and a 196-bed self-contained Intensive Management Unit which provides programs, housing and control for maximum-custody male inmates who pose a substantial threat to staff and other inmates. It also houses those inmates under a sentence of death.

During the early 1900s, there were reports of extreme brutality, floggings, negligent doctors and drinking among the guards.

From the early days on, it was a policy that the prisoners did better when they had work they could do. As early as 1917, some were allowed to work outside the prison, on road construction and other jobs. Governor Oswald West was a strong proponent of the plan. When they weren't closely supervised, many chose not to return to the prison, so Governor James Withycombe decided to find ways for them to work jobs within the prison. A flax plant was begun and eventually the prison had the largest flax-scutching mill in the world.

Today, penitentiary inmates are allowed to work in Oregon Corrections Enterprises shops – furniture factory, metal shop, upholstery shop and a commercial laundry that all bring in money for the state.

Like many other prisons, the penitentiary has had riots, escapes, strikes, tunnel-digging, accusations of racial discrimination, work stoppages and discontent.

"The Oregon State Penitentiary" by Jo-Brew:

"During the late 1940s, while I was still in high school and living at home, my family occasionally visited another family who had moved from Ashland to Sa-

Special trolleys that took visitors to the Oregon State Penitentiary and the State Mental Hospital before 1927. *Courtesy of the Lane County Historical Society*

lem where the father, another electrician, had taken a job as the electrician for the Capitol building. He urged my father to drive by the penitentiary before we went home. We did and were surprised to see the shrubs, bushes, and some of the trees on the grounds had been shaped into animals and shaped like fantasy towers and all manner of interesting sculptures. We never left Salem without a drive by after the first time we saw them. Dad's friend Ed told us they were done by one of the prisoners who could be trusted outside the wall."

Other State Prisons

The prison system in Salem also includes the Mill Creek Correctional Facility, a minimum-security prison housing 310 inmates who are within three years of release and have completed correctional programs. It provides inmates with work programs and training opportunities.

The Oregon State Correctional Institution near Salem is a men's medium-security, transitional release facility. The 892-bed facility focuses on providing transition programs and work skills to inmates with less than three years to serve, but who are not suitable for housing in a minimum-security environment. They are offered work and skills-training opportunities including printing and telecommunication services for state agencies.

Also in Salem, the Santiam Correctional Institution is a minimum-security prison that accommodates 400 male inmates within six months of release in four dormitories. Transitional programs and work experience are provided.

The Women's Correctional Center in Salem closed its crowded and obsolete prison for women at the Oregon State Penitentiary during the late 1990s and women prisoners are now housed at the new Coffee Creek Women's Correctional Facility and prisoner intake center in Wilsonville, Oregon.

Opened in 2001, Coffee Creek is a 1,684-bed facility on a 108-acre campus. It is a minimum- and medium-security facility with several programs designed to teach skills to inmates. One program involves teaching parenting skills since many of the incarcerated women are mothers. It is the only women's prison in Oregon, but has, at times, been so overcrowded that some prisoners have been shifted to other facilities. The old correctional facility in Salem, which was being used as a minimum security placement for men, has, at times, served as a backup to Coffee Creek.

Oregon State Hospital for the Insane

The Oregon State Hospital for the Insane was also begun in the Hawthorne District of Portland in 1862. In 1865, the legislature authorized the purchase of 147 acres east of Salem for the construction of a State Mental Hospital. In 1880, they established the Oregon State Insane Asylum Fund and a Board of Trustees.

The main building was completed in the summer of 1883 with much of the labor force and bricks coming from the penitentiary. Dr. Horace Carpenter, a local physician, was hired as the Superintendent of the new facility and a staff was hired to handle the 412 patients the hospital could accommodate. An extension of the north wing was built in 1899, and over time, seven separate new buildings were added.

In 1912, construction began on the dome building where the movie, "One Flew Over the Cuckoo's Nest," was filmed. In 1913, a crematorium was installed on the grounds for all patients who died with no family members to provide services. The facility also operated a large garden which provided food for the patients.

It should be noted that, historically, a person convicted of criminal activity "by reason of insanity" must also be housed and cared for in this facility. For many years the patients also included elderly suffering from dementia and often alcoholics.

The groups of buildings were connected by tunnels. Most of the government buildings in Salem used tunnels to aid in transporting supplies and people between them. These buildings include the State Capitol and often the larger hospitals in other parts of the state. The system at the State Mental Hospital used a narrow-gauge railroad with carts made of bamboo to transfer food, laundry and sometimes patients from one building to another.

Always underfunded and overcrowded, there were times when 3,000 patients needed to be fed, cared for and kept healthy by very low-paid caregivers with few qualifications. Real efforts were made to treat the inmates with the commonly-used methods of the time, some of which are not acceptable now.

In 2005, an architectural assessment of the facility determined that the site was unsafe. Construction of a 620-bed replacement hospital in Salem has been completed.

The Kirkbride building in Salem now houses a Mental Health Museum with history about many of the sometimes barbaric and discontinued practices no longer considered appropriate.

Another hospital with 174 beds, located in Junction City, is under construction with a third scheduled for the Portland area.

Like other communities and cities along the Willamette River, Salem has suffered major floods over the years. In 1890, Salem lost its only bridge across the Willamette River to the floods, while the young Oswald West, a future Oregon governor watched.

On New Years Day in 1943, the flooding water lifted the Mellow Moon, a dance hall and roller skating rink at the eastern end of the city's new Willamette River Bridge and floated the building downstream. It lodged against the bridge's piers and began collecting debris. Afraid that Salem might again lose its only Willamette River Bridge, Oregon Governor Charles Sprague ordered the Oregon Highway Department to dynamite the building. Workers were setting the charges when the building disintegrated, sweeping away workers, Archie Cook and Michael Maurer. The bridge was closed while crews searched in vain for the missing men.

The closed bridge left a thousand soldiers from Camp Adair, who were in Salem for the New Year's celebration, stranded. They were absent-without-leave (AWOL) and completely cut off from the base. After two days, the Southern Pacific Railroad supplied a special train to take the soldiers across the intact railroad bridge back to their camp.

Agriculture has always contributed much to the city's economy. Salem was considered the *"hop center of the Willamette Valley and the state"* and noted for its cherries, prunes, grapes, berries and other fruits and vegetables. There were fruit and vegetable canneries, lumber mills, a brewery and a flax factory. By the 1950s, Salem was also the largest food-preservation center in the nation.

Following World War II, the production and preservation of food was one of the predominant occupations in the Willamette Valley. The Salem area had eleven canneries, some quite large and often working double shifts. In addition, with the availability of home

Resurfacing U.S. Highway 99 between Albany and Salem in 1947. *Courtesy of the Oregon Department of Transportation (ODOT) History Center*

Drilling holes for traffic sign posts in Salem, Oregon, 1951. *Courtesy of the Oregon Department of Transportation (ODOT) History Center*

Meeting of the Oregon Development League at the Marion Hotel in Salem, 1910. *Courtesy of the Oregon Historical Society*

refrigeration and refrigerator freezers too small to store much frozen produce or meat, freezing plants also began to appear. All throughout the state, at least one market in most towns would have frozen food lockers for rent. Many people purchased meat in larger amounts or hunted game to supplement their diet. They now had the option of freezing it rather than canning it in mason jars.

The changing demands of the market where foods and products were brought from all over the world made major changes in the culture of Salem by the turn of the 21st century. The production and preservation of food was no longer the major occupation. The state itself became the largest employer with the Salem Hospital being the largest private employer.

As the population of the state grew, and new ways of running the state's business were developed, more rules and regulations were needed. This meant that, among other things, more departments were needed to inspect and enforce. Some started out sharing space, but they outgrew the space. The Real Estate Division needed their own building and so did the Department of Transportation and that's only two that touch our lives often. The list of departments and agencies covers most aspects of life for Oregonians. Since many of the different departments need to work together and to have state records easily accessible, they are now clustered in the same general area as the courthouse.

Salem is home to Willamette University, Corban University, the main campus of Chemeketa Community College, the Chemawa Indian School and the Oregon Schools for the Blind and Deaf.

Willamette University, founded in 1842, is the oldest university in the western United States. It was originally named the Oregon Institute and was an outgrowth of the early Methodist Mission founded by Jason Lee. It was co-educational from the onset and had the first School of Medicine and the first School of Law in Oregon. The School of Medicine later merged with the University of Oregon program and moved to Portland. The first Law School was opened in 1883, and Willamette University has made the study of law one of its specialties. It also has a College of Liberal Arts, the Atkinson Graduate School of Management and the School of Education. The beautiful campus is located near the Oregon State Capitol and other State buildings with a somewhat restricted space. There are several Greek houses on the cam-

"Housewife Special" bus is being boarded by women who were helping to save the Marion County bean crop during World War II. *Courtesy of the OSU Special Collections & Archives Commons*

pus as well as residence halls.

Willamette was one of the colleges and universities during World War II that offered students a path to a Navy commission during World War II. One very special story that is part of the history of Willamette University is of the football team which traveled to Hawaii to play the University of Hawaii in December 1941. Many football fans and students accompanied the team by passenger ship. The game was played on December 6. On December 7, many of the students witnessed the bombing of Pearl Harbor from their Waikiki Beach hotels. The return trip was delayed many weeks. Some had to return by troop transport ships. Many of the team members stayed with football players on the island until they could get transportation home.

Leaving Salem and heading north on Highway 99E, the traveler passes signs for the Chemawa Indian School.

The school was first established in the 1870s when the U.S. Government decided to establish a school to educate Indian children so that they could be integrated into white society. There were two on the East Coast, but Chemawa was the first to be established in the west. It was first built near Forest Grove, Oregon on four acres of land leased from Pacific University. An operating budget of $5,000 was provided to U.S. Army Lieutenant Melville Wilkinson who was put in charge. In 1880, he chose eight Puyallup boys to help him construct the buildings and the first enrollment consisted of 14 boys and 4 girls, all but one from the Puyallup Reservation in Washington. The other boy was also from Washington, from the Nisqually Reservation. They were taught *"blacksmithing, shoemaking, carpentering, wagon making, girl's industries and advancement in studies,"* according to Chemawa history.

By 1883, more funding was going to be made available for the school, and a move to another site was planned. Several factors played into the decision including a need for more land so that farming could be taught. Also, there was local resistance to the school in the Forest Grove area and the girls' dormitory burned down in 1884.

A search commenced and three possible sites were made available to them as donations. One was a 100-acre parcel near Newberg, but it was heavily timbered. Another 75 acres of pastureland, located only about four miles from the original site, was offered to them. They accepted the third option. It was a partially cleared and sparsely timbered parcel made up of 171 acres north of Salem that would be served by a spur of the railroad going through the Willamette Valley.

The school moved to the new site in 1885 and began building wooden structures that were later torn down and replaced with brick buildings. The buildings were halfway completed when half of the student body moved to the new location to help complete the construction while the other half stayed in Forest Grove. The new school was called the Salem Indian Training School at the time. After the remaining three buildings were completed, the rest of the students moved to Salem and the first 6th grade class graduated in 1886. By 1900, there were 453 students enrolled and more courses in vocational training were made available to them, but farming was one of the primary areas of interest.

By 1922, there were 70 buildings on the 40-acre campus and the enrollment had grown substantially. In 1927, it became a fully-accredited high school.

During the 1930s, leading up to the Depression, the possibility of a school closure hung over the school, but thanks to a newspaper campaign led by local journalists as well as the Oregon Delegation, the school remained open with 300 students. In the 1940s and 1950s, special programs were developed for Navajo students and tribal members from Alaska who were welcomed.

In the 1970s, the school moved its campus to an adjacent property. Currently, the Chemawa Indian School is over 125 years old and is the oldest, continuously-operated Native American boarding school in the United States. It is now in use as a resource for troubled Native American youths and is not open to the general public.

"An interview with Betty Orr of Albany, September 5, 2013" by Jo-Brew:

"Two sets of Betty Orr's ancestor's came to Oregon on the 1843 wagon train led by Peter Burnett. Their arrival in1843 makes her family one of the earliest to come to Oregon by wagon train. The wagonmaster, Peter Burnett, who led the train became a senator in Oregon and later a governor of California. On that same train was the equally prominent Holman family, who were friends of the Burnetts.

"When Betty was six, her father worked for the government and taught agriculture at Chemewa Indian School, a boarding school five miles north of Salem. Some of the Indian children were brought there as young as six, so Betty had playmates and friends, but government regulations stated that employees weren't allowed to go to school with the Indians even though the school was home to their family. Her father had been a football quarterback in school, so he did some coaching at Chemawa and encouraged Betty to exercise regularly.

"When the State Capitol building in Salem burned in 1935, they could see the flames from a big water tower that was on the school property. The next day, Betty and her father went into Salem and walked around on the grounds. She said they saw important papers, wet and ruined, scattered. There were policemen there on guard.

"Betty remembers, also, that across U.S. Highway 99 from Chemewa, there was a wooded area where gypsies came and camped every year.

"Although the family continued to maintain their home at Chemewa, they spent time on the Warm Springs Reservation where her father also worked. She says that it was a wonderful life, especially since they were able to ride horses all day. At Warm Springs, as it was at Chemewa, the employees were not allowed to attend school with the Indians, so the parents got together and hired a teacher. All of the grades were in one classroom. Since there were no other children in the sixth and seventh grades, Betty was put in with the eighth grade students.

"After that year, they returned to Chemewa, and Betty began attending junior high school in Salem. Commuting from Chemewa, she went to a couple of junior highs and eventually finished up at Parrish Junior High. Up until she entered junior high, all of her friends had been Indian, so acclimating to the Salem schools was a whole new experience for her. The other children didn't understand why she wasn't in school with the Indians, assuming she must also be Native American.

"After leaving Parrish Junior High

School, Betty attended the old Salem High School. It was a three-story building located where the Meier and Frank store once was. It is now Macys.

"Salem High was a school with secret societies in charge of the social order. It was not welcoming to a newcomer – especially one with no social connections. It was not a happy experience for Betty. Still, Chemewa was her home until she married, although she was away at school much of the time.

"After high school, with the help of a pair of nurses at the school who believed in her abilities, she was able to get a scholarship to attend Linfield College in McMinnville. There she had an entirely new experience. She was selected as the lead in a play and she also did some writing. It was at Linfield that she met John Orr, who came from a family of educators.

"With World War II looming, John and Betty married and had a daughter, Betty Lee, before he left for the South Pacific. With her mother, Betty and six-month-old Betty Lee, rented and shared a little house in Salem. Betty's father was also in the Seabees and stationed in the South Pacific."

Section 9

U.S. HIGHWAY 99E - SALEM THROUGH EAST PORTLAND

Leaving Salem, heading north on N.E. Portland Road, gets the traveler back onto Highway 99E.

HAYESVILLE

In 1849, Adam Stephens traded a gun, a horse and $30 to Anton Presley for 585.33 acres of land where the unincorporated community of Hayesville was located.

A schoolhouse was built in 1858 from lumber donated by Adam Stephens. That same year, the Hayesville Cemetery was established on land he donated following the death of Stephens' infant son, Adam Landrum Stephens.

The town was named in honor of President Rutherford B. Hayes in 1877, and by 1882, a Sunday School was organized and held at the school. Adam Stephens was president and founder of the Prohibition League that was organized in Hayesville, and later, on March 18, 1888, the First Baptist Church of Hayesville was founded. Apparently, services were first held in the school, but by 1891 a new church building had been built.

In 1939, due to low membership, the church merged with the First Baptist Church of Salem and in 1941, the building was destroyed by fire. A new building, the Halbert Memorial Baptist Church was constructed and dedicated on Easter Sunday in 1949. In

1890 Hayesville Church. *From the History of Hayesville, Oregon website.*

1999, the name was changed to the North Salem Baptist Church and it was acquired in 2008 by the New Harvest Church.

Today, Hayesville has been absorbed within the urban-growth boundary of North Salem.

BROOKS

Brooks, Oregon, an unincorporated community, was founded by and named after early settler, Linus Brooks, who came to Oregon from Illinois in 1850. A post office was established in 1871 at the time that the Oregon & California Railroad was built through Linus Brooks' donation land claim. Platted in 1878 with 30 blocks of land, it was located seven miles north of Salem in what is called the French Prairie region of Marion County. French Prairie was named for the many French Canadians who were some of Oregon's earliest settlers. Most were employed by the Hudson's Bay Company. French Prairie is a large flatland prairie located between the Willamette River and the Pudding River.

When it was platted, Brooks had about 135 residents. Besides the post office, it had a freight depot, store, blacksmith shop, hotel and a church for all denominations.

According to Linus Brooks' obituary, printed in an unidentified newspaper – probably the Portland, Oregon *Bee*:

"Mr. Brooks was a good man, a man of more than ordinary intelligence and considerable literary taste, a kind friend and neighbor, and in every respect a good citizen. He had a deep religious faith that actuated his life and added to his usefulness. His surviving children are honored and influential citizens of Oregon and Washington and do credit to his name.

"He was one of the pioneers who made homes on French Prairie at an early day, and his death, even at the ripe age attained, will be felt as a loss by many..."

Brooks, Oregon. *Courtesy of the Brooks Historical Society*

Today's Wheatland Ferry. Note the cables that operate it. *Courtesy of Wikimedia Commons*

Before bridges were built in the area, the Wheatland Ferry was used to transport travelers across the Willamette River, which is located about 9 miles to the west of Brooks. The first ferry was started by Daniel Matheny in the 1850s. It was a wooden raft powered by men with wooden poles. The Wheatland Ferry is still operating today to transport cars across the river since the nearest bridges are about 15 miles in either direction.

According to Wikipedia, today's ferry *"is powered by two electric motors connected to an on-board diesel generator. It is supported by two steel cables, one under water on the downriver side, and one overhead on the upriver side. The ferry also uses the overhead cable for steering."*

In 1900, the Southern Pacific Railroad had taken over the O&C holdings and a new depot was built in Brooks. It served the community from 1900 to 1963 and provided both freight and passenger service and also telegraph and mail service. Much of the freight that it shipped were products grown on the local farms and manufactured goods.

As with other communities along the track, the Southern Pacific picked up and delivered mail to Brooks even if it didn't schedule a stop there. The outgoing mail sacks were hung from an arm next to the depot and it would be snagged as the train passed by. The canvas sack of incoming mail was thrown out of the train at the station, hopefully hitting a clear area along the tracks. If the sack happened to get sucked under the train and run over, it was the job of the postmaster to walk along the tracks picking up the scraps to piece together. He usually had help if it contained something important, like money.

Before 1940, the mail could be taken care of by anyone, usually the store owner who also served as postmaster. After 1940, however, the job was reclassified and the postmaster needed to pass a Civil Service exam.

Brooks was, and still is, a farming community. In 1912, nearby swampland of Lake Labish was drained. A huge drainage ditch project was begun in 1911 and completed in 1915. The ditch ran from Lake Labish to the Willamette River, draining the west end of the swampland. The east end is controlled by a dam that was built on the Pudding River. This caused a controversy between those living upstream from the dam and those downstream.

A short history of Brooks, written by Dorene Isham Standish, and provided to us by the Brooks Historical Society, tells about the controversy:

"If the water was dammed, then the upstream farmers would be flooded. If the water was allowed to flow freely, the downstream farmers would be flooded out. Eventually, a compromise was reached and the dam was allowed to remain, but it had to be regulated so as not to flood either set of farmers.

"Even though there is this deep and wide drainage ditch spanning the entire Lake Labish area and a controlled dam, the area floods every winter. This flooding most likely maintains the nutrient content created by the natural swampy conditions, but the road running across the lake is inaccessible during certain periods of heavy rain every year due to flooding."

Early on, the 1,400 acres of nutrient-rich peat soil was planted primarily with Yellow Danver onions. When harvested, they were shipped throughout the Pacific Northwest between Alaska and California. Until ready for shipment, they were housed in former grain warehouses that stretched over a quarter of a mile along the Southern Pacific tracks near Brooks.

By 1918, celery became the predominant, commercially-grown crop for the area and remained so until high shipping rates cut the production drastically. Vast acres of lettuce, cane berries, strawberries, fruit trees, hops and other field crops, as well as dairy and poultry, also added to the agricultural economy in the Brooks' area.

When the U.S. Highway 99E was built a short ways from the Brooks' city center, many businesses moved closer to the highway.

Left vacant for the next 17 years, the Brooks depot building was scheduled to be demolished when two Brooks citizens bought it. It proved too expensive to maintain, however, so it was moved to Keizer where it was placed on top of a garage as a second story unit and used for various businesses and personal use. In 1984, it was offered to the Brooks Historical Society and in 1989, it was once again moved back to Brooks to the grounds of the Antique Powerland site where the restored building now serves as the Brooks Depot Museum.

During that move, it was discovered that the Southern Pacific Depot had been built from a kit with numbered boards so that it could be reassembled on site.

According to the Antique Powerland website:

"Antique Powerland, which opened in 1970, was originally established by a group of enthusiasts dedicated to the preservation, restoration and operation of steam-powered equipment, antique farm machinery and implements. Today, it encompasses an impressive collection of

The Brooks Depot Museum of the Brooks Historical Society located at the Antique Powerland site. *Courtesy of the Brooks Historical Society*

A functioning trolley gives visitors a ride around the Antique Powerland site. *Courtesy of Antiques Powerland*

museums dedicated to preserving Oregon's rich agricultural heritage.

"...The public will be able to appreciate the heritage of early-day machines and better understand the history of technology upon which modern machines, vehicles and farm equipment is based."

The 17 museums and organizations represented on the site include the Antique Powerland's own museum; the Antique Caterpillar Machinery Museum; the Antique Implement Society; the Blacksmith Shop; Branch 15 Early-Day Gas Engine and Tractor Association; the Brooks Historical Soci-

Edna Jones Ramp in front of the Howard Ramp store in 1905. This store was torn down and the energy plant (aka the Brooks garbage burner) is now at that location just west of the Southern Pacific railroad tracks. *Courtesy of Jeff Ramp*

The building in Brooks described by Sam Ramp. There was a recreation center upstairs where the kids skated and had dances. *Courtesy of Jeff Ramp*

ety; Curtis Heritage Education Center; the Northwest Vintage Car & Motorcycle Museum; the Oregon Electric Railway Museum; the Oregon Fire Service Museum; the Oregon Vintage John Deere Museum; the Pacific Northwest Chapter of the National Railway Historical Society; the Pacific Northwest Logging Museum; the Pacific Northwest Truck Museum; Western Steam Friends Association; Willow Creek Railroad Museum; and the Willamette Valley Railroad Club and Museum.

In an on-line video and audio interview, George Samuel Ramp, a descendant of one of the original settlers in Brooks, gave a class presentation to the local high school in approximately 1987. It was difficult to make out some of his stories, but they were quite interesting and thanks to his family's generosity, they are being shared here.

Sam, as he was known, was born in 1912. His father, Howard Ramp, bought his first store in Brooks in about 1905. Sam said that another large two-story building was nearby where, over the years, young and old alike would go to dance, rollerskate and play basketball upstairs.

He said that the railroad provided the best transportation during that time. It brought and picked up groceries, mail and passengers. Sam said that there were groups of "hobos" that passed through town, and occasionally, they broke into the store to steal groceries until his father began putting a couple of dogs in there at night.

Sam's son, Jeff Ramp, added his own remembrances about the store:

"That old store later became the Brooks Post Office for a time. I remember riding my bike over there to mail letters in the 1950s and 1960s until they built a new one which still stands today and is about a block to the west of Highway 99E."

The Brooks Mercantile Co. Another of the Ramp's stores, perhaps? *Courtesy of the Brooks Historical Society*

In his interview, Sam said that in about 1925, his father's store sold everything that the local residents could possibly need – groceries, hardware, nails, shoes... In fact, he said that the shoes that the store carried were high-top boots as well as ankle boots – the kind that farmers and loggers wore – not the Nikes of today. They sold for about $20 a pair which was a lot of money in 1925, but he remembered one day his father sold 48 pair of them... definitely a record number.

The businesses carried a lot of credit in those days. Farmers never were paid until their crops were harvested and sold each year, so they charged all of their groceries and other purchases and paid the bill in full at the end of the harvest.

In 1935, his father built a new store and gas station *"down at the corners where the activity was."* Sam and his cousin ran that gas station for awhile. Eventually, by the 1960s, the competition from large grocery and gas chains killed the local business and the store was vacated and torn down. According to the Brooks Historical Society, it was the fifth Ramp store in the area.

One of the students asked Sam what the roads were like before Highway 99E was built. He said that from Salem on past Brooks, it was gravel. There were low spots in the road where cars would get bogged down and a farmer made a business out of pulling them out to the top of the next rise with his team of horses – a 3-4 hour endeavor.

"He made good money doing that."

There were also corduroy roads built across the swampy areas. These were log roads made by laying logs side by side across the expanse of swamp. It made for a bumpy ride, but it provided a means to get across otherwise impassible areas.

He also talked about crews dredging a drainage ditch that was put in from Brooks to the Pudding River, near Aurora, because the ground was so swampy that the crops couldn't do well.

His uncle, George Ramp, raised and trained harness race horses. He had a track nearby and would often "run" his horses in the trotting races at the fairs in the area. Another of his Ramp relatives and members of the early Boyce family were good baseball players.

One of the students asked Sam about the local stills that were active in the area during Prohibition. Sam acknowledged that there were a few. If you knew where they were, you'd knock on the door of the house and they would go out into the field and bring back a jar which was sold for about $1 a quart.

That led Sam to tell about John Moore's tavern. Somewhere between 1930 and 1935, John Moore opened his tavern/restaurant. Sam said that it had the best breakfasts around, and they were very inexpensive. John did not use the restaurant as a means to make money, but as a way to attract customers. His main business during a 6-month period was to run his very large and sophisticated casino in the upstairs room every Saturday night. According to Sam, there were roulette, crap and blackjack tables, slot machines and everything that a casino in Reno would have. Guards were posted at the doors. Before the law shut him down, the parking lots all over town were filled with between 400-500 cars and the upstairs room was absolutely packed.

"He paid for that place in a very short while."

The next question had to do with the Japanese-American residents who were brought in to work on the local farms by a farmer named Jones, to harvest celery and lettuce before World War II. Whole families worked the ground by hand and picked the crops.

Sam's voice softened when he told about having gone to school with many kids of the 50-or-so families that lived in the area, some owning their own property.

"They were a hard-working group – good people and they had the support of almost everyone in Brooks."

After the Pearl Harbor attack, the local Japanese-Americans were confined within a few miles of their homes. They could come into town, but they were not allowed to circulate. When camps were established, they were loaded on buses and transported to camps in Ontario, Vale and Tulelake, California (among others) where some of their descendants later settled permanently.

Jones, who was in politics, went to bat for the people who worked for him, and because of it, he lost the next election.

"I trusted them. Most didn't want them to leave (Brooks). Many (of their descendants) *are good farmers in that area today."*

George Samuel Ramp passed away in January 1998 at the age of 86 years.

WACONDA / HOPMERE / QUINABY / CHEMAWA / CONCOMLY

Waconda, Hopmere, Quinaby, Chemawa and Concomly were stations along the Oregon Electric Railway line when the railway was built in 1907, but Waconda had also been a stagestop along the way.

In an early 1900s newspaper article on the well-known stagecoach driver, "Old Cal," aka Colonel Scovell, he is quoted as saying,

"The stage left Portland at 5 o'clock in the morning and reached Salem at 4 o'clock in the afternoon. Horses were changed at Oregon City, Dutch Town (Aurora) and Waconda, near the present site of Gervais. The stage left Salem for Eugene at 4 o'clock in the afternoon and reached the latter place at 3 o'clock next morning. The fare from Portland to Salem was $5 and this included the transportation of 150 pounds of baggage."

From "Waconda, Hopmere And Quinaby Stations" by Wes Sullivan on Salem Public Library's "Salem History On-Line":

"Looking ahead as we leave Concomly, we find we are approaching Waconda, Hopmere, Quinaby and Chemawa.

"...Waconda was an old name in the Willamette Valley, originally applied to a community about a mile south of present-

The Hopmere Station. *Courtesy of Bruce Fingerhood, Flickr*

day Gervais. However, that little village disappeared, only to be resurrected in the name applied by the Oregon Electric to one of its rural stations. The name apparently was brought to Oregon from the language of the Sioux Indians, meaning, roughly, a consecrated place. Waconda never lost its rural flavor, although a post office was established there in 1912 and its population in 1915 was listed as 177.

"The Oregon Electric decided to use famous Indian names in locating the stations along its route. So how did Hopmere get in there? Well, that's a story in itself, but first, we've got to get to how the Oregon Electric attached the name Chemeketa to its next station. Chemeketa is the original Indian name for Salem and for the band of Indians who lived there. The people around the new station disliked the name, however, and insisted on calling their area Hopmere, after its principal crop. Lewis A. McArthur, in Oregon Geographic Names, calls the name Hopmere 'a silly mongrel.'

"Every year about harvest time, the travel to Hopmere was heavy, as people loaded their baggage and tents on the Oregon Electric and went to Hopmere and adjacent stations to spend the harvest season in the field picking hops.

"Just down the track is Quinaby, named after one of the most colorful Indians in the region. In 1854, when all the Indians in the Valley were removed to the new reservation at Grand Ronde, Quinaby decided life was much more comfortable in Salem. So, despite regulations to the contrary, Quinaby, who was about 50 at the time, mounted his old horse and headed for Salem on the Fourth of July. He arrived shouting praises of the Great White Father in Washington, D. C.

"Actually, he expected to share in the barbecue he knew was held annually on that date. Unfortunately, it wasn't held that year. That didn't stop Quinaby, who scrounged food from his white friends, reminding them of how he had stood up for the whites in the early days. He lived in Salem for about 30 years, cadging food, conducting Indian gambling games and being generally accepted by the populace. He died about 1885 from overeating."

GERVAIS

Said to be the founder of the town of Gervais, Samuel Brown and his wife Elizabeth came to the area from the California gold fields where he is said to have made a $20,000 profit from digging 62 pounds of

The Sam Brown House in 1800s. It has been listed on the National Register of Historic Places. *Courtesy of Wikimedia Commons.*

gold. They bought the Peter Depot donation land claim and added to it with their own DLC in French Prairie, giving them a total of 1,000 acres in the Gervais area. They had 12 children, many of whom were said to have attended Willamette or Pacific Universities. He was a state senator for eight years, from 1866 to 1872, and a son, Samuel Brown II, was a state senator, sponsor of the popular $5 auto license fee, and ran for governor in 1936. The Sam Brown House, located just west of the town of Gervais, was built in 1857 and is believed to be the first in the area to be built by an architect. It was known as a stagestop at one time and housed three generations of the Brown family. The house, also known as "The Willows," is still standing and is sometimes open to visitors.

About 5 miles north of Brooks, Gervais sits to the west of Highway 99. The city is named for pioneer Joseph Gervais who was one of the first settlers on French Prairie.

As with many of the towns in the early days, Gervais was destroyed by fire and rebuilt. In 1902, all but two businesses in Gervais were burned to the ground. The local fire department was not able to handle the large fire and before help could arrive from Salem or Portland, the business district was gone.

According to Melinda Jette for the extensive on-line Oregon Encyclopedia Project:

"...During the 1830s, Gervais family members were supporters of Jason Lee's Methodist mission, located just south of the Gervais farmstead, and they allowed the missionaries to hold services at their home. Joseph Gervais later supported the efforts of the French-Indian community to secure a French Canadian Catholic mission to Oregon."

Since the 1960s, Gervais has become the home of a colony of Russian Old Believers that is considered to be the largest in the U.S.

BELPASSI / BELLE PASSI

Belpassi/Belle Passi, located about a mile south of Woodburn, Oregon on the Pacific Highway/U.S. Highway 99E, was settled in 1851 by the Reverend Neill Johnson when he and his wife, Esther, took out a donation land claim in the area. They named the fledgling town "Belpassi" or "Belle Passi," meaning "beautiful place of peace," after an Italian town which he had read about in one of his theology books.

That same year, Rev. Johnson organized the Cumberland Presbyterian Church, which became the flagship of the Oregon Presbyterian Church organization. Its Sunday services were held in the same log schoolhouse

A unique Woodmen of the World grave marker at the Belle Passi Cemetery. *From the Brew family collection*

that their 12 children attended. Gervais resident, Sam Brown, oversaw the Sunday School classes. A new two-story building was constructed in 1857 to house the church on the first floor and the school on the second and contained a library stocked with books. Students came from other areas to board in Belle Passi and attend school there.

The Belle Passi Post Office was established in 1870, but when the Oregon & California Railroad bypassed it, building its tracks about a mile away, the town began to die. As with most towns that the railroad bypassed, the post office was moved, in this case to neighboring Woodburn, and Belle Passi became a ghost town.

Reverend Johnson died at the age of 87. Even though he and Esther apparently spent their later years near McMinnville in Yamhill County, he and his family are buried in Belle Passi Cemetery. It and the old schoolhouse are the only remnants of a once-prosperous community.

The Belle Passi Chapter of the Daughters of the American Revolution (DAR) was organized on February 24, 1934. The Organizing Regent was Mrs. W. J. Wilson, and on the same day in 1942, the organization placed an historical marker on the site of the Belle Passi Community. The rock with the DAR marker was relocated to the Belle Passi Cemetery and rededicated on February 16, 2002.

HALSEY / WOODBURN

The City of Woodburn, in Marion County, was first platted in 1871 after the railroad came through the area. It lies on the eastern edge of the French Prairie region.

One of those settlers, Jean B. Ducharme, was forced to sell his donation land claim in 1862 by foreclosure and the 214 acres was bought by a farmer and nurseryman, Jessie Holland Settlemier, from neighboring Mt. Angel. Settlemier moved to the new property in 1863 and established the Woodburn Nursery Company. It grew to be one of the largest nurseries on the West Coast.

Jessie Settlemier built a beautiful family home in 1892, that still sits on almost three acres of landscaped grounds at the corner of Settlemier Avenue and Garfield Street in Woodburn. The Jessie H. Settlemier House, built in 1892, was proclaimed the "Grandest Mansion in Marion County," and was recorded in the National Register of Historic Places in 1974.

After offering 85 acres of his land to the Oregon and California Railroad on which to build its tracks, the railroad accepted and built its line in 1871 near where the first four blocks of the city were platted. Jessie Settlemier also offered a free lot to any business that would build on it, a quarter lot to the church and a full block for a new school. The town was first called Halsey, but the name was changed to Woodburn when a town further south chose that name.

The name, "Woodburn," was selected by a railroad employee after witnessing an 1880s

The Settlemier House in Woodburn, Oregon, 2007 – *Courtesy of Wikimedia Commons (Andrew Parodi)*

An old-fashioned, neighborly barn-raising near Woodburn, Oregon. Courtesy of the Gerald W. Williams Collection, OSU Archives Commons

out-of-control slash fire that burned a nearby woodlot. Woodburn was incorporated by the Oregon Legislative Assembly on February 20, 1889.

The route of the Pacific Highway/U.S. Highway 99E, heading north, goes through the French Prairie lowlands and crosses a bridge over the Pudding River, passing through the east side of the current town.

Like its neighbors, Woodburn is a farming community, but many of its commercial businesses have also added to its economy.

In an article written for Oregon.com, titled "Little Mexico in Woodburn," Vicente Guzman-Orozco wrote:

"Fifty years later, Settlemier's gamble had grown over ten times its original size, and it had become the "World's Berry Center". The Arch commemorating that fact only stood 10 years along the highway leading into town, before it had to be removed to make room for the road's expansion in 1933.

"Then, in the 60's, a series of developments changed the face of the town in a radical way. Migrant workers from Mexico and Central America who started coming through as part of the Bracero program over a decade earlier began settling. A wave of Russian and Turkish Old Believers (an Orthodox Christian sect), fleeing further persecution in their former refuge within Communist China, started arriving and also taking root. The opening of Senior Estates brought an influx of more than 2500 people over 50, creating Oregon's largest retirement community. By 1970, it was reported that 'strictly speaking, there are no minorities in Woodburn.'"

Through the years, Woodburn has hosted several festivals and community events. One of those, La Fiesta Mexicana, is the most important Hispanic event in the area. It began as a way for ranchers and merchants in the town to recognize the importance of the bicultural relationships that have resulted with the increased Hispanic population.

Highway 99 near Woodburn during the 1964 flood as it goes through French Prairie, "La Biche," and the bridge over the Pudding River. *Courtesy of the Oregon Department of Transportatin (ODOT) History Center*

In 2014, its 50th anniversary was celebrated. Most years, a Queen and/or Princess is crowned. In 1964, Francisca Gonzalez was the first to be selected. At that time, it was a one-day event that was held in downtown Woodburn, but it has grown in popularity and currently sponsors activities that last for almost a week. The more recent schedules include a large, well-attended parade, food booths in Settlemier Park, talent shows, dances, entertainment of all kinds and always, gaily-colored costumes. The festival is geared to all ages and the Kids' Zone features games and piñata-bashing, taco-eating contests. There are mariachi bands, salsa dancers and soccer games.

Other festivals have included the annual Tulip Festival which is now centered around the Wooden Shoe Tulip Farm which hosts its "Tulip Fest" during the spring from late March to May when their 40-acres of tulips are blooming.

Woodburn is also well-known for its dragstrip and outlet malls.

Almost synonymous with the name of the town, Woodburn has been known for two or three generations as Oregon's home of the boys "reform" or "correctional " school. The facility had originally been in Salem, but it was plagued by scandal over the alleged neglect of those wards of the state.

The renamed Oregon State Training School was moved to a site near Woodburn in 1926. Four cottages housed 45 boys each, according to age, mental capacity and the offense they were charged with. During the 1930s, the boys were paroled when the school officers felt their attitude had improved enough to warrant their release. Vocational experience was its primary focus and the length of stay was generally about 100 days. During that time, the daily population was about 120 boys.

In 1951, the school was renamed the MacLaren School for Boys in honor of Reverend William MacLaren, who devoted his life to working with troubled youth. The facility resembled a large working farm and ranch. Husband and wife teams, referred to as "houseparents" lived and worked there alongside the boys. They grew and raised most of their own food and provided some for other facilities, as well.

According to "History of Juvenile Justice in Oregon" on the Oregon.gov website:

"In 1975, Senate Bill 703 decreed that status offenders could no longer be held or committed to the training schools. Commitments were limited to youth having committed felonies and misdemeanors. A class-action lawsuit was filed against MacLaren School in 1977, alleging cruelty to students, unfair disciplinary actions, no due process and citing other issues. The lawsuit was settled in 1989, following the implementation of numerous changes. The 1977 Legislative Assembly approved monies for diversion beds to keep youth out of the training schools. In 1978, thirty community beds were added to transition youth back to the community."

"...During the 1980s, offense-specific treatment models for sex offenders, drug/alcohol abusers, and violent offenders were developed. Programs to serve minority youth were also introduced into the array of close-custody treatment services.

"In 1985, the Legislative Assembly put a 'cap' on the number of youth who could be committed to close-custody, reducing that population from 728 to 513 over the next two years. Savings were invested in contracts with county juvenile departments to serve youth in the community."

Today, various programs have been developed to ease the way back to life outside of the juvenile justice system for the young men who are incarcerated there. One of them, called "Project POOCH," encourages MacLaren youth to care for and train shelter dogs. The experience not only helps homeless pets learn good manners and find new homes, but it instills compassion and self-respect in the boys who work with them.

Many of the products designed and made in the MacLaren's vocational and educational programs are made available for sale to the public. These programs, including wood crafting, horticultural, welding and laser engraving and sandblasting, produce products and teach valuable skills that can be used for meaningful employment later on.

The on-site William P. Lord High School is a fully accredited, comprehensive high school and provides the educational needs of the young men incarcerated at MacLaren.

The Woodburn Volunteer Fire Department at one time. (date unknown) *Courtesy of Oregon State Library*

HUBBARD

Charles and Margaret Hubbard came to Oregon from Illinois in 1847. When they reached Oregon City in 1848, they stayed there while they considered where they would settle. Another couple in the area, Thomas and Maryann Hunt, encouraged them to rent their land and maintain their squatter's property near Mill Creek. It was located where Wolfer's Mineral Springs, developed by George Wolfer, was later located.

Leaving their son, William, to develop the Hunt property which they later bought from Margaret Hunt, Charles and Margaret moved back to Oregon City where he established a gristmill.

William Hubbard married Helen Cooley and they built a log cabin near what is now First and G Streets in Hubbard.

A second son, Charles Hubbard, Jr., also settled in the same area and when he heard that the Oregon and California Railroad was planning a route through the area, he offered it right-of-way through his property where he agreed to plat the town. The O&C accepted his offer, the railroad arrived in 1871 and the town began to grow.

A few miles north of Hubbard, the Aurora Colony commune of Christians led by Wilhelm Keil had formed and another freedom-seeking religious group, the Mennonites, settled east of Hubbard.

The book, *On the Road of a Thousand Wonders; The History of Hubbard, Oregon* by Leslie Ulven includes the story told to her by Virgil Hostetler, whose ancestors were among the arriving Mennonites:

"My, grandad, John Egli, came here from Iowa. They bought the place at the end of Miller Road, the last place before it runs into Barlow Road at the east end. They got off the train in Hubbard, Thanksgiving week. My mom, Mary Ann, was six years old, right near her seventh birthday. There was snow on the ground. She told me she remembered going through the giant trees. She said the trees were so big she couldn't see around them and mud was up to the axle of the wagon in places.

"They were Mennonites. Amos Troyer was a bishop of the Zion Church. It was the church of the neighborhood and Mom's family were charter members. Mennonites are conscientious objectors, raised on nonviolence. My mother told me the Mennonites had moved from Germany to Holland to Russia, looking for a country where they would not have to serve in the military. The United States government made an agreement with them that if they would come here and help establish farming, they wouldn't have to go to war, but could serve the country otherwise. They are some of the people who established wheat farming in Kansas, super farmers.

"Louis Mishler's kin, also Mennonites, were craftsmen and business owners. He reminisces: 'The Mishlers came from Indiana in 1889. My uncle Jim had a stock and butchering business. He lived in Hubbard. Then my grandfather moved here about the same time. I also had an uncle, Jus Mishler, who was a carpenter. Dad got the meat market.'"

The Hubbard Historical Society provided some nuggets of information on other ways that the town developed:

"The first jail in Hubbard was constructed in 1870 in back of the site of

Hubbard's first school located on U.S. Highway 99E and J Street. *Courtesy of the Willamette Heritage Center*

the present jail, which was built in 1923. The first jail was made of 2x4s nailed on top of each other, and the sides were covered with tin which looked like brick. There were two small cells and a small office in the original building.

"...Mrs. Tillie Williamson, Hubbard's fire and police telephone operator, was the Village's first policewoman. The Village Council approved the appointment of Mrs. Williamson. Her name was submitted to council by former Mayor Joseph J. Baldine who told Council members 'Without Mrs. Williamson's help, Hubbard would have been handicapped throughout these years.' Former Mayor Baldine told council members, 'All Hubbard should express thanks and appreciation for the wonderful work Mrs. Williamson has done.' After Council approved the appointment, Former Mayor Baldine pinned a gold badge on Mrs. Williamson, and the first policewoman in the history of Hubbard smilingly said, 'Thanks, members of Council.'"

The Hubbard Volunteer Fire Department was first organized in 1875, and the first streetcar in Hubbard ran in 1901.

There was quite a lot of agriculture around Hubbard. The main crop for quite some time was hops, one of the main ingredients used in the making of beer.

In her book, Leslie Ulven included memories of dozens of local residents on life in Hubbard, too. Vera Kocher Yoder told about picking hops as a child:

"The hop yard was always a social activity as well as a money-raising one. Seems like everybody went to the hop yard. Part of the time we got less than a cent a pound for picking hops. Probably a dollar or dollar and a half a day was about as much as I could expect to make.

"When I was little, I had to have on gloves, and every little hole had to be taped so that I didn't touch a vine at all. As I got older, I started just taping my thumb and first finger and found that I could pick better and really didn't irritate my hands as much as when I wore gloves. The vine is rough, not a thorn, but very abrasive, so that especially if it was wet it would cut into your hands badly.

"We picked into baskets. Years before, when my mother was young, they picked into a hopper that was a long canvas container. When we were picking, we'd fill a basket and then call for a hop sack, and one of the field crew would bring a sack and empty the basket into it. When you got your second basket, you'd call for the weighman then he'd dump the second basket into the bag and weigh them. Two baskets would weigh approximately 50 pounds. They would be tied and you'd get a ticket and that could be cashed in at the end of the season. As the day progressed, the team and wagon would come and pick up the hop sacks. Later there was a tractor.

"The hop is the flower and when we were picking by hand, the wires were not as high as now. The vine was trained to the wire and then along the wire. Arms would hang down from the wires. These arms were the easiest to pick. You'd always get leaves, too, and of course the faster pickers picked more big leaves and stems than the slow pickers did.

"We'd normally not cash in our ticket until the end of the season, or if we'd move from one grower to another. When one field was finished they'd payoff. We'd hold our tickets until that time. Usually several growers would share a crew and the ones that had the earlier hops would pick first and then we might go to another grower.

"When it was rainy, we'd quit picking, but if it just started to shower, we'd take a hop sack and stick one corner back into the other corner and put it over our head like a hood and cape and try to stick it out. If it looked like it was going to rain a while and then clear up, we'd go into the hop house and huddle around the stove and wait until we could go back out and pick.

"I always wore overalls. Long-sleeved shirts of course, because the vines would scratch your arms. I liked a straw hat to keep the sun off if it was hot."

As important as harvest is in an agricultural community, social life and recreation were not ignored in the town of Hubbard. City Hall, built in 1892 at 2nd and C Streets, served also as a performing arts center. Known as the Armory, it proved to be a popular community gathering site.

Each year since 1973 on the third Saturday in July, the community of Hubbard and the Hubbard Volunteer Fire Association has sponsored their Hubbard Hop Festival. The annual event provides the community a way to celebrate the impact that the early hops harvests had on the economic and social history of the area as well as a means to fund local community projects, scholarships and charities. Community members and visitors can partake and participate in a parade, beer garden, fun-run, community breakfast, vendor booths, kids' play areas, musical entertainment, horseshoe tournament and food and craft booths.

AURORA COLONY / AURORA

Moving further north along the route later taken by U.S. Highway 99E, was the Aurora Colony Stage Station, aka Aurora Mills Station or "Dutch Town" near the town of Aurora.

William Kraus of Aurora was interviewed on May 15, 1939 for the *WPA's American Life Histories Collection: Manuscripts from the Federal Writer's Project, 1936-1940* project. His interviewer was Howard M. Corning:

"In those early years there was a stage route through town. They had a station *here. They had a station every twelve miles; there was one at Salem, at Gervais, here at Aurora, at Oregon City, and then Portland. They changed horses at each place. The stage made the run from Portland to Salem in a day and always stopped here at noon. People, as well as the stage drivers, liked to eat here. That was all changed when the railroad came through.*

"No, the mail route didn't go through the lower part of town. It went over the hill there back of Finck's place, a little to the northwest. We walked up there for our mail."

In an article called *Railroading in the Lower Willamette Valley*, originally published in the Horner Museum Tour Guide Series in 1979, authors Lowry, Munford and Moore told about the Aurora Colony stage stop:

"The 500 or so Germans who formed Dr. Keil's communal colony became famous in stage-coach days for the meals served to passengers when drivers stopped to change horses. Before trains had dining cars, railroad passengers and crews also enjoyed the bounteous tables of 'Dutch Town.'"

In 1853, Wilhelm Keil, leader of the Bethel Colony of Missouri, a German commune, was concerned about changes taking place in the attitude of the north toward the southern states, so he sent a scouting party to look for opportunities in the new northwest territory. The group traveled across the country and chose a forested coastal area in Washington, north of the Oregon border on Willapapa Bay. Much of the colony, led by Keil, formed a wagon train to make the journey.

Before the group left, Dr. Keil's son, Willie, died and the father did not want to leave his son behind. A special lead coffin was built and filled with Golden Rule Whiskey that had been produced at the colony, to preserve the body for the cross-country trip.

From *The Well-Traveled Casket: A Collection of Oregon Folklore* by Tom Nash and Twilo Schofield:

"Willie did not live to see the train on its way. Four days before embarking, Willie Keil became sick with fever. In two days he was dead. His grief-stricken father knew he must somehow keep his word to the boy; and with the Bethelites' help, Willie Keil led the wagons west. The artisans built a lead coffin and filled it with Golden Rule whiskey. [A type of whiskey that the commune made to fund their activities.] At the head of the column of thirty-four rigs was a special hearse with open sides, the wagon containing Willie Keil's coffin and several gallons of whiskey. Over the coffin was a crossbar outfitted with hundreds of bells, which rang as the wagon rumbled across the prairie.

"In 1855 the train moved away from Bethel with the emigrants playing guitars, zithers, flutes, and drums. The Bethelites accompanied the train to the tune written by Keil for his son's funeral 'Das Grab ist Tief und Stille.' The procession was led by a brass band and a schellenbaum, an umbrella-like structure with bells attached. When the wagons arrived in Fort Kearny, they found that the Sioux and other Plains Indians were attacking virtually every wagon to cross the Oregon Trail. Without fear Keil said, 'The Lord will preserve and guide us.'

"Shortly beyond Fort Kearny, a small party of Sioux halted the procession, but

The Aurora Colony, 1889, looking southeast from one of the balconies on the 114-foot tall church bell tower in Aurora, Oregon. Although the original communal colony known as Aurora was officially dissolved in 1877, many of the colony's members continued to live and work there. Structures in the center of the photo include a sawmill, gristmill and spinning mill. Those in the back include various workshops, retail businesses, stables and living quarters of the colony's craftsmen and tradesmen.
Courtesy of the on-line Oregon History Project, Oregon Historical Society

not to raid the wagons. The hearse was fascinating to the Indians. They came to investigate the music and the bells and wanted to see what was inside the lead-lined box. Dr. Keil, without any objection whatsoever, opened the casket and showed the Indians Willie Keil's body floating in alcohol. The Indians were petrified; they wondered what kind of god would allow such things.

"After that first incident, the Bethelites were assured safe passage. As they traveled from town to town on the journey west, they heard repeated tales of atrocities and massacres; but the Indians who approached the wagon train came only to view the body. At one point, a huge band of warriors lined up alongside the hearse, riding single-file past Willie's body while the Germans sang their dirge. Every once in a while, the Bethelites would round a small hill or pass a bluff and find newly killed buffalo or elk – a gift to pacify these strange people, the Bethelites."

When the group arrived at the chosen site in Washington, neither the members nor Dr. Keil liked the area. It was heavily forested, dark and much too damp. They decided to move further south, but Dr. Keil decided to bury his son there.

The colony's final destination ended on rich farmland in Oregon, near the Pudding River which would provide a source of energy to run their mills.

Under his strong leadership, they formed a Utopian commune and named it Aurora Mills after his daughter who died in a smallpox epidemic in 1862 along with three of his other children. The colony grew in numbers and almost every aspect of life in the area was influenced by Dr. Keil's revivalism and utopianism philosophies.

The Aurora Colony is considered one of the most successful early Christian communes in Oregon. They developed a society that was known for its orchards, food, music and artisans who specialized in textiles, furniture and other German crafts and traditions, but they no longer had a distillery.

Keil was credited with bringing the railroad to Aurora in 1870. The colony built a hotel near the tracks and the trains stopped for a noon meal. It became famous for its good German food. When a train was due in, the colony band was often on the roof of the hotel to greet the passengers as they got off the train. The band also took part in nearby parades and other events.

After Wilhelm Keil's death in 1877, the Colony trustees assumed ownership of Aurora Colony and Bethel, the previous site set up by Keil's group in Missouri. His death left a power vacuum and the trustees proceeded to dissolve the two colonies. The final settlement of the dissolution was declared on January 22, 1883 and the City of Aurora was incorporated in 1893.

As occasionally happens, a modern day event opens a door to the past. One such event cast a spotlight on the Aurora Colony.

In the early 2000s, Jane Kirkpatrick, a well-known Oregon author of historical fiction, began a new series of novels called *Change and Cherish*, based on the Aurora Colony. Her extensive research into life in the

Main Street, Aurora, Oregon. (The term, *"The Road of a Thousand Wonders"* was used for railroad advertising and is sometimes incorrectly applied to the Pacific Highway as is evidenced in the photo.) *Courtesy of the Clackamas County Historical Society*

colony and literary popularity makes a visit to the old colony important to a large number of readers. That interest, and the money spent in the area, has helped the Aurora Colony Historical Society create a museum and begin some restoration. The museum displays many of the colony's collected items – musical instruments, handwoven clothing, various crafts and much more. In addition, they have developed an educational program for children where schools from the area visit to learn methods and experiences of the past including lessons on how to make candles and plan a quilt.

In an interview on May 12, 1939 for the Works Progress Administration (WPA) Folklore Studies, Elias Keil told his story:

A description of the Keil home was included by Eilias' interviewer, Howard M. Corning, in 1939:

"The large old frame house in which Eli Keil lives is perhaps the most distinctive architecturally of those now standing in Aurora. It faces east, toward the town, is quite tall and has a great-pillared front porch, with upper and lower levels, covering the entire face of the building. It was built in the middle 1860s from lumber cut at the local mill, long since burned down. The house measures probably 55-feet across the front, which is its longest dimension, for it is only about 30 feet deep, front to back. A chimney towers at the north end. A glimpse through the front windows shows that some partitions have been thrown in, dividing rooms that once were large, particularly the main living room. The fireplace does not appear impressive.

"Although the house sets well back from the highway, on a slight rise, it now has little frontyard; a strip about 20 feet deep runs before the house. Between that and the road is a garden patch. At the front south corner of the tall structure stands the most massive cherry tree I have ever seen, itself a landmark, possibly as old as the house. It throws a dense shade. Shrubbery grows wildly in the north yard. Other fruit trees stand about the home premises.

The Dr. Wilhelm Keil home in 1963 after it was renovated. It was built in the 1850s and was used as an inn until a hotel was built. *Courtesy of the on-line Oregon Encyclopedia Project, Oregon Historical Society*

A constant stream of water flows from beneath the small water tower at the back, pumped there by the water that runs at the foot of the slope to the south. Sheds and barns are spaced about the sprawling irregular area.

"The whole place is in general and sad disrepair and neglect. The owner's sole interest in life seems to be in caring for his cultivated acreage, berries, young orchard, and wheat lands, lying to the north and west. These fields climb the slope to the old Keil burial plot where the owner's parents and grandparents, the founders of the town, lie buried."

The text of Keil's interview follows:

"No, this wasn't the old William [Wilhelm] Keil house; my father built this some time in the [18]60s. Yes, my father was Frederick Keil, one of William's sons. The lumber was all cut down at the mill on the millrace. That was the second mill. The first mill was a small up-and-down one, it stood right down on Mill Creek. Sometimes when there was high water, in the winter or the spring, the first mill would be flooded so they couldn't work it. But that didn't happen very often. There were a few times, I guess, when the water was too low for the saw to operate. So they built the new mill. They built a dam back up over there to the south about a half mile, and dug a mill-race from it down to the creek. That gave them plenty of water force. The new mill set up too high to be under high water. Oh we had some high water in the spring. You could take a rowboat from right in front of the house here and boat clear over to the other side of town. That was nothing. We did it lots of times. Water stood all over the low parts. But that never happens now.

"...Those spokes in the banisters of the porch, you mean? They were turned out down at the mill, just like the main pillars of the church were. They had a turning lathe. It was run by a horse walking around in a circle. So were the porch pillars. They did some good work then.

"The big mill 'burned off' one night, some years ago.

"That half-moon window in the side of the barn there? That's only one of them; there's another on the south side. They were from the old Colony church, when it was torn down. The two of them were over the front doors.

"No, I don't seem to remember many of the old stories. There were things happened, of course. We had some visitors. The old stage route from Portland to Salem ran through here. There was where one of the old hotels stood – see that excavation over there? (He pointed several hundred yards to the south). A lot of travelers stayed there. A good many more stopped in town after the railroad came through [1873].

"Things were lively during the time they were building the railroad. Most of the work was done by the Irish – red-bearded Irish. They were a noisy bunch, always getting drunk, Saturday nights, especially. I remember once there was one got pretty drunk and started yelling 'There ain't no Dutchman can lick me.' Well, we had a teamster in town, a great big fellow. He stood this Irishman's bragging for a while, then he went up to him and said, 'See here, you better quit yellin' so loud; somebody might hear you.' But this Irish fellow kept on; 'I'd like to see the Dutchman can lick the Irish.' Well, this teamster – Schaefer was his name – he grabbed this red-bearded fellow around the shoulders

like he was wrestling with him, and laid him down on the mill platform, where they were standing. Schaefer wasn't mad; just telling him to quiet down. That fellow just turned his head to one side and sunk his teeth into Schaefer's arm. Right here in the muscle of the upper part. That made Schaefer mad. He just picked that Irishman up and threw him out into the millrace. That quieted him down. He floundered out and never said another word. There were a lot of people saw it happen and everybody laughed. I'll never forget that... Oh, I don't think of many stories like that.

"About the work gangs on the railroad: The Chinamen came in next; there were quite a lot of them for awhile. After that there were a lot of Jap[anese]. No, not many Italians, but Greeks. Only Americans work on the tracks now.

"In the early years, the wagon roads were kept up by the people owning property. In the spring the men all got out and worked the roads.

"But I missed most of the Colony life; I was five years old when it broke up. I do remember the fine music we had; two of the best bands in Oregon. My father belonged to one. He always said old John Ehlen was as good a musician as Finck (Henry Conrad Finch). He may not have been any better but he was just as good. We had festivals and picnics up in the park, and the band would play. To get there you go up the gravel road to the house on the hill, then turn west. The park's pretty much grown up now.

"...No, there were only three bells in the old church; not five. One was exhibited at Portland a few years ago and is somewhere downtown; I don't know where it's stored now. It hung in the fire hall until they bought the siren. One of them is up here in the schoolhouse. The other hangs in a church at Sherwood, I believe.

"You can photograph this house if you want to. Some people came out from the Historical Society some years ago and measured it and everything. I live here alone now, in this (south) side of the house. I had a family living in part of it for awhile. But now people seem to like to live by themselves. In the old Colony days there were several families to a house.

"Yes, that's a water ram. It pumps half a gallon every minute. It's a spring stream; comes from back up the ravine a short ways. It's good water. Sure, it pumps clear up here..."

The following is the text from Keil's second interview obtained in the lower field which the informant and a second man were plowing with a tractor and a walking plow...

"...See, I intend to irrigate this piece down here. Most every other year there has been enough overflow water from the tank above to keep it moist. But not this year. I'll do some troughing and run some ditches around and keep it watered. Yes, the water-ram will pump it around.

"Any more stories? Well, I don't know. Yes, I remember way back when Aurora had an old soldiers' lodge. All the old soldiers belonged to it; you know, there were American soldiers and some who had fought in foreign wars. All of them were together. They would all get together on Decoration Day and on the Fourth of July. One of them was my uncle (great uncle); he was the brother of my grandfather (Dr. William Keil, founder of the colony). Oh, I think he came about the same time in 1855, when the first settlers came across the country. He fought in the war against Napoleon. Let's see, when was that?

About 1812. That would make him 15 or 20 years older than his brother, I guess that was right.

"Well, you know, they were all up at the park for the celebration one Fourth of July; all these old soldiers, you know. And you know, my uncle was there and he'd been drinking. He'd got just enough to talk big and strut around. He was all dressed up, you know; had on his uniform and sabre and everything. Well, they were all talking, and my uncle he pulled out his sword and thrust it in the ground in front of him, exclaiming 'Well I fought Napoleon. I was in the wars and I fought Napoleon.' Well, he had his sword out and he wasn't very sober, so the rest of the old fellows took hold of his arms, you know, and patted him on the back, and said, 'Yes, Henry, you fought Napoleon.' He put his sword back then.

"Yes, I used to play the piano. I still have it up at the house. But they don't play the good music now. They play 'The Firefly and The Bumblebee,' and they're good. But Bennett wrote some pieces were just as good, but they don't play him any now. I don't know why. The radio [is now] mostly noise."

Interviewers comments: *"The informant talked with thoughtful composure, carefully, with little sense of drama but also with little carelessness of speech. He seems well content with life, making few demands of it. We stood in the sunny south yard, where he pointed out the landmarks and sites of a vanished life. To the south and east the scattered structures of the village, many of them painted white, as many more deeply weathered, sprawl in the bottomlands of the creek and of Pudding River, and climb the surrounding slopes. Much of the acreage about is cleared and cultivated, or lying fallow. There are scattered clumps of woodland.*

"...As we talked, a passenger train passed through the town, the track nearly a half-mile from the Keil house; yet the engine's whistle blasted against the hills with such force that the interviewer, who was speaking at the moment, had to leave his sentence temporarily unfinished..."

William Kraus of Aurora was interviewed on May 10, 1939 for the *WPA's American Life Histories Collection: Manuscripts from the Federal Writer's Project, 1936-1940* project. His interviewer was Howard M. Corning:

"...No, I don't seem to think of much right now. There used to be plenty of standing water around here in the winters. When we dug the millrace back of my place, that carried some of it off. Then we have tiled a good deal of the land around. When they first started to tile I didn't think it would do any good, but it did. It takes some of the water off just as soon as it falls and if there is any left standing it keeps taking that off; it doesn't stand in the ground the way it used to before we had the tile. The Colony had a dam back of my place a ways, you know; that was for the millrace.

"...The religious life of everyone here was in the hands of Dr. Keil. He directed it. When he died it died. Yes, we've always been Republicans hereabouts. No, there was no distillery; we didn't make liquor.

"You see, I came here after the colony was pretty well-established. Then as I say, I went to Prineville in 1878 and when I come back everything was changed, the colony life was gone. So I don't remember much about it.

"...The old buildings over town? There's the old newspaper office, and the house across from Arthur Keil's store. You have pictures of those? Well, let's see. Oh, that big building on the east side? No, that wasn't a store. (Chuckle) That was Keil's old ox barn. The Hurst's have a trucking service there; they fixed one end of it up for a residence.

"...I don't remember any German medicines that we used. The Doctor (Keil, undoubtedly) used a little machine; he put in on the arm here (forearm); it pricked the skin. It was used for most everything - smallpox, different things. Oh, I don't know what it was called. I don't think it had an American name, the German name was "schropfe" machine. I don't know that it drew the blood, but they used it a lot.

"Yes, there were some shops in the old colony. There was basket weaving. My wife's father Henry Ehlen handled all that. He did lots of weaving. They wove with oak splints. I can show you a bushel basket he made. We use it for a kindling basket, we've used it for fifty years...

"Yes, the colony made their own clothes and furniture, and I guess they had a glove factory.

"You're right, the earliest school was held in a little building up in the colony park. But that was a private school, mostly for the Keil children. The public school was built later. I went to the public school.

"No, I don't remember just when rural delivery came; later than in the eastern parts, I know. After 1900.

"...I know old Halladay used Chinese workers when he first started grading for the tracks. You can see the grade he started at the back of my place, only 300 or 400 feet from here, in those trees. It was too low and below high water. He had to begin all over, building higher up. Later there were some other nationalities worked, but I don't know what ones. Well, I remember there was an accident to a work train just north of town once. The cars were spilled over into the ditch and some of the crew were killed...

"Yes, in those days we all worked the roads. All the able-bodied men. If you were under 50 years you had to work two days each year. Then there was a poll tax of $1 for each man, I think. Besides that you were taxed $1 for each $1000 of property assessment."

BARLOWS / BARLOW

Samuel Barlow, who founded the Barlow Road, an extension of the Oregon Trail, first settled in the area now known as Barlow, Oregon, and bought the donation land claim of Thomas McKay on September 17, 1850 and later sold it to his son, William, for whom the town is named.

The Oregon & California Railroad built its tracks through Barlow in 1870 and soon after, on February 7, 1871, the Barlow Post Office was established. It closed on January 3, 1975.

The Italianate-designed William Barlow House, that was called Barlow Station, is still standing and is located south of Barlow between Canby and Aurora on Highway 99E. It was listed on the National Register of Historic Places on February 15, 1977. The house was built in 1885 and has been converted into a privately-owned museum that is open by appointment only.

From an article entitled "First Black Walnut Trees Planted in Oregon" in the *Sunday Oregonian*, October 8, 1905; a history written by Miss Mary S. Barlow:

The newspaper photo that accompanied the *Sunday Oregonian* article about the Barlow black walnut trees. The caption reads: "Residence of the late William Barlow, showing black walnut trees planted in 1859

"In 1858, Mr. John C. Dement, of Oregon City, went East to collect Indian War claims. He was requested by William Barlow to secure a bushel of black walnuts and butternuts and to send them by Adams' Express by way of the Isthmus. Mr. Dement obtained them in Indiana, Mr. Barlow's native state, and prepaid the charges on them to San Francisco. From there, they came direct to Oregon City by steamer, thence by private conveyance to their present habitat.

"The entire expense was just $65. The sack contained 665 black walnuts and 100 butternuts. One of each kind was eaten, tested and found preciously good, reminding the partakers of childhood's happy days in their far-away Eastern homes. The remaining 763 were put into a big box of earth and kept moist all Winter. By Spring the shells had opened and tiny little white sprouts began the tale of a century and more perhaps. The sprouted nuts were planted in well-fertilized soil, and 760 of them shot up their tender green [shoots],

Oregon - A December day on Barlow's Prairie. From Portland's *The West Shore* magazine, January 1, 1888

first, however, fixing for themselves a foundation of roots three three times the height of the little trees. They grew and grew all Spring and Summer.

"In the Fall of 1859, the birthyear of Oregon, 100 of them were planted on each side of the 450-foot avenue leading from the old stage road up to the old home, with its long, wide double porch, its large pillars and low sloping roof. About 200 were given to particular friends, and large trees from them are to be seen in many parts of the state today. The remainder, 510, were sold on commission by nurserymen at a profit to the prime mover in the venture of $500 and the highly-prized avenue at Barlow. Twenty years ago, the entire crop of nuts was sold to Eastern Oregon farmers. Those trees are now supplanting the mother orchard in supplying the Portland market with good well-filled nuts.

"In 1870, the 23rd year of their growth, the Barlow trees formed a beautiful vista, the length of the avenue, lending a perspective view and making a picture very Southern in type.

"But the progress of the West, which was so forcefully projected by the advent in that year of the first continental iron road of National domestic commerce, demanded that nature give way to its march. Nine large trees were leveled to the ground, where now the main track and two switches of the Southern Pacific Railroad carry to and fro products of a busy mart.

" Ben Holladay, the pioneer railroader, refused $50 for a tree that was confiscated by the iron king, and sent two flat cars and 20 men to carry it bodily to Portland. It now stands on what was once the Cunningham block, Holladay's Addition.

Mr. and Mrs. William Barlow have passed; a new house has risen from the ashes of the old home for the second generation; the thrifty Norwegians are fast converting the broad fields into small tracts; a hundred small homes are spring up over the 1,400 acres that once paid their tribute to the welfare and comfort of one man and his family: but – with all the changes, progressive or retrogressive, the walnuts planted by William Barlow 47 years ago still stand, and will stand for many, many years as monuments to the memory of one who made to grow the pioneer walnuts of Oregon."

The Barlow walnut trees that once lined the avenue to the family home have all given way to damage and age.

In an interview on February 7, 1939 for the Works Progress Administration (WPA) Folklore Studies, Mrs. Clyde B. Huntley told her story:

"I think it shows how well worth while is the work you are doing, when we of the third generation here in Oregon can remember so little of the stories we must have heard our grandmothers tell. I've been more interested than the average, I believe, yet only a few incidents can I relate, aside from what has been already related in some of the histories of the State. Everybody knows, for instance, about my great-grandfather, Samuel Kimbrough Barlow, his building of the Barlow Trail, and all that sort of thing. But perhaps this story of his burial place may not be so well-known. It seems to me it well reflects the character of the man. When he died in 1867, he was buried in the small burial plot in one corner of his farm. Here also his wife was buried, and some members of the family of Bowers, adjoining neighbors. The little burial ground was fenced off and over the graves of my great-grandfather and great-grandmother a tombstone was erected. On the tombstone is this inscription:

> "'Do not disturb the repose of the dead;
> Behold the pure spirit has arisen and fled!
> Nor linger, in sadness, around the dark tomb,
> But go, where flowers forever will bloom.'

"The inscription was composed by great-grandfather, who directed that it should be placed on his tombstone, with full directions also as to where and how he should be buried.

"In later years, Colonel Rinehart, who had married a great-aunt of mine, and was brother-in-law of my grandfather, William Barlow, wished, or rather my great-aunt wished, to move the remains of great-grandfather and great-grandmother to Seattle, where they were living, and had a family burial plot; but the inscription halted them, and the graves were not disturbed. Aunt Mollie Barlow Wilkins was similarily influenced, when, on visiting the graves, she found the tombstone deteriorating from time and weather, and the surrounding fence falling into decay. She felt that it was, perhaps, the wish of great-grandfather that his dust should be absorbed by Mother Nature and be forgotten. But I am not so sure. I am going up some day soon, and see what I can do about it. The D.A.R. Chapter at Oregon City is, as you perhaps know, named for great-grandmother Susannah [Lee] Barlow."

BAKER PRAIRIE / CANBY

Canby was founded in 1857, platted in 1870 and incorporated on February 15, 1893. It was named for Edward Richard Sprigg Canby, a Civil War general who was later killed in the Modoc War by Captain Jack and his group of warriors.

From an interview of Myra Weston, Peggy Sigler wrote an article of Myra's memories of early-day Canby. It is being reprinted here courtesy of the Canby Historical Society:

"On the high plateau, bordered by the Willamette and Molalla Rivers, Canby was once the seasonal meeting place for tribes of local Indians and was well-known for

Canby's Main Street (date unknown). *Courtesy of the Oregon Department of Transportation (ODOT) History Center*

its annual crop of wild strawberries. The area known as Baker Prairie was an open expanse of ground in the dense fir forest that stretched for miles.

"Baker, one of the earliest white settlers in Oregon, arrived in the area in 1832 with a cattle drive from California, took an Indian wife and was soon farming. The land he 'squatted' on was what is now north Canby. Other settlers arrived, including Philander and Anna Lee in 1848, who bought 'squatter's rights' beside a spring-fed creek on what is now S.E. First Avenue. The family's long-time home nearby was on the site now owned by Package Containers, Inc.

"Lee began growing apples on 80 acres of land and shipped them to the gold miners in California. In 1850, the Lees gained title to their 647 acres through the Donation Land Claim Act which brought many more settlers over the Oregon Trail to Baker Prairie and surrounding areas.

"Joseph Knight and four sons moved to Baker Prairie in 1868. They were instrumental in Canby's early development as they opened one of the first general stores, built many local buildings, served as postmaster, school clerk, sheriff, druggist, blacksmith, carpenter and more. William Knight's 1874 home still stands at 525 S.W. Fourth Avenue as does the 1890 Knight Building on N.W. First Avenue, the original meeting place of City Council and first home of Carlton & Rosenkrans, 'Clackamas County's largest department store.'

"Along with a meager network of dirt roads and trails, some still visible, such as Territorial Road with its tall fir trees lining the road, the Willamette River served as main transportation. Steamboats took produce into the markets of Oregon City and Portland from the little local communities of Baker Prairie, Barlow, New Era, Riverside, Macksburg, Mundorf, Lone Elder, Mark Prairie and others.

"While pushing the Oregon and California Railroad line from east Portland to San Francisco, promoters approached Philander Lee for land in 1870. For $2,960, he sold 111 acres for the 24-block city, 12 lots per block. The Knight family and others sold the remainder of the 300 acres to the railroad. Lee would only sell land for a town if the streets were wide enough for two span of oxen and a wagon to turn. So, Philander's son, Albert, hitched up the oxen and turned the team and wagon, measuring the diameter of the turn to be 80 feet, which became the width of Canby's original streets. The City's plat was filed in Oregon City on August 9, 1870.

"Major General Edward R.S. Canby, hero of the Civil and Indian Wars, had arrived in Oregon only one week earlier to assume command of the U.S. Army's Department of the Columbia and the new town was given this hero's name. Rails were laid in 1870 and in 1873 the depot was built near what is now N.W. First and Grant. Albert H. Lee, Philander's eighth child, was the first railroad agent.

"The first post office and depot was in the drug store across from the depot, and druggist Charles 'Doc' Knight, who came in 1870 and also built the first hotel, was the first postmaster.

"Canby was incorporated on February 15, 1893, making it the second oldest city in Clackamas County. Herman A. Lee, Philander's second son, served as the first mayor. By 1890 Canby boasted three hotels and a bank, and by 1910, the population was 587. The railroad tracks were quickly lined with warehouses as the agriculture industry grew in the Canby area. Local crops included grain, hay, potatoes, dairy products, turkeys, flax, prunes, rhubarb, asparagus, berries, nuts, livestock, lumber, bulbs, flowers and nursery stock. For many years, three covered bridges crossed the Molalla River from Canby and in 1914, local businessmen established ferry service across the Willamette River.

"Prior to 1920, the 'Road of 1000 Wonders,' now N.W. First Avenue, was the main route through Canby, running northeast to Oregon City and west to Barlow and up the valley. That year marked the arrival of the Pacific Highway (U.S. Highway 99E) to the south of the railroad tracks, making the beginning of yet a new era of transportation and development in Canby. Canby has grown from 998 people in 1940, to 1,286 residents by 1945. Now Canby boasts a population of over 13,000, and the city covers a three-square mile area. Many of the early buildings and homes in the original 24-block town site still exist and the city is surrounded by early farmhouses and barns, reminders of Canby's early pioneer, railroad and agricultural heritage."

The Clackamas County Fairgrounds in 1915. It shows "the original pavilion, a 1913 Model "T" touring car/taxi with a sign saying 'Fairgrounds 10¢,' a horse-drawn water wagon and a tall ladder from which a little dog did a crowd-thrilling leap into a small net." *Courtesy of the Clackamas County Fair History website and the "Where Memories are Born" pamphlet.*

Author's note: The term, "The Road of a Thousand Wonders" was used for Southern Pacific Railroad advertising and is sometimes incorrectly applied to the Pacific Highway as in the reference above. It actually refers to the railroad itself, not the highway.

With fertile soil and a location close to Portland, Canby has grown into a small city with a population of about 16,000. The Willamette River is on the north and the Molalla River on the west. It is still possible to cross the Willamette River to Wilsonville by ferry much of the year depending on the weather.

Canby has been the host of the Clackamas County Fair for over 100 years – since 1909. For the first two years, the fair was held in nearby Gladstone, but the Clackamas County Fair Association was organized in 1908 and began selling membership certificates at $5 per share to provide funds to purchase property in Canby. The parcel, located on the estate of Aaron Wait, was purchased for $3,692.50 with a contribution from the Clackamas County Court of $250.

According to the pamphlet, "Where Memories are Born," put out by the Clackamas County Historical Society:

"...The earliest buildings were a livestock barn and temporary grandstand. The race track was laid out and graded."

By 1915, *"...a small carnival was brought in by Browning's Carnival. It included a ferris wheel, a tent housing a "Spanish Bull Fight" and what appeared to be several games of chance."*

In 1925, state law required that fairs be placed under the jurisdiction of the counties and it was taken out of the hands of the Clackamas County Fair Association.

In 1929, *"...county fair representatives from Clackamas and four other counties met and formed an organization called the Oregon County and District Fairs. The organization rather quickly gained members in order to better represent the fairs of Oregon."*

The Clackamas County Fair has continued to grow in popularity and its site in Canby has expanded to provide one of the most popular county fairs in Oregon. With the exception of a curtailment during World War II in which the fair was limited to just a youth show, it has operated continuously since 1909.

The fairgrounds are also used for other events year round. Next to it is the oldest railroad depot in the state. It's not in the original location, but it is now refurbished and serves as the Canby Museum. There are additional remnants of the railroad history including signals and a caboose.

Even though the railroad tracks run right through the center of town and the Union Pacific Amtrak makes regular runs, it doesn't stop at Canby. The nearest place to hop on board is Oregon City.

The population of the area is made up of many second generation Russian Old Believers and an increasing number of Latinos.

NEW ERA

New Era is considered a "semi-ghost town," as there are still some current residents there, but not many. It was sited near the Parrot Creek which flows into the nearby Willamette River, above the Willamette Falls along the eventual U.S. Highway 99 route between Canby and Oregon City.

Joseph Parrot first settled in the New Era region in 1845, and was soon followed by neighbors, John G. and Elizabeth (Ensley) Gribble in 1846 and a widow, Elizabeth Alprey in 1849.

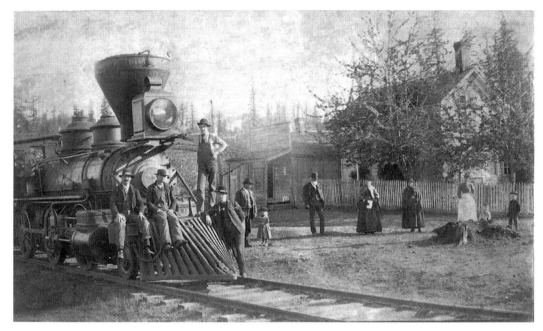

The New Era Store, Post Office and the Dustin home are in the background. The man standing next to the little girl is John C. Newbury and Laura Newbury-Thompson, ca 1891. According to Southern Pacific records, this locomotive, #33, was built at SP's Sacramento shops in 1873 and was scrapped in 1900. It was of 4-4-0 design and registered 74,000 lbs. loaded weight. *Courtesy of Stephanie McGuire*

According to the Oregon History Project biography of Ben Holladay:

"On Christmas Eve 1869, the first train from Portland arrived in the small town of New Era, twenty miles away on the east side of the Willamette River. Benjamin Holladay, a driving force behind the road, was one of the passengers. A year and a half earlier, two railways had begun construction in Portland. One, on the west side of the river, was supported by attorney Joseph Gaston and Portland city officials, while the other had the support of the Central Pacific Railroad and Holladay. Competing for both traffic and a federal land grant, the two sides agreed that whichever company first built twenty miles of line would buy out the other. Holladay won the race and expanded the east and west side lines until his finances collapsed in 1873..."

On the ghosttowns.com website, Peggy Sigler writes:

"Communities sprang up along streams where water power allowed industrial development. A post office was established in the early 1850s (original name unknown at this time), at the confluence of Beaver and Parrot creeks, now known as New Era. The New Era Rolling Mill was established in 1868, continuing operation until 1935. The origin of the name New Era is unclear, however, some inaccurately relate it to the Spiritualist Camp, founded in 1873, located near the mill site. James Washington Offield, a child when his family arrived via the Barlow Road in 1850, stated that he named 'New Era' when he

The New Era Store and Post Office. *Courtesy of Stephanie McGuire*

Inside the New Era Store and Post Office with Jennie and Wyman Dustin, owners. *Courtesy of Stephanie McGuire*

New Era, Oregon. The Brown School is the white building on the top of the hill. The Sevcik Mill pond is on the far right. *Courtesy of Stephanie McGuire*

Coalca Pillar or "Balance Rock" is located near New Era. *Courtesy of Stephanie McGuire*

built a commission warehouse circa 1860 at the same site where his mother's oxen died en-route to their donation land claim in the Macksburg area years earlier."

New Era was once a prosperous town. It was the home to the New Era Spiritual Society, a religious group that settled on a hill near the town. It's very possible that the town's name was derived from the spiritual society even though the camp may not have been formed until 1873. As early as 1854, the Boston *New Era* spiritualist periodical was listed as one of the foremost magazines devoted to the American Spiritualist Movement according to the *Family Herald* on September 2, 1854. The modern American Spiritualist Movement was begun in about 1848 and is related to the Shakers and similar religious groups. There is still a New Era Christian Spiritualists Church on New Era Road with a Canby address.

In the book, *Oregon Geographic Names* by Lewis A. McArthur, the author suggests that the name came as the result of the construction of the railroad as far as the mouth of Parrott Creek which made it possible for Willamette River boats to stop there and deliver produce. This was hailed as a new era in river transportation as boats would not have to go to the falls below at Oregon City. He comments that it has the ring of truth, but one correspondent has informed him that a local family were spiritualists and devoted to a publication called the *New Era* and named the place on that account.

The town of New Era was also a farming community. The rich soil was ideal for raising potatoes and other crops and according to Henry Chenoweth on the ghost town website, *"Shipments were made by wagon to Oregon City, transferred to boats below the falls and on to Portland. After a system of locks was built, boats could put in at New Era and after the arrival of the railroad, the produce was shipped by train."*

Stephanie McGuire, who provided the pictures for the New Era segment, is the great-great granddaughter of Jennie Dustin.

Jennie's first husband, John C. Newbury, became the first postmaster of the New Era Post Office when he and Jennie arrived from Montana in 1890. Upon his death in 1900. Jennie took over the position of not only postmaster, but Wells Fargo and Southern Pacific agent and storekeeper. In 1905, she married Wyman Dustin who helped her run the store.

When Jennie retired as postmaster of the

Next to the Sevcik Grist Mill pond located behind the New Era Store and Post Office, ca 1890. John C. Newbury is standing in the middle.
Courtesy of Stephanie McGuire

New Era Post Office and Store on January 31, 1940, she was recognized as the holder of "one of the longest records of postal service in Oregon." She served the New Era Post Office for 49½ years, 33 of those as postmaster and, by U.S. Postal Service requirements, was forced to retire at the age of 74, four years after the 70-year-old mandatory retirement.

The Southern Pacific tracks ran directly in front of the New Era Store and the Dustin home which sat next door to it.

In an article written for his Wells Fargo blog, Steve Greenwood adds more to the story:

"...At the time, New Era was a thriving community with river steamboats on the Willamette River, and railroad cars picking up or dropping off passengers. The town had a water wheel that ground flour and feed for shipment, a sawmill, and a warehouse full of hundreds of tons of potatoes bound for California. Twice a year the town attracted meetings of Spiritualists. New Era even had a one-room school with 60 students.

"Hundreds of settlers visited Jennie's store by rowboat, wagon, and horseback to buy goods, get mail, and hear the latest news. Her largest customer was the Doernbecher Manufacturing Company, which owned a sawmill on the Willamette. Today, the Doernbecher name is better known as one of Oregon's premier children's hospitals..."

When the Pacific Highway was built, it had to be cut into the bluff in front of the buildings in order to pass through the area.

As the surrounding towns began to grow, they drew more business away from the store and post office. One year after Jennie retired as postmaster, the New Era Post Office was closed.

Jennie ran the store for a few more years before it, too, closed in 1947.

After Jennie passed away in 1952, the property was sold, and in 1964, new owners had the old store torn down to make way for the widening of Highway 99.

It was truly an end of an era for New Era.

CANEMAH

We know that the stagecoach routes went through Oregon City, possibly

The Canemah Boardwalk. *Courtesy of the Clackamas County Historical Society*

Canemah, from the various mentions in the research we've already done. Feaster's Station which was mentioned in *Knights of the Whip* could have been in the Canemah (Oregon City) area, as there were Feasters living in the area at that time.

Canemah, meaning "the canoe place" was another small community that sat along the Willamette River and was a station along the O&C railroad line. It was an important boat-landing, not far south of Oregon City. Several sternwheelers were built there.

It was at Canemah that the steamer, "Gazelle" was lost in 1854. Gazelle was an early sidewheeler on the Willamette River. Only a month after her maiden voyage took place, she was destroyed in a catastrophic boiler explosion.

Gazelle was built by the Willamette Falls Canal, Milling and Transportation Company at Linn City, now called West Linn, Oregon. It was located on the west side of the Willamette River across from Oregon City. Gazelle was driven by two steam engines, each one turning one of her sidewheels.

Although it was built below Willamette Falls, Gazelle was to be used on the Willamette River above the falls. To reach the upper part of the river, Gazelle was lifted above the falls and launched on the upper Willamette at Canemah.

On April 8, 1854, at 6:30 a.m., Gazelle had come over to Canemah from the long wharf built above the falls on the western side of the river above Linn City. Its destination was said to be Corvallis. Apparently, in order to make a speedy departure, the engineer, Moses Toner, had tied down the safety valve to build up steam. About ten minutes later, Toner was seen jumping off the boat and running down the dock. About a minute later, both boilers exploded, killing over 20 people and injuring many more, four of whom died within a short while. Sixty people were on board at the time. Another sidewheeler, the Wallamet, had been lying alongside Gazelle. It was badly damaged and her pilot, J.M. Pudge was killed. Captain Hereford, the pilot of the Gazelle, was injured but survived.

There is a plaque on an outcropping of rock overlooking the Willamette River at the former Canemah landing that reads:

Willamette Falls at Oregon City. Caption from ODOT photo reads: "Oregon City - Willamette Falls, 1878" *Courtesy of the Oregon Department of Transportation (ODOT) History Center*

Near the Willamette Falls at Oregon City, January 21, 1953. *Courtesy of the Oregon Department of Transportation (ODOT) History Center*

*"600 yards south of this point
Explosion of Steamer Gazelle
April 8, 1854.
Loss of twenty-four lives.
May 18th, 1933
by Multnomah Chapter D.A.R."*

OREGON CITY

The town was built in two levels at the confluence of the Clackamas and Willamette Rivers in order to take advantage of the power that could be generated for a lumber mill from the nearby Willamette Falls. Since Oregon City had essentially the only source of power for the area, it became the natural site for the territorial government after a treaty was signed with Britain in 1846, establishing United States' interests.

In 1845, it was the first U.S. city west of the Rocky Mountains to be incorporated and from 1848 until 1851, it served as the capital of the Oregon Territory and was the terminus of the Oregon Trail.

In an interview on March 1, 1939 for the Works Progress Administration (WPA) Folklore Studies, Mrs. Sarah L. Byrd told her story:

"Bein' so little I can't remember very much about crossin' the plains. When we first got here we went to Oregon City an' stayed for a while. When we started from I-o-way father meant to go to Californy, but when they got to wher the roads parted to Oregon an' Californy, he came to Oregon. When we wuz in Oregon City we wuz perty close to where Doctor McLoughlin lived. I remember seein' a squaw out in his yard. She wore dresses, but she had bare feet. I remember thet, an' I remember hearin' 'em say thet wuz Doctor McLoughlin's wife. Ther wuz a man named Jewett in Oregon City thet father knew in I-o-way, an' he got to tellin' father 'bout the Clatsop Plains country, so father decided he'd go down ther. Ther wuzn't any roads then, o'course – jest Indian trails. Finally it wuz decided father an' my oldest brother would drive the stock down over the trail. I think he hed a cow, a yoke o' oxen an' two horses, an' Mr. Jewett tuk mother an' the rest of we young'uns down the river. We went in a big Indian canoe, with two Indians to paddle it. Goin' down the Willamette we passed a place where ther wuz a few cabins, an' Mr. Jewett sed, 'That's Portland.' Mother al'ays laughed when she tol' that. Oregon City wuz a lot bigger then. I wish I c'd remember thet trip down the Columbia. Jest mother, we three young'uns, thet strange man, an' the two siwashes, in a canoe on that big, lonesum river."

In 1846, when Britain and the United States signed a treaty setting the 49th parallel as a boundary between their interests, settlers began arriving in increasing numbers.

In 1848, the United States' Congress organized the Territory of Oregon as a temporary government. More emigrants came.

In Kay Atwood's excellent book, *Chaining Oregon; Surveying the Public Lands of the Pacific Northwest, 1851-1855*, she describes the major job of surveying the vast Oregon Territory which is also featured in the Oregon City Historic Museum.

Congress passed the Oregon Donation Land Claim Act on September 17, 1850. It had three key provisions, two of which are not often mentioned years later. The first was the selection of a surveyor general; the next, the initiation of public land surveys west of the Cascade Range; and the award of land claims to settlers who met specific requirements.

Through this act, the government offered 320 acres to any white male over eighteen years of age who was a citizen or had declared his intention to apply, who resided in the Territory on or before December 1, 1850, and who had cultivated his fields for a least four years. A settler's wife could claim 320 acres in her own name. This was the first federal legislation to grant women property in their own right.

Single men who settled in Oregon between December 1, 1850 and December 1, 1853, could claim 160 acres and a similar amount of land for their wives should they marry. It was one way to assure there would be women in Oregon.

After each settler submitted proof of settlement, cultivation, and citizenship – and after the U.S. government had surveyed the land, the General Land Office issued him/her a certificate. By the spring of 1851, thousands of people lived south of the Columbia River on lands they measured by creeks, hills, rivers and sometimes by agreements with others. People who claimed more ground than they could farm wanted to divide and sell. They pressed for surveys and official designation of boundary claims.

In November 1850, President Millard Fillmore appointed John B. Preston, an experienced engineer, to the position of Oregon's first surveyor general. He had studied bookkeeping, mathematics and surveying. He had trained as a civil engineer and an attorney.

Preston began looking for top-ranked surveyors to work for him. He required that they be experienced, must be ready to leave for Oregon almost immediately, and that they must be skilled in operating Burt's Improved Solar Compass. This compass used the sun to precisely locate due north and was important because iron ore deposits distort magnetic needle compass readings. In 1850, the General Land Office adopted the solar compass for surveying major boundary lines.

Preston had less than a month to meet with General Land Office Commissioner, Justin Butterfield, in Washington DC and buy all the equipment needed – transits, sextants, four solar compasses – and meet with Dr. John Evans, the newly-commissioned U.S. Geologist for Oregon who would travel to the Oregon Territory the following summer. Preston was given a ten-year-old sketch map of the land west of the Cascades that had been drawn by an explorer who had visited the Oregon Country in 1841. He was also given several leather-bound copies of the *Manual of Surveying* instructions.

Preston chose William Ives of Michigan and James Freeman of Wisconsin as his lead surveyors. They both had solid reputations as accurate, honest engineers. It should be noted that these two would be working on contracts for sections of land. They were to be paid when each section was completed and each would hire their own crew. William Ives asked his youngest brother to be his deputy surveyor. The group, including John B. Preston, the Surveyor General, one of the two lead surveyors and several recruits for the crew, traveled to Oregon by ship, transferring several times before arriving in San Francisco. They left San Francisco on the steamship Columbia for Astoria and then boarded the *Lot Whitcomb* for the journey on the Columbia River. From there, they traveled the Willamette River as far as Milwaukie and then boarded a flat, open "whale boat" for the rest of the trip to Oregon City. The whale boat got stuck on a sand bar, however, so some of the passengers walked to Oregon City and got help to rescue the rest of the passengers.

John Preston's first job was to find housing and a place for an office while he waited for the two lead surveyors to set up crews and obtain supplies. The instructions from the General Land Office in Washington advised him to establish the initial point – the place at which the Willamette Meridian and Base Line intersected – so that the base line running east would cross south of the Columbia River and north of Mount Hood. It would then run west, crossing the Tualatin Plains.

According to Kay Attwood:

"The Willamette Meridian, the commissioner directed, should pass between Vancouver Lake and the Columbia River

to keep the line out of these two waterways. The meridian's northerly terminus was set at Puget Sound."

For the time being, they were to survey only the Willamette and Umpqua valleys.

So, John Preston, with the advice of John McLoughlin and other Oregonians, determined that it would be necessary to go to the Cascade Mountains to run the line from the most southerly point in the River west to the meridian line in order to designate the starting point for the Base and meridian lines.

With his two lead surveyors, William Ives and James Freeman, John Preston hired a Hudson's Bay Company batteau, which is a shallow-draft, flat-bottomed boat, for a three-day trip up the Columbia. None of the men were familiar with the mountains at this elevation or the scenic wonders along the river banks. The three noted the location of the river's southern-most bend north of the present-day Corbett. They went ashore and established that point as the baseline. They returned to Fort Vancouver where Preston and Freeman left for Oregon City. Ives, joined by two of his crew, bought a skiff to establish an optimum location for the meridian line. They boated down the Columbia to the mouth of the Willamette River, hiked a mile-and a half north to make sure the line would pass on the west side of Vancouver Lake and surveyed a line back to the Columbia River. It was the first principal meridian in Oregon Territory south of the Columbia River.

"On May 28, 1851, Surveyor General Preston gave James Freeman the first federal survey contract in Oregon to faithfully survey the Willamette meridian from its intersection with the baseline south to the Umpqua Valley. William Ives received the second contract to run the baseline from its intersection with the Willamette meridian, west to the Pacific Ocean and east to the summit of the Cascade Range of mountains and also to run the Willamette meridian north of the baseline to the Puget Sound. They would have three months to complete their contract. Their expeditions were to be paid for with bonds that were about double the contract amount."

If a surveyor did not have a lot of money himself, he had to find an established businessman or landowner who would put up a bond for him. In other words, he would guarantee the work equal to an amount about double what was provided for in the contract. In this case, the contract amount specified in the Donation Land Claim Act itself was $8. So, for each mile run, marked and recorded in this case, the bond needed to be for $20.

The surveyors were to keep a detailed record of everything noted in measuring their line. They were required to also present a full and complete topographical description of the country surveyed, and to follow special instructions attached to their contracts.

These special instructions dealt with rivers too wide to be surveyed and inaccessible mountain ranges. They had to keep separate field books for the base and meridian lines and for the township and section lines. The Donation Land Claim Act required the geodetic survey as well as the rectangular survey which required even more specialized equipment.

The two lead surveyors assembled their crews of about nine. The survey teams began a major undertaking, using techniques quite different than those used today. All of the crew members had titles suggesting specific jobs, but all knew they would often have other chores.

The axemen cut trees to mark the way or chopped brush to blaze the pathway for the chainmen.

The chainmen carried the chains and poles through brush, swamps, sloughs, creeks, forests and up steep mountain sides. Their equipment included a 100-foot chain to stretch out, marking each 100 feet traversed with a steel stake or pin. They also carried 11 steel chaining pins, not longer than 14 inches, with a ring at the top.

The front chainman carried a flag pole. He would hold the chain as taut as possible to keep it horizontal and the rear chainman held the chain over a pin. To communicate with each other, they had to shout – there were no radios or walkie-talkies on which they could talk back and forth – so they used a code. When the chain was tight, the rear chainman called out, "Stick!" The front man would then repeat the call and a flagman would mark the position. The two chainman would slowly begin to move forward. They repeated their measurements three times for every hundred yards.

The second chain duo would verify the accuracy.

They continued to do this by walking back and forth from the Columbia River south to the steep canyon past Canyonville. They slept outside on the ground, in tents if it rained. There were no air mattresses. They had to carry their own food and supplies. There was no nearby store. Quite often, supplies were a long distance away. When it was feasible, they used mules to transport the supplies, but sometimes they used a boat, sending members of the crew back for supplies in the them. If the crew member who was charged with replenishing the supplies couldn't get back for an extra day or two, they went without.

When they were on land that had already been settled, they were sometimes housed inside, but because most of the small cabins were filled with the settlers and their families, they frequently continued to sleep outside or in the animal barns and sheds.

The completions of those first two contracts by William Ives and James Freeman and their crew led to the prospect of more surveying jobs. The slowness of the project, however, caused distress for the settlers and national government politics delayed payment. As squabbling and complaints increased, Native American problems escalated and their jobs became more difficult and time-consuming. Eventually, however, their work became the basis for the townships, land claims, railroads and even highways that formed the infrastructure of what we now have today on the lands on which they painstakingly measured and surveyed.

According to the 2011-2012 *Oregon Blue Book*, *"...By the end of the time period, 7,437 claimants could register their claims, use the surveys to divide and sell, and reduce or increase their land holdings to what they could farm or sell."*

The toil and dedication of these men allowed donation land claims to be defined and their work created the framework for all the engineers that came after.

Excerpts from published reminiscences of James Meikle Sharp, who, at the age of eight, crossed the plains with his father and mother in 1852. Obtained from the Interview with Mrs. J.R. Bean on January 31, 1939:

"...During the succeeding days, up to October 16th, we crossed the Clackamas River, arrived at Oregon City, and crossed the Willamette River, thence continued westerly into the Chehalem Valley, and arrived

Paper plant at Willamette Falls across the river from U.S. Highway 99.
Courtesy of the OSU Special Collections & Archives Commons

Main Street, Oregon City.
Courtesy of the Clackamas County Historical Society

The Oregon City Interurban.
Courtesy of the Clackamas County Historical Society

at Mr. George Nelson's place on the 16th...

"In Oregon City father secured a loan or donation of five dollars from a worthy gentleman by the name of R.R. Thompson, which must have been another life saver.

"Mr. Nelson's house was built on a gently rising ground, and as we drove so slowly up the hill, the sun was about to sink behind the western mountains. Mother, and most of us children were walking. Father had not been feeling well for some days and was riding in the wagon. As we pulled up alongside the front gateway, a woman came out and asked 'Isn't there a sick man in the wagon?' and learning there was, had us come into the house. She put father into bed, where they kept him for about two weeks. We think now he must have had typhoid fever. 'Uncle George' and 'Aunt Peggy,' as the Nelsons were known far and wide, were well-advanced in years, and had been living in Oregon since 1848. Their house was a large double affair, with a roofed-over open section between.

"As soon as father was able to move, we secured a house not far from Mr. Nelson's, from a Mr. Morris, into which we moved November 2, 1853. It was a structure built of small logs, about twelve by sixteen feet. I believe it had a fireplace, because we could hardly have survived a cold winter otherwise. There was a loft or attic, reached by a ladder, and here was the boys' dormitory during the winter. In this small building the nine of us spent the time from November 2, '53 to February 21, '54. There was a snowfall of about two feet during most of this period. Our food was a steady diet of boiled wheat, which was bought at $5.00 per bushel, or about 8 cents per pound. Strong and wholesome food, but rather monotonous."

John McLoughlin, fondly referred to some years later by the Oregon State Legislature as the "Father of Oregon," established Fort Vancouver in 1825 and was put in charge of the British Hudson's Bay Company. He was an astute businessman and made a lot of money for the Hudson's Bay Company and treated all of those he dealt with – trappers and natives, alike – fairly.

When exhausted, starving American settlers began arriving on the Oregon Trail, McLoughlin provided assistance by giving them supplies to help them survive their first winter in Oregon.

According to the McLoughlin House website:

"...His kindness to them would eventually cost him his job with the HBC. He had purchased HBC's land claim at Willamette Falls (Oregon City), and he and his family moved into his newly-built mansion in 1846 after being forced to retire. He died in this home in 1857."

The McLoughlin House was designated by Congress as the first National Historic Site in the West and serves as a museum today.

"In 1909, it was threatened with demolition, but a group of concerned local citizens formed the McLoughlin Memorial Association to preserve and protect the house and the legacy of Dr. McLoughlin. They moved the house from its original location by the river up to its present location atop the bluff, restored it, and turned the house into a museum. The McLoughlin Memorial Association continues to actively support the McLoughlin House, in partnership with the National Park Service. It was also added to the National Park System in

2003, as a unit of Fort Vancouver National Historic Site.

"The home opened as a museum in 1910, and it continues to draw thousands of visitors each year from all over the world. It is one of several historic homes in Oregon City which are open to the public."

The city of Oregon City is situated in a unique location. The town formed on two levels. The first level is a narrow strip, only a few blocks wide, that is wedged between the Willamette River and a towering 90-foot basalt cliff. The second level sits at the top of the cliff. Various stairways that joined a stone promenade were built to accommodate foot traffic between the levels, but they weren't a satisfactory solution.

In 1912, the voters passed a referendum to construct a 130-foot municipal water-powered elevator to transport people up and

Courthouse in Oregon City built in 1884 (not the original). *Courtesy of the OSU Special Collections & Archives Commons*

down the cliff between the two levels. It was completed in 1915 and took three minutes to go from the bottom to the top. In 1924, it was converted to an electrical drive and the trip took only 30 seconds to complete.

In 1952, after 40 years of service, another bond election was passed for $175,000 to build a replacement. The specifications called for "no-frills." The new elevator, designed by Gordon E. Trapp, has an observation deck on top, and now takes 15 seconds to ascend. It is still used today and is the only outdoor municipal elevator in the United States and one of only four in the world.

Barbara Dare of Lorane, Oregon shared some memories of U.S. Highway 99:

"In the summer of 1962, my sister-in-law, Nancy Dare, age 18, took a trip from Bakersfield, California to the Seattle World's Fair. With her was her little sister,

A photo postcard of the Oregon City elevator.

Trisha, age 14. Her grandmother, Mabel Mahan, chaperoned the girls. They don't remember a whole lot about the road trip itself, but told about an outdoor elevator that they used in Oregon City to get from the bottom of a steep cliff where one part of the town was located to the top level.

"At one point the luggage was packed in the car in such a way that it blocked the trunk from being opened, so they were stranded with what they wore. It was a Sunday, so no garages were open, but they managed to talk a gentleman into opening his shop long enough to get the tool needed to open the trunk.

"I often take Highway 99 north from Cottage Grove, area where I live, and I marvel at what the traffic must have been like on that little two-lane winding road. But it's kind of neat to think of the family traveling over that same road so many years ago."

"**In excerpts from an article *1931-1956: Hard Times & Recovery* by Eileen G. Fitzimons in *The Sellwood Bee* on October 4, 1956.**

"Slowly a few federally-funded government projects began to provide occasional short-term employment. Two of these impacted the Eastmoreland and Westmoreland areas. The first was the construction of the 'super highway,' also called McLoughlin Boulevard which began in Oregon City and gradually moved north to Portland."

Construction on Highway 99E provided jobs and quicker access between towns lying on the east side of the Willamette River.

When leaving Oregon City as McLoughlin Blvd., the original Pacific Highway route crossed over to the west side of the Willamette River on the 1922-vintage Oregon City Bridge. The route that is now Oregon Route 43, went through West Linn and Lake Oswego. From there the Pacific Highway followed what is now the Capital Highway, then Terwilliger Blvd. on its way through downtown Portland, but so much of that portion has been buried or rerouted, it is now nearly impossible to trace. We do know, however, that it crossed the river on the Broadway Bridge to get to the Interstate Bridge that crosses the Columbia River into Washington.

After U.S. Highway 99W was built, the east route which was renamed, U.S. Highway 99E, no longer crossed the river into West Linn and Lake Oswego. Now named the Martin Luther King Blvd., it stayed on the east side of the Willamette River as it en-

Pacific Highway at Oregon City taken "from overhead crossing of the Southern Pacific Railroad tracks - South." *Courtesy of the Oregon Department of Transportation (ODOT) History Center*

Oregon City's first automobile. *Courtesy of the Clackamas County Historical Society*

tered downtown Portland. The route still continues through Gladstone and Milwaukie before eventually merging with Highway 99W/Barbur Blvd., now known as Interstate Avenue, just before the entrance to the Interstate Bridge near the Portland Meadows Race Track.

As with the rest of the area, the Christmas flood of 1964 was *"the most severe rainstorm to ever occur over central Oregon, and among the most severe over western Oregon since the late 1870s,"* according to the National Weather Service office in Portland.

According to Rachel Dresbeck's *Oregon Disasters: True Stories of Tragedy and Survival*:

"At Oregon City, Willamette Falls was unrecognizable as a waterfall, and the city was flooded by several feet of water. In Portland, the lower deck of the Steel Bridge was underwater and had also been hit by a log raft consisting of around 1,000

Walking on the frozen Willamette River at Oregon City, 1919. *Courtesy of the Clackamas County Historical Society*

A Gladstone trolley headed south. *Courtesy of the Clackamas County Historical Society*

logs. The impact of the raft severely damaged the Hawthorne Bridge, closing it for a year. At 12 feet above flood stage, the flooding of the Willamette River at Portland in 1964 was second only to the 1948 flood that wiped out Vanport City. It was reported that the water rose to the top of Portland's seawall at its peak.

GLADSTONE

The City of Gladstone is located at the confluence of the Clackamas and Willamette rivers just across the Clackamas River from Oregon City.

According to the City of Gladstone website:

"The white settlers lived alongside the area's Indians who operated a ferry across the Clackamas River. The famous "Pow-Wow" maple tree marked the place where the different Indian tribes, mainly Clackamas and Multnomahs, met to make trading agreements, settle community affairs, and conduct wedding ceremonies. The tree still stands on Clackamas Boulevard, though a little battered. Adjacent to the "Pow-Wow" tree was an Indian racetrack that Peter Rinearson later used as an exercise and training ground for the racehorses he bred. In 1861, it was used as a parade ring for the First State Fair held on the Rinearson property, with the "Pow-Wow" tree marking the entrance.

"Soon after the arrival of the white settlers, the Indian ferry was replaced by a toll bridge across the Clackamas River where the present Park Place Bridge stands. This bridge was washed out by the waters of the 1856 flood, but it was soon rebuilt and finally purchased in 1861 by Ad Cason who operated it as a toll bridge. Ad's gun shop at the north end of the bridge

served as a coach stop for stages traveling between Portland and Oregon City.

"The same Ad Cason built the first school for Gladstone, Park Place and the Clackamas area, on his father's property in 1871. The district was formed with 27 taxpayers."

It wasn't until after 1900 that Judge Harvey Edward Cross founded the town of Gladstone by laying out the first streets. It was incorporated in 1911. Cross chose the name Gladstone to honor Sir William Ewart Gladstone, the Prime Minister of England who he admired greatly.

When planning the layout east of what is now Portland Avenue, the surveyor suggested Cross name the streets running north and south toward the Clackamas River after American colleges and those crossing them, east and west, for English dukes, earls and universities. Names including Cornell, Columbia, Dartmouth, Exeter, Gloucester, among others, are still prominent in that area of the city.

In 1894, at the urging of Eva Emory Dye, an Oregon City author and proponent of Chautauqua, and with the desire to enhance the community, Judge Cross granted a fifty-year lease of his land to the Willamette Valley Chautauqua Association. The popular Chautauquas were annual summer assemblies that offered lectures, concerts and theatrical events. The first outdoor Willamette Valley Chautauqua was held in Gladstone on July 24–26, 1894. It was well-attended by people from all over. They arrived by many forms of transportation – horse and buggy, trolley, the Oregon and California Railroad and the Oregon Electric Railway.

A ladies physical culture class in 1904 at Chautauqua Park in Gladstone. The Chautauqua Festival was a summer tradition of theater, concerts and lectures that started in 1894. *Courtesy of the Gladstone Historical Society*

July 4, 1914 competition held in Gladstone Park

The men's wheelbarrow race.

The women's foot race.

The men's sawing contest.

Eventually, the competition with nearby Portland, which provided better transportation and better stage acts, as well as the advent of radio, began eating into its attendance and, sadly, the Willamette Valley Chautauqua Association was bankrupt by 1927.

Judge Cross died that same year and the park, buildings and Chautauqua Lake were sold to the Western Oregon Conference of Seventh-Day Adventists where the group has held their annual camp-meetings on the site each July.

In 1907, Gladstone hosted the first official Clackamas County Fair. It was held in Gladstone Park which later was known as the Seventh Day Adventist campground.

In 1908, however, the Clackamas County Fair Association organized and began selling membership certificates at $5.00 per share to provide funds to purchase property in Canby, and the Clackamas County Fair was moved to the new site the following year.

CREIGHTON / CENTER / OAK GROVE

The town of Oak Grove was first platted as a townsite in the 1890s. The developers hired a surveying party to lay out the town. Among the crew was Edward W. Cornell, who, while having lunch with his co-workers in a stand of oak trees in the northwestern part of the tract suggested that the town be named Oak Grove. The name, however, caused some problems.

At first, the town was served by the Milwaukie Post Office, but by 1904, the community had its own post office which was called Creighton, named after Susan Creighton on whose donation land claim the building stood. It was also not named Oak Grove in the beginning because of a conflict

The Oak Grove Station. *Courtesy of the "Trolley Trail" website*

with a former post office in Josephine County by the same name.

Even the railroad avoided calling the station that it located there "Oak Grove." It was originally named Center, but by 1907, the post office had agreed to rename the post office Oak Grove and the name of the Center railroad station was changed, as well.

According to the "Trolley Trail" website:

"After the rail line was built, development along the corridor flourished. Oak Grove and Jennings Lodge both expanded to include more residences, public buildings and stores. Houses adjacent to the corridor were built with their porches facing the rail. In the late 1890s, typical homes surrounding the street were simple wood-frame buildings commonly referred to as Vernacular or Western Farmhouse styles."

In 1904, the first postmaster at the Creighton Post Office was noted Oregon botanist Thomas J. Howell. His parents had first taken a donation land claim on Sauvie Island in 1854. He and his brother, Joseph, both self-taught with little education, developed an interest in botany. In 1877, Thomas built an herbarium and catalogued 2,152 spe-

The Oak Grove Station was a busy place. *Courtesy of the Milwaukie Historical Society*

cies of plants in it. In 1878, he named an aquatic plant *Howellia aquatilis* in honor of his brother. He published his first catalog of regional plants in 1881. Other, more comprehensive books followed and today, over 30 species of plants are named *howellii*. He donated his collection of approximately 10,000 plants to the University of Oregon and in 1903-1904, before coming to Oak Grove to serve as its postmaster, he cataloged the collection of the university.

Today, Oak Grove is home to the Portland Aquarium and a Library Information Network of Clackamas County (LINCC) library operated by Clackamas County.

MILWAUKIE

Milwaukie, sited on the Willamette River, mostly in Clackamas County, was founded in 1848 by Lot Whitcomb, a businessman and entrepreneur who served in the Illinois House of Representatives before making the trek to Oregon. He settled on a donation land claim on which he built a sawmill and gristmill. He named the new town for Milwaukee, Wisconsin, using the frequent misspelling of the name for its Oregon namesake.

Lot Whitcomb saw the potential of a waterway and the possibility of an ocean port. He began building boats – coastal sailing ships and the first steamboat constructed on the Willamette River, which he called the *Lot Whitcomb*. It was considered to be *"the finest steamboat plying the river in its day."* It soon proved too expensive to run on the river, so it was eventually sold for use in San Francisco.

In 1849, Joseph Kellogg, Lot Whitcomb, and William Terrance built the 22-ton schooner *Milwaukie*. They loaded it with provisions and sent it to San Francisco where the sale of ship and cargo yielded sufficient funds to enable her builders to purchase the brig

Forrest. They ran their newly-acquired vessel between Milwaukie and San Francisco on a regular basis, and Lot Whitcomb advertised for *"Goods, Wares, Merchandise, Lumber and Agricultural Products to transport for sale."*

Milwaukie prospered for several years, but by 1850, it was abandoned as a port for sea-going vessels because the Port of Portland was so much more accessible. A few hundred people were settled in Milwaukie by then and it still had riverboats and sawmills. A post office was established in 1850 with Whitcomb as the first postmaster.

Lot Whitcomb also founded the local newspaper, *Western Star,* as a means to promote Milwaukie. It was the first Oregon newspaper founded after the formation of the Oregon Territory. In 1851, it moved to Portland as the *Oregon Weekly Times*.

In 1847, with Lot Whitcomb as the wagonmaster, Henderson Luelling, his brother Seth (who spelled his name "Lewelling") and other family members brought 700 one-year-old fruit trees by ox-team from Iowa. Upon settling in what was to become the Milwaukie area, they established Oregon's first nursery. They began grafting the trees and by 1853, had over 100,000 trees for sale. Their orchards provided homesteaders throughout the Oregon Territory with apple, cherry, pear, peach, black walnut and shell-bark hickory trees as well as quince, grape, currant and gooseberry plants to begin their own home orchards.

In 1854, Henderson left Oregon and its nurseries for California where he started the fruit industry of that state. He died in San Jose in 1878.

In the 1860s, Seth Lewelling developed two varieties of black cherries called the "Black Republican" and the "Bing." Within the next decade he also developed other new varieties including the Lincoln and Willamette cherries, the Lewelling grape, the Golden prune, the Sweet Alice apple and the Lewelling almond.

A former employee and neighbor, Joseph Lambert, was the developer of the Lambert cherry. He had also tried gold mining in California and then returned to Milwaukie and became active in local government and various business endeavors.

In an interview on January 12, 1939 for the Works Progress Administration (WPA) Folklore Studies, Mr. Harvey Gordon Starkweather told his story:

The wooden Milwaukie trestle bridge in 1907. *Courtesy of the Milwaukie Historical Society*

"You asked about my religious activities back there, reminds me of an old-time exhorter. He used an ox-team as a simile, where one of the oxen was balky. A balky ox, as you probably don't know, is just about the balkiest animal the Creator made. The good ox will pull with all his might while the balky one is stubbornly standing in his tracks, or, to make matters worse, retreating in the other direction. It's a pretty bad situation for the driver, any way you take it. So this exhorter was shouting, 'If my Baptist ox and my Presbyterian ox and my Methodist ox will only all pull together, we can pull a mighty load.' That's the way I've always felt. I'll just pull along with each and any of them, without waiting to see which is Presbyterian, Methodist or Baptist.

"Well, you want folklore. Folklore, they say, comes out of history, so perhaps I'd better give a little of that first. I've lived almost all my life in Milwaukie, as I told you back there. Same folks say Milwaukie is so spelled because the people who incorporated the town misspelled, making the last syllable 'ie' instead of 'ee,' as the town in Wisconsin is spelled. As a matter of fact, according to what I have been able to learn, 'ie' is correct rather than 'ee.'

"While Lot Whitcomb platted Milwaukie, he wasn't the first settler. Milwaukee's first settler was a man named Fellows, who built his cabin close to the edge of the Willamette river, near the foot of what is now Jefferson street. The site of the cabin washed away in the floods long ago. Where Fellows came from, when he built this cabin, or where he went after disposing of his squatter's right, nobody ever knew. Later on, Lot Whitcomb filed on the donation land claim that afterwards included the townsite.

"Lot Whitcomb was quite a man. A Yankee, born in Vermont, in 1807, he came to Oregon, in 1847, as captain of a train of 147 wagons, that included the wagons of Henderson and Seth Luelling – the name that is always associated with our famous Oregon cherries. Whitcomb was influenced in coming to Oregon by a pamphlet written by old Joel Palmer, and that he wasn't a poor man is evidenced by the fact that his own equipment consisted of six wagons, with five yoke of oxen to each wagon, and a family carriage drawn by four horses. That was quite a caravan in itself – six wagons, thirty oxen, and a four-horse carriage. In addition, he had an ample stock of provisions, furniture, bedding, new carpets, and a set of sawmill irons, such as were in use in that day. The trip across the plains to Oregon, by Whitcomb's party, took seven months and twenty-one days. They arrived at Oregon City in November 1847. The next spring, Whitcomb filed on his donation land claim, and then built the first sawmill – near the mouth of Johnson Creek, where the lumber for Milwaukie's first schoolhouse was sawed.

"Along with Whitcomb in the building of Milwaukee, then the rival city of Portland, were the Kelloggs, father and sons, Orrin and Joseph, and the brothers, Henderson and Seth Luelling, mentioned above.

"The Luellings brought the first cherry trees to Oregon. Henderson it was, who took the initial step in bringing that first good variety of grafted fruit trees, the details of which are interesting, Henderson, planning to come to Oregon in the spring of 1846, secured the cooperation of a neighbor, by the name of John

Fisher, for his plan. First, they procured a stout wagon, then they made two boxes, 12 inches deep and of sufficient length and breadth that when placed in the wagon-box, side by side, they filled it completely. The boxes were then filled with a compost, or soil, consisting principally of charcoal and earth, and in this 700 small trees were planted. The trees were from 20 inches to four feet high, protected by light strong strips of hickory bolted on to posts, set in staples on the wagon box. For that wagon alone, three yoke of oxen were detailed. Can't you see those men working and planning to the utmost detail, that Oregon might have in time the wonderful cherries and other fruit for which it is now famous? And there are those today who dare to say the pioneers had no vision, that they were mere adventurers. Well, to go on with our story. The Luelling caravan, which consisted of three wagons for the Luellings, one for the Fisher family, two for Nathan Hockett's family, and the Nursery Wagon itself – seven wagons in all – started on its long journey across the plains, on April 17, 1846. It traveled about fifteen miles a day, and every day, no matter how scarce the water, nor how far the distance between watered camps, each and every one of those little 700 trees were carefully sprinkled with water. Each little tree was a saga in itself. The Dalles was reached about October 1st. Two boats had to be constructed to bring the families and their goods, not forgetting the cherry trees, down to the Willamette Valley. It was November 1st, when they left The Dalles. They got down as far as Wind River, where the boats were unloaded and reloaded (north bank), until finally, at the Upper Cascades, the wagons were again set up and everything hauled to the Lower Cascades (north bank). Meanwhile, the boats had been turned adrift and went bumping down the current to the Lower Cascades, where they were captured, reloaded, and poled and paddled to Fort Vancouver. At The Dalles, the fruit trees had been taken out of their boxes and wrapped in cloths to protect them not only from the handling, but from frost. They were nursed carefully the next six months and more until their owner found what he thought the proper place for their final planting. About one-half of the original 700 trees survived and grew.

"Some idea of the importance of fruit in those days may be realized from the fact that a box of apples brought by Mr. Luelling to Portland, in 1852, sold as high as $75.00. Four bushels shipped to the California gold mines brought $500.00.

"Before leaving the story of the Luelling fruit trees, while it was Henderson Luelling who instigated the bringing of the first fruit trees, it is to his brother Seth that we are indebted for the toothsome Black Republican, Royal Anne and Bing cherries. Henderson left Oregon for California, in 1854, where he started the fruit industry of that State, dying in San Jose in 1878. But Seth remained true to his first love. He stayed in Oregon. A great admirer of Abraham Lincoln, Seth belonged to the 'Black Republican' party, and, saying he would make the people relish Black Republicans, he gave his newly propagated cherry that name. The Bing cherry he named in honor of his faithful old Chinaman, Bing, who cultivated the test rows of his nursery.

"The old home of Seth Luelling still stands on Front Street of Milwaukie, shaded by the great Babylon weeping willow that Seth's first wife, Clarissa, planted

as a cutting so long ago; a cutting that, tradition says, was brought originally from Mount Vernon. Every spring the old tree, as if in celebration of the start of its long journey more than ninety years ago, transforms itself almost overnight from a waving gray mass of skeleton branches into a magical fountain of vivid, living green."

In an interview on January 26, 1939 for the Works Progress Administration (WPA) Folklore Studies, Mrs. Herman Ledding told his story:

Mrs. Ledding was described by her interviewer, Sara Wrenn, as *"clever and well-educated"* and that her biography included *"kindergarten work (learned under Kate Douglas Wiggin); Practiced law. For a year or so owned and operated the Clackamas County Independent, a newspaper. First woman in the United States appointed as referee in bankruptcy. First secretary Oregon Democratic Legislative League."*

The text of Mrs. Ledding's interview begins:

"Oh, I'm afraid I can't tell you very much. I'm not a pioneer, you know, and neither were my peoples since we came here in 1881. Of course I am a stepdaughter of Seth Lewelling, and I might be able to tell you a few little things regarding him and his early life here.

"You passed the old house down on the corner, that is known as the Lewelling house, on your way here, did you not? The one with the big weeping willow tree? You perhaps already know that was built by Elisha Kellogg in 1851, and leased by him to a man named Noah Hablar, for use as a tavern. In 1852, when the Lewellings arrived, there wasn't a house to be had, and it was too late in the year for them to build. They were not poor, so finally they prevailed on Habler, whose lease ran another year, to let them move in his tavern, after which they hired him to work for them, and eventually they bought the house.

"Oh, as to the various forms of spelling my stepfather's name. His ancestors originally came from Wales, where the family of Lewellyn, as it was then spelled, was the head of the clan, with the royal prerogatives of that long ago period. Later, when the faith of the Quakers was embraced, it was considered seemly to adopt a simpler form, and the name was reduced to plain 'Lueling.' Here in Oregon it was spelled 'Luelling' by Henderson. After a misunderstanding between the two brothers, Seth and Henderson, Seth arrived at the spelling of 'Lewelling' and that, I think, is the way the name is generally spelled today.

"...A story my stepfather was fond of relating is the one when he was taking a woman visitor through his nursery one day during the cherry season. They came to a tree where there were some particularly luscious cherries hanging just within reach. There were only a few of these cherries. The woman reached up, picked them, and all before my stepfather had fully comprehended, had plopped them all into her mouth. She exclaimed over their exquisite flavor, and step-father, with a somewhat wry smile, asked if she would kindly give him the pits, which she did. Afterwards he heard that the visitor said, 'Why, that Seth Lewelling is the stingiest man I ever heard of. He asked me to give him the pits from a few cherries I ate in his old orchard.' She did not see the string hanging on the

particular branch of that tree, to show where the process of polonization had been effected a year before, and the result of which my step-father had been eagerly omitting all these months. Under the circumstances he was thankful he got the pits, since he had to take his visitor's word for the new fruit's taste.

"I do not know if it is generally known, but according to the old timers, the channel of the Willamette River used to be along the east side of Rose Island in the early days. The sea-going vessels used to come into harbor loaded down with rock ballast, and Couch, of the Couch donation land claim at Portland, as it was said, would pay the captains and crew so much to dump their ballast between the island and the east shore of the river.

"To get back to the Lewellings and their nursery, that the Bing cherry was named in honor of a Chinese workman, is fairly well known, but not much has been told about the Chinese himself. He was a northern Chinese, of the Manchou race, the men and women of which are large, and very unlike the usual Cantonese Chinese with which we are familiar. Bing was close to six feet tall, if not more, He was foreman of the gang of thirty or more Chinese usually working in the orchards, and he worked here on contract for some thirty years. But he had a family back in China, or at least he had a wife there, to whom he sent money regularly, and this wife had adopted six or seven boys, so that Bing was sure to have sons to provide for the traditional ancestor worship. Bing was always talking about his family; he wanted to go back and see his wife and sons. Finally in '89 or '90 he went, and while he was in China, the Oriental exclusion law was passed, and Bing was never able to return to the United States. He was very fond of the song, 'Ol' Black Joe,' which he would sing over and over again in a low minor key, Chinese fashion.

"The manner in which the cherry was named for him happened thus: He and my step-father were working the trees, every other row each. When they discovered this tree with its wonderful new cherry, someone said, 'Seth, you ought to name this for yourself.'

"'I've already got one in my name,' Seth responded, 'No, I'll name this for Bing. It's a big cherry and Bing's big, and anyway, it's in his row, so that shall be its name.'

"The Lewelling cherry was a prize-winner at the Philadelphia Centennial Fair, or the Philadelphia International Exhibition, as it is named on the bronze medal, which we have. The cherry sold for a dollar a pound in Philadelphia that year.

"The Lewellings were strong for the Union. In 1866 Ezra Meeker worked during the winter for Seth, and when spring came Seth grub-staked him with 1,500 one-year old trees, with which he left for Northern California and Nevada. Amongst these trees was one called the Lincoln cherry. Ezra Meeker must have sold trees to quite a number in Carson City, for on one of the old show places of that town there are Lincoln cherry trees still in existence and still bearing fruit – the only cherry tress of that name that do exist. Other fine fruit trees Seth Lewelling propagated, of which nothing is now known, was the golden prune – yellow with pink spots, and a pear, called 'Mother's Favorite.'

"The first commercial prune orchard on the Pacific Coast was that of Seth Lewelling's in 1857."

An automobile inspection station located on S.E. Powell and Milwaukie, 1939. Incredibly, the building and all the other major buildings visible are still with us today, although the church is now without its steeple. *Courtesy of the City of Portland Archives A2009-009.910*

In 1870, the Oregon and California Railroad named their station "Milwaukee," but corrected it to "Milwaukie" in 1892. In 1893, an electric streetcar line between Oregon City and Portland was built. The streetcar ran north on McLoughlin Blvd. (U.S. Highway 99E) to a 'car house' at the corner of McLoughlin Blvd. and Jackson Street. It then turned left at Jackson Street and continued across Johnson Creek to Portland, connecting Oregon City with Portland. The electric rail tracks were moved to the west of McLoughlin Blvd. in the mid-1930s to make way for the completion of the McLoughlin Blvd. segment of U.S. Highway 99E.

According to Lewis A. McArthur's *Oregon Geographic Names - Seventh Edition*, "*As the city center grew further from the railroad and a branch line was built across the Willamette to Oswego, Milwaukie station was replaced and renamed Lambert for Joseph H. Lambert... The name of the station was changed to East Milwaukee in 1913 and corrected to East Milwaukie in 1916.*"

When World War II began and the local shipyards were desperate for workers, the surrounding farming areas were obtained by the county to provide housing for the needed workers. The Housing Authority of Clackamas County built the Kellogg Park housing development where several hundred temporary houses were built. After the war, between 1946 and 1950, the site was sold to the City of Milwaukie. It was then leveled and converted to the Milwaukie Industrial Park which was annexed to the city in 1956.

In the 1950s and 1960s, the Milwaukie

waterfront was dominated by a log dump and other various industrial uses and the downtown area was cut off from the river by U.S. Highway 99E/McLoughlin Blvd. The last electric interurban trolley route through Milwaukie ended in 1958.

For years Milwaukie was the home of "the Bomber," also known as "Lacey Lady," an authentic World War II B17G bomber located on McLoughlin Boulevard, on top of a gas station, which eventually grew to 75 gasoline pumps and a restaurant.

According to the Bomber's history posted on its website:

"Our World War II B-17G Bomber was originally flown to Oregon by Art Lacey. From 1947 until its closing, the 'Flying Fortress' you see in Milwaukie, OR. sheltered one of the nation's largest filling stations.

"The family's Bomber is now in [the hands of] *a non-profit group, The Wings of Freedom. This B-17G Bomber is being restored along with the personal veteran stories that she represents.*

"The memorabilia displayed in the family restaurant are reminders of a history not to be forgotten. The Bomber family is dedicated to the preservation of this 'flying Fortress' christened the 'Lacey Lady.' She stands in honor of the men and woman who fought so valiantly during WWII to save our freedom."

Marylhurst University

In 1893, Saint Mary's Academy and College was established by a teaching order in Portland to serve Catholic women. By 1898, it became the first liberal arts college in the Pacific Northwest to award bachelor degrees to women.

In 1908, the Sisters purchased land a little south of Portland, along the east bank of the Willamette River, between West Linn and Lake Oswego. There they established Marylhurst Normal School. In 1930 Marylhurst College moved to the site and by 1950 the normal school and college were combined. The school became co-educational in 1974 and began offering graduate programs in the mid-1980s. Since 1998, as Marylhurst University, it has specialized in night and weekend courses for adult education.

Reed College

In 1855, Simeon Gannett Reed came to Oregon with his wife Amanda and became a clerk for Portland merchant Williams S. Ladd. That job led to a partnership with Ladd and

Art Lacey's "Bomber" Gas Station on U.S. Highway 99E. *Courtesy of the Montana Pioneer and Classic Auto Club*

then with others to form the Oregon Steam Navigation Company. It did well and made Reed wealthy. His venture at iron-making at Lake Oswego didn't do well, but he owned several farms where he raised blooded horses and cattle in the Willamette Valley, in California and other areas. He and Amanda moved to California and he died there in 1892. His estate went to Amanda and with it the suggestion that she use some of the money to contribute to the intelligence, prosperity and happiness of the inhabitants of Portland. Amanda took this to heart and worked with the Rev. Thomas Lamb Eliot, establishing a board of trustees which proceeded to lay the plans for Reed College. The future campus was acquired from the Ladd Estate Company. The school's focus was to be on intellectual rigor and educational innovation. Fraternities and sororities were not to be part of campus life, and the administration was to downplay intercollegiate athletics. The Reed's vision was successful. Reed College has produced many Rhodes scholars and future graduate students over the years.

The beautiful campus can be glimpsed from Highway 99E toward the south edge of Portland.

STUMPTOWN / PORTLAND EAST

Oaks Amusement Park

The Oregon Water Power & Railway Company built the large Springwater hydroelectric project on the Clackamas River in the early 1900s. The project included an electric-powered interurban railway from downtown Portland, which skirted the Willamette River's east bank and crossed Oaks Bottom near the Sellwood district. Here the company built an amusement park on 44-acres which opened on May 30, 1905, just before the opening of the Lewis and Clark Centennial Exposition. It featured a giant water slide, a skating rink, bathing in the Willamette River, picnic areas, a roller coaster and other rides and concessions. Visitors could also listen to free band concerts on the grounds. It was immensely popular.

In 1925, the park was sold to Edward H. Bollinger; in 1943 he bought the land surrounding it, as well. His son operated the park until 1985, when it was turned over to a non-profit corporation formed to perpetuate the enterprise. The park includes groves of oak trees with picnic facilities, a huge skating rink with organ music that has operated continu-

The Oaks Park Avenue looking south, Jolly Gladway. © *Oaks Park Association*

The Oaks Park taffy pulling machine. *Coutesy of the Oregon Historical Society*

ously since 1905, a 1920 Herschell-Spillman carousel, and a variety of other rides which have changed over the years. Admission has been free since opening day.

Oregon Museum of Science and Industry

On the Willamette River waterfront, a major attraction, the Oregon Museum of

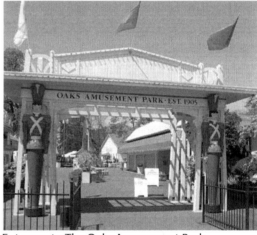

Entrance to The Oaks Amusement Park – *Courtesy of Wikimedia Commons (Tedder)*

The Blue Streak roller-coaster at Oaks Park. © *Oaks Park Association*

Science and Industry, better known as OMSI, brings visitors from all over the state – usually not once, but frequently.

Its beginnings were in the early 1900s when displays of natural science exhibits were showcased in the hallways and alcoves throughout Portland City Hall. When the collection was evicted in 1936, the artifacts were stored away due to lack of funds. In 1944, a Museum Foundation was incorporated and the legislature gave some initial funding to allow a display area in the Portland Hotel with additional displays in the U.S. National and First National banks.

By 1949, the collection had grown and the fate of the hotel was in doubt. It would again be without a home. Later in 1949, the museum moved into an old house owned by Ralph Lloyd next to the land that was later developed as The Lloyd Center. OMSI's new home was a success. A year later, the first planetarium in the Northwest was opened on the front lawn, but by 1957, the Lloyd Corporation was growing and needed the property for expansion. OMSI was again without a home. By then the yearly attendance had grown to 25,000.

In August 1957, the first-ever "museum raising" was held. With volunteer union labor under the guidance of the director, Dr. Samuel Diak, the walls went up on a new site in Washington Park where it shared a parking lot with the then-new site of the Portland Zoo. Plans for a planetarium were again included with donated funds.

By the mid-1980s, 600,000 people per year were visiting the building, designed for only 100,000 and expansion at the Washington Park site was not feasible. In 1986, it was decided that, once again, OMSI would move to a new location on the east bank of the Willamette River where a much larger building would be constructed. Property that included the Station L power plant was donated by Portland General Electric and a fundraising campaign began. In 1992, OMSI once again opened at a new site that has allowed it to display some additional unique and special attractions.

It is now home to the U.S. Navy submarine, USS Blueback, which was decommissioned on October 1, 1990. Blueback arrived in Portland in February 1994, and her propeller was removed and installed outside the museum as a National Submarine Memorial. Now, OMSI offers guided, interactive tours of the submarine several times a day. In September 2008, the vessel was added to the National Register of Historic Places.

The new site for the museum also allows it to offer boat tours on the Willamette River.

Since the basis of science and industry includes change, the exhibits and activities at OMSI frequently do not stay the same for long, although the scientific principles do.

Inside, there is an exhibit hall used for temporary exhibits, some traveling and some created by OMSI. There is the two-story Turbine Hall with smaller exhibits emphasizing physics on the mezzanine; a hands-on wet chemistry lab with themes that rotate weekly. It has a Physics Lab exhibit and a Technology Lab which investigates the impact of technology on society.

The Life Sciences Hall on the second floor offers exhibits about biology. The Earth Science Hall, also on the second floor, features geology-oriented exhibits and two specialized laboratories.

It also has a Science Playground, the early-childhood education area designed for families with newborn to six-year-old children. The area is fully enclosed and designed to keep children visible and secure while giving them freedom to explore. It includes a giant sandbox, a water area, a reading area and physical science exhibits.

Its giant Omnimax theater allows the showing of films which fit the theme of the museum. There are campouts available at the museum for school groups or organizations such as Scouts as well as ordinary field trips.

It is indeed a mecca for all ages and a proud resident of the Portland area.

In an interview for the *WPA's American Life Histories Collection: Manuscripts from the Federal Writer's Project, 1936-*

***1940**, J.J. Kadderly told of life in Portland. He was interviewed by Sara B. Wrenn on January 2, 1939:*

"School? I only went to school four years, in a little old log school house in Wisconsin. Then my father died and I had to get out and earn some money. Gosh ding it, I can smell that school house yet. There was about forty kids and I don't think they ever took a bath. I can smell it just as plain as if it was yesterday.

"I came to Oregon in 1878. It was September 1, when we, my wife and me, first set foot in Portland. We came by way of San Francisco and we came up from there on the old steamship George W. Elder. God dang it, but that old ship could roll! I was doing pretty well in Wisconsin too. I had learned the tinners trade. I had enough to get married. But we had gosh danged thunderstorms back there. One day I was settin' with some of the boys and there was a bigger storm than usual – thunder and lightnin' like blazes, and I sez, 'Gosh dang it, if I knew a place where they didn't have any such storms as this I'd go there right off,' and just then somebody spoke up and sez, 'Young man, I kin tell you where to go. Go to Portland, O-re-gan. They don't have no sich storms there.' O-re-gan, he sez, just like that.

"I looked 'round and there was an old circus clown of Forepaugh's Circus. I knew him right away. 'Heh,' I said, 'I know you. I carried twenty-two buckets of water to one of your little old elephants once.' He laughed. Sure 'nough, it was that same old clown. He told me some more about Oregon, and finally I jumped up and said 'I'm goin' out there, gosh ding! I'm goin' right away.' And I did, too.

"When me and my wife landed in Portland I had just eighteen dollars, and as I sez I was awful seasick. I felt just like a fellow does when he's been on a drunk. Somebody on the boat told us where to go so it wouldn't cost so much, and the very next day here came a man wanting to know if there wasn't a young fellow just arrived who was a tinner. He played a cornet or something, and he was going up to the State Fair at Salem, and he wanted me to take his bench. I said I would if I'd got over my drunk and he said, 'Oh jest drink a lot of coffee and you'll be alright.' I wasn't all right. I felt pretty bad; but I had to get some money, so I went down to

Early day Portland. *Courtesy of the OSU Special Collections & Archives Commons,*

where he worked next morning, and right away the boss sent me out to put on a drain pipe on a new house. It was hard work, that first job, out on Union Avenue. But I did a good job. Why gosh ding it, the last time I went by there that old house was still standing, and I bet that same drain pipe was still there.

"Well, pretty soon I had enough to start a little shop of my own. I went over to East Portland. I had just enough to pay my first month's rent. It was eighteen dollars. There was only 350 people in East Portland then. Rents were a lot lower than on the West Side. God dang it, on First Street, in 1878, they asked as much as $60 or $70 a month. I had my tinner's tools and some tin and sheet iron. Right away I made a coffee pot and painted it red and hung it out for a sign, and pretty soon I was doing a fair trade. It was a good while later that I came over to the West Side.

"I bet I've sold more cook stoves to bride and grooms than anybody in this town. In 1888 I bought four carloads of cook stoves and wood ranges, and I think I sold 'em all to bride an' grooms. I don't make so much money these days, but I keep goin'.

"And say, you asked some back there what I like best to do. Well, horses, that's what I like best. I've had some fine horses and I've got some now. There ain't anything any better than a horse.

"Portland's first race track was out at Sellwood. It was a mile track. I mind me the world's first 2:10 trotter showed on that track. It was in 1880, and his name was Alteo, out of Altamont, the greatest sire the world ever knew. I used to drive my own horses in the matinees. One of the most successful drivers of those days was a race track man named George Meisner. He used to drive for Charlie Lohmire. Charlie was some driver himself. Once at a Fourth of July meet he challenged me to drive a big mare I owned, known as Bessie Lovelace, against a trotter of his called Redskin, I could out-drive Lohmire and I knew it. Otherwise I wouldn't have been such a gol darned fool as to have accepted his challenge. That was out on the old Rose City track. We drove in carts. They're something like a sulkey, only a little heavier. Matinee races used to be always driven in carts.

"Well, Lohmire and I pulled out on the track. Redskin was a lot faster than my big filly. But Bessie was steady – an' I could drive. It was a half-mile track. Lohmire lead after the first quarter – an' I let him. I jest eased 'round after him on that first lap. After we got goin' good on the second lap I gave Old Bessie the word – I never teched a whip to any of my horses. We pulled up even with Redskin and I let Lohmire think I was makin' an awful effort. Then on the last quarter I begin to draw away easy like. At the finish I was sixty feet in the lead. Lohmire never did get over that.

"The first macadam road in this part of the country was the stretch along the river, of what is now called the Riverside Drive. It was always called the Macadam Road in early days, and everybody with any kind of a harness horse went out there to speed it. Pretty speedy folks some of them were too, and maybe they'd finish up at a tavern or roadhouse known as the White House, at the end of the speedway, where there was a little track – I think it was a quarter-mile. I wasn't much interested in that sort of drivin'.

"Yep, I've had some good horses, and gosh ding it I've got some now. Wife sez we'll go broke on horses, but we haven't yet."

Electric Interurban Railway

A special electric railway car named Helen, made her first run from her terminal at Second and Madison Streets in Portland heading toward Oregon City on February 16, 1893. It was the beginning of one of the first electric interurban railway lines in the United States. Its fourteen miles made it one of the longest such railway lines in the world. The East Side Railway Company was underway. It began regular operation with fifteen cars leaving Portland on the hour from eight to five daily. The cars were fast, comfortable, they ran on time, and they were inexpensive. They were used for transport to work, for business and family needs and scenic outings for family travel.

In 1903, the company reorganized into the Oregon Water Power and Railroad Company to build power sites on the Clackamas River and expand the rail system. The trains were moved closer to the river to serve companies interested in freight hauling from the waterfront by the electrics. More trains were added, weekend discount tickets offered, and special events sponsored. People loved the electric cars – they were the easiest transport available.

In 1906, the interurban owners merged Portland Railway and Portland General Electric which formed the company that later became Portland General Electric (PGE) Power Company. The company continued to grow. Finally, in 1908, a line was built to Salem and Forest Grove. Soon it had 38 trains running daily on the east side of the Willamette. By 1915, Oregon Electric had a line to Eugene and Springfield and the Southern Pacific's Red Electrics came from Portland on the west side of the river down to Corvallis, later into Junction City and Eugene.

Soon, however, the popularity of the automobile made a serious dent in the ridership of the electric lines and the Depression finished the job. The Southern Pacific moved from the Red Electrics to bus transportation and the Oregon Electric shut down passenger service, but continued as a freight line into the 1990s.

Fred Meyer

A man named Fred Meyer opened his first Oregon variety store in downtown Portland in 1920 with an offer to pay the overtime parking tickets for customers. He collected their names and home addresses and in doing so, he conducted early market research. He then chose the Hollywood District of Portland for his first suburban one-stop shopping center in 1931. The store combined a complete grocery supermarket, and incorporated drug, clothing, shoe, jewelry, home decor, home improvement, sporting goods, electronics, toy departments and more under one roof. In the Hollywood store, rooftop parking was included in the 1950s.

He based his store locations on planned highway construction, so the stores often show up along the U.S. Highway 99 route. Many of the stores have fared well and the chain expanded, building stores as far south as Medford, Oregon.

In 1978, Mr. Meyer died at the age of 92. Until his death, he played an active role in the company. In 1999, Fred Meyer, Inc. merged with Kroeger of Ohio and many stores have been updated. The Oregon stores, however, retain much of the original Fred Meyer feel and layout.

Fred G. Meyer (on right) and another man at the Sunshine Division warehouse in 1964. *Courtesy of the City of Portland Archives A2002-009*

Portland International Airport

In the 1920s, Broomfield Airstrip occupied the Westmoreland Park property in Portland. Before that, airplanes used the golf courses to land and take off. By the mid-1920s an airfield was badly needed. In 1926, an empty spit of land skirting the Willamette's eastern shore was selected. When the new Swan Island strip opened in 1927, Colonel Charles Lindbergh, flew his Spirit of St. Louis onto the new airfield on September 14 of that year. The deco air terminal was completed in May 1930 with the belief that the conveniently-located facility would serve Portland's needs for at least a decade. By the mid-1930s, however, the use of the large DC3 airplanes made a new site imperative. Recently-filled land behind the Columbia River levee was chosen and the airfield moved. That decision left the Swan Island site available for Kaiser Shipyards during World War II.

Construction began on the new airport site in 1937, but it was not fully operational until May 1940. In October 1940, it included the Portland Columbia Airport, a $200,000 United Airlines facility, a passenger terminal, administrative offices, maintenance hangars and a flight kitchen. United and Northwest Airlines were the first major carriers. West Coast Airlines built an adjacent facility; Pan Am operated from the United building; and Northwest Airlines shared its facilities with Western.

On May 30, 1948, the Vanport Flood inundated the entire airfield. The service was switched to Salem and then Troutdale. It wasn't until October that the field could be used again.

By then, the faster and larger planes were flying, not just coast to coast, but around the globe. The addition of "International" to the Portland Columbia name was not enough, however. It was falling behind and needed to keep up with the additional air traffic, increased aircraft sizes and speed.

In October 1955, the Port of Portland, now in charge of the airport, announced plans for expansion of the airport along the south shore of the Columbia. Acres of drainage and landfill were required for the 11,000-foot main runway which would serve the largest aircraft. The modern terminal was dedicated in 1958. Total outlay exceeded $9 million. Within five years, it was evident the terminal itself could not accommodate the large aircraft and heavy traffic. The field was renovated and the terminal expanded in 1977.

Portland International Airport, located four miles northeast of Portland, is the largest in the state. It not only accounts for 90% of the air travel in Oregon and connects with major airport hubs throughout the United States and hubs for flights to other countries, it also provides connections to smaller cities in the Western U.S.

The East Hills

The east side of Portland had more flat land than the west, but it also had its own hills, with an entirely different history. Mt. Tabor, Rocky Butte, Powell Butte and Kelly

Aerial view of the Swan Island Airport in Portland, 1929. *Courtesy of the City of Portland (OR) Archives, A2004-001.524*

Aerial view of the Portland Airport under construction (looking west) in 1940. *Courtesy of the City of Portland Archives A2005-005*

Butte are all dormant volcanoes. Mt. Tabor even has its own cinder cone. Each also has a city park, but they are used for other purposes and have residential or business areas approaching the summits.

Mt. Tabor was originally seen as an ideal place to store water for the growing city. Water came into reservoirs there from Bull Run. At first there were two, and then four, and even another small one, underground. The reservoirs were built between 1894 and 1911 of reinforced concrete designed to look like stonework. They had wrought-iron fencing, lamp posts and attractive gatehouses. All are uncovered. Reservoir #2, on the corner of 60th and Division Streets was decommissioned in the 1980s and sold to a developer, but the gatehouse remains. The rest have been ordered to be out of use by 2015 to meet government requirements. The park itself is maintained primarily by neighborhood volunteers.

Rocky Butte, which rises above Interstate 205, is the site of Joseph Hill City Park. A rotating beacon at the summit can be seen for miles. The slopes of Rocky Butte are home to the Rocky Butte Natural Area. In the 1940s, it was also home to the Multnomah County Jail and the Judson Baptist College. The City Bible Church campus, the Portland Bible College and the City Christian School are now located there.

Kelly Butte has a natural park area of 25.6 acres. During the Cold War era (1955-1956), the Kelly Butte Civil Defense Center was built. It was an underground bunker complex located on top of Kelly Butte. It was to be a secondary government headquarters in

The Kelly Butte Civil Defense command room, 1960. *Courtesy of the City of Portland Archives A2001-033*

the event of a nuclear attack or other emergency situation. It was 18,820 square feet and could house 250 people for up to two weeks. It contained food, water, back-up power, purified air, showers and other basic necessities. When the threat of nuclear war eased, it was updated and used for different purposes including an emergency "911" call center and classrooms for emergency training programs that were held there until 1995.

By 2008, the center had been dismantled. Once all contaminate material and external equipment was removed, the entrance was backfilled and buried.

Powell Butte Nature Park is a popular hiking site, but it will also be the site of the new 50-million gallon reservoir system that is planned to meet the needs of the growing city. The construction plans include another reservoir and a new public restroom facility, maintenance shed and a caretaker's house. Some of the hiking trails will be open during the construction.

In an interview for the *WPA's American Life Histories Collection: Manuscripts from the Federal Writer's Project, 1936-1940*, Cyrus B. Woodworth told of life in Portland. He was interviewed by Sara B. Wrenn on December 30, 1938:

"...It's funny how places get their names. One day in the late 70s, there was an excursion [of young] people coming down the Willamette. The banks of the river at that time were practically virgin forest, with little groves here and there, and a stream coming in. The young folks got to picking out places for themselves. One of them would say, 'I'm going to have that spot for my house;' another would shout 'That's my future home over there!' and so on, till they came to an island, when one of the girls jumped up and said, 'That island's mine. I always did want an island.'

"At that, a young man called out, 'Well if you want that island, you'll have to take me along with it, for I already own that island.'

"'I'll take you,' the girl replied, and they shook hands on it then and there. Afterwards they were married. The island was what is known as Ross Island today. The young man was Sherry Ross, and the girl's name was Deardorff."

Section 10

U.S. HIGHWAY 99W - JUNCTION CITY TO CAMP ADAIR

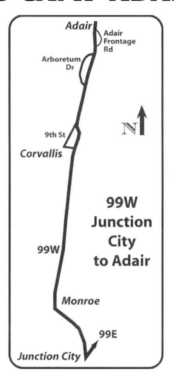

We came to the end of the U.S. Highway 99E route in the previous section, so we are heading back to Junction City to pick up the beginning of U.S. Highway 99W, which was built somewhat later. We'll take you northward, up its route on the west side of the Willamette River until it joins with U.S. Highway 99E before heading over the Interstate Bridge into Washington as a single roadway, once again.

While Oregon was still a territory, many settlers, mule trains and stagecoaches on the west side of the Willamette River traveled the "Old Territorial Road." It was also called the "Gold Mine Road" because it was used to reach the gold fields of California. It ran along the hills to avoid the mud on the valley floor during the winters. Some parts of the Old Territorial Road from Monroe were used for U.S. Highway 99W.

Heading northwest on Highway 99W from Junction City, prime farmland surrounds the highway as it passes from Lane County into Benton County. About four miles from Junction City, on the right side of the road, is

Washburne wayside "Blue Star" sign honoring World War II veterans. *From the Brew family collection*

Washburne State Wayside, the earliest wayside in Oregon. It was created and named for Junction City businessman C.B. Washburne who donated the land in 1926 when the Parks Department was part of the Oregon Department of Transportation. Located in a stand of Douglas fir trees, it is an oasis amidst vast fields of corn and other crops that surround it. The wayside provides a shady reststop where travelers can picnic, walk a nature trail and view wildlife and birds. It also was an interpretive center for the Applegate Trail that passed through the area, but the sign has recently been removed.

A little beyond Washburne State Park, on the left side of the road is the former Benton-Lane Amusement Park that was a popular local attraction for years.

A dance club called Idylwood was in business at that location between 1927-1947. In 1927, Sharkey Moore's Orchestra was a favorite and from 1939-1947, the Eldred Glaspy Orchestra played regularly.

A November 15, 1940 ad in the *Eugene Register-Guard* declared, *"Every Saturday Nite. Party favors. Music by Glenn Sill's Orchestra. Always a good time at Idylwood."*

The owner, Bob Boger, eventually converted it to a skating rink which became one of the main attractions at Benton-Lane Park.

The popular roller skating rink had a wavy floor and a stylish "Rock 'n Roll '50s" soda fountain with a red, black and white decor.

The Benton-Lane Skating Rink, formerly the Idylwood Dance Club, ca 1950. *Courtesy of Gregory Schultz. Photo taken by F.R. Schultz*

Benton-Lane pool. *"This shows the grove of trees surrounding the pool. School-age children would come for swimming lessons while their parents (mostly mothers) sat in the bleachers and watched. I'm in this group of kids. The pool was later covered. The skating rink is visible at the left."* Courtesy of Gregory Schultz; Photos taken by F.R. Schultz, 1950

The park featured a large Olympic-size pool in the days before public pools were commonplace. It was staffed with Red Cross-funded swimming instructors that taught many area children to swim.

There was a miniature train to ride around the grounds and a pole around which swings on long chains would rotate in a circle with wildly screaming children on board. Later, a motocross race track was very popular.

An Interview with Judy and Mel Parmenter by Jo-Brew:

"Judy Parmenter worked at Benton-Lane Park the summer after she gradu-

Courtesy of Gregory Schultz

Gregory Schultz: *"The penny arcade, the skating rink, and restaurant/soda fountain were in the building called Idylwood.* Photo courtesy of Judy Parmenter

ated from Monroe High School in 1966. She ran the amusement park, the carnival rides, the train, go-carts and cotton candy machine. At that time, it was a flourishing and popular place with a swimming pool, skating rink, go-cart race track, baseball diamonds, barbeque pits and places to picnic. Over the years, families used it for reunions, gatherings and afternoons of fun. Schools booked it for end-of-the school-year field trips, and businesses scheduled summer picnics for their employees.

"Judy left the area soon after that summer. With fond memories of the property, she was shocked to find it stripped, deserted and neglected when she returned in 1986. It had been denuded of its beautiful trees and everything that could be sold was gone. The roof had leaked and the floors of the skating rink were ruined.

"With the intention of staying and finding a home, Judy and Mel negotiated with the county to obtain the derelict property, knowing that there was a big project ahead of them.

"With an interest in history, Judy and Mel provided some of the story of its past. The original property was 65 acres. Although the pool property was not under the same ownership, it was run in conjunction with the park property much of the time.

"The original Olympic-sized outdoor pool was poured and built by John Mallory in 1926. At one time, it was covered by a domed metal roof. The pool remains in the possession of Dobbie Stadt who bought it from her brother-in-law, Bob Boger, the owner of the original property. She and her husband Leonard put the dome on the pool, built the dressing room, lounge and bleachers, and ran it for many years, even after the park was closed. Dobbie Stadt closed the pool for good in 1978.

"The property on which Benton-Lane sat also used to have cabins, a gas station and a grocery store.

"The large building was originally built as a dance hall. It was called Idylwood and it hosted local swing-bands and singers. It was later converted to a skating rink.

"The Parmenters have remodeled the building into a spacious and comfortable home where they can have large gatherings of family and church friends. Judy also does some childcare on site. Mel has a beautiful oversized yard and grounds to maintain. The remodeling, which was tastefully done, has obviously been costly and required a lot of work.

"The skating rink had a popular snack bar, and the original counter and stools are still there, with knotty pine walls and booths for groups. Judy and Mel have salvaged what they could of that and brought back the decor of a 1950s diner, with the red and chrome dinette set and matching barstools and black and white tile flooring.

From where I was sitting at the red and chrome dinette table, I could view places where the old knotty pine wall is still visible. The entry room with its black and white tile floor is a reminder of life in 1940s. Inside and out, there are scattered remnants of the past – the direction signs that had once been posted around the grounds, much of the original structure of the skating rink and the park-like grounds. It's a comfortable home with echos of another life. I didn't ask to see the collection of roller skates, but maybe I will next time I visit."

LICK SKILLET / STARR'S POINT / MONROE

Continuing north, the highway passes through farmland, punctuated with groves of trees, and some divided into small parcels. A small park that honors the Wilhelm Mill is on the right just as the road approaches the bridge over the Long Tom River at the entrance to the town of Monroe.

Monroe lies along the Long Tom River. During the few years that the river was navigable, a steamboat could pull up to the dock at the Wilhelm Mill to load and unload flour and supplies.

The townsite is part of the donation land claim of Joseph White, who built a sawmill there in 1850. The town was first settled in 1853 as Starr's Point, named for Sam Starr, head of a large pioneer family group who came by wagon in 1852.

Mrs. Laura Porter Coffee was interviewed in September 1939 for the Benton County *WPA's American Life Histories Collection: Manuscripts from the Federal Writer's Project, 1936-1940* project:

"...My first schooling was on Beaver Creek and my first teacher was Sam Henderson. Another teacher was Ida Dun, sister of Madge and Alwilda, who taught school so long in this county. Another was sister Hayes. Then I went to school in Philomath. My first school there was in a private dwelling and Miss Bowen was the teacher. This was shortly after the grade school had been separated from Philomath College. [For about ten years after its founding the grade school had been a part of the college.] *The students at the College called us swamp angels and we called them Brighamites. This is because President Walker was said to be rather fresh with young women.*

"Then father [Isaac Porter] *moved down by Monroe. I was about sixteen then. We lived for a while at the old stage station at Starr's Point, about a mile north of Monroe. Later father ran a livery stable in Monroe and mother had a boarding house. She had no rooms or lodgers or transients, but served meals, family style, to all who came."*

The original community of Starr's Point was located two miles north of Monroe proper near the current Alpine cut-off road.

In an interview as part of the *Historical Records Survey* project, Martha Burnett Huston told about her mother, Martha Hinton and Starr's Point:

"Martha Hinton came from Missouri with her parents, Roland and Elizabeth Hinton in 1846. They passed the first winter near McMinnville in Yamhill County. In 1847 they took a donation land claim of 640 acres just north of Monroe. There they built just a tiny log cabin at first. Later, when the Territorial Road was established past the place, grandfather built quite a pretentious frame house and conducted a tavern and stage station. Starr's Point post office was established there and for years grandfather was tavern keeper and postmaster."

In general, there weren't a lot of settlers in the area, but many of the early arrivals were from southern states and supported the South's successionist movement. Others were from groups that leaned toward the Unionist view. There were also groups of emigrants from European countries adapting to

The McFarland Church. The stained glass windows are now part of the Monroe Methodist Church. *Courtesy of the Benton County Historical Society*

new cultures who were not involved in either.

Early on, farmers had to make the long wagon trip to Lancaster or Peoria to ship their products and supplies by steamship when the Long Tom was not navigable. With no definite time-table, the goods going out would be left sitting on wharves or in warehouses until the next boat came. Sometimes the goods disappeared when a form of piracy developed.

During the rainy season, the Long Tom, usually sluggish, frequently overflowed its banks in the Starr's Point/Monroe area, as well as in other low-lying places along its course. Freight costs by horse and wagon were high and nearly impossible after the rains started and the clay soil turned muddy.

A local congressman, Representative Willis Hawley, secured a government grant to replace the Monroe Bridge with a drawbridge and improve the channel of the Long Tom River. With a drawbridge and a ferry, Monroe became a river port. The steamboat, Gypsy, took products to market. It was a short-term arrangement, as the channel soon became impassable again and Willis Hawley was not reelected.

When the flood of 1861 changed the course of the Willamette River and Lancaster was no longer a shipping point, the farmers and settlers were required to go to Harrisburg, a much longer trip, requiring the use of a ferry. Monroe needed the railroad.

The town became a farmers' trading center in the Long Tom River Valley. The flour mill, owned by Adam Wilhelm, was established in 1903. It produced flour shipped under several different names. Wilhelm established another mill in Harrisburg, a mill and bank in Junction City, and built the A.C. Wilhelm and Sons General Mercantile in Monroe.

Wilhelm also invested in other properties and businesses. At one time, he owned all but nine houses in Monroe.

In July 1911, the Corvallis and Alsea Railroad was sold to the Portland, Eugene and Eastern Railway. That railroad planned to link the system from Portland to San Francisco and considered the line from Monroe to Eugene essential. The railroad came from the north through Monroe and continued

The refurbished Adam Wilhelm house in Monroe, Oregon. *From the Brew family collection*

The Monroe Public School built 1902. *Courtesy of the Benton County Historical Society*

along Territorial Road through Alvadore and connected to the Eugene-Coos Bay line. On September 4, 1913, the golden spike connection of the railroad was driven in front of the Wilhelm house with a big crowd there to watch.

When the railroad came through, small waystations were built at every crossroad between Eugene and Corvallis where people could sit to wait for a train. The railroad was a boon to farmers with products to sell and later, the trains were able carry logs out to mills and to market.

The town was renamed Monroe after President James Monroe in 1914 when it incorporated. Some of the old buildings remain, but many are gone. There was once a weekly newspaper, a hotel, a bank, the flour mills, the creamery and several historic homes.

In 1940, the Oregon Apple packing plant (OAC) provided employment and there were some years when the opening of school needed to be delayed while the bean crop was harvested.

With the construction of Pacific Highway, however, things began to change. In 1920, the highway was blacktopped and railroad passenger and local freight service came to a halt. The freight service to sawmills continued to operate, but then stopped when the mills closed. All service was abandoned and rails from this section were removed in 1936.

Even though trains no longer come through the town, the old railroad cargo depot remains. Located across the street from the high school, it has been restored and has found a new purpose as a beautiful library, City Hall and community building.

Edward Bennett was interviewed in August 1938 for the Benton County, Oregon WPA's American Life Histories Collection: Manuscripts from the Federal Writer's Project, 1936-1940 project:

According to his interviewer, *"Mr. Bennett was interviewed at his office in the village of Monroe, where he has been practising medicine for 43 years..."*

Edward Bennett: *"...I went to school at Bellfountain with Will Taylor, Alwilda Dunn, Heman Gragg, Isobel Gray, and Maria Starr. I also attended grade school in Philomath for a year or so and had part of a year at Philomath College. I spent some time at Monmouth, but never taught school. My medical training I received at the California Medical School at San Francisco and the St. Louis College of Physicians and Surgeons. I have the first diploma ever issued in the United States for a course in Railway Surgery. It is signed by one of the professors of the St. Louis College who was also a Railway Surgeon.*

"I was graduated in 1895 and for forty-three years, I have practiced medicine here in Monroe and have been the local doctor for the S.P. Railroad. In the early days, I used to make trips for long distances back into the hills. There were no doctors there and it was a part of the work. Usually I went on horseback because there was no other way of getting there. All the doctors in that day did the same thing, but we are too old now to do it and the young doctors are too soft."

The present high school was built on U.S. Highway 99W in 1929 and became Monroe Union High School in 1938 to serve a larger area, including Bellfountain, Alpine, Cheshire and Poodle Creek.

Barbara Stroda Wright, who attended Monroe Grade School and Monroe Union High School, believed that consolidating the schools was an especially good solution for the students living in Cheshire and Poodle Creek. The road going from those areas to Junction City was often flooded.

Monroe Brick and Tile Company began in 1911 and was a major business for many years. The kilns can still be seen from the highway just past the beautiful brick high school which fronts the road. The brickyard made brick, drain tile and building blocks. As late as the 1990s, bricks could still be purchased by area residents from the yard itself.

Several of the old downtown buildings are still in use. The South Benton Community Museum has made its home along Highway 99W and just a short distance off the highway, the beautiful old Wilhelm house has been preserved as a private residence.

Elsie Hill spent the summer driving a tractor at the Benton County Flax Grower's Cooperative plant near Monroe, Oregon. *Courtesy of the OSU Special Collections & Archives Commons*

Before the United States was actually involved in World War II, the problems in Europe caused a shortage of flax for linen. It was used for twine, in parachutes and other goods that were needed by the U.S. in its preparation for war. With some urging from the government, flax was planted throughout the Willamette Valley. The processing was slow and involved several steps. A flax plant in Monroe was one of ten that were in the valley.

In the 1950s, the Willamette Valley was also growing high-grade Hannchen barley, popular with American brewers.

Hull-Oakes Sawmill

About 3½ miles north of Monroe on Highway 99, is the Dawson road turn-off. About six miles further west is a unique find that many travelers don't know about.

"Hull-Oakes Sawmill, Bellfountain, Oregon" by Michael J. "Hoss" Barker, author of Out of Oregon; Logging, Lies & Poetry:

"One gets the feeling they've happened upon a very special place when they round the corner from atop a small rise and get their first glimpse of the historic Hull-Oakes Sawmill. It's nestled in a picturesque little valley on the east side of Oregon's coast range, just outside of the once-booming community of Bellfountain, Oregon. This is Buzz Martin's old stompin' ground folks.

"Hull-Oakes is not your everyday 'run of the mill' sawmill. It is, in fact, the only remaining steam-powered sawmill in full-time operation in these here United States.

"Its founder, Ralph Hull, started out in the sawmill business in 1934 when the country was still reeling from the Great Depression. His creation has survived fires, unstable and unpredictable markets, supply problems and a host of other timber industry-related pitfalls to claim its rightful place on the registry of National Historic Sites, as well as being recorded with the Historic American Engineering Record and the U.S. Park Service. Its rich history is stored in the Library of Congress.

"The mill's claim to fame is a 1906 Ames steam engine employing a pair of 16" diameter cylinders putting out close to 450HP, delivered to the mill in a series of wheels and belts that compliment the ingenuity of its creators and operators. The engine is fueled by sawdust, generated onsite and belt-fed into masonry fireboxes that run at about 2,000 degrees F.

"Mr. Hull passed on in 2002 and left the mill in the capable hands of his grandson, Todd Nystrom, who does an admirable job of preserving an important part of our history, yet keeping up with the necessary demands and changes required to keep a sawmill afloat in one of today's most complicated and controversial natural resource industries.

"The logs begin their journey through the mill from the pond, which still has the old A-frame dumping device in place, although these days, it's for show only. In its heyday, the loaded trucks would lumber beneath the towering structure and it would pluck their loads from them and deposit the logs into the pond. Across the pond from the A-frame, the old wigwam burner stands guard over the mill like a stoic sentinel from the past. Above it, near the top of the hill, is the water tank supplying the steam engine.

"A boat has replaced the nimble pond men bristling with their pike poles to herd

the logs to the conveyer chain that takes them up into the mill and to the ring barker, which can accommodate a 72"-diameter stick of wood. From the barker it's to the head rig, where the air-operated machinery slams the log onto the carriage with such force, the whole building shakes and shimmies from its labors.

"Once the log is dogged on to the rig, the ratchet-setter and sawyer talk back and forth with hand signals like a pitcher and catcher; the carriage feeds the log through the double-edged band saw screaming for more wood to feed its insatiate appetite.

"The slabs are off-beared on to a series of chains and rollers, which guide them to their ultimate demise through the edgers, trim saws and planers that are the inner workings of the mill. From here it's on out to the green and planer chains where they are hand-pulled and stacked into units. From there, 1960s-circa lumber carriers, looking a lot like a big roller skate with a radical lift kit, pick the stacked units up and shuttle them to temporary storage or the kilns before they are shipped off to market.

"The mill's specialty are custom-ordered timbers, and they ship them all over the world. Their timber supply comes largely from the private sector, but on occasion, they get a BLM sale in the bidding process. In 2003, they had two logging sites of their own operating, and also run a few of their own trucks.

"The beauty of this place and what makes it a cut above the rest is due to a number of things. First of all, it's built from wood – old growth timbers to be more precise – and they have an ambience and character that only time and wear can conjure up. They can't be imitated or copied; they're the real McCoy. There's not a plumb wall or level floor or deck on the claim, and rightly so. That along with its sounds and odors are its persona and charm.

"The electric lines look eerily out of place amid the backdrop of steam clouds and rusting tin roofs supported by stout legs of timber. It's not just the mill itself that refuses to change with the times. The office sets the visitor up for their trip back into yesterday by its simple cheerfulness. The steps and small deck are listing to the port side and are being slowly crowded out by an ancient oak tree, gradually trying to reclaim the ground the office was built on. The pictures adorning the office wall are like a portal through the windows of time, back to a simpler, slower place – it's almost contagious.

"The old water truck rumbles by on its mission to keep the dust at bay. I'm guessing it's a 1960 something, but I could be off by ten years; it can go just as fast backward as it can forward, narrowly missing the carrier as it hurries past and snatches up another unit of lumber bound for market, leaving a hint of anti-freeze on the air to mix in with the other olfactory delights of the old mill.

"As I left the office and headed for my car, old Thelma, wondering if she would start without a jump, I saw a 20-something kid walking across the lot on his way back to the mill, talking on a cell phone. I think that, for a moment, I almost got mad at him. He'd done nothing wrong, but it just seemed so out of place. Is nothing sacred?!

"Thelma fired up all on her own, and as we sputtered our way back into 'the world,' I wondered to myself if that kid

had any idea how lucky he is to be working there. It was a good life, and for a lucky few, it still is.

"The management is very accommodating and offers group tours for the public. Anytime spent at this special place is well-spent and shouldn't be deducted from one's time here on Earth."

From Monroe to Corvallis, U.S. Highway 99W traced the old stage route in later years.

The Stannis Station is believed to be one of the next stage stops on the west side of the road according to Jesse Houck in another *Historical Records Survey* project interview. *"It was owned at first by Sam Stannis and later run by a family by the name of Zearoff."* It was probably the next stop north of Starr's Point, but we've been unable to get further information on it.

Possibly the next stagestop heading north was Gird's Twelve-Mile House. Gird's place was located 12 miles south of Corvallis in Benton County near the Finley National Wildlife Refuge. In a *Historical Records Survey* project interview included on Ancestry.com's "RootsWeb" genealogy site, Mrs. Anna Reeves Starr said, *"I remember that Bill Gird kept a stage station on the Franklin place, north of McFarland Church."*

In another interview, Jesse Houck also mentioned, *"Bill Gird had a stage station about a quarter of a mile east of what is now Bruce's Corner, on the south side of the crossroad."*

Also located off the stretch of Highway 99W north of Monroe is the William L. Finley National Wildlife Refuge, nestled along the Coast Range at the western edge of the Willamette Valley. It encompasses 5,325 acres including forest, upland prairie, wet prairie, wetlands and farm fields. It provides habitat for wintering the Dusky Canada Goose and other native species. It was acquired in the 1960s and has populations of several endangered and threatened animal and plant species. A herd of Roosevelt elk can be found in the bottomland forests or fields on the refuge.

JENNYOPOLIS

Apparently, Jennyopolis was not much more than a rest stop with a trading post and a post office north of Starr's Point. It was situated on the stage route that later became U.S. Highway 99W, between the current William L. Finley Wildlife Refuge and Greenberry. The Jennyopolis post office was established March 24, 1852. Richard Irwin, who owned the trading post, was its first postmaster, but the service was discontinued on April 18, 1857.

An excerpt of *Nimrod: Courts, Claims, And Killing On The Oregon Frontier* by Ronald B. Lansing tells of an interesting part of the Jennyopolis history:

"That large hill two miles north is Winkle's Butte, called such because settler Isaac Winkle was the first to lay claim to it. At the foot of the butte and to the west was Winkle's neighbor, Richard Irwin. Irwin had a store at trailside. They called it Jennyopolis. Headed south, the trail came upon the Starrs Point store four miles away. Farther south, the trail passed Yapo-ah Butte and Skinner's post office..."

In 1852, Benton County, Oregon's first recorded murder took place two miles south of Jennyopolis, and the trial that is outlined in the Lansing book was widely publicized.

The local store-owner, Richard Irwin, was appointed coroner and oversaw the proceedings of the trial of Nimrod O'Kelly in the death of Jeremiah Mahoney. The sheriff, Sam Starr, was in charge of assembling the jury of local settlers.

The story was a long one, and those readers wishing to learn more about the outcome of the Jennyopolis murder and trial are encouraged to locate a copy of the Lansing book.

GREENBERRY

Greenberry is a community south of Corvallis. It bears the combined given names of Green Berry Smith, a pioneer who settled in Benton County in 1846, and who, for a time, lived on his farm near there. Smith was generally called Greenberry, despite the fact that he had two given names.

In his 1885 book, *History of Benton County, Oregon*, David Fagan talked a bit about Green Berry Smith:

"Having wintered at the mouth of Washougal some fifteen miles above Fort Vancouver, in the month of March, 1846, Mr. Smith and his brother [Alexander] came to Benton county and he took up his residence in the Luckiamute Valley, about 12 miles north of Corvallis, and embarked in farming and stock-raising. His original claim of 640 acres he still owns. In 1862 he became domiciled in Corvallis, but at the end of four years removed to a farm to the south of the city, where after 16 years he returned in 1883, to Corvallis, of which he is now a most respected citizen.

"Mr. Smith is now one of the most prosperous of Benton county's residents. He owns no less the 8,000 acres of land located within her confines and that of the neighboring county of Polk; while he is considered to be a man of superior intelligence and marked individuality of character. He has been twice married, in the first instance in 1849, to Miss Eliza Hughard, a native of Missouri, who died two years after. By this union there is one son, Alexander; and secondly, in 1851, to Miss Mary Baker, a native of Tennessee, by whom he has one son, John."

Judd Smith was interviewed on May 23, 1938 for the Benton County, Oregon *WPA's American Life Histories Collection: Manuscripts from the Federal Writer's Project, 1936-1940* project:

A comment from his interviewer, Mark Phinney: *"Mr. Smith was interviewed at his farm about eight miles south of Corvallis and about one and one-half miles from the Peoria Ferry. Mr. Smith is a successful farmer and while his knowledge of the early times is limited, what he tells is dependable."*

Judd Smith's story begins: *"'My father, Terry W.B. Smith, came around the horn in 1850. With him came my grandfather, Jerry Myer Smith. Grandfather was a brother of Green Berry Smith who came to Benton County, I think, before 1850. Green Berry Smith (the two names are distinct, but many people today think his name was Greenberry) was at one time one of the largest landowners in Benton County. He owned a strip a mile wide and extending south from Corvallis to his original claim at Greenberry station, a distance of eight miles. Then he owned land in other parts of the county. He had more than nine thousand acres on Soap Creek in the north end of the county. It was he who owned and vacated the site of Tampico, the ghost town.'"*

The Willamette Community Grange in Greenberry. *Courtesy of the OSU Special Collections & Archives Commons*

More of Green Berry Smith's interesting story will continue in the Tampico, Oregon segment later in this section.

The former town of Greenberry is still marked by its beautiful old Willamette Grange building and the not-so-beautiful Greenberry Tavern and Store.

The historic Willamette Community Hall and Grange, a rectangular Georgian Revival building, was constructed in 1922 and sits on Greenberry Road on nearly two acres, encompassing approximately 4,750 square feet. In 2009, the two-story hall was listed on the National Register of Historic Places for Benton County, Oregon.

The Grange Movement

The National Grange fraternal organization, founded in 1867 by Oliver Hudson, was named The Patrons of Husbandry. Founded in 1867, it was commonly called the "Grange." It developed during the Civil War and exerted a good deal of influence on farmers and agriculture at the time. Oliver Hudson Kelley, a Mason who appreciated the benefits of fraternity, wanted to create a secret order to advance the social needs and combat the economic backwardness of farm life while furthering the industrial reconstruction of the South and the advancement of the agricultural class throughout the country.

The Grange movement was introduced to Oregon farmers in 1871. The purpose was to represent the interests of farmers and encourage education, extension services, rural free delivery and the farm credit service. It was a strong political force in each community and often in the state as a whole. In Oregon, many of the local Granges in the northern part of the state opposed any public funding for the building of the Pacific Highway for several years. They had access to both water and railroad transportation and didn't see the need.

The Granges were popular sites for social gatherings as well. The buildings were used to host dances, musicals, quilting bees, community gatherings, often classes, speakers and rallies favorable to farming interests.

The Greenberry Tavern and Store is a familiar sight and stop along the highway on the corner of Highway 99W and Greenberry Road This marks a fairly popular turn-off for a back entrance to Philomath and a shortcut to the coast.

An interesting side note is that Green Berry Smith was strongly against alcohol use and other "vices," and would probably have rolled over in his grave if he knew that a tavern, bearing his name, was operating on land he once owned.

Theodore P. Bevens, interviewed in May 1938 for the Benton County, Oregon WPA's *American Life Histories Collection: Manuscripts from the Federal Writer's Project, 1936-1940* project, shared a remembrance of Green Berry Smith:

"There were many southern sympathizers during the Civil War and clashes were frequent, but generally these were not very serious. The southern men were organized into groups or circles. My father was leader of the group in our locality, Elijah McDaniel at Independence and another man at Soap Creek. McDaniel was badly beaten up at one time. At another time, my father, carrying the Confederate flag, led a horseback parade through the streets of Corvallis. Green Berry Smith brought his boy John to the gathering. My father had the only horse that would carry double, so he took the boy behind him. In later years John told me that was the proudest moment of his life."

MARYSVILLE / CORVALLIS

In 1845, Joseph Avery purchased land from the Kalapuya Indians on the west bank of Mary's River just below its confluence with the Willamette River. He erected a small cabin, harvested crops, built a log granary, then hustled off to the California gold fields. He was able to purchase a stock of goods in San Francisco which was shipped by boat to Portland. Ox teams brought the goods from Portland to his homesite and the granary became a store. He had already platted the first lots and streets of the town and he also operated a free canoe ferry across Mary's River, hoping to encourage more settlers.

Avery called the town Marysville and opened his store in 1849. By 1851, steamboats started arriving, bringing people and manufactured goods and exporting produce, furs and lumber. His neighbor, William Dixon, platted part of his own claim as a townsite. Two stores, two blacksmith shops, a school and a saloon were established in 1851 on the two properties.

From *Willamette Landings* by Howard McKinley Corning, Oregon Historical Society, 1947:

"From earliest years, Marysville was on the road through the west Willamette Valley, by way of Yamhill Falls and across the Rickreall, Luckiamute, and Long Tom Rivers to the upper Willamette and Umpqua country. From there the road proceeded through the Southern Oregon settlements and over the Siskiyou Mountains into California. Along that route in the gold-crazed years of the Gold Rush, freight wagons and pack trains moved, carrying the commerce that made

Marysville an important way-point. Transportation of commodities employed hundreds of animals and drivers."

In 1850, Charles Ray purchased the first mail route in Oregon Territory on which wheeled vehicles were used, a line that ran between Oregon City and Salem. In 1869, he extended the route to Corvallis and inaugurated the first Concord stagecoach service in the Pacific Northwest.

From *Oregon: End of the Trail* by the Writers' Program, page 159:

"The California and Oregon Stagecoaches soon took over and rumbled over the crude roads with a Corvallis station for respite, and in 1856 workmen strung the city's first telegraph line to the state metropolis."

The Marysville Post Office was established in 1850, but in 1853, because Marysville, California, was on the same stage line, postal authorities requested that the name of Marysville, Oregon Territory, be changed. It was renamed Corvallis from the Latin phrase *"cor vallis,"* meaning "heart of the valley" by the legislative assembly.

Industry flourished along the river with flour, lumber and planing mills, a creamery and an ice-making plant providing jobs for residents. In 1851, the town was officially platted and designated the seat of the newly-created county of Benton.

When the territorial government first selected Salem as the new capital, the legislators objected to the move from Oregon City and particularly to Salem which seemed to be lacking in facilities. After one meeting there, in 1855, the government was literally kidnapped. Several legislators, very unhappy with the facilities in Salem, took the needed

Territorial capitol bulding at Corvallis, ca 1855. *Courtesy of the Oregon State Library*

official documents to Corvallis by steamboat to conduct the legislative business in a primitive hotel there. The young editor of the *Oregon Statesman*, Asahel Bush, packed his printing press and accompanied them. They did not have a regular meeting place in Corvallis and moved from one building to another. The federal government stepped in to refuse funds to any location but Salem, so after one year, the government was moved back to Salem.

During the 1850s, Corvallis was an agricultural shipping center, located on the Willamette River, and it was the most southerly ferry landing for men headed to the gold fields in Southern and Eastern Oregon.

It was incorporated as a city in 1857, and a jail was built in 1859. The steamboats moved freight up the river from Portland at $40 a ton. Local farmers engaged in dairying and raised fruit. The city had a fruit and vegetable cannery and a prune dryer as well as several creameries.

William A. Buchanan, interviewed in May 1939 for the Benton County, Oregon WPA's *American Life Histories Collection: Manuscripts from the Federal Writer's Project, 1936-1940* project:

"...I came to the Agricultural College from 1878 to 1881, but did not graduate. I took a course in agriculture. Then I was married and began farming. I lost my right arm when I was 29, but farmed for three years longer. Then I came to Corvallis and operated a dairy for some years. I was appointed deputy recorder in 1894 and elected County Treasurer in 1896. I served as treasurer continuously until 1921. I am now retired and living with my sister. I am clerk of the local lodge of the Woodmen of the World and active in the work of the Methodist Church, South.

"Life in my boyhood was much simpler and with fewer luxuries than now. Men's clothing was homemade and women's heavier clothing was often homespun. The prints and ginghams were not the delicate fabrics we see today. As a great treat, we children used to have an orange on the Fourth of July.

"There would be social gatherings in our neighborhood every two weeks or so in the winter time. We would play 'weevily wheat' and other like games... Warren Starr used to hold singing schools on Sunday P.M. Then there were the camp meetings at the Bellfountain Park and Campground. Dances were common on the Long Tom and in the Soap Creek neighborhood. There was more or less drunkenness and rough conduct at these affairs. They were not approved by the more strict people.

"I have hauled grain to the warehouse at Booneville. Much grain was shipped from there. There was no town there. The grain was shipped by steamer to Portland. I have heard father tell that the Indians used to burn off the old grass in the valley every year

"I am an optimist, and have always believed that our country would come out right in the end. I have been interested in public affairs and have had a part in them. But I will tell you, I fear for the future of our country. We can't go as we are now going for very long without meeting disaster."

Henry Gerber, interviewed on February 22, 1940 for the Benton County, Oregon WPA's *American Life Histories Collection: Manuscripts from the Federal Writer's Project, 1936-1940* project:

"Grandfather Entz left his family in Missouri and came alone to the Willamette Valley and settled in Salem. In 1850, or perhaps a little earlier, he sent for his family. The children were John, Kate, Rachel, Mary, and my mother, Victoria. They came by water by way of the Isthmus of Panama. While crossing the Isthmus Grandmother Entz was struck by lightning and died as a result of the shock. The captain of the steamer on which they had engaged passage brought the children safely to Portland and put them in charge of Captain Bennett who commanded one of the Willamette River boats. Captain Bennett was acquainted with Grandfather Entz and brought the family on to Salem. Grandfather did not think it best to try to keep his family together.

"Captain Bennett, who had brought the children to Salem, was childless, and

Bridge over Mary's River, Corvallis in 1910. *Courtesy of Gerald W. Williams Collections, OSU Special Collections & Archives Commons*

he and his wife took Mary. Kate was cared for by a family named Ferguson. My mother found a home with the Bennett family, who were pioneers of Benton County. The brother, John, was interested in mining and dropped out of sight. It is supposed he was killed by Indians or met some other such lonely fate.

"Grandfather later came to Benton County and bought the farm that included the hills northwest of town and part of what is now included within the limits of Corvallis. He was a devout Catholic and donated the ground on which the Catholic Cemetery is located. His daughters were all adopted by people from the south and none of them grew up in their father's faith. After some years, grandfather turned the place over to his children and my parents bought out the other interests.

"...Although Father [Henry Gerber] owned the farm near town, he never farmed himself, but rented it out to others. He himself did whatever other work offered. He and a partner named Tim Donahue dug many wells here in Corvallis before the days when there was a water system. The rate charged was a dollar per foot, and the work was profitable. Tim worked under ground and father worked on the surface.

"Then there was a granite quarry on the farm from which they took out much stone for foundations of buildings in Corvallis and for bases for tombstones. There were no persons living here who were skilled in shaping stone for finer uses.

"I attended school at the old North School at Fifth and Harrison Streets. I remember Minnie Lee used to teach there and a Mr. Bennett whose father at one time was pastor of the North M.E. Church. At the Evangelical Church Mr. Bowersox was pastor. When he took down the bell rope to keep the boys from ringing the church bell on New Year's Eve, we climbed a balm tree whose limbs spread to the belfry window. But Mr. Bowersox had the last laugh for he was waiting for us at the base of the tree with a heavy switch and we had to come down that way.

"Most of the merchants in the early days were Jews. I remember Jacobs & Neugass, Kline, Stock, Harris, and Max Friendly, all had drygoods stores here. There was no racial feeling and no social discrimination.

"There were also many Chinese here then. The Chinese worked as laundrymen or as railroad laborers. They were not socially recognized.

"There used to be a planing mill at Third and Jackson and a tannery on Adams Street, but the tannery never operated after I was old enough to remember. In the seventies there was a fruit drying plant on First that dried quantities of apples. Almost every farm had a good-sized orchard and as there were no pests then to injure the crop there was always a good supply of apples. Pears were plentiful, too, and there were some peaches along the river. Father had a block or more of land here planted to cherries. They were the old fashioned kinds, but were a very profitable crop.

"The big business in my younger days was wheat raising. There were four large warehouses on the river bank, owned by Mr. Avery, Mr. Nicholas, Mr. Cauthorn, and Mr. Blair. These were built chiefly for the storing and shipping of wheat, which was of course transported by river steamers. During the harvest seasons the teams would extend in an unbroken line for half a mile, all waiting turn to unload, while across the line waiting to cross the ferry they extended as far up the road as one could see.

"Father used to go out to the farm on thrashing day and not come back until all the wheat was in. I remember one time he returned in the middle of the night in such a bad humor he wouldn't speak to mother. Finally she said to him 'What is the matter with you? Did you have a fight with John?' (John was the tenant.) He replied, 'No. A damned sight worse than that. The wheat made only fifty bushels to the acre. We'll all starve to death. We had better sell the old farm.' Sixty bushels to the acre was a common yield at first, but the farmers kept raising grain year after year and putting nothing back until the soil was worn out. The thrashing machines had no blowers or stockers of any kind and the straw was bucked away from the machine in all directions by a boy with a team. Then a strip was plowed around the field to protect the fences and when the first sprinkle of rain started, the straw piles were fired and straw and stubble were burned off the whole field. You could almost read at night from the reflected glare of all the straw piles burning at once.

"Joseph Avery had a flour mill below the mouth of Mary's River, built before my time. Mr. Wilson and others built another mill on First street. Then Mr. Fisher, who ran the mill here so long, bought both mills and removed the machinery from the one on First Street.

"The old ferry was at the site of the Van Buren Street bridge. St. Clair and Isaac and Reuben Moore operated at first, and then Brookhart bought it. The County bought out Mr. Brookhart's interest and operated the ferry until the bridge was built. There has been no brick yard right in the town since I can remember, but there were great pits at Ninth and Van Buren, at Tenth and Harrison, and at Seventh and A Streets, where clay had been dug out and made into brick. These pits would fill with water and make excellent skating ponds whenever we had a cold winter.

"There was a saw mill on the river bank about a block below this house, which was built in an early day. Before I was a man in years I began to work there and continued to work in the engine room until the mill burned and was not rebuilt in 1911. As I recall, the different men who owned it, in succession, were H. P. Harris, Mr. Robinson, Mr. McCullough, Max Friendly, and Mr. Strong. It burned in 1889, but Max Friendly rebuilt it. The only man

Ferry docking at Corvallis. *Courtesy of the OSU Special Collections & Archives Commons*

who really made it pay was Strong, who bought it for $8,000 and after operating it a few years, sold to a group of men from Texas for $75,000.

"I have never married, and since my parents died, mother in 1923 and father in 1910, I have lived alone. At present I am not working, except as caretaker of the Odd Fellows Cemetery.

"I was about to enlist in the Oregon Regiment in the Philippine War. When I asked father what he thought about it he said: 'You have a good job now, at good wages, a good place to sleep and regular meals. You do more or less as you please and when you go out in the morning you are reasonably sure of coming back safe. If you join the army you'll work for Uncle Sam at a dollar a day, do what you are told and nothing else, eat what is offered to you when you can get it, and sleep where night finds you.' I thought it over and didn't enlist."

A new group of emigrants came into Oregon after the Civil War – more than 10,000 of them – veterans from both sides who were restless, broke or just looking for a way to build a new future. The presence of many of them had a lasting effect on the young state.

Corvallis Academy, Corvallis College, Oregon State Agricultural College, Oregon Agricultural College, Oregon State College and Oregon State University:

The Southern Methodist Church established Corvallis College in 1865, but it struggled. When it needed a new president in the summer of 1872, the bishops of the Methodist Episcopal Church South asked Professor Arnold, a Confederate veteran, to go west. President Arnold changed the name of Corvallis College to Corvallis State Agricultural College and then to Oregon Agricultural College. He served as president of the college for 20 years and remains a giant figure in the history of the school. It became a state institution in 1886, and has since developed as Oregon State University. In 1869, the legislature designated the school as its land grant agricultural college and supplied the required funding to meet the federal requirements.

Arnold introduced the study of scientific agriculture at the school and authorized experiments for the purpose of helping farmers in the state. Faculty and students spent eight hours a day in the classroom and were required to work on the college's farm during after-school hours. He also established an alumni association for the school and introduced intercollegiate athletics when he allowed the formation of a baseball team. Before that, debate had been the only authorized student social activity allowed outside the classroom.

The mission of the "land-grant" college as set forth in the 1862 Morrill Act was to focus on the teaching of practical agriculture, science, military science and engineering without excluding classical studies. Other acts passed since have further defined the mission to include research and sharing, but the basics are much the same.

It is that status which has allowed Oregon agricultural experiment stations and sent cooperative extension agents into rural areas to spread the results of their research and other programs with matching federal and state funds. Some of these include 4-H, Master Gardening and Food Preservation.

Arnold also introduced military science to the curriculum and hired an active-duty U.S. Army officer to lead the cadet corps. This was the precursor to the modern ROTC.

Early in his tenure, Arnold asked his army colleague, Professor B.J. Hawthorne, to join the faculty. Hawthorne accepted the offer and, as the first chairman of the Agriculture Department, he taught horticulture, botany, zoology, care of domestic animals and stockbreeding. Other Confederate veterans on the

Oregon Agricultural College, Corvallis, ca 1915. *Courtesy of Gerald W. Williams Collections, OSU Special Collections & Archives Commons*

Oregon Agricultural College were the mathematics professor, John Letcher and Reverend J.R.N. Bell, a member of the Board of Regents.

While Arnold was involved in his career, Reverend Bell, who had been commandeered from theology college by the Confederacy, arrived on the scene. As a private, he had been a captured prisoner of war and later was discharged, taught school, married and then went back to finish his education. Moving to Ashland, he was ordained in the Methodist Episcopal Church South and given charge of the church at Ashland. With several stops along the way and ordained by both the Presbyterians and Methodists, Bell ended up in Corvallis. He performed the marriage rites for more than a thousand couples, and was a guest preacher in hundreds of churches, regardless of denomination. He was the best-known minister in the state. He also purchased and published several newspapers over the years, served as the Masonic Chaplain and began serving on the Board of Regents of Oregon Agricultural College with Arnold after 1874.

When intercollegiate athletics began, Bell was one of the program's ardent supporters. He was among the spectators at the first football game between Oregon Agricultural College and the University of Oregon. In 1921, Oregon Agricultural College named the football stadium in his honor and Bell Field was the home of the Beavers until 1953.

Arnold moved the campus from Fifth Street to the present location of Oregon State University and supervised the fundraising and construction of the first college building on the new site. He died in 1892 at just 52 years

Tug 'O War at Oregon Agricultural College. Class of 1917 vs 1918 at Fischer's Millrace (1918 won). *Courtesy of the OSU Special Collections & Archives Commons*

OAC Campus, Corvallis. *Courtesy of the OSU Special Collections & Archives Commons*

Downtown Corvallis. Jefferson Street is the cross street in the forefront. *Courtesy of the Benton County Historical Soceity*

The Benton County Courthouse in Corvallis as it looks today. *Courtesy of Greg Keene, Wikimedia Commons*

of age. He was succeeded as college president by another Civil War veteran, John McKnight Bloss, a Union man.

Railroad service from Portland reached Corvallis in 1880 and, during the following decade, railroads reigned king. Lines were built to Yaquina Bay and were projected eastward across the Cascade Range to the midwest.

The nationwide financial troubles of the early 1890s halted the rail expansion. However, during the period of "railroad fever," Corvallis built a new courthouse. Today, it is the oldest courthouse in Oregon still in use. They also built a city hall, a new flour mill, an electric light plant, a brick hotel, a new school and Benton Hall, the first building on the present Oregon State University campus. The

Corvallis Depot. *Courtesy of the OSU Special Collections & Archives Commons*

courthouse that was built in 1888, is well-maintained and a popular subject for tours and photographs.

From "The Arrival of the Automobile in Corvallis." *Corvallis Daily Gazette-Times,* April 19, 1918:

"In Corvallis, the arrival of the automobile is usually dated to July 4, 1904, when Mark Rickard, the first person to own an automobile in Benton County, drove his car into Corvallis. He arrived in a shining 1-cylinder Reo-touring car. It had leather upholstery, but there was no top and no windshield—one had to pay extra for those. The cost for this beautiful machine was $1,450. The crank to start the automobile was located on the side of the car, so in case the car leapt forward, no one would be run over. Mr. Rickard reported that the car traveled about twenty miles an hour, but expenses were high. The car took a gallon of gas every ten miles, and gas wasn't as plentiful as it is today. Gasoline was sold in drugstores and other places. Drivers bought a quart here, or a pint here. Usually it was impossible to get more than a gallon at any one place..."

Mr. Rickard made several memorable trips in his Reo. One night, he left Corvallis at midnight and traveled all night reaching Newport at noon.

"...The roads weren't very good, and we had to drive slow – going down Pioneer mountain we had to cut a fir tree and drag it behind to keep below the speed limit."

He drove to Portland from Corvallis in only six hours.

Corvallis Airport located on Grant Street looking west, 1930. *Courtesy of the OSU Special Collections & Archives Commons*

Lyndon Airfield on Hebert Road, Corvallis, 1939. *Courtesy of the OSU Special Collections & Archives Commons*

"He also drove his car to the top of Skinner's Butte in Eugene. A large crowd assembled to see the first car get to the top of the Butte."

Before gasoline pumps and stations, Corvallis was one place where large metal barrels of gasoline with a hand pump were grouped along the road in front of a store where an automobile tank could be filled. The barrels were also used at the early air fields.

The Southern Pacific Red Electrics were running from Portland with an extension to Corvallis which was the southern terminus before World War I. The line was abandoned in 1929. Even a slow automobile was preferable.

By the 1920s, the Pacific Highway /U.S. Highway 99W ran right through Corvallis, ten years after U.S. Highway 99E on the east side of the Willamette was built.

At the mid-century, Corvallis was expanding its civic center, improving its public parks and rerouting U.S. Highway 99W along the scenic Willamette riverfront.

LEWISTON / LEWISBURG

The station, Lewisburg, which is a little further north in Benton County, was named for Haman Lewis. After settling on a 640-acre donation land claim in the area, Haman was elected as a free-state delegate to the Benton County Constitutional Convention. When the final vote was taken for the adoption of the constitution, Haman was absent, so his signature doesn't appear on the document. Haman also served as one of the directors of the first school in Benton County.

"First Male Child Born of White Parents in Benton, County Tells of Joys and Troubles of Pioneer Times" (From *Gazette-Times*, May 7, 1928):

"Mr. Lewis' father and mother came across the plains with an emigrant train in 1845. The elder Mr. Lewis was born in New York state and his wife in Missouri and both were southern sympathizers who stood out valiantly for state rights. The Lewis' settled on a donation land claim of 640 acres in Benton County two and a half miles from Corvallis.

"Here the husband built, first a log cabin without windows and made it strong to resist attack, for the Indians were none too friendly. [On] *November 29, 1847, the Whitman massacre* [took place] *and everywhere settlers were on the alert for more*

trouble. Shortly before Haman Lewis was born, a party of Calapooya Indians raided the Lewis ranch, led by chief Ringnose. Their interpreter demanded what he called a 'beef.' Two Indians thrust their guns into holes they made in the log cabin, but did not fire. The elder Lewis' gun was not in working order, but one defender ran for a hatchet. One Indian entered the Lewis home and moved toward Mrs. Lewis, but she beat him with her fists. The hatchet was getting into action when the Indian, accompanied by his fellows, ran off to their reservation in Yamhill County.

"Jan. 21, 1847, Haman Lewis was born on the ranch stormed by the Indians and when he was a baby, he says men workers were hired at 25 cents a day and wheat rose from 25 cents a bushel to $4.00. B.B. Smith, a neighbor of the Lewis's, had a drove of cattle which he bought for $12 a head and shortly afterward sold for $75 a head.

"Men then wore buckskin pants.

"Like a dream, Haman Lewis remembers the Indian Wars of 1854-56 and saw volunteers with guns on their shoulders leaving for the fighting in eastern and southern Oregon. Oregon City, in the 1850s was the most important town in Oregon and baby Portland was spoken of as 'that village.'

"'In 1859, says Mr. Lewis, my father drove to Portland to collect $3,000 for beef which he had sold and I went with him. Portland was then only a small place. We got the $3,000 in gold coin.

"'Did you put the money in the bank?' asked the reporter.

"'No,' replied the veteran, 'there wasn't any bank in our country in those days. We dumped the $3,000 into a sack, the same as we would handle potatoes, threw the sack into our wagon and drove home.

"'When the Civil War raged in 1861, supporters of the Union and those who favored the South were sharply divided in Oregon and especially in Benton County where southern people had settled.

"'And about 1863, I remember things got hot out our way. We thought the south was right and said so. We met on the quiet and talked about what might happen to us. Folks said we might be attacked. About 150 of us men formed what we called the Knights of the Golden Circlet, a secret organization. Oh, yes, we had guns and ammunition, but were never attacked and nothing ever came out of it.'"

Interview of Haman Lewis by Mark Phinney, October 30, 1937, for the *WPA's American Life Histories Collection: Manuscripts from the Federal Writer's Project, 1936-1940* project:

"...The neighbors got together and built a schoolhouse about four miles north of Corvallis. It was a studding building, weather-boarded on the outside with rough lumber. The floor also was rough, the roof covered with shakes and sealed up a few feet with shakes. A fireplace in one end served as a heater. For furniture, we had a board for a desk along each side of the room and benches. The first teacher was James H. Slater who afterwards became U.S. Senator from Oregon."

"...When I was twenty-one, father ran a packing house in Corvallis for a number of years. I worked with him all this time and it was there I learned to make bacon. In 1853, father drove a band of horses to Umatilla Landing to sell and I went with him. It was my first real trip away from home. It took us a month to

Lewisburg, Oregon. *Courtesy of the St. Anne Orthodox Church website*

Lewisburg, Oregon music group in the Lewisburg Hall. *Courtesy of the St. Anne Orthodox Church website*

make the complete journey and during this time we lost two horses in Portland. We never expected to see them again, but when we got home there they were, having swum the Tualatin and Yamhill Rivers and made it through all alone..."

C.R. (Dick) Ballard, interviewed in August 1938 for the Benton County, Oregon WPA's *American Life Histories Collection: Manuscripts from the Federal Writer's Project, 1936-1940* project:

"One of the dangers to the traders and travelers was from the highwaymen. These were mostly toughs from the Willamette Valley who robbed and killed without mercy. Father never talked of these things except with old timers, but there was a man named Bill Igo, who had worked at freighting at the same time father was in the business and who used to stay at our house for quite a while at times. I have heard them talk about the highwaymen and how they were punished.

"There was a man in the Willamette Valley who had taken in a homeless lad and raised him as one of his own. Later this boy went to the mines and fell in with the outlaw gang. Through their confederates in town the gang would learn of some man starting out with a large amount of gold and would then waylay and kill him.

This man who had befriended the lad was in the mines. He sold out this holdings and because he had a large sum with him, he left on a round-about way, avoiding the main road. In spite of the precaution, the highwaymen met him and he recognized the boy he had helped. This boy promised to do his best to save him and finally helped him to escape. He had seen and recognized the whole party and immediately returned to Lewiston and raised a posse. Such law and order as there was then was mostly enforced by the Vigilantes. The criminals were brought in and placed in a wooden building under guard. The tough element in the saloons and gambling halls were in sympathy with the prisoners and immediately started a move to set them free. While the mob were drinking and otherwise working themselves up to the point of making a jail-delivery, the vigilantes took the gang out and hung them on a hurriedly-made scaffold. The leaders of the highwaymen were Dave English from the Soap Creek district in this county and Three-fingered Pete. There were eight or ten others. Father and Bill Igo knew most of them. Igo was in Lewiston when they were hung, but he never admitted having anything to do with the dead."

Today, the most visible marker for the community of Lewisburg is the 1911-vintage Lewisburg Hall and Warehouse Company building. It was once the Mountain View Grange No. 429 and is currently owned and cared for by the St. Anne Orthodox Church as a church and community center. It is listed on the National Register of Historic Places.

One of the special features of the Lewisburg area today is the establishment of the Lewisburg Old Growth Trail. The 2½ mile trail goes through an OSU Research Forest and is said to be the best place to see stands of old growth trees that are sheltered by a steep valley and untouched by modern man.

CAMP ADAIR

Just past Lewisburg, going north out of Corvallis, a large cocoa-brown building on the left side of the highway, is the old Lakepark Skating Rink. It was built in 1922 to entertain members of the Army Corps of Engineers stationed nearby.

The large structure was used heavily during the 1930s with Civilian Conservation Corps recruits and in the 1940s when Camp Adair was filled with soldiers. It saw such heavy use, a new floor had to be installed after the war. It continued to be used for both skating and community dances through the turn of the century.

As the war in Europe heated and it became obvious we were going to become involved, the United States Government knew we needed training facilities. It began the process of planning what was needed, based on where our soldiers would likely be fighting. Three cantonments, or temporary camps, were planned for Oregon, two affecting U.S. Highway 99, the major north-south highway at that time. One was out of Medford – Camp White – and the other was Camp Adair north of Corvallis. Although funding had yet to be approved, they were selected in July 1941, in farm country that somewhat resembled Germany.

The true size of the camp was never visible from the road, but the specifications called for an area of about 65,000 acres with 2,000 to be level ground and the balance to be rolling hills with light woods.

Only five days after the December 7,

1941 Japanese attack on Pearl Harbor, funding was approved and construction began in early 1942.

The Corvallis Chamber of Commerce and nearby communities had been pushing to bring the cantonment to this area. The effects of the recession were still being felt, and the additional population surge would bring in great benefits to local business. Still, rural land owners in the Corvallis area nervously awaited word that their farms would be spared. They were producing much-needed crops and they were hoping that it should give them some protection.

In "Remembering Camp Adair," a 1995 class project for the Oregon State University Extension's Home Economics Mini College, Janice Barclay wrote:

"When the official word that they must move finally reached them, they were shocked, angry, sad and, above all, they were helpless."

The news came to the landowners being dispossessed in the form of a postcard, dated July 1, 1942, that said, *"This farm will be vacated by October 1, 1942."*

No mention was made of any monetary amount. The physical act of moving was only part of the problem. Where could a farmer go when there was no money for a down payment on another farm? Then there was the rest... All household belongings had to be moved and anything not moved was to be abandoned.

"Camp Job is Starting," an article in the *Monmouth Herald*, February 26, 1942:

"Acquiring of farm land will start Monday. Farmers may have homes, building, fences or anything they can move off.

The cantonment area will be bounded on the east by the Corvallis-Independence Road and approximately on the north by the Suver-Airlie Roads. It will form a rectangle six miles wide and 10 miles long, being longer east and west."

Several additional acquisitions took place over time. The headlines on another newspaper article, dated September 21, 1942, stated that, *"20,500 Acres of Land North of Present Adair Taken by U.S."*

From the *Monmouth Herald*, September 3, 1942:

"Farmers in this community are going in all directions, looking for farms to replace theirs taken over by the government. In traveling elsewhere they report that land of comparable quality is considerably higher than they are being paid."

The building of the camp displaced 250 families – farmers in particular – some of whom had been on their property for three generations. 414 graves were moved from eight cemeteries, and two family plots. The Lewisville rural school and fourteen others as well as the settlement of Wells were also taken over. More than 50,000 acres were assembled from farm properties at a cost of $17,000,000.

Camp Adair was designed to house 33,000 men and support staff at a time. Four infantry divisions would train at the camp, with more than 100,000 G.I.s passing through. It was named for Lt. L. Henry Rodney Adair, a West Point graduate from Astoria, Oregon who was killed during the Mexican Revolution Border War on June 21, 1916.

The construction of the camp physically involved major portions of both Benton and Polk Counties, but it also brought in 40,000 residents on a temporary basis, some of whom also brought families.

One volunteer in the Polk County Historical Museum pointed out that Camp Adair had been created in a three-month period; another source said that it took six months. A poster in the Polk County Museum said it had taken 8,000 workers to build 1,800 structures including 500 barracks, 11 chapels, eight movie theaters, 13 post exchanges, two service buildings, a hospital, two guest houses, a bank, two phone exchanges, a post office, a field house with three full-size basketball courts, a bakery that could produce 45,000 loaves of bread every day, a wastewater treatment plant, a fresh water treatment plant, a model German village, coal yard, firing ranges, airfield, orderly rooms... and, the list went on.

During the early part of Camp Adair construction, U.S. Highway 99W, the main highway between Corvallis and Portland, was extensively rebuilt and straightened and the road work added to the chaos that was going on. Day and night, tons of construction materials of all kinds arrived at the site and were stockpiled along the highway, making it virtually impassable most of the time.

Sunday drives became a major problem. The huge undertaking drew a great deal of interest from people living in the area and they frequently drove out the congested highway to see the progress. At times, the highway became completely blocked by sightseers. Eventually, the U.S. Army had to put notices in the newspapers asking people not to come.

The troops came for training in waves that eventually slowed, but totaled in the neighborhood of 100,000 before the last ones deployed in 1944.

Not long after the last division left Camp Adair and headed overseas for combat, the U.S. Navy took over the camp hospital for use as a major West Coast medical facility to treat Navy and Marine casualties from the Pacific Theater of Operations. As many as 3,600 wounded servicemen could be treated simultaneously at the Camp Adair hospital complex.

The camp was also used for Italian and German prisoners of war until May 1946. In the Willamette Valley, it wasn't unusual to see German POWs with "PW" emblazoned on their clothing, working in the bean and hop fields while being guarded by soldiers with machine guns. With the shortage of workers available for labor, many of the POWs worked in agricultural harvests.

Under terms of the 1929 Geneva Convention, the prisoners were paid eighty cents a day for their labor. If they chose not to work, they were paid ten cents per day. The funds were redeemable at the base canteen or in cash when the war ended. It was well into 1946 before the captives were repatri-

The Adair hospital units that were converted into apartments for Oregon State College between 1946-1951. Highway 99W runs past in the foreground. *Courtesy of the OSU Special Collections & Archives Commons*

The caption on this photo from the OSU Archives says that these are "soldiers" on their way to the Terhune Hop Yard, but they may be German POWs. *Courtesy of the OSU Special Collections & Archives Commons*

German POWs picking beans in the Oregon fields. *Courtesy of the OSU Special Collections & Archives*

ated, nearly a year after Germany's surrender.

"Fighters on the Farm Front: Oregon's Emergency Farm Labor 1943-1947" from the Oregon State University Archives:

"From 1944 to 1946, over 3,517 prisoners of war, mostly Germans, were utilized on Oregon farms. Although they constituted a small percentage of the total number of farm labor placements, they provided valuable assistance throughout the state. In Malheur County alone, they were largely responsible for the 7,500 acres of potatoes, 3,500 acres of onions, and 3,000 acres of lettuce planted and harvested in 1945. That same year they harvested nearly a half million bushels of pears in Jackson County and 3.8 million pounds of hops in the Willamette Valley.

"The U.S. Army operated six POW camps from which farm workers were obtained. Jackson, Benton, Marion, and Polk counties each housed a camp, while Malheur County maintained two.

"In his unpublished memoirs, Willi Gross, a former German sergeant and prisoner of war, reflected positively on his experience harvesting crops in Oregon during his imprisonment. While stationed

at Camp Adair, Gross 'took every opportunity to seek work details outside the camp,' where he was expected to fill a harvest quota, but was able to enjoy scenery 'very much like Germany.' When Camp Adair closed, Gross suffered from 'a certain amount of sadness,' yet continued working the land in Nyssa, Oregon. While Gross was sent to many POW camps throughout his time in the United States, like many other POWs, he spent most of his time stationed in Oregon, living in relative ease, and helping to keep not only Americans, but Germans in American-occupied territories, fed."

At the end of the war, much of the farmland was offered for sale back to the original owners and, if not taken, to any buyer. Those who did buy back their land found the buildings, roads, fences, electric and telephone lines gone.

The camp was decommissioned in 1946. Many of the buildings were dismantled and sold for scrap or relocated – but not the 11 chapels. They were set aside and distributed to religious organizations from around the region.

Gary Richards, of Suver, Oregon, took the time to research where the chapels are now located. Nine of them are still in Oregon in the towns of Colton, Corvallis, Dallas, Lincoln City, Reedville/Aloha, Rocky Butte/Portland, Silverton, Sweet Home and West Linn. The tenth chapel was found in Crescent City, California, but the eleventh chapel is still missing. Most have been incorporated into churches at each site.

Oregon State College received large blocks of timberland that remained on the vacated Camp Adair site. The area occupied by the main camp was deeded to the State of Oregon and became the home of the E.E. Wilson Wildlife Preserve and the Regional Headquarters of the Oregon Fish and Wildlife Department. The U.S. Government also retained some of the land.

The former hospital was converted into apartments that were used for 370 married veteran students and 30 faculty members who attended and worked at Oregon State College. Some barracks were sold and transported to other places, even as far away as Eugene and Springfield where some are still in use today. As the housing shortage eased by 1951, the apartment buildings were sold, cut apart and moved to various locations in the local area.

After the Korean War, the U.S. Air Force built a large air-conditioned concrete building – a Semi Automatic Ground Environment (SAGE) – at Adair as part of the Western Air Defense Command. It housed two massive computers. A powerhouse was constructed behind the blockhouse. Support buildings, including headquarters, barracks, mess hall, motor pool, supply, and base exchange were added. By 1960, Adair Air Force Station was fully operational. The primary purpose of the Air Force operation at that time was as a radar base to detect and identify all aircraft entering U.S. airspace from the Oregon-Washington border south to Red Bluff, California. If identification was not made, fighter-interceptor aircraft were dispatched.

A long-range anti-aircraft missile base was also constructed a couple of miles north of the SAGE center. It was built, but never manned because the missiles had become obsolete and ineffective. The site was supposed to be restored to its original condition, but the concrete foundations and launch pads are still present. The SAGE center was in operation until 1969 when it also became obsolete and the equipment moved.

After the Air Force ceased operation, the Adair property, including individual houses, were sold. Adair Village was incorporated as a city in 1976 and began functioning as a suburb of Corvallis.

A few older structures remain, including the original smokestack and a few remaining barracks. The present AV Market and Pub was once the original fire station.

New uses have also been found for some of the available land and buildings. A historic museum is evolving. The Santiam Christian Academy is located on the grounds and it is now adding a new classroom building. On playgrounds where troops once trained, school age children run and play or take part in physical activities.

Not far from Santiam Christian Academy, there is a large and beautiful county park with space and facilities for many activities, ball fields and picnic areas. Separately, there is also a field for model airplane enthusiasts.

West of Adair Village, across Highway 99W, is the Peavy Arboretum. The 80-acre Oregon Agricultural College arboretum was established in 1925 and includes 160 species of trees and shrubs. It also serves as the gateway to the university's adjacent McDonald research forest where hikers, bikers and horseback riders find miles of trails.

On the current Highway 99W, you drive past the subdivision of homes of Adair Village. Past that, still on the right, Adair Frontage Road is a mile-long section of the oldest highway with concrete peeking up through the asphalt and just beyond that, a historic site plaque commemorates the camp.

The building of Camp Adair displaced U.S. Highway 99. Just beyond the Camp Adair marker, past a blinking light, the original route can be picked up again. The old highway route went west of what became the camp entrance, heading toward Helmick Park. It then crossed the Helmick Bridge over the Luckiamute River, through farm country and into downtown Monmouth.

From this road, as it nears Monmouth, the hillside community cemetery that was enlarged to include the gravesites moved from Camp Adair, is visible. It's also an area where the width of the old highway can be seen.

At Orr's Corner, it takes a right-angle turn east to the current Highway 99 to continue north.

A section of the new highway was laid to the east of the old route. It was wider and allowed for entrances to the camp itself. It did not go into Monmouth itself, but traveled

One of the few remnants of the old Camp Adair. The smokestack can be seen in the photo on the opposite page. *Courtesy of Curt Deatherage, Cottage Grove*

east of the town until it reached the junction with the main street, rejoining the original road.

TAMPICO

According to legend, the colorful and eccentric Green Berry Smith was very much against "alcohol, carousing and loose morals." Tampico, a thriving, boisterous town, was well-known for all of those activities. Mr. Smith, being a very wealthy man, bought the whole town and burned it to the ground. There is virtually nothing left of Tampico today.

Mrs. Annie Brown was interviewed in July 1938 for the Benton County, Oregon *WPA's American Life Histories Collection: Manuscripts from the Federal Writer's Project, 1936-1940* project:

"Tampico was a great place for recreation and amusement. People would come there from all directions on Saturday to hear the news. Some would have letters from the East and any bit of news was passed around. Then some diversion was always planned, or at least something diverting happened. One day there would be a horse race. Another time there would be a shooting match with, perhaps, a pig for a prize. Sometimes when men had a serious difference of opinion they would arrange to settle it at Tampico on a Saturday afternoon.

"I remember the story of one famous fight my father had before he was married. We had a neighbor, Jim Wheeler. This man had the habit of saying false and slanderous things about anybody and everybody. He told some falsehood about my father and refused to make the demanded retraction and apology. They agreed to fight it out at Tampico. On the appointed day, the men present formed a large ring and the two combatants were placed inside. They were both strong, husky young men and very evenly matched. They fought until they could not stand and then fought lying on the ground. Finally Wheeler said he had enough. Wheeler later wanted to be friends and I remember when he was an old man he used to visit us. Father would treat him civilly but he always disliked and distrusted him because 'if he lied once he will lie again.' I remember one time he asked father, 'How did you feel the next morning after our fight?'

"'All right, I guess,' said father, for he never liked to talk about the matter.

"'Well,' said Wheeler, 'I was so stiff and sore I could hardly walk. I went out to the barn and called my hogs as loud as I could so that the neighbors would know I was alive.'"

Mrs. Eunice Brown Flickinger was interviewed in July 1938 for the Benton County, Oregon *WPA's American Life Histories Collection: Manuscripts from the Federal Writer's Project, 1936-1940* project:

"Most of what little education I have was gotten at Tampico school. The terms were only three months long and sometimes, on account of bad weather and bad roads we did not get to go more than half of the time. Sam Berry taught one term. Mr. Price had a school one year for boys. Then there was a man named Noschker. I do not remember the others. My sister and I and brothers Jim and Frank had four months at Philomath College elementary school one winter.

"Some of our neighbors were John Wiles, Wrightsman, Modie, Blake,

An old tavern at Tampico, Oregon, 1905. *Courtesy of the OSU Special Collections & Archives Commons*

Calloway, Thomas Read, Judge Moore, Sam Tetheroe and Joseph Morris.

"Green Berry Smith owned a lot of land near Tampico, but his home was south of Corvallis. Tampico was considered a tough town but I was so young I never knew much about it. There was a saloon there and a store. Billy Picketts kept the store. There used to be camp meetings at Tampico and I can remember when I was quite small, my parents would take us there for a day. But the town didn't last long. There was church and Sunday School regularly at Gingles Schoolhouse and we went there when we could, once or twice a month at least. Dr. Hill, who preached there was a tall slim man. The young people called him the old jay-bird."

In his 1885 book, *History of Benton County, Oregon,* David Fagan shed a little light on Tampico:

"Who of the 'old-timers' is there that does not remember Tampico, situated just south of the old Soap Creek crossing on the old pack trail? A quarter of a century ago, this was a place of considerable importance and famous for the 'high-jinx' held within its bar-rooms. But, the glory of Tampico has departed, and for years past, it has been a pasture for browsing cattle and nibbling sheep; only a few dilapidated houses remain. Ichabod! Ichabod!"

SOAP CREEK / SUVER / NEW SUVER / SUVER JUNCTION

Joe Wellington Suver first settled near the area that bears his name in 1845 when he took out a donation land claim. His father-in-law, George W. Pyburn settled on the actual site where the town was later built. When the Oregon & California Railroad passed through the area, Joe Suver bought Pyburn's claim and platted a town on it in 1881. The Southern Pacific Railroad named the station, Suvers. It was originally called Soap Creek, but when the post office was established in 1881, it took the name, Suver. Sam Cohen was its first postmaster and the post office served the community until it was closed in 1935.

According to *Inventory of Historic Properties Historic Resource Survey Form*:

"Suver grew to include a store, a sawmill, two warehouses, a grain elevator, a dance hall, a train depot, a blacksmith shop, a shoe repair shop, and several residences by the mid-1890s. In 1895, the Suver School was built.

"Between 1895 and 1925, Suver continued as a rural shipping facility and community center for the surrounding population."

When U.S. Highway 99W was built through the area in the 1920s, the town began to decline along with the decrease in railroad shipping. In order to take advantage of the automobile and truck traffic being generated by the new highway, Fred Stump moved his store in Suver to the new site near U.S. Highway 99W. This site began to be referred to as "New Suver" or "Suver Junction."

Mrs. Annie Brown was interviewed in July 1938 for the Benton County, Oregon WPA's *American Life Histories Collection: Manuscripts from the Federal Writer's Project, 1936-1940* project:

"... 'Uncle' Joe Suver in 1845 built the first cabin between the Luckiamute River and the California line. He had started west with a large outfit, but his animals all died but one. With what that one could draw on a cart he forded the Luckiamute, liked the looks of the country, and staked out his claim. Others followed where he had forced a trail through the high grass on the river bottom and a ford was established at the place.

"When he first came over the country was lonely and very quiet. One morning he heard an ax and said to himself, 'Now I have a neighbor.' He followed up the sound and five or six miles away on the Willamette River bottom he found Bob Russell cutting logs for a cabin.

"Suver was my father's partner for a time and married my cousin, Delilah Pyburn. Their children were Caroline, Carolena, Greenberry and Marshall.

"...My father, Henry Flickinger, came from Pennsylvania around the Horn to the mines of California in 1852. He remained there for a year or so and, although he made no rich strike, he prospered – then he came north to Benton County. For a while he was a partner of Joseph Suver, and together they drove cattle and then hogs to the mines at Yreka, California. The hogs were rangy animals of the razor back type, could stand the trip and were not hard to drive, but so many were lost by 'cutting their throats' with their sharp fore hoofs while swimming the streams that they changed their plans. They slaughtered and cured the animals in Benton County and freighted the bacon to the mines.

"From the proceeds of this work and the money he had made in the mines, father bought and paid cash for 210 acres of land here at Suver. I am still living on the place. Father could have taken claim back next to the hills but he did not like the soil there.

"The only kind of fencing practical then was the rail fence and there was no timber near for rails. Father bought an acre of timber several miles away on the east side of the river. He would drive to the river in the morning, row across in a boat, split rails and ferry them across the river, and each evening bring home the rails he had split that day. Working in this way, he fenced his whole farm with an eight-rail, stake-and-rider fence. What man would do that today?"

Section 11

U.S. HIGHWAY 99W - CAMP ADAIR TO TIGARD

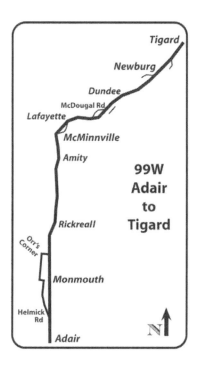

MONMOUTH

A group of Disciples of Christ emigrants, led by Elijah Davidson, arrived in Polk County, Oregon Territory in 1853 from Monmouth, Illinois. Most of the group were of Davidson's family. He was a devout advocate of prohibition. Under the sponsorship of the Christian Church, the group laid claim to 640 acres of land with the goal of establishing a town and a college. It was probably the first Oregon town founded with that as its primary purpose. The land was deliberately selected to be away from well-traveled routes, rivers, streams or other natural attributes normally considered positive factors in establishing a town.

After the townsite was surveyed in 1855, lots were sold and the proceeds were used to fund the college which was named Monmouth University. A post office opened in 1859 and the town of Monmouth was incorporated. In February of that year, Davidson's and other trustees' efforts to prohibit the importation, exportation, sale and consumption of alcohol in Monmouth became a reality.

The college struggled to survive and merged with another nearby institution, Bethel College to become Christian College. In 1882, ownership was transferred to the State of Oregon and it was renamed Oregon State Normal School at Monmouth. The term, "normal school" refers to an institution specifically designed for teachers' training. Prince Lucien Campbell was president of the Oregon State Normal School in 1890 and obtained the first public funds to operate the school. The school didn't receive any actual state funding until 1910, partly due to the opposition of Harvey W. Scott, the powerful editor of the *Portland Oregonian*. His opposition to government-funding of high schools and colleges slowed their development in Oregon for years. It might also be mentioned that he led an equally-determined campaign against letting women vote.

Harvey Scott and the anti-normal school group, including Governor Chamberlain, succeeded in stopping the state-funding, and the school struggled along with community contributions. Students paid double tuition, the staff took reduced wages and the president took no salary. It finally closed, but was reopened in 1911 with 138 students enrolled under the new name of Oregon Normal School. John Henry Ackerman, state superintendent of schools, was chosen as its president.

The consequences of Harvey Scott's campaign had far-reaching effects beyond just Monmouth. The normal schools at Drain and Ashland were abolished or closed. The one at Drain transferred to Monmouth and the Ashland school did not reopen until 1926; another was opened once again at LaGrande in 1929.

W.H. (Captain) Hembree was interviewed on April 25, 1938 for the *WPA's* *American Life Histories Collection: Manuscripts from the Federal Writer's Project, 1936-1940* project. His interviewer was Andrew C. Sherbert:

"I was born in Monmouth, Polk County, Oregon, October 7, 1864, and was christened William Harry Hembree. My father's name was Houston Hembree. He was named for the illustrious Sam Houston and was born in Texas, though his family later moved to Missouri. My mother's name was Amanda Bowman and she was born in Iowa, coming to Oregon in 1848. My father left Missouri for Oregon in one of the first emigrant trains of the great migration of the 1840s, arriving in the Willamette Valley sometime in 1843. The train that my father came to Oregon with is said to have been the first 'wheels' ever to make the entire journey from the east to The Dalles.

"The wagon train of which my father and his kinfolks were members was more fortunate than the parties which followed the old Oregon Trail in the years immediately after. The Indians did not trouble the earlier emigrants, were friendly in fact, according to accounts given me by my father. It was not until the later emigrants came through that the Indians began to attack travelers – in 1844, 1845, and thereafter. Father's train arrived at The Dalles with exactly the same number of members as it had when it left Missouri. There had been, however, a death and a birth on route, both occurring simultaneously at a place now called Liberty Rock, Idaho. The one who died was a second cousin of mine, whose name I have forgotten. The child that was born, was my aunt, Nancy Hembree.

"Though there had been gold stam-

pedes, land grants from the government, and all sorts of empire-building activities in Oregon after my father arrived from the east, he had not yet struck it rich when I squalled onto the scene 10 years later. When I am asked to recall incidents of my early life and to describe the games we played in my childhood, I can truthfully answer that there was no childhood, in the sense meant. There were no games. All that I remember about my childhood is 'work, work, and work.' Work, long before the sun came up. Work, long after the sun had set. When I was eight years old I was doing real labor – labor that today would draw a man's wages. Union working hours? Sit down strikes? Such things were not dreamed of then.

"My father and older brothers used to make shingles every day in the week except Sunday. They made them by hand, riving them out of cedar bolts with a tool called a 'frow.' If you've never seen one, a frow is a steel, wedge-shaped cleaver-like blade with a sharp edge, with a handle set at right angles from one end of the blade. You hit the frow with a mallet, driving through the shingle bolt, cleaving the bolt with the grain of the wood. Only the best, the very best straight-grained cedar was used for these shingles. The manufactured shingles of today have a useful life of about ten years or so, but I'm willing to wager that some of the shingles my family made – if there was any possible way of identifying them – are still giving service somewhere in Oregon. They were made to be practically everlasting.

"At the tender age of eight years, I worked right along with the rest of the men of the family. Being the youngest, my job was to keep the shavings all raked up into piles, and to bundle the shingles as fast as my father and brothers made them. That was no easy job for a youngster so small, for they contrived to fashion a surprisingly large number of shingles each day and the piles of shavings grew prodigiously large as the day wore on. No sooner would I arrange and tie one bundle of shingles than it seemed another was ready to tie. We used to work well on into the evening. That's when the piles of shavings were put to use. I would set fire to the shaving piles, one after another as each burned out, and we worked by the light of these pungent fires. It was not at all unusual for us to work 14 or 16 hours from

Corner of Broad and Main Street in Monmouth.
Courtesy of the Polk County Museum

the time we started in the morning until we gave up and called it a day. I was always a pretty tired youngster when I had tied off the last bundle and was mighty glad when my father would say, 'Alright boys, let's put out the fire.'

"I worked along with the family, riving shingles until I was 12 or 13 years old when I began to work out for others. Boys in those days seemed to mature earlier than they do now. As soon as a lad had a sign of fuzz on his cheek he was considered a man and was expected to fill any place that a man could. I was no exception. At 15, I was riding the range, and at 17 had been pretty much all over the great plains of central and eastern Oregon.

"As I said before, we worked every day but Sunday, and except for chores, Sunday really was a day of rest, and a very welcome one. The day was really a quiet and holy day in those times. My family was not what one would consider over much pious or religious, for those times, but it seemed that every family embraced some sort of faith. God did not seem so far away as he does today. He seemed mighty close to us. We seemed to see evidence of His works all around us and were mightily awed by His power. I noticed that folks in general don't have that sort of religious consciousness in them of late years.

"Our home was typical of a pioneer Oregon family. Mother made home-spun. I can see her at the spinning wheel, treading out the yarn that was to go into the things that we would be wearing a few months later. Today women of the age she was then, use the same toe my mother used on the treadle, to step on the accelerator as they drive to a department store for machine-made cloth and ready-made garments. Our work clothes, shirts and pants, were usually made of home-tanned buckskin. This stuff wore like iron, and though it was not very beautiful to look at, was extremely serviceable. When a man – and I mean by that, any male person over 16 or thereabouts – was able to accumulate the required number of dollars, one of his most important investments would be in a Sunday-go-to-meeting outfit made by eastern tailors, and consisting of a swallow-tail coat, a fancy, light-colored vest, and a striped pair of pants. He would top this elegant attire with a high, beaver hat.

Downtown Monmouth. *Courtesy of the Polk County Historical Society*

Central High School in Monmouth, 1910. *Courtesy of the Heritage Museum Society, Independence, Oregon*

He was then ready for – and considered properly dressed to be acceptable in – the most dignified and formal gathering, or social function."

Throughout its history, the college at Monmouth has gone through several name changes including Christian College, Oregon Normal School, Oregon College of Education, Western Oregon State College and finally, Western Oregon University.

According to Kyle Jansson for the Oregon Encyclopedia Project:

"In 1940, the City of Monmouth started one of the few city-owned electrical utilities in Oregon and began providing city residents with electricity. During World War II, the city grew with families who had been removed from land taken for the construction of the Camp Adair training base and with some of the tens of thousands of soldiers who trained there. After the war, Oregon College of Education expanded as veterans used the GI Bill to attend college, bringing the town's population to several thousand.

"The post-war population surge overwhelmed public schools in Independence and Monmouth, and in 1949 the two cities and surrounding communities formed the Central School District to deal with overcrowding. The college continued to operate a campus elementary school as a training school for its teacher education students until 1984."

The neighboring towns of Monmouth and Independence, Oregon, although separate entities, are linked. They lie directly across Highway 99 from each other – Monmouth on the west side and Independence about a half mile on the east – and their boundaries have grown together. For years, the most marked difference between the two towns was that Monmouth was dry and Independence was not. Those who wanted to buy a six-pack of beer or a bottle of wine, had to go to Independence to get them.

Inspite of the struggles of several local merchants to repeal prohibition, the religious community managed to keep it in force for decades. The event that finally changed the tide for the voters of the town to pass a repeal was the closure of the last market in town because it could not sell alcoholic beverages. The repeal went into effect in 2002, ending its long tenure as the *"Driest Town in the U.S."*

On Columbus Day 1962, Monmouth felt the effects of the major wind storm that slammed through Oregon. It caused deaths and destruction throughout the western part of the state. One of the most famous pictures of that day was taken by Wes Luchau, an unsuspecting student who was handed a camera as the storm began. He captured the picture of the Campbell Hall Tower on the Western Oregon College of Education just as it was coming down in front of him. The photo was featured in the October 26, 1962 issue of *Life* Magazine.

For the people in town who lost roofs, trees, windows, power and often much more, most don't need a photograph to bring back the memory.

THORP'S TOWN/ HENRY HILL'S TOWN OF INDEPENDENCE/ INDEPENDENCE

Located east of Highway 99, Independence, Oregon is the third largest urban area in Polk County, Oregon according to the city's historical website. Whereas the founders of neighboring Monmouth chose to locate away from main travel routes and rivers, Independence was built on the west bank of the Willamette River.

Parade on Main Street in Independence in the 1880s. *Courtesy of the Heritage Museum*

"The Peanut," a small gas-powered trolley. *Courtesy of the Heritage Museum*

Ferry crossing the Willamette River at Independence in 1915. *Courtesy of the Heritage Museum*

The K.C. Eldridge Creamery. *Courtesy of the Heritage Museum*

Elvin Thorp took out a donation land claim north of the present town of Independence where he platted a small townsite which was named Independence after the Missouri town that was also the staging point for wagon trains heading west. It was also Elvin Thorp's hometown. Thorp's Town began to grow. It was located in a strategic shipping location because of its proximity to the Willamette River, but after the devastating 1861 flood, the town was moved to higher, flatter ground located on the donation land claim of Henry Hill who had earlier opened a log cabin store there. He called the new site "Henry Hill's Town of Independence." On February 26, 1885, the two "Towns of Independence" were merged and incorporated.

According to the City of Independence website, *"Independence settled into the business of being a quiet, yet prosperous Willamette Valley river town. Its strategic location made it a valuable transportation point for the burgeoning lumber industry. But, during the 1920's and '30's, Independence saw a hop industry grow to such large proportions, that by 1946 Independence was known as being... the center of the most concentrated hop district in the world. During hop harvesting season, the population of Independence swelled by 40,000 – 50,000 hop pickers. Unfortunately, the bottom of the hop market dropped out and Independence settled back into peaceful existence.*

"In 1989, a Historic District was formed in the City of Independence, and this District was placed on the National Register of Historic Places. This 30-block area is located on the west bank of the Willamette River and retains much of the early character and architecture from the 1880s to the 1920s."

DIXIE /RICKREAL /RICKREALL

A creek, which was named "LaCreole River," ran through an area of what was to become Polk County, Oregon when John E. Lyle arrived there in 1845 from Illinois. Almost immediately, he opened a school in what would become the town of Rickreall. The origin of the name "Rickreall" which was also given to a nearby creek has been imbedded in controversy from as far back as 1915.

On August 8, 1915, J.T. Ford submitted a poem that he had written to *The Sunday Oregonian*. It was titled "Sparkling Rickreall." Ford, however, revised it and had it republished on July 23, 1916 with this explanation:

"The following is a revised copy of a former poem under the above title. The author hopes that his presentation is an improvement over the original and his only excuse for publishing it is to help perpetrate, in so far as he can, the euphonious and significant Indian name of this beautiful little stream."

However, a letter to the editor written by Mac Mahon on July 26, 1916, begged to differ with Ford's premise.

"I always understood the name was originally French and was written "La Creole" but afterwards blended into "Rickreall" by those who did not speak or understand the French language.

"This, at least, is the derivation given by Colonel Nesmith who lived by the stream and knew something about French Canadian... Mac Mahon, Letters to the Editor, The Sunday Oregonian, July 26, 1916."

This was followed by lengthy debates on the pages of the newspaper between advo-

Sparkling Rickreall

Leaping from dark canyons,
    Thy bright waters flow,
Roaring down the mountains,
    Where the tall firs grow.
Waltzing through the valley,
    So proudly, I ween,
Garlanded in the Springtime's
    Witchery of green;
Sparkling 'midst the meadows,
    Singing 'mongst the trees,
Wafting sweet melody
    On the soft sea breeze.
And kissing the pale moon
    When painted softly bright
On thy limpid bosom
    In the clear, calm night;
Rippling o'er the pebbles,
    Splashing through the lea
Flowing on forever
    To the moon-mad sea.
O gay, rollicking Queen
    Of the West-Side streams,
Thou mystical enchantress
    Of my boyhood's dreams!

Rushing o'er glacial drifts,
    Piling up the floe,
Leaping down Cambrian fens,
    Aeons long ago;
Carving thy rugged path
    Through sandstone and laom,
O'er the Pliocene plain
    Where the giant herds roamed,
Ere human thought was here
    To reason and plan,
The wild world to conquer,
    The infinite scan;
Strange voices were chanting
    The triumphant lay,
That intellectual man
    Was coming some day.
On thy shady green sward,
    One bright Summer moon,
A coy, dusky maiden
    Hummed a sweet love tune;
A gallant warrior bold
    Came at her low call,
And they softly name thee,
    "Sparkling Rickreall."

O lovely mountain stream,
    Limpid as the air,
Playing the cosmic game
    Impartial and fair;
Purling through vernal groves,
    And luring the wild birds
With sylvan joy calls,
    Rushing down the gorges,
Gloaming in deep pools
    And swirling in eddies,
Where the game trout schools;

Rickreall, Rickreall,
    "Swift flowing water,"
Thy Indian synonym
    Will live for ever!
Flow on, beautiful stream
    Flow on to the sea;
Untold generations
    Will sing paeons to thee!
Flow on, beautiful stream,
    Down the aisles of Time;
No vandal hand shall still
    That sweet voice of thine.

~ J.T. Ford, Dallas, Oregon
The Sunday Oregonian,
July 23, 1916

Birdseye view of Rickreall, Oregon. *Courtesy of Gerald W. Williams Collections, OSU Special Collections & Archives Commons*

cates for the theory that "Rickreall" was an Indian word and those who believed it was created from the French term, "La Creole" meaning 'native.'

Among those who believed it was derived from the French word, "La Creole," was Frank M. Sebring who worked it into his letter by saying, *"Now it seems a little sacrilege to shatter so pretty a fancy when presented in so entertaining a guise, but a strict regard for cold facts impels me, however distasteful the task, to shatter the pretty legend of the 'shy dusky maiden' and 'gallant warrior bold,' to smithereens..."*

Sebring contended that the native languages did not allow for the pronunciation of the letter "R" in their speech and there was no way that the name could have once been an Indian word.

Ford countered by telling the story of his grandfather, Colonel Nathanial Ford, and father, Mark Ford, who settled on the Rickreall Creek in 1844.

His grandfather *"was curious to learn the Indian names of the mountains and streams of the Willamette Valley, and especially the names of the streams in his immediate vicinity. Each stream was the hunting and fishing grounds, the 'Illihee' of some petty tribe. The little tribe inhabiting the environs of the stream upon which the Fords had located was called the 'Rickrealls,' the Indians so designating their tribal affinity...*

"Among the Rickrealls was an Indian familiarly known to the pioneers as 'Steve,' an old fellow of more than average native intelligence and with whom my father had many curious and interesting 'wahwahs.'' Old Steve said that Rickreall was the Indian name of the little stream which his tribe claimed as its 'Illihee,' and that the name meant 'hiac chuck, hiac chuck,' and he would motion with his arms in imitation of running water. 'Hiac chuck' is jargon for 'run-

ning or flowing water,' which is a marked characteristic of the Rickreall..."

There were several back-and-forth discussions, some quite humorous, between Misters Sebring and Ford between July 26, 1916 and August 24, 1916 and they reference others who entered the discussion, too. It seemed to be a standoff, although Ford seemed to have made more valid points than Sebring in our estimation. On August 24, however, Lewis A. McArthur sent a letter to the editor on the subject.

"...As a matter of fact, written records indicate that the name 'Rickreall' was certainly used before the words 'LaCreole,' as applied to the stream in question.

"George H. Himes has seen a diary written in May 1843, by James John which refers to the stream as the 'Rickreall,' and [I] have in my possession a copy of Joel Palmer's Journals written in 1845-46 which use the name 'Rickreall' and not 'LaCreole.'

"Many of the earliest settlers along the Rickreall were Southerners, and these people had known and heard of the Creoles of Louisiana long before they came to Oregon, and it is rather hard to imagine that such Southerners would so mispronounce LaCreole and make it Rickreall. Creole was a familiar word with them. [I] do not believe that Rickreall was ever a changeling from LaCreole..."

The post office was established in 1851 with the name, "Rickreal" with one "L." The post office was discontinued in 1857, but re-established in 1866 with the spelling "Rickreall" and is still operating.

During the Civil War and after, the town was nicknamed Dixie, evidently because of the number of Southern settlers in the community, but it was never an official name. Even a wooden sign with Dixie painted on it was posted on a tree near the wagon road.

The *Oregon Spectator*, published at Oregon City, was the first newspaper published in the Oregon Territory. The March 19, 1846 issue carried this notice:

"[The] Jefferson Institute is located in the Rickreall Valley, one mile west of the residence of Col. N. Ford. The first session of this school will commence on the second Monday of next April and continue twenty-four weeks. Scholars from a distance can be accommodated with boarding in the neighborhood. Terms of tuition, $8.00 per scholar. John E. Lyle, Teacher."

The Jefferson Institute

The Jefferson Institute located in Rickreall, was the original school by that name. A later one was formed near the town of Jefferson, Oregon in 1856.

On the *Genealogy Trails* website, Julia Veazie Glenn relates the story of the Jefferson Institute in Rickreall as remembered by Mary Embree Hayter, daughter of Carey Embree, before her death in 1925:

"Jefferson Institute was held in a log cabin built expressly for a schoolhouse on the land claim of Carey Embree... Benches made of long planks were placed along the walls and the children sat facing the wall, using for a desk a puncheon, a wide board, propped against the walls. Pens were made of sharpened goosequills, many of them kept in readiness by Mr. Lyle.

"The first pencils were lead bullets hammered flat and long. Ink was made by squeezing the juice from oak balls and

The home of James W. Nesmith, an early settler, politician and lawyer in the Rickreall area. *Courtesy of the Polk County Museum*

letting it stand on iron fillings. The writing paper was blue and probably purchased of the Hudson's Bay Company. The pioneers had brought school books; Carey Embree bought enough to keep the children advancing for three years. The Bible was read in the morning, each child reading a verse. There was a lunch period, also recess, during which the boys played ball with knitted balls on one side of the house, while on the other side the girls jumped the rope with ropes made of braided rawhide.

"A pulpit was placed in Jefferson Institute. The cabin was used for Church and for all general gatherings. Lyle was a Presbyterian. Denominational differences were ignored, and missionaries of all churches were welcomed. Mac Waller preached there, as did John Boone and Glen O. Burnett. People came from miles away and through the Sabbath morning in those early days could be heard the men's voices urging on their ox teams as they approached the Institute. Hospitable cabins welcomed the arrivals and happy hours of visiting followed the religious services before the slow moving oxen were turned homeward.

"In summer, additional shelter for the congregation was provided by setting forked tree limbs upright across the front of the building and covering them with fir boughs. The young girls sometimes decorated the room by filling the fireplace with greens and inserting yew boughs in cracks along the log walls. When they had finished, says Mrs. Hayter, they carefully swept all litter from the doorway with branches of snow-berry..."

The school/church was also used as a courthouse when needed. The first provisional county circuit court was convened there on September 6, 1846.

AMITY

Amity, Oregon is a small agricultural town in Yamhill County, six miles south of McMinnville on Highway 99W. It was one of the earliest settlements in Oregon with homesteaders arriving as early as the late 1840s. The town itself was established in 1849 when area families decided to establish a school. The site of the school, however, was the subject of an on-going controversy. While the families were arguing over where to build the school, Jerome B. Walling and a group of the local farmers approached Ahio S. Watt about being the administrator of the school as well as its first teacher. Although Watt, had been planning to leave for the California gold fields, he agreed to stay under the condition that the local families would settle their disagreement amicably.

According to Richard Engeman in his piece for the Oregon Encyclopedia Project:

"...He consented to remain on the condition that the community 'would then and there settle a long controversed question of the location of the school, and should all go to work and build the schoolhouse.'

"The condition was met, and Ahio christened the school Amity."

After the post office was established on July 6, 1852, Jerome Walling became the postmaster and the community began to grow.

In 1853, the Methodists built Amity's first church.

In 1859, Walling laid out the townsite for Amity around Trade Street which was the main street through town and later became part of the Pacific Highway/U.S. Highway 99. Joseph Watt established the first woolen mill in Oregon there, and the Oregon Central Railway from Portland laid tracks through the town in 1879. Amity was incorporated as a city the next year.

Like its neighbors, Amity was principally an agricultural community. Many crops including fruit, prunes, hazelnuts (aka filberts) and hops grew well there as well as the English walnut orchards planted on the hills to the east of the town.

Fields of grain and green pastureland spawned dairies which supplied milk and

Main Street, Amity, Oregon. *Courtesy of Gerald W. Williams Collections, OSU Special Collections & Archives Commons*

A muddy Amity street following a snow-melt. *Courtesy of the Oregon Department of Transportation (ODOT) History Center*

dairy products. The abundance of grain harvests kindled a need for milling centers and warehouses for the harvests and much of the wheat was shipped by railroad to ports, bound for markets far and wide. In 1910, the Meeker Seed and Grain mill was built. It served the area for 92 years before being dismantled in 2002.

From the Salem, Oregon *Daily Capital Journal*, May 4, 1910 (no by-line):

The 1910 newspaper article was quite lengthy, but extremely interesting. The writer had a great sense of humor and details a lot of the businesses and people in Amity in 1910:

"There is no part of Oregon that is making more rapid advancement or adding values and making improvements more rapidly than this part of Western Oregon – Amity – Yamhill county. This is a live lot of business men back of Amity and it is no longer the sleepy place that it was for 40 years. It has awakened and will never be let sleep again. The city is surrounded by a semi-circle of hills, and has splendid drainage and the richest soil in the valley.

It has a splendid class of people, who are hospitable and glad to welcome additions to their community. With such advantages, there is a future for the city and county. New industries are being organized, and those already in existence are being enlarged and Amity will be a city of 1,000 people inside of two years.

"Amity has a progressive city government at the hands of Walter S. Fuller, mayor. He is also the treasurer of the condensery, and man of spirit and enterprise... Amity has electric lights and up-to-date jail with two cells.

"...The best proof of the growth in prosperity of any community is found in the amount of shipments of produce and business furnished the railroads. The record of Amity for carloads shipped out and in for the year 1910 is 140 carloads out and 76 carloads in. Of this, 35 carloads were condensed milk, 45 cars stock and about as many of hay. The express shipments include poultry, eggs, cream, dressed meat and fruit. Dr. Blackburn, the Southern Pacific agent at present says the indications are favorable to large shipments of lumber from the Roth sawmills.

"... The Yamhill Valley Condensed Milk Company has a $50,000 plant here. It employs 16 persons and has 210 patrons. It was established May 6, 1908... The product of the condensery is sold under the label, 'Holly Brand,' and is marketed in Portland, Spokane, Montana and California.

"...Amity has a good high school with 11 grades taught, P.M. Stroud, principal. He is a Monmouth graduate, and had to work his way through the State Normal School. He has taught seven years and has three assistants. It is hard to imagine what a pitiful state of affairs will prevail in Or-

1912 Oregon State Fair Champion Mare owned by Felix Comegys of Amity. Courtesy of Gerald W. Williams Collections, OSU Special Collections & Archives Commons

egon when the normal schools are all killed off, and high school grades will be taught by girls holding eighth grade diplomas.

"Amity has a Methodist, Baptist and Christian church... Rev. Gittins [of the Methodist Church] is not one of the harsh type, but mingles with all kinds of sinners, hotel keepers, livery stable men, and newspaper reporters. He has been well-treated by the people of Amity who seem to have no prejudices against preachers. There are several lodges at Amity and in all respects it is a pretty well-balanced community day and night, work days and Sundays."

From the Portland *The Sunday Oregonian*, November 12, 1911:

"Statistics just compiled show that the town of Amity has made rapid strides in the last three years, having more than twice doubled its population in that time and buildings to the number of 60 having been erected. Amity has never been promoted by a Commercial Club or a proposed railway scheme, but had relied entirely on its resources, which are among the richest in the Willamette Valley..."

After the construction of the Pacific Highway through Amity in 1910, it was finally paved in 1920, but in the 1930s, much of the long-distance traffic between Portland and Junction City began using the U.S. Highway 99E route rather than the more rural Highway 99W route. Business and commerce slowed markedly in Amity and the other towns in the area.

Today, Amity is still an agricultural area. Wineries have flourished, bringing in tourists who help support the economy. They come for other Amity attractions through the year, as well.

"Since the late 1960s," according to the Engeman piece, *"Amity has held a popular annual summer pancake breakfast, and Amity High School has sponsored an Amity Daffodil Festival each spring since 1995. The Brigittine order of contemplative monks established the Priory of Our Lady of Consolation in 1986 at a former farm near Amity. The monks have acquired a reputation for producing a fine fudge confection, and the priory is now a tourist attraction."*

McMINNVILLE

Sitting at the confluence of the North and South forks of the Yamhill River in the

Oregon -- Public, Educational and Business Structures in McMinnville, Oregon. *From the West Shore magazine, April 26, 1890.*

Willamette Valley, McMinnville is the county seat and largest city in Yamhill County. It is entered by crossing the 1921-vintage North Yamhill River Bridge. The earliest route of Highway 99W, taking a right on 3rd Street, a left on Irvine, a right on Lafayette and back to the current Highway 99W – included dangerous railroad crossings. It was rerouted to the current couplet through town in 1938.

John Baker and his family settled on their claim in 1844. He soon was appointed the first sheriff in the Yamhill district.

William T. Newby, a 1843 Oregon Trail emigrant from Tennessee, settled on a claim next to the Baker's. In 1853, he established a grist mill and began milling grain for local farmers. Because of the traffic going across his land on the way to connect with the main trails leading to California, Newby was encouraged to use some of his land as a townsite. Samuel Cozine located a blacksmith shop close by the mill and Soloman "Dutch" Beary opened a store next to the blacksmith shop. In 1854, William Newby hired Sebastion C. Adams to lay out a townsite in exchange for half a block of the new city. The town was platted in May 1856 and named McMinnville after Newby's birthplace of McMinnville, Tennessee.

However, according to Dan Linscheid for the Oregon Encyclopedia Project:

"The plat was not recorded in the

county clerk's office in Lafayette until July 1865, even though Newby received his U.S. patent in October 1858.

"By 1866, McMinnville had 300 residents, two doctors, two churches, a flour mill, a photography studio, a silversmith, a shoe shop, and two wagon shops."

The Oregon Central Railroad built its tracks near McMinnville in 1871, linking the area to Portland. The town was incorporated in 1876 and became a city in 1882. The railroad line was extended to McMinnville proper in 1879, and south to Corvallis in 1880. In 1886, after a bitter fight, Yamhill County residents voted to move the county seat from Lafayette to McMinnville.

From *The Works of Hubert Howe Bancroft, Volume XXX; History of Oregon*, Volume II by Hubert Howe Bancroft, 1888.

"The origin of McMinnville and its college was as follows: In 1852-1853, W.T. Newby cut a ditch from Baker Creek, a branch of the Yamhill River, to Cozine Creek, upon his land where he erected a grist mill. In 1854, S.C. Adams, who lived on his donation land claim 4 miles north, took a grist to mill, and in the course of conversation with Newby, remarked upon the favorable location for a town which his land presented, upon which Newby replied that if he, Adams, would start a town, he should have half a block of lots and select is own location, from which point the survey should commence.

"In the spring of 1855, Adams deposited the lumber for his house on the spot selected, about 200 yards from the mill, and proceeded to erect his house, where, as soon as it was completed, he went to reside. Immediately after he began to agitate the subject of a high school as a nucleus for a settlement and, as he and most of the leading men in Yamhill were of the Christian Church, it naturally became a Christian school.

"James McBride, William Dawson, W.T. Newby and Adams worked up the matter, bearing the larger part of the expense. Newby gave six acres of land. The building erected for the school was large and commodious for those times. Adams, who was a teacher by profession, was urged to take charge of the school, and taught it for a year and a half. But there had not been any organization, or any charter asked for, and Adams, who found it hard and unprofitable work to keep up the school alone, wished to resign, and proposed to the men interested, to place it in the hands of the Baptists who were about founding the West Union Institute. To this they made no objection, as they only wished to have a school, and were not sectarian in feeling. Accordingly, Adams proposed the gift to the Baptists and it was accepted, only one condition being imposed and agreed to in writing, to employ at least one professor in the college department continuously. It was incorporated in January 1858 as the Baptist College at McMinnville..."

Baptist College / Linfield College

The Baptist College at McMinnville was chartered in 1858 by the Oregon Territorial Legislature, and later became McMinnville College. Through the early years, the college also served as McMinnville's secondary school and didn't award its first baccalaureate degree until 1884.

In 1922, the school was struggling financially, until Frances Eleanor Ross Linfield, the

Dean of Women, made the college the beneficiary of a large donation that included property that she and her late husband owned in Spokane, Washington. Following the sale of the Washington property, the college realized more than $250,000 and the trustees, at the request of Mrs. Linfield, named the college in honor of her late husband, the Rev. George Fisher Linfield. Six years later, Linfield College was fully accredited by the Northwest Association of Schools and Colleges.

In 1998, Linfield acquired 115 more acres of land from the Hewlett-Packard Company, increasing its size from 78 to 193 acres.

The area around McMinnville became a center of the agricultural district that raised fruit, poultry, dairy cattle, sheep and Angora goats. The farmers shipped prunes and walnuts, wool and mohair. They had a milk condensary, a fruit evaporator and a lumber planing mill.

In 1938, a turkey barbecue was held downtown by turkey farmers when the main source of wealth in the county was based on the turkey-farming industry. The TurkeyRama became a three-day festival including rides, booths and outdoor entertainment. Eventually, turkey farms and the turkey processing plant disappeared from McMinnville, but the festival is still celebrated to a lesser degree.

Other livestock production continued, and by the 1950s, the area around McMinnville boasted 150,000 acres of land and livestock in production including veal, lamb and pork.

Other crops included fruit and nut production, nurseries, grains, vegetables and melons. Filberts have long been a major crop, but McMinnville, at one time, was known as "Walnut City" for the 100,000 walnut trees growing in the area. The Columbus Day storm of 1962 nearly wiped that industry out in a single day.

The vicious Columbus Day Storm hit McMinnville, like much of Oregon, hard. Three local people died, eight more were injured. Warehouses, barns and cars were destroyed. Wind speeds reached over 100 miles per hour through the town. Many roofs and whole portions of homes were ripped off. Estimates were that 170,000 prune and 50,000 walnut trees toppled. On nearly every farm in Yamhill County, between one and eight structures were destroyed.

A strong argument can be made that the Oregon wine industry began in Yamhill County. At least a dozen vineyards are now located in and near McMinnville.

West Pacific Bridge into McMinnville, 1949. *Courtesy of the Oregon Department of Transportation (ODOT) History Center*

In 2011, Linfield College developed "The Oregon Wine History Archive." According to the site's description:

"The Linfield archive showcases the colorful and sometimes quirky history of what was once an upstart industry. Early growers in this region planted grapes against the advice of experts, with what one called 'more guts than brains.' One grower lived in a lumberjack shack with his family; another built his first winery with a leftover chicken-house roof. They lost crops to shoulder-high weeds and one frantically bought garden hoses in an attempt to save grapes planted in August.

"What eventually emerged was a close-knit community of hardy idealists. Yamhill County wine pioneers helped initiate the national movement toward green agriculture and established Oregon as North America's home for Pinot noir. It's a story worth preserving..."

"Oregon Wines" by Rich Schmidt and Rachael Woody of the Oregon Wine History Archives at Linfield College:

"The story of Oregon wine dates back to the time of the Oregon Trail when settlers brought vines across the country and planted them in the fertile soil they found upon arrival. Henderson Luelling planted the first grapes in the Willamette Valley in around 1847. In spite of doubts about commercial viability, Peter Britt founded Valley View Vineyard in Southern Oregon in 1852, which was the first recorded commercial vineyard in the state. Though it hasn't been a continuous run, Valley View Vineyard exists today along with more than 500 other wineries in the state.

"HillCrest Vineyard in Roseburg, founded by Richard Sommer in 1961, was the first post-Prohibition winery to commercially plant and bottle pinot noir in Oregon. Sommer's winery was a common stop for the 1960s Oregon wine pioneers like Dick Erath, Dick and Nancy Ponzi, David Lett and Charles Coury, all of whom set up wineries in the Willamette Valley and planted pinot noir. Their contention that Oregon would be an ideal location for world-class pinot noir, much like Britt's idea to open a commercial vineyard 100 years earlier, was met with much derision. And, as with Britt, the naysayers were proven wrong as wine has become one of Oregon's biggest industries and a source of much income and pride as Oregon's pinot noir has become internationally recognized.

"In 2011, Linfield College established

"Good Roads" near McMinnville, Oregon. *Courtesy of Gerald W. Williams Collections, OSU Special Collections & Archives Commons*

the Oregon Wine History Archive (OWHA), which chronicles the Oregon wine industry and will grow to include historical documents from all aspects and regions of the Oregon industry. Located in McMinnville in the heart of Oregon's pinot noir country, Linfield has a relationship with the wine industry going back to the 1980s when it was chosen as the home of the annual International Pinot Noir Celebration (IPNC). The relationship has grown impressively in recent years, and OWHA has started to collect documents, photographs, interviews and all sorts of materials to tell the thousands of individual stories that make up Oregon wine history.

"Sharing these stories is the best part of what the Oregon Wine History Archive is doing. With the mission to collect and preserve all aspects and regions of the Oregon wine industry, OWHA helps to reveal the narrative of Oregon wine. OWHA has more than 20 collections from winery owners, winemakers, grape-growers, wine marketers and sommeliers, as well as organizations like the Oregon Wine Board, IPNC and the ¡Salud! healthcare program."

McMinnville is now the home of Howard Hughes' famous "Spruce Goose" airplane which is on exhibit at the Evergreen Aviation and Space Museum. This facility, which houses dozens of unique and historic aircraft, is located just north of the McMinnville Municipal Airport, at the southeastern outskirts of town along Oregon Highway 18. The Spruce Goose, which was built mostly of birch, has the largest wingspan of any aircraft in history. In 1993, it was moved in pieces by barge and lowboys to McMinnville, where it underwent a restoration effort and awaited construction of a new building large enough to house it.

An historic attraction in McMinnville is the Hotel Oregon, constructed in 1905 and now operated as a McMenamins pub and hotel. McMenamins sponsors a UFO festival each year to commemorate the reported 1950 sighting of an unidentified flying object by the Trent family near their farm between Sheridan and McMinnville.

On June 9, 1950, the McMinnville *Telephone-Register* published two photographs of a purported unidentified flying object – UFO – taken at a local farm by Mr. and Mrs. Paul Trent. The photos were published by the *Oregonian* and then by *Life* magazine. An international debate raged and resulted in a UFO Festival being held in McMinnville each year.

LAFAYETTE

Lafayette is a historic town located in the northern Willamette Valley in Yamhill County. It sits along Highway 99W, five miles northeast of McMinnville along the Yamhill River. It was founded in 1846 by Joel Perkins who laid out a townsite on the main Indian trail that traversed the Willamette Valley at a point on the Yamhill River known for years as Yamhill Falls.

"Joel Perkins" by Joan Momsen. *Grants Pass Daily Courier*, January 3, 2012:

"...Joel Perkins was born in New York State in 1821 and migrated to Oregon with his parents, Eli and Sally Perkins, older brother John and threes sisters and their spouses, in 1844, only the second year after the Oregon Trail was 'officially' opened. The immigration of 1844 consisted of 800 people, 235 of whom were listed as 'able-bodied men.' Among the list of these able-bodied men, one finds Joel

Perkins, Sr., Joel Perkins, Jr. and John Perkins. The Perkins' family left New York, having moved there from Massachusetts. In 1832, they left New York and moved to Tippecanoe County, Indiana.

"In 1845, Joel Perkins, filed a land claim in Yamhill, Oregon. He soon became the county clerk and in the time period of 1846-47, he is given credit for founding the community of Lafayette, Oregon, named for Lafayette, Indiana, the county seat of Tippecanoe County.

"...Joel Perkins was an entrepreneur, which in today's terms probably meant he was a real go-getter, and had his hands in many endeavors. This is neither good nor bad, but was what one had to do to survive in the wilderness. In the early 1850s, Oregon was still sparse in its settlements and forms of government.

"Joel Perkins made several trips to California in the 1840s and 1850s. Departing Oregon in 1849 during the Gold Rush of '49, he headed south to California and bought land in Sacramento where he set up a trading post. He was only there nine months and returned to Lafayette where he ran a ferry on the Yamhill River with his brother-in-law, James Johnson, who he had previously been partners with in a general store. In the 1850 census, he is listed as we know him as Joel Perkins, age 29, born in New York and working as a merchant. The census says he was living in the Hawn residence. Jacob and Harriet Hawn ran the local tavern and hotel and several single men resided at the hotel. Laura Hawn helped her parents with chores around the hotel and tavern. On July 23, 1850, he married Laura Hawn, age 15, in Lafayette, Oregon. At 29, Joel Perkins was twice the age of his 15-year-old bride, but this was not unusual for the groom to be several years older than his

Bridge across the Yamhill River near Lafayette, Oregon. *Courtesy of OSU Special Collections and Archives Commons*

bride and for the bride to be in her early teenage years. Lafayette was on the main Indian trail that crossed the Willamette Valley and grew quickly after gold was discovered in California.

"Lafayette was the county seat of Yamhill County [from] when it was founded until 1878. While Lafayette was growing, Joel Perkins and his new bride were always coming and going, not staying long at any location..."

The Perkins family eventually moved to the Grants Pass area of Oregon where their later history has been recorded and it was where Joel Perkins was murdered at the age of 35 by John Malone who was purportedly Laura Perkins' lover. The story of the murder, the trial and Laura's part in the murder can be found in the Grants Pass segment of this book. It continues here, however, because after Laura was not held on charges as the instigator of the murder, she moved back to Yamhill County where her family still lived.

Joan Momsen's story continues:

"...Her [Laura's} parents whisked her back to Yamhill County. On December 31, 1856 she gave birth to a daughter, Joan. Who was the father? We will never know.

"The surviving Perkins in Yamhill seldom mentioned Joel. No one wanted to bring up the story and so not much was clarified about his death. It seems as if nobody really knew the details and if they did, they were not sharing with the general public.

"Laura Hawn Perkins' daughter, Harriet, died in about 1870 and Joan in 1873. Laura remarried at least twice again and gave birth to eight more children, totaling 11 children. She outlived seven of her children and was asked several times by news reporters to tell the story of the murder of Joel Perkins. She refused to talk and passed away in Portland in 1921."

Oregon's first circuit court met in Lafayette in 1847. It had a post office by 1851. In the 1850s, Lafayette was one of the most prosperous towns in Oregon. The river was navigable part of the time and flatboats, and then steamboats, connected Lafayette to Oregon City until the 1880s.

Lafayette's early growth was so impressive that, Ruth Stoller, a well-known Yamhill County historian remarked in a speech, *"...By 1850, Lafayette, with more business than Portland, had 800 people while Portland had only 700."*

The second of Lafayette's courthouses was built in the 1860s. It was described in an 1866 *Lafayette Courier* newspaper article as *"the best public building in the state, except the one in Linn County, which has quite recently been completed..."*

The editor of the Portland *Oregonian* newspaper in 1866 remarked on the rich fertile soil around the town of Lafayette. He observed that, *"The only objection of a serious character, that we can offer [of Lafayette], is the farms are too large. Men own too much of Mother Earth... For grain and stockgrowing we have seen but little to equal and nothing to surpass North Yamhill anywhere on the Pacific coast."*

The city was incorporated in 1878, and served as the county seat until 1889 when it was moved to McMinnville through the vote of the county residents.

Locks were installed around the Yamhill Falls in 1900 and operated until 1954. Although the locks were built for shipping, they

Intersection of the Tualatin Valley Highway and Pacific Highway, 1929. *Courtesy of the Yamhill County Historical Museum*

were later used to float logs downstream to sawmills.

Famous women's rights advocate, newspaper editor and writer, Abigail Scott Duniway, spent part of her youth and some of her adulthood in Lafayette, Oregon.

In 1853, as a young woman, Abigail taught school in Eola, Oregon. She met and married Benjamin Charles Duniway and in 1857, they moved back to Lafayette, where her parents first settled. After Benjamin was disabled in a wagon accident, Abigail established a small boarding school in Lafayette, but in 1867, the family moved to Albany where she ran a millinery shop. Many of her customers came into the store and confided to her about the abuse and inequality that they lived with at home. It angered her to the point that Benjamin encouraged her to use her education and passion in helping women find a respected place in not only their own households, but in their communities, as well. She moved to Portland in 1871 and established her own weekly newspaper, *The New Northwest*, which became a vehicle for her campaign for women's rights and suffrage issues.

Her influence was evident early-on in Lafayette. She had not forgotten her friends there and organized a group of local women to assert their rights. Local meetings, normally the domain of the male gender in the community, were attended by the group, headed by Ms. Duniway. They were first met with hisses and boos upon their arrival, but soon they were accepted as citizens who could contribute to the decision-making of the town.

In a letter-to-the-editor to Abigail Duniway's *The New Northwest*, published on December 4, 1874, the writer who signed with the initials A.J.D. (Abigail, herself?) told of the meetings that she had been to since her last correspondence in the paper.

"Captain Miller very kindly brought us up from Dayton to Lafayette, making an extra trip for the purpose; the first instance on record of a steamer being proffered, free of charge, to take women to a Suffrage Convention. Verily, the world moveth.

"Evening session well-attended, but stormy. The representative from Yamhill who had said in the Legislature that the leaders of the Suffrage Movement were all women of bad character, and that the

women of Lafayette who wanted to vote were not first-class women, bitterly denied his own words, and interrupted us furiously with the LIE.

"After we had finished our story, giving the ladies a faithful account of the way they had been misrepresented in the Legislature by the men's Representative, we yielded the floor, the President stating that any one desiring to discuss this question in a polite and respectful manner had opportunity. Hoodlums called for Bradshaw, the ex-Representative aforesaid. That sex-protector who thinks 'women have nothing to complain of,' you know, mounted the rostrum and declared that we had lied when we said that a rising vote was taken upon admitting us to the floor of the Lower House as a reporter. President called him to order in vain. He pounded the desk, roared and bellowed like an infuriated bovine, and attacked our reputation in a most shameful manner. He declared that the vote upon the resolution to amend the Constitution by striking out the word 'male,' was lost by a vote of 13 to 47. Mrs. Coburn ventured to correct him, stating that the vote stood 27 to 33. He denied it again. We'll publish the ayes and noes on that next week..."

Abigail's own brother, Harvey W. Scott, at the time was the editor of the Portland *Oregonian*. His editorials became strong opposition to his sister's efforts and to the women's rights movement. Women's suffrage referendums met political opposition and consistently failed on state ballots for several years.

Abigail Scott Duniway's determination and hard work, however, paid off when in 1912, Oregon became the seventh state in the U.S. to pass a women's suffrage amendment and she was the first woman to register to vote in Multnomah County.

Lafayette has been an agricultural community where hops and apples were grown and dairy cattle provided milk products. Today, lying in a fertile area for growing grapes, it is surrounded by vineyards and wineries.

One of two Yamhill County Historical Societies and a museum are the keepers of Lafayette's considerable heritage. The Lafayette site sits on 12 acres, and three buildings make up the Yamhill Valley Heritage Center. It includes the Poling Memorial Church that was built in 1892 and was included on the National Register of Historic Places in 2002. The church building houses thousands of artifacts from the 19th and 20th centuries. The Miller Log Cabin Museum, that was specifically built in 1994 to house the Ruth Stoller Research Library, contains many photos, genealogical and archival materials and books by local and regional authors. There is also a large metal building, constructed in the 1970s, which houses the Center's collection of antique farm equipment, a sawmill and blacksmith shop.

There's been a bit of folk legend enshrouding the Lafayette community for many years. It has taken on many forms, but according to the legend, the cemetery is inhabited by a witch... or was it a ghost witch? Anna Marple, purported to be a gypsy, is said to have put a curse on the town of Lafayette when her son was hanged for a murder which he committed there in 1887. She is said to have also been hanged as a witch and that her ghost still haunts the cemetery. But, the authors of the NewLafayette.org website are also quick to debunk the legend. There was, indeed a hanging – and a hanging tree – in Lafayette. Anna's son, Richard 'Gus' Marple, was the second and last person to be hanged in Yamhill County, but Anna was also accused of being an accomplice in the murder for which her son was hung. She was said to have allegedly provided her lover, the murder victim, David L. Corker, with a sleeping potion before her son robbed and killed him.

According to the website, *"If she was a witch or a kind of gypsy with 'super-natural' abilities, she probably wouldn't be haunting the Lafayette cemetery because Anna Marple was not buried in Lafayette.*

"After the hanging, Anna Marple eventually moved to Jacksonville, Oregon where she lived many more years until she died on March 11, 1916 of liver cancer at the age of 73. She was buried at the Jacksonville Cemetery."

Information at the Yamhill County Historical Museum, however, indicates that when the family cabin was later demolished, the murder weapon that was used to kill David Corker, was discovered.

EKINS / DUNDEE JUNCTION / DUNDEE

The small community of Dundee was settled by emigrant farmers beginning in the 1840s, but the community was established after William Reid of Dundee, Scotland brought financial investments to the area in order to save the Oregon Railway, a narrow-gauge rail line that was being planned to connect Willamette Valley farmers with Portland. Dundee was located at the junction of two of these narrow-gauge rail lines.

In 1881, the first post office was named Ekins. It was closed in 1885 and a new office opened in 1887 named "Dundee Junction." The "Dundee" portion of the name was given to it by William Reid to honor the city of his Scottish investors. The "Junction" was derived from plans to build a bridge across the Willamette River for the railroad, which would have called for a junction at Dundee between the west railroad and the new east railroad. The bridge was never built, however, so the post office was shortened to "Dundee" in 1897 and the town of Dundee was incorporated in 1895.

In the early 1890s, the Southern Pacific Company acquired the fragmented narrow-gauge lines, converted them to standard gauge, and merged them into their network of Willamette Valley rail lines.

Prunes, filberts and walnuts were the major agricultural crops grown in the vicinity of Dundee, and fruit and nut dryers and packing plants were prevalent. Wine is now the leading product of the area.

In an October 3, 2013, article on OregonLive.com titled "Dundee in Heart of Oregon Wine Country Offers Reasons to Pull off Busy 99W." Terry Richard, a travel writer for the Portland *Oregonian*, talked about Dundee:

"Dundee lies at the epicenter of Oregon's wine industry, where a short drive into the hills at the west edge of town leads to some of the state's largest and most beautiful estate wineries.

"But in town, the highway is everyone's worst traffic nightmare. The Dundee crawl results from Oregon 99W scrunching from four to two lanes, carrying traffic to wine country, casinos, colleges and the coast.

"Despite the slow traffic, or perhaps because of it, Dundee is encouraging visitors to park the car and explore the town on foot. If you love wine, you will love Dundee.

The Willamette River at Newberg, Oregon. *Courtesy of OSU Special Collections and Archives Commons*

Rex Hill near Newberg. *Courtesy of the Oregon Department of Transportation (ODOT) History Center*

"The Yamhill County city of 3,200 residents is located 26 miles southwest of Portland, via Tigard, Sherwood and Newberg, or is just a short hop across the Chehalem Hills from Beaverton, Hillsboro and Forest Grove.

"A new tourist placard published this summer, called 'Walk Dundee,' lists 36 businesses and a walking map on the other side. A dozen of the businesses are wine tasting rooms; another 10 serve food.

"With the Willamette River on one side and the world-famous Dundee Hills, on the other, this small town has one of the most beautiful locations in the Willamette Valley. In 10 years, national magazines will be placing Dundee near the top of those ubiquitous lists of best small towns in America.

"By then, the city will have been skirted by a new highway. Construction began in June, with the first phase of the Newberg-Dundee Bypass to be complete in 2016. Next spring/summer will see sidewalk and street lighting improvements in town on Oregon 99W. The highway will be resurfaced and Dundee will get its second traffic light.

"Future traffic rerouting will spur development of walking trails and bike paths, connecting the 16,000-square foot homes in the hills to the river. Vacant lots, rundown ramblers and businesses of today will be too valuable to remain that

way. The street project will make further development less costly.

"Viticulture and hospitality services will drive the transformation. Even if Oregonians continue to drive past without stopping, wine lovers far and wide will flock to Dundee..."

GRUBBY END OF THE CHEHALEM VALLEY / CHEHALEM /ROGER'S LANDING / NEUBERG / NEWBURGH/NEWBERG

Newberg, Oregon, in Yamhill County, lies on the west bank of the Willamette River close to the mouth of Chehalem Creek.

One of the first settlers in the area was not a welcome one in the eyes of the Hudson's Bay Company. Ewing Young was an American trapper and fur trader from Tennessee who migrated to the Oregon Territory via what was then Northern Mexico and California in the 1830s. While in Northern Mexico and California, he joined with Peter Skene Ogden of the Hudson's Bay Company and they sold their pelts in San Francisco. He soon became one of the wealthiest Americans in Mexican territory. When he and another associate, Oregon Territory promoter, Hall J. Kelley, arrived at Fort Vancouver in 1834, he was discouraged by the Hudson's Bay Company from settling in the Oregon Territory. One of the reasons given was that after the Young party left Mexico, the Mexican government accused his group of stealing 200 horses. Although Young denied that he was a part of the theft, Dr. John McLoughlin blacklisted him from doing business with the Hudson's Bay Company. The company also had a history of discouraging settlers and other traders in the American region.

Despite everything, Ewing Young settled on the banks of the Chehalem Creek near the current site of the town of Newberg. His home is believed to have been the first one built by a European American on the west bank of the Willamette River.

In 1836, once settled on Chehalem Creek, Young decided to go into the business of distilling whiskey. Jason Lee, leader of the nearby Methodist Mission, had formed the Oregon Temperance League. The OTL with the help of John McLoughlin, whose Hudson's Bay Company prohibited the sale of liquor to the Indians. Together, they fought Young's efforts to establish the distillery. Eventually, because of the opposition from near and far, Young gave up the proposed project. Young later became involved in the cattle business and added to his considerable fortune through the sale of beef.

Curiously, as successful as Ewing Young became in his lifetime, it was his death that made a much bigger impact on the region. Young died in February 1841. He had no family or heir and he left no will to manage his vast fortune. In order to settle the estate, his situation created the need to set up some type of government to probate it. Partly because of his intestate death and the need to probate his estate, the first provisional government located in neighboring Champoeg was established in 1843.

Of course, the area was settled by other farming families in the 1840s, too. Joseph Rogers was one of the first settlers in 1848. In the early days, the area was called the "Grubby End of the Chehalem Valley," and for awhile, Rogers' Landing, but in 1869, according to one source, the first postmaster, Sebastian Brutscher, named it "Neuberg" for a town in his homeland of Bavaria. Another source shows the early spelling to have been "Newburgh."

After visiting the area in the 1870s, Quaker minister William Hobson settled there and began preaching. Other Quakers from mainly Indiana and Iowa soon followed. The religious group also established Friends Pacific Academy which later became George Fox College/University. Dr. Henry John Minthorn was the first headmaster of the academy after having served as the school superintendent at the Indian School, later "Chemawa," in neighboring Forest Grove.

Minthorn's orphaned nephew, Bertie, joined him there. Bertie, more commonly known as Herbert Hoover, later became the 31st President of the United States.

It was Dr. John Minthorn who resuscitated 2-year-old Bertie and saved his life during a bout of croup before his move to Oregon. Bertie was orphaned at the age of nine, and went to live first with his grandmother and then another uncle, Allen Hoover, in Iowa. He then moved to Oregon in 1885, to be raised by his uncle, John Minthorn. Minthorn was a practicing physician and businessman. He wrote a "liquor clause" into the deeds of lands sold through his real estate company, restricting sale or manufacture of alcohol. He was deeply involved with the native tribes of Oregon, too, and provided medical care to them. He was even rumored to have adopted some of the Indian children as his own.

"Bertie," (Herbert Hoover), did not attend high school, but instead took night school classes to learn bookkeeping, typing and mathematics, and attended the Friends Pacific Academy for 2½ years. He also worked in John Minthorn's Oregon Land

Hoover-Minthorn House Museum in Newberg, 1928. *Courtesy of the Herbert Hoover Presidential Library & Museum, West Branch, Iowa*

A filbert sweeper participates in a Newberg parade in 1953. *Courtesy of the Yamhill Historical Society*

Company office in Salem before enrolling at Stanford University.

Today, the boyhood home of the former President and Quaker activist Henry John Minthorn in Newberg is now the Hoover-Minthorn House Museum.

Newberg was platted in 1881 and incorporated in 1889. In 1915, a farming community, Newberg was the center of an area known for dairying, livestock, orchards of prunes and walnuts and fields of strawberries and loganberries. It was also noted for lumber production and the manufacturing of tile and brick. It hosted a large sawmill, a milk condensing plant, a fruit drier, two flour mills and a cooperative canning association.

Frequent interurban electric trains, the Southern Pacific Reds, connected Newberg with McMinnville and Portland.

After World War II, Newberg prospered with a large newsprint paper mill and a redirection of agriculture into grape growing and wine-making.

BUTTE / EAST BUTTE / TIGARDVILLE / TIGARD

According to Sean Garvey in his Tigard history for the Oregon Encyclopedia Project, Tigard *"is located in Washington County in the lower Willamette Valley, a region that for thousands of years was the territory of the Atfalati Kalapuya, a band that nineteenth-century settlers called the Tualatin. The Tualatin resided in permanent villages during the winter and spent the remainder of the year roaming the valley to hunt and gather. In the early 1830s, a deadly malaria epidemic struck the band, decimating it and killing as much as 97 percent of the population."*

Along with other families looking for a place to live, raise a family and grow some crops. Wilson M. Tigard and his family settled there in 1852, buying the claim of another settler.

Known as East Butte, the area was made up of rich farm land. Wilson Tigard and his neighbors established the first school there, building a larger new one in 1869 which they

John W. Tigard house in Tigard, Oregon.
Courtesy of Wikimedia Commons (M.O. Stevens)

called East Butte School. Soon, there was the Butte Grange, which organized in 1874, and a general store, built by Wilson's son, Charles Tigard, that in 1886, began hosting a post office which was named Tigardville.

That same year, the Emanuel Evangelical Church was built at the foot of Bull Mountain and in the 1890s, John Gaarde opened a blacksmith shop. There was a rather large influx of German immigrants arriving in the 1890s and a new East Butte School needed to be built to house the children of the new families.

In 1880, Wilson's son, John, built his family's Carpenter Gothic Victorian home on the corner of what is now Pacific Highway and Gaarde Street. It was scheduled for demolition when the Tigard Historical Association began a successful campaign in 1970 to save it. They had it restored and it was later moved to the corner of S.W. Canterbury Lane and S.W. 103rd in Tigard where it now serves as a museum. It was added to the National Register of Historic Places in 1979.

In 1907, the name of the post office was changed to Tigard because the planned railroad through the area wanted to distinguish it from the neighboring town of Wilsonville. Also in 1908, a large two-story commercial building called Germania Hall was built to accommodate a restaurant, grocery store, dance hall, a new post office, rooms to rent and a livery stable. Telephone service also arrived that same year.

In 1910, the Oregon Electric Railway opened its line between Portland and Salem making the town a commuter suburb. Many heads of households chose to live in Tigard and commute by train to jobs in Portland and Salem. The depot was built north of Tigard, causing much of the commercial district to shift to that area.

Originally a farming community, Tigard was known for its agricultural bounty of fruit, mainly prunes, walnuts, dairy cattle, livestock and poultry. Many of the farms became truck gardens that raised produce for Portland markets. There was a sawmill outside of town, also.

Electricity was introduced to the community in 1911 when the Tualatin Valley Electric Company added Tigard to their service grid.

By the 1930s, Tigard welcomed U.S. Highway 99W (aka Barbur Blvd.), the major highway between Portland to Corvallis and points south. One of the first gasoline stations was established at the William Ariss blacksmith shop which he started in 1912. More and more of its residents became commuters. Buses and private automobiles soon took the place of the railway and trolleys to take commuters to city jobs.

Although it had become primarily a bedroom community for Portland, Tigard was incorporated in 1961.

Sean Garvey continues his narration of the area's history:

"One of Tigard's many historic homes

is the John Tigard House, a Carpenter Gothic Victorian house built in 1880 by Wilson Tigard's eldest son. The Tigard Historical Association saved the house from demolition and restored it in the late 1970s; it was listed in the National Register of Historic Places in 1979.

"Annual family-oriented events include the Festival of Balloons in June and the Family Festival in September."

Section 12

U.S. HIGHWAY 99W - TIGARD TO THE INTERSTATE BRIDGE

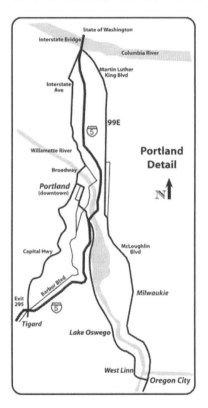

STUMPTOWN / PORTLAND WEST

William Overton and Asa L. Lovejoy jointly claimed land on the west side of the Willamette River which was the site of Portland's earliest beginnings. The decision between naming the spot "Boston," or "Portland" was settled by a coin-toss. Overton later sold his interest to Francis Pettygrove. For several years it was also known as "Stumptown" for the stumps in the middle of its mud streets.

Captain John Couch, a sea captain, filed on an adjacent land claim and helped establish Portland as the effective head of navigation on the Willamette River. He also became the treasurer of the provisional government and the commissioner of Multnomah County.

Portland had a post office by 1849 and was incorporated in 1851. During the 1850s, the *Oregonian* newspaper was established, as was Portland's own department store, Meier and Frank.

The settlement was surveyed and platted by early pioneer Jesse Applegate using a

Located in Portland, Dr. Ralph Wilcox ran the first day school in Oregon, which opened in 1847. The cost was $10 per pupil per academic quarter.
Courtesy of the OSU Special Collections & Archives Commons

magnetic compass which didn't reflect true north, so some of the early streets aren't in line with those platted after Oregon became a Territory of the United States..

The early settlers settled along the banks of the Willamette River near the confluence of the Columbia and Willamette Rivers. The west bank offered the best place for the bigger ships to dock, so early business generally grew in that area. As more settlers arrived and began to spread out, more space was needed. The problem was, there wasn't a lot of flat land. To the west, the Tualatin Mountains bordered the city. To the south was Council Crest, then Marquam Hill and, to the north, the West Hills. Gradually, the residences and businesses began to be built on the hills.

When more settlers came and the east side began to develop, a ferry was used to transport people and commodities across the river into the city.

In an interview for the *WPA's American Life Histories Collection: Manuscripts from the Federal Writer's Project, 1936-1940*, Miss Mary Agnes Kelly told of life in the Portland area. She was interviewed by Sara B. Wrenn on February 27, 1939:

"My father's people came to Oregon across the plains in 1848. Father's father was Clinton Kelly, the one who filed on all this country round-about as a donation land claim. See, up there on the hill is the house grandfather built after the burning of his big log house. The house is used now as a sanitarium. There are five cherry trees growing there that grandfather bought from that famous nursery brought across the plains by the Lewellings. Joseph Watt, who afterward started the first woolen mill in Oregon, at Salem, was captain of my people's train. He had come across earlier in 1843, and so was well qualified for his responsibilities as captain.

"Are you interested in Indian stories? If so, here is one that may be interesting because, if you have imagination, you can see something of the picture on the hill over yonder. It was the Indian trouble of 1855 and 1856 when the word went out over the country that the Indians were going to wipe out the whites – the Cayuse and Yakima Indians, I think they were. Of course everybody was panic-stricken, and all the outlying settlers began to pour in, by whatever means they could, to the more closely settled community, which seemed to be in this vicinity.

"Grandfather had built a huge loghouse. I've been told it was 80 by 100 feet. The house was built on the order of some of the old southern plantation homes, in two different sections, roofed over between. As the house and outbuildings were on an eminence, it formed a fairly strong place for protection. So it was here the frightened settlers began to congregate. They came from every direction, especially from the Columbia River and Powell Valley, and they came in every sort of conveyance. The hill up there was practically covered with horses, oxen and wagons, and they stayed for days. The men were busy fortifying and getting their arms and ammunition ready, and the women, of course, were more than busy cooking and caring for the many children. One woman – a Mrs. Duvall from the vicinity of what is now Gresham – had given birth to a baby the very day she had to be moved. How to carry her and the tiny baby safely over the more than ten miles of rough road was a problem that had to be solved quickly. But a man by the name of Jacob Jackson Moore, who owned the land where the Gresham cemetery now is, was quick-witted. Boring holes in the sides of a wagon-bed, he then stretched ropes across, and on the mattress formed by the ropes he placed a feather bed. On this improvised ambulance, mother and babe rode to safety.

"A week or so later troops were ordered out against the Indians, and with them went Plympton Kelly, grandfather's oldest son.

"Grandfather, Clinton Kelly, did considerable preaching for some time after coming to Oregon, not so much professionally as from a sense of duty. The tradition is that he preached the second sermon in Portland – and that in a cooperage. Elsewhere he preached at Mount Tabor, Lents, Foster's Milwaukie and Oregon City. Dr. Samuel Nelson, a physician, had built a small house on the western slope of Mount Tabor, only it wasn't then named, but it must have been an attractive spot, for during the summer grandfather and his family would go with their ox team and wagon, and Sunday would be put in with, first, Sunday school, then a sermon, and then a class meeting, all in succession. It must have been pretty hard on the youngsters, but all the people in the community came. It was on one of these occasions that somebody suggested naming the mountain. Grandfather's first thought was Mount Zion, but one of his sons, who had been reading history, spoke up and said, 'Father, this reminds me of what I have been reading about Mount Tabor. Let's call it that.' So Mount Tabor it has been called ever since, though nobody then dreamed they were on an extinct volcano – that they were so close, as you might say, to hell fire and brimstone, even if centuries ago.

"Thomas Kelly, the youngest brother of Clinton, took up a homestead on land where the Grant High School now stands. It was a very remote and lonesome place then. Great-uncle Thomas was a bachelor. He built himself a little log house, and did the various other improvements required by law; but he probably didn't work as hard as he would had he been driven by the necessity of supporting a wife and several children. He liked to hunt and he had time for it. He had been hunting one day, and, late in the evening, was carrying home the deer he had shot – carrying it slung over his shoulder, with the head hanging down his back. Dusk had fallen when he realized that he was being followed by something or someone. It didn't take him very long to know that it was a mountain lion or cougar. Knowing the beast's proclivities, that if he hastened his steps attack would be precipitated, he forced himself to hold back when every impulse was to run. Finally, after what seemed to him an eternity, he reached his cabin door. He had no more then dropped the heavy bar inside, when, bang! came the full weight of the cougar on the door. Luckily the door was strong and well-fastened, for again and again the animal lunged, snarling at the barrier. Then it sprang on the roof, and all night long, maddened by the smell of the deer's blood, it yelled and howled and scratched at the frail shakes, only a few feet above his head. With daylight, the big cat slunk away, and never was daylight more welcome to great-uncle Thomas, so I've been told.

"And here's another cougar story of the early days. Grandfather Marquam, for whom Marquam Hill is named, came to Oregon from California in 1851. He wanted some land cleared, so he hired a man by the name of Latham to do the work. Latham had a wife and three or four little children. The clearing was on the crest of Marquam Hill, where a little house or cabin was built in which the family might live. Latham was absent from home one night. Early in the evening one of the children was taken sick with some childish ailment, probably colic, for it cried and cried. With darkness, shut in as the cabin was by towering trees, the child's complaining cries grew louder, or so it seemed to the frightened and lonely mother. Presently, to her horror, there came an answering cry from just outside in the little clearing. By this time all the children were frightened and whimpering, and the sick child screamed both with fear and pain. For every scream it gave the cougar or panther answered. Then it, too, leaped on the frail roof, scratching and tearing to get through. Mrs. Latham had no gun, and wouldn't have known how to fire it if she had. But she did have a washboiler, and she had, it appears, plenty of water and plenty of wood. So all night long she kept the water boiling, her only weapon if the snarling, hungry beast broke through in the midst of her little brood. This time, also, daylight served as a rescuer, but never again did Mrs. Latham spend the night up there on Marquam Hill alone. She said afterward she thought her hair would be white when morning came.

"There is a story, the details of which I wish I could remember better. It is about what we always called the 'great-grandfather of all the wolves' story, that was too smart to take any of the trap baits put out by grandfather Kelly. Time after time calves and sheep and pigs were taken, and time after time grandfather set his traps and his baits – all to no purpose. This 'great-grandfather of all the wolves' was just too clever for him. Grandfather grew more and more disgusted at his failure. Then, if I remember the story correctly, he built a little pen, in which he placed a live sheep, yet so protected that the wolf couldn't reach it. Just outside the pen he put some poisoned bait that he had been careful enough to literally 'handle with gloves.' The next day grandmother and father and all the rest of the young Kellys were taken out by grandfather to see the 'great-grandfather of all the wolves' stretched out stark and stiff, and dead as a stone.

"Grandfather Marquam had a rather keen sense of humor and loved his little jokes. He got a big laugh from the story of the sanctimonious minister – we won't mention the name – who, on returning home from church one Sunday, when the weather was bitter cold, and all the ponds round about were covered with ice, met a little boy with his skates slung over his shoulder. This, thought the sanctimonious minister, is a good time to deliver a moral lecture. He spoke to the little boy, who responded in gay, good humor. Then he said, 'Sonny, do you know where little boys go, who carry their skates on Sunday?'

"'Yes, sir,' the little boy answered, with a bright smile, 'some of 'em goes to Couch's Lake, and some of 'em goes to Carruthers Pond.'

"In Grandfather's day, the family never went to bed, nor left the house for the day, without first having family prayers, for which the entire family, including such hired man as there might be, congregated in the living room. It was all very patriarchal, and any hired man who refused to comply with this household custom did not long remain in grandfather's employ. First he would read a chapter from the Bible, followed by singing in which all took part, and then there would be a prayer by grandfather.

"Another custom in our family, which my brother and I maintain today, is to say on parting for the night, 'Goodnight, and bless you.'

"A farewell salutation of grandmother's was 'I wish you well.'

"Yes, I remember well the Chinese gangs my people employed in clearing land, as well as in cultivating it for garden purposes. They were always very fond of children and would bring us presents. As a rule they were both industrious and honest. But I remember once when father found under the big flat bamboo hats, which they had left on the ground near their work, a number of potatoes, several to each hat. They were planning to take them to their camp, no doubt. So father simply had their boss pick the potatoes all up, and then he gave them to the gang, reminding them at the same time it was unnecessary for them to steal."

In an interview for the *WPA's American Life Histories Collection: Manuscripts from the Federal Writer's Project, 1936-1940*, George Estes told of life in the Portland area. He was interviewed by Andrew C. Sherbert on November 28, 1938:

"...My work in the field of telegraphy brought me early to Portland. I have seen this sprawling metropolis grow from a compact little village skirting the banks of the Willamette. In my earlier days I contacted socially, many of the aging pioneers who have long since passed from the scene. Right here I should like to interject the statement that Portland's history, as set down by each historian in turn (including my old friend, John Gaston), seems to me to be entirely wrong. Too much stress is laid on the part played by Lovejoy and Pettygrove in the founding of the city. Perhaps they did stake out the town plot – perhaps they did flip a coin and give the town its name, but I contend that whatever else they contributed to the establishment of the city of Portland was of minor importance. I fully believe that I would not be sitting here in this office building, that you would not be here to interview me – for there would be no building here – if it were not for Captain John Couch. Captain Couch took a small group of primitive dwellings in a setting of stump-cluttered clearings and through his own efforts and determination, gave Portland the impetus that made it a city. Surely, Portland's future was extremely doubtful had it not been for one man alone – John Couch. It irritates me to see him treated historically as an incidental figure.

"I have seen the coming of the first horse-cars – and what a luxury and improvement over shank's mares they seemed! I have seen the advent of the electric streetcar, hailed the coming of the first chugging automobile – and now, trackless trolleys. I have seen Portland's first squat buildings share ground with tall structures. Airplanes dot the sky. Change, change, change, always change, and no end in sight.

"...As a young telegrapher in Portland, I had a great many acquaintances. At the time of which I speak, Burnside Street was a busy thoroughfare – the crossroads of the Oregon country, where one might meet anyone he had ever met or known before. In those few short blocks there congregated people of all types, from the more or less dandified Portland sophisticates, to the rough, uncouth wranglers of the hinterland. The gold miner from Eastern or Southern Oregon rubbed elbows with the almond-eyed Chinese. The farmer from Tualatin Valley walked the length of Burnside Street a time or two, before he started for home with the new plow he had purchased. There was only one Burnside Street on the face of the earth, and that was in Portland.

"...My whole life has been just like that. Just luck that my father decided to settle at the foot of the Calapooia Mountains, instead of taking up residence in the far-heralded Willamette Valley, as so many other immigrants did. Just luck that the stage line found it necessary to cross my father's homestead claim. Just luck that the first telegraph line followed the stage route through our place during my infancy, causing me to know the Morse code almost as soon as I had learned my letters. You might say it was luck that placed me at the head of all the railroad telegraphers of the English-speaking world, for a time..."

In 1854, Portland became the county seat of Multnomah County, though portions of the city also lie in Clackamas and Washington Counties.

By 1860, Portland was the largest town in the new State of Oregon, which had earned its statehood in 1859. During the 1860s, the Oregon Steam Navigation Company was formed, making access to products from the productive Willamette Valley possible.

At the end of the Civil War, Oregon had a new wave of immigrants, not by wagon train, however. Some 10,000 veterans from both sides of the Civil War began arriving. There are generalizations about where they settled, probably with some truth. In general, it's said the northerners were more apt to find the business centers most comfortable and sought out city life while the southerners sought out land that could produce crops. It's equally true that there was no hard and fast division.

In an interview for the *WPA's American Life Histories Collection: Manuscripts from the Federal Writer's Project, 1936-1940*, Mrs. John H. James told of life in Portland. She was interviewed by Sara B. Wrenn on February 6, 1939:

"Did brother Charlie tell you about how our half-brother John's girl, up from California, got him to spruce up and take dancing lessons? He did. Well I bet he didn't tell you what a rag-a-muffin the old dancing teacher, Cardinell, was. That was in 1868 or 1870, and old Charlie Cardinell would go around over the country in a little old wagon, drawn by one horse, picking up every cast-off thing he could find. My! My! but he looked like an old beggar! But he could certainly dance, and what with teaching everybody in town to dance, and gathering up every old rag and bottle and stuff like that, and selling it for a few cents, he died pretty well off, owning all of Cardinell Hill, up on the Canyon Road.

"Of course we went to all the revival meetings in those early days, but I don't remember much in particular about them. I remember when the old tabernacle was built in the early '80s, at 12th and Taylor Streets. It was built for a series of meetings conducted by the revivalist, Mrs. Hanson, and she was a wonder. I guess she drew the biggest crowds Portland had up to that time. The tabernacle was packed every night, and nearly everybody in town got religion. Later on the tabernacle was moved to 12th and Morrison Streets. B. Fay Mills, Chapman, Billy Sunday, and all the big evangelists held meetings there."

The Centennial Block. 2nd Street between Yamhill and Morrison, 1878. *The West Shore*

In Portland, as in other communities in the state, organizations began to form as like-minded people came together for social contact and to do as a group what couldn't be done individually. Throughout the state, the names of different groups show up on buildings, projects, and even cemeteries. One of

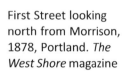

First Street looking north from Morrison, 1878, Portland. *The West Shore* magazine

those that didn't come west with the pioneers but after, when it was needed, was the Grand Army of the Republic.

In 1866, the United States was facing a new challenge – recovery from the ravages of war – with the veteran warrior one of the most important parts of the challenge. In earlier wars it was the family or the community who stepped up for the returning veterans. Soldiers were friends, relatives and neighbors who went off to fight.

The Civil War was different; the men from different communities or states were forced together where new friendships and trusts were forged. At the end of the war, the communities couldn't deal with the needs of widows and orphans and the needs of the veterans, as well. Many of those veterans needed jobs – and the same need was often felt by the new group of veterans – the "colored" soldier and his whole newly-freed family. State and federal leaders had little knowledge of how to accomplish the needed care and there was little political pressure to see it happen.

In time, friendships forged in battle survived the separation, and the knowledge that banding together could win those struggles began to assert itself. With that as background, groups of men began joining together – for camaraderie and connection as well as for political power.

Various organizations of veterans formed, but most didn't last for long. Emerging as most powerful of these veteran organizations was the Grand Army of the Republic (GAR). Many honorably-discharged veterans of the Union Army, Navy, Marine Corps or the Revenue Cutter Service who had served between April 12, 1861 and April 9, 1865, joined. The community-level organization was called a "post" and it was part of a department, usually a state or region. They also formed auxiliary groups including Sons of Union Veterans of the Civil War and Ladies of the Grand Army of the Republic. There were posts in every corner of Oregon.

The GAR founded soldiers' homes and was active in relief work and pension legislation. Using political pressure, it established a national Memorial Day and provided cemeteries for deceased Union soldiers. The peak year for the organization was 1890, with a membership of about 500,000 nationwide.

The final Encampment of the Grand Army of the Republic was held in 1949, and the last member, Albert Woolson, died in 1956 at the age of 109 years.

The bear pit at Washington Park, ca 1935. *Courtesy of the City of Portland Archives*

The new Portland Railroad Bridge, 1887. *From the* West Shore *magazine*

The 1870s brought the beginning of the railroad construction with the Oregon & California Railroad linking Portland with the Willamette and Umpqua Valleys. By1880, the railroad had connected to California through the auspices of the Southern Pacific Railroad. By 1890, three bridges crossed the Willamette with streetcars connecting to East Portland and Albina. The three cities merged into one and continued to grow.

Among the Civil War veterans who traveled west for new opportunities was Isaac W. Smith, a Confederate engineer. He had worked for the government, often in the State of Washington before the war, but the attack on his native Virginia sent him to fight for the south. He built pontoon bridges for General Robert E. Lee, constructed the fortifications at Petersburg and, after the war, spent some time in Mexico. He was then hired by North-

1917 Interstate Bridge and ferry. *Courtesy of the Oregon Historical Society*

ern Pacific Railroad to conduct surveys in California, Oregon and Washington. In 1872, he was in Oregon City where he built the canals and locks around Willamette Falls. He worked other jobs in Tacoma, Canada, Peru and California. In 1885, the City of Portland hired Smith as its first chief engineer and superintendent of the Water Committee.

For the next decade, Colonel Smith developed the infrastructure for the growth of modern-day Portland. His work included finding a route and constructing a pipeline and reservoir from the Bull Run watershed to Portland. The route was through untouched wilderness, old growth forest and brush, building all the roads and bridges needed for the pipeline as they went, then overseeing upgrades of the city's mains and distribution pipe and coordinating the construction of reservoirs.

Portland Park System

During the 1860s, Portland's civic leaders discussed creating a forest preserve in the hillside woods near northwest Portland. That idea led to the creation of a municipal park commission in 1903. The commission hired a landscape architectural firm to develop a plan for the Portland parks. The firm, Olmsted Brothers, proposed creating linking parks and parkways, Many, such as Forest Park, did not come into being until years later. Acquiring land through donations, transfers from Multnomah County and tax foreclosures, the city eventually combined parcels to create the Forest Park preserve in 1948 with 4,200 acres. The park has walking trails which link to many other Portland parks. It also connects to well-known Washington Park, the home of the Oregon Zoo, the World Forestry Center, the Portland Japanese Garden, the Rose Garden and the Hoyt Arboretum. On the northwest corner of Washington Park, near where West Burnside becomes Barnes Road, there is another small park called the Willamette Stone Park. It is the starting point for all Oregon Surveys.

The Oregon Zoo

In 1871, the city of Portland purchased 40 acres from Amos King for its first municipal park. It was small, but it was a beginning.

In 1887, a Portland pharmacist who collected animals as a hobby, appealed to the city for permits to keep his two bears. The city presented him with cages and allowed him to display the animals to collect funds. A year later, he was back and offered to donate the bears and other exotic animals to the city. The city accepted, and the oldest zoo west of the Mississippi was created in Washington Park. Underfunded, one person served as the park supervisor and zoo keeper. In 1905, the zoo acquired a lion, leopard and polar bear from the Lewis and Clark Fair. By 1894, there were over 300 animals in the collection. In 1925, the zoo moved to the site of the Portland Japanese Garden that was located in another section of Washington Park.

It moved again in 1958-59 to its current site within Washington Park. The Portland Zoo Railway opened at the same time and the Oregon Museum of Science and Industry (OMSI) was a neighbor.

The zoo has changed names over the years – Portland Zoological Gardens, then the Washington Park Zoo, and now the Oregon Zoo.

According to the 2012 *Oregon Blue Book*:

"The Oregon Zoo is nestled on 64 acres in the forested hills of Washington

The Council Crest trolley, ca 1920. *Courtesy of the City of Portland Archives A2012-005*

Park. It is home to more than 2,000 animals from around the world. It has settings that recreate the environments of various animals who live there.

"They are also committed to conservation, research and education. They have joined with other conservation organizations to partner in more than 40 breeding programs and have also increased their educational programs to involve participants from three years old to senior citizens."

On Memorial Day in 1907, Council Crest Amusement Park opened southwest of Portland on the hill by the same name. It had its own trolley and trolley station to bring visitors to the Roof Garden on the Mountaintop. It also had a scenic train ride, a boat ride around the park, a ferris wheel, a carousel and a Big Tree Observatory which had an elevator to the top. There was also a midway and popular Crest Dance Pavilion. Unfortunately, it became a casualty of the Depression, and the park was closed on Labor Day in 1929 and torn down in 1941. Now the area is a community park.

Council Crest, the tallest of the hills surrounding Portland at over 1,000 feet, is a perfect host. There are incredible views, a picnic area, a four-mile hiking trail and a statue with a history...

In 1956, "Joy," a welded, sheet-bronze drinking fountain sculpted by Frederic Littman in 1954 was installed in the park. It was made possible by a bequest from Florence Laberee, widow of a local contractor. It depicted a young mother joyfully lifting her baby above her head. Sadly, vandals cut the statue off at her ankles with a hacksaw and stole it. A decade later, the police involved in a narcotics raid in northeast Portland, found the statue. It has been repaired and is once again displayed near the entrance to the park.

The settlement of "Stumptown," or Portland, along the banks of the Willamette River

Frrederic Littman's sculpture, "Joy."

Flooded downtown Portland street in 1894. *Courtesy of the City of Portland Archives*

near the confluence with the Columbia, was growing and spreading. There were homes and businesses on both sides of the river that were served by a ferry, and as time went on and the river became busier, a wider area for growth was needed. However, because of the shortage of flat land, other solutions had to be found. On the west, the foothills of the Tualatin Mountains presented challenges, but they still offered scenic locations for expansion. The slopes of Marquam Hill, West Hills and Forest Park all began to be settled. On the east side of the river, Mt. Tabor, a cinder cone, and Rocky Butte offered more possibilities.

The University of Oregon Medical School / Oregon Health & Science University/ Oregon Health Sciences University

Phillip A. Marquam, from Baltimore, Maryland, came to Portland in 1851. He

The first traffic signal on Third and Morrison in Portland (no date available). *Courtesy of the City of Portland Archives*

Barbur Blvd./ U.S. Highway 99 approaching Portland, 1954. *Courtesy of the Oregon Department of Transportation (ODOT) History Center*

practiced law and invested in real estate. He became a judge in 1862 and a State Legislator in 1882. He was prominent in the legal, economic, sporting, educational and theatrical history of Portland.

Marquam Hill which lies just southwest of downtown Portland was named for him. It's one of the very steep promontories of the Tualatin Mountains.

The parcel of land encompassing Marquam Hill was donated to the University of Oregon Medical School in 1917. The Oregon-Washington Railroad & Navigation Co. donated the first 20 acres and C.S. "Sam" Jackson, the former publisher of the *Oregon Journal* newspaper donated another 89 acres.

The first building of the medical complex, Mackenzie Hall, was built on it in 1919. By 1950, the campus of the University of Oregon Medical School located along Sam Jackson Road included Multnomah County Hospital, Doernbecher Children's Hospital, the Medical School, a Tuberculosis Hospital, a Veterans Hospital, the medical fraternity house and a student nurse dormitory. The buildings made a half circle around a deep gully which was wooded, but had a walking bridge over it. The major buildings comprising the hospitals had tunnels between them for easy passage back and forth.

Since that time, many changes have taken place. In 1955, the medical school became a teaching hospital and the name was changed to the Oregon Health & Science University (OHSU). With another slight change in name to the Oregon Health Sciences University, it is now the state's only medical and research university. It services nearly 200,000 patients a year and has over 11,000 employees and is the largest employer in the City of Portland. It is also recognized as one of the premier trauma centers in the United States.

The lack of space for the scientific research laboratories on the steep hillside was limiting its growth, so alternative sites were considered. But, the increased travel time between the research facilities and the hospital caused problems when major connecting highways were already built and clogged with traffic. The only nearby empty space was a large waterfront area which had been zoned industrial. With detailed engineering studies and much city involvement, it was decided to put the research department along the waterfront area, connecting the two with a tram that wends its way up the hill, passing over Barbur Boulevard /Highway 99W and Interstate 5. The transport time between the two units is just over twelve minutes.

The number of employees and visitors arriving and departing at OHSU during rush hour traffic in and out of Portland is a major problem, and the city has tried to mitigate the situation. Extra TriMet buses run from Marquam Hill to Tigard and other areas in southwest Portland during rush hours.

Above the hospital complex and a residential area on Marquam Hill, Sam Jackson Park is linked by trails to other city parks.

In 1891, a port district was created to improve navigation on the Willamette and lower Columbia Rivers. It also kept both land and water carriers from monopolizing the wharves. As international trade grew, so did business along the Willamette River.

In 1887, the Morrison Street Bridge was built across the Willamette, forecasting the impending demise of the ferry. It was a wooden toll bridge and was privately-owned. The city eventually bought it and replaced it with another wooden bridge. In 1888, The railroad built a steel bridge nearby where the trains could cross.

In 1894, the Madison Bridge was added, but it too was privately owned with tolls. The city purchased it and had to replace it in 1900. In 1910, it was replaced once again and renamed the Hawthorne Bridge.

In 1894, the Burnside Bridge was added to the family of bridges. It was replaced in 1926. Some of the material from the original, however, was reused for the Bull Run water project.

There was a pause in bridge building until 1913 when the double-leafed Broadway Bridge was constructed.

In 1913, the responsibility for the construction and maintenance of bridges was switched to the jurisdiction of Multnomah County. The reassignment occurred, however, at about the same time that the popularity of the Klu Klux Klan was renewed throughout Oregon. It had even infiltrated Multnomah County politics. When the county built three more bridges during the early 1920s – the Sellwood Bridge, the new Burnside Bridge and the Ross Island Bridge, the least impressive of the three, the Ross Island Bridge, was the only one free of corruption. In the building of the other two, the construction contracts and methods were so blatantly corrupt and over-budget, that a strong citizen outcry resulted, bringing down the commissioners who had KKK backing and removing them from office.

The last of the major bridges, the St. Johns Bridge in northwest Portland, was built in 1931.

In 1911, the licensing of motor vehicles began. E. Henry Wemme of Portland was the first in line and registered his 32-horsepower Pope-Hartford touring car, receiving Oregon license plate #1. Graduated fees were based on horsepower. Revenue from the fees was placed in the state's General Fund and dedicated to road building and maintenance. During that year, there were 6,428 motor vehicles registered in the state and gasoline cost 16-cents per gallon.

During the early days of automobiles, the Portland Automobile Club, with 40 owner-members, complained loudly about the dusty dirt roads during the summer when it was the time to enjoy the autos. In 1905, they raised enough funding to oil one stretch of Linnton Road to access a popular restaurant they wanted to visit. By the next year, they raised enough money to oil a return road on the other side of the Willamette, crossing the new bridge to make a loop. Their numbers grew rapidly and they pushed for more useable roads.

The next decade brought the development of the Columbia Highway and the beginnings of the Pacific Highway to connect Oregon to Washington and California.

Traveling north through Portland on U.S. Highway 99W, the highway also headed east in order to cross the Willamette River to merge with U.S. Highway 99E. From there, for the short distance to where the route takes it over the Interstate Bridge spanning the Columbia River into Washington, it once again became a single highway.

From "The Burial of 'Old Man Detour,'" *The Oregon Motorist*, November 1923. Eugene, Oregon:

"Thursday, October 25, 1923, marked an epoch in the history of highway construction in the Pacific North, for it was on this day that 'Old Man Detour,' the bugaboo which has been making life miserable for motorists traveling over the Pacific Highway in Oregon and Washington, was buried for keeps. The obsequies were conducted by the Governors of Oregon and Washington, assisted by many other prominent citizens of the two states and British Columbia. Frank Branch Riley, the silver-tongued orator who has done more than any other one man to attract visitors to the Pacific Wonderland, delivered the funeral oration at the great Interstate bridge which spans the majestic Columbia. A military band from the army post at Vancouver rendered fitting music for the occasion, and hundreds of motorists from up and down the Pacific Coast joined in making the event one long to be remembered in the annals of motordom.

"It was a celebration rather than a ceremony, joy taking the place of solemnity throughout the proceedings. The affair began Thursday morning in Olympia, the capital of Washington, where, after appropriate opening exercises had been held, the lifeless form of the 'Old Man' was loaded on a hearse and the journey south to the Oregon line was begun. A caravan of several hundred cars made up the funeral cortege. This caravan was met at Longview, Washington by some thirty cars that had journeyed north from Portland, and, after lunch had been served, the whole procession moved on south to the Interstate bridge where the funeral service was held."

A cement base line road mile marker near Portland. *Courtesy of Curt Deatherage*

"After Mr. Riley had concluded the eulogy, the military band played a solemn dirge, the military bugles sounded taps and the troublesome 'Old Man' was rather unceremoniously dumped over the railing into the deep waters of the Columbia. To be sure he was planted forever, his body was weighted down with blown-out tires, smashed fenders and broken automobile springs. As the body splashed into the water, the word was flashed throughout the world that the Pacific Highway in Oregon and Washington had been completed, a 700-mile stretch of hard-surfaced pavement beginning at Vancouver, British Columbia and ending at the California line.

"The Pacific Highway stands today as the longest paved highway in the world, and world travelers pronounce it to be the most scenic."

The Lewis & Clark Exposition Bandstand and Government Building in Portland, 1905. *Courtesy of the on-line Oregon Encyclopedia Project*

During the 1920s, an open-air farmers' produce market, located in the 3rd and Yamhill blocks of southwest Portland, drew shoppers from all over the area. That success caused the city to look toward a huge enclosed structure to serve the same purpose, but in a more sanitary and less-congested manner. Financing the project proved difficult, slow and again some local self-interests became involved. Eventually, the city bought property on Front Street and tried to fund it in a private stock sale which failed to bring in the amount needed. The project eventually proceeded with a Depression-era Reconstruction Finance Corporation loan. The Portland Public Market opened just prior to Christmas 1933, but didn't gain acceptance from merchants or customers. The $1.4 million market closed, buried in debt and abandoned by the Portland City Council.

In World War II, the U.S. Navy leased the former Portland Public Market building and, in 1946, the *Oregon Journal* bought it. It became one of the most visible and photographed buildings along the Portland waterfront and was used by the newspaper until it closed down in 1968. The building was later demolished and the property it sat on is now a popular waterfront park.

1908 Fire engine decorated for the Portland Rose Parade. *Courtesy of the City of Portland Archives*

The Portland Rose Festival

Following the close of the 1905 Lewis and Clark Centennial Exposition, Portland mayor, Henry Lane, proposed that the City of Portland host a similar annual event. The proposal took root and by 1907, the first Portland Rose Festival became a reality.

The Grand Floral Parade, similiar to the one held in Pasadena, California on New Years Day each year, has become the main event of the week-long celebration. Intricately-designed floats are decorated with flowers, many of them roses, and a Queen is chosen to promote and publicize the other events. One of those events is "Fleet Week" where U.S. Navy, Coast Guard, U.S. Army Corps of Engineers and Royal Canadian Navy ships are displayed along the Tom McCall Waterfront Park.

There are also fireworks displays, dances, carnival rides, boat races, air shows and a plethora of other fun and entertaining activities.

"Lucy Lee Thomas to Others, but Nama to Me" by Kandice Carsh Bartels:

"This is a story of my grandmother, Lucy Lee Thomas whom I affectionately referred to as 'Nama.' I am writing from my own recollections, from scrapbooks she kept and from stories passed down to me. And then there is the eternal bond I feel – for all she was to me, and how iconic her grace and leadership was in an era when women were overlooked as potential business leaders. Her picture hangs in my office; a snapshot in time of a tearfully-happy seventeen-year-old girl, just crowned the Portland Rose Festival

The coronation of Lucy Lee Thomas, 1923 Rose Festival Queen. *Courtesy of Kandice Carsh Bartels*

Queen of 1923. It doesn't hang there just because I'm proud she held that title; it is there to remind me that women can be pageant royalty and beautiful and still be respected for their intelligence and leadership. My grandmother blazed the trail for women to become respected business leaders, and her picture reminds me to push through setbacks and adversity with the same grace and determination she displayed during some of the most challenging times of her life.

"My grandmother was born on September 6, 1905, in Jackson, Kentucky to a Spanish-American War Veteran, Robert B. Thomas and his wife Lucy Lee Thomas, for whom she was named. They lived in Kentucky and West Virginia before settling in Portland, Oregon when she was 4-years-old. It interests me to read of her personality from the newspaper clippings in 1923, the year Roosevelt High School voted her to be their Rose Festival Queen candidate. It was a day when she was absent from school, proof of the high-regard her peers, teachers and school officials had for her. One newspaper article described her as follows: 'She is a beautiful girl of the brunette type, modest, a leader of her classes and one of the popular girls of the graduating class of Roosevelt High this session. She is surpassed by none in beauty, tact and talent.' Several newspapers used the word 'piquant' to describe her – a term I was unfamiliar with. Upon looking up the definition, I now understand that four generations of daughters (my grandmother, my mother, myself and my daughter) could all be characterized as 'piquant.' Its definition: intriguing, stimulating, colorful; but when used to describe food: spicy, tangy, peppery! We all possess a wee bit of tenacity that has served us well in getting our point across!

"In the spring of 1923, the process for becoming a Rose Festival Queen was handled differently than it is today. The candidates themselves were not allowed to garner votes, but each had a campaign manager to promote them and be present to assist in the tabulation of votes. Ballot boxes were distributed to all the leading stores and public libraries around the city, and each vote cost 1-cent. This money was used to bring credit to the schools, the Rose Festival and the City of Portland. Immediate family members were not allowed to buy votes and vote solicitation was not to occur at the seven high schools from which the candidates were chosen.

"At the start of the campaign, and at the direction of the Portland Publicity Bureau, each of the seven candidates posed for photographs wearing the royal velvet and ermine robe and the beautiful 1,700-gemmed crown while holding a bouquet of roses. These photographs were sent to all of the publications throughout the nation and upon the Queen's election, the Portland Publicity Bureau would send a 'flash' allowing them to release the picture of the Rose Festival Queen already dressed in royalty. They were then asked to destroy the other photos – Media foresight, even in 1923!

"The vote for Queen of the Portland Rose Festival really came down to who the residents of the City of Portland, wanted. Lucy Lee Thomas won by over 7,000 votes (136,959), astounding if you consider the entire population of the City of Portland was roughly 258,000 that year. Her stammering press statement upon winning: 'I, I, I – I am very glad and yet, I'm sorry too. Sorry that the other girls had to lose. But most of all I'm glad for my school, Roosevelt High.'

"Her most poignant memory of being the Queen of the Rose Festival was the 20-gun salute she received by the Seattle flagship of the American Fleet of the Navy. To that she said: 'I didn't think too much about it at the time, but later found out that the Secretary of State only rates a 17-gun salute and the President of the United States gets a 21-gun salute.'

"The Royal Ball of the Rose Festival was on the same night as her high school graduation, so she put on her graduation dress, received her diploma, came home, put on her royal robe and crown and was met at her front door by a royal horse-drawn carriage to be whisked away to the Royal Ball. Sounds like a fairytale doesn't it?

"After graduating from high school, Lucy Lee taught primary school in Stayton while completing a business course and was later offered a job with the Peninsula State Bank in the Commercial Department.

"She became Mrs. Robert D. "Marnell" Helser in 1924. Marnell worked, with his brother in the family trucking business, Helser Brothers Transfer Company which was established in Portland in 1902.

"The couple welcomed their first child, Robert, on August 6, 1925, and would not have their second and last child, Marna (my mother) until 16 years later, in the spring of 1941.

"Throughout that time, Lucy Lee helped her husband operate the transfer company until Marnell died suddenly of a heart attack at the age of 42, leaving Lucy Lee a widow and single mother of a 7-year-old child.

"A respected business woman emerges… it is here that I give pause and reflection to my grandmother for not only being brave enough to carry on the family business, but to operate a business that was male dominant – trucking. She didn't open a clothing boutique or become an interior designer; she ran a trucking company – Go, Lucy Lee!

"She took over my grandfather's share of the business after his death and partnered with a woman named Mrs.

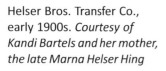

Helser Bros. Transfer Co., early 1900s. *Courtesy of Kandi Bartels and her mother, the late Marna Helser Hing*

Maude Rowley who bought out Marlow Helser's interest. Two strong-minded, intelligent, capable businesswomen owned and operated the business and did it so well that they were awarded four of the six contracts in the Detroit Dam Project, serving as a modern day 'pony express,' delivering replacement parts, tools, materials and machinery over the duration of the project. Shipments would vary from an electronic instrument weighing 1.5 pounds to huge 15-ton pieces of machinery. They provided services from Seattle shippers to the dam-site contractors by having Interstate Freight Lines transfer urgently-needed parts to their trucks 'with a speed that would make even a Wells Fargo circuit rider blush with his inadequacy' as quoted in a Daily Journal of Commerce article published in 1951. The firm was tasked with furnishing parts and materials on split-second schedules where loss of a few hours of time in delivery can run into thousands of dollars of extra cost to the contractors on the job.

Maude Rowley and Lucy Thomas in front of a Helser Bros. truck. *From a* Daily Journal of Commerce *article.*

"When my grandmother had enough of the trucking business, she went into real estate. She became a charter member of the Quota Club for Women Executives and was an active member of the Portland Board of Realtors. She did well for herself and became a leading businesswoman in the Portland area, always impeccably dressed in business suits, hand-tailored by a close friend.

"For me, my grandmother, Lucy Lee, was larger than life. My memories of her were spent watching her sit at her make-up vanity, readying herself for the business day ahead, dabbing on perfume and red lipstick, sliding into patent leather heels and heading out the door, with me by her side. It was an honor to accompany her to her real estate office that was located in the Clackamas Center. The Center had an ice-skating rink and a candy store – which made it double the fun, especially at Christmas time when everything was bathed in twinkling, colorful lights. I distinctly remember her large wooden desk and the crystal prism that sat at the front of the desk, elegantly displaying her name. I knew I wanted to be just like her, someday.

"Sadly, I lost my grandmother when I was 14-years-old, an age when girls need good mentors. While my own mother was a wonderful role model, I was crushed to no longer have my icon in my life. In that short time, however, I emulated many of her qualities that have served me well in my own career as a businesswoman in an industry that is male-dominant.

"When I feel an unprofessional moment about to overtake me, I look at her picture and remind myself that it is always better to exude positivity than to waste energy being negative. It is always better *to step back and exhale than to be reactionary and say words you can't take back. In matters of business, it is the elements of our character that determine our success: integrity, empathy, tenacity and 'piquant-ness' seems to be a good mixture of traits to have.*

"Thank you for inspiring me to reach my dreams, no matter the peaks and valleys, Nama – Lucy Lee."

The Richfield Beacon in Portland

The Sunday *Oregonian* reported in its September 29, 1928 edition, *"In selecting Healy Heights as the site of the gigantic new air beacon for the Northwest, the Richfield Oil Company has given to Portland the distinction of being the largest electric sign in the world. Each letter is 60 feet high, while the entire sign is more than 725 feet long and uses more than 3,000 feet of Claude Neon tubes, giving it a viability of more than 100 miles.*

"The new Richfield Beacon will be officially dedicated tonight, Saturday, September 29th, at 10 p.m. by Mayor George Baker, who will preside at the ceremony. Current will be turned on by telegraph from Kansas City by Major Clarence M. Young, Director of Aeronautics for the Department of Commerce."

On September 30, 1928, an advertisement in the *Morning Oregonian* declared, *"There goes the gong! Now look out your windows, folks, and see the largest electric sign in the world lighted for the first time, exclaimed Mayor Baker through the microphone of radio station KGW."*

The *Oregonian* reported that at *"10:15 o'clock last night, ceremonies dedicating and inaugurating the colossal Richfield air beacon spanning Healy heights"* brought the celebration to a climax.

"...Radio parties of listeners throughout Portland and environs flocked to windows, porches and yards and gazed toward the southwesterly heights to see the unprecedented mass of color, formed by 3,000 feet of the orange-colored lights formed by the neon gas-charged glass tubing, the whole spelling the word 'Richfield.'

"Forests of Oregon were combed for the enormous straight timbers that form the framework supporting the Richfield sign, some of which are 140 feet in length. The background of the letters of glass tubing, is formed by cross pieces of heavy planking, which makes a lattice-work painted a bright orange color to conform to the electrical effect. The present schedule is for the sign to burn nightly from dusk to midnight, but in summer when there is much late touring, the hours probably will be extended."

In the beginning, a few letters to the editor in the *Oregonian* indicated that the blinking orange light on the tower wasn't popular with everyone, but they soon stopped. The July 1, 1932 edition of the *Morning Oregonian*, announced that the world's largest sign, the Richfield sign on Portland Heights, would be relighted.

On July 24, 1932, the Richfield sign on Council Crest was also relit, at the request of the Portland Chamber of Commerce, in order to have the lights flashing for the American Legion Convention.

Francis Pettygrove and Asa Lovejoy's original 1845 townsite plat had just 16 blocks, 200-square-feet in size with 60-foot-wide streets. There were only three north-south streets and nine going east-west. During the 1930s, the growing city of Portland

Aerial view of waterfront area - Portland, Oregon; Steel bridge looking downriver. ©*Thomas Robinson*

Damascus Milk Co. - N.W. 3rd & Hoyt St., Portland, Oregon. ©*Thomas Robinson*

Envoy Apartments - W. 23rd & West Burnside, Portland, Oregon; Kienow Foods, Town House, shopping center, 1952. ©*Thomas Robinson*

Chinatown - N.W. Portland, Oregon; Chinese merchants from all parts of the U.S. are meeting in Portland, 1920s. ©*Thomas Robinson*

Iconic White Stage, Made in Oregon sign, 1975. ©*Thomas Robinson*

"A Darker Portland" - Portland at night - S.W. Broadway from *Oregonian* building; Paramount and Broadway theaters, 1948. ©*Thomas Robinson*

Historic Portland, S.W. Broadway, July 4, 1958. ©*Thomas Robinson*

had absorbed several smaller suburbs, a problem faced by other cities, making the street addresses only usable by renumbering everything. The city was divided into N.E., N.W., S.E. S.W. quadrants. North-south became named streets; east-west were numbered avenues. It also assigned 100 addresses per block. It is one of the few large cities where you can determine where to go by the address. You can spot the N.E and know the numbering will be consistent with where you want to go. A traveler can get on one street and follow it across the city with no name change and he can count on numbered streets being one block apart.

Lewis and Clark College

The Montieth family of Albany, Oregon donated land for the Albany Collegiate Institute founded by the Presbyterian Church in 1867. It was a single building, co-educational school. In 1934-38, it moved to Portland as a junior college. In 1942, the trustees acquired the 137-acre Fir Acres Estate on Palatine Hill in southwest Portland that had been owned by Lloyd Frank of Meier & Frank department stores, and the name of the college was changed to Lewis and Clark College.

The Lewis and Clark School of Law descended from a state law school which moved to the University of Oregon in 1915. Some faculty decided against moving to Eugene and formed the Northwestern College of Law which became affiliated with Lewis and Clark in a new facility in 1967.

Portland During World War II

Although increasing hostilities in the war in Europe led the United States to begin preparing to join the Allies in the 1930s, it was the attack on Pearl Harbor by the Japanese in 1941 that jolted our country into the war.

In February 1942, West Coast citizens of Japanese descent were ordered to evacuation centers to wait until they could be relocated, even if some of them had family serving in our military. The evacuation center in Portland was located at the cow barn at the Exposition center. The Japanese people were transferred from there to other isolated places, often in Eastern Oregon. Those who were removed lost homes, crops, farm animals, property, bank accounts and personal possessions.

The people of Portland went through the same changes as others in Oregon and the rest of the country – food shortages, rationing, air raids, time served in the Civil Air Patrol, etc. In addition, in Portland and Vancouver, Henry J. Kaiser's shipyards employed some 100,000 workers. Men and women worked together to build "Baby Flattops" and "Liberty Ships" for the war effort.

In Portland, the African-American population grew from 2,565 in 1940 to 25,000 in 1944. Newcomers coped with inflated rents, shantytown camps and trailer parks.

In 1942, Edgar Kaiser built Vanport on the south bank of the Columbia. With 35,000 residents, the community was one of the largest towns in Oregon, but Camp Adair to the

One of the internment barracks where citizens of Japanese descent were sent during WWII. *Courtesy of the OSU Special Collections & Archives Commons*

south was even bigger at times.

By 1943, 12,000 women were working in the shipyards and one third of those were mothers. In addition to training women in new skills and paying good wages for the time period, Kaiser recognized some other needs for the women he employed in the work force. He set up a clinic that offered good health care and then went one step farther. He set up childcare centers in two special buildings, one at each shipyard. They had safe play areas inside and out, special child-sized bathrooms, and the children were provided nutritional meals, health care and teachers 24-hours a day so mothers working any shift had access to them. They even offered hot, prepared meals that a mother could purchase at the end of her shift. For many coming out of the Depression, this was a big step toward getting and staying healthy.

Later, industrialist, Henry J. Kaiser, expanded his empire, forming Kaiser Aluminum and Kaiser Steel and organizing Kaiser Permanente Healthcare for his workers and their families. He was the manufacturer of Kaiser-Frazer automobiles through his Kaiser Motors Company. With his wealth, he also set up the Kaiser Family Foundation to address major health care issues facing the U.S. and to work towards developing a global health policy.

KAISERVILLE / VANPORT / VANPORT CITY

Vanport City was built in 1942 on a wetland area between Portland and the Columbia River by Edgar Kaiser. The 640 acres on which it was built was once low-lying farmland.

According to the Museum of the City website:

"In the mid 1800s, the area of today's Vanport Wetlands was a mixture of lakes, sloughs, and marshes. Prior to the 1920s, the largest lake in the area was called Force Lake. The lake was named after George W. Force, an early Portland settler. In 1920, Force Lake was drained to create more farm land. Farming continued on the land until the mid-1960s. Today's maps show Force Lake to be a small lake on the northeast side of the Heron Lakes Golf Course. In the early 1920s the KGW radio tower was built on the property. After the 1948 flood which destroyed the nearby city of Vanport, the area was referred to as the 'radio tower site.' In 1999 the Port of Portland purchased the area to create wetlands as a trade for their filling the wetlands near the Portland International Airport..."

When the Henry Kaiser shipyard began increasing its production of ships for World War II, the 100,000 workers who worked there needed somewhere to live. There was a housing shortage, so Kaiser obtained the property and within 10 months had built a town of 35,000 people, almost half of them blacks and other minorities. It was built on the floodplain of the Columbia River and was meant to be protected by levees and dikes.

The newly-built town soon had a library, post office, police station, several fire stations, an infirmary, businesses of all kinds, five elementary schools and a 750-seat movie theater. After the war, Vanport College was created to provide the returning veterans with educational benefits as part of the G.I. Bill.

On Memorial Day, May 30, 1948, it was all washed away when 200-feet of dikes along the river gave way after the Columbia River rose 15-feet above flood stage. It destroyed in one day what had taken less than a year to build. Fifteen people were killed.

Aerial view of the Vanport flood waters, looking west from N. Denver Avenue, 1948. *Courtesy of the City of Portland Archives*

Portland State College/University

Unlike the other state universities, Portland State did not exist prior to 1946. It began as the Vanport Extension Center at Vanport to meet the needs of returning veterans. Then it was soon the Vanport College. It grew so fast that it took up any unoccupied space available. It was destroyed in the Vanport flood and was forced to move to Grant High School in the summer of 1948. Soon, it occupied converted buildings at the Oregon Shipyards, earning the nickname of the "U at the Slough."

In 1953, it moved to downtown Portland, occupying the former Lincoln High School.

In 1955, after moving to yet another area, and as it grew into a four-year, degree-grant-

Aftermath of the 1948 Vanport flood. *Courtesy of the City of Portland Archives*

ing institution, it was renamed Portland State College. The tenacity and growth that it continued to show earned the school its second nickname of "The College that Wouldn't Die."

Masters-level programs were added beginning in 1961 and doctoral programs in 1968. In 1969, the Oregon State System of Higher Education designated it Portland State University.

The Jantzen Story

In 1910, three friends, John Zehntbauer, his brother, Roy, and Carl Jantzen, a Danish emigrant, founded the Portland Knitting Company. They began producing heavy woolen sweaters, hosiery and gloves which they retailed from their own store at S.W. 2nd and Alder Streets.

In 1913, Carl Jantzen developed a special lightweight rib stitch for sweater cuffs and when he showed it to a fellow rowing-club member, the man asked if a swimming suit could be made from the same material. It was the beginning of their success story. By 1915, the company was the leader in a new and expanding market of knitted swimwear.

In 1918, the company changed its name to Jantzen Knitting Mills and introduced the diving girl in a red swimsuit as a logo. It became famous across the country and was synonymous for fashionable swimwear.

From *Oregon, the End of the Trail*, a project published in 1940 on the Jantzen Knitting Mills:

"The knitting department has seventy-five machines, each with about 1,500 needles. Following the knitting, the fabric is shrunk, cut into shape by electric cutting machines, and sewed on power-driven machines. In its Portland mill, the company employs 700 workers. The buildings are modern, well-lighted and ventilated, and the grounds beautifully landscaped."

The company grew and later introduced sweaters, and then sportswear. As it grew and its fame spread, a separate business venture got underway that grew and flourished.

On May 26, 1928, Jantzen Beach Amusement Center on Hayden Island opened and thrilled Portland for more than four decades.

A popular local joke was that Jantzen Knitting had grown so large, it needed a place to hold its picnics.

Among the featured elements was the

The Jantzen Knitting Mill, ca 1940s. *Courtesy of the OSU Special Collections & Archives Commons,*

The Big Dipper roller coaster at Jantzen Beach Park. *Courtesy of Steve Kenney (pdxhistory.com)*

swimming pool complex – two 500,000 gallon Olympic-size pools and a kids' wading pool about a fourth the size. Many times, the complex had up to 4,000 swimmers on a hot day.

The amusement park had a beautiful carousel, said to be the largest ever built, the Big Dipper Roller Coaster, a bumper car ride, the very popular fun house and tunnel of love and a midway with cotton candy and carnival-type games of chance among so many other features that provided fond memories for those of us lucky enough to partake in them.

For many, the highlight was a large, big-band-era ballroom. Nearly every important big band in the country played there at least once. As a nursing student at the time, Jo-Brew danced to the band of Charlie Barnett in that ballroom.

The ballroom, funhouse, roller coaster and all of the games are gone now. In their place is a large and popular shopping mall which still houses the popular merry-go-round near the food court.

"The Coney Island of the West" by Clara Shepard, *The Spectator*, July 1942:

"*Portlanders with a merry-making mood coming on, always head toward Jantzen Beach park on the Columbia River. While there are no orange trees around it... it has the biggest area of improved amusement park facilities (under one ownership) in America. (O.K., Coney Island is made up of many parks...lumped into one.) It is the picnic place par excellence; it really has what it takes for family entertaining en masse; and there are three special private areas for groups, with their own softball grounds and horseshoe courts.*

"*There are 16 kinds of ways to snap one groggy by rides at Jantzen Beach. There is the giant dipper with its soul-wrecking and perfectly safe...crashes; the loop-o-plane where one is at the mercy of the single arm...and the rollo-plane which adds the final ga-ga trick of turning while looping; there are the buzzer, the scooter, the giant swing...thrills and chills and spills.*

"*Then, as one gradually returns to earth and sanity, there is the boat ride through a dark tunnel where the bars to boy-meets-girl are entirely let down; and the pastoral boat ride through the park designed for grandpa and little Sally.*

"*There is the Ferris wheel offering its private seat in the sky; the merry-go-round* decked with tinsel which suddenly takes on the gold of "really true" right before one's eyes.

"There is the newest thing in anti-aircraft guns (and any small boy in town can explain that beam of light principle)...and the strength testers and love meters in the penny arcade.

"If a young man about town says dancin' to a girl, he might just as well say Jantzen Beach at the same time...for they are synonymous as far as she is concerned. The golden canopied ballroom features the sweetest swing in the county every night of the park's season, with a parade of 'big name' dance bands moving across its boards... in engagements of a night to a fortnight. The sixth season of Dad Watson's calling off old time square dances is in full swing. The old timers know that he holds forth every Sunday afternoon.

"And anybody could be suited with a swim (or for a swim) at Jantzen. There are four crystal-clear, outdoor swimming pools... two for diving and swimming, and two for the small fry to wade in. There is complete natatorium service; the water is tempered; the diving equipment is all of the most modern type; there is a life guard on duty all the time that the pools are being used..."

"Merry-go-rounds, Rollercoasters and Daddy" by Margie Buell McNutt

"Daddy (Leslie W. Buell) began his career at Janzten Beach Amusement Park/ Hayden Island Corporation in 1962. Prior to that, he was the administrator for the Riverdale School District in Portland. In the Riverdale area there were many successful people; among them was John Zentbauer, founder of Jantzen Knitting in Portland. Mr. Zehntbauer and his brother had established the amusement park with its two Olympic-size swimming pools to promote the clothing business's swimwear line and he offered Daddy a position with their company.

Daddy decided to make the transition in order to take advantage of the opportunity to develop Hayden Island where Jantzen Beach was located. Over the years, he enlarged the island by dredging the Columbia River, eventually connecting Tomahawk Island with Hayden.

"I was 11 when Daddy went to Jantzen Beach. It was an exciting time, having my father running an amusement park! Along with the excitement came summer jobs for my two older sisters, Jeanie and Maridi, and me. My first job was working in the office running the change machine, rolling coins. I soon was sent out into the park to sell ride tickets or run the miniature golf and balloon stand.

As the boss's daughters, we were protected by the security and carnival workers. Many of the carnival workers also had careers as carnival entertainers. There was Eddie who could throw his voice and make anything sound like it was talking. One of his claims to fame was marrying his wife in a block of ice in an old time carnival show!

"One of my fondest memories of that time was spending my entire lunch hours on the Big Dipper, a wooden roller coaster that was a mile long! Another is of the carousel. The famous carousel carver by the name of C.W. Parker had made it for the World's Fair in the early 1900s. Each horse was a work of art! For my fortieth birthday, Mom and Daddy gave me a horse *from that carousel. It is now a sentimental treasure in our home.*

"In 1970, the park was torn down to develop Jantzen Beach Shopping Center. Because the 'Island' was across the river from Washington, many came into Oregon to shop to avoid the sales tax. Over the next few years, condos, motels, apartment buildings and more were built. As he ran out of room on the Island, Daddy set his sights on Portland Meadows and in later years began building shopping centers throughout the state along with a few high-rise buildings in downtown Portland.

"Daddy built up stock in Hayden Island, buying up shares as they became available, and he soon became the majority stockholder. Over the years, the stock went public, dividing several times until Hillman Corporation out of Pennsylvania purchased the business, retaining Daddy as CEO until 1990.

"After he retired, Daddy joined the Board of Directors for Oaks Park on the east side of the Willamette River. The Oaks was owned by a trust for Oregon State College and run as a non-profit. Daddy retained that position until his death in 2012.

"The development of Hayden Island was a boon to North Portland, creating jobs and an inclusive environment for people to live. There was a Safeway store, shopping center, bowling alley, movie theater, marina, hotels, houseboats, condominiums and apartments.

"The amusement park was long gone but the I-5 corridor benefited by all that replaced it.

"And the young girls who spent their lunch hours riding merry-go-rounds and roller coasters are very proud of the father who had a major part in making it all happen."

A combination of events served to doom the park; an accidental death on the roller coaster and the ensuing court battle; then the fun house and tunnel of love caught fire and burned. Two consecutive years of cool, wet summers kept swimmers out of the pools and finally, the 1969 planned freeway expansion put the finishing touches to Jantzen Beach Park. But, none of these events will ever erase the wonderful memories of the girls and boys

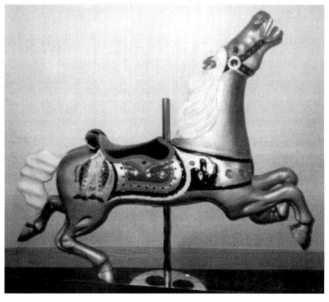

Margie McNutt's 40th birthday present... an original C.W. Parker carousel horse from the original Jantzen Beach carousel. *Courtesy of Margie Buell McNutt*

who had the privilege to experience its magic.

Portland, with its seven hills, a seaport at the confluence of the Willamette River with the Columbia, a mix of old and new businesses, old and new settlers, innovation next to tradition, millionaires and paupers, cozy neighborhoods and large industries, all stirred together in one sprawling center is a fitting place for Oregon's two main streets, Highway 99 E (Union Avenue, now Martin Luther King Avenue) and Highway 99W (Interstate Ave) to come together again. They do – almost at the Columbia River and the Interstate Bridge, just past where Jantzen Beach Amusement Park was on the west and Portland Meadows Race Track is on the east. The traffic is heavy enough, as the two states connect, that a driver going on to the Interstate Bridge won't be watching the scenery – but, if he or she could, there would be a lot to see with ships beneath, airplanes above and history spread on either side.

The lighthouse at the junction of the Columbia and Willamette Rivers, 1911. *Courtesy of the OSU Special Collections & Archives Commons*

Traveling the Pacific Highway in 1913 from North to South

From *The Sunday Oregonian*, Portland, October 19, 1913

"Building a Model Highway. Pacific Highway in Oregon is to be Ideal Course for Commerce & Tourists!" proclaimed a major article in *The Sunday Oregonian*, Portland, October 19, 1913.

These were the headlines from the first part of a series of articles on the Pacific Highway in Oregon, printed in *The Sunday Oregonian* that year. It was an exciting prospect and one with a lot of support from the whole state.

"...The picturesque beauty of the Willamette Valley, the quaintness of Oregon forests and the ruggedness of Southern Oregon mountains are to be exhibited to the world by way of a model highway. The wealth in farm, forest and mining products in the vast stretch of country between the Washington and California lines west of the Sierra Nevadas is to drain into Portland markets over a highway free from heavy grades and attractive for its sustainability and excellence."

The articles discussed the "common-cause" work being done by the various counties and communities in Oregon to complete a road from the Canadian border to Mexico as a model for Washington and California to follow.

The imminent completion of the Panama Canal, which officially opened on August 15, 1914 – only months away – was expected to bring in thousands of "homeseekers" to Oregon.

"...As the Pacific Highway stands today, it can be coursed by automobile or team from Portland to the California line, but the trip is not a pleasant one, owing to the fact that for many miles the road has not been improved further than for use as a mere rural route from farming communities to small settlements.

"Oregon probably is busier on the highway than any of the other states interested, which is taken as an indication that the people here realize more fully than

do the people elsewhere the benefits and advantages to be derived."

The Interstate Bridge between Washington and Oregon was the beginning point at the north section of the new highway. The *Sunday Oregonian* article takes us in the north-to-south journey of the new road as opposed to our south-to-north layout, but it gives some insightful observations as to the conditions and expectations in 1913.

The highway *"...extends over the paved arterial streets of the East Side into the business heart of Portland.*

"It then proceeds on the West Side, down the Whitehouse Road through Multnomah County to Oswego.

"...Leaving Multnomah County near Oswego, the road proceeds south and east to Oregon City. Proceeding south, the road has been made good for two miles where it strikes a stretch of rough road. From Canby, near this point to the Marion County line near Aurora, the highway is in good condition... Towns in Clackamas County where the Pacific Highway improvement fever is strong are New Era, Canby, Barlow and Aurora."

Improvements in Marion County, however, were not going quite as well as in other counties. At the time the article was written the county was hoping to pass a tax levy.

"...Between Aurora and Salem, the highway passes through Hubbard, Woodburn, Gervais, Brooks and Chemawa.

"...From Salem, the highway leads south [the article says "north"], encountering in one place a 10% grade and in a number of places, bad stretches of road.

"Leaving Marion County, the road enters Linn County at the south end of the bridge across the Santiam River at Jefferson and follows south to Albany. This portion has been improved considerably. Passing through Albany, where the highway is much favored as an arterial, it leads south in a somewhat irregular course to Eugene. Between these two cities, it passes through Tangent, Shedd's, Halsey, Harrisburg and Junction City. As the main-traveled highway of Linn County, the road is receiving a great deal of attention from the road-building era. It is said that Linn County will be well toward the top of the list of counties finally completing the highway through the state, a large amount of work already having been done, and much more being contemplated year by year until the highway is made the best road in the county.

"Leaving Linn County by way of a ferry over the Willamette River at Harrisburg, the highway passes into Lane County, proceeding south to Eugene with only here and there a place which is in poor repair. The city of Eugene has taken pride in improving the highway, and Lane County has done its share of improvements. The road is now in fairly good shape from Eugene southward to Drain, passing through Goshen, Creswell, Walker, Saginaw, Cottage Grove, Latham and Divide.

"...At Divide, the road passes into Douglas County and continues south by west to Drain, with comparatively good going a great part of the distance. Passing through Drain, the road continues on through Yoncalla, Oakland, Sutherlin, Wilbur, Winchester and Edenbower to

Roseburg. From there it goes through to the Josephine County line."

In Douglas County, the article discusses a couple of "serious problems" along the route that needed special attention... namely the Pass Creek Canyon and the Cow Creek Canyon areas. Because of the terrain the road went through, the road-building process met with exceeding difficult problems despite its "beautiful mountain scenery."

"...For many years, tourists complained of the Pass Creek road and, upon numerous occasions, warnings were issued in the newspapers against the use of the road by tourists. Realising the monetary value of tourist traffic, the county got busy... It was decided to build a permanent road inasmuch as the course was a part of the Pacific Highway... a class A macadam road second, probably to none in the state."

The road was about four miles long and was consider the main link between Douglas County and Lane County.

The other major problem at Cow Creek Canyon, which is located between Canyonville and Glendale, was that a much longer route was considered to be at that time an easier solution.

"...There is plenty of rock available while the surface is of rock formation and furnishes an excellent foundation."

"...In Josephine County, improvements are of a general nature. The highway enters the county seven miles southeast of Grants Pass and follows a winding course to Grants Pass. There are few hills and the road is in good shape, so the drive can be made in about 20 minutes. From Grants Pass, the road goes to Wolf Creek, a distance of about 30 miles over the mountains. This part of the road is on a good base, and is in good condition most of the way. The grade out of Grave Creek, about 17 miles from here, is short, about a quarter of a mile in length, and comparatively smooth. From Grave Creek to Wolf Creek, the road is in good condition for automobiles, but will need some attention as to grade. At Wolf Creek, the road leads over a mountain with a steep grade with no turnouts. The hill is about a mile in length and is dangerous. It is proposed to improve this by changing the course when practical."

The October 19, 1913 article in the *Sunday Oregonian* ended at this point, but there was more to come in the 2-part series which tells about the highway's route through Jackson County, beginning at the top of the Siskiyous – reversing directions from south to north. On November 30, 1913, the story resumed:

"Pacific Highway Will Take This Course Through Stately Siskiyous. Jackson County Will Spend Half Million on Great Scenic Route:

"MEDFORD, Or. Nov. 28 – A graceful, hard-surfaced road leading down through the picturesque scenery of Southern Oregon from the dizzy heights of the Siskiyous to the gradeur of the scenic forests and valleys is to be Jackson County's contribution to the Pacific Highway in Oregon. Work is to commence at once and is to be finished by June 1, 1915. The road in Jackson County will be the model for the rest of Oregon and the other states coursed by

the highway to follow.

"For two miles the new road will follow in a winding course the crest of the Siskiyous. For many miles it will follow the easiest grades down through the hills to the valleys rich in scenic wonders, opportunities and activity. At the top of the Siskiyous, 5000 feet in the air, the road with a foundation of concrete will carry the traveler into the clouds. On the one side of the course will be the beautiful Rogue River Valley, Mount Pitt and Southern Oregon Valleys in full view in clear weather. On the other will be the expansive Siskiyou County with Mount Shasta looming in the background.

"...In selecting the route where two ways were found to be equally safe and equally short, the more scenic has been chosen so that not only will this new highway offer the first easy and convenient route ever built between California and Oregon, but it will in itself attract hundreds of tourists who are interested in beautiful country and aspiring views.

"...There will be three concrete bridges constructed and about 500 concrete culverts. A novel feature will be a complete loop where the highway will go over the railroad, turn a circle and pass under itself. A 60 foot span concrete bridge will be constructed at this point."

Thank you for making the trip with us!

OREGON'S MAIN STREET: U.S. Highway 99
"The Folk History"

BIBLIOGRAPHY

Attwood, Kay; *Chaining Oregon; Surveying the Public Lands of the Pacific Northwest, 1851-1855.* McDonald & Woodward Publishing Company, 2008.

Bancroft, Hubert Howe; *The Works of Hubert Howe Bancroft, Volume XXX:"History of Oregon*, Volume II. San Francisco, California: The History Company, 1888

Barclay, Janice; *Remembering Camp Adair*. Unpublished Manuscript for a class at Oregon State University Mini College; Summer 1995

Barker, Michael J.; *My Time in Paradise*. Eugene, OR: *Groundwaters* Publishing, LLC, expected publication, 2015.

Barker, Michael J.; *Out of Oregon: Logging, Lies and Poetry*. Eugene, OR: Dunlogin Enterprises. 2003

Barrett, Carol; *As It Was*. Ashland, OR: Jefferson Public Radio, 1998

Bartley, Ron; "Canyonville Mail Plane Crash;" *Pioneer Days in the South Umpqua Valley*. Vol. 26, 1992

Barton, Lois, Ed.; *One Woman's West*. Eugene, OR: Spencer Butte Press, 1997.

Battaile, Connie Hopkins; *The Oregon Book Information A to Z*. Newport, OR: Saddle Mountain Press, 1998

Baum, Gerald; "Seely Hall," *Southern Oregon Heritage Today*. Spring 2007, Vol. 9 No. 2

Beckham, Stephen Dow; *Land of the Umpquas; A History of Douglas County, Oregon.* Douglas County Commissioners, 1986

Bolz, Eleanor; "Main Street, Phoenix Over The Years," *The Gasburg Gazette*, Phoenix, OR, February 2006

Booth, R.A. "History of Umpqua Academy," *Oregon Historical Quarterly*, March 1918

Bottenberg, Ray and Jeanna; *Images of America: Vanishing Portland*. Charleston SC: Arcadia Publishing, 2008

Brady, Marie; Johns, Jennene; "Azalea Telephone Exchange," *Pioneer Days in the South Umpqua Valley*. 1996, Vol. 29, p. 40

Brown, Elizabeth Esson; "*History of the Sam Brown House*," Marion County Historical Society Vol 1. p.6-8

Bureau of Land Management; "O&C Sustained Yield Act: the Law, the Land, the Legacy, 1937-1987.

Carey, Charles Henry; *History of Oregon*, Chicago-Portland: The Pioneer Historical Publishing Company,1922

Chandler, Stephen; "Cow Creek Valley: from Mi-wa-leta to New Odessa," *The Drain Enterprise*, Drain, OR, 1981

City of Eugene Landmark Application; Brunner-Schmitz House

Claflin, Dorothy; "Phoenix, Oregon 1950s," *The Gasburg Gazette*, Phoenix, OR, February 2006

Corning, Howard McKinley; *Willamette Landings*. Oregon Historical Society, 1947, 2004

Corning, Howard McKinley; *Dictionary of Oregon History*. Hillsboro, OR: Binford & Mort Publishing, 1956, 1989

Cornutt, John M.; *Cow Creek Valley Memories: the Early Settlers of Riddle, Oregon*. Eugene, OR: Industrial Publishing Co., 1971

Culp, Edwin D.; *Early Oregon Days*. Caldwell, ID: The Caxton Printers, LTD., 1997

Deatherage, Curt; "It Happened in Oregon," *Creswell Chronicle*, Thursday, June 16, 2011, p. 11

DeCosta, Stephen; "Joseph Stewart: Father of the Commercial Fruit Industry in the Rogue Valley," *Southern Oregon Heritage Today*, June 2003, Vol. 5 No. 6

Dietz, Diane, "And Still Soaring." *Register-Guard*, Eugene, OR, 2013

Dietz, Diane, "Sweet Memories: The Brunner Fruit Dryer." *Register-Guard*, Eugene, OR, 2012

Dole, Phil; "Farmhouses and Barns of the Willamette Valley," in *Space, Style and Structure: Building in Northwest America*, 78-140. Portland, OR, 1974

Douglas County Museum; *Images of America: Land of the Umpqua*. Charleston SC: Arcadia Publishing, 2011, p. 21-23

Dresbeck, Rachel; "The Willamette River Flood." *Oregon Disasters: True Stories of Tragedy and Survival*, Guilford, Connecticut: Insiders' Guide, 2006

Ellis, Lucia; *Wild Water: The Story of the Far West's Great Christmas Week Floods*. Portland, Oregon: Overland West Press, 1965

Engeman, Richard H.; *the Oregon Companion*. Portland, OR: Timber Press, 2009

Fagan, David D.; *The History of Benton County, Oregon: Including its Geology, Topography, Soil and Productions*; 1885.

Fattig, Paul; "Fond Memories of the Farm;" *Medford Mail Tribune*. November 6, 2011

Fattig, Paul; "Life on the Farm," *Medford Mail Tribune*. November 7, 2011

Favrholdt, Visti; *Junction City to Denmark, a Boyhood Journey*. Danish American Society, 1996

Ferguson, Bruce; "Biographical Sketch," *Pioneer Days in the South Umpqua Valley*. 1994, Vol. 27, p. 14-18

Fortt, Inez; "From Sacramento to Portland in Seven Days. *Lane County Historian*. Eugene, Oregon: Lane County Historical Society, Vol XVI, No. 1, 1971

Friedman, Ralph; *In Search of Western Oregon* (2nd ed.). Caldwell, Idaho: The Caxton Printers, Ltd, p. 516, 1990. ISBN 0-87004-332-3.

Fuller, Tom; Ayre, Art; *Oregon at Work 1859-2009*. Portland, OR: Ooligan Press, 2009

Fuller, Tom; Van Heukelem, Christy; Mission Mill Museum; *Images of America: Salem*. Charleston SC: Arcadia Publishing, 2009

Gaston, Joseph; *The Centennial History of Oregon 1811-1912*, page 510

Gatke, Robert M, and Robert D. Gregg; *Chronicles of Willamette*. Portland, Oregon: Binfords & Mort, 1943

Genaw, Linda Morehouse; *Gold Hill and its Neighbors along the River*. 1988

Guyer, R.J.; *Douglas County Chronicles; History from the Land of One Hundred Valleys*; American Chronicles, A History Press Series, 2013

Hall, John; "Fifty Years by the Side of the Road," *Pioneer Days in the South Umpqua Valley*. 1978, Vol. 11, p. 31

Hallman, Tom, Jr.; "A Barn Bequeathed to an Oregon Cat Will Have a 2nd Life as Community Hall in Tangent," *The Oregonian* on October 05, 2012

Hart, Deanna Hart; "Going to the next level," *American City and County Magazine*, June 2008

Hartley, Laura; "Tribute to Dr. Robert Kinoshita," *Pioneer Days in the South Umpqua Valley*. 2001, Vol. 34

Hauser, Susan; "Oregon City – The town at the end of the Oregon Trail is still a destination for travelers." *VIA*, the bimonthly travel magazine of the California State Automobile Association, 2004

Holmes, Kenneth; *Ewing Young: Master Trapper*. Portland, Oregon: Binsford & Mort, 1967

Horner, John B.; *Oregon: Her History, Her Great Men, Her Literature*. Portland, Oregon: The J.K. Gill Company, 1921

Hussey, John A.; *Champoeg: Place of Transition, A Disputed History*. Oregon Historical Society, 1967

Jackson, Kerby, editor; "Female Miners in Southern Oregon." *Oregon Gold: Finding Gold in Oregon. Mining Review*, May 1904. Web. 16 Apr. 2014. "Medford as a Mining Center." Jefferson Mining District. Feb. 1912. Web. 16 Apr. 2014.

John, Finn, J.D.; "Offbeat Oregon History." *Creswell Chronicle*, Thursday, Feb. 14, 2011, p. 8

Johns, Jennene; "Azalea," *Pioneer Days in the South Umpqua Valley*. 1996, Vol. 29

Jonasson, Jonas A.; *Bricks Without Straw: The Story of Linfield College*. Caxton Printers, 1938

Keefer, Bob; *Register-Guard*, January 20, 2013

Kinoshita, Richard; "Hey Doc, Remember Me?" *Pioneer Days in the South Umpqua Valley*. 2002, Vol. 35

Klooster, Karl; *Round the Roses: Portland Past Perspectives.* Portland, OR: Karl Klooster, 1987

Kramer, George & Chappel, Jill A.; *Historic Resources Survey and Inventory of Central Business District"* The City of Grants Pass, 1992

Kravets, David; "May 5, 1945: Japanese Balloon Bomb Kills 6 in Oregon." Wired.com, May 5, 2010

Kreisman, Arthur; *Remembering: A History of Southern Oregon University*. Eugene, OR: University of Oregon Press, 2002

Lane County Historical Society; *Lane County Historian*, Vol X, No. 2, 1965

Lang, H.O., Editor; *The History of the Willamette Valley*. Portland Oregon: Himes & Lang Publishers, 1885

Lansing, Ronald B.; *Nimrod: Courts, Claims, and Killing on the Oregon Frontier.* Pullman, WA: Washington State University Press, 2005

Livingston, Jill; *That Ribbon of Highway III: Highway 99 Through the Pacific Northwest.* Klamath River, CA: Living Gold Press, 2003

Lovelace, Anna McKirdy; *Annie's Story: Life in Early 20th Century Western Oregon*. Grants Pass, OR: Sisters Publishing, 2000

Lowell, Regina; "Excerpts from Memories of Leroy (Bud) Lowell," *Pioneer Days in the South Umpqua Valley*. 1994, Vol. 27, p. 23

Lowry, Robert, Munford, Kenneth and Moore, Harriet; *Railroading in the Lower Willamette Valley*, originally published in the Horner Museum Tour Guide Series, 1979

Mangold, Scott; *Tragedy at Southern Oregon Tunnel 13*, History Press, 2013

Marschner, Janice; *Oregon 1859; A Snapshot in Time*. Portland, OR: The Timber Press, 2008

Mather, Ruth E. & Boswell, F.E.; *Vigilante Victims: Montana's 1864 Hanging Spree.* Oklahoma City, OK: History West Publishing Co., 1991

McArthur, Lewis A.; *Oregon Geographic Names - Seventh Edition*. Portland, Oregon: Oregon Historical Society Press, 2003

McArthur, Lewis; *Oregon Geographic Names - Fifth Edition: Western Imprint*. Press of the Oregon Historical Society, 1982

McClintock, Thomas C.; "Henderson Luelling, Seth Lewelling and the Birth of the Pacific Coast Fruit Industry," Oregon Historical Quarterly 60, No. 2, June 1967

McIntyre, Ann (Martin), Ed.; *Memories of Growing up in Ashland, Class of 1958*. 2008

McLane, Larry L.; *First There Was Twogood: A Pictorial History of Northern Josephine County*. Sexton Enterprises, 1995

Metzler, Ken, Ed.; *Yesterday's Adventure: A Photographic History of Lane County, Oregon*. Eugene, OR: Lane County Historical Society, 1998

Miller, Bill; "Fourteen Miles of Trouble." *Medford Mail Tribune*, September 19, 2010, p. 8A

Mills, Randall V.; *Sternwheelers up Columbia – A Century of Steamboating in the Oregon Country*. University of Nebraska, Lincoln, NE. (1977 reprint of 1947 ed.)

Moore, Lucia W.; McCornack, Nina W.; McCready, Gladys W.; *The Story of Eugene 1846-1946*. New York: Stratford House, 1949; Eugene, OR: Lane County Historical Society, 1995.

Moulton, Larry; *History of Douglas County Sawmills*, unpublished manuscript

Mount Hood Territory History, Museums, Historic Sites and Transportation. Clackamas County Tourism Development Council, 2006

Munford, Kenneth; *Pioneer Trails from Benton to Douglas Counties. Horner Museum Tour Guide Series, 1982*

Nash, Tom, Scofield, Twilo; *The Well-Traveled Casket: A Collection of Oregon Folklife.* Salt Lake City: University of Utah Press, 1992.

Newton, Sidney W.; *Early History of Independence, Oregon*, 1971

Nichols, Jim and Mildred; "Ranching in Riddle."*Pioneer Days in the South Umpqua Valley*. 2003, Vol. 36, p. 9

Norman, James, etc.; *Oregon Main Street: A Rephotographic Survey.* Oregon Historical Society Press, 1994

O'Donnell, Terrance; Vaughan, Thomas; *Portland: An Informal History & Guide.* Oregon Historical Society, 1984

O'Harra, Marjorie Lutz; *Ashland: the First 130 Years.* Southern Oregon Historical Society, 1981

ODOT History Committee; *Oregon on the Move: A History of Oregon's Transportation Systems.* 2009

Oregon Pacific Highway Association; *Drive 99 in Oregon: A Travelogue of the Oregon Pacific Highway (U.S. Highway 99) with a Directory of Accommodations and Service.* Published sometime between 1926 and 1939.

Oregon City Municipal Elevator; End of the Oregon Trail Interpretive Center, 2006

Paul, Alex; "Morse Bros. Provided Rock-solid Foundation." *Albany Democrat-Herald*, December 15, 2013.

Pintarich, Dick; *Great and Minor Moments in Oregon History.* New Oregon Publishers, Inc., 2003, 2008.

Pioneer Heritage - Linfield College. Archived from the original on August 1, 2008.

Plude, Betty Chapman; *Columbus Day Storm, 1962: Memories.* 2012, p. 212-214

Polk County Museum Association; *Camp Adair Memories: 1941-1993,Volume II.* Dallas, OR, 1993

Polk County Historical Society; *Camp Adair, World War II: Volume I.* Polk County Museum Association, 1992

Polk County Historical Society; *History of Polk County Oregon*, 1987

Portrait and Biographical Record of Western Oregon. Chicago: Chapman Publishing Co., 1904

Portrait and Biographical Record of the Willamette Valley, Oregon. Chicago: Chapman Publishing Co., 1903

Proctor, Virginia; "Dedication of the South Douglas Community Building." *Pioneer Days in the South Umpqua Valley.* 1997, Vol. 30, p. 10-13

Proctor, Bob and Virginia; "Twentieth Century Man ...Oregon Style." *Pioneer Days in the South Umpqua Valley.* 1997, Vol. 30, p. 25-31

Pugh, Lance; "Omar's: Ashland's Best Secret Revealed." *Ashland Daily Tidings*, Monday, May 16, 2005

Register-Guard; *Looking Back. Lane County: A Pictorial Retrospective of Lane County, Oregon, the Early Years: Mid-1800s to 1939.* 2005

Robinson, Wayne & Maybell, *Two Teachers Wore A Dozen Hats*; An unpublished manuscript.

Rosecrans, Charles E.; *the Gold Hill Cement Plant.* 1997

Ross, George W.; Campbell, Joan; Wilson, Sandra; *the Blue Valley: a History of Creswell.* Creswell, OR: Creswell Area Historical Society, 1993, 2004

Rowles, Genevieve; Christianson, Alice; *Slabtown... the Other Cottage Grove.* Cottage Grove Historical Society, 2010

Shannon, Red; "Triumph and Tragedy: Where Heroes Are Forged." *Bleacher Report, Gonzaga Newsletter* (http://bleacherreport.com/articles/279848-Triumph-and-tragedy-where-heroes-are-forged)

Sherman, Barbara; "Nearing the Century Mark, Curtis Tigard Reflects on His Namesake City". *The Times*, 2009

Siskiyou Pioneers: Siskiyou County, California 1885 Directory

Smith, John B.; "Excerpts from the Way it Was." *Pioneer Days in the South Umpqua Valley*. 1994, Vol. 27, p. 19-21

Sol, Ilana; "On Paper Wings." Documentary Film, http://www.onpaperwingsthemovie.com, 2008

Staff; "Ford's Restaurant," *Pioneer Days in the South Umpqua Valley*. 2003, Vol. 36, p. 20-21

Starr, Frank W.; "Myrtle Creek Fire Department," *Pioneer Days in the South Umpqua Valley*. 1993, Vol. 26

Strobridge, Elaine M.; "Founding to Boom Days." *Pioneer Days in the South Umpqua Valley*. 1993, Vol. 26, p. 1-8

Sullivan, William L.; *Oregon's Greatest Natural Disasters*. Eugene, OR: Navillus Press, 2008

Sund, Cheryl Martin; *Images of America: Rogue River*. Charleston SC: Arcadia Publishing, 2009

Suver, Oregon; *Inventory of Historic Properties Historic Resource Survey Form* Polk County. Oregon State Historic Preservation Office.

Swett, Theodore M.; "New Odessa Colony," Oregon Historical Society's Oregon History Project, February 2014

The Rogue River Valley, Southern Oregon; Ashland, OR: *Ashland Tidings* Newspaper and Job Printing Office, 1885

Timmen, Fritz; *Blow for the Landing – A Hundred Years of Steam Navigation on the Waters of the West*. Caldwell, ID: Caxton Printers, 1973

Toye, Donald C.; "Mexia's Pie Shop," *Pioneer Days in the South Umpqua Valley*. 2002, Vol. 35, p. 27

Truwe, Ben; Southern Oregon Media Group; Southern Oregon Historical; *Jackson County: Looking Back: The Early Years 1800s Through 1939*. 2011

Tweedt, Bess; *Historic Harrisburg: A Little Town on the Willamette River*. Eugene, OR, 1994; 2nd Edition. Harrisburg Historical Museum, 2012

Ulven, Leslie Carol; *On the Road of a Thousand Wonders; The History of Hubbard, Oregon*, 1991

Unknown; "Canyonville 1922," *Pioneer Days in the South Umpqua Valley*. 2008, Vol. 41, p. 36

Unknown; "The Alpine Lodge," *Pioneer Days in the South Umpqua Valley*. 1992 Vol. 25, p. 23

Van Orden, Linda; *Junction City, Lane County, Oregon: A Compiled History*. 1991, 1999, 2006

Waddle, Susan; "Emergency Landing Strips in Douglas County," *Pioneer Days in the South Umpqua Valley*, 2002, Vol. 35, p. 24

Waldron, Sue; *Siskiyou Mountain Toll Road: Passing Through the Gap*. Southern Oregon Historical Society #2574, 1991

Walling, A.G.; *Illustrated History of Lane County, Oregon*. Portland, Oregon, 1884.

Walling, A.G.; *History of Southern Oregon, Comprising Jackson, Josephine, Douglas, Curry and Coos Counties Compiled from the Most Authentic Sources*. Portland, OR: A.G. Walling, 1884

Weich, Bob; "A Brief Introduction to the Civilian Conservation Corps," *Pioneer Days in the South Umpqua Valley*. (From Notes by Bob Weich and the 1939 Annual of the Medford District, North Corps Area. CCC) 1997, Vol. 30, p. 26-31

Weich, Bob; "Fond Memories," *Pioneer Days in the South Umpqua Valley*. 2002, Vol. 35, p. 31

Westbrook, Vera; "A Family Tradition Deserving Recognition." *River Road/Santa Clara Tribune*, Dec. 1, 2010

Wilde, Chris T.; *Early Days of Junction City, Oregon*. 1978

Will, Clark Moor; *The Clark Moor Will Papers, 1877 to 1981*. Special Collections and University Archives, University of Oregon Libraries,

Winkler, Allan M.; *Home Front USA: America During World War II*. Arlington Heights, IL: Harlan Davidson, Inc., 1986

Workers of the Writers' Program; *Oregon End of the Trail, 1940*. American Guide Series, Work Projects Administration in the State of Oregon. Portland: Oregon State Board of Control, 1940; Portland, OR: Binfords & Mort Publishers, 1951

Wright, Jan; *Images of America: Talent*. Charleston SC: Arcadia Publishing, 2009

OREGON'S MAIN STREET: U.S. Highway 99
"The Folk History"

WEBLIOGRAPHY

(This listing is not meant to be comprehensive. It does not include a complete compilation of web sources used in this book, but is only meant to recognize some of our on-line resources as we have documented them.)

Albany, Oregon: http://www.el.com/to/albany/; http://web.archive.org/web/20070411003443/ http://www.ci.albany.or.us/about/history-hubcity.php; http://www.cityofalbany.net; http://www.oregonencyclopedia.org/entry/view/albany

American Life Histories: Manuscripts from the Federal Writers' Project, 1936-1940 http://memory.loc.gov/wpaintro/

Amity, Oregon: http://www.oregonencyclopedia.org/entry/view/amity/

Aurora, Oregon: http://www.bentoncountymuseum.org/research/Railroading.cfm; http://www.oregonencyclopedia.org/entry/view/aurora/

Benton County Museum: http://www.bentoncountymuseum.org/research/Railroading.cfm

Brooks, Oregon: http://www.antiquepowerland.com/index.html; http://www.willowcreekrr.org/; http://www.oregonpioneers.com/marion/BrooksHistoricalSociety.htm; http://vimeo.com/28166182

Camp Adair: http://www.adairvillage.org/; http://campadair.webs.com/chapels.htm; https://osulibrary.oregonstate.edu/archives/omeka/exhibits/show/fighters/topics/pow

Canby, Oregon: http://www.ci.canby.or.us/cityhall/history.htm; http://www.clackamas.us/fair/history.html

Canyonville, Oregon: http://www.southernoregon.com/canyonville/index.html; http://www.cowcreek.com/; http://www.canyonville.net/

City of Dillard, Oregon: http://www.oregoncities.us/dillard/index.htm

Civilian Conservation Corps (CCC) Legacy: http://www.ccclegacy.org/CC_Brief_History.html

Corvallis, Oregon: http://www.bentoncountymuseum.org/timeline/print_timeline.cfm; http://www.corvalliscommunitypages.com/Americas/US/Oregon/corvallis/outlawstop.htm; http://scarc.library.oregomstate.edu/chronology/chron_1880.html

Cottage Grove, Oregon: http://hawleyranch.com/the-story/; http://bohemiamineownersassociation.webs.com/history.htm; http://www.highbeam.com/doc/1G1-215813344.html

Creswell, Oregon: http://home.centurytel.net/gunderson/cres/cresmuse.htm;

Donation Land Claims: http:www.ccrh.org/comm/cottage/primary/claim.htm; http://www.ohs.org/education/oregonhistory/historical_records/dspDocument.cfm?doc_ID=2D6350BC-CC5A-E143-2EB7E422E9DFE9A7; http://www.ohs.org/education/oregonhistory/historical_records/dsp; http://www.historylink.org/index.cfm?DisplayPage=output.cfm&file_id=9501

Douglas County, Oregon: http://oregonlookouts.weebly.com/douglas-county.html
Drain, Oregon: http://www.drainoregon.org/; http://www.cityofdrain.org/; http://www.drainoregon.org/history.htm; http://nwda.orbiscascade.org/ark:/80444/xv92932; http://www.drainoregon.org/victorian_houses.htm; http://nwda.orbiscascade.org/ark:/80444/xv92932; http://oregongiftsofcomfortandjoy.blogspot.com/
Dundee, Oregon: http://www.oregonlive.com/travel/index.ssf/2013/10/dundee_in_heart_of_oregon_wine.html
Eugene, Oregon: http://www.aaroads.com/guide.php?page=s0099or; http://news.google.com/newspapers?nid=1310&dat=19911227&id=l_tQAAAAIBAJ&sjid=OOoDAAAAIBAJ&pg=5012%2C6209100; https://www.eugene-or.gov/Archive/ViewFile/Item/664; http://allthingsquackenbush.weebly.com/quackenbush-hardware-store-eugene-oregon.html; http://registerguard.com/; http://bluebook.state.or.us/cultural/history/history16.htm; http://www.waymarking.com; http://freepages.genealogy.rootsweb.ancestry.com-jtenlen/OR.Bioshttp/frankbrunner; http://www/thefreelibrary.com/OBITUARIES.-a0106434883 Joseph Brunner; http://www/tjefree library.com_/Printarticle.aspx?id= 120486995 *The Register-Guard*
Galesville, Oregon: http://www.bentoncountymuseum.org/research/MinersTrail.cfm
Garrett House Station: http://www.historicgarretthousestation.com/about_us
Gervais, Oregon: http://www.waymarking.com/waymarks/WMHDGJ_Samuel_Brown_House_Gervais_Oregon; http://www.oregonpioneers.com/1846.htm
Gladstone, Oregon: http://www.ci.gladstone.or.us/history.html
Grants Pass, Oregon: http://www.visitgrantspass.org/Index.aspx?page=319; https://www.grantspassoregon.gov/Index.aspx?page=704; http://www.offbeatoregon.com/o1101c-oregon-backcountry-rich-in-legends-of-buried-treasure.html; http://bleacherreport.com/articles/279848-triumph-and-tragedy-where-heroes-are-forged; http://oregondigital.org/cdm4/item_viewer.php?CISOROOT=/gwilliams&CISOPTR=1576&CISOBOX=1&REC=11
Greyhound Historical Timeline: http://www.greyhound.com/en/about/historicaltimeline.aspx
Halsey, Oregon: http://www.halseyoregon.com/
Harrisburg, Oregon: http://www.ci.harrisburg.or.us/; http://www.gazettetimes.com/news/local/morse-bros-provided-rock-solid-foundation/article_2c687d90-654f-11e3-9931-001a4bcf887a.html
Hayesville, Oregon: http://www.freewebs.com/hayesvillechurch/;
Holt International: http//pages.uoregon.edu/adoption/people/holt.htm; http://www.nytimes.com/2000/08/02/us/bertha-holt-96-a-leader-in-international-adoptions.html; http://ohs.org/education/oregonhistory/historical_records/dspDocument.cfm?doc_ID=F291CCF6-BC9C-D516-3E0E11C6611335B7
Independence, Oregon: http://www.ci.independence.or.us/historic/local-history; http://www.herimuseum.org/
Jackson County Roads: http://id.mind.net/~truwe/tina/roadwork.html
Jefferson, Oregon's Looney Station: http://archiver.rootsweb.ancestry.com/th/read/LOONEY/1998-03/0889384357; http://jeffersonchronicles.homestead.com
Jennyopolis, Oregon: https://www.osbar.org/publications/bulletin/06jan/heritage.html
Josephine County, Oregon: http://www.oregongold.net/?s=wisenbacher
Lafayette, Oregon: http://www.ci.lafayette.or.us/; http://www.newlafayette.org/lafayette-history/old-myth-of-lafayette-can-rest-in-peace/; http://www.newlafayette.org/lafayette-history/lafayettes-glory-days-when-the-west-was-still-wild-part-two/
Lewisburg, Oregon: http://arcweb.sos.state.or.us/pages/exhibits/1857/during/bios/lewis.htm; http://wc.rootsweb.ancestry.com/cgi-bin/igm.cgi?op=GET&db=benton&id=I2677; http://www.everytrail.com/guide/old-growth-trail; http://www.staoc.com/
Linfield College: http://www.linfield.edu/;
Logging: Logging: http://oregondigital.org/

Lookouts in Oregon: http://www.firetower.org/

Louse Creek Station: http://www.offbeatoregon.com/o1101c-oregon-backcountry-rich-in-legends-of-buried-treasure.html

McMinnville, Oregon: The Oregon Encyclopedia by Dan Linscheid: http://www.oregonencyclopedia.org/entry/view/mcminnville/; http://www.linfield.edu/linfield-news/owha/

Medford, Oregon: http://id.mind.net/~truwe/tina/timeline.html; http://id.mind.net/~truwe/tina/histories.html; http://www.harryanddavid.com/

Millersburg, Oregon: http://www.katu.com/news/local/International-Paper-Albany-implosion-163339146.html

Milwaukie, Oregon: http://en.wikipedia.org/wiki/Milwaukie,_Oregon;http://thebomber.wix.com/bomb#!history; http://www.b17WingsofFreedom.org

Miscellaneous: http://www.foresthistory.org/ASPNET/Policy/Fire/Lookouts/Lookouts.aspx; http://www.oregonhistoryproject.org/articles/biographies/ben-holladay-biography/; http://home.comcast.net/~bygonebyways/Oregon_99.htm; http://geonames.usgs.gov/; http://www.oregoncylopedia.org/

Monroe, Oregon: http://www.eugenemusicians.com/history-local-scene/history-music-venues/; http://wc.rootsweb.ancestry.com/cgi-bin/igm.cgi?op=GET&db=benton&id=I3183; http://www.bentoncountymuseum.org/research/munford.cfm

Myrtle Creek/Tri-City: http://myrtlecreekchamber.com/; http://www.southernoregon.com/myrtlecreek/index.html

Newberg, Oregon: http://geog.uoregon.edu/edge/gs_documents/Projects/2009/Gault/Digging_for_Friends/HJ_Minthorn.html; https://www.newbergoregon.gov/newberg/history

New Era, Oregon: http://www.usgennet.org/usa/or/county/clackamas/timeline2.html; http://www.ghosttowns.com; http://www.ohs.org/the-oregon-history-project/biographies/Ben-Holladay.cfm

New Odessa: http://ohs.org/education/oregonhistory/historical_records/dspDocument.cfm?doc_ID=07F38A5E-B06B-B65B-0320EC03EBE61D30

Oak Grove, Oregon: http://www.hhpr.com/trolleytrail/history.html

Oakland, Oregon: http://www.historicoaklandoregon.com/

Oregon WPA Folklore Project: http://lcweb2.loc.gov/wpaintro/orcat.html

Oregon Electric Station Restaurant: http://www.oesrestaurant.com/oeshistory.htm

Oregon City, Oregon: http://www.el.com/to/oregoncity/; http://www.mcloughlinhouse.org/; http://www.historicoregoncity.org

Oregon Historical Society: http://ohs.org/education/oregonhistory/historical_records/dspDocument.cfm?doc_ID=07F38A5E-B06B-B65B-0320EC03EBE61D30

Oregon Libraries Digital Collection: http://oregondigital.org/digcol/archives/; http://oregondigital.org/digcol/

Phoenix, Oregon: http://en.wikipedia.org/wiki/Phoenix,_Oregon;http://www.phoenixoregon.gov/

Portland, Oregon: http://montanapioneerandclassicautoclub.org/gasstations/earlygasstations.html; http://pdxhistory.com/html/council_crest.html;http://kellybutteunderground.blogspot.com/; http://pdxhistory.com/html/council_crest.html; http://www.portlandoregon.gov/parks/finder/index.cfm?&propertyid; http://www.ohsu.edu/about/facts/; http://www.marylhurst.edu/about-marylhurst/history; http://airport-portland.com/; http://www.portlandoregon.gov/water/53622

Richfield Beacon Stations: http://www.livinggoldpress.com/sisksum.htm ; http://richfieldbeacons.blogspot.com/; ttp://richfieldbeacons.weebly.com/oregon.html

Rickreall, Oregon: http://ncbible.org/nwh/orhistbc.html; http://genealogytrails.com/ore/polk/biographies/polkcountypioneers1.html

Riddle, Oregon: http://www.riddleoregon.com/RiddleHistory.html

Rock Point, Oregon: http://www.aaroads.com/guide.php?page=s0099or http://structurae.net/structures/data/index.cfm?ID=s0008512

Roseburg: http://uvarts.com/uvaa-history/; http://www.tfff.org/; http://www.cityofroseburg.org/visitors/1959-blast/;

Siskiyous: http://home.comcast.net/~bygonebyways/Oregon_99.htm; http://www.callahanslodge.com/

Southern Oregon: http://id.mind.net/~truwe/tina/s.o.history.html; http://www.faqs.org/docs/air/avfusen.html; http://www.airvectors.net/idx_wmil.html;

Starlite Drive-in Theater, Medford: http://cinematreasures.org/theaters/33641; http://cinematreasures.org/members/william/photos/23189)

Talent, Oregon: http://www.cityoftalent.org/Page.asp?NavID=41; http://www.talenthistory.org/

Tangent, Oregon: http://www.cityoftangent.org/; http://www.oregonlive.com/pacific-northwest-news/index.ssf/2012/10/a_barn_bequeathed_to_an_oregon.html

Tampico, Oregon: http://www.geocaching.com/geocache/GC2ZNNH_lost-but-not-forgotten-tampico-oregon?guid=8779cabd-e065-4571-953f-6d2743750180

Tigard, Oregon: http://www.ci.tigard.or.us; http://www.oregonencyclopedia.org/articles/tigard/#.U2m80SjwKJU

Tiller, Oregon: ; http://www.foresthistory.org/ASPNET/Policy/Fire/Lookouts/Lookouts.aspx

Umpqua Dairy History: http://www.umpquadairy.com/page/about-us

USDA Forest Service: http://www.fs.usda.gov/umpqua/; http://www.fs.usda.gov/rogue-siskiyou/

Vanport City, Oregon: http://www.museumofthecity.org/the-history-of-the-land-of-vanport-oregon/

Waconda, Oregon: http://www.salemhistory.net/transportation/electric_railway_waconda.htm

Wells, Fargo & Co.: http://blogs.wellsfargo.com/guidedbyhistory/2007/04/stagecoaching-in-oregon/

West Coast Trailways Bus Line: http://cw42.tripod.com/Jon-6.html

Wikipedia.com: http://en.wikipedia.org (The references that contributed to the Wikipedia articles are usually researched and cited separately.)

Wilbur, Oregon: http://my.umwestern.edu/Academics/library/libroth/MHD/vigilantes/VV/pursuit.html

Winchester, Oregon: http://www.winchesteroregon.com/

Winston-Dillard, Oregon: http://www.winstonoregon.net/HistoricalBackgrnd.html

Wolf Creek, Oregon: http://www.rogueweb.com/wolfcreekinn/

Woodburn, Oregon: http://commons.wikimedia.org/wiki/File:Tulipfarm.jpg;http://www.oregon.com/metro_portland_attractions/little_mexico_in_woodburn; http://www.oregon.gov/oya/pages/history.aspx

Yoncalla, Oregon: http://www.motherearthnews.com/organic-gardening/one-mans-apples.aspx#axzz2lcJiU4ao; http://www.seattletreefruitsociety.com/nick-botner%E2%80%99s-place-is-for-sale; http://www.opb.org/television/programs/ofg/segment/apple-detectives-try-to-save-worlds-largest-apple-collection/

OREGON'S MAIN STREET: U.S. Highway 99
"The Folk History"

CONTRIBUTORS

Alexander, Mary
Andersen, Teresa L.
Attwood, Kay
Barclay, Janice
Barker, Michael J. "Hoss"
Barnett, Carol
Bartels, Kandice Carsh
Bartley, Ron
Beckham, Stephen Dow
Binus, Joshua
Booher, Chuck
Brown, Beverly
Campbell, Joan
Chapman, Mike
Card, Douglas
Corning, Howard McKinley
Craven, Jim
Dare, Ken & Barbara
Deatherage, Curt
Dixon, Virginia P.
Dresbeck, Rachel
Dyer, Dora
Engemann, Richard
Fattig, Paul
Favrholdt, Visti
Fitzimons, Eileen G.
Fletchall, G.F.
Foster, Dianne
Friedman, Ralph
Garvey, Sean
Glen, Julie Veazie
Griggs, Joe
Guzman-Orozco, Vicente
Hartley, Laura
Hobijn, Jon
Hollyer, Helen
Horton, M.B.
Hoyt, Bill
Hulin, Gil
Jackson, Kerby
Jansson, Kyle
Jensen, Jeff
John, Finn J.D.
Jones, Gil "Gene"
Johns, Jennene
LaLande, Jeffrey
Lamster, Margaret
Lansing, Ronald B.
Lowry, Robert
Malchow, Dee
Mangold, Scott
Marschner, Janice
McCornack, Nina W.
McCready, Gladys W.
McGuire, Stephanie
McNutt, Margie Buell
Meier, Gary & Gloria
Miles, Anita J.
Miller, Bill
Momsen, Joan
Moore, Harriett
Moore, Lucia W.
Munford, Kenneth
Nash, Tom
O'Harra, Marjorie (Lutz)
Orr, Betty
Parmenter, Judy & Mel
Paul, Alex
Petty, Glyn
Pierce, Sandy
Pintarich, Dick
Proctor, Bob & Virginia
Richard, Terry
Rogers, Ron
Ross, George W.
Schmidt, Rick
Schofield, Twilo
Shaffer, George
Shannon, Red
Sigler, Peggy
Stevenson, Lillian (Bartley)
Strobridge, Elaine M.
Suiter, Jim
Sullivan, Wes
Thompson, Gary
Thompson, Richard
Toy, Eckhard, Jr.
Truwe, Ben
Ulven, Leslie
Van Prooyan, Ada
Waddle, Susan
Waldron, Sue
Warnock, Dan
Weich, Robert H.
Weston, Myra
Wilde, Chris T.
Wilson, Sandra
Woody, Rachael
Wright, Jan

OREGON'S MAIN STREET: U.S. Highway 99
"The Folk History"

PHOTO CREDITS

Albany Regional Museum
Antiques Powerland
Applegate Family Collection
Barnes, Mike, Gene Jones' *Jefferson Chronicles*
Bartels, Kandice Carsh
Bean Team Waymarking
Benton County Historical Society
Booher Family Collection
Brew Family Collection
Britt, Peter Photograph Collection, Hannon Library Special Collections, Southern Oregon University
Brooks Historical Society
Chapman Family Collection
Clackamas County Historical Society
Clackamas County Fair History ("Where Memories are Born" pamphlet)
Cox, Arlene Poole
Creswell Area Historical Museum
Deatherage, Curt Collection
Dot Dotson Photography
Douglas County Historical Society
Dustin & Newbury Family Collection
Edwards, Pat, *Sawdust and Cider* collection
Edwards Family Collection
Eugene Register Guard Archives
Fingerhood, Bruce Collection
Forest History Society, Flickr Commons
Gaston's *The Centennial History of Oregon*
Gavotte, Jane Collection
Gladstone Historical Society

Grants Pass Park & Recreation Department
Griggs Family Collection
Hamby, Ellis, Gene Jones' *Jefferson Chronicles*
Hawley Family Collection
Hayesville, Oregon website
Heritage Museum Society, Independence, Oregon
Hing, Marna Helser
Hobijn, Jon History Corner website
Hoover, Herbert Presidential Library & Museum, West Branch, Iowa
Irish, Curtis Collection
Jones, Gene, *Jefferson Chronicles*
Josephine County Historical Society
Keene, Greg, Wikimedia Commons
Kenney, Steve, pdxhistory.com
Kunkle, Joe Collection
Lancaster, George Collection
Lane County Historical Society
Leach Family Collection
Letsom Letters Collection- (Jody Johnson and Kathy Matthews)
Lookout Sites Registry
Mangold, Scott
Maxwell, Ben Collection, Salem Public Library Historic Photograph Collections
McCartney, Tim
McGrew, Jerry
McGuire, Stephanie, Dustin & Newbury Family Collection
McNutt, Margie Buell

Miles, Anita J.
Milwaukie Historical Society
Montana Pioneer and Classic Auto Club
North Douglas School District
Oaks Park Association
Obst, Rick Collection
Oregon Encyclopedia On-Line, *Oregon Historical Society*
Oregon Historical Society
Oregon State Library
Oregon Historical Quarterly
Oregon Department of Transportation Archives (ODOT)
OSU Special Collections & Archives Commons
Parmenter, Judy
Parodi, Andrew, Wikimedia Commons
Polk County Museum
Portland, City of, Archives
Ramp Family Collection
Robinson, Thomas
Rose, Russell C. Collection, *Lebanon Express*
Roseburg, City of
Ross, Joe, Bureau of Land Management, Roseburg District
Runk Family Collection
Salem Public Library, Salem , Oregon
Schultz Family Collection
Smith, Stan Family Collection
Smith/Edwards Family Collection
Southern Oregon Historical Society
St. Anne Orthodox Church
Sunday Oregonian (public domain)
Talent Historical Society
Tangent, City of
Thompson, Richard
Tiller Ranger District
Tri County Chamber of Commerce
Trolley Trail website
Truwe, Ben
UO Libraries Archives Commons
Walling, A.G., *History of Southern Oregon*, 1884
West Shore, The magazine (public domain)
Wikimedia Commons – (Cacophony)
Wikimedia Commons (Tedder)
Wikimedia Commons (Visitor 7)
Willamette Heritage Center
Williams, Gerald W. Collection, OSU Special Collections & Archives
Woodard Family Collection
Wright, Barbara Stroda
Yamhill County Historical Museum

OREGON'S MAIN STREET: U.S. Highway 99
"The Folk History"

MUSEUMS AND HISTORICAL SOCIETIES ALONG THE WAY

Take time to visit and support these wonderful portals into the history of the communities lying along the route of U.S. Highway 99!

- Albany Regional Museum
- Antique Powerland Museum
- Applegate Trail Interpretive Center
- Benton County Historical Society and Museum
- Bohemia Gold Mining Museum
- Brooks Historical Society and Depot Museum
- Calapooia Reflections Museum – Sutherlin
- Canby Depot Museum
- Clackamas County Historical Society's Museum of the Oregon Territory
- Cottage Grove Museum
- Creswell Historical Museum
- Douglas County Museum of Natural & Cultural History
- Gold Hill Historical Society
- Harrisburg Area Museum
- Heritage Museum Society - Independence
- Hoover-Minthorn House Museum - Newberg
- Jackson County Museum
- John Tigard House Museum – Public Library, History Room
- Josephine County Historical Museum and Research Center
- Junction City Historical Society
- Lane County Historical Society & Museum
- Linn County Historical Museum - Brownsville
- McLoughlin House - Oregon City
- Miller Log Cabin Museum - Lafayette
- Milwaukie History Museum
- Museum of Mental Health - Salem
- Museum of the Oregon Territory - Oregon City
- Oakland Museum
- Oregon History Museum
- Phoenix Historical Society and Museum
- Polk County Museum
- Samuel Barlow House Museum - Barlow
- South Benton Community Museum - Monroe
- South Umpqua Historical Society Museum - Canyonville
- Southern Oregon Historical Society
- Talent Historical Society and Museum
- Woodburn Historical Museum
- Woodville Historical Museum (Rogue River)
- Yamhill County Historical Society & Museum

About the Authors...

Jo-Brew is the author of the companion book to this one called *OREGON'S MAIN STREET: U.S. Highway 99* "The Stories." In addition, she has written six novels. These include *Preserving Cleo, Cleo's Slow Dance, Finding Clarice, What Next Ms. Elliott?* and *Marge, Back on Track, Anne Marie's New Melody* and *La Femme*, a collection of short stories.

She decided that she was ready to leave fiction behind, so she embarked on a new road, drawing on her interest in Oregon and its history which led to the publication of these two Highway 99 books.

Jo is also an active member of The Association of University Women and for seven years, she wrote a weekly column for the *Creswell Chronicle*.

"When I'm not writing, thinking about writing, or talking about writing, I garden, keep a house and spend time with my friends. My husband Ken and I both like to travel and go when we can. We also combine activities with our grown children and their families as often as possible. School concerts, ball games, ultimate frisbee, picnics and camping are all part of our lives."

Pat Edwards is the author of two books on the history of her home community of Lorane, Oregon. The first, *Sawdust and Cider; A History of Lorane, Oregon and the Siuslaw Valley*, was written with co-authors Nancy O'Hearn and Marna Hing in 1987 to help celebrate the community's centennial. In 2006, Pat wrote a major revision of the book called *From Sawdust and Cider to Wine*.

She and Jim own the Lorane Family Store and Pat spent 15 years as Administrative Coordinator for the Institute of Neuroscience at the University of Oregon.

Since then, Pat has taken on the role of Managing Editor for the literary quarterly, *Groundwaters*, which is distributed throughout all of Lane County, Oregon. The magazine is now in its 11th year of publication. Pat also is the community correspondent for two small Lane County weeklies, the *Fern Ridge Review* and the *Creswell Chronicle*.

Her work with *Groundwaters* has led her into the field of editing and publishing the works of others. It's how she and Jo-Brew met.

"I'm blessed with a large, loving family. Jim and I celebrated our 50th wedding anniversary in 2014 and our family and home are our highest priorities."

Index

A

A.L. Woodard Lumber and Dry Wood 215, 217
Abernethy, George 246
Adair Village 436
African-American 253, 495
Aircraft Observation 37, 238
ALBANY 9, 18, 37, 98, 104, 220, 258, 274, 278, 281, 284, 287, 299-300, 302-310, 312, 324, 332, 335, 463, 495, 505
Albany Collegiate Institute 303
Albany Democrat Herald 296
Albany Regional Museum 305-307
Albany Timber Carnival 306
Albany Veteran's Day Parade 308
Albina 480
Alexander, Mary L. 230
Allen Elizabethan Theatre 32
ALMADEN 110, 112
Alpine Lodge Resort 124
Ambrose Station 178, 186
Amerman, James V. 54
AMITY 452-455
Anderson, John 6
Angus Bowmer Theatre 32
ANLAUF 176, 192-195, 200
Anlauf, Frank and Robert 192
Antique Powerland Museums 340-341
Applegate, Charles 179-180, 183
Applegate, Hortense 153, 167, 169, 181
Applegate Trail Interpretive Center & Museum 108
Applegate, Jesse 108, 178-179, 183, 186, 472
Applegate, Lindsay 14, 177, 179
Applegate Trail 1-2, 8, 16, 108, 123, 147, 166, 178, 274, 406
Applegate's Cut-off 1

ASHLAND 2, 11, 13-14, 17-19, 21-22, 25-44, 46-51, 57, 60, 64, 66, 68, 74, 76, 81, 98, 148, 160, 179, 188, 232, 312, 330, 425, 442
Ashland Academy, 29-30
Ashland College and Normal School 29-30
Ashland Mills 28
Ashland Springs 34
Ashland Tidings 25, 33, 38-42, 48-49
Attwood, Kay 49, 376
AURORA 6, 10, 312, 343-344, 351, 353-361, 505
AURORA COLONY 351, 353-357
Aurora Colony Historical Society 357
Aurora Mills 353, 356
Aviation 24, 69, 140-141, 238, 271, 308, 457
AZALEA 117, 120-122, 139

B

Bagley Canning Company 50
Bailey, Beth 204
BAKER PRAIRIE 364-365
Baker, John 456
Baker, Thomas & Elizabeth 273
Ballard, C.R. "Dick" 430
Bancroft, Hubert Howe 457
Bangs, Eli Livery 8
Banister, Manly M. 58, 183
Banks, Llewellyn 72
Barbur Blvd. 382, 470, 484
Barclay, Janice 432
Barker, Michael J. "Hoss" 99, 101, 225, 228, 413-414
BARLOW 322, 351, 361-366, 370, 505
Barlow, Samuel 361
Barlow, Samuel House Museum 361
Barnard, Charles P. 8

Barnett, Carol 55
Barron, Martha 15
Barron's Ranch/Station 11, 14-17, 27, 71
Bartley, Ron 67, 123, 137, 140
Base Line 376, 486
Bates, Sidney 20
Bean, J.R. 247, 291, 379
Bear Creek 46-47, 53, 55, 59-61, 63, 90
Beaver Portland Cement Company 81-82
Becker, Ray D. 238
Beckham, Stephen Dow 172
Beekman, C.C. and Benjamin 58-59
Beeson, Lewis 49
Beeson, Welborn 50
BELLE PASSI / BELPASSI 346-347
Ben Maxwell Collection 257
Benton-Lane Park 280, 406-408
Berkley Hot Sulphur Springs 34, 43
Beverly, John 126
Binus, Joshua 119
Blackford, Grace Griggs 198
BLM 10, 139, 414
Blue Ruin 286
Boger, Bob 406, 408
Bohemia Mining District 211, 214
Bomber (The) 394
Bonanza Mine 174
Booher, Charles 185, 194-197, 199
Booher, Mike & Dolores 185
BOOTH aka AZALEA 120
Booth-Kelly Lumber Company 177, 190, 192, 207, 234, 244
Booth, R.A. 167-168
Booth, Robert 177
BOSTON, BOSTON MILLS aka SHEDD 299-300
Boston Flour Mill 300
Boswell Springs 184
Bowmer, Angus 32
Braceros 62
Brew 29, 35, 37, 43-44, 53, 77-79, 87, 103-104, 125, 264, 269, 273, 291, 293, 300, 312, 329, 335, 346, 407, 410, 499
Britt, Peter Photograph Collection 25, 459
Broadway Bridge 382, 485

BROOKS 338-344, 346, 505
Brooks Depot Museum 340
Brown, Annie 437, 439
Brown, Beverly 106
Brown, Eunice Flickinger 437
Brown, J. Henry 321-322
Brown, Samuel 345-347
Brown, Will Q. 140
Bruce's Corner 415
Brunner Commercial Dryer 266-267
Brunner, Ernest 266
Brunner, Frank & Bertha 266
Brunner, Joe 267
Brunscheon, Ralph & Orine 281
Buchanan, William A. 420
Buell, Leslie W. 500
Bunton, Bill 165-166
Bunton, Elijah 165-167
Bunton's Gap 165, 167-168
Bureau of Land Management 9, 110, 139
Burnett, Peter 335
Burnside Bridge 485
Burt, Ella 183
Burt, George 177
Burt, Mary 181
Butler, Gwin 34
Byrd, Charles 204
Byrd, Sarah L. 374

C

Calapooia 167, 174, 177, 180, 186, 190, 299-300, 302, 307, 477
Calapooya 180, 186, 203, 211, 237, 429
California & Oregon Stage Company 2, 4, 13, 29, 58, 108, 111, 117, 174, 201, 284, 286, 303, 313
California and Oregon Railroad 9-10
California Trail 1, 2, 8
California-Oregon Trail 16, 28, 86, 125, 141, 174, 186, 249
Callahan's 26, 28
Callahan, Don 26
Camas 1, 116, 173, 181, 247, 252
CAMAS SWALE 171-172, 246
CAMP ADAIR 253, 306, 331, 431-436, 445, 496

Camp Baker 56
Camp White 52, 62, 74-75, 431
Camp Wimer 87
Campbell, Joan 236
Campbell, Prince Lucien 252, 442
CANBY 10, 361, 364-368, 370, 372, 386, 505
Canby Depot Museum 367
CANEMAH 372-373
Canyon Creek 109, 122-123, 125-126
Canyon Creek Arch Bridge 123
CANYONVILLE 9, 90, 109, 117, 121-130, 135-136, 138, 140-141, 149, 153, 377, 506
Canyonville Christian Academy 127-128
Canyonville Hotel 126
Canyonville Museum 130
Card, Douglas 247
Carnegie Library 97-98, 260-261, 308, 326
Carsh, Kandice Bartels 488-492
Cartwright House 186, 201, 203, 256
Casey, Henry & Elizabeth 17
Caveman Bridge 92, 98-99, 106
CCC 32, 73-74, 87, 110, 129-130, 135, 137
Centennial Toll Bridge 80
CENTER 386
Central Linn School District 299
Central Oregon Normal School 187
CENTRAL POINT 31, 60, 64, 66, 77-81, 151
Chambers, J.H. 224
Chapman, Charles, Nefa & Nancy 204
Chapman, Clare, Sherman & Leslie 204
Chautauqua 31-32, 34, 155, 293, 384, 386
Chavner, Thomas 80-81
Chehalem 379, 466-467
CHEMAWA 333-335, 344, 468, 505
Chemawa Indian School 333-335
CHEMEKETA 318, 321, 333, 345
Chenoweth, Henry 370
Cheshire 202
Chief Sam 80
China Ditch Project 143-146

Chinese 59, 94, 143, 145-146, 190, 304, 361, 392, 421, 476- 477, 493
Civil Air Patrol 495
Civil Defense 37, 39, 403
Civil War 29, 56, 152, 156, 171, 179, 229, 249, 253, 276, 303, 364, 417-418, 423, 426, 429, 451, 477, 479, 480
Civilian Conservation Corps (CCC) 32, 73-74, 87, 110, 130, 135, 431
Clackamas County Fair 366-367, 386
Clackamas County Historical Society 356, 367, 372, 378, 382-383
Clarke, Kathryn 119
Clean Air Act 79
Clinkinbeard, James L. 168
Clyman, James 237
Coffee Creek Women's Correctional Facility 330
Coffee, Laura Porter 409
Cole, Rufus C. 15
Coles' Mountain House/Station 6, 14-16, 21, 166
Columbia College 249
Columbia River 11, 248, 375-377, 382, 401, 474, 485, 496, 499-500, 502
Columbus Day Storm 53, 192, 241, 265, 281, 328, 446, 458
Colver, Samuel 55-56, 58
COMSTOCK 192, 195, 197-201, 210
Comstock, James J. 198
CONCOMLY 344
Conser, Jacob 311-313
Cooper Creek Reservoir 173-174
Corbett, H.W. 4, 6, 320
Corey, Chester 34-35
Cornell, Frances 312, 316
Corning, Howard McKinley 284, 353, 357, 360, 418
Cornwall, Josephus A. 176
CORVALLIS 4-5, 9, 175-176, 258, 274-275, 277-278, 286, 297, 306, 319, 323, 372, 400, 410-411, 415-416, 418-429, 431-433, 435-436, 438, 457, 470
COTTAGE GROVE 44, 190, 195-196, 199, 200-201, 205-206, 208, 210-236, 281, 436, 505

Cottage Grove Museum 218
Couch, John, Captain 472, 477
Coulter, Frank E. 324
Council Crest 473, 482, 492
Cow Creek 115-118, 120, 121-122, 125-127, 129, 138-139, 141, 506
Cox, Arlene Poole 23, 36
Cox, Thomas 322
Crater Lake 64, 68, 71, 74, 98, 161
Crater Rock Museum 78
Craven, Jim 85
Creed Floed House 152
CREIGHTON 386-387
CRESWELL 210, 229, 235-241, 246, 505
Creswell Area Historical Museum 237
Cross, Harvey Edward, Judge 384, 386
Crowley, Martha Leland 107
CROW'S NEST 287
Croxton, Thomas 92
Croxton's Station 92, 107
CURTIN 194-197
Curtin, Daniel 194

D

Dare, Ken & Barbara 161, 381
DariMart 280, 298
Daugherty, Stan 233
DAYS CREEK 129-130, 136, 138
Deatherage, Curt 232, 235, 436, 486
DEER CREEK 151-153
Del Rio Orchards 81, 85
Depot, Peter 346
Detering, Gerald & Marie 294
Detering Orchards 294
DILLARD 109, 149-150, 221
Dimmick, Eb 92
DIVIDE 136, 195, 203-206, 217, 505
DIXIE 448, 451
Dixon, Virginia P. 157
Doernbecher Children's Hospital 371, 484
DOLE 149
Dollarhide 14, 17, 26-27, 47
Dollarhide, Dudley 26
Dollarhide, Jesse 14
Dollarhide Toll Road 17, 26-27, 47

Dot Dotson Photography 172, 174-175, 191, 252-253, 259-261, 264, 266, 279
Dougherty, Elvyn 20
Douglas County Fair 155
Douglas County Historical Society 142, 144, 145-148, 152
Douglas, David 129
Dow, Stephen Beckham 172
DRAIN 10, 79, 184-194, 197-198, 200-201, 220-222, 442, 505
Drain Academy 187
Drain Black Sox 191
Drain, Charles and Anna 187-188
Dresbeck, Rachel 383
Driver, W.C. 65
DUNDEE 465-467
Duniway, Abigail Scott 30, 57, 463-464
Dustin, Jennie 368-371
Dutch Town 6, 312, 344, 353-354
Dyer, Dora 142
Dyer, Moses True 142

E

EAST BUTTE 469-470
East Side Railway Company 9, 400
EDEN 46, 51
EDENBOWER 505
Egli, John 351
EKINS 465
Elmer, Julian Nelson 108, 119
Elsinore Theatre 326, 328
Emigrant Creek 1, 50
Emigrant Lake 17, 27-28, 44, 51
Enders Block 32-33
Enders, Henry 32
Engeman, Richard 453, 455
Estes, Elijah T. & Susan 186
Estes, George 186, 189-190
Estes Ranch 186, 205
Eubanks, C.L. 93
EUGENE 4, 6, 8-9, 36-37, 69, 98, 105, 146, 156-157, 161, 175, 184, 188-190, 194, 197, 200-202, 205, 210, 216, 221, 229, 234, 236-238, 240-275, 277-278, 280-281, 285-286, 288, 290-292,

EUGENE *(cont'd)* 294, 297, 308, 312, 344, 400, 406, 410-411, 428, 435, 486, 495, 505
Eugene Airport 271-272
EUGENE CITY 9, 202, 205, 236, 245-248, 254, 256, 257, 260, 275, 285
Eugene Fruit Growers 266
Eugene Register-Guard 215, 247, 253-254, 258, 264, 267, 406
Evan's Ferry 86
Evergreen Aviation and Space Museum 460

F

Fagan, David 416, 438
Fattig, Paul 18, 83
Favrholdt, Visti 278
Felzer, William 300
Ferry Street Bridge 246, 254
Finley National Wildlife Refuge 415
Finley, Richard 299
Fitzimons, Eileen G. 381
Flint, Addison R. 163
Fletchall, Gale F., Dr. 281-282
Flight Patterns 272
Floed-Lane House 152
Flood 2, 16, 28, 50, 53, 72, 83-84, 90, 106, 119, 148-149, 230, 254, 256, 269-270, 279, 285-288, 320, 326, 331, 340, 349, 358, 382-384, 389, 401, 410, 412, 448, 483, 496-497
Force, George W. 496
Force Lake 496
Ford Family Foundation 163
Ford, J.T. 448-449
Ford, Kenneth W. & Hallie 150, 163
Fort Grant 56
Fort Lane 80
Fort Leland 108
Fort Umpqua 151
Fort Wagner 46
Foster, Dianne 147
Frank, Lloyd 495
Franklin 202
Franklin Boulevard 242, 244-245 261-262, 265

Frazier, Roy 36
FREEDOM 284
Freeman, James 375-377
French Prairie 338, 346-349
Fresno Free Speech Fight of 1910-1911 19
Friedman, Ralph 285-286

G

GALESVILLE 117
Galice Ranger District 110
GASBURG 54-57, 312
Gaston, Joseph 3, 321, 368
Gavatte, Jane 287-288, 293
George Fox College 468
Gerber, Henry 420-421
Germania Hall 470
GERVAIS 6, 344-347, 348, 349, 354, 505
Gervais, Joseph 346
Giants 94-95, 143-145
Gibson, Gladys & Howard 280
Gilbert, L.D. 276
Gilbert, Royal 270
Gilbert Shopping Center 270
Gird, Bill 415
Gird's Twelve-Mile House 415
GLADSTONE 367, 382-386
Gladstone Historical Society 384
GLENDALE 18, 108, 114-115, 118-120, 149, 222, 506
GLENWOOD 242, 244-245, 256
Glenn, Julia Veazie 451
GOLD HILL 79-85, 87
Gold Mining 55, 66, 81-83, 86, 92-93, 95, 109, 112, 143-145, 225, 322-323 365, 389-390, 405, 477
Gold Ray Dam 81
GOLD RIVER 86
Gold Rush 86, 94, 179, 246, 418, 461
Golden Rule Whiskey 354
Good Government Congress 72
Good Roads 11, 21, 459
Goodel, Warren 186
Gorst, Vern 66-67, 70-72
GOSHEN 203, 241-242, 244, 505
Grand Army of the Republic 479

Grange 57, 78, 103, 235, 290-291, 298, 300, 326, 417, 431, 469
Granite Hospital 32, 36
GRANTS PASS 18, 26, 35, 37-38, 46, 48, 77, 81-82, 86-87, 89-98, 100, 102-108, 110, 118, 122, 147, 177, 222, 264, 312, 460, 462, 506
Grants Pass Irrigation District 97
Grants Pass Station 92
GRAVE CREEK 100, 107-110, 117, 312, 506
GREENBERRY 416-418, 437
Greenwood, Steve 2, 371
Greer, Bert 33-34
Grey Eagle Mining Co. 82-83
Grey, Zane 98-100
Greyhound 105, 121, 148, 158-159, 263, 313-314
Gridley, Zora 204
Griffon, Wiley 253-254
Griggs, Joe 198, 200
Griggs, John Allen & Sarah 198, 200-201
Griggs, Lloyd 201
Grist Mill 28, 57, 64, 126, 142, 169, 172, 213, 257, 293, 299-300, 303, 351, 355, 371, 387, 456-457
Grubby End of the Chehalem Valley 467
Guzman-Orozco, Vicente 348

H

Hackleman, Abner 302-303, 308
Hall, Seely 70-71
HALSEY 292, 298-299, 347, 505
Halsey State Bank 298
Halsey, William T. 298
Harkness, McDonough 107-108
HARRISBURG 10, 237, 248-249, 256, 278-279, 284-296, 298, 410, 505
Harrisburg Historical Museum 293
Harrisburg Sand & Gravel Company 295-296
Harry and David 61-62
Hartley, Laura 135
Hasard, Charles 187-188
Hatfield, Roy V. 140-141
Hawley, Ira B. 204-205

Hawley's Ranch/Station 203, 205-206, 236
Hawthorne Bridge 383, 485
Hayden Island 498, 500-501
Hayes, Rutherford B. (President) 111, 126, 153, 337
HAYESVILLE 337-338
Hayter, Mary Embree 451-452
Hedrick, Myra 190
Helser Trucking 490-491
Hembree, W.H., Captain 442
Hentze Family Farm 269
Heritage Museum Society 445-447
Hileman, W.W. 236
Hill, Fleming R. 166
Hill, Sam 11-12, 23
Hing, Marna Helser 490
Hinton, Martha 409
Hobijn, Jon 159
Hobson, William 468
Hodges, Duane D. 238-239
Holladay, Ben 9, 237, 249-250, 276, 288, 290, 319-320, 363, 368
Hollyer, Helen 238
Holt, Harry & Bertha 239-241
Home Guard 37, 39, 238
Hoover, Herbert 468-469
Hoover-Minthorn House 468-469
HOPMERE 344-345
Hops 95-96, 237, 242, 294, 306, 313, 340, 345, 352-353, 434, 453, 464
Horton, M.B. 216
Hotel Oregon 31, 460
Houck, Jesse 415
House of Mystery 82-83
Howard Prairie 50-51
Hoyt, Bill 205
HUBBARD 351-353, 505
Hudson's Bay Company 1, 13, 89, 125, 128, 151, 338, 374, 376, 379, 452, 467
Hulin, Gilbert Marshall 274-275
Hulin, Lester Gilbert 273-275
Hulin, Wilbur & Daye 275
Huntley, Clyde B. 363
Huston, Margaret Hayworth 291
Huston, Martha Burnett 409
Hyatt Creek 50

I

Idylwood 406-408
INDEPENDENCE 418, 432, 445-448
Indian 1, 14, 46, 56, 80, 86, 91-92, 107-108, 111, 116-118, 126-128, 138, 151, 153, 156, 161, 166, 171, 177, 190, 237, 246, 316, 320, 333-335, 345-346, 351, 354-355, 362, 365, 374, 383-384, 418, 420-421, 428-429, 442, 448-450, 460-462, 467-468, 473-474
Indian Wars 46, 56, 153, 365, 429
Industrial Workers of the World 18
Interstate 5 / I-5 2, 14-15, 26-28, 106, 109, 112, 123, 125, 162, 177, 181, 194-195, 197, 203, 242, 281, 310-311, 318, 484, 501
Interstate Bridge 382, 405, 480, 485-486, 502, 505
Interurban Railway 394, 396, 400, 469, 478
Irish, Curtis 189, 230, 234
Iron Mike 42
Irvine, B.F. 71
Irwin, Richard 417
Ives, William 375-377
IWW 18-19

J

Jackson County Poor Farm 54-55
Jackson County Rebellion 72
Jackson, Kerby 93, 95
Jackson, Sam 484
JACKSONVILLE 4, 6, 9, 16, 20, 28, 47, 58-60, 64, 66-67, 70, 75-77, 81, 90-91, 93, 122, 153, 174, 248, 312, 465
James, John H., Mrs. 477
Jansson, Kyle 445
Jantzen Beach 498-502
Jantzen, Carl 498-499
Jantzen Knitting Mills 498-500
Jantzen, Roy 498
Japanese 39-41, 69, 135, 275, 294, 343-344, 432, 481, 495
Jeddeloh Brothers Sweed Mill 82
JEFFERSON 311-319, 427, 453-454, 505
Jefferson Institute 311, 313, 316, 451-452
Jenks Century Farm 300-302
JENNYOPOLIS 415-416
Jensen, Jeff 14
Jerry's Home Center 271
Jessel, Susie 37
John, Finn J.D. 93
Johns, Jennene 120, 122
Johns, T.B. 122
Jones, Gene (Gil) 313-315, 317
Joseph Hill City Park 403
Josephine County Historical Society 99, 112
Josephus A. Cornwall 176
Joyce, David & Kacey 272
Judkins Point 261-262
JULIA 118
JUNCTION CITY 18, 202, 237, 260, 265, 268-270, 272-286, 289, 298, 331, 400, 405-406, 410, 412, 455, 505
Junction City Historical Society 277

K

K & R Drive In 177
Kadderly, J.J. 398
Kaiser, Edgar 495-496
Kaiser, Henry J. 495-496
Kaiser Shipyards 295, 401
KAISERVILLE 496
Kalapuya 180, 210, 237, 418, 469
Keil, Wilhelm 351, 354-361
Kelly Butte 402-403
Kelly, Mary Agnes 473
Kingsbury's Soda Springs 17, 28
Kinoshita, Robert 135-137
Kirkpatrick, Jane 356
Kitty Kat 301
Klamath Junction 28
Knife River 297
Knight, Joseph 365
Kraus, William 353, 360
Ku Klux Klan / KKK 68-69, 485
Kuni, Dale 238
Kunkle, Joe 280, 290
Kuykendall, George B. 168, 171

L

Lacey, Art 394
LaCreole 448, 451
LAFAYETTE 6, 90-92, 127, 456-457, 460-465
Lake Labish 6, 319, 339-340
LaLande, Jeffrey M., Dr. 1
Lamster, Margaret 224
LANCASTER 202, 269, 277, 284-286, 292, 410
Lancaster, George 213
Lane County Historical Society 273-274, 282, 326-327, 329
Lane, Henry 488
Lane, Joseph 151-152, 248
Lansing, Ronald B. 415
LATHAM 210, 218
Latham, Milton 210
Leach, Ralph & Nureen 44
Ledding, Herman 391
Lee, Jason 320-321, 333, 346, 467
Lee, N.L., Dr. 277
LELAND 107-108, 110, 112
LEMATI 210, 213
LEONA 192-193
Levens, Daniel 117, 126
Lewelling, Henderson & Seth 325, 388-389, 391-393, 473
Lewis and Clark Centennial Exposition 396, 481, 487-488
Lewis and Clark College 303, 495
Lewis, Haman 428-429
LEWISBURG 428-431
LEWISTON 428, 431
Lindberg, Charles 24, 102, 401
Linfield College 336, 457-460
Lithia Park 31-36, 41-42, 44, 232
Littman, Frederic 482
Lloyd Center 397
Lochmead Farm 280, 298
London, Jack 111, 114
Long Tom River 248, 273, 286, 409-410, 418
Looney, Jesse 312-314, 316-317
Lot Whitcomb 375, 387-390
Lou and Ev's 270-271
Louse Creek 92-93, 95
Lovejoy, Asa 472, 476, 492
Lovelake Road 269, 285
Lowry, Robert 354
Luce, Henry 172
Luckiamute 416, 418, 436, 439
Luelling, Henderson 388-391, 459
LUPER 273
Luper, James 273

M

Mackay, Cleal 204
MacLaren School for Boys 349-350
Madison Bridge 485
Mahlon Sweet Field 271-272, 275
Malchow, Dee 215, 219
Mallory, John 408
Mangold, Scott 188-189
Marquam Hill 473, 475, 483-484
Marquam , Phillip A. 483
Marschner, Janice 166
Maryhill Museum 11
Marylhurst 395
Mary's River 418, 421-422
MARYSVILLE 176, 418-419
Maxwell, Ben 257
McCall, Tom 21, 488
McCartney, Tim 27, 35-36, 42-43
McCue, Wilbur & Wayne 204
McCullough, Conde 144, 312-313
McDonaugh, James 92
McGrew, Jerry 16
McGuire, Stephanie 368- 371
McLane, Larry L. 112
McLaren, John 34-35
McLoughlin House 379-380
McLoughlin, John, Dr. 321, 374, 376, 379, 467
McMINNVILLE 6, 9, 98, 277, 336, 347, 409, 452, 455-460, 462, 463, 469
McNutt, Margie Buell 500-501
McQueen, G.H. 276
McReynolds, Kathleen & George 204

Meadowview 260, 272-273
MEDFORD 21-22, 26, 37-38, 41, 47-48, 52, 54-55, 58-78, 81, 90, 93, 95, 98, 100, 104, 123, 135, 137, 151, 223, 265, 401, 431, 506
Medford Mail Tribune 18, 26, 67, 71-73, 83, 85, 123
Meier, Gary & Gloria 84, 178, 201
Meier, Julius 70, 336, 472, 495
Menke, Arnold S. 17
Mental Health, Museum of 331
Meridian 376-377
Merlin Hill 92
Methodist Mission 320-321, 333, 346, 467
Mexia's 125
Miles, Anita J. 240-242
Miller, Bill 123
Miller Log Cabin Museum 464
Miller's Gulch 85
MILLERSBURG 310-311
Milliorn 202, 275-276, 284-286
Milliorn Station 275-276
Milliorn, Thomas A. 276
Milliron (misspelling of Milliorn) 276
MILWAUKIE 169, 375, 382, 386-395, 474
Minthorn, John Henry 468-469
Mission Bottom 320-321
Missouri Bottom 139-140, 144
Momsen, Joan 90, 460, 462
MONMOUTH 187-188, 412, 432, 436, 441, 443-446, 454
MONROE 248, 274, 277, 293-294, 405, 408-413, 415
Monteith, Thomas & Walter 302-303, 308
Morrison Street Bridge 485
Morse, Benjamin 237
Morse, Bill 296-297
Morse Bros. 295-297
Morse, Clinton & Lydia 295
Morse, Forrest 296-297
Morse, Frank 296
Morse, Joe 296-297
Morse, Sherman 237
Mostachotti, John & Amerigo 204
Mountain House 6, 15-17, 186, 201, 203

Mt. Tabor 402, 474, 483
Mulkey, John 286
Mulkey, Philip 248
Mullaly, Larry 17
Mullen, Jay 18
Mulligan, Charnel 246, 248
Multnomah County Hospital 484
Munford, Kenneth 354

N

Nash, Tom 354
National Register of Historic Places 110-112, 146, 176, 179, 187, 264, 313, 345, 347, 361, 397, 417, 431, 448, 464, 470-471
National Soldiers' Home for the Pacific Northwest 155-156
Native American 1, 14, 78, 80, 83, 86, 89-90, 151, 161, 180, 242, 253, 320, 335, 377
Natron Cutoff 36
Nelson, Julian Elmer 108-109, 119
NEW ALBANY 302
NEW ERA 9, 365-372, 505
NEW ODESSA 119-120
NEWBERG 18, 98, 334, 466-469
Newbury, John C. 368, 370-371
Newell Barber Field 70-72
Newman, John Henry 262-263
Newman's Fish Market 262-263
Nickel Mountain 138-140
Nielsen, A.C. 278
Norris, W.B. 25-26
Northwest Art and Air Festival 308
Northwestern Turkey Show 175

O

O&C 9-10, 59-60, 153, 177, 237, 339, 351, 372
OAK GROVE 149, 386-387
OAKLAND 4, 9-10, 123, 142, 166, 174-176, 178, 183, 189, 220-221, 223, 286, 505

Oaks Park 395-396, 501
Oatman, Harvey 54
Oatman's Station 54
Obst, Rick 282
ODOT (Oregon Department of Transportation) 12, 54, 58, 78, 113, 157-158, 176, 183, 185, 268, 285, 289-290, 298-300, 317, 332, 349, 364, 373, 381, 454, 458, 466, 484
Ogden, Peter Skene 14, 467
O'Harra, Marge 38-42
OHSU 484
Old Cal 4-5, 320, 344
Old Highway 99S 24, 27-28
Old Siskiyou Highway 27
Omar's 43
OMSI 397-398, 481
Oregon & California Railroad 10, 17, 47, 59, 81, 86, 93, 118, 138, 142, 153, 172, 177, 184, 186-187, 198, 210, 288, 298-299, 304, 313, 338, 347, 361, 438, 480
Oregon Caves 96, 98, 100, 222
Oregon Central Railroad 9, 457
OREGON CITY 5-6, 9, 19, 63, 90, 98, 153, 184, 205, 246, 256, 276, 278, 312, 319, 321-323, 344, 351, 354, 362, 364-370, 372-384, 386, 390, 393, 400, 419, 429, 451, 462, 474, 481, 505
Oregon City Historic Museum 374
Oregon Electric Railway 258-260, 262, 273, 290-291, 313, 342, 344-345, 386, 400, 470
Oregon Encyclopedia Project 1, 49, 68, 75, 305, 346, 357, 445, 453, 456, 469, 487
Oregon Health & Science University 483-484
Oregon Health Sciences University 483-484
Oregon Militia 29, 238
Oregon Museum of Science and Industry 397-398, 481
Oregon Normal School 29-30, 32, 187-188, 398, 442, 445

Oregon State College / University 34, 252, 295, 423-426, 433, 435, 445, 501
Oregon State [Mental] Hospital for the Insane 316, 328, 330-331
Oregon State Penitentiary 328-330
Oregon State Police 23-24
Oregon State Seal 323
Oregon State Soldier's Home 155-157
Oregon Temperance League 467
Oregon Territory 2, 89, 151, 165, 176, 179, 253, 374-376, 388, 419, 441, 451, 467
Oregon Trail 1, 16, 28-29, 86, 210, 268, 275, 354, 361, 365, 374, 379, 442, 456, 459-460
Oregon Vortex 82-83
Oregon Wine History Archive 459-460
Oregon Zoo 481-482
Oregonian 21, 30, 66, 72, 313, 362, 442, 448-449, 455, 460, 462, 464-465, 472, 492-494, 504-506
Orem, Jerry 271
Orr, Betty 335-336
OSU Special Collections 22, 24, 27, 34, 107, 118, 129, 156-157, 188
OSU Special Collections [Commons] 33-34, 42, 61, 63, 80, 90, 97, 113, 118, 122, 143, 152, 154, 178, 191, 211-212, 214, 236, 252, 259, 278, 324, 327, 333, 378, 380, 398, 412, 417, 421, 423-425, 427-428, 433-434, 438, 450, 453, 455, 459, 461, 466, 473, 495, 498, 502
Overland Mail 2, 8, 322
Overton, William 472

P

Pacific Air Transport 67, 70-72, 123-124, 271
Pacific College 249
Pacific Greyhound Lines 158-159, 263
Pacific Railway Act of 1862 9
Palmer, Joel 86, 116, 389, 451
Panama Pacific International Exposition 34, 61, 64, 67

Parker, C.W. 500-501
Parmenter, Judy 407
Pass Creek 186, 192, 195, 199, 201, 205, 506
Paul, Alex 296
Pearce, Greenberry C. 210
Pearl Harbor 39-40, 275, 294, 334, 344, 432, 495
Perkins, Joel 90-92, 460-462
PERKINSVILLE 89-92
Perozzi, Domingo 34
Petrie, Jost & Jerusha 254-256
Petty, Glyn 147-149
Pettygrove, Francis 472, 476, 492
Pheasant Creek 192
Phinney, Mark 416, 429
PHOENIX 54-58, 312
Phoenix Historical Society and Museum 56
Pierce, Sandy 297
Pintarich, Dick 246
Pioneer Bridge 123
Pipes, J.P. 94-95
Polk County Museum 433, 443, 452
Poole, Arlene Cox 23, 36
PORTLAND 1-6, 8-11, 14, 17-19, 21, 23, 30, 34, 36-37, 48, 52, 57-59, 61, 63, 69-71, 75, 81-82, 84, 98, 104-105, 111, 120, 123-124, 135-137, 148, 153, 155, 160, 168, 182, 184, 186, 189, 201, 205, 208, 210, 237, 246, 249, 254, 257-258, 260-261, 267, 269, 274-276, 278, 287-288, 290, 295, 303-304, 312, 318-320, 324, 325-326, 328, 330-331, 333, 337-338, 344, 346, 354, 358-359, 362-363, 365, 367-368, 370, 374, 381-384, 386-388, 390, 392-393, 395-404, 410, 418-420, 426-430, 433, 435, 442, 453-455, 457, 462-466, 469-470, 472-502, 504-505
Portland Airport 401-402
Portland Meadows 382, 501-502
Portland Park System 481
Portland Public Market 487
Portland Rose Festival 488-492
Portland State College 497-498
Portland Zoo 397, 481-482
Powell Butte 402-403

Powell Butte Nature Park 403
PRAIRIE CITY 287-288
Prather, Martin Lair 188-189
Preston, John B. 375-376
Proctor, Bob & Virginia 141

Q

Quackenbush, J.W. & Sons 263-264
QUINABY 344-345

R

Ramp, George Samuel "Sam" 342-344
Ramp, Jeff 341-342
Rand National Historic Site 110
Red Electrics 258, 400, 428
Reed, Calvin 169
Reed College 395
Reed, Simeon Gannett 395
Reynolds, Jackson 126
RICE HILL 176-177
Rice, Isadore F. 177
RICE VALLEY 176-177
Rice, William Street 177
Richard, Terry 465
Richards, Gary 435
Richfield 24-26, 72, 102-104, 160, 266-267, 492
RICKREALL 237, 418, 448-452
RIDDLE 138-141, 148
Riverdale School District 500
River Road 85, 229, 256-257, 265-270, 275, 285
Robinett, James 236-237
Robinett Station 236
Robinson, Thomas 92, 493-494
Robinson, Wayne & Maybell 173
ROCK POINT 81, 84-85
Rocky Butte 402-403, 435, 483
Rogers, Ginger 73
Rogers' Landing 467
Rogers, Ron 242
Rogue River Courier 96, 110

Rogue River / Valley 1, 11, 22, 64, 68, 71, 75, 79-81, 83-84, 87, 90, 93, 97-99, 102, 110, 114, 126, 167, 179, 225, 237, 274, 507
ROGUE RIVER, Oregon 74, 77, 81, 86-87
Rogue River Indians 56, 80, 116-117
Rogue River Valley Railway 66, 76
Rollins, Floyd 92
Rollins, Josephine Ort 92
Rose, Aaron 152-153
Rose, Russell C. 296
ROSEBURG 8-10, 18, 26, 37, 47, 55, 63, 90, 103, 105, 123, 125, 136-137, 139-141, 147-163, 166-167, 171, 177-178, 182, 184, 188, 192, 221-222, 237, 248, 250, 313, 459, 506
Roseburg Explosion 161-162
Roseburg Lumber Company 150
Roseburg News Review 123-124, 145, 160
Roseburg Plaindealer 184, 192,
ROSEBURGH 153
Rosenberg, Harry & David 61-62, 139
Ross, George W. 236
Ross Island 404
Ross Island Bridge 485
Ross, Sherry 404
Rowley, Maude 491
Ruby's Kitchen 26
Ruckles, Matt 149
Ruhl, Robert 72
Runk, Jacob 201-202
Ruth Stoller Research Library 462, 464

S

SAGINAW 192, 205-206, 233-235, 505
SALEM 2-6, 9, 20, 37, 63, 69, 91, 98, 109, 148, 168, 216, 257-258, 260, 287, 297, 310, 312, 314, 316-338, 343-346, 349, 354, 358, 399-401, 419-420, 454, 469-470, 473, 505
Salem Capital Journal 69, 238
Salem Public Library 257, 327-328, 344
Sams, Kermit 224
Sams Valley Highway 84
Sauvie Island 387

Savage Rapids Dam 97, 99
Sawdust and Cider 173, 175, 202
Scandinavian Festival 269, 281-283
Schmidt, Rich 459
Schmitz, Peter & Marie 266-267
Schofield, Twilo 354
Schultz, Gregory 277, 280, 406-407
Scott, Harvey 30-31, 442, 464
Scott, Levi 108
Scotts Valley 181-182, 185
Scottsburg 1, 46, 63, 107, 142-143, 151, 165, 167, 175, 184, 193
Scovell, Colonel L.C. 4-5, 319, 344
Seng, Marvin 20
Settlemier, Jessie Holland 347
Seward, Norby, Clovy, Lillian, Milan, Peachy & Roxie 204
Shaffer, George 127
Shakespearean Festival 32, 37, 74
Shannon, Red 104-106
Sharon, Jennie 233-234
Sharp, James Meikle 247, 379
SHEDD 299-300, 505
Shedd, Frank Captain 300
SHEDD'S STATION 300
Shepard, Clara 499
Sherbert, Andrew C. 186, 442, 476
Sigler, Peggy 364, 368
Siskiyou Mountain Wagon Company 14
Siskiyou Mountains 6, 10, 14, 16-17, 19, 23, 25, 28, 179, 418
Siskiyou National Forest 68, 110
Siskiyou Pass 11-12
Siskiyou Summit 20, 24, 26
Six Bit House 110-111
Skidmore, Henry 30
SKINNER 245-246, 274, 415
Skinner, Eugene 245-247, 274
Skinners Butte 246, 260, 428
SLAB TOWN 210-212
Smith, Francis 235
Smith, Green Berry 416-418, 437-439
Smith, Isaac W. 480
Smith, Jedidiah 151
Smith, Stan 30
Smith, Vera 271

Smith, W.G. 112
SOAP CREEK 416, 418, 420, 422, 431, 438
Sommerville, Thomas 292
Southern Emigrant Road 1
Southern Oregon Historical Society 13, 15, 18, 64
Southern Oregon Normal School 29-30, 32
Southern Oregon University 18, 25, 28-31, 33, 35, 43, 75, 157
Southern Pacific Railroad 10, 17, 19, 23, 29, 36-37, 48, 51, 55, 59, 60-61, 67, 75, 81, 136, 139, 144, 153, 156, 158, 176, 188, 190, 192, 194-195, 200, 214, 235, 237, 250, 257-258, 262-263, 275, 279-280, 291, 308, 312, 331, 339-341, 363, 367-368, 371, 381, 400, 428, 438, 454, 465, 469, 480
Spaulding, Charles K. Logging Company 257
Spencer Butte 256
Spencer, Nettie 321
SPRINGFIELD 18, 177, 190, 200, 216, 241-245, 249, 257-258, 260, 263, 265, 267, 270-271, 288, 400, 435
Spruce Goose 460
St. Charles Hotel 247, 250
St. John's Bridge 485
Stage Terminal Hotel 253
Staging Days 2, 85, 107, 153
Stannis Station 415
Starkweather, Harvey Gordon 322, 389
Starr, Frank W. 146
Starr, Sam 409, 416
Starr's Point 409-410, 415
STARVOUT 120
State Hospital 20, 316, 328, 330
State Traffic Force 23
Steel Bridge 93, 97, 138, 382-383, 485, 493,
Steinman Bridge 27
Sterling, Jas. A. 192-193
Stevenson, Lillian 128, 140
Stewart, Joseph 60-61
Stewart, Faye H. 226-228
Stewart, Loran LaSells "Stub" 215, 225
"Stri-ped Horse" Station 186

Strobridge, Elaine M. 138
STUMP TOWN / JULIA / GLENDALE 119
STUMPTOWN / PORTLAND, 395, 472, 482
Suffrage 30, 57, 96, 180, 463-464
Suiter, Jim 194
Sullivan, Wes 344
Summit Ranch Lodge 25-26
Sunny Valley 105, 107-110, 112
SUNNYSIDE 318
SUTHERLIN 171-174, 505
Sutherlin, John & Sarah 171
SUVER 432, 435, 438-439
Suver, Joe Wellington 438
Swan Island 295, 401-402
Swedenburg, Francis G., Dr. 32-33
Sweed Mill 82

T

Table Rock 26, 86, 151
Table Rock Sentinel 13
Table Rock Reservation 86
TAILHOLT 86
TAKENAH 302
TALENT 28, 44, 46-54, 57, 74
Talent, Aaron Patton 47
Talent Historical Society 47-49 51-53
Talent Irrigation District 28, 50-51
TAMPICO 416-417, 437-438
Tamulonis, John 244-245
TANGENT 71, 295, 300-302, 505
Taylor, Henry Wells 210
Territorial Road 201, 203, 365, 405, 409. 411
Thomas, Lucy Lee 488-492
Thomas, Michael 14
Thomas Theatre 32
Thompson, D.P. 5
Thompson, Gary 193
Thompson, Richard 75-76
Thompson's Mills State Heritage Site 300
THORP'S TOWN 446, 448
THURSTON 287-288, 292
TIGARD 260, 466, 469-471, 484
Tigard, Charles 470
Tigard, John 470

Tigard, Wilson 469, 471
TILLER 129-130, 135-138
Tiller Ranger District 129-130
Tiller Trail Highway 129
Tonole, Mac & Toni 204
Torrent Creek 26
Tower of Lights 24
Toy, Eckhard, Jr. 68
Trapp, Gordon E. 381
Tri-City 140-141
Tri-County Chamber of Commerce 289
True, Moses Dyer 142-143
Truwe, Ben 22, 24-25, 31, 33, 49, 52, 56-57, 68, 70, 72, 77, 82-83, 85, 87, 97, 100, 105, 108-109, 111, 152, 155
Tualatin Valley 463, 470, 477
Tualatin Mountains 473, 483-484
Tucker, Louis 6
Twogood, James H. 107-108, 112

U

U.S. Bureau of Mines 93, 306, 310
U.S. Forest Service 70, 110, 129-131, 137, 236, 252, 259
Ulven, Leslie 351-352
Umpqua Academy 167-170
Umpqua Community College 163
Umpqua Dairy 160-161
Umpqua River 1, 46, 55, 90, 99, 115, 120, 125, 128, 136, 138, 141-144, 149-152, 157, 162, 169, 176, 203
Umpqua tribe 116
Universal Mental Liberty Hall 49-50
University of Oregon 188, 228, 240, 251-253, 261-262, 265, 274-275, 333, 387, 425, 483-484, 495
University of Oregon Medical School 483-484

V

Van Prooyan, Ada 190, 206
Van Scoy, W.T. 188
VANPORT / VANPORT CITY 383, 401, 495-497

Vanport College 496-497
Veteran's Hospital 155, 163
Victor, Frances Fuller 2
Villard, Henry 251-252

W

WACONDA 6, 344-345
Waddle, Susan 130
WAGNER CREEK 46, 49-50
Wagner, Jacob 46, 92
Waldron, Sue 13
WALKER 205, 235-236, 505
Wall Creek 26
Walling, A.G. 117, 176
Ward, Robert H. 205
Ward's Toll Road 205
Warnock, Dan 242-243, 245
Washburne State Park 406
Washington Park Zoo 479, 481
Watkins, Hortense 250
Weasku Inn 87
Weich, Robert H. 136
Weisenbacher, T. 95
Wells, Fargo & Co. / Wells Fargo 2-4, 6, 8, 15, 58-59, 153, 166, 177, 371, 491
Wells Fargo Bank 303
Welsh, John P. 202
Welsh Changing Station 201-202
West Hills 473, 483
West, Oswald, Governor 11-12, 329, 331
West Side Company 9
Wheatland Ferry 339
Whitcomb, Lot 387-390
White, Joseph 409
Whiteaker, John 29
Whiteley, Opal 228-229
Wikimedia Commons 10, 127, 187-188, 191, 197, 304, 339, 345, 347, 382, 396, 426, 470
WILBUR 154, 165-170, 174, 181-182, 196, 505
Wilbur, James H. 167-168, 170
Wild and Scenic 100, 102, 110
Wilde, Chris 276, 281
Wildlife Safari 150-151

Willamette Falls 368, 372-374, 378, 379, 383, 481
Willamette Meridian 376
Willamette River Bridge 290, 331
Willamette University 93, 168, 277, 316, 321, 333-334
William L. Finley Wildlife Refuge 415
Williams, Charles & Lucy Ann 302
Williams, Gerald W. 22, 24, 27, 33-34, 42, 97, 107, 113, 118, 122, 129, 152, 154, 156-157, 178, 191, 211, 212, 214, 252-253, 259, 278-279, 304, 348, 421, 424, 450, 453, 455, 459
WILLIS CREEK 149-150
Wilson, Sandra 236
Wilson, W.H. 183
Winburn, Jesse 32-33
WINCHESTER 9, 152-153, 163, 169, 505
Wine / Wineries 85, 155, 174, 235, 455, 458-460, 464-467, 469
Winkle's Butte 415
Winn, Loson 125
Winslow, Walker 93
WINSTON 149-151
Winston, W.C. 150
Wobblies 18-19
WOLF CREEK 108-115, 506
Wolf Creek Tavern 109-111
Wollenberg, Hyman & Julia 120, 144
Woodard, Ambrose (A.L.) & Ella J. 215-224
Woodard Family Collection 213, 215-217, 224, 229, 233, 244
Woodard Family Foundation 216
Woodard, Walter A. 215-216
WOODBURN 18, 98, 346-350, 505
Woodmen of the World 57, 103, 346, 420
WOODVILLE 86
Woodworth, Cyrus B. 403-404

Woody, Rachael 459
WOODY'S LANDING 284-286
Works Progress Administration 35, 86, 104, 250, 291, 316, 321-322, 324, 357, 363, 374, 389, 391
World War I 24, 68-69, 208, 242, 294, 428
World War II 37-39, 42-43, 52, 62, 74, 79, 104, 123, 131, 138, 140, 150, 175, 191, 207, 209, 214, 230, 238, 245, 252, 266, 270, 275, 294, 303, 306, 313, 331, 333-334, 336, 343, 367, 394, 401, 406, 413, 445, 469, 487, 495-496
WPA 35, 58, 64, 79, 86, 93, 153, 167, 169, 181, 183, 186, 247, 250, 291-292, 311, 316, 321-322, 324, 353, 357, 360, 363, 374, 389, 391, 398, 403, 409, 412, 416, 418, 420, 429, 430, 437, 439, 442, 473, 476-477
Wrenn, Sara B. 153, 167, 169, 247, 312, 324, 391, 398, 404, 473, 477
Wright, Jan 49
Wright, Barbara Stroda 412

Y

Yamhill Historical Society and Museum 90, 469
YONCALLA 10, 177-185, 195, 197, 505
Yoncalla Kalapuya 180
Young, Ewing 467

Z

Zearoff 415
Zehntbauer, John A. 498, 500
Zoo 35, 151, 268, 397, 481

If you enjoyed

OREGON'S MAIN STREET: U.S. Highway 99
"The Folk History"

you're sure to like its 2013 companion book

OREGON'S MAIN STREET: U.S. Highway 99
"The Stories"

by Jo-Brew

You can now find both books in your local bookstore, library, museum or on-line or you can order directly from the authors at:

Groundwaters Publishing, LLC
P.O. Box 50, Lorane, OR 97451
edwards@groundwaterspublishing.com